lonely planet

Andalucía

John Noble
Susan Forsyth

LONELY PLANET PUBLICATIONS
Melbourne • Oakland • London • Paris

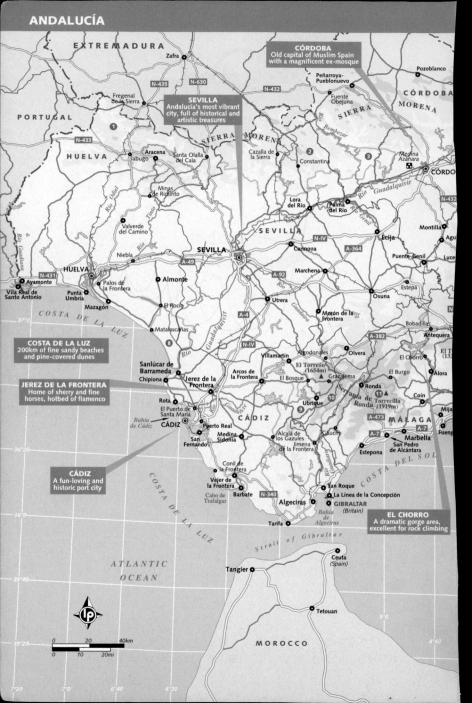

ANDALUCÍA

EXTREMADURA

Zafra

N-435 N-630

Fregenal
de la Sierra

PORTUGAL

N-433

HUELVA

Aracena
Jabugo

Santa Olalla
del Cala

Minas
de Riotinto

Valverde
del Camino

Niebla

HUELVA

N-431

Ayamonte

Vila Real de
Santo António

Punta
Umbría

Palos de
la Frontera

Almonte

Mazagón

El Rocío

COSTA DE LA LUZ

Matalascañas

COSTA DE LA LUZ
200km of fine sandy beaches
and pine-covered dunes

Sanlúcar de
Barrameda

Chipiona

JEREZ DE LA FRONTERA
Home of sherry and fine
horses, hotbed of flamenco

Rota

El Puerto de
Santa María

*Bahía
de Cádiz*

CÁDIZ

Puerto Real

San
Fernando

Medina
Sidonia

Conil de
la Frontera

CÁDIZ
A fun-loving and
historic port city

Vejer de
la Frontera

*Cabo de
Trafalgar*

Barbate

N-340

COSTA DE LA LUZ

**ATLANTIC
OCEAN**

CÓRDOBA
Old capital of Muslim Spain
with a magnificent ex-mosque

Pozoblanco

Peñarroya-
Pueblonuevo

N-432

Fuente
Obejuna

CÓRDOBA

SIERRA

MORENA

Cazalla de
la Sierra

Constantina

Río Bembézar

Medina
Azahara

CÓRDO

N-432

SEVILLA
Andalucía's most vibrant
city, full of historical and
artistic treasures

SIERRA MORENA

Lora
del Río

Palma
del Río

Río Guadalquivir

Montilla

Agu

SEVILLA

Carmona

Écija

N-IV

Puente-Genil

Luce

A-364

SEVILLA

Marchena

Río

Utrera

A-92

Osuna

Estepa

A-4

Morón de la
Frontera

Bobadilla

Río Guadaira

A-382

Antequera

Villamartín

Algodonales

Olvera

El Chorro

EL T
(13.

N-IV

Arcos de
la Frontera

El Torreón
(1654m)

Grazalema

El Burgo

Álora

El Bosque

CÁDIZ

Ubrique

10

*Serranía de
Ronda*

Ronda

Torrecilla
(1919m)

Coín

Mija

Alcalá de
los Gazules

Gaucín

A-473

MÁLAGA

A-7

A-7

Fueng

Jimena
de la Frontera

9

Estepona

Marbella
San Pedro
de Alcántara

COSTA DEL SOL

San Roque

La Línea de la Concepción

Algeciras

GIBRALTAR
(Britain)

*Bahía
de
Algeciras*

EL CHORRO
A dramatic gorge area,
excellent for rock climbing

Tarifa

Strait of Gibraltar

Ceuta
(Spain)

Tangier

Tetouan

MOROCCO

0   20   40km

0   10   20mi

Contents – Text

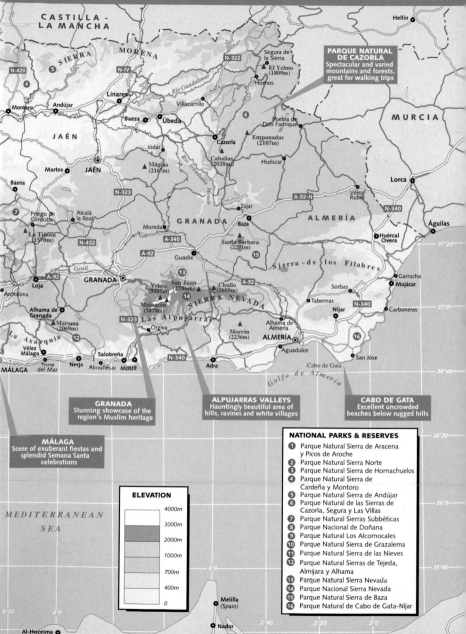

PARQUE NATURAL DE CAZORLA
Spectacular and varied mountains and forests, great for walking trips

GRANADA
Stunning showcase of the region's Muslim heritage

MÁLAGA
Scene of exuberant fiestas and splendid Semana Santa celebrations

ALPUJARRAS VALLEYS
Hauntingly beautiful area of hills, ravines and white villages

CABO DE GATA
Excellent uncrowded beaches below rugged hills

ELEVATION

	4000m
	3000m
	2000m
	1000m
	700m
	400m
	0

NATIONAL PARKS & RESERVES

1. Parque Natural Sierra de Aracena y Picos de Aroche
2. Parque Natural Sierra Norte
3. Parque Natural Sierra de Hornachuelos
4. Parque Natural Sierra de Cardeña y Montoro
5. Parque Natural Sierra de Andújar
6. Parque Natural de las Sierras de Cazorla, Segura y Las Villas
7. Parque Natural Sierras Subbéticas
8. Parque Nacional de Doñana
9. Parque Natural Los Alcornocales
10. Parque Natural Sierra de Grazalema
11. Parque Natural Sierra de las Nieves
12. Parque Natural Sierras de Tejeda, Almijara y Alhama
13. Parque Natural Sierra Nevada
14. Parque Nacional Sierra Nevada
15. Parque Natural Sierra de Baza
16. Parque Natural de Cabo de Gata-Níjar

Andalucía
2nd edition – January 2001
First published – January 1999

Published by
Lonely Planet Publications Pty Ltd ABN 36 005 607 983
90 Maribyrnong St, Footscray, Victoria 3011, Australia

Lonely Planet Offices
Australia Locked Bag 1, Footscray, Victoria 3011
USA 150 Linden St, Oakland, CA 94607
UK 10a Spring Place, London NW5 3BH
France 1 rue du Dahomey, 75011 Paris

Photographs
All of the images in this guide are available for licensing from
Lonely Planet Images.
email: lpi@lonelyplanet.com.au
Web site: www.lonelyplanetimages.com

Front cover photograph
Making a stand – a toros de Osborne, Cádiz province (Dushan Cooray)

ISBN 1 86450 191 X

text & maps © Lonely Planet Publications Pty Ltd 2001
photos © photographers as indicated 2001

GR and PR are trademarks of the FFRP (Fédération Française de la Randonnée Pédestre)

Printed by The Bookmaker International Ltd
Printed in China

Contents – Text

CÓRDOBA PROVINCE 297

GRANADA PROVINCE 315

JAÉN PROVINCE 354

ALMERÍA PROVINCE 385

LANGUAGE 403

GLOSSARY 411

INDEX 418

MAP LEGEND back page

METRIC CONVERSION inside back cover

Contents – Maps

MAP LEGEND – SEE BACK PAGE

MAPS

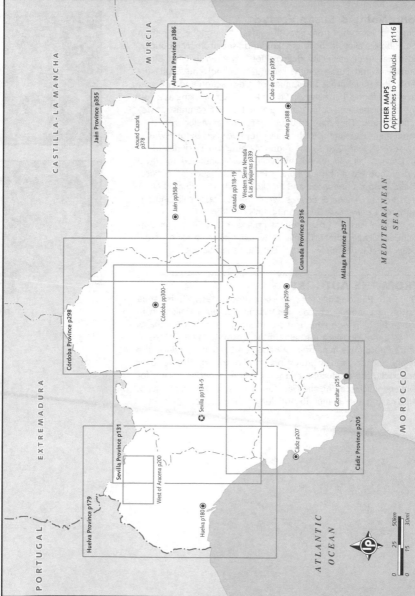

PORTUGAL

EXTREMADURA

CASTILLA-LA MANCHA

MURCIA

Huelva Province p179

Sevilla Province p131

West of Aracena p200

Huelva p180

Córdoba Province p298

Sevilla pp134-5

Córdoba pp300-1

Jaén Province p355

Around Cazorla p378

Jaén pp358-9

Almería Province p386

Cabo de Gata p395

Almería p388

Granada pp318-19

Western Sierra Nevada
& Las Alpujarras p339

Granada Province p316

Málaga Province p257

Málaga p259

Cádiz p207

Gibraltar p251

Cádiz Province p205

MOROCCO

ATLANTIC
OCEAN

MEDITERRANEAN
SEA

0   25   50km
0   15   30mi

The Authors

John Noble & Susan Forsyth

John and Susan hail from opposite sides of the globe – he from the Ribble Valley in northern England, she from Melbourne, Australia. After university degrees John worked in Fleet Street journalism and Susan taught secondary school and adult students. But travel proved too much of a distraction and one year they both found themselves in Sri Lanka – Susan working as a volunteer teacher and John carrying out his first commission for Lonely Planet. They married three years later in Melbourne, then based themselves in the Ribble Valley for five years before switching several years ago to the more Melbourne-like climes of an Andalucian hill village. All the while they continued to travel widely, both co-authoring Lonely Planet titles such as *Mexico*, *Spain*, *Australia*, *Indonesia* and *Sri Lanka*. John coordinated *USSR* and *Russia, Ukraine & Belarus*, wrote *Baltic States* solo and co-authored *Central Asia*. Susan and John's children Isabella and Jack go many places with them, but still manage to attend their Andalucian village school, thanks to which their command of the local dialect is definitely more fluent than their parents'.

FROM THE AUTHORS

Thanks to Patricia Luce for a constant flow of tasty titbits; Anna Sutton in London, Jen Loy in Oakland and Julia Wilkinson in Lisbon for help with getting-there information; Karen Abrahams in Los Caños de Meca for help on the Costa de la Luz; Mariano Cruz, a hospitable mine of information on Granada province; the helpful and increasingly professional staff of tourist offices all over Andalucía; the production team in London, especially Claire for some beneficial editing and Gadi for nice maps; and Kiko Veneno, Niña Pastori and Raimundo Amador for their music.

This Book

John Noble and Susan Forsyth wrote the first edition of *Andalucía* and updated this second edition.

From the Publisher
This edition of *Andalucía* was edited and proofed in Lonely Planet's London office by Claire Hornshaw, with invaluable assistance from Michala Green; thanks to Christine Stroyan for her help in the early stages and to Quentin Frayne, who compiled, updated and found time to make last minute changes to the language chapter. Gadi Farfour co-ordinated the design and cartography; Adam McCrow designed the cover and Jim Miller created the back cover map. Lonely Planet Images provided photographs and illustrations were drawn by Jane Smith, Kate Nolan, Martin Harris, Mick Weldon and Nick Kelly. Jane Smith also illustrated the special sections. Many thanks to John and Susan for their extremely thorough work.

Thanks
Many thanks to the following travellers who used the last edition and wrote to us with helpful hints, useful advice and interesting anecdotes:

Alan Thornton, Alberto Larocca, Alejandro Contreras, Alfred Shaw, Bernhard Raps, Bjorn Furumark, Beth Connors, Camille Credeville, Carlos P Moran, Caroline Raphael, Charles Moberley, Charles William Kersey, Christian Armbruester, Christian Bowers, Claudia Balzer, Cormac Bracken, Cynthia Gehan, Daniel A Brown, David Gibbons, Dirk Jan van der Kaa, E Sarlet, Emma Morgan, Eric Roche, Felice, Felix Weickmann, Geoff Walker, George Hawkins, George Musser, Georgia Carr, Gerhard Zarbrock, Gillian Sutton, Hannah Main-van der Kamp, Hanneke Fialka, Harold Zuberman, Helen Sundhaug, Isabel Noriega, Janessa Maria-Diego, Jim Alexander, Johan Andersson, John O Donoghue, Laura Edmunds, Leya Nelson, Linda Highton, Lisa Rozenbes, Malcolm Love, Mark and Kath, Mary Lewis, Mary Ryan, Melanie America, Mike Shen, Mikole Liese, Milly Dudley-Owen, Mostapha Karim, Mrs. MG Savage, Nadja Peachey, Nico Morgan, Nicole Fabisch, Paul McGrath, Peter Cliefe, Piero Facchinetti, RA Zambardino, Ray Singer, Richard Lewis, Rob Azarcon, Robert Mason, Ron Faris, Rose Brannen, Ruth MacGintie, Sandy Wubben, Sarah Woolston, Scott Slayton, Sean Donegan, Sebastian Lechel, Sergei Strid, Sheila & Roman Russek, Stefan Rukatukl, Susie Roy, Swantje Paula Pohlmann, Terry D Schoessow, Tim Hoy, Tim Reid, Ton Renders, Tricia Harrison, Valerie

Foreword

ABOUT LONELY PLANET GUIDEBOOKS

The story begins with a classic travel adventure: Tony and Maureen Wheeler's 1972 journey across Europe and Asia to Australia. Useful information about the overland trail did not exist at that time, so Tony and Maureen published the first Lonely Planet guidebook to meet a growing need.

From a kitchen table, then from a tiny office in Melbourne (Australia), Lonely Planet has become the largest independent travel publisher in the world, an international company with offices in Melbourne, Oakland (USA), London (UK) and Paris (France).

Today Lonely Planet guidebooks cover the globe. There is an ever-growing list of books and there's information in a variety of forms and media. Some things haven't changed. The main aim is still to help make it possible for adventurous travellers to get out there – to explore and better understand the world.

At Lonely Planet we believe travellers can make a positive contribution to the countries they visit – if they respect their host communities and spend their money wisely. Since 1986 a percentage of the income from each book has been donated to aid projects and human rights campaigns.

Updates Lonely Planet thoroughly updates each guidebook as often as possible. This usually means there are around two years between editions, although for more unusual or more stable destinations the gap can be longer. Check the imprint page (following the colour map at the beginning of the book) for publication dates.

Between editions up-to-date information is available in two free newsletters – the paper *Planet Talk* and email *Comet* (to subscribe, contact any Lonely Planet office) – and on our Web site at www.lonelyplanet.com. The *Upgrades* section of the Web site covers a number of important and volatile destinations and is regularly updated by Lonely Planet authors. *Scoop* covers news and current affairs relevant to travellers. And, lastly, the *Thorn Tree* bulletin board and *Postcards* section of the site carry unverified, but fascinating, reports from travellers.

Correspondence The process of creating new editions begins with the letters, postcards and emails received from travellers. This correspondence often includes suggestions, criticisms and comments about the current editions. Interesting excerpts are immediately passed on via newsletters and the Web site, and everything goes to our authors to be verified when they're researching on the road. We're keen to get more feedback from organisations or individuals who represent communities visited by travellers.

Lonely Planet gathers information for everyone who's curious about the planet – and especially for those who explore it first-hand. Through guidebooks, phrasebooks, activity guides, maps, literature, newsletters, image library, TV series and Web site we act as an information exchange for a worldwide community of travellers.

Research Authors aim to gather sufficient practical information to enable travellers to make informed choices and to make the mechanics of a journey run smoothly. They also research historical and cultural background to help enrich the travel experience and allow travellers to understand and respond appropriately to cultural and environmental issues.

Authors don't stay in every hotel because that would mean spending a couple of months in each medium-sized city and, no, they don't eat at every restaurant because that would mean stretching belts beyond capacity. They do visit hotels and restaurants to check standards and prices, but feedback based on readers' direct experiences can be very helpful.

Many of our authors work undercover, others aren't so secretive. None of them accept freebies in exchange for positive write-ups. And none of our guidebooks contain any advertising.

Production Authors submit their raw manuscripts and maps to offices in Australia, USA, UK or France. Editors and cartographers – all experienced travellers themselves – then begin the process of assembling the pieces. When the book finally hits the shops, some things are already out of date, we start getting feedback from readers and the process begins again …

WARNING & REQUEST

Things change – prices go up, schedules change, good places go bad and bad places go bankrupt – nothing stays the same. So, if you find things better or worse, recently opened or long since closed, please tell us and help make the next edition even more accurate and useful. We genuinely value all the feedback we receive. A well travelled team reads and acknowledges every letter, postcard and email and ensures that every morsel of information finds its way to the appropriate authors, editors and cartographers for verification.

Everyone who writes to us will find their name in the next edition of the appropriate guidebook. They will also receive the latest issue of *Planet Talk*, our quarterly printed newsletter, or *Comet*, our monthly email newsletter. Subscriptions to both newsletters are free. The very best contributions will be rewarded with a free guidebook.

Excerpts from your correspondence may appear in new editions of Lonely Planet guidebooks, the Lonely Planet Web site, *Planet Talk* or *Comet*, so please let us know if you *don't* want your letter published or your name acknowledged.

Send all correspondence to the Lonely Planet office closest to you:

Australia: Locked Bag 1, Footscray, Victoria 3011
USA: 150 Linden St, Oakland, CA 94607
UK: 10A Spring Place, London NW5 3BH
France: 1 rue du Dahomey, 75011 Paris

Or email us at: talk2us@lonelyplanet.com.au

For news, views and updates see our Web site: www.lonelyplanet.com

HOW TO USE A LONELY PLANET GUIDEBOOK

The best way to use a Lonely Planet guidebook is any way you choose. At Lonely Planet we believe the most memorable travel experiences are often those that are unexpected, and the finest discoveries are those you make yourself. Guidebooks are not intended to be used as if they provide a detailed set of infallible instructions!

Contents All Lonely Planet guidebooks follow roughly the same format. The Facts about the Destination chapters or sections give background information ranging from history to weather. Facts for the Visitor gives practical information on issues like visas and health. Getting There & Away gives a brief starting point for researching travel to and from the destination. Getting Around gives an overview of the transport options when you arrive.

The peculiar demands of each destination determine how subsequent chapters are broken up, but some things remain constant. We always start with background, then proceed to sights, places to stay, places to eat, entertainment, getting there and away, and getting around information – in that order.

Heading Hierarchy Lonely Planet headings are used in a strict hierarchical structure that can be visualised as a set of Russian dolls. Each heading (and its following text) is encompassed by any preceding heading that is higher on the hierarchical ladder.

Entry Points We do not assume guidebooks will be read from beginning to end, but that people will dip into them. The traditional entry points are the list of contents and the index. In addition, however, some books have a complete list of maps and an index map illustrating map coverage.

There may also be a colour map that shows highlights. These highlights are dealt with in greater detail in the Facts for the Visitor chapter, along with planning questions and suggested itineraries. Each chapter covering a geographical region usually begins with a locator map and another list of highlights. Once you find something of interest in a list of highlights, turn to the index.

Maps Maps play a crucial role in Lonely Planet guidebooks and include a huge amount of information. A legend is printed on the back page. We seek to have complete consistency between maps and text, and to have every important place in the text captured on a map. Map key numbers usually start in the top left corner.

Although inclusion in a guidebook usually implies a recommendation we cannot list every good place. Exclusion does not necessarily imply criticism. In fact there are a number of reasons why we might exclude a place – sometimes it is simply inappropriate to encourage an influx of travellers.

Introduction

Andalucía – the south of Spain, barely a stone's throw from Africa – has fascinated foreign travellers since the early 19th century when Romantic voyagers and writers were captivated by its people's love of colour, music and fiesta; by its state of picturesque decay from an exotic past; by its dramatic mountains, sparkling seas and southern heat; and by its unique flamenco music and dance.

Though modernity has arrived in Andalucía with a bump in recent decades, much of what gripped those early travellers lives on. Andalucians remain gregarious, relaxed and in love with life, still with a distinctly flexible notion of time. Their multitudinous fiestas are always full-blooded affairs, full of colour, noise and spectacle – be it the relatively solemn processions of Semana Santa (Holy Week) or the unadulterated hedonism of night-long music, dancing and drinking at summer fairs.

The Islamic civilisation that swept the Iberian Peninsula in the 8th century flourished longest (until 1492) in the south, and Andalucía is still perhaps the least European part of Western Europe. The Muslim era left behind not only magnificent buildings such as the Alhambra in Granada and the Mezquita in Córdoba, but also a deep imprint on the landscape, townscapes, people and even the food of modern Andalucía. Flamenco, the music that says 'Spain' to the outside world but which is Andalucía's own, has clear Islamic roots too, though it emerged only later as flamenco per se. The guitar, another Andalucian invention, also had its origin in Islamic times.

The recent Christian centuries have given Andalucía a great deal of its fascinating folklore and a superb legacy of Gothic, Renaissance and baroque architecture. The great artists Velázquez, Murillo and Picasso all came from Andalucía, as did the great writer Federico García Lorca and Spain's most celebrated composer, Manuel de Falla. In the 18th century Andalucía was one of the birthplaces of that

quintessential Spanish activity, bullfighting, which continues to thrive there today.

Sevilla, Granada, Málaga, Córdoba and Cádiz are cities with a fascinating heritage of history, art and architecture. They also provide a vibrant entertainment scene which often kicks on until dawn. A great start to a night out is to do the rounds of a few bars to sample the delicious snacks known as tapas. An excellent accompaniment to many tapas is sherry, which is produced only in Andalucía.

The region's climate – sizzling in July and August, temperate in winter – is another part of its appeal. The potent combination of sun, sea and sand has turned the Costa del Sol, west of Málaga, into one of the world's most densely developed package tour destinations. You'll be delighted to discover that other stretches of the Andalucian coast, such as Cabo de Gata in the east and the Atlantic Costa de la Luz in the west, have better beaches and far fewer people.

Away from the cities and beaches, much of Andalucía is rugged mountain chains and picturesque white villages where for centuries time has at best ambled along. From the mysterious Las Alpujarras valleys and the green and damp Sierra de Grazalema to the rocky crags of beautiful Parque Natural de Cazorla, you'll find a wealth of excellent walking and a profusion of beautiful flora and unusual fauna. Seventeen per cent of Andalucía is now under environmental protection.

Almost anywhere you go in Andalucía, fascinating surprises await. And the more you explore it, the deeper its fascination grows.

Facts about Andalucía

HISTORY

Andalucía stands where the Mediterranean Sea meets the Atlantic Ocean and Europe gives way to Africa. From prehistoric times to the 17th century, this critical location put Andalucía at the forefront of Spanish history – and at times made a mover of European and even world history. Then Andalucía became a backwater, a condition from which it has only emerged since the 1960s, helped by its leading place in Spain's tourism industry, the regeneration of the Spanish economy after the Franco dictatorship and the prominent roles played by Andalucians in national politics since then.

In the Beginning

A bone fragment found in 1976 near Orce, in Granada province, could be the oldest known human remains in Europe. It is probably one to two million years old and is believed to be from the skull of an infant *Homo erectus* – an ancestor of modern *Homo sapiens*. From the much later Neanderthal era comes 'Gibraltar Woman', a skull dating from about 50,000 BC, found in 1848.

The Palaeolithic or Old Stone Age, which lasted beyond the end of the last Ice Age to about 8000 BC, was somewhat less cold in Andalucía than in more northerly regions. Thick forests and varied fauna developed, permitting hunter-gatherer humans to live here in reasonable numbers. Many traces of their presence remain, notably some impressive rock art (see Painting, Sculpture & Metalwork in the Arts section later in this chapter).

The Neolithic or New Stone Age reached eastern Spain from Egypt and Mesopotamia in around 6000 BC, bringing a host of innovations such as the plough, crops, livestock raising, pottery, textiles and permanent villages. Between 3000 and 2000 BC, what was probably Spain's first metalworking culture arose at Los Millares, near

Almería. The ability to smelt and shape local copper deposits was a big agricultural and military breakthrough. This Copper or Chalcolithic Age saw the emergence in Andalucía of megalithic culture, during which tombs known as dolmens were built of large rocks. Spain's best dolmens are near Antequera.

The next big technological advance was bronze – an alloy of copper and tin, and stronger than copper. In about 1900 BC, El Argar, near Antas in the Almería province, became probably the first Bronze Age settlement on the Iberian Peninsula (modern Spain and Portugal). Between 1700 and 1200 BC, bronze technology spread throughout Andalucía.

Tartessos

By about 1000 BC, a flourishing culture, rich in agriculture, animals and metals, had arisen in western Andalucía. Phoenician traders, largely from Tyre and Sidon in present-day Lebanon, came to exchange luxuries such as perfumes, ivory, jewellery, oil, wine and textiles for Andalucian silver and bronze. The Phoenicians set up trading settlements on the coast at Adra (west of Almería), Almuñécar (which they called Sex), Málaga (Malaca), Cádiz (Gadir) and Huelva (Onuba). Cádiz, possibly founded as early as 1100 BC, may be the oldest city in Europe. In the 7th century BC the Greeks came too, trading much the same goods.

The culture of western Andalucía in the 8th and 7th centuries BC, influenced by the Phoenicians and Greeks, is known as the Tartessic culture. The name comes from Tartessos, a place somewhere in this area which was described centuries later by Greek, Roman and biblical writers as the source of fabulous riches. Whether Tartessos was a city, a state or just a region no-one knows. Some argue it was a trading settlement on the site of modern Huelva, others believe it may lie beneath the marshes near the mouth of the Río Guadalquivir, and yet others equate it with the lost continent of Atlantis.

The Phoenicians and Greeks brought Andalucía the potter's wheel, writing, the olive tree, the vine and animals such as the donkey and hen. Tartessic culture in the lower Guadalquivir valley gave rise to improved methods of working gold, a new religion with Phoenician-type gods, and the replacement of bronze by iron as the most important metal.

Iberians

From the 6th century BC the Phoenicians and Greeks were pushed out of the western Mediterranean by Carthage, a former Phoenician colony in modern Tunisia which came to dominate regional trade. Tartessic culture weakened and the people known as Iberians, from farther north in Spain, set up a number of small, often one-village statelets in Andalucía.

Romans

The Carthaginians inevitably came into conflict with a new Mediterranean power, Rome. After losing the First Punic War (264–241 BC), fought against Rome for control of Sicily, Carthage conquered southern Spain. The Second Punic War (218–201 BC) not only saw the Carthaginian general Hannibal march his elephants over the Alps towards Rome, but also brought Roman legions to Spain, to end Carthaginian ambitions on the Iberian Peninsula with a victory at Ilipa (Alcalá del Río, near Sevilla) in 206 BC. The first Roman town in Spain, Itálica (Santiponce, near Sevilla), was founded near the battle site soon afterwards. Hannibal was finally routed by the Roman general Scipio in North Africa in 202 BC.

Although it took Rome 200 years to finally subdue the rest of the Iberian Peninsula, Andalucía settled quickly into Roman ways and became one of the most civilised and wealthiest areas of the empire outside Italy. Local products such as wheat, vegetables, grapes, olives, copper, silver, lead, fish and *garum* (a spicy seasoning derived from fish) were exchanged for luxury goods from Rome. Andalucía also gave Rome two emperors – Trajan and Hadrian, both from Itálica.

Initially, Rome divided the Iberian Peninsula into two provinces, Hispania Citerior and Hispania Ulterior, with their capitals at Carthago Nova (Cartagena) and Corduba (Córdoba). In the 1st century BC these were reorganised into three: Baetica, covering most of Andalucía, southern Extremadura and south-western Castilla-La Mancha, with its capital at Corduba; Lusitania (Portugal and northern Extremadura); and Tarraconensis (the rest, including far eastern Andalucía). The Via Augusta road ran from Rome to Gades (Cádiz), passing through Tarraco (Tarragona in Catalunya), Corduba, Astigi (Écija), Carmo (Carmona) and Hispalis (Sevilla).

Rome gave Andalucía aqueducts, temples, theatres, amphitheatres, circuses and baths. It also bequeathed Spain its language (Castilian Spanish is basically colloquial Latin 2000 years on), the basis of its legal system, a sizeable Jewish population (Jews spread throughout the Mediterranean part of the Roman Empire), and Christianity, which probably arrived in the 3rd century AD with soldiers from North Africa and merchants. The new religion took root in Andalucía – initially among the wealthier urban classes – before Emperor Constantine made it the empire's official religion in AD 313.

Visigoths

By the late 3rd century, the Roman Empire was weakening and under attack from the north and east. In 324 Constantine made Byzantium (renamed Constantinople) his new capital, and in 395 the empire split into eastern and western halves. When the Huns arrived from Asia in the late 4th century, displaced Germanic peoples moved west, some overrunning the Iberian Peninsula. One Germanic group, the Visigoths, took Rome in 410. Having spared the emperor, they made a pact with him to rid the Iberian Peninsula of other invaders in return for lands in southern Gaul (France). But early in the 6th century, yet another Germanic people, the Franks, pushed the Visigoths out of Gaul. The Visigoths then settled in the Iberian Peninsula, and Toledo, in central Spain, became their capital.

The long-haired Visigoths, who numbered about 200,000, had little culture of their own and tended to ape Roman ways. Their rule over the relatively sophisticated Hispano-Romans was precarious, and undermined by strife among their own nobility. Ties between the Visigoth monarchy and the Hispano-Romans were strengthened in 587 when King Reccared converted to Catholicism from the Visigoths' Aryan version of Christianity (which denied that Christ was God). This probably helped the Visigoths expel, in 622, Byzantines who had conquered southern Spain in the mid-6th century.

The Muslim Conquest

By 700, with famine in Toledo, strife among the aristocracy and chaos throughout the peninsula, the Visigothic kingdom was falling apart. This paved the way for the Muslim invasion of 711, which set Spain's destiny quite apart from the rest of Europe.

Following the death of the prophet Mohammed in 632, Arabs had spread through the Middle East and North Africa, bringing Islam with them. If you believe the myth, they were ushered onto the Iberian Peninsula by the sexual exploits of the last Visigoth king, Roderick. Ballads and chronicles relate how Roderick seduced young Florinda, the daughter of Julian, the Visigothic governor of Ceuta in North Africa; and how Julian sought revenge by approaching the Muslims with a plan to invade Spain. In dull fact, Julian probably just wanted help in a struggle for the Visigothic throne.

In 711 Tariq ibn Ziyad, the Muslim governor of Tangier, landed at Gibraltar with around 10,000 men, mostly Berbers (indigenous North Africans). He had some of Roderick's Visigoth rivals as allies. In the same or the following year, probably near the Río Guadalete in Cádiz province, Roderick's army was decimated and he is thought to have drowned as he fled. Visigothic survivors fled north.

Within a few years, the Muslims had taken over the rest of the Iberian Peninsula except for small areas in the Asturian mountains in the far north.

Al-Andalus

The Muslims (often referred to as Moors) were to be the dominant force on the Iberian Peninsula for nearly four centuries, a potent force for 170 years after that and a lesser one for a further 250 years. Between wars and rebellions, the Muslim areas of the peninsula developed the most cultured society of medieval Europe. The name given to the Muslim territories, Al-Andalus, was probably an Arabisation of the Visigothic name for their kingdom, *landa-hlauts*, and lives on in the modern name of what was always the Muslim heartland – Andalucía.

Al-Andalus' frontiers were constantly shifting as the Christians strove to regain territory in the stuttering 800-year Reconquista (Reconquest). Up to the mid-11th century, the frontier stretched across the Iberian Peninsula roughly from just south of Barcelona to what's now northern Portugal. The small Christian states that developed north of this frontier were too weak and quarrelsome to pose a major threat to Al-Andalus for 350 years. Al-Andalus itself also suffered internal conflicts, and Muslims and Christians even struck up alliances against their own kind.

Muslim political power and culture centred first on Córdoba (756–1031), then Sevilla (c. 1040–1248) and lastly Granada (1248–1492). In the main cities, the Muslims built beautiful palaces, mosques and gardens, established large, bustling *zocos* (markets) and opened universities. Sticklers for cleanliness, they built numerous public bathhouses, which most people attended about once a week. In the countryside, they built on the Hispano-Roman agricultural base by improving irrigation and introducing new fruits and crops, such as oranges, lemons, peaches, sugar cane and rice.

Although military campaigns against the northern Christians could be bloodthirsty affairs, the rulers of Al-Andalus allowed freedom of worship to Jews and Christians under their rule. Jews, on the whole, flourished, but Christians in Muslim territory (Mozarabs; Spanish *Mozárabes*) had to pay a special tax, so most either converted to Islam (to be known as *Muladíes*, or Muwallads) or left for the Christian north.

The Muslim ruling class was composed of various Arab groups prone to factional friction. Below them was a larger group of Berbers, holding mainly second-rank positions and living on second-grade land. The Berbers rebelled on numerous occasions.

The Arabs and Berbers didn't bring many women with them and, before long, Muslim and local blood merged. There was even frequent royal and aristocratic intermarriage with the northern Christians, for tribute, appeasement or alliance.

Cordoban Emirate (756–929) Initially, Muslim Spain was a province of the Emirate of Ifriqiya (North Africa), part of the Caliphate of Damascus, which ruled the Muslim world. In 750 the Omayyad caliphal dynasty was overthrown by a rival clan, the Abbasids, who soon shifted the caliphate to Baghdad. One Omayyad escaped the slaughter and somehow made his way to Córdoba, where in 756 he managed to set himself up as an independent emir, Abd ar-Rahman I. It was he who began the construction of Córdoba's great Mezquita (mosque).

Abd ar-Rahman I's Omayyad dynasty more or less unified Al-Andalus for long periods. Muslim leaders near Christian frontiers often resisted central Cordoban authority, but some of the most prolonged resistance was waged by Omar ibn Hafsun, a Muwallad bandit based at the hilltop hideout of Bobastro (Málaga province). Ibn Hafsun gained a large following – partly, it's said, because he defended the peasants against taxes and forced labour – and at one stage controlled territory from Cartagena to the Strait of Gibraltar. His rebellion was carried on by his sons for 10 years after his death in 917.

Cordoban Caliphate (929–1031) In 929 Abd ar-Rahman III (912–61) bestowed

upon himself the title caliph (meaning supreme religious, political and military leader of the Muslim world) to assert his authority in the face of a rival Muslim state in Tunisia, ruled by the Shiite Fatimids. Thus he launched the Caliphate of Córdoba, during which Al-Andalus reached its greatest power and lustre. At its peak, the caliphate encompassed most of the Iberian Peninsula south of the Río Duero, plus the Balearic Islands and some of North Africa. Córdoba at this time was the biggest, most dazzling and most cultured city in Western Europe, thriving on agriculture and the work of its skilled artisans. Astronomy, medicine, mathematics, philosophy, history and botany flourished, and one of the greatest Muslim libraries was established in the city. Abd ar-Rahman III's court was frequented by Jewish, Arabian and Christian scholars. Even Christians from northern Spain came to be treated by its renowned doctors.

Later in the 10th century, the fearsome Cordoban general Al-Mansour (or Almanzor) terrorised the Christian north with 50-odd *razzias* (forays) in 20 years. In 997 he destroyed the cathedral at Santiago de Compostela in north-western Spain – home of the cult of Santiago Matamoros (St James the Moor-Slayer), which was a crucial inspiration to Christian warriors. Al-Mansour also conquered Morocco and, though not caliph, effectively ruled Al-Andalus. But after the death of his son in 1008, the caliphate imploded in a devastating civil war. In 1031 it disintegrated into dozens of *taifas* (small kingdoms), ruled by local potentates, often Berber generals.

Rise of Sevilla Such was the disintegration that for Andalucía alone the list of the largest of the small kingdoms totals 12: Algeciras, Almería, Arcos, Carmona, Córdoba, Granada, Huelva, Málaga, Morón, Niebla, Ronda and Sevilla. Granada and Sevilla were the strongest.

Sevilla's Abbasid dynasty, with access to the trading and agricultural wealth of the lower Guadalquivir valley, was soon able to start absorbing other kingdoms – they did this by a variety of means, including

MARTIN MOOS

DAN HERRICK

SARA-JANE CLELAND

OLIVER STREWE

OLIVER STREWE

DAN HERRICK

It's not often that you see people hurry in Andalucía. The pace of life is slow and time is a fluid commodity. It's a region to be savoured – visitors and locals take time to catch up on the news and soak up their surroundings.

OLIVER STREWE

MARTIN MOOS

MARTIN MOOS

SARA-JANE CLELAND

MARTIN MOOS

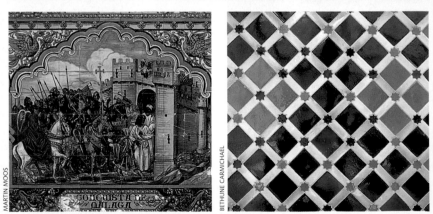
BETHUNE CARMICHAEL

A region at the forefront of thousands of years of Spanish history, Andalucía is steeped in the cultural legacies of its occupiers. Intricate tiles and lavish shrines on palaces and private houses illuminate this tumultuous past.

suffocating the rulers of Morón, Arcos and Ronda in the bathhouse of Sevilla's Alcázar. By 1078, Sevilla's writ ran all the way from southern Portugal to Murcia, restoring a large measure of peace and prosperity to Andalucía.

Almoravids Meanwhile, the small northern Christian states were getting themselves into more threatening shape. Castile (Castilla), originally a small principality within the kingdom of León, emerged as the dominant force in the 11th century. When Toledo fell to Alfonso VI of Castile in 1085, Sevilla begged help from the Almoravids, a fanatical Muslim sect of Saharan Berbers who had conquered Morocco. The Almoravids came, defeated Alfonso in Extremadura (Sagrajas) in 1086, and went back to Morocco. They then returned in 1091 to help themselves to Al-Andalus too.

Aghast at what they saw as the decadence of Al-Andalus, the Almoravids ruled it from Marrakech as a colony, and persecuted Jews and Christians (many fled north into Christian territory). But the charms of Al-Andalus seemed to relax the austere grip of the Almoravids. A wave of revolts spread across the region from 1143 and within a few years it had again split into kingdoms.

Almohads A new, strict Muslim Berber sect, the Almohads from the Atlas Mountains, displaced the Almoravids in Morocco and then started nibbling at Al-Andalus. So too did the Christians: Portugal, an emerging kingdom in the west of the Iberian Peninsula, took Lisbon in 1147. Alfonso VII of Castile and the kingdom of León took Córdoba in 1146 and Almería in 1157, but quickly lost them to the Almohads, who invaded Al-Andalus in 1160. They brought it under full control by 1173, but what they ruled was considerably less than the Al-Andalus of its 10th-century heyday: the frontier now ran from south of Lisbon to north of Valencia.

The Almohads made Sevilla capital of their whole realm (which included Algeria, Tunisia and Morocco) and revived arts and learning, building Sevilla a big new mosque.

In 1195, King Yousouf Yacoub al-Mansour successfully thrashed Castile's army at Alarcos, south of Toledo, but this only had the effect of uniting most of the increasingly strong Christian states against him. In 1212 the combined armies of Castile, Aragón-Catalunya and Navarra routed a large Almohad force at Las Navas de Tolosa in north-eastern Andalucía – the beginning of the end for Al-Andalus.

The Almohad state cracked in a succession dispute after 1224, and the Christians took full advantage. Castile's Fernando III (El Santo, the Saint) took the strategic town of Baeza, in north-eastern Andalucía, in 1227. León took the key towns of Extremadura in 1229 and 1230, while Aragón-Catalunya took the Valencia region in the 1230s. Fernando III took Córdoba easily in 1236, and won Jaén in 1246 by agreeing to respect the frontiers of the Emirate of Granada, a wedge of territory carved out of the disintegrating Almohad realm by one Mohammed ibn Yousouf ibn Nasr. Ibn Nasr agreed to pay half his income in tribute to Castile and sent a troop of cavalry to join Fernando's attack on Sevilla, which fell, after a two-year siege, in 1248.

Nasrid Emirate of Granada Portugal's defeat of the Muslims in 1249 left the Granada kingdom, known as the Nasrid emirate after ibn Nasr, as the only Muslim state on the Iberian Peninsula. It comprised roughly the modern provinces of Granada, Málaga and Almería, plus bordering bits of Cádiz, Sevilla, Córdoba and Jaén, and had a population of about 300,000, of whom some 50,000 were in Granada itself.

The Nasrids ruled from Granada's lavish Alhambra palace. The city saw the final flowering in Spain of Muslim culture and the state prospered with an influx of refugees from conquered Muslim lands. In between bouts of fighting, Granada traded with Christian Spain, selling silk, dried fruits, sugar and spices, and buying salt, oil and other staples. The emirate reached its greatest glory in the 14th century under Yousouf I and Mohammed V, both of whom contributed to the splendours of the Alhambra.

Castilian armies eventually began nibbling at the emirate in the 15th century. Granada's final downfall was precipitated by two things. One was Emir Abu al-Hasan's refusal in 1476 to pay any more tribute to Castile. The other was the unification in 1479 of Castile and Aragón-Catalunya, the peninsula's biggest and most powerful Christian states, through the marriage of their monarchs Isabel and Fernando (Isabella and Ferdinand). The Reyes Católicos (Catholic Monarchs), as Isabel and Fernando are known, launched the final crusade of the Reconquista – against Granada – in 1482.

By now, Granada's rulers were riven by harem jealousies and other feuds. Matters degenerated into a confused civil war, allowing the Christians to push across the emirate, besieging towns and devastating the countryside. They captured Alhama de Granada in 1482, Málaga (whose people were mostly sold as slaves) in 1487, and Granada itself, after an eight-month siege, on 2 January 1492.

The surrender terms were fairly generous to Boabdil, the last emir, who got the Alpujarras valleys south of Granada as a personal fiefdom. He stayed there only a year, however, before leaving for Africa. The Muslims were promised respect for their religion, culture and property, but this didn't last long.

13th- & 14th-Century Christian Andalucía

Much of the Muslim population from areas that fell to the Christians in the 13th century fled to Granada or North Africa. The new Christian rulers gave smallholdings to Christian settlers in an attempt to repopulate the countryside. They also handed out large tracts of land to the nobility and to the knightly crusading orders – such as the Orden de Santiago (Order of Santiago) and Orden de Calatrava – who had played a part in the Reconquista. This was the origin of the *latifundia* (large estates), which have been a problematical feature of rural Andalucía ever since. Muslim raids from Granada often made the lesser settlers flee or sell their lands to the nobility and orders, whose land-holdings thus increased. By 1300, rural Christian Andalucía was almost

The Muslim Legacy

The Muslims left a deep imprint on Andalucía – and not just because of the palaces, castles, mosques and bathhouses which rank among the greatest monuments today. For a start, many, if not most, Spaniards are, through medieval interbreeding, partly descended from the Muslims.

The typically narrow, labyrinthine street plan of Andalucian villages and towns is of Muslim origin, as are the predilection for fountains and running water and the use of plants as decoration. Muslim architectural tastes and crafts were adopted by Christians in and outside Al-Andalus (the Muslim territories), and many of these techniques and motifs remain in use in Spain today. Flamenco song, though brought to its modern form by *gitanos* (Roma people) in post-Muslim times, has pretty clear Islamic roots. The Spanish language contains numerous words of Arabic origin – including *arroz* (rice), *alcalde* (mayor), *naranja* (orange) and *azúcar* (sugar). Many of the foods eaten in Andalucía today were introduced by the Muslims, and in many places the irrigation and terracing systems on which foods are grown date back to Muslim times. Lots of Andalucian churches are converted mosques.

It was through Al-Andalus that much of the learning of ancient Greece was transmitted to Christian Europe. The Arabs, during the course of their conquests in the eastern Mediterranean, had absorbed the Greek scientific and philosophical traditions, translating classical works into Arabic and refining and enlarging such sciences as astronomy and medicine. There were two meeting points in southern Europe between the Islamic and Christian worlds where this knowledge could find its way north – one was southern Italy, the other was Al-Andalus.

empty. The landowners turned much of it over to sheep, ruining former food-growing land.

Fernando III's son Alfonso X (El Sabio, The Learned; 1252–84) made Sevilla one of his capitals and launched something of a cultural revival, gathering around him scholars, particularly Jews, who knew Arabic and Latin and could translate ancient texts into Castilian Spanish.

Initially, Mudéjares (Muslims who remained in Christian territory) faced no reprisals. But in 1264 the Mudéjares of Jerez rose up against new taxes and rules that required them to celebrate Christian feasts and live in ghettoes. After a five-month siege they were expelled to Granada or North Africa, along with the Mudéjares of Sevilla, Córdoba and Arcos.

Alfonso was plagued by further uprisings and plots, even from within his own family. The Castilian nobility, rich from wool production on their huge estates, went on challenging the crown until the 15th century. Meanwhile, their preoccupation with wool allowed Jews and foreigners, especially Genoese, to dominate Castilian commerce and finance.

The Black Death and a series of bad harvests ravaged Christian Andalucía in the 14th century. Discontent eventually found its scapegoat in the Jews – resented for their involvement in tax collecting and money-lending – who were subjected to pogroms around the peninsula in the 1390s. As a result, some Jews converted to Christianity (they became known as *conversos*); others moved to Granada.

The Catholic Monarchs

The pious Isabel and Machiavellian Fernando (see the earlier Nasrid Emirate of Granada section) were an unbeatable team. The Granada campaign was just one of the steps they took to cement their subjects' loyalty. They checked the power of the Castilian nobility, excluding them from the royal administration and granting Andalucian land to their own supporters. They also reformed a corrupt clergy. By the time Fernando died in 1516 (12 years after Isabel –

KATE NOLAN

Through marriage and belief, Isabel, Catholic crusader, united Spain under a single rule.

both are buried in Granada), Spain was united under a single rule for the first time since Visigothic days.

Jews & the Inquisition The urge for unity was not just territorial. The Catholic Monarchs revived the Inquisition – originally founded in the 13th century to deal with heretics in France – to root out those who didn't practise Christianity as the Catholic church wished them to. The Spanish Inquisition focused most of all on conversos, accusing many of these converted Jews of continuing to practise Judaism in secret. Despite Fernando's part-Jewish background and Jewish loans for the Granada war, Jews were considered Muslim allies. The Inquisition's first tribunal was held in Sevilla in 1481. In its three centuries of existence, the Inquisition was responsible for perhaps 12,000 deaths, 2000 of them in the 1480s.

Under the influence of Grand Inquisitor Tomás de Torquemada, in 1492 Isabel and Fernando ordered the expulsion from their territories of every Jew who refused

Christian baptism. Some 200,000, the first Sephardic Jews (Jews of Spanish origin), left for other Mediterranean destinations. Around 50,000 to 100,000 Jews converted, but the bankrupt monarchy seized all unsold Jewish property. A talented urban middle class was decimated.

Persecution of the Muslims Cardinal Cisneros, Isabel's confessor and overseer of the Inquisition, was given the task of converting the Muslims of the former Granada emirate. He carried out forced mass baptisms, had Islamic books burnt and banned the Arabic language. This, combined with expropriations of Muslim land, sparked a revolt in 1500 in the Alpujarras valleys which spread right across the former emirate, from Ronda to Almería. Afterwards, Muslims were ordered to convert to Christianity or leave. Most, an estimated 300,000, underwent baptism and stayed. They became known as Moriscos (converted Muslims), but their conversion was barely skin-deep and they never assimilated to Christian culture.

Sevilla & the Americas
In April 1492 the Catholic Monarchs granted the Genoese sailor Christopher Columbus (Cristóbal Colón to Spaniards) funds to sail across the Atlantic in search of a new trade route to the Orient. Isabel and Fernando were motivated by the urgent need to fill their empty coffers, as well as the possibility of more Christian conversions.

Columbus' finding of the Americas (for his story, see the boxed text 'The Four Voyages of Christopher Columbus' in the Huelva Province chapter) opened up a whole new hemisphere of opportunity for Spain, and especially for the river port of Sevilla. The Casa de la Contratación, a government office controlling commerce with the new colonies, was soon established in Sevilla.

During the reign of Carlos I (Charles I; 1516–56), the first of the new Habsburg dynasty, Spain occupied vast tracts of the American mainland. Ruthless but brilliant conquerors such as Hernán Cortés and Francisco Pizarro, who subdued the Aztec and Inca empires respectively with small bands of adventurers, were, with their mix of brutality and bravery, gold lust and piety, the natural successors to the crusaders of the Reconquista.

The new colonies sent huge quantities of silver, gold and other treasure back to Spain, where the crown was entitled to one-fifth of the bullion (the *quinto real*, or royal fifth). Sevilla became the hub of world trade, a cosmopolitan melting pot of money seekers, and remained Spain's major city until late in the 17th century, even though little Madrid was made the national capital in 1561.

The prosperity was shared to some extent by Cádiz and the lower Guadalquivir area, and less so by cities such as Jaén, Córdoba and Granada. But eastern Andalucía still depended on technologically backward agriculture and craftsmanship. Those peasants who still lived off the land lacked any way of improving their lot, while a small number of big landowners did little with large tracts of territory except raise sheep on them.

Sevilla's cosmopolitan status opened up Andalucía to new European ideas and artistic movements. Lavish Renaissance and, later, baroque buildings sprouted and Sevilla became a focus of Spain's artistic golden age. New universities in Sevilla (1505), Granada (1531) and Baeza (1542) spread the humanist ideas of the Renaissance, which led to a questioning of Roman Catholic dogma by so-called *protestantes* or *alumbrados* (enlightened ones) in a few centres. These nascent flickers of Protestantism were soon snuffed out by the Inquisition.

Morisco Revolt & Expulsion
Felipe II (Philip II; 1556–98) was, among other things, a fanatical Catholic who, as well as spurring the Inquisition to renewed persecutions, in 1567 forbade Moriscos (ex-Muslims) to use the Arabic language, Arabic names, Morisco dress or practise certain Morisco customs. The Moriscos were blamed – with reason – for some of

the frequent raids on Spanish coasts from North Africa. A Morisco revolt in the Alpujarras spread across southern Andalucía and took two years to put down, resulting in the expulsion of the Moriscos from the rebel areas and Granada to western Andalucía and more northerly parts of Spain. Among other things, this ruined the Granada silk industry. The Moriscos were finally expelled from all of Spain by Felipe III between 1609 and 1614.

Decline

Even under Carlos I, Spain had been spending much of its new wealth on European wars, which wrecked any chance of the country developing into an early industrial power. There was no plan to absorb the American wealth, or to cope with the inflation it caused. The gentry's disdain for commerce and industry allowed Genoese and German merchants to dominate trade, and left the countryside full of sheep and cattle ranches, with Spain running a trade deficit because grain had to be imported.

In the 17th century, under the last three ineffectual Habsburg kings, Spain's European wars continued while silver shipments from the Americas shrank disastrously. In Andalucía, epidemics and runs of bad harvests killed some 300,000 people – including half of Sevilla in 1649. Coming after the expulsions of the Jews and Moriscos, this left Andalucía distinctly under-populated. The lower Guadalquivir, Sevilla's lifeline to the Atlantic, became increasingly silted up and in 1717 the Casa de la Contratación (see the earlier Sevilla & the Americas section) was transferred to Cádiz.

The gentry and the church apart, most Andalucians had no land or property, and the cities had to pay heavy taxes and send soldiers to fight in the kings' wars.

The 18th Century

Under the new Bourbon dynasty – still in place today – Spain made a limited recovery in the 18th century. This was the age of the Enlightenment, with its faith in reason, science and social planning. The monarchy financed incipient industries, such as Sevilla's tobacco factory. A new road, the Carretera General de Andalucía, was built from Madrid to Sevilla and Cádiz. Along the Andalucian section, Carlos III's reforming minister Pablo de Olavide founded a couple of dozen new towns, with straight streets, broad squares and German and Flemish settlers. The idea was both to repopulate empty and rather lawless areas and to modernise Andalucía's agriculture. But the project was opposed by the big landowners (who didn't like releasing land) and the church (because many of the settlers were Protestants), and had little effect.

New land was opened up for wheat and barley, however, and trade through Cádiz (whose heyday this was) grew. Free trade decrees in 1765 and 1778 made it legal for additional Spanish ports to conduct commerce with the Americas, which stimulated the growth of Málaga. New settlers from other parts of Spain had by 1787 boosted Andalucía's population to about 1.8 million.

Napoleonic Invasion & the Cádiz Cortes

When Louis XVI of France (a cousin of Spain's Carlos IV) was guillotined in 1793, Spain declared war on France. Two years later, with French forces occupying northern Spain, Spain switched sides, pledging military support for France against Britain in return for French withdrawal from Spain. In 1805 a combined Spanish-French navy was beaten by the British fleet under Nelson off Cape Trafalgar (which lies between Cádiz and Gibraltar). This terminated Spanish sea power.

Two years later, Napoleon Bonaparte and Spain agreed to divide Portugal, Britain's ally, between them. French forces poured into Spain, supposedly on the way to Portugal, but by 1808 this had become a French occupation of Spain, with Napoleon forcing Carlos IV to abdicate to his brother, Joseph Bonaparte (José I). In the ensuing Spanish War of Independence, or Peninsular War, the Spanish populace took up arms in guerrilla fashion, and with help from British and Portuguese forces led by the Duke of Wellington, drove the French out by 1813.

During the war, few Spanish cities kept the French at bay, but Cádiz withstood a two-year siege from 1810 to 1812. A national parliament which convened in the city during the siege adopted a new constitution for Spain which proclaimed sovereignty of the people and reduced the rights of the monarchy, nobility and church.

Liberals v Conservatives

The Cádiz constitution set the scene for a century of struggle between Spanish liberals, who wanted vaguely democratic reforms, and conservatives who wanted to maintain the status quo. Fernando VII, son of Carlos IV, revoked the new constitution, persecuted opponents and even reestablished the Inquisition. In 1820 in Las Cabezas de San Juan, Sevilla province, Colonel Rafael de Riego made the first of 19th-century Spain's many *pronunciamientos* (pronouncements of military rebellion) in the name of liberalism. But French troops put Fernando back on the throne in 1823 (Riego was captured in Jaén and hung, drawn and quartered in Madrid).

Meanwhile, Spain's American colonies had taken advantage of its problems to strike out on their own. Mexico and most of South and Central America achieved independence between 1813 and 1825 – desperate news for Cádiz, which had been totally reliant on trade with the colonies.

The Disamortisations of 1836 and 1855, when liberal governments ordered church and municipal lands to be auctioned off to reduce the national debt, pleased the bourgeoisie, who could build up new estates. But they were a disaster for the peasants who lost municipal grazing lands.

Despite being home to one-quarter of Spain's 12 million population in 1877, Andalucía declined into one of Europe's most backward, socially polarised areas. At one social extreme were the bourgeoisie and the very rich, often absentee, aristocratic landowners. At the other were a small number of poor people with regular jobs and a large number of even poorer *jornaleros* – landless agricultural day labourers who were without work for a good half of the year and who, with their families, probably comprised three-quarters of the population. Illiteracy, disease and hunger were rife. The Industrial Revolution had reached northern Spain in the late 18th century, but barely touched the south. The few successful industries – such as the Río Tinto mines and the Jerez and Málaga wineries – owed much to British investment and management.

In 1873 a liberal government proclaimed Spain's First Republic – a federal grouping of 17 states. The republic was totally unable to control its provinces, where numerous cities and towns declared themselves independent states. Some even declared war on each other, as happened between Sevilla and nearby Utrera! The First Republic lasted only 11 months, with the army restoring the monarchy.

Anarchism & Socialism

In the face of lost grazing lands, erratic, miserably paid work and hunger, some Andalucian peasants emigrated to Latin America. Others staged uprisings, always savagely put down, from the mid-19th century onwards. The anarchist ideas of the Russian Mikhail Bakunin gained a big following in Andalucía, especially in the lower Guadalquivir area, where the estate owners monopoly on cultivable land was most complete. Bakunin advocated strikes, sabotage and revolts as the path to a spontaneous revolution of the oppressed that would usher in a free society in which autonomous groups of people would voluntarily co-operate with each other.

The powerful anarchist union, the Confederación Nacional del Trabajo (CNT, National Labour Confederation), was founded in Sevilla in 1910. Anarchist trade unionists, known as syndicalists, saw the general strike as the main weapon to achieve an anarchist society. But major anarchist actions in Andalucía, such as the occupation of Jerez de la Frontera by 4000 labourers armed with sticks one day in 1891, brought violent repression which sent the movement back underground for years at a time. Waves of anarchist strikes occurred in 1902–5 and 1917–18.

Socialism, with its aim of steady change through parliamentary processes, won less support in Andalucía. By 1919, the CNT had 93,000 members in Andalucía, compared with the 12,000 of the socialist Unión General de Trabajadores (UGT, General Union of Workers), and 7000 in Catholic unions.

In 1923 an eccentric general from Jerez, Miguel Primo de Rivera, launched a mild military dictatorship, which won the co-operation of the UGT, while anarchists went underground. Primo achieved more industrialisation, better roads, punctual trains, new dams and power plants. He was unseated in 1930 by an economic downturn and by discontent in the army, with King Alfonso XIII taking the chance to dismiss him.

The Second Republic

When a new republican movement scored sweeping victories in Spain's municipal elections in April 1931, Alfonso XIII departed to exile in Italy. The Second Republic that ensued (1931–6) was an idealistic, tumultuous period that ended in civil war.

The Left in Charge (1931–3) La Niña Bonita (the Pretty Child), as the Second Republic was called by its supporters, was welcomed by leftists and the poor, but conservatives were alarmed. Elections in 1931 brought in a mixed government including socialists, centrists and Republicans, but the Cortes (Parliament) contained few workers and no-one from the anarchist CNT, which preferred strikes and violence to bring on the revolution.

A new constitution in December 1931 outraged Catholics by stopping government payment of priests' salaries, legalising divorce and banning clerical orders from teaching. The constitution promised land redistribution, which pleased the Andalucian landless, but failed to deliver much.

The Right in Charge (1933–6) Anarchist disruption, an economic slump, the alienation of big business and disunity on the left all helped the right win the 1933 election. A Catholic party, Confederación

Española de Derechas Autónomas (CEDA, Spanish Confederation of Autonomous Rights) won the most seats. Another new force on the right was the fascist Falange, led by José Antonio Primo de Rivera, son of the 1920s dictator. The Falange practised blatant street violence. The left, including the emerging Communists (who, unlike the socialists, supported the Russian Revolution), called increasingly for revolution.

By 1934 violence was spiralling out of control. When workers' committees which had taken over the northern mining region of Asturias were viciously quashed by generals Millán Astray and Francisco Franco, along with the Spanish Foreign Legion (set up to fight Moroccan tribes in the 1920s), the whole country was polarised into left and right.

Popular Front & Army Uprising In the February 1936 elections the Popular Front left-wing coalition narrowly defeated the right-wing National Front. Violence continued on both sides of the political divide. The CNT now had over one million members and peasants were on the verge of revolution.

On 17 July 1936 the Spanish garrison in Melilla in North Africa revolted against the leftist government, followed the next day by some garrisons on the mainland. The leaders of the plot were five generals. On 19 July one of them, Francisco Franco, flew from the Canary Islands to Morocco to take command of his legionnaires. The civil war had begun.

The Civil War

The Spanish Civil War split communities, families and friends. Both sides committed atrocious massacres and reprisals, in the early weeks especially. The rebels, who called themselves Nationalists, shot or hanged tens of thousands of supporters of the Republic. Republicans did likewise to those they considered Franco sympathisers, including some 7000 priests, monks and nuns. Political affiliation often provided a convenient cover for settling old scores. Around 350,000 Spaniards died in the war.

In Republican areas, anarchists, Communists or socialists ended up running many towns and cities. Social revolution followed. In Andalucía this tended to be anarchist, with private property abolished and churches and convents often burned and wrecked. Large estates were occupied by the peasants and around 100 agrarian communes were established. The Nationalist campaign, meanwhile, quickly took on overtones of a holy crusade against the enemies of God.

Nationalist Advance The basic battle lines were drawn within a week of the rebellion in Morocco. Cities whose garrisons backed the rebels (most did) and were strong enough to overcome any resistance fell immediately into Nationalist hands – as happened at Cádiz, Córdoba, Algeciras and Jerez. Sevilla was in Nationalist hands within three days and Granada within a few more. Hugh Thomas, in his authoritative work *The Spanish Civil War*, estimates that 4000 people were executed by the Nationalists in and around Granada after they had taken the city, saying that this was probably characteristic of Nationalist Spain generally. There was slaughter in Republican areas too. An estimated 2500 people were murdered in a few months in anarchist Málaga. A gang from Málaga killed over 500 people in Ronda in the first month of the war.

From Sevilla, Nationalist troops mopped up most of western Andalucía by the end of July and relieved Granada in August. Málaga fell, with little resistance, to Italian and Spanish Nationalist troops in February 1937. When the Nationalists captured Republican towns they exacted bloody revenge for any supposed atrocities carried out there: thousands were executed after they took Málaga.

After the fall of Málaga there was little shift in the military position in Andalucía for the rest of the war. Almería and Jaén provinces, the eastern half of Granada province and the north of Córdoba province all remained Republican until the end of the war in 1939.

General Franco emerged as the undisputed Nationalist leader in late 1936, styling himself Generalísimo (Supreme General). Before long, he also declared himself head of state and adopted the title Caudillo, roughly equivalent to the German Führer.

Foreign Intervention The scales were tipped in the Nationalists' favour by support from Nazi Germany and Fascist Italy – weapons, planes and 92,000 men (the majority from Italy). The Republicans had some Soviet planes, tanks, artillery and advisers, and 25,000 or so French and as many other foreigners in the International Brigades, fought on their side.

Republican Quarrels, Nationalist Victory The Republican government moved from besieged Madrid to Valencia in late 1936. The diversity of political persuasions on the Republican side erupted into fierce street fighting in Barcelona in May 1937, with the Soviet-backed Communists crushing the anarchists and Trotskyites. The Republican government moved to Barcelona in autumn 1937.

In 1938 Franco swept eastward, isolating Barcelona from Valencia, and the USSR withdrew from the war. The Nationalists took Barcelona unopposed in January 1939 and Madrid in March. Franco declared the war won on 1 April 1939.

Franco's Spain (1939–75)

After the civil war, instead of reconciliation, more blood-letting ensued. An estimated 100,000 Spaniards were killed, or died in prison, after the war. Spanish Communists and Republicans continued their hopeless struggle in small guerrilla units in the Andalucian mountain ranges and elsewhere until the 1950s.

Franco kept Spain out of WWII, but afterwards Spain was excluded from the United Nations until 1955 and suffered a UN-sponsored trade boycott which helped turn the late 1940s into the *años de hambre* (years of hunger) – particularly hungry in poor areas like Andalucía where, at times, peasants subsisted on soup made from grass and wild herbs.

From 1939 to 1975 General Francisco Franco ruled over every aspect of Spanish life.

Franco ruled absolutely. He was commander of the army and leader of the government and the sole political party, the Movimiento Nacional (National Movement). Army garrisons were maintained outside every large city and the jails were full of political prisoners. Catholic orthodoxy was fully restored, with most secondary schools entrusted to the Jesuits; divorce was made illegal and church weddings compulsory. Crime rates were low and strikes were illegal.

In the late 1950s a new breed of technocrats in government engineered an economic boom. In Andalucía, despite some new industries and the take-off of tourism on the Costa del Sol, many villages still lacked electricity, reliable water supplies and paved roads to the outside world. Between 1950 and 1970 some 1.5 million Andalucians left to find work elsewhere – some went to other European countries, but more to Barcelona, Madrid and other Spanish cities. Although tourism certainly created jobs for some Andalucians, it also brought culture shock to what was still an old-fashioned, traditional society.

New Democracy

Franco chose as his successor Alfonso XIII's grandson, Prince Juan Carlos, who took the throne, aged 37, two days after Franco's death in 1975. Much of the credit for the ensuing transition to democracy goes to the king. The man he appointed prime minister, Adolfo Suárez, pushed through the Francoist-filled Cortes a proposal for a new, two-chamber parliamentary system. In 1977 political parties, trade unions and strikes were all legalised, the Movimiento Nacional was abolished and Suárez's centrist party won nearly half the seats in elections to the new Cortes. The left-of-centre Partido Socialista Obrero Español (PSOE, Spanish Socialist Workers' Party), led by a young lawyer from Sevilla, Felipe González, came in second.

Personal and social life, too, enjoyed a sudden liberation after Franco. Contraceptives, homosexuality, adultery and divorce were legalised, and it was during this era that the *movida* – the late bar and club scene that enables people almost anywhere in Spain to party till dawn or after – emerged.

Government by the PSOE & PP

In 1982 Spain made a final break with the past by voting the PSOE into power with a big majority. Felipe González was to be prime minister for 14 years, taking several other Andalucians into high office with him. The party's young, educated leadership came from the generation that had opened the cracks in the Franco regime in the late 1960s and early 1970s. It made big improvements in education, launched a national health system, and legalised the use of narcotics in 1983 and abortion in 1985 (in the face of drug and alcoholism problems, public use of narcotics was banned in 1992).

In 1986 Spain joined the EC (now the EU), which brought on its second post-civil war economic boom, lasting until 1991, and cut unemployment to 16%. The PSOE, however, began to figure in a series of scandals. Questions were asked about how the party got hold of its substantial funds. González's long-standing number two, another *sevillano* (citizen of Sevilla), Alfonso

Guerra, resigned as deputy prime minister in 1991 over an affair involving his wheeler-dealer brother's use of a government office. Most damaging was the GAL affair, named after the Grupos Antiterroristas de Liberación, death squads that had murdered 28 suspected Basque terrorists in the mid-1980s. Eventually, in 1998, a dozen senior police and PSOE men were jailed in connection with GAL.

In the face of all this and a post-1991 economic slump, the PSOE lost the 1996 general election to the Partido Popular (PP, People's Party), a centre-right party under the leadership of a former tax inspector, José María Aznar. After four years of steady economic progress and no scandals, Aznar and the PP won again in 2000.

Andalucía since Franco PSOE government at national and regional level eradicated the worst of Andalucian poverty with a series of grants and community works schemes and a much more generous dole system. The left-of-centre party dominated Andalucía's regional government in Sevilla from its inauguration in 1982. The 1992 Expo world fair in Sevilla – held the same year as the Barcelona Olympic Games, exactly five centuries on from the pivotal year of Spanish history, 1492 – brought hundreds of thousands of visitors and a big boost to the international image of Sevilla and Andalucía, plus the new high-speed Alta Velocidad Española (AVE) railway from Madrid to Sevilla, and a big improvement in Andalucía's roads.

Tourism and gradual industrial growth have helped the economic picture too, as has the overall improvement of the Spanish economy since the mid-1990s. Andalucía still lags behind most of Spain, but it has an air of growing prosperity and confidence which would surprise any Andalucian returning home today after 40 years on Mars – as would the bright lights and high-rise public housing blocks in the cities, the transformation of long stretches of formerly useless, barren coast into international honey (and money) pots, the relaxation of old codes of dress and morality, the loud

new music, the motorcycles instead of donkeys, the rarity of hunger, the universal schooling, youth literacy and large numbers of university students. Yet not everything would be unfamiliar. Andalucians remain a close-knit bunch, oriented first to their family, second to their village or town, third to their district, fourth to their province, and finally, about equally to Andalucía and Spain. They know they must still stick together because the relatively good times have not lasted long enough to obliterate the memory of the bad ones.

GEOGRAPHY
Andalucía stretches 550km from east to west and between 90 and 250km from north to south. Its 87,000-sq-km area – about the same size as Portugal – comprises 17% of Spain. The region has 460km of coastline along the Mediterranean Sea, and a 240km seaboard on the Atlantic Ocean. The two meet at the Strait of Gibraltar, where the town of Tarifa, just 15km from Africa, is continental Europe's most southerly point.

Andalucía has four main geographic regions, all running roughly east-west across it – the Sierra Morena, the Guadalquivir valley, the mountains and the coastal plain.

The Sierra Morena
The Sierra Morena, a range of low and mostly rolling hills that rarely tops 1000m, stretches across the north of Andalucía, straddling the borders with neighbouring Extremadura and Castilla-La Mancha. The area has a few mining towns, but most of it is very sparsely populated and divided between evergreen oak woodlands and scrub and rough pasture used for grazing. Different bits of the Sierra Morena have their own names, such as the Sierra del Viento in Sevilla province and the Sierra de Aroche and Sierra de Aracena in Huelva province.

Guadalquivir Valley
Across Andalucía, south of the Sierra Morena, stretches the fertile valley of the 660km Río Guadalquivir, Andalucía's longest river. The Guadalquivir flows approximately westward from Jaén province

through Córdoba, then turns south through Sevilla to enter the Atlantic at Sanlúcar de Barrameda. From the lower Guadalquivir, a broad plain stretches west across Huelva province and south-east into Cádiz province. Before entering the ocean, the Guadalquivir splits into a marshy delta known as Las Marismas del Guadalquivir, which includes the Parque Nacional de Doñana.

The Guadalquivir is navigable as far upstream as Sevilla, and used to be navigable up to Córdoba. These two cities, amid rich agricultural country, have been the main seats of political power in Andalucía since Roman times. The name Guadalquivir derives from the Arabic Wadi al-Kabir (Great River): the Romans called it the Betis and the ancient Greeks the Tartessos.

The plains rolling north and south from the river as far downstream as Sevilla are known as la campiña. From about Córdoba downstream, the valley is referred to as the lower Guadalquivir basin: this is the territory of huge estates, which have been the source of some of Andalucía's greatest social problems.

The Mountains

Between the Guadalquivir valley and the Mediterranean coast rises the Cordillera Bética, a band of rugged mountain ranges which widens out from its beginnings in south-west Andalucía to a breadth of 125km or so in the east. Beyond Andalucía, the mountain chain continues across the Murcia and Valencia regions, then re-emerges from the Mediterranean as the Balearic islands of Ibiza and Mallorca.

In Andalucía, the cordillera divides into two main chains: the more northerly Sistema Subbético and the southerly Sistema Penibético. Both begin in the green, rainy hills south and south-west of Ronda. The two chains are separated by a series of valleys, plains and basins, such as the Llanos de Antequera, the Vega de Granada, the Hoya de Guadix and the Hoya de Baza.

In the north-east of Andalucía, the Sistema Subbético turns into the picturesque and complicated collection of 2000m-plus ranges – here running almost north-south –

which make up the Parque Natural de Cazorla in Jaén province, source of the Río Guadalquivir.

The Sistema Penibético incorporates the 75km-long Sierra Nevada, south-east of Granada, with a series of 3000m-plus peaks, including Mulhacén (3478m), the highest mountain on mainland Spain.

The Coast & Coastal Plain

Andalucía's coastal plain varies in width from 50km in the far west to virtually nothing in parts of Granada and Almería provinces, where the Sierra de Contraviesa and Sierra de Cabo de Gata drop away in sheer cliffs to the Mediterranean. Where the plain is wide enough, it supports much vegetable and fruit growing.

Andalucía's most important ports are Almería, Málaga, Algeciras, Cádiz and Huelva. Tourist development has turned the 75km-long Costa del Sol from Málaga to Estepona into one almost continuous built-up strip. Elsewhere, the coast runs between smaller fishing, farming or resort towns, with – especially around the Cabo de Gata promontory east of Almería and along the Atlantic coast (called the Costa de la Luz) – plenty of fine, long, sandy beaches which for much of the year are distinctly under-populated. As well as the Marismas del Guadalquivir, further wetlands mark the mouths of several rivers along the Atlantic coast.

Dams & Desert

Nearly all Andalucía's rivers are dammed at least once in their course to supply water and hydroelectricity. You'll come across large reservoirs almost throughout the region. The exception is the very dry Almería province, which contains extensive semi-desert areas of bare, eroded terrain with enough resemblance to the Arizona badlands to have been used as the location of many Western movies!

CLIMATE

There's a marked difference between the coastal and interior climates. Inland, the weather can be pretty inclement from

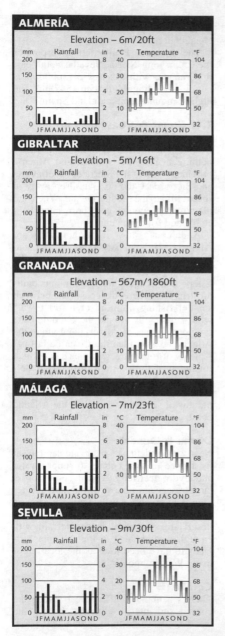

November to February and frying hot in July and August. On the coasts, temperatures are temperate in winter and not quite so hot in summer.

In July and August, daytime temperatures typically reach 36°C in Sevilla and Córdoba and only a little less in Granada and Jaén. Along the coasts, expect about 30°C. Winter weather (November to February) is unpredictable but, overall, cyclical: dry, warm winters (and drought) in the early 1990s were followed by wet, cool winters between 1995 and 1998. Then the 1998–9 and 1999–2000 winters were again dry, prompting renewed worries about drought. From December to February, average daytime highs hover round 16°C on the coasts and in Sevilla, and around 13°C in Granada and Jaén. Granada gets close to freezing at night.

Rain falls mainly between October and March, and during that period Andalucía, on average, receives a similar amount of rain to London. There's little rain from June to September. With the prevailing winds coming from the Atlantic Ocean, western Andalucía is damper than the east. In fact, the Sierra de Grazalema, west of Ronda, is the wettest part of Spain and the town of Grazalema receives over 2200mm of rain per year. Meanwhile, the Cabo de Gata promontory in Almería province is the driest place in Europe, with just 100mm a year.

Tarifa, situated at Andalucía's southernmost point, where the Atlantic Ocean meets the Mediterranean Sea, has strong winds most of the time – a mecca for windsurfers.

In the mountains, temperatures are always several degrees cooler than down on the plains and you can expect more rain and, in winter, some snow. The Sierra Nevada is snow-covered above about 3000m most of the year.

Sea temperatures hover around 20°C along most of the coast from July to October, and around 15°C from December to April.

ECOLOGY & ENVIRONMENT

Andalucía's relative lack of industry and, until recently, its fairly traditional agriculture have left it with a pretty clean environment. Each year, around 60 or 70 Andalucian beaches are awarded EU blue flags for hygiene and facilities.

There are, however, a few black spots, such as air pollution by industry in the Huelva area and large amounts of untreated sewage entering the sea along the coast east of Málaga. There have also been occasional disasters, such as the damage to areas around the Parque Nacional de Doñana in western Andalucía caused by a big leakage of poisonous mining wastes in 1998 (see the boxed text 'Aznalcóllar: The Aftermath' in the Huelva Province chapter), and scares over fertilisers which may have polluted the drinking water of the lower Guadalquivir basin.

Andalucía's environment has been significantly altered by human activity. It was the Romans who began to cut its extensive woodlands and forests for timber, fuel, weapons and space for agriculture. The Romans and Muslims opened up large areas to agriculture through irrigation and terracing of the hillsides. Later, overgrazing by huge sheep flocks brought substantial topsoil erosion – most of the Guadalquivir wetlands have been formed by deposited sediment in the past 3000 years – and imperial Spain's demand for shipbuilding timber decimated many native forests. Many animal species have been drastically depleted by hunting. Protection given to many animal and bird species has helped some, but it's probably too late for others.

Conservation

Environmental awareness in Spain took a quantum leap forward in the 1980s under the PSOE government, which gave regional administrations responsibility for most environmental matters. In 1981 Spain had 35 environmentally protected areas, covering 2200 sq km. Today there are over 400, covering more than 25,000 sq km, and Andalucía is the leader in this field (see National Parks & Reserves later in this chapter). Not that protected areas are always perfectly protected. Environmentalists have to stay alert against corrupt officials turning a blind eye to illicit building, quarrying,

hunting and so on in protected areas. The Parque Nacional de Doñana, whose wetlands are a bird habitat of huge international importance, has battled since its creation in 1969 against agricultural and tourism schemes around its fringes which threaten to reduce or pollute its water supplies. At the time of writing, an odd combination of ecologists, Andalucía's political far left and Spain's right-of-centre national government was fighting a legal battle against the Andalucian regional government to try to stop a 2-sq-km luxury holiday complex near Sanlúcar de Barrameda, on the park's fringes.

Drought

Potentially, Andalucía's worst environmental problem is drought, which struck in the 1950s and 1960s and the early 1990s and was threatening again as the 21st century dawned. This is despite huge investment in reservoirs (which cover a higher proportion of the land in Spain than in any other country in the world).

FLORA

The variety of Andalucian flora is astonishing, as anyone who witnesses the spectacular wild-flower displays in spring and early summer will testify. Andalucía has around 5000 different plant species, of which some 150 are unique to it. This abundance is largely due to the fact that the last Ice Age was relatively temperate at this southerly latitude, allowing plants which were killed off farther north to survive here. According to the Junta de Andalucía (the regional government), 46,000 sq km – more than half of Andalucía – is still forested.

High-Altitude Plants

The mountain areas are responsible for a lot of Andalucía's botanical variety. The Parque Natural de Cazorla alone has 2300 plant species (24 of them found nowhere else) and the Sierra Nevada 2100 (about 60 unique to it). When the snows melt, the alpine and subalpine zones above the tree line bloom with small, rock-clinging plants and high pastures full of gentians, orchids, crocuses and narcissi.

Mountain Forests

Many of the lower slopes are clothed in forests of pine, often commercial. The rare *pinsapo* (Spanish fir), a relic from forests of millions of years ago, exists only in the mountains around Ronda and in northern Morocco. According to the Junta de Andalucía, pines grow on 10,000 sq km of Andalucía – but they're threatened by the hairy, pine-needle-devouring caterpillars of the pine processionary moth, best steered clear of (see Cuts, Bites & Stings under Health in the Facts for the Visitor chapter).

Lowland Forests

Along river valleys you'll often find a rich variety of deciduous trees, such as poplar, ash, willow, maple, elm and alder.

In some areas, especially in Jaén and Córdoba provinces, there's nothing but lines of olive trees as far as the eye can see (see the boxed text 'Essential Oil' in the Jaén Province chapter). Another widely cultivated tree, though now unfashionable because of its insatiable thirst, is the eucalyptus. But arguably the most characteristic

The Dehesas of Andalucía

In areas such as the Sierra Morena, Sierra de Grazalema and Parque Natural Los Alcornocales, you can't help noticing the extensive woodlands-cum-pastures known as *dehesas*. Two types of useful evergreen oak predominate: the *alcornoque* (cork oak) and the *encina* (holm or ilex oak).

The cork oak's thick outer bark is stripped every ninth summer for cork – you'll see the scars on some trees, a bright terracotta colour if they're new. The holm oak can be pruned about every four years and the offcuts used for charcoal. Meanwhile, livestock can graze the pastures, and in autumn pigs are turned out to gobble up the fallen *bellotas* (acorns) – a diet considered to produce the best ham of all. Dehesas were mostly created long ago by the felling or burning-off of the original Mediterranean forest for pasture which was replanted with these useful trees.

of all Andalucian trees are the cork oak and the holm or ilex oak. By Junta de Andalucía figures, these cover 13,000 sq km of Andalucía.

Beneath Andalucía's trees sprout, in autumn, some 2000 species of fungi, many of which are edible and appear on country menus and in markets. Others are poisonous – and decisions on which are safe are best left to the local experts!

Scrub & Steppe

Where there are no trees and no agriculture, the land is likely to be either scrub or steppe-like. Scrub occurs where forests were felled and the land was later abandoned. Herbs like lavender, rosemary, fennel and thyme are typical plants, as are shrubs of the cistus family and gorse, juniper and heather. Orchids, gladioli and irises may flower beneath these shrubs, some of which are themselves colourful in spring.

Steppe is produced by overgrazing or occurs naturally in hot, very dry areas such as the south-east of Almería province. Here, plant life is sparse, often with cacti, but the area blooms with colour after rain.

FAUNA

Andalucía's wildlife is among the most varied in Europe, thanks to its wild, varied terrain, which has allowed the survival of several species that have died out in other countries – though some are now in perilously small numbers. Many animals are nocturnal and you need to be dedicated and/or lucky to track down even the more common ones. Naturally they tend to be most common in the wilder country areas, especially protected areas.

Mammals

A small number of wolves survive in the Sierra Morena (in Jaén province, the northeast of Córdoba province and neighbouring areas of Castilla-La Mancha). In 1986 the wolf was declared in danger of extinction in Andalucía and, in an effort to protect it from hunters, farmers are now awarded compensation if their animals are attacked by wolves. But the wolf population – probably not more than 100 – continues to diminish dangerously. Around 1500 wolves survive in other parts of Spain.

Things are better for the ibex, a stocky mountain goat, about 10,000 strong in Andalucía, whose males have distinctive long horns. It spends summer hopping agilely around high-altitude precipices and descends lower in winter. Around 5000 ibex live in the Sierra Nevada, 2000 in the Parque Natural de Cazorla, 1000 in the Sierra de las Nieves and a few hundred each in the Sierra de Grazalema and Sierra Almijara.

The Pardel or Iberian lynx, unique to the Iberian Peninsula and smaller than the lynx of northern Europe, is considered the world's most endangered feline. Its numbers have been reduced (to less than 600 in Spain and under 50 in Portugal) by hunting and by a decline in the number of rabbits, its staple diet. Around 50 lynx remain in Andalucía's Parque Nacional de Doñana. Other individuals survive in the Sierra Morena.

Less uncommon beasts include the mainly nocturnal wild boar, which likes thick woods, marshes and farmers' root crops; the red deer, roe deer and fallow deer in forests and woodlands of all types; the nocturnal genet, rather like a short-legged cat with a black-spotted white coat and a long, striped tail, in woodland and scrub; the red squirrel, in mountain forests; the nocturnal badger, in woods with thick undergrowth; the mainly nocturnal Egyptian mongoose, in woods, scrub and marshes; the fox, common in scattered areas; the otter; and the beech marten, in deciduous forests and on rocky outcrops and cliffs. The *mouflon*, a wild sheep, has been introduced to the Parque Natural de Cazorla and a couple of other areas for hunting.

Gibraltar is famous for its colony of Barbary macaques, the only wild monkeys in Europe. The Bahía de Algeciras and Strait of Gibraltar harbour plenty of dolphins (common, striped and bottle-nosed) and some whales (pilot, killer and even sperm), and boat trips to see them are an increasingly popular attraction from Gibraltar.

Birds

Andalucía is a magnet for bird-watchers (see Bird-Watching under Activities in the Facts for the Visitor chapter for details).

Raptors Andalucía has 13 resident raptor (bird of prey) species and several other summer visitors from Africa. You can see some of them circling or hovering over the hills in many parts of Andalucía.

The Sierra Morena is a stronghold of Europe's biggest bird, the rare black vulture. The few hundred pairs in Spain are probably the world's biggest population, and one of the biggest colonies of these birds is in the Sierra Pelada, south of Aroche in Huelva province.

Another emblematic and extremely rare bird is the Spanish imperial eagle, found in no other country. Its white shoulders distinguish it from other imperial eagles. Of the 130 pairs remaining, about 30 are in Andalucía, of which seven (at the last count) are in the Parque Nacional de Doñana. Poisoned bait put out by farmers or hunters is the imperial eagle's greatest enemy.

Other large birds of prey include the golden eagle and several other eagles, and the griffon vulture and Egyptian vulture, all found in mountain regions. Among smaller birds of prey, many of them found around deciduous or lowland woods and forests, are the common kestrel and buzzard, the sparrowhawk, harriers, and the acrobatic red kite and black kite. Black kites may be seen over open ground near marshes, rivers and rubbish dumps.

Storks The large, ungainly white stork, actually black and white, nests from spring to summer on electricity pylons, trees and towers – sometimes right in the middle of towns – in western Andalucía. Your attention will be drawn to it by the loud clacking of beaks from these lofty perches. The much rarer black stork, all black, also nests in western Andalucía, typically on cliff ledges. Both types migrate from Africa across the Strait of Gibraltar in flocks of up to 3000 to breed in Spain.

Water Birds Andalucía is a haven for water birds, mainly thanks to large wetlands along the Atlantic coast, such as the Parque Nacional de Doñana and Paraje Natural Marismas del Odiel. Hundreds of thousands of migratory birds, including an estimated 80% of Western Europe's wild ducks, winter in Doñana, and many more call in during spring and autumn migrations.

Laguna de Fuente de Piedra, near Antequera, is Europe's main breeding site for the greater flamingo, with as many as 16,000 pairs rearing chicks in spring and summer. This beautiful pink bird can also be seen in several other places, including Cabo de Gata, Doñana and the Marismas del Odiel.

Other Birds Among the most colourful of Andalucía's birds are the golden oriole, seen in orchards and deciduous woodlands

JANE SMITH

Time it right and you'll see the sky turn pink as the flamingoes head for warmer climes.

in summer (the male has an unmistakable bright yellow body); the orange-and-black hoopoe, with its distinctive crest, common in open woodlands, on farmland and golf courses; and the gold, brown and turquoise bee-eater, which nests in sandy banks in summer. Various woodpeckers and owls inhabit mountain woodlands.

Other Fauna

From spring to autumn, Andalucía is a paradise for butterfly and moth enthusiasts. Most of Europe's butterflies are found in Spain. There are several bat species, salamanders, chameleons (most numerous in the Axarquía region), numerous lizards, and snakes. See Cuts, Bites & Stings under Health in the Facts for the Visitor chapter for information on dangerous beasts.

NATIONAL PARKS & RESERVES

Much of Spain's most spectacular and ecologically important countryside is under some kind of official protection, and Andalucía has over 60% of the total protected area in Spain – over 90 protected areas covering some 17,000 sq km (20% of Andalucian territory). All these can be visited, but degrees of conservation and access vary. The most interesting usually have visitor centres with ample information on features of interest, and on where you can and can't go.

Parques Nacionales

National parks are declared by the national parliament and administered by the national and regional governments. At the time of writing, mainland Spain has seven, of which two, the Parque Nacional de Doñana and Parque Nacional Sierra Nevada, are in Andalucía.

National parks are areas of exceptional importance for their fauna, flora, geomorphology or landscape and are the most strictly controlled protected areas. They tend to have sparse human population and may include reserves, which are closed to the public, and restricted areas, which can only be visited with permission. Camping inside national parks is banned.

Parques Naturales

Natural parks are declared and administered by regional governments – in Andalucía's case this means by the Junta de Andalucía's Consejería de Medio Ambiente (Environmental Department). The 23 in Andalucía account for most of the region's protected territory and include its most spectacular countryside – ranging from the great cork oak forests of Los Alcornocales to the beautiful mountains and valleys of Cazorla (at 2140 sq km the largest single protected area in Spain) and the Sierra de Grazalema, or the rolling Sierra Morena country of the Sierra de Aracena.

Natural parks are intended to protect not only nature but also human cultural heritage. They are also designed to promote economic development that is compatible with conservation. Many of them include roads, villages or even small towns, with accommodation often available within the park. Camping is usually not allowed outside organised camp sites. In some parks there are networks of marked walking trails. Like national parks, they may include areas which can only be visited with permission.

Other Protected Areas

The two other types of protected areas in Andalucía are Paraje Natural (Natural Area; there are 31 of these) and Reserva Natural (Nature Reserve; numbering 28). These are smaller, usually little-inhabited areas, with much the same goals as natural parks. Natural areas include many of the lesser Atlantic coast wetlands. Nature reserves are the smallest areas and include many inland lakes.

Reservas Nacionales de Caza

Some wilderness areas – about 900 sq km in Andalucía – are National Hunting Reserves. These are usually well conserved for the sake of the wildlife that is to be hunted – which has to be exploited in a 'rational' manner. Hunting, though subject to restrictions, is a deeply ingrained aspect of Spanish life. Public access to the reserves is usually pretty open and you might walk or drive across one without even knowing it. If you hear shots, though, it is advisable to be cautious!

GOVERNMENT & POLITICS

Since 1978 Spain has been a constitutional monarchy. The national parliament, the Cortes Generales, comprises the Congreso de los Diputados (lower house) and Senado (upper house). Both houses are elected by free universal suffrage.

The 1978 constitution provided for substantial devolution of power to Spain's regions. As a result, Spain is now divided into 17 autonomous communities, each with its own parliament, government and supreme court. Andalucía's parliament sits in Sevilla and its 109 members are chosen by universal suffrage every four years. The executive government, called the Junta de Andalucía, is headed by a president. The parliament and executive *(junta)* have been controlled by the PSOE ever since autonomy began in 1982 – although recently the PSOE has been governing without an absolute parliamentary majority after the break-up of a coalition with the communist Izquierda Unida (IU, United Left), which usually gets around 15% to 20% of the vote. Manuel Chaves has been the junta's president since 1990.

The policy areas that are controlled at autonomous-community level vary. Andalucía, the most populous autonomous community, has more powers than most, including over industry, agriculture, tourism, education, health, social security, environmental conservation and non-national roads and railways. But, since the national government has a far larger budget than that of the autonomous community, many of the important decisions are still made in Madrid.

Each autonomous community consists of one or more provinces. Andalucía has eight, all named after their capital cities – Almería, Cádiz, Córdoba, Granada, Huelva, Jaén, Málaga and Sevilla. The provinces are further subdivided into city, town and village administrative units called municipalities *(municipios)*, each with an elected council headed by a mayor.

ECONOMY

Spain's entry in 1986 into the European Community (now the European Union) opened new export markets and brought a flow of funds into infrastructure projects (such as roads, railways and airports). An economic boom resulted, and the fact that the left-of-centre national government of the time was dominated by Andalucians did Andalucía no harm at all. But the EC also opened Spain up to competition from outside. Boom eventually changed to slump, with national unemployment reaching 24% during 1994, and joblessness among under-26-year-olds running at an even higher rate. Growth has since returned, and by 2000 unemployment was down to 15% – still the highest in the EU but perhaps a misleading figure since far more housewives register as unemployed than in other EU countries.

Andalucía has followed the curves of the national economy, at a distance. Things are better than they were – the most obvious evidence being the widespread building boom of the late 1990s and early 2000s – but worse than in most of Spain. Average Andalucian wages, at around 200,000 ptas a month, are well below the national average. Unemployment in Andalucía – officially 27% in 1999 – is the highest in Spain. Within Andalucía, Cádiz province has the highest unemployment rate, at 33%, and Almería province has the lowest, at 13%. According to figures from La Caixa bank in 2000, Spain's seven poorest cities are all in Andalucía, five of them in Cádiz province.

Such statistics may conflict with the impression many visitors get of Andalucía, whose people on the whole appear, if not fabulously rich, not desperately poor either. One explanation is that tourists don't generally frequent the rougher areas of cities or the more desolate country towns and villages. It's also true that the dole and other help for the unemployed has eradicated most of the worst poverty. The strength of the family helps too – several generations may share housing and whatever income they get. And, undoubtedly, many people get away with registering as unemployed (to qualify for dole) and working at the

same time! According to the organisation Pro Derechos Humanos in 1999, the 'submerged' economy accounts for 26% of Andalucian income.

Just 2% of Andalucian landowners still own about half of Andalucía's land, and the 'big five' – the Duques de Arcos, Infantado, Medinaceli, Medina Sidonia and Osuna – retain vast estates. The estates now tend to be efficiently farmed, but mechanisation has not provided many new jobs. There are still perhaps 200,000 *jornaleros* – landless, seasonally employed agricultural day-labourers.

The Expo '92 world fair in Sevilla brought Andalucía big improvements in road and rail communications, but failed to spark a take-off of high-tech industries in Andalucía, and the region remains under-industrialised. Such industry as exists is concentrated mainly in the western Sevilla–Huelva–Cádiz triangle, with some in Málaga, Córdoba and Granada.

Agriculture still provides one job in seven (one in five in some provinces). Successful intensive hothouse farming is now practised under acres of plastic sheeting, especially in the Almería province. Traditional agricultural products include pork, wool, beef, wine, grains, cork and olives (Andalucía produces about 10% of the world's olive oil; see the boxed text 'Essential Oil' in the Jaén Province chapter for details). Fishing is still important – Andalucía has one of the biggest fishing fleets in Spain – but the value of Andalucian production, per head of population, is little more than half that of prosperous Spanish areas such as Catalunya and Madrid.

Tourism accounts for over 10% of the Andalucian economy, and provides over 100,000 jobs directly. Fifteen to 20 million tourists a year come to Andalucía, just over half of them foreigners. Málaga province, where the Costa del Sol lies, gets nearly half this business.

POPULATION & PEOPLE
Population

Andalucía has a population of 7.24 million – almost exactly one for every foreign tourist per year. The population comprises 18% of the Spanish total and Andalucía is the most populous of Spain's 17 regions. Of Andalucía's eight provinces, Sevilla has the most (1.7 million), Málaga (1.24 million), Cádiz (1.11 million), Granada (801,000), Córdoba (767,000), Jaén (646,000), Almería (505,000) and Huelva (454,000).

The population is very much weighted to the provincial capitals. The cities of Sevilla (population 702,000), Málaga (528,000), Córdoba (310,000), Granada (241,000), and Huelva (140,000) are all at least five times as big as any other town in their provinces. Only two non-capital cities – Jerez de la Frontera (182,000) and Algeciras (102,000) – top the 100,000 mark. This urban concentration reflects a drift in recent decades from the countryside to the cities. Andalucians like to live together, in cities, towns or villages. Country farmsteads and cottages are rarely actually lived in these days – their owners will travel out to them daily from their villages by car, motorcycle, mule or donkey, or just use them at weekends.

Spain has one of the lowest birth rates in the world (1.07 children per fertile woman) and it has been predicted that its population will fall from around 40 million to 30 million by 2050. Some pundits argue that it must encourage immigration in order to maintain its workforce, its production and its tax and welfare systems. Despite high unemployment, there are relatively few Spanish takers for low-paid jobs on fruit farms, building sites or in domestic service.

People

The ancestors of today's Andalucians include prehistoric hunters from Africa; Phoenicians, Jews and Arabs from the Middle East; Carthaginians and Berbers from North Africa; Visigoths from the Balkans; Celts from central Europe; Romans; and northern Spaniards, who were themselves descended from a similar mix of ancient peoples. By the time the remaining identifiable Jews and Muslims were expelled in the 15th to 17th centuries, all these influences were intermingled. In the past 1000 years there have been just two major additions to the Andalucian ethnic picture: the *gitanos*

(Roma, formerly called Gypsies), who arrived in the 15th century, and the northern Europeans, whose 19th-century trickle turned into a tide in the 1960s. Spain never received any significant numbers of immigrants from its overseas empire.

Gitanos About half of Spain's 500,000 to 600,000 gitanos live in Andalucía. Their origins are uncertain, but they are thought to have come from India, from where they headed west in the 9th century AD. One migration route led to Istanbul and then into Europe, where some eventually reached Spain in the 15th century, most heading to the south – perhaps, it's postulated, because of some kind of affinity with the Muslims of the Emirate of Granada. Another route from the east, it's thought, led to Egypt (hence, some reckon, the word Gypsy) and across North Africa to Andalucía.

Spain began enacting laws against the gitanos in 1499 and went on doing so for a long time. Early ones were chiefly intended to stop them wandering. Others tried to extinguish the gitano identity by forbidding them to own horses, work as blacksmiths or use gitano names, language or dress. King Carlos III in 1783 permitted gitanos to do whatever work they could on the impossible condition that they abandon their customs. They remained on the fringes of society. Along the way they created flamenco music, which emerged in something like its current form in the 19th century (see the Flamenco special section).

Today, most Andalucian gitanos lead a settled life in cities, towns and villages across the region, though the heartland of flamenco is in and around Sevilla, Jerez de la Frontera and Cádiz. Gitano quarters are often the poorest parts of town. Gitanos rub along all right with other Spaniards, but still tend to keep – and be kept – to themselves. Marriages between gitanos and non-gitanos, for instance, are unusual.

For more information on Spanish gitanos, a good place to start is at the trilingual (English, Spanish and Romani) Web site of the gitano organisation Unión Romaní (www.unionromani.org).

Foreigners Officially, Andalucía has 96,000 foreign residents, mostly from Britain, Germany, Scandinavia and France. About half of them live on the Costa del Sol and a good proportion are retired. In addition, there are perhaps twice that number living in Andalucía temporarily or part-time who don't appear on the censuses.

Africans An estimated 100,000 Africans (possibly approaching 200,000), chiefly from Morocco and neighbouring countries, live in Spain. Most of them enter the country through Andalucía and head north in search of work. The province of Almería, with its seasonally labour-intensive horticultural industry, has the highest numbers of Africans in Andalucía – and sees occasional outbreaks of racial conflict.

Many of the Africans come to Spain illegally, and hundreds each year die in the attempt – most often by drowning when their overloaded small boats capsize in the treacherous Strait of Gibraltar, or when they can't manage to swim the last few hundred metres to the shore after their boats dump them. Thousands more each year are intercepted by the police and sent back.

EDUCATION

Seven of Spain's 17 regions have taken charge of their own education systems, and Andalucía is one of them. Schooling is compulsory throughout Spain from the age of six to 16. Children move from primary to secondary school at the age of 12. Two-thirds of children attend free state schools; most of the rest go to state-subsidised Catholic coeducational schools. About 90% of four- and five-year-olds attend nursery school (state or private). In very general terms, Spanish education can be characterised as well-organised and fairly thorough, but not particularly imaginative. Extracurricular activities are few.

Around 55% of school leavers go on to vocational training or to the *bachillerato*, a two-year academic course leading to higher education or higher-grade vocational studies. As well as the more academic disciplines, qualifications for professions such as teaching, nursing and physiotherapy have to be gained at university, and around 40% of Spaniards now attend university (up from 20% in the early 1980s before badly needed improvements in education were launched by the PSOE government). However, the dropout rates are high: only 10% to 12% of students complete their courses successfully.

Each of Andalucía's eight provincial capitals has a publicly run university. To enter university, students must obtain their bachillerato and pass a university entrance exam. They can then do either a three-year course leading to the degree of *licenciado* or *diplomado* (roughly equivalent to bachelor's degrees), or a five- or six-year course leading to a *licenciatura, arquitecto* or *ingeniero superior* degree (roughly equivalent to a master's degree). University fees vary between about 50,000 and 80,000 ptas a year, and around one-seventh of students get grants. Higher education is also available in institutes devoted to fields such as physical education, tourism and the performing arts.

Reliable literacy figures for Andalucía are hard to find, but the one certain thing is that illiteracy is much less widespread than it was 30, or even 15, years ago, thanks to universal schooling, adult education and job training schemes. According to one report in 1995, illiteracy levels among people aged over 16 in Andalucía's eight provinces ranged between 5.5% (Granada) and 11.1% (Jaén). Around 60% of illiterates are women and nearly all illiterates were born before 1960. Their school years passed in an era when even primary school attendance was far from universal.

ARTS

The constellation of creative forms known as flamenco is Andalucía's most characteristic art; see the Flamenco special section for details.

Music

The flamenco tradition so permeates Andalucian sensibilities that relatively few performers or composers make much sense outside the flamenco context.

See Public Holidays & Special Events in the Facts for the Visitor chapter for information on music festivals.

Pop & Rock The Spanish music scene is busy and vibrant. Andalucian summers are filled with happy, danceable pop. Los del Río, a duo from Dos Hermanas near Sevilla, had a world disco hit with *Macarena* in the mid-1990s, but with many of its best young musicians drawn to flamenco fusion, Andalucía has produced less than its share of pop and rock stars. Things may be changing: Málaga province, according to official statistics, now has 250 'young musical groups', and Granada claims to be home to 300 rock bands.

One of the most interesting characters is the singer-songwriter Kiko Veneno. Born in Catalunya in 1952, Kiko has spent most of his life around Sevilla and Cádiz. Though also a practitioner of flamenco fusion (see the Flamenco special section), he's more in a rock/R&B camp now. After his 1970s collaboration with Raimundo Amador, Kiko accompanied El Camarón de la Isla for a while (writing Camarón's classic rumba *Volando Voy*; I Go Flying), then disappeared from the music scene for a while. He eventually found his way back, and to success, with four 1990s albums, *Échate un Cantecito* (Sing Yourself a Little Song), *Está muy bien eso del Cariño* (The Love Thing's Going Fine), *Punta Paloma* and *Puro Veneno* (Pure Poison). Now, again collaborating with Raimundo Amador and others, Kiko mixes rock, blues, African and flamenco rhythms with lyrics that range from humorous, *simpático* snatches of everyday life to Lorca poems.

Granada band Lagartija Nick, whose music has been described as 'technopunk' and a 'tyrannical storm of sound', made waves through a partnership with flamenco ace Enrique Morente that included the 1996 album *Omega*. Then came *Val del Omar* (1998), inspired by the eccentric *granadino* (native of Granada) of that name – inventor, experimental cineaste and 'electronic poet' – who died in 1982. This was followed by *Space: 1999* and *Lagartija Nick* (2000). Of this last, one reviewer commented that the band deprived pop of such basics as melody or refrain.

Other groups worth watching out for include Hermanas Sister, a Málaga-based *madrileño*-and-Englishwoman duo whose repertoire includes Janis Joplin and Red Hot Chilli Peppers numbers; Los Perdidos from Fuengirola, with a powerful mix of rock, Latin, reggae, rap, psychedelia, flamenco and anger; Sevillan punk rockers Amphetamine Discharge; Los Hermanos Dalton, an energetic pop/punk trio from San Fernando; Latin/rock/reggae band Hyperbórea from Marbella; Málaga mainstream group Danza Invisible; Granada-based indie band Los Planetas; and Tabletom, an avowedly hippy band who have been mixing blues, jazz, Frank Zappa and Málaga hedonism since the 1970s and have accumulated several generations of admirers.

Andalucian performers apart, there's often a chance to see other top Spanish bands at the many concerts and festivals staged in summer. Keep an eye open for the likes of Madrid quartet Dover, the most successful Spanish indie band of the 1990s; Barcelona rock/blues outfit Jarabe de Palo; hip-hop exponents Mastretta; Asturian bagpipe rockers Hevia; Barcelona techno provider An Der Beat; heavy rockers Extremoduro from Extremadura; Celtas Cortos from Valladolid, reminiscent of the Pogues; and the Javier Vargas Blues Band (who come with a Carlos Santana recommendation).

One genre that is truly untouched by flamenco, born outside Spain but perfectly suited to the Spanish propensity for dancing all night, is electronic dance music in its varied guises. A growing number of *salas* (halls; some of them very late-night, for example opening at 6 am) and festivals are devoted to DJs playing techno, house and their sub-genres. Names to watch for include Javy Unión from Sevilla (Detroit-style techno), and Sambafonker (house), DJ Killer and Jordi Slate (Electro-Break Beat) and F Volumen (techno-house), all from Málaga.

Classical Arguably the finest Spanish classical composer of all, Manuel de Falla, was born in Cádiz in 1876. He grew up in Andalucía before heading off to Madrid and Paris, then returned in about 1919 to live in Granada until the end of the civil war, when he left for Argentina. His three major works, all intended as ballet scores, have deep Andalucian roots: *Noches en los Jardines de España* (Nights in the Gardens of Spain) evokes the Muslim past and the sounds and sensations of a hot Andalucian night, while *El Amor Brujo* (Love, the Magician) and *El Sombrero de Tres Picos* (The Three-Cornered Hat) are rooted in flamenco. *El Amor Brujo*, a gitano love story with a supernatural touch, was the mainstay of Spanish dancers for decades.

Falla's friendship with Federico García Lorca was instrumental in the staging of the 1922 Concurso de Cante Jondo in Granada (see the Flamenco special section). One guitarist who played at the *concurso* – but not flamenco – was Andrés Segovia from Jaén province, who was en route to becoming one of the major classical guitarists of the 20th century.

That, however, exhausts the list of important Andalucian contributions to classical music. The region is more notable for the music it has inspired from others – such as Rossini's opera *Il Barbiere di Siviglia* (The Barber of Seville) and Mozart's *Don Giovanni*, which drew on a 17th-century Spanish play by Tirso de Molina that presented the immortal character of Don Juan (see the boxed text 'Andalucía Through Romance-Tinted Spectacles' in the next section). Falla's friendship in Paris with the French composers Ravel (of *Bolero* fame) and Debussy *(Ibéria)* no doubt encouraged their Hispanic leanings.

Literature

Roman Andalucian literature began with two Cordobans, the Stoic philosopher Seneca and his poet-historian nephew Lucan. Both rose high in imperial circles in Rome, but both were condemned to death by suicide for their parts in an AD 65 conspiracy against Emperor Nero, their former mentor.

Muslim Period The 11th century saw a flowering of both Arabic and Hebrew poetry. The Arabic was chiefly love poetry (platonic and otherwise), by such as Ibn Hazm and Ibn Zaydun from Córdoba, and Ibn Ammar and Al-Mutamid, a king, from Sevilla. The latter pair, initially friends, fell out, and Al-Mutamid hacked Ibn Ammar to death with an axe. Of the Jewish poets, Judah Ha-Levi, considered one of the greatest of all post-biblical Hebrew writers, divided his life between Granada, Sevilla, Toledo and Córdoba, before deciding that a return to Palestine was the only solution for Spanish Jews. Samuel Ha-Nagid's work dealt a lot with war because he was also Granada's top general.

Of the many Muslims who wrote on themes other than love, the philosopher Averroës, or Ibn Rushd (1126–98), from Córdoba, stands out. He expressed the Almohads' inward, spiritual approach to Islam, and his commentaries on Aristotle, trying to reconcile science with religious faith, had a great influence on European Christian thought in the 13th and 14th centuries. This remarkable polymath was also a judge, astronomer, mathematician and personal physician and adviser to two Almohad rulers.

Siglo de Oro In Andalucía the Spanish literary Golden Century, roughly the mid-16th to the mid-17th centuries, began with the circle that gathered in Sevilla around Christopher Columbus' great-grandson Álvaro Colón. It included the playwrights Juan de la Cueva and Lope de Rueda, as well as Fernando de Herrera, who addressed his love poetry to Colón's wife.

Córdoba's Luis de Góngora (1561–1627) is considered the greatest Spanish sonneteer and, by many, the greatest Spanish poet. Góngora manipulated words with a majesty that has defied attempts at critical explanation; his metaphorical, descriptive verses are above all intended as a source of sensuous pleasure. Some of them celebrate the more idyllic aspects of the Guadalquivir valley.

Góngora's contemporary Miguel Cervantes (1547–1616) was not an Andalucian but he did, in the course of an eventful life, spend 10 troubled years here procuring oil and wheat for the Spanish navy and as a collector of unpaid taxes. Cervantes also procured for himself an indecent number of lawsuits, spells in jail and even excommunications – no doubt grist to the mill of the inventor of the novel. Cervantes' *El Ingenioso Hidalgo Don Quijote de La Mancha* (The Inventive Hidalgo Don Quixote of La Mancha) started life as a short story designed to make a quick peseta, but Cervantes had turned it into an epic tale by the time it appeared in 1605. Quixote and his compan-

ion, Sancho Panza, conducted most of their deranged ramblings on the plains of La Mancha, but did stray into the Sierra Morena for a few crazed episodes. Some of Cervantes' short *Novelas Ejemplares* (Exemplary Novels) chronicle turbulent 16th-century Sevilla.

19th Century Andalucian literary creativity didn't flower again until the time of José María Blanco White (1771–1841), who was born into an Irish Catholic merchant family in Sevilla but fled from the Napoleonic invasion to England. His *Letters from Spain* (1822), widely read in England, chronicled

Andalucía Through Romance-Tinted Spectacles

The very backwardness and poverty of 19th-century Andalucía spurred travellers from northern Europe to develop, in a kind of escape from the realities of their own lands, the Romantic image of Andalucía – a mysterious, sensuous, materially poor but spiritually rich land of almost oriental adventure. The picturesque decay of Andalucía's cities and monuments; its gitano flamenco music and dance; its semi-oriental, legend-filled past; its people's love of pageant, fiesta, fun and bullfighting; its narrow, crooked streets; its rugged mountains; its heat; its dark-haired, dark-eyed people; even the brigands who roamed its remoter regions – all these contributed to an exotic image that's hard to shake off even today. Many Andalucians themselves are prey to it – which is hardly surprising, really, because it's partly accurate, and the more acceptable now because much of the poverty which the early Romantics sublimated has gone.

One of the first Romantic writings to be set in Andalucía (Sevilla, in this case) was *Don Juan*, the masterpiece of Britain's Lord Byron, who came to Andalucía in 1809 and wrote the mock epic near the end of his life in the early 1820s. In 1826 France's Viscount Chateaubriand published a melancholic novella, *Les Aventures du Dernier Abencerage* (The Adventures of the Last Abencerraj), in which a Muslim prince of Granada returns to his city after the Christian conquest. The Alhambra was established as the quintessential symbol of exotic Andalucía in *Les Orientales* (1829), by Victor Hugo (who didn't visit Granada), and *Tales of the Alhambra* (1832), by the American Washington Irving (who lived in the palace for a few months). Frenchman Théophile Gautier made the Alhambra his focus in *Voyage en Espagne* (1841). *Carmen*, a violent story of gitano love and revenge in Sevilla, written in the 1840s by another Frenchman, Prosper Mérimée, added subtropical sensuality to the Andalucian mystique. Georges Bizet's 1875 opera based on Mérimée's novella watered down the plot but fixed the stereotype of Andalucian women as full of fire, guile and flashing beauty.

Russian composer Mikhail Glinka went to Granada in 1845 and, fascinated by gitano song and guitar, returned home to write Spanish-flavoured music that influenced many of his successors. Among them was Rimsky-Korsakov, who popped into Cádiz for three days' shore leave from the Russian navy – resulting in his delightful *Capriccio Espagnol* (1887; Spanish Caprice).

Alexandre Dumas came close to summing it all up when he characterised Andalucía as a 'gay, lovely land with castanets in her hand and a garland on her brow'. But English missionary George Borrow, author of *The Bible in Spain*, though less of a Romantic, was perhaps pithier than any of them when he commented 'It is impossible to be sad in such a land.'

Andalucian life and customs in a detail that didn't disguise his contempt for their 'superstition' and 'fanaticism'. The one place in Andalucía that he remembered favourably was liberal Cádiz – 'one of the few Spanish cities which for their good taste can be compared with the English of the second rank'.

The so-called *costumbrista* writers (a costumbrista is a writer or artist who tries to depict the characteristic customs, manners and habits of a region) Serafín Estébanez Calderón, with his *Escenas Andaluzas* (1846; Andalucian Scenes), and Fernán Caballero (actually a Swiss-born sevillana called Cecilia Böhl de Faber Morges), with her novel *La Gaviota* (1849; The Seagull), portrayed Andalucian customs in a manner influenced by the foreign Romantics' interest in 'exotic' Andalucía (see the boxed text 'Andalucía Through Romance-Tinted Glasses' on the previous page).

Generations of '98 & '27 The Generation of '98 was a loose collection of intellectuals whose common thread was a deep disturbance about the national decline symbolised by Spain's loss of its last overseas colonies in 1898. Its best-known figure was the northern novelist, poet, academic and political writer Miguel de Unamuno. Antonio Machado (1875–1939), the leading poet of the group, was born in Sevilla but spent most of his adult life outside Andalucía, except for a few years as a teacher in Baeza, where he completed *Campos de Castilla* (Fields of Castile), a set of poems evoking the landscape of Castile, home of his beloved wife who had died young, and ruminating on the national malaise.

Antonio Machado's friend Juan Ramón Jiménez (1881–1958), from Moguer near Huelva, touchingly and amusingly brought to life his home town in *Platero y Yo* (Platero and I). This prose-poem tells of his childhood wanderings around Moguer with his donkey and confidant, Platero. Juan Ramón, winner of the 1956 Nobel literature prize, stands as a kind of bridge between the Generation of '98 and the last great wave of Andalucian writers in the Generation of

'27. The name comes from the readings and talks they organised in Sevilla in 1927 for the tercentenary of the death of their icon, Luis de Góngora. The loose-knit grouping included the poets Rafael Alberti, from El Puerto de Santa María, and Vicente Aleixandre (the 1977 Nobel laureate) and Luis Cernuda, both from Sevilla. The composer Manuel de Falla was also closely associated with them, but the outstanding figure – for many, the major Spanish writer since Cervantes – was Federico García Lorca, from Granada.

Federico García Lorca Lorca (1898–1936) was a musician, artist, theatre director, poet, playwright and more. Though charming and popular, he felt alienated – by his homosexuality, his leftish outlook and, probably, his talent itself – from his stuffy home town Granada (which in 1936 he called 'a wasteland populated by the worst bourgeoisie in Spain'), and from contemporary Spanish society at large. Lorca identified with Andalucía's marginalised gitanos and empathised with women stifled by conventional mores. He longed for spontaneity and vivacity and he eulogised both Granada's Islamic past and what he considered the 'authentic' Andalucía (to be found in Málaga, Córdoba, Cádiz – anywhere except Granada).

As a student in Madrid in the early 1920s Lorca met Jiménez, Alberti and others associated with the Generation of '27, including the artist Salvador Dalí and the film-maker Luis Buñuel. Lorca won major popularity with *El Romancero Gitano* (Gypsy Ballads), a colourful 1928 collection of verses on Andalucian gitano themes, full of startling metaphors and with the simplicity of flamenco song. This was followed between 1933 and 1936 by the three tragedies for which he is best known: *Bodas de Sangre* (Blood Wedding), *Yerma* (Barren) and *La Casa de Bernardo Alba* (The House of Bernardo Alba) – brooding, dark but dramatic works dealing with themes of entrapment and liberation, passion and repression. Lorca was executed by the Nationalists early in the civil war.

Architecture

Apart from a few Phoenician tombs (as at Almuñécar) and megalithic dolmens, such as those at Antequera, Andalucía's most significant pre-Muslim structures are Roman – notably at Itálica, near Sevilla, which possesses the biggest of all Roman amphitheatres, a bathhouse and a theatre. The Roman town sites of Baelo Claudia and Ronda la Vieja are worth a visit, as is the necropolis at Carmona. The Romans bequeathed to Andalucía the happy invention of the interior patio, an idea later taken up by the Muslims.

Muslim Architecture Muslim cities had at their heart a main *mezquita* (mosque) and a large market, around which would spread the tangled streets of the *medina*, or inner city. A mosque has three main parts: the minaret, a tower (always square in Andalucía) from which the faithful are called to prayer; the prayer hall; and the ablutions courtyard, for ritual washing before entering the prayer hall.

Relatively few major Muslim buildings in Andalucía survived the Christian era intact, but those that did include some of the most beautiful in the world: the Mezquita in Córdoba, the Alhambra palace in Granada, and La Giralda minaret in Sevilla. A fourth great construction, the Medina Azahara palace-city outside Córdoba, has been partly restored. Muslim artisans also take credit for much of the Alcázar in Sevilla, including its superb Palacio de Don Pedro, created in the 14th century for a Christian king. The Mezquita in Almonaster la Real, Huelva province, is a marvellous example of a well-preserved small mosque. This is one of the many Andalucian churches that are either converted mosques or were built on the sites of ruined mosques. Many of today's church towers were originally minarets.

Numerous impressive Muslim castles and fortifications survive in varying states of preservation at places like Almería, Málaga and Baños de la Encina. Many other Andalucian castles and forts are of Muslim origin, though rebuilt by later rulers. In civil architecture, dozens of town centres and villages retain their labyrinthine Muslim-era street plans. Granada's Albayzín district is just one case in point.

The most characteristic architectural feature of the Muslim period was the arch shaped like a horseshoe – perhaps brought from the Middle East, perhaps developed from similar Visigothic arches. Other common Muslim threads are the use of beautiful, decorative tilework and, from the 10th century onwards, the carving of stucco into intricate geometric or plant patterns or calligraphic verses from the Qur'an.

Muslim architecture in Andalucía falls into two broad periods. First was the imposing, confident caliphal style emanating from Córdoba and brought by the Arabs from the Middle East. The Córdoba Mezquita is the pre-eminent example of this, with its double rows of arches supporting the roof.

The second period was that of the Maghreb style, developed by Muslims in North Africa, brought to Spain by the 12th-century Almohad invaders and developed in contact with North Africa over the next three centuries. The Giralda, built in 1184–98, with its beautiful proportions and trellis-like brick patterning, is the finest of all Maghreb minarets. The style became increasingly elaborate, culminating in the Alhambra's Palacio Nazaries and Sevilla's Palacio de Don Pedro.

Mudéjar & Mozarabic These are the names given to the derivatives of Muslim architecture developed by, respectively, Muslims in Christian areas and Christians in Muslim areas.

Some Mudéjar buildings are almost indistinguishable from Muslim buildings, as is the case with Sevilla's Palacio de Don Pedro (see Muslim Architecture). However, Mudéjar builders did develop a few tricks of their own. One was the use of brick for many churches and mansions. Elaborately carved timber ceilings are also a mark of the Mudéjar hand. *Artesonado* is the word used to describe ceilings with interlaced beams leaving regular spaces (triangular, square or polygonal) for decorative insertions. True Mudéjar ones generally bear floral or simple geometric patterns, but later Renaissance variations with less oriental patterns also abound. Mudéjar and Christian Gothic styles are often found side by side in the same building.

The only significant remaining Mozarabic structure in Andalucía is the rock-cut church at Bobastro. There's much more Mozarabic architecture in northern Spain, constructed by Christians who fled north from Al-Andalus (see the earlier History section).

Gothic The pointed arches, ribbed ceilings, flying buttresses and fancy window tracery of the Gothic style (nothing to do with the Visigoths) began to infiltrate Christian Spain from France in the 12th century and reached northern and western Andalucía with the Reconquista in the 13th. It was dominant until the 16th century. Gothic's technical innovations enabled the building of much bigger structures – notably big cathedrals. Sevilla's cathedral, the biggest in Spain, is almost entirely Gothic in structure.

Spanish Gothic cathedrals have a number of differences from French and English ones. They tend to be wider (in some cases because they were built on the sites of square mosques), to place the choir (*coro*) and a chapel containing the high altar (*capilla mayor*) in the middle of the church, to have many side chapels off the aisles, and to feature retables (*retablos*; see the boxed text later in this chapter).

There are dozens of Gothic or part-Gothic churches in Andalucía, and many of the innumerable castles and town mansions were built or rebuilt in Gothic times. Many buildings that began life in Gothic times were finished or added to later, so that they ended up as (often successful) stylistic hotchpotches. Such are the cathedrals at Jerez de la Frontera (Gothic, baroque and neo-classical, with a Mudéjar belfry) and Málaga (Gothic, Renaissance and baroque).

The final flourish of Spanish Gothic was Isabelline Gothic, from the time of the Catholic Monarchs, whose own burial

chapel – the Capilla Real in Granada – is probably the supreme work in this style. Isabelline Gothic features sinuously curved arches and tracery, and facades with lace-like ornament and low-relief sculptures (including lots of heraldic shields). Another fine example is the facade of the Palacio de Jabalquinto in Baeza.

Renaissance The Renaissance in architecture was an Italian-originated return to disciplined ancient Roman and Greek ideals of harmony and proportion, with columns and classical shapes such as the square, circle and triangle predominating. Many Andalucian Renaissance buildings feature elegant interior courtyards lined by two tiers of wide, rounded arcades.

In Spanish architecture, the Renaissance can be roughly divided into three distinct styles. First came plateresque, a genre more of decoration than of structure, taking its name from the Spanish for silversmith, *platero*, because its decorative effects resembled those of silverware. Facades were given round-arched portals bordered by classical columns and stone sculpture (often including heraldry, in a carryover from Isabelline Gothic).

Next came the more purist Renaissance style that has its maximum expression in the Palacio de Carlos V in Granada's Alhambra, designed by the Rome-trained Pedro Machuca.

The last and plainest phase was Herreresque, after Juan de Herrera (1530–97), creator of the grand and austere palace-monastery complex of San Lorenzo de El Escorial, near Madrid, and Sevilla's Archivo de Indias.

All three phases were spanned in Jaén province by Andrés de Vandelvira (1509–75), who gave the town of Úbeda one of the finest ensembles of Renaissance buildings in the country (see the boxed text on Vandelvira in the Úbeda section of the Jaén Province chapter). Vandelvira was much influenced by the Burgos-born Diego de Siloé (1495–1563), who had studied in Italy and was chiefly responsible for the cathedrals of Granada, Málaga and Guadix.

Hernán Ruiz, who specialised in 'improving' on surviving Islamic buildings, stuck a Renaissance bell tower atop Sevilla's Giralda, and plonked an entire cathedral *inside* the Mezquita at Córdoba.

Baroque The reaction to Renaissance sobriety came in the form of the colours, sense of motion and dramatic, top-heavy effect of baroque, a movement which gathered steam in the later 17th century and reached a peak of elaboration (some say over-elaboration) in the 18th century. Andalucía was one of the places where baroque blossomed most brilliantly.

Baroque was at root classical, but crammed a great deal of ornament onto facades and stuffed interiors full of ornate stucco sculpture and gilt paint. Retables reached their apogee of opulence.

Before full-blown baroque, there was a kind of transitional stage from the Renaissance, exemplified by more sober works such as Alonso Cano's 17th-century facade for Granada cathedral. Then came an outburst of greater exuberance, of which the most elaborate work is termed Churrigueresque after a family of sculptors and architects from Barcelona, called Churriguera.

Sevilla has probably as many baroque churches per square kilometre as any city in the world, and elaborate is certainly the word for many of them. However, the Monasterio de La Cartuja in Granada, by Francisco Hurtado Izquierdo (1669–1728), is one of the most lavish baroque creations in all Spain. Hurtado's followers adorned the small town of Priego de Córdoba with seven or eight baroque churches. Écija is another small place that received a disproportionate share of baroque attention because of its prosperity at the time.

Neo-classicism Throughout Europe in the mid-18th century, the cleaner, restrained lines of neo-classicism came into fashion – another return to Greek and Roman ideals, in keeping with the Enlightenment philosophy that prevailed in learned circles. Cádiz, whose heyday was in the 18th century, has

the biggest neo-classical heritage in Andalucía. But the single most notable neo-classical building is Sevilla's very large, almost monastic Antigua Fábrica de Tabacos (Old Tobacco Factory), built to house an early state-supported industry.

19th & 20th Centuries Neo-classicism survived into the early 19th century, to be followed by revivals of all sorts of earlier styles, in a sort of yearning for past glories at a time of decline. Andalucía experienced some neo-Gothic, and even a bit of neo-baroque, but most prevalent were neo-Mudéjar and neo-Islamic. Mansions such as the Palacio de Orleans y Borbón, in Sanlúcar de Barrameda, and public buildings ranging from railway stations in Sevilla and Almería to markets in Málaga and Tarifa were constructed in imitation (often pleasing) of past Muslim architectural styles. For the 1920s Exposición Iberoamericana fancy buildings in almost every past Andalucian style were constructed in Sevilla.

During the Franco era, historic buildings in Sevilla were demolished to make way for new roads and developments. Drab, Soviet-style blocks of workers' housing sprang up in many cities. New public buildings exhibited a bit of Stalinist classicism here, a touch of Art Deco there.

Since Franco, the major impetus has been Expo '92 in Sevilla, which brought the city several spectacular new bridges over the Guadalquivir and a sea of avant-garde exhibition pavilions on the Isla de la Cartuja.

Painting, Sculpture & Metalwork
Andalucian art goes back to the Stone Age and reached its creative high point during the 17th-century baroque era.

Early & Muslim Art Stone Age hunter-gatherers left impressive rock paintings of animals, people and mythical or divine figures in caves such as the Cueva de la Pileta near Ronda, the Cueva de los Letreros near Vélez Blanco and the Cueva de los Murciélagos near Zuheros. The later Tartessians were notable goldsmiths, and their successors, the Iberians, left fine stone sculptures of animals, deities and other figures, often with Carthaginian or Greek influence. Fine Iberian collections are on display in the archaeological museums in Sevilla and Córdoba, and Jaén's Museo Provincial.

The Roman artistic legacy is at its best in the form of mosaics, with some wonderful examples at Itálica, Carmona and Écija (all in Sevilla province), and in Córdoba's Alcázar de los Reyes Christianos and the archaeological museums in Córdoba and Sevilla.

Visigothic artistic output was limited. Gaudy Visigothic jewellery appears in some museums, and a few Visigothic-era carvings or fonts are incorporated into later buildings.

Islam frowns on the artistic representation of living beings, so the art of Muslim Andalucía – and of the Mudéjares (Muslims living or working under Christian rule) – is chiefly a matter of intricate carved or tilework geometric and plant patterns, or calligraphic inscriptions from the Qur'an. Stupendous work of this type is to be seen in the Alhambra in Granada and the Alcázar in Sevilla.

Gothic & Renaissance Art Sevilla, the most powerful and richest city of post-Reconquista Andalucía, was long the region's artistic epicentre. One of the earliest masterpieces of Andalucian Christian art is the huge Gothic main retable in Sevilla's cathedral. Designed and begun by a Flemish sculptor, Pieter Dancart, in 1482, it's carved with more than 1000 gilded and painted biblical figures.

Around Dancart's time, the Frenchman Lorenzo Mercadante de Bretaña and his local disciple, Pedro Millán, began to work a new naturalism and detail into Sevillan sculpture. Then Sevilla's boom in the 16th-century opened it right up to the humanist and classical trends of the Renaissance. Alejo Fernández (1470–1545), an artist of probable German origin who moved to Sevilla in 1508, ushered in the Renaissance in painting; the Italian Pedro Torrigiano (1472–1528), a former rival of Michelangelo in Florence, did the same for sculpture.

Southern Spain, however, produced no-one in the 16th century of the stature of El Greco, the great Greek-born painter who spent his career in Toledo.

A 16th-century master artisan known as Maestro Bartolomé created some of Spain's loveliest *rejas* (wrought iron grilles) in churches in Granada and Jaén province.

Siglo de Oro The late 16th century was the era of the stiff, idealised schemes of Mannerism, the transition from Renaissance to baroque art. But early in the 17th century – the dawn of Spain's artistic *Siglo de Oro* (Golden Century) – a more naturalistic approach, heralding baroque, was taken by Sevillans led by Juan de Roelas (1560–1625), who travelled in Italy, and Francisco Pacheco (1564–1654). Pacheco's studio was the centre of a humanist circle that influenced most of Andalucía's leading artists of the century. Pacheco advised his pupils to 'go to nature for everything'. Roelas' 'two-level' style – depicting heavenly realms in the upper parts of his large canvases and earthly matters below – was very influential.

The great Sevillan artists of the 17th century are well represented in the city's Museo de Bellas Artes, which is Andalucía's best art museum.

The mystically-inclined Francisco de Zurbarán (1598–1664), a Basque born in Extremadura, lived most of his life in and around Sevilla, though he eventually died in poverty in Madrid. Zurbarán's clear, spiritual paintings of saints, churchmen and monastic life are often highlighted by strong light/shadow contrasts comparable with the work of two contemporaries, the Italian Caravaggio and José de Ribera, a Spaniard who spent most of his life in Italy. Notable Zurbarán collections are to be seen in Sevilla cathedral and the Museo de Cádiz.

Francisco Pacheco's son-in-law, Sevilla-born Diego Rodríguez de Silva y Velázquez (1599–1660), also showed a strong naturalistic leaning and used masterly light/shadow effects in the early works he painted in Sevilla – religious scenes (using models drawn from the Sevilla streets), kitchen scenes and portraits. Velázquez left Sevilla in 1623 to become an official court painter in Madrid and, ultimately, the major artist of Spain's cultural golden age.

Velázquez's friend Alonso Cano (1601–77) also studied under Pacheco. In the course of a turbulent life he moved to Madrid, which he left after being tortured for the murder of his wife (which he didn't commit), and later to Granada. Cano was a gifted painter, sculptor and architect. Some of his best work is in Granada and Málaga cathedrals.

Bartolomé Esteban Murillo (1618–82) and his friend Juan de Valdés Leal (1629–90), both Sevilla-born, led the way to full-blown baroque art. With its large, colourful, accessible images, the baroque movement took deep root in Andalucía. The prolific Murillo, youngest of 14 children, was orphaned at the age of nine. His fine technique and soft-focus beggar images and religious scenes (he did seemingly dozens of versions of the *Concepción Inmaculada*, the Immaculate Conception) were very popular in a time of economic decline and gained him many artistic disciples. He died from injuries received in a fall while painting a retable in Cádiz.

The greatest works of the passionate Valdés Leal, who could be both humorous and bitterly pessimistic, can be seen – alongside several Murillos – in Sevilla's Hospital de la Caridad.

Baroque Sculpture Sevilla's Juan Martínez Montañés (1568–1649) carved such dramatic and lifelike sculptures in polychromed wood that contemporaries called him 'El Dios de la Madera' (The God of Wood). His work crops up in many Andalucian churches and, as his career coincided with the first organisation of Sevilla's Semana Santa (Holy Week) along something like its current lines, many of the statues still carried by the city's processional brotherhoods are the work of his hands. Martínez Montañés' Crucifixions, Immaculate Conceptions, infant Christs and retables with diverse carvings of saints served as models for generations of sculptors. Among his many disciples, Juan de Mesa stands out for the pathos of his images, particularly his crucifixions.

The leading Sevillan sculptor of the second half of the 17th century was Pedro Roldán (1624–99). Some of his work (in wood) was painted by Valdés Leal and, like the latter, Roldán's best work is in the Hospital de la Caridad. Several of Roldán's children and grandchildren were sculptors too. It was his daughter María Luisa Roldán, or La Roldana (1654–1704), who, according to tradition, created La Macarena, the powerful Virgin image that takes the place of honour in Sevilla's Semana Santa.

Pedro de Mena (1628–88), the most sought-after Andalucian sculptor of his age, produced a welter of saints, child Christs and other religious work. The last major Andalucian baroque sculptor was Granada's José de Mora (1642–1724), who seems to have had only one model for his numerous Virgin sculptures – his wife, Luisa de Mena.

18th & 19th Centuries An impoverished Spain in this period produced just one outstanding artist – the great Francisco Goya (1746–1828). Though hailing from Aragón, in northern Spain, Goya recorded bullfights at Ronda. Tradition has it that he painted his famous *La Maja Vestida* and *La Maja*

Retables

A retable *(retablo)* – a Spanish invention in church adornment – is a large, often three-part, sculptural altarpiece, elaborately carved and/or painted with biblical scenes, saints, angels and so on. A church's main retable can fill the whole width of the nave behind the altar, and there are often smaller ones for side altars too. The retable's basic function is to illustrate Christian stories and teachings for the benefit of worshippers.

The first retables appeared in the 14th century, in Gothic style, and they reached their peak of lavish, gilded, colourful elaboration in the baroque era.

Desnuda – identical portraits of one woman, clothed and unclothed – at a royal hunting lodge in what is now the Parque Nacional de Doñana. It was also on a visit to Andalucía, in 1792, that Goya went deaf – an event which presaged the bleaker aspect of his later work. A few Goya works are on view in Andalucía in places such as the cathedral in Sevilla and the Oratorio de la Santa Cueva in Cádiz.

The 19th-century costumbrista painters of Sevilla – chief among them José Domínguez Bécquer – turned out sentimental pictures of gitanos, dancers and so on for tourists.

The 20th Century Like Velázquez (see the earlier Siglo de Oro section), Pablo Picasso (1881–1973) was born in Andalucía (Málaga) but didn't stay long. When Picasso was nine his family moved to Galicia and then a few years later to Barcelona. He revisited Málaga for annual holidays from 1891 to 1900, painting landscapes and fishing scenes, but never returned thereafter. He settled in France for good in 1904. Picasso's career involved many abrupt changes. He showed prodigious aptitude at an early age and quickly absorbed techniques from Goya, Velázqucz and El Greco, then, in Paris, from Gauguin, Toulouse-Lautrec and Van Gogh. His sombre Blue Period (1901–4) was followed by the merrier Pink Period; later, with Georges Braque, Picasso pioneered cubism. His best known work is *Guernica*, portraying the horror of war and inspired by the German bombing of the Basque town of Gernika in 1937. A new Picasso museum is due to open in Málaga in 2002, with a large collection of his works donated by his daughter-in-law, Christine Ruiz-Picasso, finally giving the city of his birth a slice of the Picasso pie.

Two of the more notable 20th-century artists who actually worked in Andalucía were Julio Romero de Torres (1880–1930) from Córdoba, a painter of dark, sensual female nudes, and Huelva's Daniel Vázquez Díaz (1882–1969), a portraitist who also did a set of murals on the Columbus story in the Monasterio de La Rábida.

SOCIETY & CONDUCT

Andalucians have a big capacity for enjoying themselves, but their reputation for being lazy seems entirely unjustified. As someone put it, they work, but they don't have a work ethic.

They can be economical with etiquette and thank-you's, but this does not signify unfriendliness. One small way in which you may notice people expressing their fellow-feeling is a general *'Buenos días'* to all present when they enter a shop or bar, or an *'Adiós'* when they leave. Andalucians are generally tolerant and easygoing, often welcoming towards the millions of foreigners who descend upon their land each year, and now have several decades' experience in making life easy for them. They don't expect foreigners to speak much Spanish, but nor do they expect more than superficial communication with transient visitors. Invitations to their homes are something special.

Andalucians are gregarious and the family is of paramount importance, with chil-

MICHAEL WELDON

The life and work of Andalucía's most famous son, Pablo Picasso, is celebrated in Málaga.

dren always a good talking point. At the same time, they're an individualistic, proud people. But short of blatantly insulting someone, it's not easy to give offence. Disrespectful behaviour in churches – including excessively casual dress – is something that doesn't go down well.

Gender roles are more defined in Spain than in northern Europe and north America, and perhaps particularly so in Andalucía. While a respectable number of women have jobs outside the home, they tend to do most of the domestic work too. Things are less extreme in the bigger cities and among the young, but in the villages you'll notice that nearly all motorcycle riders are men and nearly all pushchair pushers are women and you won't see many men shopping for food or women sitting at bars. It still seems to be the case that many men can get away with extramarital affairs, while their wives are expected to remain 100% faithful – even to the point of not being seen to converse with unfamiliar men.

Most people like to look their best and take every opportunity to dress up – though not often to the extent of a formal suit and tie. They know that foreigners don't go to quite the same lengths, but you may feel uncomfortable in an un-fresh T-shirt, jeans and trainers in some restaurants or discos – some wouldn't let you in, in any case.

Time

The Spanish, and perhaps especially the Andalucian, attitude to time is more relaxed than in most other Western cultures. But things that need a fixed time – trains, buses, cinemas, bullfights – get one, and it's generally stuck to. Waiters may not always be in a hurry, but they come in the end.

What is different is the daily timetable. The Spanish *tarde*, usually translated as afternoon, doesn't really start until 4 or 5 pm and goes on to 9 or 10 pm or later. In the hot summer months, people stay outside till very late at night, enjoying the coolness. At fiestas, don't be surprised to see a merry-go-round packed with tiny children at 3 am. And Friday and Saturday nights year-round barely begin until midnight for those doing the rounds of bars and discos.

Siesta

Contrary to popular belief, most Andalucians do not sleep in the afternoon. The siesta, if taken, is generally devoted to a long lunch and lingering conversation. Then again, if you've stayed out until 6 am...

Treatment of Animals

Dangerous though it is to generalise, and leaving aside the issue of bullfighting for a moment, Andalucians appear to respect animals about as much as most other Western Europeans – but they rarely mollycoddle them. They value them above all for their usefulness – as beasts of burden or farming help (horses, mules, donkeys), as guardians (dogs) or ratcatchers (cats), and above all, of course, as food – and will treat them well as long as they remain useful.

Hunting wild animals and birds (with a gun, for food) is a very popular country pursuit, but is controlled fairly closely so that populations are not depleted. Spaniards eat more meat than any other people in the EU – 103.5kg per person a year in 1997, over half of it pig meat. But vegetarianism is increasing, especially among the young.

As for bullfighting, it's so ingrained in the culture as a sport-cum-art-cum-fiesta that the question of whether it's cruel or not just doesn't frame itself to many Andalucians (except perhaps in terms of the very real danger to the bullfighters). Plenty of people are uninterested in the activity, but few actively oppose it. If pressed, they might comment that the bulls live a particularly good life before they die in a fight, and that they wouldn't have been bred at all if there was no bullfighting. The main anti-bullfighting organisation in Spain is the Asociación para la Defensa de los Derechos del Animal (ADDA, Association for the Defence of Animal Rights), Calle Bailén 164, Local 2 interior, 08037 Barcelona. ADDA, with a Web site in English and Spanish at www.inter com.es/adda/, also opposes practices such as intensive farming, animal captivity and cosmetic testing on animals, and is involved in international anti-bullfight campaigns. Another anti-bullfighting organisation is the World Society for the Protection of Animals, a network of animal protection societies from over 80 countries, with its headquarters (☎ 020-7793 0540) at 89 Albert Embankment, London SE1 7TP, UK. It has a Web site at www.wspa.org.uk.

RELIGION
Roman Catholicism

It's impossible not to notice the importance of the Roman Catholic church in Andalucía, as throughout Spain. So many of the big occasions are religious fiestas; so many of the finest buildings are cathedrals or churches, lovingly tended by the faithful. The great majority of Spaniards have church baptisms, weddings and funerals. According to surveys, around 85% of them say they are Catholics. This is hardly surprising in a country whose very existence is the result of a series of medieval anti-Muslim crusades.

Under Franco, the government granted the church numerous privileges, including lots of money. Since 1978 Spain has had no official religion, but the government still subsidises the church heavily, and many schools are still run by religious orders and groups.

The country also has a deep-rooted *anti*-clerical tradition, going back to the days when the church and nobility were very rich and most other people very poor. The church was considered one of the main enemies by the Andalucian anarchists and other 19th-century Spanish revolutionaries. This hostility reached a bloody crescendo in the civil war, when some 7000 priests, nuns and monks were killed in Spain. The revolutionary spirit lives on in Andalucía (around 10% of people vote communist) and so does the anti-church tradition – especially among men. One villager said: 'Look at the people who go to church. They're the *bad* people.'

Despite avowing Catholicism, only some 40% of Spaniards now go to church once a month or more. Those who do are often old, poor, female and live in rural areas. But Catholicism is so ingrained that men who hardly ever go to church vie for membership of the brotherhoods that carry holy images in Easter processions, and families spend an average of 300,000 ptas on special clothes and festivities for a child's first communion. There's still plenty of truth in early-20th-century philosopher Miguel Unamuno's quip: 'Here in Spain we are all Catholics, even the atheists'.

Other Faiths

Protestantism was eradicated by the Inquisition in the 16th century. Today, the few Protestants in Andalucía nearly all come from northern Europe. The Jehovah's Witnesses have a sizeable presence.

Muslims and Jews played an enormous role in medieval Spain, but were firmly stamped on at the end of that period (see the earlier History section). Today, mainland Spain has perhaps 100,000 Muslims. Most are African immigrants and live outside Andalucía – though there are a few hundred native-born converts living in Granada's old Muslim quarter, the Albayzín.

The Jewish community numbers a few thousand people, many of them from Morocco. In 1982 Sephardic Jews (Jews of Spanish origin) were officially invited to return to Spain, 490 years after expulsion by the Catholic Monarchs.

LANGUAGE

Spanish is spoken throughout Andalucía. Most Spaniards who encounter foreign tourists on a regular basis speak at least a little English and/or German, and those who speak them well generally prefer to use them rather than put up with a foreigner stumbling along in pidgin Spanish. Away from the main tourist routes, however, you must be ready to use a little Spanish. See the Language chapter at the back of the book for details and local pronunciation.

Flamenco: The Gitano's Lament

MARTIN MOOS

DAMIEN SIMONIS

STEVE DAVEY

Flamenco has an
Andalucian soul. The
passionate song and
dance reverberates
around the region.
(Title page: photograph
by Steve Davey)

Spain pulsates with music and Andalucía is, in many ways, the country's musical heart. Flamenco, the music that outsiders most readily associate with Spain, was an Andalucian invention and Andalucía remains its home ground.

Flamenco is a type of song, music and dance that emerged among *gitanos* (Roma people, formerly called Gypsies) in the lower Guadalquivir valley in the late 18th and early 19th centuries. It grew out of existing musical forms and its forerunners may have included music and verses of medieval Al-Andalus, songs brought to Andalucía by the gitanos themselves and even the Byzantine chant used in Visigothic churches.

The earliest form of flamenco was *cante jondo* (deep song), an anguished lament that grew from the experience of the marginalised gitano. *Jondura* (depth) is still the essence of flamenco, and some of the early jondo forms are still sung – notably the *martinete*, whose only accompaniment is the sound of a hammer striking an anvil, an echo of the smithies where many gitanos worked.

A flamenco singer is known as a *cantaor* (male) or *cantaora* (female); a dancer is a *bailaor/a*. Most of the songs and dances are performed to a blood-rush of guitar from the *tocaor/a*. *Coplas* (flamenco songs) are made up of short, rhyming bursts called *tercios*, permitting some improvisation. The underlying rhythm is called the *compás*. Flamenco sounds 'different' to most Western ears because it uses the Phrygian mode, in which the interval between the first and second notes of an eight-note scale is a semitone. In conventional Western music the interval is a whole tone. Flamenco's scales and rhythms can be a little difficult for the uninitiated to deal with, but it's hard to remain indifferent to its emotional intensity.

Andalucians have always loved dancing, and it was only natural that dance (called *baile* in flamenco contexts) should soon accompany song.

The origin of the guitar, the third component of flamenco, lies in an ancient Middle Eastern stringed instrument, the cithara, which the Arabs developed into a four-string lute. The 9th-century Córdoba court musician Ziryab added a fifth string and this instrument was widespread in Spain for centuries. Around the 1790s a sixth string was added, probably by a Cádiz guitarmaker called Pagés. In the 1870s Antonio de Torres of Almería brought the instrument to its modern shape by enlarging its two bulges and placing the bridge centrally over the lower one to give the guitar its carrying power. In flamenco, *toque* (guitar-playing) for a long time functioned solely as accompaniment to singing and dance.

From the mid-19th to early 20th centuries, establishments called *cafés cantante* literally gave flamenco its first platform – a small, low stage in a bar. This was when castanets first made an appearance (they're not essential to flamenco, percussion being provided by tapping feet or clapping hands). Typical 19th-century clothing – for women, the long, frilly *bata de cola* dress, the shawl and the fan; for men, flat Cordoban hats and tight black trousers – became fixed as flamenco costume.

Song Forms

There are several song types, or *palos*. The *siguiriya*, a song of intense despair about loss or death, is considered the biggest test of a singer's ability. It's thought to have originated in Jerez de la Frontera, one of the three key cities of flamenco's lower Guadalquivir heartland. The *soleá*, marginally less anguished, probably came from the Triana district of Sevilla, for centuries a gitano *barrio* (quarter). The happier, livelier *alegría* is a contribution from the third city, Cádiz. Jerez is also the home of the *bulería*, the fastest, most upbeat palo.

Non-jondo, lighter forms (though they can still be intense) include the *tango*, originally from Cádiz, and its derivatives the *guajira*, *rumba* and *colombiana*, all with roots in music brought back from Latin America. The home of the *fandango* is Huelva, but other areas have their own varieties of fandango – such as Malaga's *malagueña*, Granada's *granaína* and Ronda's *rondeña*. Almería's *taranta* is not dissimilar.

The *saeta*, an outburst of religious adoration by an onlooker at a Semana Santa procession, was not originally a flamenco form but was flamenco-ised around the start of the 20th century. Saetas, traditionally spontaneous, are these days usually stage-managed.

The very popular *sevillana* is not, most pundits agree, flamenco at all. This dance with high, twirling arm movements, consisting of four parts each coming to an abrupt halt, is probably an Andalucian version of a Castilian dance, the *seguidilla*.

Legends of Flamenco

The first person to make a living from flamenco was El Fillo, from the Cádiz area, born about 1820. His name lives on in the term *voz afillá*, which refers to the classic raw, powerful, booze-and-baccy-soaked jondo voice.

The first two great singers of the café cantante era were Silverio Franconetti, from Sevilla, and Antonio Chacón, from Jerez. Their successors in the early 20th century were Sevilla's La Niña de los Peines, the first great cantaora, and Manuel Torre, from Jerez, whose singing could, legend has it, drive people to rip their shirts open and upturn tables.

La Macarrona, from Jerez, and Pastora Imperio, from Sevilla, the first great bailaoras, took flamenco to Paris and South America.

From the flamenco of the cafés cantante developed, in the 1920s, a type of light, operetta-like show called *opera flamenca*. The singer Pepe Marchena, its chief exponent, went on until the 1960s. In 1922 the composer Manuel de Falla, the writer Federico García Lorca and others organised a famous Concurso (competition) de Cante Jondo in Granada to try to revive pure jondo singing. Though the event launched the career of Manolo Caracol, the leading jondo singer of the mid-20th century, it did not stop cante as a whole from continuing to get more commercial and less jondo.

The baile, meanwhile, flourished in the persons of La Argentina and La Argentinita, two female dancers of Argentine origin who made it a theatrical show, forming the first Spanish dance troupes and triumphing in Paris and America in the 1920s and '30s. Their contemporary Vicente Escudero was the first great male dancer. The fast, dynamic, unfeminine dancing and wild lifestyle of Carmen Amaya (1913–63), from Barcelona, made her the gitano dance legend of all time. She too toured abroad successfully, as did Antonio (Antonio Ruiz Soler; 1921–96), from Sevilla, famous for his footwork but also the first bailaor to really use his arms.

Sabicas, a long-time partner of Carmen Amaya, was the father of the modern solo flamenco guitar, inventing a host of techniques now considered indispensable. He never returned to live in Spain after having left during the civil war.

During the 1950s and '60s the flame of pure flamenco was kept alive by Antonio Mairena, from Sevilla, who not only sang cante jondo but campaigned for it, recording old songs and spurring a wave of competitions and festivals. At the same time, however, the lightweight strand of flamenco reached its most debased form with the *tablaos* set up to entertain foreign tourists – 'clubs' with second-rate shows emphasising the sexy and jolly elements.

Since the late 1960s, *flamenco puro* has had a new lease of life. Singers who flourished in the 1970s include Terremoto (Earthquake)

Right: A renewed interest in the true art of Flamenco has saved it from becoming just a tourist attraction.

JULIET COOMBE

and El Chocolate, both from Jerez; Enrique Morente, from Granada, with a clear, tenorish voice; and La Paquera, from Jerez, a stormingly powerful bulería singer.

However, the 1970s was, above all, the decade of El Camarón de la Isla, the 'Shrimp of the Island' – the island being the Isla de León on which Cádiz and Camarón's home town, San Fernando, stand. Camarón's screaming, raucous voice, his great range of styles and his wayward unreliability made him a legend well before his early death in 1992, after years of an uncontrollable drug problem. He was one with *duende* (the spirit), an undefinable transforming magic possessed by the great flamenco performers – the kind of thing that made Manuel Torre's listeners tear open their shirts.

The one flamenco name likely to be known to the uninitiated is that of Paco de Lucía (born 1947), from Algeciras. De Lucía absorbed forms and techniques with such Picasso-like rapidity that by the time he was 14 his teachers had nothing left to do. Since then he has transformed the guitar, formerly the junior partner of the flamenco trinity, into an instrument of solo expression with a raft of new techniques, scales, melodies and harmonies which have taken him far beyond the limits of traditional flamenco. De Lucía, who has attained great international acclaim, can sound like two or three people playing together. In the 1970s, he accompanied El Camarón de la Isla, with several joint albums resulting. Since then, de Lucía has, among other things, collaborated with jazz players such as John McLaughlin and Larry Coryell, and (on the 1990 album *Ziryab*) looked back to the Islamic roots of Andalucian music. The double album *Paco de Lucía Antología* is an excellent introduction, ranging from 1967 to 1990.

Flamenco Today

Several of those mentioned above – de Lucía, Chocolate, Morente, La Paquera – are still going very strong. Morente, in fact, is the leading figure of contemporary male cante. But new generations of artists continue to broaden flamenco's audience.

Song Big-name singers today include José Mercé, from Jerez, whose *Del Amanecer* (1999) is one of the most exciting cante albums of recent years, and versatile Carmen Linares, from Linares, whose 1996 double album *Carmen Linares en Antología* is a journey through the past 150 years of female cante. Other top-notch singers include Remedios Amaya and Aurora Vargas among women, and El Cabrero, José 'El Duende', José Menese, Juan Peña 'El Lebrijano', Calixto Sánchez, Chano Lobato and Vicente Soto 'Sordera' among men.

Dance Always the readiest of the flamenco arts to cross boundaries, dance has reached its most adventurous horizons in the person of Joaquin Cortés, born in Córdoba in 1969. Cortés says he is not really a flamenco dancer but a gitano who dances. His immensely popular touring ensemble fuses flamenco with contemporary dance, ballet and jazz, to music at rock-concert amplification; Cortés himself often dances naked from the waist up, and sometimes in women's clothes.

Antonio Canales, born in Sevilla in 1962, is more of a flamenco purist. His company has done successful shows on bullfight and gitano themes, and in 2000 unveiled the new *Cenicientas* (Cinderella).

Perhaps close to joining Cortés and Canales as a megastar is teenager Farruquito, grandson of the great traditionalist Farruco, who died in 1997. Grandpa used to say that young Farruquito was the only '*puro masculino*' bailaor left.

Classy flamenco dance companies are led by Sevilla's Cristina Hoyos, a big name since the 1970s, and Sara Baras, born in Cádiz in 1971, with a female ensemble formed in 1998.

Individual bailaoras to watch for include Manuela Carrasco and Concha Vargas (both from Lebrija), Juana Amaya and the innovative Belén Maya and Eva la Yerbabuena.

Guitar Look out for the top-flight soloist Manolo Sanlúcar; Manuel Morao, who has played with many great singers and now leads a successful flamenco show company – Manuel Morao y Gitanos de Jerez; Moraíto Chico; Juan Habichuela and Pepe Habichuela, from Granada's voluminous Montoya family of flamenco performers; and Tomatito, from Almería, who accompanied El Camarón de la Isla after Paco de Lucía.

Flamenco Fusion Given a cue, perhaps, by Paco de Lucía, since the 1970s a new wave of musicians has adventurously mixed flamenco with jazz, rock, blues, rap and many other idioms. This *nuevo* (new) flamenco has greatly broadened flamenco's appeal.

The seminal work was a 1977 flamenco/folk/rock album, *Veneno*, by the group of the same name centred on Kiko Veneno (see Pop & Rock under Music in the Facts about Andalucía chapter) and Raimundo Amador, both from Sevilla. The album, virtually ignored at the time, has since acquired legendary status (it was re-released by Sony in 1995).

Right: Whether played solo or as an accompaniment, the Flamenco guitar keeps the rhythm of the dance.

DAN HERRICK

Amador and his brother Rafael formed Pata Negra, which produced four fine flamenco/jazz/blues albums culminating in *Blues de la Frontera* (1986). Raimundo now performs solo, staging some memorable mixed blues and flamenco concerts with the likes of BB King – the album *Noche de Flamenco y Blues* (1998) preserves one such event for posterity.

The group Ketama, whose key members are all from the Montoya flamenco family, are named after a Moroccan hashish town and mix flamenco with African, Cuban, Brazilian and other rhythms. Two of their best albums were *Songhai* (1987) and *Songhai 2* (1995).

The latest generation is led by artists such as Cádiz's Niña Pastori, who arrived in the late 1990s singing jazz-influenced flamenco. Her albums *Entre dos Puertos* (1997), *Eres Luz* (1999) and *Cañailla* (2000) are all great listening. Tomasito, from Jerez, *'el breaker flamenco'*, does electronic bulerías with an avalanche of rumba and hiphop rhythm. Navajita Plateá, two brothers from Jerez, are somewhere between flamenco and pop: their *Desde Mi Azotea* was easily the biggest-selling flamenco album of 1999.

Established flamenco artists are experimenting too. Guitarist Tomatito has enjoyed a successful partnership with Dominican jazz pianist Michel Camilo (check out their 1999 album *Spain*). Manolo Sanlúcar encompasses, like Paco de Lucía, rock, jazz and classical modes. Perhaps most startling was Enrique Morente's 1996 collaboration with the Granada 'wall of sound' metal rockers Lagartija Nick on *Omega*, an interpretation of Lorca's poetry collection *Poeta en Nueva York* (Poet in New York) and songs by the Lorca-influenced Leonard Cohen.

Oddly, perhaps the most successful flamenco-style music of all is the rumba-rock of the Gipsy Kings – who happen to be from southern France, not Spain.

Flamenco Films

Carlos Saura, one of the leading Spanish film makers since the early 1970s, has dedicated several films to flamenco, including flamenco versions of Lorca's *Bodas de Sangre*, Bizet's *Carmen* and de Falla's *El Amor Brujo*. Saura's *Flamenco* (1995) is an exciting review of the best artists in the field – among them Paco de Lucía, Manolo Sanlúcar and Joaquín Cortés. A double CD set of the music is available.

Seeing Flamenco

See under Entertainment in this book's city and town sections, and also Public Holidays & Special Events and Entertainment in the Facts for the Visitor chapter, for tips on where and when to catch live flamenco in Andalucía.

Alma 100, a monthly magazine available free at tourist offices and flamenco venues in places such as Granada, Córdoba, Sevilla and Jerez, has long listings of upcoming flamenco performances, and adverts for flamenco tuition. The Web site of the Centro Andaluz de Flamenco in Jerez (http://caf.cica.es) includes a calendar of flamenco events and is an excellent place to surf the Internet for flamenco information.

Facts for the Visitor

SUGGESTED ITINERARIES

Where you should go in Andalucía depends entirely on what you're interested in and what you like doing: admiring the marvellous monuments from its fascinating past; enjoying its beaches, seas and rugged coasts; exploring its spectacularly beautiful mountain and country areas; or living it up after dark in its vivacious cities. Have a look at the Highlights boxed text for suggestions of destinations you shouldn't miss. If you're still at a loss, here are a few suggestions to help you get as broad a taste of Andalucía as possible in limited time.

One Week

You have to travel fairly hard to get much of a taste of Andalucía in just one week. For the major monuments and three contrasting and fascinating cities, make a beeline for Sevilla, Córdoba and Granada. Alternatively, make an eastern or western circuit. An eastern trip could combine Granada with Las Alpujarras, a beautiful slice of mountainous, rural Andalucía. In the west, Sevilla can be combined with the historic port of Cádiz, or the sherry capital Jerez de la Frontera, or a couple of days on Cádiz province's Costa de la Luz (Coast of Light). Córdoba or Málaga, another rewarding city, could complete the week in either case.

Two Weeks

The Sevilla-Córdoba-Granada axis should be the hub of your trip. You could easily devote two weeks to those three cities alone, maybe with a few trips out to places such as Carmona, Sanlúcar de Barrameda or Jerez de la Frontera from Sevilla; Zuheros from Córdoba; or Las Alpujarras and the Sierra Nevada from Granada. A wider-ranging trip might include either western or eastern add-ons to the basic trio of cities: in addition to those destinations already mentioned, in the west consider Ronda, Tarifa, the Costa de la Luz, Cádiz, the Sierra de Grazalema, the Parque Nacional de Doñana and the Sierra de Aracena. In the east, the architectural splendours of Jaén, Úbeda and Baeza and the beautiful, mountainous Parque Natural de Cazorla merit several days – or go for a laid-back beach stint on the spectacular Cabo de Gata. The city of Málaga makes an interesting and lively start or end to any trip.

One Month

Travelling consistently, you could cover most of the 'Two Weeks' options in one trip. Or, select a limited number of destinations and give yourself time to savour them properly.

Two Months

With this sort of time you can cover everywhere we've mentioned above at a fairly relaxed pace, select some off-the-beaten track destinations of your own, and throw in some genuine relaxation time too. Don't worry about running out of variety – the more you know of Andalucía, the more you'll probably want to know.

PLANNING
When to Go

Andalucía can be enjoyable any time of year, though the weather between November and February is a hit-or-miss affair. Climatically, the ideal months to visit are April, May, June, September and October. At these times the countryside is at its most colourful and you can rely on good to excellent weather, yet you avoid the sometimes extreme heat and the main crush of tourists of July and August, when temperatures may climb to 45°C inland. July and August are also the high season for room prices in most places – but, to compensate, they're the peak months for colourful fiestas too, though there are plenty of these at almost any time between Semana Santa (Holy Week) and October.

Most museums and places of interest stay open year-round. If you plan to pursue some specific activity such as walking or skiing, choose your season carefully – see Activities later in this chapter and regional chapters for more information.

Maps

Small-Scale Maps Michelin's 1:400,000 *Southern Spain* is excellent for overall planning and touring. A new edition is published each year. It's widely available in and outside Andalucía: within Spain, petrol stations and bookshops are the places to look. The map costs around 900 ptas.

Highlights

Most parts of Andalucía are well worth visiting. Here are a few highlights to help start your explorations.

Cities & Towns
Sevilla is Andalucía's most vibrant city. Málaga is not far behind in terms of its people's capacity for fun, though it lacks Sevilla's range of great historical and artistic treasures. Granada is a must because of its Muslim heritage. It has perhaps the most international atmosphere of Andalucía's cities thanks to its many foreign students and travellers. Córdoba too has an unmissable Muslim heritage.

Among the smaller cities and towns, our favourites include down-to-earth, fun-loving Cádiz; Jerez de la Frontera, the sherry capital also famed for its horses and flamenco; Ronda, astride a dramatic gorge with beautiful hill country close by; Arcos de la Frontera, a white town spilling over a rocky ridge; and Cazorla, an old-fashioned place that's also the gateway to the beautiful Parque Natural de Cazorla. All these places, except Cádiz, have a clear imprint from the Islamic past. Near Cazorla, Baeza and Úbeda are full of lovely architecture from the early post-Reconquista (Reconquest) centuries.

Coasts
Andalucía's best coasts are near its extremities. East of Almería, the dry, sparsely populated Cabo de Gata promontory is strung with excellent and, by Spanish standards, under-populated beaches, backed by stark, rugged coastal hills.

In western Andalucía, the 'Costa de la Luz' (Coast of Light) stretches almost 200km from Tarifa to the Portuguese border. The slightly cooler Atlantic waters and breezes are a small price to pay for many fine, long, sandy beaches, backed by pine-covered dunes. Small places like Tarifa itself (with

---

Road Atlases See under Car & Motorcycle in the Getting Around chapter for details.

City Maps For finding your way around cities and towns, the maps provided by tourist offices are often adequate. If you want something more comprehensive, most cities are covered by one of the Spanish series such as Telstar, Alpina and Everest, with street indexes – available in bookshops. Be sure to check their publication dates.

Large-Scale Maps The Centro Nacional de Información Geográfica (CNIG), the publishing arm of the Instituto Geográfica Nacional (IGN), covers most of Spain, including about three-quarters of Andalucía, in 1:25,000 (1cm to 250m) sheets, most of which are recent. The CNIG and the Servicio Geográfico del Ejército (SGE, Army Geographic Service) both publish 1:50,000 series; the SGE's tends to be more up to

date. Other CNIG maps include a *Mapa Guía* series of national and natural parks, mostly at 1:50,000 or 1:100,000 and published in the 1990s. CNIG maps may be labelled CNIG, IGN or both. Some of the *Mapa Guía* were produced in collaboration with the Junta de Andalucía, Andalucía's regional government.

The Junta also publishes a range of Andalucía maps of its own. Most are pretty recent, including a fairly widely available natural and national parks *Mapa Guía* series at 1:75,000, which started appearing in 1998. These are less good for walking than 1:50,000 maps but perhaps better for vehicle touring. Other Junta maps include 1:10,000 and 1:20,000 sheets covering the whole of Andalucía – good maps but sales outlets for them are few.

The best maps for walkers in the Sierra Nevada, Las Alpujarras and Parque Natural de Cazorla are the 1:40,000 maps recently produced by Catalunya-based Editorial Alpina.

Highlights

its international windsurfing scene), Bolonia, Zahara de los Atunes, Los Caños de Meca, Sanlúcar de Barrameda and La Antilla are among the most enjoyable and laid-back resorts of the region – most of them relatively unknown to the outside world, though popular enough with Andalucians. The beaches and resorts are interspersed with cities and ports such as Cádiz, Huelva and Isla Cristina and with extensive wetlands that are vital to wildlife – most famously the Parque Nacional de Doñana.

Hill Country

Andalucía has some beautiful mountain and hill areas, great for walking, mountain biking or just cruising around. The thickly forested Parque Natural de Cazorla in Jaén province is perhaps the most stunning – its mountains are among the most rugged and spectacular, and in Segura de la Sierra you'll find one of the most dramatically located villages in Spain.

The Alpujarras valleys on the southern flank of the Sierra Nevada, south-east of Granada, form an otherworldly, hauntingly beautiful zone of arid hillsides and ravines, dotted with oasis-like white villages. The Sierra Nevada itself contains mainland Spain's highest peak and is a major goal for energetic walkers.

The Sierra Morena, rolling along Andalucía's northern rim, rarely more than 1000m high, attains surprising verdure and beauty in areas like the Parque Natural Sierra Norte and especially the Parque Natural Sierra de Aracena y Picos de Aroche. These areas are far off the regular foreign tourist's trail.

Further very beautiful and green mountainous areas lie around the town of Ronda, mostly in the Parque Natural Sierra de Grazalema and the Serranía de Ronda. A little farther east, Andalucía's most awesome gorge, El Chorro, has been carved out by the Río Guadalhorce.

Obtaining Large-Scale Maps You may or may not come across large-scale maps in or near the areas they cover – you're more likely to find the *Mapa Guía* and Alpina maps than the others – so it's best to try to obtain them in advance.

Edward Stanford (☎ 020-7836 1321, fax 7836 0189), 12–14 Long Acre, Covent Garden, London WC2E 9I P, UK, has a good range of Spain maps and an efficient mail order service. In Spain, seek out any specialist map or travel bookshops in cities you pass through. LTC (☎ 95 442 59 64, fax 95 442 34 51, ✉ ltc-mapas@sp-editores.es), Avenida Menéndez Pelayo 42–44, 41003 Sevilla, is the best map shop we have found in Andalucía, selling most Junta maps as well as SGE and CNIG maps. At LTC the 1:10,000 and 1:20,000 Junta sheets cost just 284 ptas each. LTC can send maps to Spanish addresses, using the *reembolso* (pay-on-delivery) system, or to other countries by post (for which prior payment by bank transfer is required) or by more expensive

delivery service enabling payment on receipt. Another excellent shop selling the 1:10,000 and many other maps is Atlante Mapas in Málaga (see under Bookshops in the Málaga section for contact details).

The CNIG has sales offices in Andalucía's eight provincial capitals, including:

Granada (☎ 958 29 04 11) Avenida Divina Pastora 7 & 9
Málaga (☎ 95 231 28 08) Avenida de la Aurora 47, 7º
Sevilla (☎ 95 464 42 56) Avenida San Francisco Javier 9, Edificio Sevilla 2, 8º (módulo 7)

The CNIG's head office (☎ 91 597 95 14, fax 91 553 29 13), Calle General Ibáñez de Íbero 3, 28003 Madrid, will send you a free catalogue of its maps, which you can then order by fax or mail: the 1:25,000 and 1:50,000 maps cost 500 ptas each plus postage (tell them which maps you want and they'll tell you how much they will cost and how to pay).

The SGE's only map shop in mainland Spain (☎ 91 711 50 43; fax 91 711 14 00) is at Calle de Darío Gazapo 8 (Cuartel Alfonso X), 28024 Madrid, open 9 am to 1.30 pm Monday to Friday. Once you have established which maps you want, you can place an order by fax or mail. The SGE will then send you a bill which you have to pay by bank transfer within Spain or by peseta cheque from outside Spain. Then they'll send you the maps. The 1:50,000 maps are 303 ptas each.

CNIG or SGE maps bought from other shops often cost more than the above prices, owing to delivery costs, mark-up and so on.

What to Bring

Everything you bring, you have to carry. You can buy most things you need in Spain.

Luggage If you'll be doing any walking at all with your luggage, a backpack is the sensible answer. One with straps and openings that can be zipped inside a flap is more secure and there's less risk of it getting trapped in escalators, caught on handles and so on. A small daypack is a useful addition.

Inscribing your name and address on the inside of your luggage, as well as labelling it on the outside, increases your chances of getting it back if it's lost or stolen.

Most Spanish train and bus stations have left-luggage *(consigna)* lockers costing 300 ptas to 600 ptas for 24 hours, depending on the amount of luggage.

Clothing In high summer (July and August) you may not need more than one layer of clothing even at 4 am. In cooler seasons, layers of thin clothing, which trap warm air and can be peeled off if necessary, are better than a single thick layer. You need a pair of strong shoes – at least strong trainers – no matter what type of trip you're making. It's a good idea to pack a set of good clothes and shoes smarter than trainers for some night spots and restaurants – they don't have to be too formal, though.

Useful Items Apart from things you might require for particular kinds of trips (such as camping, walking and windsurfing), consider the following:

• an under-the-clothes money belt or shoulder wallet, useful for protecting your money and documents in cities
• a small towel and soap, often lacking in cheap accommodation
• sunscreen lotion, which can be more expensive in Spain than elsewhere
• a small Spanish dictionary and/or phrasebook
• photocopies of your important documents, kept separate from the originals
• a pocket knife
• minimal unbreakable cooking, eating and drinking gear if you plan to prepare your own food and drinks
• a medical kit (see Health)
• a padlock or two
• an adapter plug for electrical appliances
• a torch (flashlight)
• an alarm clock
• sunglasses
• binoculars if you plan to do any wildlife spotting

TOURIST OFFICES
Local Tourist Offices

All cities and many smaller towns and even villages have at least one tourist office *(oficina de turismo)* or tourist information office *(oficina de información turística)*. On the whole, these are helpful, knowledgeable and well-equipped with give-away or for-sale printed material. There's nearly always someone on hand with some English. Opening hours vary widely.

Local tourist offices may be run by the local town hall, by some district organisation or by the provincial government or the regional government, the Junta de Andalucía. There may be more than one of these in larger cities. Each will offer information on the territory it represents (town, district, province or all of Andalucía). The Junta's environmental department, the Consejería de Medio Ambiente, has visitor centres in many environmentally protected areas – *parques naturales* and so on. If a place has no tourist office, the town hall will often be able to help with information.

euro currency converter   1000 ptas = €6.01

Tourist Offices Abroad

You can get information on Andalucía from Spanish national tourist offices in 20 countries, including:

Belgium (☎ 02-280 19 26, @ bruselas@tour spain.es) Avenue des Arts 21, 1000 Brussels

Canada (☎ 416-961-3131, @ toronto@tour spain.es) 2 Bloor St W, 34th Floor, Toronto M4W 3E2

France (☎ 01 45 03 82 57, @ paris@tour spain.es) 43, rue Decamps, 75784 Paris, Cedex 16

Germany (☎ 030-882 6036, @ berlin@tour spain.es) Kurfürstendamm 180, 10707 Berlin Branches in Düsseldorf, Frankfurt am Main and Munich

Italy (☎ 06-678 31 06, @ roma@tourspain.es) Via del Mortaro 19, interno 5, 00187 Rome

Netherlands (☎ 070-346 59 00, @ infolahaya@ tourspain.es) Laan Van Meerdervoor 8a, 2517 AJ The Hague

Portugal (☎ 21-354 1992, @ lisboa@tour spain.es) Avenida Sidónio Pais 28-3° Dto, 1050-215 Lisbon

UK (☎ 020-7486 8077, brochure request ☎ 09001 669920 at 60p a minute, @ londres@ tourspain.es) 22–23 Manchester Square, London W1M 5AP

USA (☎ 212-265-8822, @ oetny@tourspain.es) 666 Fifth Ave, 35th Floor, New York, NY 10103 Branches in Chicago, Los Angeles and Miami

Several Spanish tourist offices overseas have their own useful Web sites, to which you'll find links on the Turespaña site at www.tourspain.es.

VISAS & DOCUMENTS
Passport

Citizens of the 15 European Union (EU) member states and Switzerland can travel to Spain with their national identity card alone. If such countries do not issue ID cards – as is the case with the UK – travellers must carry a full valid passport (UK Visitor passports are not acceptable). All other nationalities must have a full valid passport.

If your passport's expiry date is only a few months away, you may not be granted a visa should you need one.

By law, you are supposed to have your ID card or passport with you at all times in Spain. You will usually need one of them for registration when you take a hotel room.

Visas

Spain is one of 15 countries that have signed the Schengen Convention, an agreement between all EU member countries (except the UK and Ireland), plus Iceland and Norway, to abolish checks at internal borders by the end of 2000. The other EU countries are Austria, Belgium, Denmark, Finland, France, Germany, Greece, Italy, Luxembourg, the Netherlands, Portugal and Sweden. Legal residents of the Schengen countries and citizens of the UK and Ireland need no visa to visit a Schengen country. Nationals of a number of other countries, including Canada, Japan, New Zealand and Switzerland, do not require visas for tourist visits of up to 90 days to any Schengen country – but it's worth double-checking this as the exemption list is subject to change. At the time of writing Belgium had reintroduced passport controls at all border crossings in an effort to control illegal immigration.

Various other nationals not covered by the Schengen exemption can spend up to three months in Spain as a tourist without a visa. These include Australian, Israeli and US citizens. Citizens of countries we have not mentioned should check with a Spanish consulate about visa requirements for any visit.

The standard tourist visa issued by Spanish consulates is the Schengen visa, valid for up to 90 days. A Schengen visa issued by one Schengen country is generally valid for travel in all other Schengen countries – but individual member countries may impose additional restrictions on certain nationalities, so it's worth checking the regulations with the consulate of each Schengen country you plan to visit.

Since passports are often not stamped on entry (unless you arrive by air from outside the Schengen area), the 90-day rule can often be interpreted flexibly, since no-one can prove how long you have been in the country.

You must apply for the visa in your country of residence, *in person* at the consulate (postal applications are not accepted), and you can apply for no more than two Schengen visas in any 12-month period. If you are going to visit more than one Schengen country, you are supposed to apply for the visa at a consulate of your main destination country, or, if you have no main destination, then the first country you intend to visit. It's worth applying early for your visa, especially in the busy summer months.

If you are a resident applying in the UK you will be required to produce a UK residence permit, proof of sufficient funds, an itinerary, return tickets and a letter of recommendation. Finally, the visa does not guarantee entry. Options include 30-day and 90-day single-entry visas (in London these cost UK£17.75 and UK£21.30, respectively), 90-day multiple-entry visas (UK£24.85), and various transit visas (those people who need a visa for Spain may do so even if just changing planes at a Spanish airport). A multiple-entry visa will save you a lot of time and trouble if you plan to leave Spain – say to Gibraltar or Morocco – and then re-enter it. Schengen visas are free for spouses and children of EU nationals.

Though it is occasionally possible for people who are required to have a visa to reach Spain and travel there without one, it is illegal and can lead to deportation. Travelling from the UK to Spain by sea and land, for example, you might not have your passport checked. Those arriving by air, however, have no such chance. Coming from Morocco, passports will almost certainly be checked on arrival in Andalucía or in Spain's North African enclaves of Ceuta or Melilla. If you go via Gibraltar, you may just sneak across at La Línea without having your passport checked – but you certainly can't count on it.

Visa Extensions & Residence Schengen visas cannot be extended. Nationals of EU countries, Norway and Iceland wanting to stay in Spain longer than 90 days are supposed to apply during their first month for a resident's card. This is a lengthy bureaucratic procedure: if you intend to subject yourself to it, consult a Spanish consulate before you go to Spain as you will need to take certain documents with you.

Other nationalities who want to stay in Spain longer than 90 days are also supposed to get a resident's card, and for them it's a nightmarish procedure, starting with a residence visa issued by a Spanish consulate in their country of residence. Start the process light years in advance.

Non-EU spouses of EU citizens resident in Spain can apply for residence too. The process is lengthy and those needing to travel in and out of the country in the meantime could ask for an *exención de visado* – a visa exemption. In most cases, the spouse is obliged to make the formal application in his/her country of residence. A real pain.

Travel Insurance

A travel insurance policy to cover theft, loss and medical problems is a good idea (see Health later in this chapter for further information on medical insurance).

A wide variety of travel policies is available and travel agents will be able to make recommendations. Check the small print: some policies specifically exclude 'dangerous activities', which can include scuba diving, motorcycling or even trekking. You may prefer a policy that pays doctors or hospitals directly, rather than you having to pay on the spot and claim later. If you have to claim later, make sure you keep all documentation. Check whether the policy covers ambulances or an emergency flight home.

Buy travel insurance as early as possible. If you buy it in the week before you leave home, you may find, for example, that you are not covered for delays to your trip caused by strikes.

Paying for your ticket with a credit card often provides limited travel accident insurance, and you may be able to reclaim payment if the operator doesn't deliver. Ask your credit card company what it will cover.

Driving Licence & Permits

All EU countries' licences (pink or pink and green) are accepted. (But note that the old-style UK green licence is not accepted.) Other foreign licences are supposed to be accompanied by an International Driving Permit (although in practice, for renting cars or dealing with traffic police, your national licence will suffice). The International Driving Permit, valid for 12 months, is available from automobile clubs in your country. For other documents needed to drive to or in Spain, see The UK under Land in the Getting There & Away chapter.

Hostel Card

A valid hostel card is needed at all 19 youth hostels of Inturjoven, the official Andalucía hostel organisation – see Accommodation later in this chapter for details.

Student, Teacher & Youth Cards

These cards can get you worthwhile discounts on travel, and reduced prices at some museums, sights and entertainments.

The International Student Identity Card (ISIC), for full-time students, and the International Teacher Identity Card (ITIC), for full-time teachers and professors, are issued by student-travel-related organisations such as STA Travel, usit Campus and Council Travel (see under Air in the Getting There & Away chapter for more on these).

Anyone under 26 can get a GO25 card or a Euro26 card. These give similar discounts to the ISIC and are issued by most of the same organisations. The Euro26 has a variety of alternative names in different countries including the Under 26 Card in England and Wales and the Carnet Joven in Spain. For information you can contact usit Campus (☎ 020-7730 7285), 52 Grosvenor Gardens, London SW1W OAG, UK.

The more useful discounts on offer for Euro26 card holders in Spain include 20% to 25% off most 2nd-class train fares, discounts at some youth hostels including 10% off lodging and meals in Andalucía's Inturjoven hostels, and discounts at some museums.

Copies

It is a wise precaution to photocopy all important documents (passport data and visa pages, credit cards, travel insurance policy,

air/bus/train tickets, driving licence and so on) before you leave home. Leave one set of copies with someone at home and keep another with you, separate from the originals.

Another option for storing details of your vital travel documents is Lonely Planet's on-line Travel Vault. You are able to create a personal Travel Vault free at www.ekno .lonelyplanet.com. It will be password-protected and accessible on-line at any time.

EMBASSIES & CONSULATES
Your Own Embassy

It's important to realise what your own embassy – the embassy of the country of which you are a citizen – can and can't do to help you if you get into trouble. Generally speaking, it won't be much help in emergencies if the trouble you're in is remotely your own fault. Remember that you are bound by the laws of the country you are in. Your embassy will not be sympathetic if you end up in jail after committing a crime locally, even if such actions are legal in your own country.

In genuine emergencies you might get some assistance, but only if other channels have been exhausted. For example, if you need to get home urgently, a free ticket home is exceedingly unlikely – the embassy would expect you to have insurance. If you have all your money and documents stolen, it might assist with getting a new passport, but a loan for onward travel is out of the question.

Spanish Embassies & Consulates

Here is a list of Spanish embassies and consulates in selected countries:

Australia (☎ 02-6273 3555, @ embespau@ mail.mae.es) 15 Arkana St, Yarralumla, Canberra, ACT 2600
Consulate in Brisbane: (☎ 07-3221 8571)
Consulate in Melbourne: (☎ 03-9347 1966)
Consulate in Perth: (☎ 09-9322 4522)
Consulate in Sydney: (☎ 02-9261 2433)
Canada (☎ 613-747-2252, @ spain@ DocuWeb.ca) 74 Stanley Avenue, Ottawa, Ontario K1M 1P4
Consulate in Toronto: (☎ 416-977-1661)
Consulate in Montreal: (☎ 514-935-5235)
France (☎ 01 44 43 18 00, @ ambespfr@mail .mae.es) 22, avenue Marceau, 75008 Paris, Cedex 08

Germany (☎ 030-261 60 81, @ embesde@mail
.mae.es) Lichtensteinallee 1, 10787 Berlin
Consulate in Düsseldorf: (☎ 0211-43 90 80)
Consulate in Frankfurt am Main: (☎ 069-959
16 60)
Consulate in Munich: (☎ 089-98 50 27)
Ireland (☎ 01-269 1640) 17A Merlyn Park,
Balls Bridge, Dublin 4
Japan (☎ 03-3583 8533, @ embesjpj@mail
.mae.es) 1-3-29 Roppongi Minato-ku, Tokyo
106
Netherlands (☎ 070-364 38 14) Lange
Voorhout 50, 2514 EG The Hague
New Zealand See Australia
Portugal (☎ 02-347 2381, @ embesppt@mail
.mae.es) Rua do Salitre 1, 1250 Lisbon
UK (☎ 020-7235 5555, @ espemblon@
espemblon.freeserve.co.uk) 39 Chesham
Place, London SW1X 8SB
Consulate in London: (☎ 020-7589 8989)
20 Draycott Place, London SW3 2RZ
Consulate in Manchester: (☎ 0161-236 1233)
Consulate in Edinburgh: (☎ 0131-220 18 43)
USA (☎ 202-452-0100) 2375 Pennsylvania
Ave NW, Washington, DC 20037
Consulates in Boston: (☎ 617-536-2506)
Consulate in Chicago: (☎ 312-782-4588)
Consulate in Houston: (☎ 713-783-6200)
Consulate in Los Angeles: (☎ 213-938-0158)
Consulate in Miami: (☎ 305-446-5511)
Consulate in New Orleans: (☎ 504-525-4951)
Consulate in New York: (☎ 212-355-4080)
Consulate in San Francisco: (☎ 415-922-
2995)

Embassies & Consulates in Spain

All foreign embassies are in Madrid, but
many countries also have consulates in
other Andalucian cities – there are nearly 40
in Sevilla. Málaga, Almería and Cádiz are
among other cities with some foreign consulates. Embassies and consulates include:

Australia
Embassy: (☎ 91 441 93 00) Plaza del Des-
cubridor Diego de Ordás 3, Madrid
Consulate: (☎ 95 422 09 71) Calle Federico
Rubio 14, Sevilla
Canada
Embassy: (☎ 91 432 32 50) Calle de Núñez de
Balboa 35, Madrid
Consulate: (☎ 95 222 33 46) Edificio Hori-
zonte, Calle Cervantes, Málaga
France
Embassy: (☎ 91 310 11 12) Calle del Marqués
de la Ensenada 10, Madrid

Consulate: (☎ 95 422 28 96) Plaza de Santa
Cruz 1, Sevilla
Consulate: (☎ 95 222 65 90) Calle Duquesa de
Parcent 8, Málaga
Germany
Embassy: (☎ 91 557 90 00) Calle de Fortuny
8, Madrid
Consulate: (☎ 95 423 02 04) Edificio
Winterthur, Avenida de la Palmera 19,
Sevilla
Ireland
Embassy: (☎ 91 436 40 95) Paseo de la
Castellana 46, Madrid
Consulate: (☎ 95 421 63 61) Plaza de Santa
Cruz 6, Sevilla
Consulate: (☎ 95 247 51 08) Avenida de los
Boliches 15, Fuengirola
Morocco
Embassy: (☎ 91 563 79 28) Calle de Serrano
179, Madrid
Consulate: (☎ 91 561 21 45) Calle de
Leizaran 31, Madrid
Netherlands
Embassy: (☎ 91 359 09 14) Avenida del
Comandante Franco 32, Madrid
Consulate: (☎ 95 422 87 50) Calle Placentines
1, Sevilla
New Zealand
Embassy: (☎ 91 523 02 26 or 91 531 09 97)
Plaza de la Lealtad 2, Madrid
Portugal
Embassy: (☎ 91 561 47 23) Calle de Castelló
128, Madrid
Consulate: (☎ 91 577 35 38) Calle Lagasca
88, Madrid
Consulate: (☎ 95 423 11 50) Avenida del Cid
s/n, Sevilla
Note: Portugal-bound travellers needing Por-
tuguese visas (at the time of writing this in-
cludes Australians) in Andalucía need to show
the Sevilla consulate their passport and proof of
adequate funds (preferably a credit card) and be
should be prepared to wait several days for the
procedure to go through. The consulate opens
9.30 am to 1.30 pm, Monday to Friday.
UK
Embassy: (☎ 91 700 82 72) Calle de Fernando
el Santo 16, Madrid
Consulate: (☎ 91 308 52 01) Calle del Marqués
de la Ensenada 16, Madrid
Consulate: (☎ 95 422 88 75) Plaza Nueva 8B,
Sevilla
Consulate: (☎ 95 235 23 00) Edificio Euro-
com, Calle de Mauricio Moro Pareto 2, Málaga
Consulate: (weekday mornings ☎ 958 27 47
24, mobile ☎ 607-87 21 98), Carmen de San
Cristóbal, Carretera de Murcia s/n, Granada

USA
Embassy: (☎ 91 587 22 00) Calle de Serrano 75, Madrid
Consular agency: (☎ 95 423 18 85) Paseo de las Delicias 7, Sevilla
Consular agency: (☎ 95 247 48 91) Apartment 1C, Avenida Juan Gómez 'Juanito' 8, Fuengirola

The above offices can tell you if their countries have other consulates nearer to where you are. Tourist offices can also usually help.

CUSTOMS

Duty-free allowances for travellers entering Spain from outside the EU include 2L of still table wine; 1L of spirits or 2L of fortified wine, sparkling wine or other liqueurs; 60ml of perfume; and 200 cigarettes or 50 cigars or 250g of tobacco. Duty-free allowances for travel between EU countries were abolished in 1999. For duty-paid items taken from one EU country into another, allowances include 90L of wine, 10L of spirits, 110L of beer and 800 cigarettes.

MONEY

You can get by easily enough with a single credit or debit card enabling you to withdraw cash from Automatic Teller Machines (ATMs), but it's sound thinking to take two cards (if you have them) and some travellers cheques too. The combination gives you a fallback if you lose a card or for some reason are unable to use it.

Currency

Spain's currency for everyday transactions until early in 2002 is the peseta (pta). This comes in coins of one, five, 10, 25, 50, 100, 200 and 500 ptas, and notes of 1000, 2000, 5000 and 10,000 ptas. A 5 ptas coin is known as a *duro*, and it's fairly common for small sums to be quoted in duros: *dos duros* for 10 ptas, *cinco duros* for 25 ptas, *veinte duros* for 100 ptas.

The euro (€), the new currency that Spain shares with Austria, Belgium, Finland, France, Germany, Ireland, Italy, Luxembourg, the Netherlands and Portugal, has been in use since 1999 for some non-cash transactions such as bank transfers. The euro will become the currency of cash transactions too in all 11 countries early in 2002, and as that time approaches, more and more prices and receipts will be denominated in both currencies together, to prepare people for the change.

Euro coins and notes will appear on 1 January 2002; then follows a two-month transition period in which pesetas and euros will circulate side by side and pesetas can be exchanged for euros free of charge at banks. After 28 February 2002 the euro will be the sole currency of Spain and the 10 other 'euro zone' countries.

The euro is divided into 100 cent (or *céntimos* in Spain). Coin denominations will be one, two, five, 10, 20 and 50 cent, €1 and €2. The notes will be of €5, €10, €20, €50, €100, €200 and €500. All euro coins of each denomination will be identical on the side showing their value, but there will be 11 different obverses, each representing one of the 11 euro zone countries. All euro notes of each denomination will be identical on both sides (the €500 note shows two of the bridges that cross the Río Guadalquivir at Sevilla). All euro coins and notes will be legal tender throughout the euro zone.

Exchange Rates

The values of euro zone currencies against the euro (and therefore against each other) were fixed permanently in 1999. Exchange rates between euro zone and non-euro zone currencies, and between the euro and non-euro zone currencies, are variable.

currency	unit		pesetas	euros
Australia	A$1	=	103 ptas	€0.62
Canada	C$1	=	119 ptas	€0.72
euro	€1	=	166 ptas	–
France	10FF	=	253 ptas	€1.52
Germany	DM1	=	85 ptas	€0.51
Japan	¥100	=	163 ptas	€0.98
New Zealand	NZ$1	=	81 ptas	€0.49
Morocco	Dr10	=	168 ptas	€1.01
Portugal	100$00	=	83 ptas	€0.50
UK	UK£1	=	266 ptas	€1.60
USA	US$1	=	176 ptas	€1.06

euro currency converter €1 = 166 ptas

Exchanging Money

You can exchange cash or travellers cheques at virtually any bank or exchange office. For those with money in the form of plastic cards, a great many banks have ATMs. If coming from Morocco, be sure to get rid of any dirham before you leave. Spain's international airports usually have bank branches and exchange offices, and seaports and road crossings into Spain will at least have one or the other close by.

Banks tend to offer the best exchange rates, and even small villages very often have one. They mostly open from about 8.30 am to 2 pm Monday to Friday, and 9 am to 1 pm Saturday.

Exchange offices – usually indicated by the word *cambio* (exchange) – exist mainly in tourist resorts and other places that attract high numbers of foreigners. Generally they offer longer opening hours and quicker service than banks, but worse exchange rates.

Travellers cheques usually bring a better exchange rate than cash, and in many places, the more money you change, the better the exchange rate you'll get.

Wherever you change, it's well worth asking about commissions first, and confirming that exchange rates are as posted (posted rates may not have been updated since yesterday, or last week). Every bank seems to have a different commission structure: commissions may be different for travellers cheques and cash, and may depend on how many cheques, or how much in total, you're cashing. A typical commission is 3%, with a minimum of 300 ptas to 500 ptas, but there are places which have a minimum of 1000 ptas and sometimes 2000 ptas. Places that advertise 'no commission' usually offer poor exchange rates to start with.

Travellers Cheques These protect your money because they can be replaced if they are lost or stolen. In Spain they can be cashed at the many banks and exchange offices and usually attract a higher exchange rate than cash. You usually can't use them like money to actually make purchases.

Thomas Cook and American Express are widely accepted brands with efficient replacement policies. For American Express travellers cheque refunds you can call ☎ 900 99 44 26 from anywhere in Spain.

It doesn't really matter whether your cheques are denominated in pesetas (euros from 2002) or in the currency of the country you buy them in: most Spanish exchange outlets will change all developed-world currencies. Get most of your cheques in fairly large denominations (the equivalent of 10,000 ptas or €100 or more) to save on any per-cheque commission charges.

It's vital to keep your initial receipt, and a record of your cheque numbers and the ones you have used, separate from the cheques themselves.

Take along your passport when you go to cash travellers cheques.

ATMs & Plastic Money Credit cards (such as Visa) are marginally more useful than debit cards (such as Maestro or Cirrus) because they can generally be used for over-the-counter cash advances at bank branches as well as for direct purchases and withdrawing cash from ATMs. They may also give you access to more money per day.

The exchange rate used for credit card currency exchanges is usually more in your favour than for cash exchanges.

You can use plastic to pay for many purchases (including meals and rooms, especially from the middle price range up, and long-distance trains), and you can use it to withdraw pesetas from banks and ATMs. Among the most widely usable cards are Visa, MasterCard, EuroCard, Eurocheque, American Express, Cirrus, Maestro, Plus, Diners Club and JCB.

Some cash cards, such as those in the Cirrus and Maestro networks, enable you to access money in personal bank accounts at home when in Spain, without any cash-advance fee. Ask your card issuer before leaving home about rates and charges. It's also advisable to ask how widely usable your card will be, how to report a lost card, whether your personal identification number

During Semana Santa, the week leading up to Easter Sunday, the streets are awash with parades. Marching bands, solemn-looking processions and floats richly decorated with holy images ensure the event will be a sensory overload. The most magnificent celebrations are held in the streets of Sevilla.

DAMIEN SIMONIS

JULIET COOMBE

STEVE DAVEY

MARTIN MOOS

JOHN M BRETTELL

JULIET COOMBE

Believed to be of Roman origin, the bullfight is entrenched with tradition and ritual. It is considered by many to be a fundamental element of Andalucían culture and, from May to October, bullfights are staged throughout the region.

(PIN) will be acceptable (some European ATMs don't accept PINs of more than four digits), and to know your withdrawal/spending limits.

American Express are among the easiest cards to replace – you can call ☎ 902 37 56 37 or ☎ 91 572 03 03 (in Madrid) at any time. Always report a lost card straight away: for Visa cards call ☎ 900 97 44 45; for MasterCard or EuroCard ☎ 900 97 12 31; for Diners Club ☎ 91 547 40 00.

International Transfers To have money transferred from another country, you need to organise someone to send it to you, through a bank there or a money-transfer service fir example Western Union (www.westernunion.com) or MoneyGram (www.moneygram.com), and a bank (or transfer-service agent) in Spain to collect it. If there are funds in your home bank account, you may be able to instruct the bank yourself.

For information on Western Union services in Andalucía, call ☎ 900 63 36 33.

To set up a transfer through a bank, either get advice from the bank at home on a suitable pick-up bank in Andalucía, or check with an Andalucian bank about how to organise it. You'll need to let the sender have full, exact details of the Spanish bank branch – its name, address, city and any contact or code numbers required.

A bank-to-bank telegraphic transfer typically costs the equivalent of 3000 ptas or 4000 ptas and takes about a week. Western Union is likely to be quicker but a bit more expensive. It's also possible to have money sent quickly by American Express.

Security
Keep only a limited amount of money as cash, and the bulk in more easily replaceable forms such as travellers cheques or plastic. If your accommodation has a safe, use it. If you have to leave money in your room, divide it into several stashes and hide them in different places.

For carrying money on the street – it's in cities and tourist resorts that you have to take most care – the safest thing is a shoulder wallet or under-the-clothes money belt.

An external money belt is only safe if it can't be sliced off by a quick knife cut. Watch out for people who touch you or seem to be getting unwarrantedly close, in any situation.

Costs
If you are extremely frugal, it's just about possible to scrape by on 3000 ptas a day; if you stay in the cheapest possible accommodation, avoid restaurants except for an inexpensive set lunch, minimise your visits to museums and bars, stay away from more expensive cities such as Sevilla and generally don't move around too much. A more comfortable economy budget would be 6000 ptas a day. This could allow you 1500 ptas to 2000 ptas for accommodation; 300 ptas for breakfast (coffee and a pastry); 1000 ptas to 1500 ptas for lunch or dinner; 600 ptas to 800 ptas for another, lighter meal; 250 ptas for public transport; 500 ptas to 1000 ptas for entry fees to museums, sights or entertainment; and a bit over for a drink or two and intercity travel.

If you've got 20,000 ptas to 25,000 ptas a day you can stay in excellent accommodation, rent a car and eat some of the best food Andalucía has to offer.

Ways to Save Two people can travel more cheaply (per person) than one by sharing rooms. You'll also save by avoiding the peak tourist seasons, when most room prices go up: these vary from region to region, depending on local festivals and climate, but they run from about July to mid-September in most places. A student or youth card, or a document such as a passport proving you're over 60, brings worthwhile savings on some travel costs and entry to some museums and sights (see the earlier Visas & Documents section for details). A few museums and sights are cheaper for EU passport holders.

Tipping & Bargaining
The law requires menu prices to include service charge, and tipping is a matter of personal choice – most people leave some small change if they're satisfied, and 5% is

usually plenty. Porters will generally be happy with 200 ptas, and most won't turn their noses up at 100 ptas.

The only places in Spain where you are likely to bargain at all are markets – though even there most things have fixed prices – and, occasionally, cheap hotels, particularly if you're staying for a few days.

Taxes & Refunds

In Spain, value-added tax (VAT) is known as IVA (**ee**-ba, *impuesto sobre el valor añadido*). On accommodation and restaurant prices, it's 7% and is usually included in quoted prices. On retail goods and car hire, IVA is 16%. To ask 'is IVA included?', say '*¿está incluido el IVA?*'.

Visitors are entitled to a refund of the 16% IVA on purchases costing more than 15,000 ptas from any shop if they are taking them out of the EU within three months. Ask the shop for an invoice showing the price and IVA paid for each item and identifying the vendor and purchaser. Then present the invoice to the customs booth for IVA refunds when you leave Spain. The officer will stamp the invoice and you hand it in at a bank in the airport or port for the reimbursement.

POST & COMMUNICATIONS
Postal Rates

At year 2000 rates a postcard or letter weighing up to 20g costs 70 ptas from Andalucía to other European countries, 115 ptas to North America and 185 ptas to Australasia. An aerogram costs 85 ptas to anywhere in the world.

Registered mail *(certificado)* costs an extra 175 ptas for international mail. *Urgente* service, which means your mail may arrive two or three days quicker, costs around an extra 270 ptas for international mail.

Sending Mail

Stamps are sold at most *estancos* (tobacconist shops with 'Tabacos' in yellow letters on a maroon background), as well as at all post offices *(oficinas de correos)*. Main post offices in cities and towns are usually open from about 8.30 am to 8.30 pm Monday to Friday, from about 9 am to 1.30 pm on Saturday. Village offices may be open shorter hours. Estancos usually open for normal shop hours.

It's quite safe and reliable to post mail in the yellow street post-boxes *(buzones)* as well as at post offices. Delivery times are erratic but ordinary mail to other Western European countries normally arrives within a week; to North America within 10 days; to Australia or New Zealand within two weeks.

Receiving Mail

Delivery times are similar to those for outbound mail (see above). Poste restante mail can be addressed to you at poste restante (or better, *lista de correos*, the Spanish name for it), anywhere in Spain that has a post office. It will be delivered to the place's main post office unless another one is specified in the address. Take your passport when you go to pick up mail. It helps if people writing to you capitalise or underline your surname. A typical poste restante address looks like this, with the name of the province following that of the town:

Jenny JONES
Lista de Correos
29780 Nerja
Málaga
Spain

Code Conduct

All Spanish addresses have a five-digit postcode, use of which may help your mail arrive a bit quicker. Villages, towns and small cities have one postcode for the whole place (for example, 29400 for Ronda). But the biggest cities each encompass several different postcodes. The postcodes given in this book for these larger places (Andalucía's eight provincial capitals, plus Algeciras and Jerez de la Frontera) are those to be used on mail addressed to the poste restante *(lista de correos)* at main post offices.

American Express card or travellers cheque holders can use the free client mail-holding service at American Express offices in Andalucía. You can obtain a list of these from American Express. Take your passport when you go to pick up mail.

Telephone

Andalucía is very well provided with street pay phones (they are blue) and they are easy to use for both international and domestic calls. The phones accept coins and/or slot-in Spanish phonecards *(tarjetas telefónicas)*. Phonecards come in 1000 ptas and 2000 ptas denominations and, like postage stamps, are sold at post offices and tobacconists.

Coin pay phones inside bars and cafes – usually green – are normally a little more expensive than street pay phones. Phones in hotel rooms can be a good deal more expensive: managements set their own rates, so it's worth asking the costs before using one.

Costs Calls from pay phones using coins or a slot-in card cost about 35% more than calls from private lines. A three-minute payphone call costs around 25 ptas within your local area, 35 ptas to numbers starting 901, 65 ptas to other places with the same province, 75 ptas to numbers starting 902, 110 ptas to other Spanish provinces, 230 ptas to other EU countries and Spanish mobile phones (numbers starting with 6), 280 ptas to North America, and 820 ptas to Australia. All these calls except those to mobile phones are cheaper from 8 pm to 8 am (6 pm to 8 am for local calls), and all day Saturday and Sunday. Calls to mobile phones are cheaper between 10 pm and 8 am Monday to Friday, 2 pm to midnight Saturday and all day Sunday. Discounts are about 50% for provincial and interprovincial calls and calls to mobile phones, and around 10% for local and international calls. Numbers starting ☎ 900 are free.

A variety of discount cards are available which can significantly cut call costs, especially for international calls. Most of these are not slot-in cards but work through special access numbers – see the later eKno section for details.

Domestic Dialling Spain has no telephone area codes. All numbers have nine digits and you just dial that nine-digit number, wherever in the country you are calling from.

For an ambulance call ☎ 061. Dial ☎ 1009 to speak to a domestic operator, including for a domestic reverse-charge (collect) call *(una llamada por cobro revertido)*. For directory inquiries dial ☎ 1003; calls cost approximately 60 ptas. The Spanish yellow pages can be found on-line at www.paginasamarillas.es.

International Dialling To make an international call from Andalucía, dial the international access code (☎ 00), then the country code, area code and number you want. For international collect calls, dial ☎ 900 99 00 followed by the code for the country you're calling: ☎ 61 for Australia; ☎ 44 for the UK; ☎ 64 for New Zealand; ☎ 15 for Canada; and for the USA, ☎ 11 (AT&T) or ☎ 14 (MCI). Codes for other countries are often posted up in pay phones. You'll get straight through to an operator in the country you're calling. If for some reason this doesn't work, in most places you can get an English-speaking Spanish international operator on ☎ 1008.

Mobile Phones Use of mobile phones *(teléfono móvil)* has mushroomed in Spain. Spain uses GSM 900/1800, compatible with the rest of Europe and Australia but not with the North American GSM 1900 or the totally different system used in Japan (though some North Americans have GSM 1900/900 phones that do work here). If you have a GSM phone, check with your service provider about using it in Andalucía, and beware of calls being routed internationally (very expensive for a 'local' call). Every Andalucian town of medium size or bigger has mobile-phone shops. MoviStar, found on almost any high street, sells phones for around 10,000 ptas, including 4000 ptas of calls. Some shops offer the phone itself for virtually nothing – you just pay for the call time that it comes credited with (maybe 5000 ptas or 10,000 ptas).

Calling Andalucía from Abroad Spain's country code is ☎ 34. Follow this with the full nine-digit number you are calling.

Phone Cards You'll notice a wide range of local and international phonecards on sale in the main travellers' centres in Andalucía such as Sevilla and Granada. Most are not meant to be slotted into the phone: they operate through special access numbers that you dial to initiate your call. If you're thinking of buying one, look closely into call costs (including any taxes payable, such as IVA) and exactly where you can use the card from.

Lonely Planet's eKno Communication Card is aimed specifically at independent travellers and provides budget international calls, a range of messaging services, free email and travel information – for local calls, you're usually better off with a local card. You can join by phone from Spain by dialling ☎ 900 93 19 51 or ☎ 900 97 15 37 or on-line at www.ekno.lonelyplanet.com.

Check the eKno Web site for joining and access numbers from other countries and updates on super budget local access numbers and new features.

Fax

Most main post offices have fax service: sending one page costs about 350 ptas within Spain, 1115 ptas to elsewhere in Europe and 2100 ptas to 2500 ptas to other countries. However, you'll often find cheaper rates at shops or offices with 'Fax Público' signs.

Email & Internet Access

An easy way of accessing the Internet and email while you're on the road is through cybercafes and other public access points. You'll find these in many Andalucian cities and towns, especially those with student populations. Some are mentioned in city and town sections of this guide; visit www.netcafeguide.com for more. Charges for an hour on-line range between 200 ptas and 600 ptas. It's easiest to use Web-based email, which you can access anywhere in the world from any Internet-connected computer. Several such email accounts are available free, such as eKno (available on-line at www.ekno.lonelyplanet.com), Yahoo! at www.yahoo.com or Hotmail at www.hotmail.com.

Travelling with a portable computer is also a great way to stay in touch with the rest of the world, but unless you know what you're doing it's fraught with potential problems. If you plan to carry your notebook or palmtop computer with you, remember that the power supply voltage in Spain may vary from that at home, risking damage to your equipment. The best investment is a universal AC adaptor for your appliance, which will enable you to plug it in anywhere without frying the innards. You'll also need a plug adaptor for Spain – often it's easiest to buy these before you leave home.

Your PC-card modem may or may not work outside your home country – and you won't know for sure until you try. The safest option is to buy a reputable 'global' modem before you leave home, or a local PC-card modem if you're spending an extended time in Spain. The telephone sockets in Spain may be different from those at home, so ensure that you have at least a US RJ-11 telephone adaptor that works with your modem. You can almost always find an adaptor that will convert from RJ-11 to the local variety. For more information on travelling with a portable computer, check out the Web sites at www.teleadapt.com or www.warrior.com.

Major Internet service providers (ISPs) such as AOL (www.aol.com), CompuServe (www.compuserve.com) and AT&T Business Internet Services (www.attbusiness.net) have dial-in nodes throughout Europe including in Sevilla, Málaga and other Spanish cities. It's best to download a list of the dial-in numbers before you leave home.

INTERNET RESOURCES

The World Wide Web is a rich resource for travellers. You can research your trip, hunt down bargain air fares, book hotels, check on weather conditions or chat with locals and other travellers about the best places to visit (or avoid!).

A good place to start your Web explorations is the Lonely Planet Web site (www.lonelyplanet.com). You'll find succinct summaries on travelling to most places on earth, postcards from other travellers and the Thorn Tree bulletin board, where you can ask questions before you go or dispense advice when you get back. You can also find travel news and updates to many of our most popular guidebooks, and the subWWWay section links you to the most useful travel resources elsewhere on the Web.

The following are among the best wide-ranging English-language Web sites on Andalucía. You'll find more specialised sites recommended in specific sections of this book.

All About Spain
The site contains sections on cities, bullfighting, flamenco, fiestas, food, nightlife and more. www.red2000.com/spain
Andalucía There's Only One
The official tourism site of Junta de Andalucía, also in French, Spanish and German; includes a calendar of events, tourist atlas with photos, locator maps and detailed information on every city, town and village, and an on-line booking facility for accommodation, activities and hire cars. www.andalucia.org
Go Spain
This site boasts over 1300 links to all sorts of things Spanish. www.clark.net/pub/jumpsam
Turespaña
The site of the Spanish overseas tourism promotion body, with links to sites of Spanish tourist offices worldwide, hotel prices and lots of other useful practical stuff. www.tourspain.es

BOOKS
Andalucía has fascinated foreign writers for two centuries, giving rise to a wealth of literature in English and other languages. For any reading material you particularly want, stock up before you go: local availability of foreign-language books is patchy. Books on Spain (☎ 020-8898 7789, fax 8898 8812), PO Box 207, Twickenham TW2 5BQ, UK, can send you mail-order catalogues of hundreds of old and new titles on Andalucía (Web site: www.books-on-spain.com).

Most books are published in different editions by different publishers in different countries. As a result, a book might be a hard-cover rarity in one country while it's readily available in paperback in another. Fortunately, bookshops and libraries search by title or author, so your local bookshop or library is best placed to advise you on the availability of the following recommendations.

Lonely Planet
You'll find detailed route descriptions for many of Andalucía's best walks (short and long), plus practical and informative background, in *Walking in Spain*. If you're travelling in Spain beyond Andalucía, the *Spain*, *Madrid*, *Barcelona* and *Canary Islands* guides will point you in the right directions. *Spain* covers the mainland and the Balearic Islands. *World Food Spain* by Richard Sterling is a trip into Spain's culinary soul, from tapas to *postres* and the *menú del día* to the *carta de vinos*, with a comprehensive culinary dictionary. The *Spanish Phrasebook* will enable you to fill some of the gaps between ¡hola! and ¡adiós!.

Guidebooks
Of the many guides in Spanish to different parts and aspects of Andalucía and Spain, those published by El País/Aguilar stand out for their concise, lively, honest coverage and handy format. They range from series of city guides and tapas bar guides to one-offs such as the excellent *Pequeños Hoteles con Encanto* (Charming Small Hotels) and *Pueblos con Encanto de Andalucía* (Charming Villages of Andalucía). See also Walking under Activities in this chapter for details of walking guides.

Travel
19th-Century Classics Washington Irving was an American who took up residence in Granada's Alhambra palace when it was in an abandoned state in the 1820s. His *Tales of the Alhambra*, easy to find in Granada, weaves a series of enchanting stories around the folk with whom he shared his life there. Irving was largely responsible, along with French writers of the

same period, for the Romantic image of Al-Andalus (the Muslim-ruled parts of medieval Spain) which persists to this day.

A Handbook for Travellers in Spain by Richard Ford, first published in 1845, remains a classic not only for telling us how things were then in places we see now, but also for its irascible, witty English author. Ford spent much of his time in Andalucía, including three summers in Sevilla. Unfortunately, the most easily available edition costs around £75.

The Bible in Spain by George Borrow is an English clergyman's view of 19th-century Spain in which he tried to spread the Protestant word. It's amusing both for the man himself and for his experiences. You stand a chance of tracking this down relatively cheaply.

20th Century Laurie Lee set off from his Gloucestershire home on foot, aged 19, in 1934. He walked from northern Spain to Andalucía, playing his violin for a living, before the civil war broke out when he was in a village he calls Castillo (probably Almuñécar) and he was rescued by the Royal Navy. *As I Walked Out One Midsummer Morning*, his delightful account of these adventures, evokes the sights, smells and contrasting moods of turbulent pre-civil war Spain. Lee returned to his old haunts in Andalucía in the 1950s, a trip recorded in *A Rose for Winter*.

Among recent writings, David Gilmour's *Cities of Spain* and Adam Hopkins' *Spanish Journeys*, both culture- and history-focused, give decent coverage to Andalucía in books ranging over all Spain. Gilmour paints perceptive portraits of Sevilla, Córdoba and Cádiz.

History

Michael Jacobs in *Andalucía* and James Woodall in *In Search of the Firedance* both admirably elucidate Andalucía's history in books of broader compass (see under Culture & Arts later in this section for more on these titles).

Most histories of Spain pay major attention to pre-1700 Andalucía, since it was the hub of Islamic Spain and then of early imperial Spain. A colourful and not over-long survey of the whole saga is *The Story of Spain* by Mark Williams. *Moorish Spain* by Richard Fletcher is a fascinating short history of the Islamic era, concentrating to a large extent on Andalucía.

Andalucía since 1700 is less written about, but Gerald Brenan works much about the region's problems and politics into *The Spanish Labyrinth*, an unravelling of the tangled political and social movements of pre-civil war Spain. See the following section for more on Brenan.

The murky story of one of the civil war's most infamous atrocities, the killing near Granada of the writer Federico García Lorca, is chillingly and fascinatingly pieced together in *The Assassination of Federico García Lorca* by Ian Gibson.

On the civil war as a whole, Hugh Thomas' *The Spanish Civil War* is probably the classic account in any language; long and dense with detail, yet readable and humane.

Life in Andalucía

In the 1920s Englishman Gerald Brenan settled in Yegen, a remote village in Las Alpujarras south of Granada, aiming to educate himself unimpeded by British mores and traditions. *South from Granada* is his classic account of local life punctuated by visits from members of the Bloomsbury set. In 1949 Brenan returned to Andalucía to explore Franco's Spain, an experience recounted in *The Face of Spain*.

Alastair Boyd's *The Sierras of the South* evokes life in the hills around Ronda in the 1950s and '60s, when foreigners were a rarity. Naturalist Nicholas Luard does a similar job for the hinterland of the coastal towns of Tarifa and Algeciras in the 1960s and '70s in *Andalucia: A Portrait of Southern Spain*. Luard also ranges quite widely around other parts of Andalucía. His wife Elisabeth Luard insightfully tells of their life with their four children in *Family Life* (1996), a book sprinkled with *andaluz* recipes she learned and which ends like a sledgehammer with a terrible family tragedy. *Inside Andalusia* by

David Baird is a lively, always interesting, 1980s collection of portraits of people and places. *Driving Over Lemons* (1999), the big hit of recent English-language writing about Spain, is the entertaining tale of drummer-cum-writer-cum-sheep-shearer Chris Stewart's small farm in Las Alpujarras.

James Michener's *Iberia*, first published in 1968, is not an epic novel in his usual mode, but an absorbing treatise reflecting a long love affair with Spain – including chapters on the Doñana wetlands, Sevilla, Córdoba and bullfighting.

Two excellent, wide-ranging introductions to modern Spain are *Fire in the Blood* by Ian Gibson and *The New Spaniards* by John Hooper, a former Madrid correspondent for the *Guardian*.

Death in the Afternoon is Ernest Hemingway's book about bullfighting.

Culture & Arts

It would be hard to better James Woodall's *In Search of the Firedance* as an introduction to flamenco. Woodall explains the different forms of flamenco, tells us about the great artists, visits all the main flamenco hubs and explores flamenco's gitano and Islamic roots. Ian Gibson's *Federico García Lorca* is an excellent biography of arguably Andalucía's greatest writer.

Andalucía, by Michael Jacobs, runs comprehensively, eruditely and irreverently through the region's culture and history, from Muslim architecture to Lorca and the Sevillan golden age to flamenco, adding informed comment on today's Andalucía, plus a 140-page gazetteer of places and sights. It's great for those of us who wonder whether the street we're staying on is named after a 16th-century playwright or a 19th-century general.

Fiction

Ernest Hemingway's gripping civil war novel *For Whom the Bell Tolls* (1941) – probably the most read of all English-language books set in Spain – only touches on Andalucía but it repays reading in any Spanish context. Hemingway experienced the war as a journalist, as did Arthur Koest-ler, who was imprisoned by the Nationalists when they took Málaga, and almost executed – an experience on which his excellent novel *Darkness at Noon* (1940) is based.

See the Literature section in the Facts about Andalucía chapter for information on works by Andalucian writers.

Fauna

Wildlife Travelling Companion Spain by John Measures covers 150 of the country's best sites for viewing flora and fauna – many of them in Andalucía – with details of how to reach them and what you can hope to see. It also contains a basic field guide to some common animals and plants. Serious birdwatchers will find *Where to Watch Birds in Southern Spain* by Ernest Garcia & Andrew Paterson invaluable, but will also want a field guide such as *Collins Field Guide to the Birds of Britain and Europe* by Roger Peterson, Guy Mountfort & PAD Hollom, or *Collins Pocket Guide Birds of Britain and Europe* by H Heinzel, RSR Fitter & J Parslow.

For botanists, there's *Flowers of South-West Europe, A Field Guide* by Oleg Polunin & B E Smythies, and *Wild Flowers of Southern Spain* by Betty Molesworth Allen.

Food

A Flavour of Andalusia by Pepita Arias gives you recipes for some 50 typical Andalucian dishes, plus interesting background on the region's food. Numerous books on the diverse field of Spanish cookery include plenty of Andalucian material: among the best are *The Foods and Wines of Spain* by Penelope Casas, *The Best of Spanish Cooking* by Janet Mendel, and *World Food Spain* by Richard Sterling (see under Lonely Planet earlier in this section for details).

NEWSPAPERS & MAGAZINES
Spanish Press

Spain has a thriving and free press. Spaniards have never taken to the idea of 'popular' newspapers so, mercifully, there's no equivalent of the *Sun* or the *New York Daily News* here. Among the major daily national newspapers, the liberal *El País* is hard to beat for solid reporting. Every sizeable city in Andalucía has at least one daily paper of its own and these are often useful for what's-on and transport information. Among the best are Sevilla's *El Correo*, Granada's *Ideal* and Málaga's *Sur*.

Foreign-Language Press

The Málaga-published weekly free newspaper *Sur in English* reviews local news and has good small ads. You can often pick it up at tourist offices, hotels and some shops, especially in Málaga province and the western half of Andalucía. *Lookout* is a glossy monthly magazine, usually with some interesting features and news on Andalucía and Spain. Look for it in bookshops and other shops patronised by English speakers. *The Coastal Gazette* from La Herradura is an expat freebie 'dedicated to the restoration of beer-drinking as a true art form'.

Newspapers from Western European countries and international press such as the *International Herald Tribune*, *Time* and *Newsweek* reach major cities and tourist areas on the day of publication.

RADIO & TV
Radio

The coastal areas have at least six English-language radio stations. Most carry BBC or British independent radio news on the hour several times a day. You'll get a mix of music and talk on Spectrum (105.5MHz), Central (98.6MHz and 103.8MHz FM), Premiere Music Radio (96.8MHz), Onda Cero International (101.6MHz FM) and Coastline (97.7MHz FM) – we've listed them in approximate ascending order of audience age. There's also Premiere Talk Radio (104.9MHz FM). Radio Gibraltar is on 91.3MHz FM. Somewhere around 99 or 100MHz FM you can often pick up BBC Radio 4 or Radio 5, broadcast for British forces.

Spanish radio stations, of which there are dozens in Andalucía, are good for music and trying to improve your Spanish. *El País* publishes local wavelength guides in its *Cartelera* (What's-on) section. The most listened-to stations in Andalucía are Canal

Sur Radio and the commercial pop and rock stations 40 Principales and M-80. The state network Radio Nacional de España (RNE) has four stations including RNE 3 (Radio d'Espop), with some excellent pop and rock programs, and RNE 2 (classical music), both on FM only. For flamenco and other exclusively Spanish music, find Radio E around 91MHz FM.

TV

Spaniards are Europe's greatest TV watchers after the British. Most TVs receive between five and seven channels – two from the state-run Televisión Española (TVE1 and La 2), three independent (Antena 3, Tele 5 and Canal Plus) and a couple of regional or local ones, including the all-Andalucía Canal Sur. Most of them broadcast round the clock, or nearly. Apart from news (of which there's a respectable amount), programing consists largely of game and talk shows, sport, soap operas *(telenovelas)* and English-language films dubbed into Spanish. Canal Plus is a pay channel: non-subscribers get bad reception on most programs.

Satellite and digital TV offer a multifarious choice and can be found in some bars, cafes and hotels. Foreign channels you may come across include BBC World (mainly news and travel), BBC Prime (other BBC programs), CNN, Eurosport, MTV, Sky News, Sky Sport, Discovery and Disney.

VIDEO SYSTEMS

If you want to record or buy video tapes to play back home, you won't get a picture if the image registration systems are different. Spanish television and nearly all prerecorded videos in Spain use the phase alternation line (PAL) system common to most of Western Europe and Australia. France uses the incompatible SECAM system, and North America and Japan use the incompatible NTSC system. PAL videos can't be played on a machine that lacks PAL capability.

PHOTOGRAPHY

Most main brands of film are widely available, and processing is fast and generally efficient. A roll of print film (36 exposures,

ISO 100) costs around 700 ptas and can be processed for around 1700 ptas – there are often better deals if you have two or three rolls developed together. The equivalent in slide *(diapositiva)* film is around 800 ptas plus 800 ptas for processing.

Your camera and film will be routinely passed through airport x-ray machines. These shouldn't damage film but you can ask for hand inspection if you're worried. Lead pouches for film are another solution.

Some museums and galleries ban photography, or at least flash, and soldiers can be touchy about it. It's common courtesy to ask – at least by gesture – when you want to photograph people.

Bright midday sun tends to bleach out your shots. You get more colour and contrast earlier and later in the day.

Lonely Planet's *Travel Photography*, written by internationally renowned travel photographer Richard I'Anson, offers expert advice and is designed to take on the road.

TIME

All mainland Spain is on GMT/UTC plus one hour during winter, and GMT/UTC plus two hours during the daylight-saving period which runs from the last Sunday in March to the last Sunday in October. Most other Western European countries have the same time as Spain year round, the major exceptions being Britain, Ireland and Portugal. Add one hour to these three countries' times to get Spanish time.

Spanish time is normally USA Eastern Time plus six hours, and USA Pacific Time plus nine hours. But the USA tends to start daylight saving a week or two later than Spain, so you must add one hour to the time differences in the intervening period.

In the Australian winter subtract eight hours from Sydney time to get Spanish time; in the Australian summer subtract 10 hours. The difference is nine hours for a few weeks in March.

ELECTRICITY

Electric current in Spain is 220V, 50 Hz, as in the rest of continental Europe, but a few places are still on 125V or 110V (sockets are

often labelled where this is the case). Voltage may even vary in the same building. Don't plug 220V (or British 240V) appliances into 125V or 110V sockets unless they have a transformer. North American 60 Hz appliances with electric motors (such as some CD and tape players) may perform poorly.

Plugs have two round pins, again like the rest of continental Europe.

WEIGHTS & MEASURES

The metric system is used. Like other continental Europeans, the Spanish indicate decimals with commas and thousands with points.

LAUNDRY

Self-service laundrettes are rare. Small laundries *(lavanderías)* are fairly common: they will usually wash, dry and fold a load for 1000 ptas to 1200 ptas. Some youth hostels and a few budget *hostales* (guesthouses) have washing machines for guests' use.

TOILETS

Public toilets are not common, but it's OK to wander into many bars and cafes to use their toilet even if you're not a customer. It's worth carrying some toilet paper with you as many toilets lack it. If there's a bin beside the toilet, put paper and so on in it – it's there because the local sewerage system can't cope otherwise.

HEALTH

Most travellers experience no health problems. Your main potential risks are likely to be sunburn, dehydration, foot blisters and insect bites, or mild gut problems at first if you're not used to olive oil.

Preparations

Immunisations It is recommended you seek medical advice at least six weeks before travel. You might consider immunisation against hepatitis A, you should have a tetanus-diphtheria booster if necessary, and you could think about hepatitis B vaccination if you might have sexual contact with the local population, stay longer than six months in southern Europe, or be exposed

Medical Kit Check List

Consider including the following (consult your pharmacist for brands available in your country):

☐ **Aspirin** or **paracetamol** (acetaminophen in the USA) – for pain or fever

☐ **Antihistamine** – for allergies, eg, hay fever; to ease the itch from insect bites or stings; and to prevent motion sickness

☐ **Loperamide** or **diphenoxylate** – 'blockers' for diarrhoea

☐ **Prochlorperazine** or **metaclopramide** – for nausea and vomiting

☐ **Antiseptic** such as povidone-iodine – for cuts and grazes

☐ **Calamine lotion, sting relief spray or aloe vera** – to ease irritation from sunburn and insect bites or stings

☐ **Bandages and Band-Aids (plasters)** and other wound dressings

☐ **Scissors, tweezers** and a **thermometer** – note that mercury thermometers are prohibited by airlines

☐ **Insect repellent, sunscreen** and **lip balm**

through medical treatment. Hepatitis B vaccine is now widespread for infants and for children aged 11 or 12 who did not complete the series as infants. For more information on hepatitis see that section under Infectious Diseases.

Health Insurance Visitors from other EU countries and Norway, Iceland and Liechtenstein are entitled to free Spanish national health emergency medical care on provision of an E111 form, which you must get in your home country before you come. You will probably still have to pay at least some of the cost of medicines bought from pharmacies, even if a doctor has prescribed them (unless you are a pensioner), and perhaps for a few tests and procedures.

An E111 is no good for private consultations or treatment in Spain, which includes all dentists and some of the better clinics and surgeries, or for emergency flights home. If you want to avoid paying for these, you'll need to take out medical travel in-surance. See Travel Insurance under Visas & Documents earlier in this chapter for more information. In Britain, E111s are issued free by post offices. Just supply name, address, date of birth and National Insurance number. You are required to provide a photocopy of the E111 if you go for treatment, so you might as well get a couple when you get the form.

Many US health insurance policies stay in effect, at least for a limited period, if you are travelling abroad. Most non-European national health plans (including Australia's Medicare) don't, so you must take out special medical insurance.

Other Preparations If you wear glasses take a spare pair and your prescription. If you need a particular medication carry an adequate supply, as it may not be available locally. Take part of the packaging showing the generic name, rather than the brand, to make getting replacements easier. It's a good idea to have a legible prescription or letter from your doctor to show you use the medication legally.

Water

Domestic, hotel and restaurant tap water is safe to drink in most of Spain. The city of Málaga, however, is one place where many people prefer to play safe by drinking bottled water. Safe bottled water is available everywhere, generally for 60 ptas to 125 ptas for a 1.5L bottle in shops and supermarkets.

Ask '¿es potable el agua?' if you're in any doubt about water quality. Water from public spouts and fountains is not reliable unless it has a sign saying 'Agua Potable'. Often there are signs saying *Agua No Potable*: don't drink here.

Natural water, unless it's straight from a definitely unpolluted spring, or running off snow or ice with no interference from people or animals, is not safe to drink unpurified.

Medical Services

For serious medical problems and emergencies, the Spanish public health service provides care to rival that anywhere in the world. Seeing a doctor about something more mundane can be less than enchanting, because of queues and obscure appointment systems, though you should still get decent attention in the end. The expense of going to a private clinic or surgery often saves time and frustration: you'll typically pay between 3000 ptas and 6000 ptas for a consultation (not counting medicines). All dental practices are private in any case.

If you need to see a doctor quickly, or need emergency dental treatment, one way is to go along to the emergency *(urgencias)* section of the nearest hospital. Many towns also have a Centro de Salud (health centre) with an emergency section. Take along as much documentation as you can muster when you deal with medical services – passport, E111 with photocopies and insurance papers. Tourist offices, the police and your accommodation can all tell you where to find medical help, or how to call an ambulance. You could contact your country's consulate for advice. For an ambulance call ☎ 061. Many major hospitals and other emergency medical services are mentioned and/or shown on maps in this book's city sections.

Pharmacies *(farmacias)* can help with many ailments. A system of duty pharmacies *(farmacias de guardia)* operates so that each district has one open all the time. When a pharmacy is closed, it posts the name of the nearest open one on the door. Lists of duty pharmacies are often given in local papers.

Environmental Hazards

Altitude Sickness Lack of oxygen at altitudes over 2500m affects most people to some extent. The effect may be mild or severe and occurs because less oxygen reaches the muscles and the brain, requiring the heart and lungs to work harder. Mild symptoms include headache, lethargy, dizziness, difficulty sleeping and loss of appetite. Acute Mountain Sickness (AMS) has been fatal at 3000m, although 3500 to 4500m is the usual range.

Treat mild symptoms by resting at the same altitude until recovery, usually a day or two. Paracetamol or aspirin can be taken

for headaches. If symptoms persist or become worse, however, *immediate descent is necessary*; even 500m can help.

Fungal Infections Such infections most commonly occur in hot weather and are usually found on the scalp, between the toes (athlete's foot) or fingers, in the groin and on the body (ringworm). You get ringworm (which is a fungal infection, not a worm) from infected animals or other people. Moisture encourages these infections.

To prevent fungal infections wear loose, comfortable clothes, avoid artificial fibres, wash frequently and dry carefully. If you get an infection, wash the area at least daily with a disinfectant or medicated soap and water. Apply an antifungal cream or powder like tolnaftate. Try to expose the area to air or sunlight as much as possible, and wash all towels and underwear in hot water, change them often and let them dry in the sun.

Heat Exhaustion Dehydration and salt deficiency can cause heat exhaustion. Take time to acclimatise to high temperatures, drink sufficient liquids and don't do anything too physically demanding.

Salt deficiency is characterised by fatigue, lethargy, headaches, giddiness and muscle cramps; salt tablets may help, but adding extra salt to your food is better.

Heatstroke This serious, occasionally fatal, condition can occur if the body's heat-regulating mechanism breaks down and the body temperature rises to dangerous levels. Long, continuous periods of exposure to high temperatures and insufficient fluids can leave you vulnerable to heatstroke.

The symptoms are feeling unwell, not sweating very much (or at all) and a high body temperature ($39°C$ to $41°C$ or $102°F$ to $106°F$). Where sweating has ceased, the skin becomes flushed and red. Severe, throbbing headaches and lack of coordination will occur, and the sufferer may be confused or aggressive. Eventually the victim will become delirious or convulse. Hospitalisation is essential, but in the interim get victims out of the sun, remove their clothing, cover them with a wet sheet or towel and then fan continually. Give fluids if they are conscious.

Hypothermia Too much cold can be just as dangerous as too much heat. It could occur in the mountains (the high Sierra Nevada can be bitterly cold even in September). Hypothermia occurs when the body loses heat faster than it can produce it, and the body's core temperature falls. It is surprisingly easy to progress from very cold to dangerously cold due to a combination of wind, wet clothing, fatigue and hunger. It's best to dress in layers: silk, wool and some of the new artificial fibres are good insulating materials. A hat is important. Carry basic supplies, including food containing simple sugars to generate heat quickly and fluid to drink.

Symptoms of hypothermia are exhaustion, numb skin (particularly toes and fingers), shivering, slurred speech, irrational or violent behaviour, lethargy, stumbling, dizzy spells, muscle cramps and violent bursts of energy. Sufferers may claim they are warm and try to take off their clothes.

To treat mild hypothermia, first get the person out of the wind and/or rain, and replace wet clothes with dry, warm ones. Give them hot liquids – not alcohol – and some high-kilojoule, easily digestible food. Do not rub victims – instead, allow them to slowly warm themselves. The early recognition and treatment of mild hypothermia is the only way to prevent severe hypothermia, a critical condition.

Prickly Heat This itchy rash, caused by excessive perspiration trapped under the skin, usually strikes people who have just arrived in a hot climate. Keeping cool, bathing often, drying the skin and using a mild talcum or prickly heat powder, or resorting to air-conditioning, may help.

Sunburn You can get sunburnt surprisingly quickly, even through cloud. Use a sunscreen (taking care to cover areas which don't normally see sun – for example, your feet), a hat, and barrier cream for your nose and lips. Calamine lotion or a commercial after-sun preparation are good for mild sunburn. Protect your eyes with good quality sunglasses, particularly if you will be near water, sand or snow.

Infectious Diseases

Diarrhoea Simple things like a change of water, food or climate can all cause a mild bout of diarrhoea, but a few rushed toilet trips with no other symptoms are not indicative of a major problem.

Dehydration is the main danger with any diarrhoea, particularly in children or the elderly. Under all circumstances *fluid replacement* is the most important thing to remember. Weak black tea with a little sugar, soda water, or soft drinks allowed to go flat and diluted 50% with clean water are all good. With severe diarrhoea a rehydrating solution is preferable to replace minerals and salts lost. Commercially available oral rehydration salts (ORS) are very useful; add them to boiled or bottled water.

In an emergency you can make up a solution of six teaspoons of sugar and a half teaspoon of salt to a litre of boiled or bottled water. You need to drink at least the same volume of fluid that you are losing in bowel movements and vomiting. Urine is the best guide – if you have small amounts of concentrated urine, you need to drink more. Keep drinking small amounts often. Stick to a bland diet as you recover.

Gut-paralysing drugs such as loperamide or diphenoxylate can be used to bring relief from the symptoms, but they do not cure the problem. Only use these drugs if you do not have access to toilets, for example, if you *must* travel. They are not recommended for children under 12. Do not use these drugs in more serious cases such as diarrhoea with fever, profuse watery diarrhoea, persistent diarrhoea not improving after 48 hours, or severe diarrhoea. In these situations you should seek medical help urgently.

Hepatitis A general term for inflammation of the liver, hepatitis is common worldwide. The symptoms include fever, chills, headache, fatigue, feelings of weakness and aches and pains, followed by loss of appetite, nausea, vomiting, abdominal pain, dark urine, light-coloured faeces, jaundiced (yellow) skin and yellowing of the whites of the eyes. Hepatitis A, transmitted by contaminated food and drinking water, can occur in Spain but is not common. There are almost 300 million chronic carriers of Hepatitis B in the world and Spanish children are routinely vaccinated against it. It is spread through contact with infected blood, blood products or body fluids, for example through sexual contact, unsterilised needles and blood transfusions, or contact with blood via small breaks in the skin. Other risk situations include having a shave and tattoo or body-piercing with contaminated equipment. The symptoms of type B may be more severe than type A and may lead to long-term problems.

HIV & AIDS Infection with the human immunodeficiency virus (HIV; in Spanish, VIH) may lead to acquired immune deficiency syndrome (AIDS; in Spanish, *sida*), a fatal disease. Any exposure to blood, blood products or body fluids may put the individual at risk. The disease is often transmitted through sexual contact or dirty needles – vaccinations, acupuncture, tattooing and body piercing can be potentially as dangerous as intravenous drug use. The number of new cases of AIDS in Spain (9.3 per 100,000 inhabitants in 1998) is now half what it was in the mid-1990s.

If you do need an injection, ask to see the syringe unwrapped in front of you, or take a needle and syringe pack with you. Fear of HIV infection should never preclude treatment for serious medical conditions.

All Andalucian provincial capitals have AIDS information and support organisations. The Fundación Anti-Sida España (☎ 900 11 10 00) can also help. It has a Web site at www.fase.es.

Sexually Transmitted Diseases HIV/AIDS and hepatitis B can be transmitted through sexual contact – see the relevant sections earlier for more details. Gonor-

rhoea, herpes and syphilis are among these diseases; common symptoms are sores, blisters or rashes around the genitals, discharges or pain when urinating. In some STDs, such as wart virus or chlamydia, symptoms may be less marked or not observed at all, especially in women. Syphilis symptoms eventually disappear but the disease continues and can cause severe problems in later years. While abstinence from sexual contact is the only 100% effective prevention, using condoms *(condones* or *preservativos)* is also effective. The different STDs each require specific antibiotics.

Cuts, Bites & Stings

Wash well and treat any cut with an antiseptic such as povidone-iodine. Where possible, avoid bandages and sticking plasters (Band-aids), which can keep wounds wet.

Insects, Scorpions & Centipedes Bee and wasp stings are usually painful rather than dangerous. However, in people who are allergic to them severe breathing difficulties may occur and require urgent medical care. Calamine lotion or a sting relief spray will give relief; ice packs will reduce pain and swelling.

Scorpion stings are notoriously painful but Spanish scorpions are not considered fatal. Scorpions often shelter in shoes or clothing, so shake these out before you put them on when camping. Some Andalucian centipedes *(escolopendras* or *ciempiés)* have a very nasty, but not fatal, sting. The ones to steer clear of are those composed of clearly defined segments, which may be patterned with, for instance, black and yellow stripes.

Also beware of the hairy, reddish-brown caterpillars of the pine processionary moth *(procesionarias)*, which live in easily discernible silvery nests in pine trees in many parts of Andalucía and have a habit of walking around in long lines. Touching the caterpillars' hairs sets off a severely irritating allergic skin reaction.

Mosquito and other insect bites can be a nuisance but Spanish mosquitoes don't carry malaria. You can avoid bites by covering your skin and using an insect repellent.

Ticks Check all over your body if you have been walking through a potentially tick-infested area (such as woodlands or fields in spring or summer), as ticks can cause skin infections and other more serious diseases. If a tick is found attached, press down around its head with tweezers, grab the head and gently pull upwards. Avoid pulling the rear of the body.

Snakes The only venomous snake that is even relatively common in Spain is Lataste's viper (*vibora hocicuda* or *víbora de Lataste* in Spanish). It's a triangular-headed creature, rarely more than 50cm long, and grey with a zigzag pattern. It lives in dry, rocky areas, away from humans. Its bite can be fatal and needs to be treated as soon as possible with a serum which state clinics in major towns keep in stock.

To minimise the chance of snake bites, wear boots, socks and long trousers when walking through undergrowth where snakes may be present. Don't put your hands into holes and crevices, and be careful when collecting firewood. If you suspect a venomous snake bite has occurred, immediately wrap the bitten limb tightly, as for a sprained ankle, and attach a splint to immobilise it. Keep the victim still and seek medical help, if possible with the dead snake for identification. Don't attempt to catch the snake if there is a possibility of being bitten again.

Jellyfish With their stinging tentacles, jellyfish *(medusas)* generally occur in large numbers or hardly at all, so it's fairly easy to know when not to go into the sea. Dousing in vinegar will deactivate any jellyfish stingers which have not 'fired'. Calamine lotion, antihistamines and analgesics may reduce the reaction and relieve the pain.

Leishmaniasis This is a group of parasitic diseases found in many parts of the Mediterranean. *Leishmania infantum*, the strain found in Spain – mainly in country areas near the Mediterranean coasts – is a form of visceral leishmaniasis which is characterised by irregular bouts of fever,

substantial weight loss, swelling of the spleen and liver, and anaemia. It can be fatal for children under five and people with deficiencies of the immune system such as AIDS sufferers. It is transmitted when sandflies bite dogs carrying leishmaniasis, then bite humans. Avoiding sandfly bites is the best precaution: cover up and apply repellent. Sandflies are most active at dawn and dusk. The bites are usually painless but itchy. If you suspect leishmaniasis, seek medical advice as laboratory testing is required for diagnosis and treatment.

Women's Health
Gynaecological Problems Antibiotic use, synthetic underwear, sweating and contraceptive pills can lead to fungal vaginal infections in hot climates. Good personal hygiene, loose-fitting clothes and cotton underwear will help prevent them. Fungal infections, characterised by a rash, itch and discharge, can be treated with a vinegar or lemon-juice douche, or with yoghurt. Nystatin, miconazole or clotrimazole pessaries, or vaginal cream, are the usual treatment.

Sexually transmitted diseases are a major cause of vaginal problems. Symptoms include a smelly discharge, painful intercourse and sometimes a burning sensation when urinating. Medical attention should be sought, and male sexual partners must also be treated. For more details see the earlier section on Sexually Transmitted Diseases. Besides abstinence, the best thing is safe sex using condoms.

Pregnancy Most miscarriages occur during the first three months of pregnancy. They can occasionally lead to severe bleeding. The last three months should also be spent within reasonable distance of good medical care. A baby born as early as 24 weeks stands a chance of survival, but only in a good modern hospital. Pregnant women should avoid all unnecessary medication, but vaccinations should be taken where needed. Additional care should be taken to prevent illness, and particular attention should be paid to diet and nutrition. Alcohol and nicotine, for example, should be avoided.

WOMEN TRAVELLERS

Women travellers should be ready to ignore any stares, catcalls and unnecessary comments, though in fact harassment is not frequent. Learn the word for help (*socorro*) in case you need to draw other people's attention. Men under about 35, who have grown up in the post-Franco era, are less sexually stereotyped than their older counterparts. But you still need to exercise common sense about where you go solo. Think twice about going alone to isolated stretches of beach or country paths, or down empty city streets at night. It's highly inadvisable for a woman to hitchhike alone – and not a great idea even for two women together.

Topless bathing and skimpy clothes are acceptable in many coastal resorts, but people tend to dress more modestly elsewhere.

For emergency services for women, see the Emergencies section later in this chapter.

GAY & LESBIAN TRAVELLERS

Gay and lesbian sex are both legal in Spain: the age of consent is 16, the same as for heterosexuals. In 1996 the conservative Partido Popular (PP) government put the brakes on a law intended to establish the legal rights of gay couples, but by 2000 some civil registrars were recording de facto gay/lesbian couples.

Andalucía's liveliest gay scenes are in Sevilla, Granada, Cádiz and Torremolinos. The Madrid-based gay magazine *Entiendes* is on sale at some newsstands for 500 ptas and has a quarterly English edition. International gay and lesbian guides worth tracking down are the *Spartacus Guide for Gay Men* (the Spartacus list also includes the comprehensive *Spartacus National Edition España*, in English and German), published by Bruno Gmünder Verlag (Mail Order, PO Box 61 01 04, D-10921 Berlin) and *Places for Women*, published by Ferrari Publications in Phoenix, Arizona, USA.

Organisations

Two good sources of information on gay places and organisations throughout Spain are Coordinadora Gai-Lesbiana in Barcelona (☎ 93 298 00 29, fax 93 298 06 18), which publishes a copy of 'Gay Spain, Feel the Passion' on its Web site (www.pangea.org /org/cgl), a guide the PP prevented being published in 1997; and Cogam, Calle del Fuencarral 37, 28004 Madrid (☎ /fax 91 532 45 17), with a Web site at www.cogam.org. Both can provide info on help groups, places to go, bars, HIV/AIDS, and just about anything else you might want to know.

Asociación Andaluza de Lesbianas y Gais (NOS) at Calle Lavadero de las Tablas 15, Granada, runs the Teléfono Andaluz de Información Homosexual (☎ 958 20 06 02). It opens 10 am to 2 pm and 4 to 8 pm Monday to Friday. You'll find details of several other Andalucian gay and lesbian groups on the Web site of the Plataforma Gay-Lesbiana de Sevilla at www.arrakis.es/~somos. Further gay links are on the Gayscape site at www .gayscape.com.

DISABLED TRAVELLERS

Some Spanish tourist offices in other countries can provide a basic information sheet with some useful addresses for disabled travellers, and give details of accessible accommodation in specific places.

Wheelchair accessibility in Andalucía is improving. Fuengirola is equipping two beaches for the disabled, with specially adapted showers and sun bed areas, reserved toilets and parking, and aluminium wheelchairs that can be taken into the sea without going rusty. Nearly all Andalucian youth hostels now have rooms adapted for the disabled, but accessibility is still rare enough in other budget accommodation. All new public buildings are now required to have wheelchair access, but most public buildings predate the law. Unfortunately, many hotels that claim to be accessible actually retain problem features.

The British-based Royal Association for Disability & Rehabilitation (RADAR) publishes a useful guide, *European Holidays & Travel Abroad: A Guide for Disabled People*, which provides a good overview of facilities available to disabled travellers throughout Europe. RADAR (☎ 020-7250 3222) is at Unit 12, City Forum, 250 City

Rd, London EC1V 8AS. Its Web site is at www.radar.org.uk. Holiday Care (☎ 01293-774535), 2nd Floor, Imperial Buildings, Victoria Rd, Horley, Surrey RH6 7PZ, UK, produces an information pack on Spain for disabled people and others with special needs. Tips range from hotels with disabled access through to where you can hire equipment and tour operators dealing with the disabled. Check out their Web site at www.freespace.virgin.net/hol.care.

SENIOR TRAVELLERS

There are reduced prices for people aged over 60, 63 or 65 at some museums and sights, and occasionally on transport (see the Getting There & Away chapter). Some of the luxurious *paradores* (see Accommodation in this chapter) sometimes offer discounts for people over 60.

TRAVEL WITH CHILDREN

Andalucians as a rule are very friendly to children. Any child whose hair is less than jet black will get called *rubia* (blonde) if she's a girl, or *rubio* if he's a boy. Accompanied children are welcome at all kinds of accommodation, and in virtually every cafe, bar and restaurant. Andalucian children stay up late and at fiestas it's commonplace to see even tiny ones toddling the streets at 2 or 3 am. Visiting kids like this idea too – but can't cope with it quite so readily.

Most young kids don't like moving around too much and are happier if they can settle into places and make new friends. It's easier on the parents too if you don't have to pack up and move on every day or two. Spanish street life and bustle, and the novelty of being in new places, provide some distraction but most children will get bored unless some of the time is devoted to their own favoured activities. Children are likely to be more affected by unaccustomed heat and need time to acclimatise. Take care to avoid sunburn.

Apart from the obvious attractions of beaches, playgrounds are fairly plentiful in Andalucía, and many places have excellent special attractions such as amusement parks (for example Sevilla's Isla Mágica, and

Tivoli World on the Costa del Sol), aquaparks, aquariums –and let's not forget Mini-Hollywood and other Western movie sets in the Almería desert (see those chapters for details).

Most children are irresistibly drawn to the ubiquitous street-corner *kioscos* selling sweets or packets of *gusanitos* (corn puffs) for a few pesetas. The magnetism of these places often overcomes children's inhibitions enough for them to carry out their own first Spanish transactions.

Nappies, creams, lotions, baby foods and so on are as easily available in Spain as in any other European country, but if there's some particular brand you swear by it's best to bring it with you.

Children benefit from cut-price or free entry at many sights and museums. Those under four travel free on Spanish trains and those aged four to 11 normally pay 60% of the adult fare.

Lonely Planet's *Travel with Children* has lots of practical advice, and first-hand stories from many Lonely Planet authors and others.

USEFUL ORGANISATIONS

The Instituto Cervantes exists to promote the Spanish language and the cultures of Spanish-speaking countries. It has branches in over 30 cities around the world, including at 102 Eaton Square, London SW1W 9AN, UK (☎ 020-7235 0353). It's mainly involved in Spanish teaching and has library and information services.

It has a Web site at www.cervantes.es.

DANGERS & ANNOYANCES

Andalucía is generally a pretty safe place. The main thing you have to be wary of is petty theft (which may of course not seem so petty to you if your passport, money and camera go missing). With a few simple precautions you can minimise the risk.

For some specific hints about looking after your luggage, money and documents, on travel insurance and on safety for women, see the sections on Planning; Visas & Documents; Money; and Women Travellers earlier in this chapter.

Theft & Loss

Most risk of theft occurs in tourist resorts, big cities, and when you first arrive in the country or a new city and may be unaware of danger signs.

The main things to guard against are pickpockets, bag snatchers and theft from cars. Carry valuables under your clothes if possible – certainly not in a bag which could be snatched away easily – and watch for people who get unnecessarily close to you at airports, at stations, on trains or buses or on the street. Don't leave baggage unattended. Avoid crushes. Be cautious with people who come up to offer or ask you something, or start talking to you for no obvious reason. These could be attempts to distract you and make you an easier victim.

Car contents are sitting ducks for thieves. When you leave the car, don't leave visible anything that looks even remotely valuable – and preferably don't leave anything at all. Even if thieves who get into your car end up taking nothing, they will probably have broken a window.

Take care with your belongings on the beach; anything lying on the sand could disappear in a flash when your back is turned. Avoid dingy, empty city alleys and back-streets, or anywhere at night that doesn't feel 100% safe.

Don't leave anything valuable lying around your room, especially in any hostel-type place. Use a safe if there's one available.

If anything valuable does get stolen or lost and you want to make an insurance claim, you'll need to report it to the police and get a copy of the report. If your passport has gone, contact your embassy or consulate for help with a replacement.

Terrorism

The Basque terrorist organisation ETA occasionally explodes bombs or commits murders in Andalucía, as in other parts of Spain. Before travelling to Spain, you can consult your country's foreign affairs department for any current warnings, by telephone or on the Internet: Australia (☎ 02-6261 3305), with a Web site at www.dfat.gov.au; Canada (☎ 613-944 6788, ☎ 800 267 67880) with a Web site at www.dfait-maeci.gc.ca; UK (☎ 020-7238 4503), with a Web site at www.fco.gov.uk; USA (☎ 202-647-5225), with a Web site at http://travel.state.gov.

Annoyances

Andalucía is a pretty mellow place and there isn't much to get annoyed about. That said, there may be a few attempts to short-change you – and you must be prepared for

---

Police – Who Does What?

Spanish police are more of a help than a threat to the average law-abiding traveller. Events such as random drug searches do occur, but not with great frequency.

There are three main types of *policía*: the Guardia Civil, the Policía Local and the Policía Nacional. If you need to go to the police, any of them will do, but you may find the Policía Local are the most helpful. Meanwhile, anywhere in Spain you can call ☎ 091 for the Policía Nacional or ☎ 092 for the Policía Local. The Guardia Civil in Andalucía are often but not always on ☎ 062. Further police numbers, and locations of main stations, are given in city and town sections of this book.

Guardia Civil The main responsibilities of the green-uniformed Guardia Civil include roads, the countryside, villages and international borders.

Policía Local Also called Policía Municipal, these police are controlled by city and town councils and deal mainly with minor matters such as parking, traffic and bylaws. They wear blue-and-white uniforms.

Policía Nacional This force covers cities and bigger towns. Those of its number who wear uniforms are in blue. There is also a large contingent to be found shuffling paper in bunker-like police stations called *comisarías*.

---

more noise than you're probably used to! There's some sort of legislation about motorcycle silencers but it's rarely enforced.

El Libro de Reclamaciones

Most public establishments have a sign up saying that they have a complaints book (*libro de reclamaciones*) available for those customers who wish to use it. If you have a serious gripe, asking for the complaints book might just bring a change of attitude from whoever you're at odds with. If you actually go as far as making an entry in the book, there'll be a copy for you and a copy for the establishment concerned. On the back of your copy will be instructions on how to take the matter further. The books are supposedly checked from time to time by government consumer agencies.

EMERGENCIES

Spain is introducing a single number, ☎ 112, for all emergency services – police, ambulance and fire. At the time of writing this was in use in parts of the country, and some parts of Andalucía, but not in others. Until ☎ 112 is universal, a variety of other emergency numbers will be useful. For police contact numbers see the boxed text 'Police – Who Does What?' on the previous page.

Medical

Call ☎ 061 for an ambulance. In many cities, ambulances or emergency medical help can also be obtained by calling the Cruz Roja (Red Cross). This and other medical emergency numbers, and locations of many hospitals and clinics, are given in this book's city and town sections.

See the Health section earlier in this chapter for more on Spanish medical facilities and health problems. If you're seriously ill or injured, someone should tell your embassy or consulate.

Fire

The fire brigade (*bomberos*) is on ☎ 080 in most cities, but ☎ 085 in Cádiz, Jerez de la Frontera and Algeciras, ☎ 953 25 15 95 in Jaén and ☎ 95 277 43 49 in Marbella.

For Women

Each province's national police headquarters has a special Servicio de Atención a la Mujer (SAM; literally Service of Attention to Women). The Comisión de Investigación de Malos Tratos a Mujeres (Commission of Investigation into Abuse of Women), Calle Almagro 28, 28010 Madrid, maintains a 24-hour free emergency line for victims of physical abuse anywhere in Spain: ☎ 900 10 00 09.

LEGAL MATTERS

If you're arrested you will be allotted the free services of a duty solicitor (*abogado de oficio*), who may speak only Spanish. You're also entitled to make a phone call. If you use this to contact your embassy or consulate, it will probably be able to do no more than refer you to a lawyer who speaks your language. If you end up in court, the authorities are obliged to provide a translator.

Drugs

Spain's liberal drug laws were severely tightened in 1992. The only legal drug is cannabis, and only for personal use – which means very small amounts. There are some bars where people smoke joints openly, although public consumption of any drug is supposedly illegal. The only sure guideline is to be very discreet if you do use cannabis. It would be very unwise in hotel rooms or guesthouses.

Travellers entering Spain from Morocco, especially with a vehicle, should be ready for intensive drug searches.

BUSINESS HOURS

In Andalucía, people generally work from about 9 am to 2 pm from Monday to Friday and then again from 5 pm for another three hours. Shops are usually open these hours on Saturday too (although sometimes without the evening session). Big supermarkets and department stores will often stay open all day Monday to Saturday, from about 9 am to 9 pm. A lot of government offices don't bother with afternoon opening any day.

The Times They Are Always A-Changing

Opening hours of museums, monuments and other sights in Andalucía change frighteningly often. Apart from different hours for different days of the week (which often include shorter opening on Sunday and no opening on Monday), many places change their hours with the seasons. Don't expect any pattern to the changes, though: summer opening could be longer than winter hours because there's more daylight, or shorter because it's too hot in the afternoon, or nonexistent because the staff have all gone on holiday. And everything can be thrown into complete confusion around public holidays.

Many tourist offices will give you a list of opening hours of local sights (horario de monumentos), but this won't always keep track of the latest changes. The only sure way to check a place's opening hours is to phone ahead, or get a tourist office to phone for you. Unfortunately, the places whose hours change more often than any others are tourist offices themselves. Well, this is Andalucía – go and have a drink and tapas while you wait for it to reopen.

PUBLIC HOLIDAYS & SPECIAL EVENTS

Everywhere in Spain has 14 official holidays a year – some are holidays nationwide, some only in one village. The list of holidays often changes a bit from year to year. If a holiday date falls on a weekend, sometimes the holiday is moved to the Monday. If a holiday falls two days away from a weekend, many Spaniards take the intervening day off too – a practice known as making a *puente* (bridge).

The two main periods when Spaniards go away on holiday are Semana Santa and the six weeks from mid-July to the end of August. At these times accommodation in resorts can be scarce and transport heavily booked, but other cities are often half-empty.

In 2000 the nine official national holidays were:

Año Nuevo (New Year's Day) 1 January
Viernes Santo (Good Friday) 13 April in 2001, 29 March in 2002
Fiesta del Trabajo (Labour Day) 1 May
La Asunción (Feast of the Assumption) 15 August
Fiesta Nacional de España (National Day) 12 October
Todos los Santos (All Saints' Day, the traditional day for paying respects to the dead) 1 November
Día de la Constitución (Constitution Day) 6 December
La Inmaculada Concepción (Feast of the Immaculate Conception) 8 December
Navidad (Christmas) 25 December

In addition, the Andalucía regional government sets three holidays and local councils a further two. In 2000 the three regional holidays were:

Epifanía (Epiphany) or **Día de los Reyes Magos** (Three Kings' Day) – children receive presents and, in many towns, Reyes Magos cavalcades (cabalgatas) tour the streets the evening before, tossing out sweets to the crowds. 6 January.
Día de Andalucía (Andalucía Day) 28 February
Jueves Santo (Holy Thursday, the day before Good Friday) 12 April in 2001, 28 March in 2002

Local holidays in some places include:

Corpus Christi late May or June (14 June in 2001, 30 May in 2002)
Día de San Juan Bautista (Feast of St John the Baptist, King Juan Carlos I's saint's day) 24 June
Día de Santiago Apóstol (Feast of St James the Apostle, feast day of Spain's patron saint) 25 July

Festivals

Andalucians indulge their love of colour, noise, crowds, pageant, dressing up and partying at innumerable exuberant local fiestas. Every little village and every city *barrio* (district or quarter) holds several festivals every year, each with its own unique twist. Many fiestas are religion-based but still highly festive.

Most places hold their main annual fair

(feria) in summer, with concerts, parades, fireworks, bullfights, fairgrounds, dancing and an all-night party atmosphere.

There's always a festival happening somewhere in Andalucía. Main local festivals are noted in city and town sections of this book, and tourist offices can supply detailed information.

The monthly what's-on magazine *El Giraldillo* also has a section devoted to upcoming fiestas. The dates of many fiestas are given on the 'Andalucía There's Only One' Web site at www.andalucia.org.

The most outstanding events include (see city and town sections for more information on many of them):

Carnaval (Carnival)
Fancy-dress parades and merrymaking happen in many places (wildest in Cádiz) in February and/or March, usually ending on the Tuesday 47 days before Easter Sunday.

Semana Santa (Holy Week)
The week leading up to Easter Sunday sees parades of lavishly bedecked holy images, long lines of *nazarenos* (penitents, who sometimes go hooded), and big crowds, in almost every city, town and village. In major cities there are daily processions from Palm Sunday to Easter Sunday; smaller places may omit Monday and Tuesday. Sevilla has the most famous celebrations; Málaga, Granada, Córdoba, Arcos de la Frontera, Jaén, Baeza, Úbeda and Huércal-Overa also stage spectacular processions. Village events can be just as unique and touching. The Web site Guía de Semana Santa (http://guia .semanasanta.andal.es) provides links to dozens of related sites.

Feria de Abril
A week-long party held in Sevilla in late April.

Romería de la Virgen de la Cabeza
Hundreds of thousands of people make a mass pilgrimage to the Santuario de la Virgen de la Cabeza near Andújar, Jaén province, on the last Sunday in April.

Feria del Caballo (Horse Fair)
This fair held in Jerez de la Frontera, Andalucía's horse capital, in early May, includes colourful equestrian activities and other festivities.

Cruces de Mayo (May Crosses)
Crosses are placed in squares and patios in many towns, notably in and around Granada, on about 3 May. They are decorated with flowers and become the focus for temporary bars, food stalls, music and dancing.

JANE SMITH

During Romería del Rocío cheerful pilgrims head to the village in gaily decorated carts.

Concurso de Patios Cordobeses
Scores of beautiful private courtyards open to the public for two weeks in early May in Córdoba.

Romería del Rocío
This festive pilgrimage of up to one million people to El Rocío in Huelva province is held on Pentecost weekend, the seventh after Easter (2–4 June 2001; 18–20 May 2002).

Hogueras de San Juan
A celebration with midsummer bonfires and fireworks, especially on beaches. It is held on 23 June.

Día de la Virgen del Carmen
The feast day of the patron of fisherfolk, when her image is carried into the sea, or paraded upon it amid a flotilla of small boats, at many coastal towns. Held on the 16 July.

Feria de Málaga
This is the most animated of all the summer fairs; it runs for nine days from about 15 August.

Moros y Cristianos (Moors and Christians)
On 14 and 15 September there is a re-enactment of the 1568 Muslim rebellion in Válor, Granada province (one of the most colourful of several events commemorating Muslim/Christian conflicts).

Fiestas de Otoño (Autumn Festival)
Jerez de la Frontera's grape harvest celebrations run from mid-September to mid-October, with horse races and parades, flamenco dancing and an air show.

Music & Dance Festivals Given Andalucians' love of music and partying, it comes as no surprise that the calendar is peppered with music and dance festivals. Every town's and village's summer fair features plenty of live performances, and in the bigger towns and cities these often include the top names of the Spanish music and dance world. Many towns stage one- or two-night *fiestas de flamenco* in June, July or August, getting going around midnight: the three big ones for aficionados are the Potaje Gitano, Caracolá Lebrijana and Gazpacho Andaluz (see below for details). Ask tourist offices for exact dates, or check the music section of *El Giraldillo*. Here's a selection of Andalucía's major music and dance festivals (you'll find more on many of them in city and town sections):

Espárrago Rock
This festival is held at Jerez de la Frontera over a weekend in late March or April, featuring indie and alternative rock – the line-up in 2000, for example, included The Cranberries, Lou Reed, Asian Dub Foundation, Celtas Cortos, Dover and Mastretta.

Festival de Jerez
This two-week fiesta of music and dance, especially flamenco, is held in Jerez de la Frontera in late April.

Potaje Gitano (Gitano Stew)
This flamenco festival in Utrera, Sevilla province, is held on a Saturday in June.

Festival Torre del Cante
Another June flamenco event, this is held in Alhaurín de la Torre near the Costa del Sol.

Caracolá Lebrijana
This Saturday night flamenco festival in Lebrija, Sevilla province, is held in June or July (*caracol* means snail).

Festival Internacional de la Guitarra
This guitar festival is held in Córdoba for two weeks in late June or the first half of July.

Festival Internacional de Música y Danza
A two-week music and dance festival is held in Granada in late June or early July.

Festival Internacional de Itálica
This two-week program of dance includes everything from classical ballet to contemporary. It is held in Sevilla in July.

Cubano y Flamenco
Top Cuban *son* bands (traditional Cuban sounds) and Andalucian flamenco stars tour Sevilla province together for two weeks in July.

Gazpacho Andaluz
This flamenco festival held in Morón de la Frontera in July or August.

Castillo de Cante
A one-night flamenco song festival is staged in Ojén near Marbella, on the first or second Saturday of August.

Bienal de Flamenco
This event attracts the largest assembly of big flamenco names. It is held in Sevilla in September of even-numbered years.

Festival Internacional de Jazz
This jazz festival is held in several Andalucian cities during November.

Fiesta Mayor de Verdiales
This exhilarating celebration of a brand of folk music unique to the Málaga area happens in Puerto de la Torre, Málaga, on 28 December.

ACTIVITIES

There's heaps to do in Andalucía apart from seeing sights and lying on beaches. Spanish tourist offices – locally and in other countries – have information or contact addresses/numbers for many activities, and the Junta de Andalucía publishes useful guides to activities such as horse riding, diving, mountain biking, sailing, fishing and golf, sold in several languages at its tourist offices for a few hundred pesetas. For information on organised activity holidays, see Organised Tours in the Getting There & Away chapter.

Walking

Andalucía's rugged landscape provides some beautiful walking areas, mostly in mountainous regions such as the Parque Natural de Cazorla in Jaén province; the Sierra Nevada and Las Alpujarras in Granada province; the Sierra de Grazalema and other hill areas near Ronda (Cádiz and Málaga provinces); the Parque Natural Sierra de Aracena y Picos de Aroche in Huelva province; the Cabo de Gata promontory in Almería province; and the Parque Natural Sierras de Tejeda, Almijara y Alhama straddling the border of Málaga and Granada provinces.

In some of these areas you can string together day walks into a trek over several days, sleeping in a variety of hostales, camp sites or occasionally mountain refuges or wild camping. Further information on walking is given in this book's regional chapters, and three weeks' worth of Andalucía's best walking is detailed in Lonely Planet's *Walking in Spain*. Tourist offices – especially visitor centres in natural parks and other protected areas – can help with walking information. Among Spanish walking guidebooks, Libros Penthalon's handy *El Búho Viajero* series includes about a dozen volumes on areas of Andalucía. Anaya Touring Club's *Ecoguía* series is good too. You may find some of these Spanish guides available in walking areas, but it's also a good idea to check out city bookshops.

For information on maps, see Planning at the beginning of this chapter.

Paths Some of Andalucía's many walkable trails are well signed with route numbers. On others just the odd spot of paint on a stone might tell you you're heading in the right direction. Elsewhere, you're left entirely to your own devices.

The two main categories of path in Spain are *senderos de Gran Recorrido* (GRs, long-distance footpaths, some several hundred kilometres long) and *senderos de Pequeño Recorrido* (PRs, shorter routes suitable for day or weekend hikes). Not all, however, are marked or maintained over their full length – or even for much of their length in some cases. There are also plenty of paths which are neither GRs nor PRs.

The GR-7, a long-distance path which is being created across Europe from Greece to Algeciras, enters Andalucía near Almaciles in north-east Granada province, then divides at Puebla de Don Fadrique, with one branch heading through Jaén province and the other through Las Alpujarras south-east of Granada. Signposting of this path throughout Andalucía is in progress.

Natural and national parks and other protected areas may restrict visitors to limited zones and routes – and ban wild camping – but usually have marked walks through some of their most interesting areas.

Seasons April to mid-June, and September through to mid-October, are generally the most pleasant times for walking, but conditions in the high Sierra Nevada are relatively easy only from July to early September. The weather in high mountains is never predictable.

Climbing

Mountainous Andalucía is full of rocky crags that invite climbing *(escalada)*. More than 3000 climbs – over half of them in Málaga province – are equipped with bolts. The sheer walls of El Chorro gorge in north-west Málaga province are the main magnet, with over 400 charted climbs of every degree of difficulty. Other climbing areas and centres include the Sierra Nevada, El Torcal near Antequera, the Sierra de las Nieves near Ronda, Casares near Estepona, the Sierra de Grazalema and the Parque Natural de Cazorla. *Andalusian Rock Climbs* by Chris Craggs is a good guide.

Cycling

Mountain bikers can test their muscles on many kilometres of good and bad tracks and roads in Andalucía. Tourist offices often have information on routes. The Spanish for mountain bike is *bici todo terreno* (BTT) or *bici de montaña*.

An increasing number of places rent out mountain bikes in Andalucía, usually for 1500 ptas to 3000 ptas a day. For some of the possibilities, see this book's sections on Tarifa; Parque Natural Los Alcornocales; El Chorro, Ardales and Around; Ronda; Sierra Nevada and Las Alpujarras; and Parque Natural de Cazorla.

Skiing

The popular Sierra Nevada ski resort southeast of Granada is Europe's most southerly, and its runs and facilities are good enough to have staged the world alpine skiing championships in 1996. The season normally lasts from December to April.

Windsurfing

Tarifa, west of Gibraltar, is one of Europe's top windsurfing spots, with strong breezes year round, a big windsurfing scene and long, sandy beaches.

Diving & Snorkelling

Some of the rockier parts of the Mediterranean coast offer interesting snorkelling. The best diving spots include La Herradura and Castell de Ferro, both near Almuñécar, and Cabo de Gata, where Punta del Plomo is good for beginners. You'll find diving trips, and gear rental, available in these places.

Sailing

Sailing is naturally a popular activity along Andalucía's coasts and over 40 marinas and mooring places are strung between Ayamonte on the Portuguese border and Garrucha in Almería province. The biggest are the flashy Puerto Banús and Benalmádena on the Costa del Sol, and Almerimar near Almería, each with over 900 moorings.

Golf

Andalucía's golfing profile was so heightened by the 1997 Ryder Cup at the Valderrama course at Sotogrande (near Gibraltar) that the Costa del Sol now subtitles itself 'Costa del Golf'. This was the first time that the illustrious Ryder Cup, a contest between Europe and the USA, had been held anywhere in Europe except Britain. (Europe, captained by the Spaniard Severiano Ballesteros, won.)

Andalucía has 54 golf courses, of which two-thirds are dotted along or near the Costa del Sol between Gibraltar and Málaga. Green fees at most clubs cost between 6000 ptas and 9000 ptas, but under 6000 ptas at courses such as Estepona and La Duquesa on the Costa del Sol, Guadalhorce near Málaga, and Añoreta at Ri-ncón de la Victoria. Top courses, such as Valderrama, Sotogrande, and Las Brisas and Aloha at Marbella, are more costly (30,000 ptas at Valderrama, the most expensive). Golf Service (www.golf-service .com) offers discounted green fees and tee-off time reservations.

Horse Riding

Chief breeding ground of the Spanish thoroughbred horse (also known as the Andalusian), Andalucía is steeped in equestrian tradition. There are plenty of fine trails to ride, and a growing number of stables which will take you on a guided ride or even a long-distance trek. Check this book's sections on Aracena, Arcos de la Frontera, Around Ronda, El Rocío, Sierra Nevada and Las Alpujarras, Parque Natural de Cazorla, Parque Natural Los Alcornocales, San José (Almería province), Tarifa and West of Aracena. The cost is usually around 3000 ptas for two hours or 5000 ptas for four hours.

Anyone with an interest in horses should put Jerez de la Frontera on their itinerary. The town holds a number of exciting annual equine events and its Royal Andalucian School of Equestrian Art and the nearby Yeguada del Hierro breeding centre are fascinating to visit at any time. Jerez hosts the World Equestrian Games in 2002.

Bird-Watching

Andalucía is a magnet for bird-watchers year round. March and April, when you can see many wintering species and some arriving summer visitors, are good times. The Strait of Gibraltar is a particularly exciting viewing site (see the boxed text 'High Fliers Over the Strait of Gibraltar' in the Cádiz Province chapter). You'll find information on other bird-watching spots – including details on the greater flamingo, perhaps Andalucía's most spectacular bird – in several other sections of this book, including Flora & Fauna (in the Facts about Andalucía chapter), Isla Cristina, Laguna de Fuente de Piedra, Paraje Natural Marismas del Odiel, Parque Nacional de Doñana, Parque Natural de Cazorla, Parque Natural Sierra de Grazalema, Parque Natural Sierra Norte and San Miguel de Cabo de Gata. See also Books earlier in this chapter. SEO/Birdlife, the Spanish Ornithological Society (☎ 959 50 60 93) has an office at El Rocío on the fringe of the Parque Nacional de Doñana.

COURSES

A spot of study is a great way not only to learn something but also to meet people and get an inside angle on local life.

Language

The Instituto Cervantes (see Useful Organisations earlier in this chapter) offers a great deal of information on Spanish-language courses in Andalucía, on its Web site and through its branches worldwide. Another

Internet source is the Spanish Directory at www.atlas.co.uk/efl/spain.

Sevilla and Granada are the most popular places in Andalucía to study Spanish, but there are also schools in most other main cities and in coastal towns such as Tarifa, Nerja, Marbella and Almuñécar. University courses often last a term, though they range from two weeks to a year. Private language schools are generally more flexible about when you can start and how long you stay. Most places cater for a wide range of levels, from beginners up. Many courses have a cultural component as well.

Costs vary widely. University courses offer some of the best value, with a typical four-week course of 20 one-hour classes a week for around 60,000 ptas. Many places offer accommodation with families, in student lodgings or in flats, if you want it – generally from around 35,000 ptas a month with no meals to about 70,000 ptas for full board.

Further information on some schools is provided in this book's city sections. Most schools can furnish detailed information on what they offer. Things to think about when choosing one include how intensive the course is (this varies at different schools), class sizes, who the other students are likely to be and whether you want organised extracurricular activities. Personal recommendation from previous students counts for a lot in selecting your school. It's also worth asking whether a course will lead to any formal certificate. The Diplomas Oficiales de Español como Lengua Extranjera (DELE) are qualifications awarded by Spain's Ministry of Education and Science (for a complete beginner approximately 40 hours of classes are required to achieve the most basic DELE qualification).

It's easy to arrange private classes in many places: check notice boards in universities and language schools, or small ads in the local press. Expect to pay around 2000 ptas per hour for individual private lessons.

Arts & Culture

Many of the universities and schools offering language courses also offer other courses in Spanish history, literature and culture. The Instituto Cervantes is, again, a good source of information. See the Sevilla and Granada sections for information on some courses in Spanish dance and guitar. The magazines *Alma 100* (see Seeing Flamenco in the earlier special section 'Flamenco: The Gitano's Lament') carries heaps of ads for flamenco classes and courses. The magazine *El Giraldillo* has a few.

Cooking & Other Courses

Pata Negra (☎ 020-7736 1959, fax 7736 1925), 28 Parsons Green, London SW6 4UH, UK, runs week-long Spanish and North African cooking courses with expert cooks at country houses in western Andalucía, starting at UK£1040 plus flights. Web site at www.patanegra.net.

Learning for Pleasure (UK ☎ 01892-668 090, UK fax 667854, @ v_parks@msn .com) offers expert-led courses in Spanish and Moroccan cooking, painting, Mediterranean gardening and herbal medicine at a country property *(cortijo)* near Jimena de la Frontera in the green hills of Cádiz province. Most courses are for pre-existing groups, but they also offer a few open-subscription courses, especially in cookery.

Cortijo Romero is a personal development and alternative holiday centre near Órgiva in Las Alpujarras, with week-long courses and workshops ranging from dance, massage and creative writing to yoga, Alexander technique and 'sunfeast weeks', led by facilitators from around the world. The typical price is UK£365; contact Cortijo Romero (☎ 01494-782720), Little Grove, Grove Lane, Chesham, Bucks HP5 3QQ, UK, or check out the Web site at www.cortijo-romero.co.uk.

WORK

With high unemployment even by Spanish standards, Andalucía doesn't exactly have a labour shortage. But there are a few possible ways of earning your keep (or almost) while you're here. If you have any contacts – perhaps among the many foreigners living in Andalucía – follow them up. Word of mouth counts for a lot.

Regulations

Nationals of EU countries, Norway and Iceland are allowed to work in Spain without a visa, but if they plan to stay for more than three months, they are supposed to apply within the first month for a resident's permit (see Visas & Documents). Virtually everyone else is supposed to obtain a work permit from a Spanish consulate in their country of residence and, if they plan to stay more than 90 days, a residence visa. These procedures are well-nigh impossible unless you already have a job contract, and you should set things rolling long before you go to Spain. That said, plenty of people do work, discreetly, without bothering to tangle with the bureaucracy.

Opportunities

Tourist Resorts Summer work, especially on the Costa del Sol, is a distinct possibility, particularly if you get in early in the season and are prepared to stay a while. Many bars, restaurants and other businesses are run by foreigners. Follow up any contacts you have, look at notice boards, and check the local press, including *Sur In English*, which carries some ads for secretaries, receptionists, salespeople, waiters, bar staff, nannies, chefs, baby sitters and cleaners as well as 'liners', 'closers' and other types required to sell timeshare properties to foreign holidaymakers. The more Spanish you can speak, the better your prospects, of course.

Language Teaching Having some relevant qualifications and a knowledge of Spanish obviously help for this option. There are several language schools in most cities and often one or two in smaller towns. Getting a job is harder if you're not an EU citizen. Giving private lessons is an option, though unlikely to bring you a living wage very soon.

Sources of information on possible teaching work – school or private – include universities, language schools and foreign-language bookshops. Some of these have notice boards where you may find work opportunities, or where you can advertise your own services. The local press is also worth scanning or advertising in. Language

schools are listed under 'Academias de Idiomas' in the Yellow Pages.

Boat Crew Gibraltar is the best place to look for a crew place on a yacht or cruiser. In high summer, a few places a week come up there on craft sailing the Mediterranean, and from November to January there's the possibility of working your passage to the Caribbean. Puerto Banús is the next best place to try. You're unlikely to be paid for this work.

ACCOMMODATION

The annual *Guía de Hoteles, Pensiones, Apartamentos, Campings y Casas Rurales*, published by the Junta de Andalucía and available from some tourist offices and bookshops in Andalucía for 800 ptas, lists most of the region's places to stay, including camp sites, and their facilities and approximate prices. Three useful Internet sites, with on-line booking, are InterHotel at http://interhotel.com/spain/en; the Junta's tourism Web site at www.andalucia.org; and Madeinspain at www.madeinspain.net.

Camping

Andalucía has over 130 officially graded camp sites *(campings)*. Some are well located in woodland or near beaches or rivers, others are stuck away near main roads on the edges of towns and cities. Very few are near city centres.

Sites are officially rated 1st class (1ªC), 2nd class (2ªC) or 3rd class (3ªC). There are also a few not officially graded, usually equivalent to 3rd class. Facilities range from reasonable to very good, though any site can be crowded and noisy at busy times. Even a 3rd-class site is likely to have hot showers, electrical hook-ups and a cafeteria. The best sites have heated pools, supermarkets, restaurants, laundry service and children's playgrounds. Sizes vary; some cater for under 100 people, others can take over 5000 people.

Camp sites usually charge per person, per tent and per vehicle – anywhere between 250 ptas and 800 ptas for each (500 ptas is typical). Children usually pay a bit less than

When the Price is Right

Accommodation prices given in this book are high-season prices unless stated otherwise – so you can expect some pleasant surprises at off-peak times of year. Many places to stay have separate price structures for high season *(temporada alta)*, shoulder season *(temporada media)* and low season *(temporada baja)*, all usually displayed on a notice in reception or close by. (Hoteliers are free to charge less than the posted prices, which they quite often do, or more, which happens less often.)

High season depends on where you are, but in most places it's summer – which can mean a period as short as mid-July to the end of August or as long as Easter to October. The Christmas–New Year period, Semana Santa (the week leading up to Easter Sunday) and local festivals, which attract lots of visitors, are also high season in many places. We note major seasonal pricing trends in Places to Stay sections, and the prices we give include the 7% value-added tax (IVA) unless stated otherwise.

Differences between low and high-season prices tend to be biggest in coastal resorts – there you'll typically pay 25% less in February than in August, but it can be 50% less. Some places to stay in Sevilla charge three times as much during Semana Santa and the Feria de Abril as they do in winter.

Many establishments, especially the cheaper ones, vary their prices according to demand. Some will forget about IVA if you don't require a receipt, and even in high season some will charge less than we quote if business is slow. At any time you may be able to obtain a discount if you stay for more than a couple of nights.

In the low season there's generally no need to book ahead, but when things get busier it's advisable to do so, and at peak periods it can be essential if you want to avoid a wearisome search for a room. At many places, a phone call is all that's needed, giving your approximate time of arrival.

adults. Many sites are open year round, but some close from around October to Easter. Here and there you come across a *zona de acampada* or *área de acampada*, a country site with no facilities, no supervision and no charge. Tourist offices can always direct you to the nearest camp site.

With certain exceptions – such as many beaches and environmentally protected areas – it is permissible to camp outside camp sites (though not within 1km of official ones). Signs may indicate where wild camping is not allowed. You'll need permission to camp on private land.

Camping Gaz is the only common brand of camping gas: screw-on canisters are near-impossible to find.

Youth Hostels

Most of Andalucía's 20-odd youth hostels (*albergues juveniles*, not to be confused with *hostales* – see the next section) are affiliated with Inturjoven, the official Andalucía youth hostel organisation. Inturjoven hostels are mostly good, modern places with a high proportion of twin rooms as well as

small dormitories with bunks. Sheets are provided and most rooms have private bathrooms. The hostels don't have cooking facilities but they do have dining rooms *(comedores)*, usually serving all meals at good prices. Inturjoven has a central booking office (☎ 902 51 00 00, fax 95 503 58 48, ✆ reservas@inturjoven.junta-andalucia.es) at Calle del Miño 24, Los Remedios, 41011 Sevilla – open 9.30 am to 2 pm and 5 to 7.30 pm Monday to Friday. You can also book with the hostels themselves.

Prices for a bed in any official Inturjoven hostel, including breakfast, are 1200/1500/1800 ptas in the low/medium/high season for under-26s, and 1500/2000/2300 ptas for people aged 26 or over – plus IVA in all cases. At most hostels it's medium season from mid-June to mid-September and for certain short peak periods at other times of year, and low season the rest of the time. But the Almería, Córdoba, Granada, Málaga and Sevilla hostels have no low season. High season rates only apply for certain short peak periods at these five and a few other hostels. Any Inturjoven hostel

euro currency converter 1000 ptas = €6.01

can supply full price information and other details for all the others – as can the Inturjoven Web site at www.inturjoven.com.

To stay in an Inturjoven hostel you need a youth hostel card. If you don't already have one from a youth hostel or hostel organisation in your own country, you can get a Hostelling International (HI) Card, valid till 31 December of the year you buy it, at any Inturjoven hostel or the Sevilla office, or at any of the 140 or so other hostels in the Red Española de Albergues Juveniles (REAJ), the Spanish affiliate of HI. For the HI card, you pay in instalments of 300 ptas for each night you spend in a hostel, up to 1800 ptas.

Some hostels are often heavily booked by school or youth groups, but inconvenient night-time curfews or daytime closing hours are rare.

The annual HI Europe hostels directory lists all Inturjoven and other REAJ hostels.

Just a few Andalucian hostels are run by organisations other than Inturjoven. Some of these do not require hostel cards.

Hostales, Hospedajes, Pensiones & Hotels

Officially all these establishments are classified as either *hoteles* (from one to five stars) or *pensiones* (one or two stars). In practice, places to stay use all sorts of titles, especially at the budget end of the market.

In broad terms, the cheapest are places which just advertise beds (*camas*), *fondas* (traditionally a basic eatery and inn combined, though one or other function is now often missing) and *casas de huéspedes* or *hospedajes* (guesthouses). All such places will be bare and basic. Bathrooms are likely to be communal. Your room may be small, possibly lacking a window, towel and (probably) soap, and it may have alarming electrical fittings and erratic hot water – but in most cases it will be kept pretty clean. The beds may make you feel as though you're lying diagonally across a bumpy hillside – or they may be firm, flat and comfortable. In winter don't hesitate to ask for extra blankets. Single/double rooms cost from around 1200/2000 ptas to 2000/3000 ptas. A *pensión* (basically a small private hotel) is usu-

ally a small step up from the above categories, in standards and price. Some cheap establishments forget to provide towels or soap or replenish the toilet paper. Don't hesitate to ask for these necessities.

Next up the scale are *hostales*, little different from pensiones except that some are considerably more comfortable, and more rooms tend to have private bathrooms. Some hostales are bright, modern and pleasant; others are less so. Prices for rooms range from around 1500/3000 ptas to 6000/8000 ptas.

Establishments calling themselves *hotel* range from simple places where a double room could cost 4000 ptas or less up to super-luxury, five-star places where you would pay 50,000 ptas. Even in the cheapest hotels, rooms are likely to have an attached bathroom and there'll probably be a restaurant.

Some of Andalucía's most charming places to stay are small or medium-sized hotels with economical or mid-range prices from around 5000 ptas to 10,000 ptas a double. Many such establishments occupy characterful old town houses or rambling country properties with pleasant gardens and pools.

Many places to stay of all the aforementioned types have a range of rooms at different prices. At the bottom end prices will vary according to whether the room has a washbasin (*lavabo*), shower (*ducha*) or full bathroom (*baño completo*). At the top end you may pay more for a room on the outside of the building or with a balcony, and will often have the option of a suite. Many places have rooms for three, four or more people where the per-person cost is much lower than in a single or double – good news for families. Checkout time is nearly always noon.

Casas Rurales

The booming interest of Spaniards in their own countryside has led to the opening of many new places to stay in rural areas, in Andalucía as elsewhere. These *casas rurales* are usually comfortably renovated village houses or farmhouses, with just a handful of rooms. Some have meals available; some

Old-Fashioned Luxury

Spain's *paradores*, officially *paradores de turismo*, are a chain of 85 high-class hotels around the country (16 of them in Andalucía). Many – such as those at Carmona, Jaén, Úbeda and Granada in Andalucía – are in converted castles, mansions or monasteries, and are wonderful places to stay. Room-only prices start at 9200/11,500 ptas plus IVA for singles/doubles in the low season and you're looking at about 14,000/17,500 ptas plus IVA for most paradors in the high season – even more at paradors such as Granada's, which is the most expensive in all Spain. Special offers can make paradors more affordable for some people: the over-60s can get 35% off room and breakfast prices at many paradors for much of the year (especially from October to June), and some paradors offer bed and breakfast for two people for less than 12,000 ptas in winter. You can find out the current offers on the parador Web site at www.parador.es, or by contacting the paradors' central reservation service, the Central de Reservas, Calle Requena 3, 28013 Madrid (☎ 91 516 66 66, fax 91 516 66 57, ✉ info@parador.es).

just provide rooms; some offer self-catering accommodation. Prices typically range between 1500 ptas and 3000 ptas per person per night.

Tourist offices can usually provide leaflets on local country accommodation and direct you to any local agencies where you can book. Rural Andalus (☎ 95 227 62 29, fax 95 227 65 56), Calle Don Cristián 10, 29007 Málaga, represents over 200 rural properties including some hotels. It's particularly strong on La Axarquía and the Serranía de Ronda in Málaga province, but houses are offered in most parts of Andalucía. Check out the Web site at www.ruralandalus.es. Red Andaluza de Alojamientos Rurales (RAAR, Andalucian Country Lodgings Network, ☎ 902 44 22 33, fax 950 27 16 78) offers over 370 rural accommodation possibilities. It has a Web site at www.raar.es.

Apartments, Houses & Villas

In many places in Andalucía there are equipped, self-catering apartments, houses and villas to rent. A simple one-bedroom apartment for two or three people might cost as little as 3000 ptas a night, though more often you're looking at twice that, and prices can jump further in peak seasons. These options are most worth considering if you plan to stay several days or more, in which case there will usually be discounts from the daily rate.

Tourist offices can supply lists of places for rent, and in Britain the *Sunday Times* carries a lot of private ads for such places. British-based house and villa agencies (don't expect low prices) include Magic of Spain (☎ 020-8748 4220), with a Web site at www.magictravelgroup.co.uk; Individual Travellers Spain (☎ 01798-869485) with a Web site at www.indiv-travellers.com; Simply Spain (☎ 020-8541 2222), with a Web site at www.simply-travel.com and Secret Spain (☎ 01527-578900).

Also see the previous Casas Rurales section.

ENTERTAINMENT

You need never go short of entertainment in Andalucía. If nothing else, just sitting in a cafe and watching the animated street life go on around you can be fun enough.

Listings

Local papers often carry fairly thorough entertainment listings. Try to pick up *El Giraldillo*, a good monthly what's-on listing for all Andalucía, from tourist offices. It's in Spanish but decipherable. Tourist offices can help with specific inquiries and may have further what's-on publications.

Bars & Discos

Wild and very late nights, especially on Friday and Saturday, are an integral part of the Andalucian scene. Even small towns often have lively scenes. Many young Andalucians don't think about going out till midnight or so. Bars, in all shapes, sizes and themes, are the main attractions until around 2 or 3 am. Some play great music, which will get you hopping before you maybe move on to a *discoteca* or electronic-music *sala* till 5 or 6 am – or later! Some discos won't let you in wearing jeans or trainers.

The word 'club' in nightlife contexts in Spain, by the way, has a somewhat different meaning from what it has in many other countries: it often refers to a sleazy pick-up joint, not a million miles from a brothel.

Live Pop, Rock & Jazz
Most towns have at least one bar or cafe with live music at the weekend. In the major cities there's something happening every night and a big choice at weekends.

The Spanish rock and pop scene is large and lively, and foreign touring bands put in fairly frequent appearances in Andalucía, especially in summer. Live music of many types is an essential ingredient of many fiestas. Jazz and blues have good followings, with venues in most big cities.

Flamenco
Flamenco is easiest to catch in the summer, when a number of towns stage flamenco festivals and others include flamenco in a wider-ranging fair or fiesta. Such flamenco nights are typically long-drawn-out open-air affairs, rarely getting going till after midnight and sometimes lasting till dawn, with copious quantities of alcohol being drunk.

The rest of the year you'll find there are intermittent big-name performances in theatres, but also regular flamenco nights at bars and clubs in some cities – often just for the price of your drinks. Flamenco fans also band together in clubs called *peñas*, which stage live performance nights – most will admit genuinely interested visitors and the atmosphere here can be very intimate.

Unless asked otherwise, tourist offices may steer you towards *tablaos*, regular shows for a tourist audience, usually with high prices. Some of these are reasonably good; others are tacky.

See Public Holidays & Special Events in this chapter for major flamenco festivals, and the Flamenco special section and city and town Entertainment sections for further information on flamenco. Sevilla, Jerez de la Frontera and Granada are flamenco hotbeds, but you'll often be able to find something in Málaga, Cádiz or Córdoba – and, erratically, in many other places too.

Cinemas
Cinemas abound and are inexpensive, though foreign films are almost always dubbed into Spanish. In the major cities a few cinemas show foreign films with Spanish subtitles – look for the letters v.o.s. *(versión original subtitulada)* in listings.

Classical Music, Dance & Theatre
Plenty of these go on in Andalucía's cities. They often take the form of festivals (see Public Holidays & Special Events earlier in this chapter). Theatre is nearly all in Spanish, of course.

Festivals
Andalucía's myriad of fiestas (see Public Holidays & Special Events earlier in this chapter) provide heaps of colourful spectacle and, more often than not, a celebratory atmosphere.

SPECTATOR SPORTS
Football
Soccer *(fútbol)* rivals bullfighting as Spain's national sport. Every weekend from September to May, millions follow the national Primera División (First Division) on TV. Spaniards take their favoured teams' fortunes very seriously!

Andalucía's three best teams are Sevilla, Málaga and Real Betis (of Sevilla). Look for them in the lower half of the Primera División table or the upper half of the Segunda División. Teams from other main Andalucian cities tend to go up and down between the Segunda División and the next league down, the Segunda División B (which is divided into four regional groups). Andalucian soccer fans often care more about Real Madrid or Barcelona than about their local club.

League games are mostly played on Sunday, with a few on Saturday. Games in the Copa del Rey (Spain's FA Cup equivalent) are held midweek at night. For upcoming fixtures see the local press or the sports paper *Marca*, or visit Planet Fútbol at www. grupocorreo.es/grupo/planetfutbol.

Bullfighting

The bullfight *(corrida)* is a pageant with a long history and many rules. It is not simply a ghoulish alternative to the slaughterhouse. Many people feel ill at the sight of the kill, and the preceding few minutes' torture is undoubtedly cruel, but aficionados will say that fighting bulls have been bred for conflict and that before the fateful day they are treated like kings. The bull is better off, it is said, dying at the hands of a *matador* (killer) than in the abattoir *(matadero)*. The corrida is about many things – a direct confrontation with death, bravery, skill and performance. Although many Spaniards themselves consider it a cruel activity, many view it as an art and there is no doubting its popularity.

Contests of strength, skill and bravery between man and beast are no recent phenomenon. The Romans probably staged Spain's first bullfights. *La lidia*, as the modern art of bullfighting on foot is known, took off in an organised fashion in Spain in the mid-18th century. Andalucía was one of its birthplaces and has been one of its hotbeds ever since. Before then, bullfighting on horseback was a kind of cavalry training-cumsport for the gentry. (Horseback bullfights, known as *corridas de rejones*, still crop up here and there – and the equestrian skills displayed can be enthralling.)

Three generations of the Romero family from Ronda in Málaga province established most of the basics of bullfighting on foot. In the 1830s King Fernando VII appointed Pedro Romero, the third of the line, director of the Escuela de Tauromaquia de Sevilla, the country's first college for bullfighters. It was around this time, too, that breeders succeeded in creating the first reliable breeds of *toro bravo* or fighting bull.

For information on anti-bullfighting organisations see Treatment of Animals under Society & Conduct in the Facts about Andalucía chapter.

El Matador & La Cuadrilla Only champion matadors make good money, and some actually make a loss. The matador must pay a supporting team *(cuadrilla)*, pay for the right to fight a bull, and rent or buy an outfit and equipment.

The cuadrilla is made up of quite a few people. Firstly, there are several *peones*, junior *toreros* (bullfighters) under the orders of the matador. They come out to distract the bull with great capes, manoeuvre him into the desired position, and so on. Then come the *banderilleros*. At a given moment one or two banderilleros race towards the bull and attempt to plunge a pair of colourfully decorated *banderillas* (short prods with harpoon-style ends) into the withers of the bull. This is intended to goad the animal into action. The horseback *picadores* play a different role. Charged by the bull, which tries to upend or eviscerate the horse, the picador shoves a lance into the withers which will greatly weaken the bull. Animal-lovers may take some consolation from the fact that, since the 19th century, the horses have been protected by heavy padding that bulls rarely manage to penetrate. Prior to that, at least as many horses as bulls died in bullfights.

Then there is the matador. The matador's dress could be that of a flamenco dancer. At its simplest, in country fiestas, it is generally a straightforward combination of black trousers or tights, white shirt and black vest. At its most extravagant, the *traje de luces* (suit of lights) can be an extraordinary display of bright, spangly colour. All the toreros (matadors, banderilleros and so on) wear the black *montera*, the hat that looks a little like a set of Mickey Mouse ears. The torero's standard weapons are the *estoque* or *espada* (sword) and the heavy silk and percale *capa* (cape). The matador alone also employs a different cape with the sword – a smaller piece of cloth held with a bar of wood called the *muleta* and used for a number of different passes.

La Corrida Bullfighting usually begins about 6 pm and, as a rule, six bulls are on the day's card, with three different matadors fighting two bulls each. If a bull is considered not up to scratch, it is booed off (to the shame of the ranch that bred it) and a replacement is brought on. Each fight takes about 15 minutes.

Fights begin with the bull charging into the arena, then being moved about and calmed down a little by the junior bullfighters. The matador then appears and executes moves *(faenas)* with the bull. The more closely and calmly the matador works with the bull, pivoting before its horns, the greater will be the crowd's approbation. After a little of this, the matador strides off and leaves the stage first to the banderilleros, then to the picadores, before returning for the final session. At various moments during the fight, a brass band will strike up, adding to the air of grand spectacle.

When the bull seems tired out and unlikely to give a lot more, the matador chooses the moment for the kill. Facing the animal head-on, the matador aims to sink the sword cleanly into its neck for an instant kill – the *estocada*. It's an awful lot easier said than done.

A good performance followed by a clean kill will have the crowd on its feet waving handkerchiefs in appeal to the president to award the matador an ear of the animal. The president usually waits to gauge the crowd's enthusiasm before finally flopping a white handkerchief onto his balcony. If the fight has been exceptional, the matador might *cortar dos orejas* – cut two ears off. And a matador who does really really well may be awarded the tail too *(dos orejas y rabo)*.

The carcass is meanwhile dragged out by a team of dray-horses and the sand raked in preparation for the next bull. The meat ends up on sale at the market or a butcher's.

Matadors If you are spoiling for a fight, it is worth looking out for the big names among the matadors. They are no guarantee you'll see a high-quality corrida, as that also depends on the animals themselves, but it is a good sign. Names to look for include: Enrique Ponce, a serious class act; Joselito; Rivera Ordóñez; Curro Romero, born in the 1920s and still fighting; Julián 'El Juli' López, a recently-arrived teenage sensation; José Tomás; and El Cordobés, one of the biggest names, although for some his style borders on mocking the animal and is considered unnecessarily cruel.

Ethics of the Fight Anyone in doubt about the danger to the human participants in this contest of bravery should remember that people *do* die in the ring. Today, however, the risk is reduced by the fraudulent practice known as the *afeitado* – the filing down of the bull's horns. Filing not only makes the bull a little bit less anxious to attack its tormentors but also impairs its judgement of distance and angle. When moves were made to stop this practice in 1997, the matadors went on strike.

When & Where The official bullfighting year in Andalucía runs from Easter Sunday to October, though it's possible to see a corrida at other times of the year on the Costa del Sol. Most corridas are held as part of a city or town fiesta. Few rings have regular fights right through the season, Sevilla being an exception.

The big bang that launches Andalucía's bullfighting year is Sevilla's Feria de Abril (April Fair), with fights almost daily during the week of the fair and the week before it. It's Sevilla, too, where the year ends with a corrida on 12 October, Spain's National Day. Here are some of the other major seasons on the Andalucian bullfight calendar:

Late April or early May
Fiesta de Jerez de la Frontera

Late May or early June
Feria de Nuestra Señora de la Salud Held in Córdoba, a big bullfighting stronghold.
Feria de la Manzanilla Held in Sanlúcar de Barrameda.
Corpus Christi Held in Granada.

June to August
El Puerto de Santa María & the Costa del Sol Fights happen most Sundays, those on the Costa del Sol tend to be frequented by tourists but most Sundays there's a respectable fight in one of the rings (such as Fuengirola, Marbella, Torremolinos and Mijas).
Fiestas Colombinas Held in Huelva from approximately 3 to 9 August.
Feria de Málaga Held in mid-August.

Feria de la Virgen del Mar Held in Almería in the last week of August.

September

Corrida Goyesca Held in Ronda – select, stylish matadors fight in costumes of the type shown in Goya's bullfight engravings. It runs from around 6 to 8 September.

Corridas in Jaén province are mostly held in mid- or late September, including at Úbeda, Cazorla and Linares, site of the 1947 death of the very famous matador Manolete.

Bullfighting magazines such as the weekly *6 Toros 6* carry full details of who's fighting, where and when. Gaudy posters advertise upcoming fights locally and give ticket information. In addition to the top corridas, which attract the big-name matadors and big crowds, there are plenty of lesser ones in cities, towns and villages. These are often *novilleras*, in which immature bulls (*novillos*) are fought by junior matadors (*novilleros*). In small places the Plaza Mayor may serve as a makeshift bullring.

If you're interested in knowing more about bullfighting, a good place to start is the Web site www.sol.com/list/toros.htm.

Other Sports

The Jerez de la Frontera Grand Prix in the World Motorcycle Championship, held in May, is one of Spain's biggest sporting events, attracting around 150,000 spectators.

Basketball is also popular. Andalucía's most successful teams in the Liga ACB national professional league are Unicaja of Málaga and Caja San Fernando.

Andalucía stages several major professional golf tournaments each year. Events, venues and dates change, but the Volvo Masters will be played in November at Montecastillo, Jerez de la Frontera, till at least 2002. In 1999, Andalucian Ryder Cup star Miguel Ángel Jiménez, from Churriana near Málaga, became the first Spaniard to win the Volvo.

SHOPPING

You can find some very attractive and reasonably priced handicrafts in Andalucía.

There's surprising variation in what you find from one area to another. Many products are sold only close to where they are made. Apart from craft shops – abundant in production and tourist areas – you may pick up crafts at markets in villages or towns, and even in department stores such as the nationwide El Corte Inglés chain. There are also flea markets (*mercadillos*) and car boot sales (*rastros*) around the region where you can at times find incredible bargains.

Pottery

This comes in many attractive regional varieties – crockery, tiles, plant pots and more – and is cheap. Islamic influence on design and colour is strong. In Granada, the dominant colours are white splashed with green and blue, often with a pomegranate as the centrepiece of the pattern. In Córdoba the product is finer, with black, green and blue borders on white. Úbeda, another noted pottery centre, typically employs a green glaze. Gaudier colours are used in some other areas. Some excellent, more individual pieces are made in Níjar near Almería.

Rugs

Inexpensive, colourful rugs and blankets are made in several areas, among them Las Alpujarras and Níjar.

Leather

Andalucian leather goods can be a bargain. You can still get good prices on jackets, bags, belts, shoes and boots in many places. Exquisite riding boots can be purchased in 'horsey' places like Jerez de la Frontera and El Rocío. Embossed, polychrome leather products such as poufs make a good, not-too-bulky present: you simply roll up the leather and insert the filling back at home.

Other Crafts

Gold and silver jewellery abound; some of the best is the filigree made in Córdoba. There's some pleasing woodwork available, such as Granada's marquetry boxes, chess sets and more. Basketwork is most evident on the coasts.

Food & Drink

OLIVER STREWE

OLIVER STREWE

OLIVER STREWE

Title page: photograph by Oliver Strewe

Top: Traditionally cured in the mountains, Huelva's hams are said to be the best in Spain.

Middle: A vegetarian option: ensalada de garbanzos y tomate (chickpea and tomato salad)

Bottom: You see food like this and it's hard to leave coastal Andalucía.

FOOD

Andalucian cooking is typically Mediterranean in its liberal use of olive oil, garlic, onions, tomatoes and peppers. Traditionally, it's simple peasant fare based on fresh ingredients and with a hint of herbs and spices, reflecting Roman, Jewish, New World and Arabic influences, the latter being the most distinctive.

Pescado (fish) and *carne* (meat) are eaten almost everywhere, and there are many excellent varieties of *mariscos* (seafood), especially from the Atlantic coast. A quick deep-fry in very hot olive oil is the most common method of cooking seafood in Andalucía. A good *sopa de mariscos* (seafood soup) can almost be a meal in itself. Note that prices for fish and seafood on menus are sometimes given by weight, which is potentially misleading.

Everywhere the fruit and vegetables are delicious and fresh, for the growing season is almost year round.

Many varieties of soaked dried beans have, for reasons of economy, traditionally made up the bulk of stews, with meat only added for flavour if available.

For a culinary glossary, see Food in the Language chapter.

Provincial Specialities

Most restaurants provide quite a range of fare, but you'll notice changes of emphasis from one area to another. Andalucía's local specialities reflect its geographical diversity. In the *sierras* (mountains), hams are cured and game dishes abound. On the coasts, seafood predominates and seafood soups, fried fish and sardines grilled on spits over driftwood fires are all common.

The following is a brief look at some of the gastronomic traditions of Andalucía's eight provinces:

Almería This arid eastern province has a simple, basic cuisine that makes use of chickpeas, grains, seafood and plenty of irrigation-grown fresh vegetables.

Cádiz The coastline has fantastic seafood, with a multitude of mouthwatering tapas. Cádiz city is home to *pescaíto frito* (fried fish). Sherry is added to meat dishes in Jerez de la Frontera. The French and English, who played a big role in the sherry industry in Jerez, have also influenced the cuisine.

Córdoba This province was at the heart of the culinary changes introduced by the Muslims. Today, some of Córdoba city's classy restaurants prepare food in the medieval Muslim and Sephardic (Jewish) styles. Few authentic recipes survive from the Muslim era, but there is enough information to approximate, especially on *cocina Mozárabe* (Mozarabic fare), the food of Christians who lived under

Muslim rule. Try the upmarket *El Caballo Rojo* (see Places to Eat in the Córdoba section for details) if you're interested in sampling Mozarabic dishes from the time of the caliphs. At grassroots level, Córdoba is strong on vegetable dishes and has good cured meats.

Granada The province of Granada includes Spain's highest peaks and a semi-tropical coastline. It is known for its mountain-cured hams and warming meat dishes, but seafood and tropical fruits feature too.

Huelva There's excellent seafood here at the western end of Andalucía – *chocos* (small cuttlefish) are a local passion. But Huelva is best known for its cured meats, especially hams from Jabugo.

Jaén On the southern slopes of the eastern Sierra Morena, Jaén is the home of olive oil, added liberally to many dishes. It's also known for its potato and game dishes.

Málaga This province is known for its fried fish and seafood, especially *boquerones* (anchovies), which are often eaten raw marinated in

From Little Acorns, Great Hams Grow

Appetising may not be the word that leaps to mind when you first set eyes on a dozen or two pigs' back legs dangling from the ceiling of a Spanish bar. But to most Spaniards there's no more mouth-watering prospect than a few thin, succulent slices of cured *jamón* (ham). Try two or three slices as a tapa, or have it in a *bocadillo* (sandwich) for 500 to 600 ptas, or get a *ración* (meal-sized serving of a tapa) for anywhere upwards of 900 ptas.

Most of these hams are *jamón serrano* (mountain-cured ham, although nowadays the climatic conditions of the mountains can be reproduced in sheds and cellars at any altitude). The best serrano is *jamón ibérico*, also called *pata negra* (black leg) from the black (or dark brown) Iberian breed of pig, and the best jamón ibérico is *jamón ibérico de bellota*, from swine fed on *bellotas* (acorns).

Considered to be the best jamón of all is the jamón ibérico of Jabugo, in Andalucía's Huelva province, which comes from pigs free-ranging in the Sierra Morena oak forests. The best Jabugo hams are graded from one to five *jotas* (Js), and JJJJJ *(cinco jotas)* hams are said to come from pigs that have never eaten anything but acorns.

For 1kg of jamón serrano in a shop, expect to pay about 2000 ptas. Ibérico can cost double that.

Ordinary, uncured cold ham, by the way, is called *jamón York*. It's dull as ditchwater after you've tasted serrano or ibérico.

vinegar, oil and garlic. Seafood soups are common. Ronda, in Málaga's mountains, has tasty game, cured meats, stews and bean dishes. Migas are a Málaga speciality: at their most basic, migas consist of crumbly fried flour and water, but they can be enlivened with fish, garlic, peppers or dried tomato.

Sevilla Cuisine here is a touch more sophisticated than elsewhere in Andalucía. Sevilla city was the first port of arrival for the new foodstuffs from the Americas that radically changed European cookery – potatoes, avocados, turkey, tomatoes, peppers, dried beans, chocolate and more. It's also the tapas capital of Andalucía.

Meals
The Spanish eating timetable is at its most extreme in Andalucía, so it's a good idea to reset your stomach clock unless you want to eat alone or only with other tourists.

Breakfast Andalucians, like most Spaniards, start the day's eating – often at around 10 am, when many take a break from work – with a light *desayuno* (breakfast), usually coffee with a *tostada* (toasted roll or slice of bread).

You can put a seemingly infinite variety of things in or on your tostada. Andalucian spreads include: *aceite* (olive oil), maybe with *ajo* (garlic); *manteca* (pork lard), maybe coloured red with paprika; *sobrasada*, a lard made from pork sausages; and *tomate frotado* (crushed tomato). Likely to appeal more to many visitors are ham, *beicon* or *tocino* (bacon), a slice of *lomo a la plancha* (grilled pork loin), a slab of *tortilla* (omelette), *queso* (cheese), or plain old *mantequilla* (butter) and *mermelada* or *confitura* (jam).

You may get the chance to specify what type of bread you want for your tostada – we thoroughly recommend *molletes*, tasty soft rolls, if they're available. You can have an *entera* (whole) or *media* (half) roll or slice of bread.

Churros con chocolate – long, deep-fried doughnuts to dip in thick hot chocolate – make a rich, calorie-laden breakfast.

If you're hungry, a tortilla is always a good option. Eggs *(huevos)* can be served *fritos* (fried), *revueltos* (scrambled) or *cocidos* (hard-boiled).

Lunch This is usually the main meal of the day, eaten between about 2 and 4 pm, and known as the *comida* or *almuerzo*. It can consist of several courses, including a soup and/or salad; then meat or fish with vegetables, or a rice dish or bean stew; followed by fruit, ice cream or dessert.

Dinner The evening meal, cena, tends to be lighter than lunch and may be eaten as late as 10 or 11 pm. People may also go out for a bigger dinner in a restaurant – though before about 9 pm you're unlikely

to see anyone but foreigners doing this. Only a few restaurants offer their *menú del día* (fixed-price meal) in the evening.

In-Between Times It's not a bad idea to go to a bar or cafe for a *merienda* (snack) around noon and again around 6 or 7 pm. Tapas (barsnacks) apart, one great Spanish snack is a *bocadillo*, a long, white bread roll filled with cheese or ham, salad or tortilla...the list goes on.

Types of Eatery

Cafes & Bars If you want to live like the locals, you'll spend plenty of time in cafes and bars. The latter come in various guises, such as *bodegas* (old-fashioned wine bars), *cervecerías* (beer bars), *tascas* (bars specialising in tapas), *tabernas* (taverns) and even *pubs*. In many of them you'll find tapas. Others may serve more substantial fare too. You'll often save 10% to 20% by eating at the bar rather than at a

---

The Menú is not Always on the Menu

In addition to the possibility of ordering from *la carta* (the main menu), you nearly always have the option of the cheaper *menú del día* (daily set meal). Some restaurants offer *platos combinados*, a kind of halfway house between the carta and the menú.

Menú del Día Most restaurants offer a menú del día – the traveller's best friend – typically costing 800 to 1200 ptas. You normally get a starter, main course, postre (dessert), bread and wine, with a choice of two or three dishes for each course. The menú is usually posted up outside – if it makes no mention of drinks, dessert, bread, coffee or 'IVA incluido', your meal may cost more.

Platos Combinados The plato combinado literally translates as 'combined plate' – maybe a steak and egg with chips and salad, or fried squid with potato salad. Don't let insipid photos of them put you off.

A la Carte You'll pay more for your meals if you order a la carte, but the food will be better. The Spanish menu (la carta – not *el menú*, which means the menú del día) begins with starters such as *ensaladas* (salads), *sopas* (soups) and *entremeses* (hors d'oeuvres). Later courses will probably be listed under headings like *pollo* (chicken), *carne* (meat), *mariscos* (seafood), *pez/pescado* (fish), *arroz* (rice), *huevos* (eggs) and *vegetales/verduras/legumbres* (vegetables). 'Vegetable' dishes may contain more than just vegetables – for example, beans with bits of ham.

Desserts have a low profile – helado (ice cream), fruit and flan (caramel custard) are often the only choices.

table. (The outside table area of a cafe, bar or restaurant is known as a *terraza* and is usually even more expensive.)

Restaurants Throughout Andalucía, plenty of *restaurantes* serve good, straightforward food at affordable prices, often featuring local specialities. There are also some woeful places, particularly in tourist haunts.

Put a Lid on it – Tapas & Raciones

The saucer-sized mini-snacks known as tapas are part of the Spanish way of life and come in infinite variety. The word *tapa* translates as 'lid'. Today's snacks supposedly originated in the sherry area of Andalucía in the 19th century, when bar owners placed a piece of bread on top of a drink to deter flies; this developed into the custom of putting a titbit, something salty to encourage drinking, such as olives or a piece of sausage, on a lid to cover the drink.

Today, tapas have become a cuisine in their own right and each Spanish region and city has its specialities. Sometimes they're free, though this custom has all but disappeared in many areas. A tapa generally costs between 100 and 200 ptas (check before you order as some are a lot more expensive). Tapas are not a cheap way of eating if you're very hungry, as you'd need half a dozen to approximate to the quantity of a dinner.

Typical tapas include olives, slices of cured meats or cheese, potato salad, bite-sized portions of fried fish, *albóndigas* (meat or fish balls), chickpeas with spinach, a small serving of pork *solomillo* (sirloin) or *lomo* (loin) with garnish, *gambas* (prawns) in garlic, and *boquerones* (anchovies) marinated in vinegar or fried in batter. There's infinite scope for adventurous chefs to combine flavours and textures. See the boxed text 'Andalucian Tapas Specialities' later in this section for more varieties of tapa.

Bars usually display a range of tapas on the counter or have a tapas menu. Otherwise, it seems you're expected to know what's available and the situation can be rather confusing. A place that appears not to have tapas may actually specialise in them! You just have to ask what tapas are available, then try to recognise a few words in the long list you're likely to get for an answer. In Andalucía, Sevilla is the greatest place to *tapear* – to tour bars to sample their tapas.

A *ración* is a meal-sized serving of these snacks; a *media-ración* is half a ración. Two different media-raciones amount to something like a full meal. A *tabla* is a board with a selection of tapas – typically hams, sausages, cheeses; like a ración, it's good for a group of people to share.

A *mesón* is a simple eatery with home-style cooking, attached to a bar, while a *comedor* is usually a dining room attached to a bar or hostal – here the food is likely to be functional and cheap. A *venta* is usually a family-run establishment, probably previously a roadside Inn, often off the beaten track – the food can be delectable and cheap. A *marisquería* is a seafood restaurant, while a *chiringuito* is a small open-air bar or kiosk, or sometimes a more substantial beachside restaurant.

Ethnic & Vegetarian Restaurants

Andalucía has many Chinese restaurants, generally mundane but cheap. Some of the bigger cities and tourist resorts have other Asian restaurants, including Indian. Italian restaurants are common and there are some good Arabic restaurants in Málaga and Granada.

Many ethnic restaurants offer more scope for vegetarians than the heavily meat-based typical Spanish eateries. There are also a few avowedly vegetarian restaurants. Vegetarians will find that salads in most restaurants are a good bet. A reliable vegetarian dish is *pisto*, a fry-up of courgettes, green peppers, onions and potatoes.

Markets

Andalucía's *mercados* (food markets) are fun places to visit. Buy a selection of fruits, vegetables, cold meat, sausage, olives, nuts and cheese, pick up some bread from a bakery, stop in at a supermarket for a bottle of wine and head for the nearest picturesque picnic spot. If you shop carefully, you could put together a filling meal for as little as 500 ptas per person.

Popular Dishes

Stews

In the past, the *cocido*, a one-pot feast of meat, sausage, beans and vegetables, was a mainstay of the local diet. It's a time-consuming dish to prepare, but in Andalucian villages the smell of cooking chickpeas still wafts through the streets around lunch time. A cocido can constitute a three-course meal, with the broth eaten first followed by the vegetables and then the meat.

More usual nowadays is a simpler kind of stew, the *guiso*, which comes in three traditional types – *las berzas*, with cabbage and either beef or pork; *el puchero*, chicken and bacon broth with turnips and mint; and *los potajes*, with dried beans and chorizo sausage.

Gazpacho

True *gazpacho*, a typical Andalucian dish, is a cold soup of blended tomatoes, peppers, onion, garlic, breadcrumbs, lemon and oil. It's sometimes served in a jug with ice cubes, with side dishes of chopped raw vegetables such as cucumber and onion. Its close relatives – all cold soups containing oil, garlic and breadcrumbs – include *salmorejo cordobés*, Cordoban gazpacho cream with hard-boiled eggs as a garnish, and *ajo blanco con uvas*, pounded almond and garlic soup with grapes, popular in Málaga province.

Gazpacho developed in Andalucía among *jornaleros*, agricultural

Andalucian Tapas Specialities

Charcutería or *chacinas* (pork products) feature everywhere. As well as straight ham, they include *lomo embuchado*, pork loin cured and stuffed in a sausage skin (also called *caña de lomo* or *cinta* in Andalucía) and *chorizo*, a marbled salami-type sausage. Offal such as *sesos* (brains), *callos* (tripe), *criadillas* (bull or sheep testicles), *riñones* (kidneys) and *hígado* (liver) may appear in a small earthenware dish, simmering in a tomato sauce or gravy, as may *albóndigas* (meatballs). Meat eaters can also enjoy *croquetas* (ham croquettes) or *flamenquines* (deep-fried, breaded veal or ham).

Seafood tapas are a highlight of Spanish cookery. Sample Andalucía's best shellfish in the sherry triangle of Cádiz province – from Atlantic *conchas finas* (Venus shell, the biggest of the clams) or *langostinos* (jumbo prawns) to *cangrejos* (tiny crabs, cooked whole) or *búsanos* (sea snails or whelks). *Langostinos a la plancha*, grilled with coarse-grained salt, can be a taste sensation.

Cádiz city has its own special array of seafood tapas. Elsewhere, standard seafood tapas include *boquerones* (anchovies), *mejillones* (mussels), *cazón en adobo* and *pavía* (chunks of deep fried fish, pre-seasoned and marinated) and *gambas al pil pil* (small prawns cooked in oil with garlic and chilli).

The plump *manzanilla* type of olives, with or without anchovy stuffing, are sometimes a free tapa. Common salad tapas include *pipirrana* (based on diced tomatoes and red peppers), *salpicón* (the same with bits of seafood), *ensaladilla* (Russian salad) and *aliño* (any salad in a vinegar-and-oil dressing).

day labourers, who were given rations of bread and oil. They soaked the bread in water to form the basis of a soup then added oil and garlic and whatever fresh vegetables were to hand. All the ingredients were pounded using a mortar and pestle. The resulting dish was relatively refreshing and nourishing.

Paella Spain's most famous dish often includes seafood and/or chicken in Andalucía. On the Costa del Sol, peas, clams, mussels and prawns, and a garnish of red peppers and lemon slices is a popular combination, while in Sevilla and Cádiz big prawns and sometimes lobster are added. Paella is cooked in a wide, two-handled metal pan – best on a wood fire outdoors. Its flavour comes from the simmering rice absorbing the juices of the other ingredients, and the yellow colour traditionally comes from saffron, but since saffron is expensive today, food colouring or *pimentón* (paprika) are more commonly used. A lot of restaurants will only serve paella to a minimum of two people as it's not worth the effort of preparing a single portion.

WINE

Wine production in Spain began in Andalucía when the Phoenicians, who founded Cádiz, possibly as early as 1100 BC, introduced vines. Vino – *blanco* (white), *tinto* (red) or *rosado* (rosé) – accompanies many a meal in Spain, where it is strong due to the sunny climate.

In general, wine remains cheap. A bottle costing 500 ptas from a supermarket or wine merchant will be better than average. The same money in a restaurant will get you an average drop. Cheap *vino de mesa* (table wine) sells for less than 200 ptas a litre in shops.

You can order wine by the glass *(copa)* in bars and restaurants: the *vino de la casa* (house wine) may come from a barrel or jug at 125 ptas (sometimes less) a glass.

Wine Terminology

You can judge the quality of Spanish wine to a certain extent from the label. DOC stands for Denominación de Origen Calificada and refers to wine from areas that have maintained consistently high quality over a very long period. Rioja, in northern Spain, is the only DOC at present, although Andalucía's Jerez (sherry) may join it. DO, Denominación de Origen, is one step down from DOC. There are 50-odd DO areas around Spain. A DOC or DO label tells you that the wine has been produced to certain supervised standards by serious wine growers, although each DOC and DO covers a wide range of wines of varying quality (usually indicated by the price).

Wine made for immediate drinking is called *vino joven*, while *vino de crianza* must be stored for certain minimum periods: if red, two full calendar years with a minimum of six months in oak; if white or rosé, one calendar year. *Reserva* requires three years' storage for reds and two for whites and rosés. *Gran reserva* is a title permitted for particularly good vintages, which must have spent at least two calendar years in storage and three in the bottle. They're mostly reds.

Sherry & Manzanilla

Jerez (sherry) is produced in the towns of Jerez de la Frontera, El Puerto de Santa María and Sanlúcar de Barrameda, plus five other areas in Cádiz province and Lebrija in Sevilla province. Manzanilla (to non-experts, effectively another type of sherry) is made only in Sanlúcar de Barrameda. There are 103 sq km of sherry and manzanilla vineyards.

A combination of climate, chalky soils that soak up the sun but retain moisture, and a special maturing process called the *solera* system (see the boxed text 'The Solera Process' in the Cádiz Province chapter) produces these unique wines.

The main distinction in sherry is between *fino* (dry and straw-coloured, with an alcohol content of around 15%) and *oloroso* (sweet, dark and 18% alcohol, with a strong bouquet). An *amontillado* is an amber, moderately dry fino with a nutty flavour and a higher alcohol content. A manzanilla is a camomile-coloured, unfortified fino: its delicate flavour is reckoned to come from sea breezes wafting into the *bodegas* (wineries) in Sanlúcar de Barrameda. An oloroso combined with a sweet wine results in a 'cream sherry', containing up to 25% alcohol. Sherry, especially fino, goes brilliantly with many tapas, but it can also accompany a meal: manzanilla is great with seafood, amontillado with white meat, and oloroso with red meat and game.

The Web site www.sherry.org provides a good introduction on the subject of sherry and the firms that make it.

Other Sherry-Like Wines

The Montilla-Moriles DO in Córdoba province, centred on the towns of Montilla and Moriles, produces a wine similar to sherry but, unlike sherry, not fortified by the addition of brandy – the fino is the most acclaimed.

Málaga Wine

For centuries, sweet and velvety Málaga Dulce pleased the palates of the famous, from Virgil to Shakespeare, as well as those of the ladies of Victorian England, for whom it was a favourite tipple. Unfortunately, the vines were blighted around the beginning of the 20th century and today the Málaga DO area is Andalucía's smallest, at only 9 sq km. You can sample Málaga wine straight from the barrel in some of the city's numerous bars.

Other Andalucian Wines

Almost every village has its own wine – cheap country wine is simply known as *mosto*. In addition to the DOs mentioned, eight areas produce distinctive, good, non-DO wines which can be sampled locally. These are Aljarafe and Los Palacios (Sevilla province), Bailén, Lopera and Torreperogil (Jaén province), Costa Albondón (Granada province), Laújar de Andarax (Almería province) and Villaviciosa (Córdoba province).

Right: Taste your way around the wine-making regions of Andalucía.

DAN HERRICK

OTHER DRINKS

Beer

The most common way to order a *cerveza* (beer) is to ask for a *caña*, which is a small draught beer, or a *tubo*, a larger draught beer (about 300mL) in a straight glass. If you just ask for a cerveza at a restaurant or cafe table you may well get bottled beer, which tends to be a bit more expensive. A small bottle of beer is called a *botellín* or a *quinto*; a bigger one (330mL) is a *tercio* or a *media*. San Miguel, Cruzcampo and Victoria are all decent Andalucian beers.

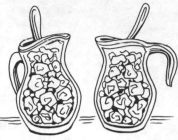

A *clara* is a shandy, a beer with a dash of lemonade.

Mixed Drinks, Spirits & Liqueurs

Sangría is a wine and fruit punch, sometimes laced with brandy. It's refreshing going down, but can leave you with a sore head. You'll see jugs of it on tables in restaurants, but it also comes ready-mixed in bottles at around 300 ptas for 1.5L. *Tinto de verano* is a mix of wine and sweet carbonated water.

Coñac (Spanish brandy) is popular and cheap. Most of it is made in Andalucía – mainly in the sherry towns, but also in Málaga and in Córdoba province. In bars, you'll notice locals starting the day with a coffee and a coñac, or a glass of *anís* (aniseed liqueur).

Spirits produced in Spain are generally much cheaper than imports. Málaga's Larios gin is an example. *Ron* (rum) is produced in Málaga and Motril (Granada province), the only areas in Europe that grow sugar cane.

Andalucía also produces a wide range of *licores* (liqueurs). Aguardiente is a colourless, grape-based liqueur. When spiked with aniseed, it becomes an anís or anisado (anisette). Pacharán, a red liqueur made with aniseed and sloes, the fruit of the blackthorn, is very popular in Andalucía – the favourite brand is Zoco.

Non-Alcoholic Drinks

Coffee Addicts should specify how they want their fix, and expect it to be strong. A *café con leche* is about 50% coffee, 50% hot milk; ask for *grande* or *doble* if you want a large cup, *en vaso* if you want it in a glass and *sombra* if you want lots of milk. A *café solo* is an espresso (short black); *café cortado* is an espresso with a little milk.

Tea In cafes and bars, *té* (tea) is invariably weak. Ask for milk to be separate *(leche aparte)*, otherwise you'll end up with a cup of lukewarm milky water with a tea bag thrown in. Many places also have *té de manzanilla* (camomile tea). *Teterías* (Islamic-style tearooms) are increasingly fashionable in some cities, serving all manner of teas and herbal *infusiones*.

Top: Sangría is a popular and punchy drink.

Chocolate Spaniards brought chocolate back from Mexico and adopted it enthusiastically. As a drink, it's served thick; sometimes it even appears among *postres* (desserts) on menus. Generally, it's a breakfast drink consumed with churros (see Food earlier in this special section).

Soft Drinks Zumo de naranja (orange juice) is the main freshly squeezed juice available, but it's not cheap at around 200 ptas a glass. Boxed juices come in all varieties in shops, and are good and cheap.

Refrescos (cool drinks) include the usual international brands of soft drinks, local brands such as Kas and expensive *granizado* (iced fruit crush).

Clear, cold water from a public fountain or tap is a Spanish favourite – but check that it's *potable* (drinkable). For tap water in restaurants, ask for *agua de grifo*. Bottled water *(agua mineral)* comes in innumerable brands, either *con gas* (fizzy) or *sin gas* (still). A 1.5L bottle of still water can cost anywhere between 60 ptas and 125 ptas in a supermarket.

A *batido* is a flavoured milk drink or milk shake. *Horchata* is made from the juice of *chufa* (tiger nuts), sugar and water: it tastes like soya milk with a hint of cinnamon. You'll come across it both fresh and bottled – Chufi is a tasty brand.

Right: Give your day a calorie kick-start with *Churros con Chocolate* (deep-fried doughnuts to dip in hot chocolate).

Getting There & Away

Andalucía is well linked to other European countries and the rest of Spain by air, rail and road. From Europe, it's often cheaper to fly than go overland or by sea.

AIR

The peak season for travel to Andalucía is mid-June to mid-September, although Easter is also busy.

Airports & Airlines

Málaga is Andalucía's main international airport and the cheapest flights available usually go there. Almería, Sevilla, Jerez de la Frontera and Gibraltar also receive some international flights. Granada airport receives internal Spanish flights only (you can get there with a transfer at Madrid or Barcelona).

Major national airlines such as Spain's Iberia (which was being privatised in 2000), British Airways (BA), Air France, Alitalia, Sabena, Swissair, Lufthansa Airlines and Scandinavian Airlines fly into Málaga and, in some cases, other Andalucian airports. They're generally an expensive way to fly, though some now offer competitively priced, advance-purchase tickets. They're also worth checking for special offers.

Other scheduled airlines include Monarch Airlines (from England to Málaga and Gibraltar), Air Liberté from France, LTU International Airways, Air Berlin and Hapag-Lloyd from Germany, and two Spanish airlines, Air Europa and Spanair, both flying from several European countries and the USA.

The cheapest fares are often to be found on no-frills airlines such as Go (London–Málaga), easyJet (to Málaga from the UK) and Buzz (London–Jerez). Charter flights provide further inexpensive options from many European countries. Most charters go to Málaga, though Almería gets some too.

If you can't find a suitable ticket to an Andalucian airport, you have the option of flying into, say, Madrid, Barcelona or Alicante and completing the journey overland.

Iberia flies domestic routes to/from all five of Andalucía's airports (not including Gibraltar). Other Spanish airlines such as Air Europa, Spanair and Binter Mediterráneo provide further domestic flights.

Buying Tickets

Start your ticket search early: some of the cheapest tickets have to be bought months in advance, and some popular flights sell out early. Look in newspapers and magazines (including any Spanish press in your home country), watch for special offers, phone around travel agents for bargains and consult the Internet. Many airlines and travel agents have Web sites offering ticket deals, which can often be bought online with a credit card. Find out fares, routes and any restrictions on the tickets (see the Air Travel Glossary in this chapter), then sit back and decide which is best for you.

You can often obtain lower fares by travelling midweek. Students with an International Student Identity Card (ISIC) and people aged under 26 often have access to special student and youth fares. Children under two years old generally travel for 10% of the adult fare (or free, on some airlines) if they don't occupy a seat. Children aged between two and 12 can usually occupy a seat for 50% of the regular fare or 67% of a discounted fare (but will probably pay full fare on charter flights and no-frills airlines).

No-frills airlines apart, some of the cheapest flights from the UK and USA are available from unbonded travel agencies. Many such firms are honest, but a few rogues will take your money and disappear. If you feel suspicious, leave a deposit of 20% or so and pay the balance when you get the ticket. Paying by credit card generally offers protection, as does buying a ticket from a bonded agent, such as one covered by the Air Transport Organisers' Licensing (ATOL) scheme in the UK. Once

Air Travel Glossary

Cancellation Penalties If you have to cancel or change a discounted ticket, there are often heavy penalties involved; insurance can sometimes be taken out against these penalties. Some airlines impose penalties on regular tickets as well, particularly against 'no-show' passengers.

Courier Fares Businesses often need to send urgent documents or freight securely and quickly. Courier companies hire people to accompany the package through customs and, in return, offer a discount ticket which is sometimes a phenomenal bargain. However, you may have to surrender all your baggage allowance and take only carry-on luggage.

Full Fares Airlines traditionally offer 1st class (coded F), business class (coded J) and economy class (coded Y) tickets. These days there are so many promotional and discounted fares available that few passengers pay full economy fare.

Lost Tickets If you lose your airline ticket an airline will usually treat it like a travellers cheque and, after inquiries, issue you with another one. Legally, however, an airline is entitled to treat it like cash and if you lose it then it's gone forever. Take good care of your tickets.

Onward Tickets An entry requirement for many countries is that you have a ticket out of the country. If you're unsure of your next move, the easiest solution is to buy the cheapest onward ticket to a neighbouring country or a ticket from a reliable airline which can later be refunded if you do not use it.

Open-Jaw Tickets These are return tickets where you fly out to one place but return from another. If available, this can save you backtracking to your arrival point.

Overbooking Since every flight has some passengers who fail to show up, airlines often book more passengers than they have seats. Usually excess passengers make up for the no-shows, but occasionally somebody gets 'bumped' onto the next available flight. Guess who it is most likely to be? The passengers who check in late.

Promotional Fares These are officially discounted fares, available from travel agencies or direct from the airline.

Reconfirmation If you don't reconfirm your flight at least 72 hours prior to departure, the airline may delete your name from the passenger list. Ring to find out if your airline requires reconfirmation.

Restrictions Discounted tickets often have various restrictions on them – such as needing to be paid for in advance and incurring a penalty to be altered. Others are restrictions on the minimum and maximum period you must be away.

Round-the-World Tickets RTW tickets give you a limited period (usually a year) in which to circumnavigate the globe. You can go anywhere the carrying airlines go, as long as you don't backtrack. The number of stopovers or total number of separate flights is decided before you set off and they usually cost a bit more than a basic return flight.

Transferred Tickets Airline tickets cannot be transferred from one person to another. Travellers sometimes try to sell the return half of their ticket, but officials can ask you to prove that you are the person named on the ticket. On an international flight tickets are compared with passports.

Travel Periods Ticket prices vary with the time of year. There is a low (off-peak) season and a high (peak) season, and often a low-shoulder season and a high-shoulder season as well. Usually the fare depends on your outward flight – if you depart in the high season and return in the low season, you pay the high-season fare.

Warning

The information in this chapter is particularly vulnerable to change: prices for international travel are volatile, routes are introduced and cancelled, schedules change, special deals come and go. Airlines and governments seem to take a perverse pleasure in making price structures and regulations as complicated as possible. The travel industry is highly competitive and there are many lurks and perks. You should check directly with the airline or a travel agent to make sure you understand how a fare (and ticket you may buy) works.

The upshot of this is that you should get opinions, quotes and advice from as many airlines and travel agents as possible before you part with your hard-earned cash. The details given in this chapter should be regarded as pointers and are not a substitute for your own careful, up-to-date research.

you have the ticket, ring the airline to confirm you are booked on the flight.

You may decide to pay more than the rock-bottom fare and opt for a better-known travel agent. Firms such as STA Travel and usit Campus, with offices worldwide, and Council Travel in the USA are not going to disappear overnight and offer good prices.

Make a note of your ticket's number, the flight number and other details. If it's lost or stolen, this will help you get a replacement.

Use fares quoted in this book as a guide only. Quoted fares do not necessarily constitute a recommendation for the carrier.

Travellers with Special Needs

If you have special needs of any sort – you're vegetarian, travelling with a baby, in a wheelchair or with a guide dog – tell the airline early so that they can make arrangements. Remind them when you reconfirm your booking and again when you check in.

Departure Tax

Air fares are usually quoted with taxes included, but sometimes you have to add them to the ticket price. Spain, Britain

and Gibraltar charge a departure tax of 1000 ptas, UK£10 and £7, respectively, on flights to other European countries. Taxes on a round-trip flight from the USA to Spain can approach US$100 in total.

The Rest of Spain

Flying can be worth the money if you're in a hurry, especially for longer or return trips.

Iberia The national airline, Iberia, flies daily (in some cases several times a day) nonstop from Madrid and Barcelona to all of Andalucía's airports, and from Bilbao and Valencia to Sevilla. An Iberia subsidiary, Binter Mediterráneo, flies from Valencia to Málaga (but not vice versa) nonstop. Normally the cheapest type of Iberia fare is the 'Estrella', which you must buy at least two days before departure and with which you must return between four and 14 days after departure; for longer stays you need a 'Supermini', which you must buy at least four days ahead. Sample Estrella/Supermini/one-way fares are 15,000/19,150/15,950 ptas for Madrid–Sevilla, and 25,300/30,600/25,750 ptas for Barcelona–Málaga. In winter you may find special deals as low as 14,500 ptas return on these and other routes.

Other Airlines Air Europa's nonstop routes include Madrid–Málaga, Madrid–Jerez, Barcelona–Sevilla and Bilbao–Málaga. Spanair flies nonstop to Málaga and Sevilla from Madrid and Barcelona. Both offer connections at Madrid to/from many other Spanish cities. These airlines' standard fares are broadly similar to Iberia's, but they're well worth checking for special offers: on Air Europa, for instance, you can often fly Barcelona–Sevilla for around 16,500/18,500 ptas, or Madrid–Málaga one way/return for around 12,500/16,500 ptas.

Youth Fares Try the student and youth travel organisation usit Unlimited (☎ 902 25 25 75), which has offices in Sevilla and Granada (see city sections). Its Web site is at www.unlimited.es.

The UK & Ireland

The weekend national newspapers often have information on cheap fares. In London try also the *Evening Standard*, *Time Out* and the free magazine *TNT*. The Internet is an increasingly useful place to find fares and book flights.

No-Frills Airlines Budget, ticketless airlines revolutionised air travel between the UK and Spain in the late 1990s. You buy flights direct from the airline, not through travel agents, and can usually obtain a small discount by buying on the airlines' Web sites. Fares on a flight increase as tickets sell, so if you book well in advance you can find some real bargains. You sometimes don't get a ticket, just a confirmation number to quote at check-in. On board, you pay for all food and drink. The no-frills market is highly competitive – one such airline, Debonair, went into receivership in 1999.

You can fly from Luton and Liverpool to Málaga and other Spanish airports with easyJet for as little as UK£37.50 one way (excluding departure tax). In slow periods (such as winter weekdays), prices have been known to drop as low as UK£19! Once fares top about UK£60 it's time to start thinking about alternatives. You can connect at Luton with easyJet flights to/from Belfast and several Scottish airports.

The BA-run Go flies to Málaga and other Spanish cities from London Stansted (a 40-minute train ride from Liverpool St station). If you comply with certain restrictions (easily done if you are planning to spend a week or more in Spain) you're usually looking at UK£50 to UK£60 one way plus taxes.

KLM's Buzz began Andalucian operations as we researched this book by flying between Stansted and Jerez de la Frontera from UK£49 one way (including tax).

The budget airlines' fare structure makes it easy to plan open-jaw flights. You pay a one-way fare to one destination and a one-way fare back from another. With other airlines, open-jaw can be very expensive.

Discount & Charter Flights Discounted tickets for scheduled flights and tickets for charter flights are sold by travel agencies, which advertise in the press and on the Internet. Most British travel agents are registered with ABTA (Association of British Travel Agents). If you have bought a flight ticket from an ABTA-registered agent that goes out of business, ABTA will guarantee a refund or an alternative. Unregistered agencies are riskier but sometimes cheaper.

Check the arrival and departure times of charter flights, as they can be inconvenient – and even more so if they are delayed. Remember that if you miss your charter flight, you have lost your money.

Some discount agencies are better established than others and have a long track record of reliability. They may sell non-discounted fares as well as discounted ones. The following sell student and youth as well as regular tickets:

STA (☎ 020-7361 6145 for European flights) 86 Old Brompton Rd, London SW7 3LQ
Glasgow: (☎ 0141-338 6000) 184 Byres Rd, G12 8SN. There are 38 other UK branches, mainly in university cities.
Web site: www.statravel.co.uk

Trailfinders (☎ 020-7937 5400) 215 Kensington High St, London W8 6BD
Glasgow: (☎ 0141-353 2224) 254–284 Sauchiehall St, G2 3EH
Dublin: (☎ 01-677 7888) 4/5 Dawson St, Dublin 2. Trailfinders also has branches in Bristol, Birmingham, Manchester and Newcastle-upon-Tyne.
Web site: www.trailfinders.com

Usit Campus (☎ 0870-240 1010) 52 Grosvenor Gardens, London SW1,
Edinburgh: (☎ 0131-668 3303) 5 Nicholson Sq, EH8 9BH.
There are about 50 other branches in England, Scotland and Wales.
Web site: www.usitcampus.co.uk

Usit Now (☎ 01-602 1600) 19–21 Aston Quay, O'Connell Bridge, Dublin 2
Belfast: (☎ 028-9032 4073) Fountain Centre, College St, BT1 6ET
It is also located in several other Irish cities.
Web sites: www.usitnow.ie and www.usitnow.com

Other agencies worth looking into include:

Spanish Travel Services (☎ 020-7387 5337) 138 Eversholt St, London NW1 1BL

Tarleton Direct (☎ 01604-633633) 353
Wellingborough Rd, Northampton NN1 4ER
It specialises in inexpensive flights to Almería
from Manchester and London Gatwick.
The Charter Flight Centre (☎ 020-7565 6755)
15 Gillingham St, London SW1 V1HN

Some ticket agencies work largely, or only,
via the Internet. You get quotes online, and
often book and pay (by credit card) online
too. Like fares in press adverts, some advertised fares don't stand up if you actually want to buy them, but plenty of good
deals are available this way. Worth checking are:

www.lastminute.com
www.dialaflight.com
www.ebookers.com
www.airnet.co.uk
www.cheapflights.co.uk

The range of discount and charter fares is
broad, but in the low season you should be
able to get a return from London to Málaga
for about UK£100 including taxes; in summer you're more likely to pay UK£150.
Discount and charter return fares to Málaga
from airports such as Manchester, Leeds/
Bradford, Bristol and Glasgow average
only about UK£20 more than from London.
From Edinburgh or Belfast you're looking
at roughly UK£150/200–225 in low/high
season. From Ireland, getting to London
first may save you money.

Flying into any Andalucian airport other
than Málaga will generally cost more.

Scheduled Airlines On BA and Iberia,
economy return fares between London and
Málaga or Sevilla range from UK£175 (low
season) to UK£270 (high season), but there
are sometimes special offers, especially in
the low season, under UK£150. BA flies
from London to Gibraltar for similar fares.
All these BA flights are operated by a fran-
chise carrier, GB Airways.

Monarch Airlines flies from Luton to
Málaga and Gibraltar and from Manchester
to Málaga. Return fares have been as low as
UK£100 in winter, rising to UK£250 in

August. Other airlines flying nonstop to
Málaga include British Midland from East
Midlands Airport and CityJet from Dublin.

Air Europa flies from London to Málaga
with a transfer at Madrid, starting from
around UK£165 to UK£200 depending on
season.

Fly-Drive Packages including flights and
pre-booked car hire can be attractive, as
local car hire prices often exceed those of
pre-booked cars. Numerous travel agents
can make arrangements.

Continental Europe

Except for very short hops, airfares often
beat overland alternatives on cost. Web sites
worth checking include www.ebookers.com
and www.etn.nl.

France It's possible to find charter or discounted return flights from Paris to
Málaga for under 1600FF. Iberia fares on
this route start at 1490FF plus taxes, and
are only slightly more for Paris–Sevilla.
Air Europa flies Paris–Málaga most days,
with a transfer at Madrid, for as little as
1140FF return.

France's student travel agencies can usually supply discount tickets to travellers of
all ages. OTU Voyages (☎ 01 44 41 38 50)
has a central Paris office at 39 Ave Georges
Bernanos (5e) and another 42 offices around
the country; its Web site is at www.otu.fr.
Acceuil des Jeunes en France (☎ 01 42 77
87 80), 119 rue Saint Martin (4e), is another
popular Paris discount agency. Other places
in Paris to look for good fares include Nou-
velles Frontières (☎ 080 333 33 33), 5 Ave
de l'Opéra (1er), with a Web site at www
.newfrontiers.com; Voyageurs du Monde
(☎ 01 42 86 16 00), 55 rue Sainte Anne (2e);
and Forum Voyages (☎ 01 53 10 50 50), 28
rue Monge. Forum Voyages has other offices across France.

Germany Return flights to Málaga from
most German airports can generally be
bought for DM500 to DM700. There are
some DM400 deals, including on LTU International Airlines and Iberia if you can

meet the conditions. However, you may need to pay DM800 in high summer or for late bookings, or for another Andalucian airport besides Málaga.

STA Travel (Web site: www.statravel.de) has branches in 18 cities including Goethestrasse 73, Berlin (☎ 030-311 09 50).

Netherlands & Belgium Return flights from Amsterdam to Málaga run from around f380 to f800. Many of the cheaper fares are on Transavia. Brussels–Málaga return flights range from about f10,000 to f20,000.

NBBS Reizen, the Dutch student travel agency, offers some good fares. You can find them at Rokin 66 (☎ 020-624 09 89), Amsterdam, in several other offices around the city, and in Brussels. Compare NBBS' prices with the unbonded agencies along Rokin.

In Belgium, try Acotra Student Travel Agency (☎ 02-512 86 07), rue de la Madeline, Brussels, or WATS Reizen (☎ 03-226 16 26), de Keyserlei 44, Antwerp.

Portugal There are no direct flights between Portugal and Andalucía, but Iberia can fly you from Lisbon to Málaga in about four or five hours with a transfer at Madrid, from around 26,000$00, one way or return.

The USA

The only direct flights between the USA and Andalucía at the time of writing are once-weekly (Thursday) scheduled flights between New York and Málaga by the Spanish airline Air Plus Comet. Plenty of flights with transfers in Madrid or another European city are available. Airlines flying New York–Madrid nonstop include Delta, Continental, Iberia and Air Europa; Spanair flies Washington–Madrid. American Airlines and Iberia fly New York–Barcelona nonstop. London and Frankfurt are other common transfer cities. Fares via other countries are not always more expensive than via Madrid.

Discount travel agents in the USA are known as consolidators. San Francisco is the country's consolidator capital, although good deals can be found in Los Angeles, New York and other big cities. Consolida-

tors can be found through the *Yellow Pages* or the major daily newspapers. The Sunday editions of the *San Francisco Times*, *New York Times* and *Los Angeles Times* advertise cheap flights. New York's free *The Village Voice* is also a good place to look. The Internet is another useful source of fare information and bookings – try www.travelocity.com, www.flifo.com and www.expedia.msn.com.

A good place to start your search for an economical ticket is the student travel organisation Council Travel (☎ 800 226 8624), which has around 60 offices in the USA. It sells youth, teacher and adult as well as student air fares. Its Web site is at www.counciltravel.com. Spanish Heritage Tours (☎ 800 456 5050), a Spain specialist, has some competitive fares (www.shtours.com). Other budget agencies include STA Travel (☎ 800 777 0112), with offices in several major cities (www.statravel.com), and Discount Tickets in New York (☎ 212-391 2313).

Some competitive fares are being offered by the scheduled airlines. Iberia's lowest New York–Málaga low-season adult return fare costs around US$600. You transfer in Madrid or Barcelona. Air Plus Comet's roundtrip fares range from around US$500 to US$750 depending on the season. Air Europa one-month returns range from about US$650 to US$920 (two-week returns are cheaper). Spanair's recent Washington–Málaga high-season fare was around US$900. High-season fares under US$1000 have been available on Swissair and Belgium's Sabena. BA's cheapest New York–Málaga return fares (via London) cost between about US$770 and US$1100 depending on the season.

One-month student return fares quoted by Council Travel started at US$589 in August and US$541 in November, plus taxes.

Price differences between the east and west coasts are generally between US$100 and US$300.

Standby & Courier Flights Standby one-way fares are often sold at 60% of the normal price. Airhitch (☎ 800 326 2009) is a specialist: one-way fares from the USA to Western Europe cost from US$169 (east coast) to US$239 (west coast) plus taxes. Its Web site is at www.airhitch.org.

On courier flights you accompany freight or a parcel to its destination. Most flights depart from New York. A New York–Madrid low-season return can cost under US$300. Arrangements often have to be made a month or more in advance. You will need to travel light, and you may have to be a US resident and be interviewed before they take you on. Now Voyager (☎ 212-431 1616), 74 Varick St, New York, NY 10013 specialises in courier flights.

Canada

Canada 3000 flies weekly from Toronto to Màlaga with return fares as low as C$800. Otherwise, the best adult round-trip fares from Montreal or Toronto to Málaga cost between C$1100 and C$1500 depending on the season. Flights are with some combination of Air Canada, Canadian Airlines and various major European and American airlines, with a transfer in Madrid or another European capital, and sometimes in the USA too. Flights from Vancouver cost anything from C$250 more.

Canada's main student travel organisation, Travel CUTS (☎ 800 667 2887), known as Voyages Campus in Quebec, has offices in all major cities. Its Web site is at www.travelcuts.com. Otherwise, scan the ads in the *Globe & Mail*, *Toronto Star*, *Montreal Gazette* and *Vancouver Sun* or check the Web sites mentioned in the USA section, above.

For courier flights, contact FB Onboard Courier Services (☎ 514-631 2077 in Toronto). Airhitch (for details see the USA section above) has standby fares from some Canadian cities.

Morocco

Iberia and Royal Air Maroc both fly from Málaga to Casablanca daily. Return fares are around 40,000 ptas with Iberia and start at 33,900 ptas on Royal Air Maroc. Morocco's Regional Air Lines flies direct from Málaga to Casablanca and Tangier daily, and from Gibraltar to Casablanca (£104 return) most days.

Spain's Binter Mediterráneo flies to Marrakesh from Granada and Málaga for around 30,000 ptas return, and to Melilla, the Spanish enclave on the Moroccan coast, from Málaga, Almería and Granada, starting at 13,000 ptas to 16,050 ptas return, depending on the departure airport.

Australia

As there are no direct connections from Australia to Spain, you will have to fly to Europe via Asia (or, less often, America) and change flights, if not airlines, at least once.

Sydney–Málaga return tickets on mainstream airlines through reputable agents can generally be bought for A$1700 to A$2000 for February departures, and A$2000 to A$2500 for August.

On some flights between Australia and major European destinations such as London, Paris and Frankfurt, a return ticket between that destination and another European city is thrown in. Madrid and Barcelona are usually possible choices in these deals, which start at around A$1750.

The weekend editions of the *Age* in Melbourne and the *Sydney Morning Herald* have many cheap fare advertisements. STA Travel (☎ 1300 360 960) and Flight Centre (☎ 13 1600) are major dealers in cheap airfares, with offices in major cities Australia-wide. Their Web sites are www.statravel.com.au and www.flightcentre.com.au, respectively. The Web site www.travel.com.au is worth consulting too. Remember that heavily discounted fares can often be found at your local travel agent.

New Zealand

Fares are advertised in the *New Zealand Herald* travel section. STA Travel (Auckland ☎ 09-309 0458, www.sta.travel.com.au) and Flight Centre (Auckland ☎ 09-309 6171) are popular travel agencies with offices around the country. The cheapest fares from Auckland to Madrid are generally via Asia or the USA. Expect to pay around NZ$2000 to NZ$2200 for a return flight during the low-season. Round-the-World

Contacting Airlines

Here are some selected airline contact details:

Air Berlin
www.airberlin.com
Spain: ☎ 901 11 64 02
Germany: ☎ 01801-737800

Air Europa
www.air-europa.com
Spain: ☎ 902 40 15 01
UK: ☎ 0870 240 1501
US: ☎ 888 238 7672
France: ☎ 01 42 97 40 00

Air Plus Comet
US: ☎ 212-983 1277,
    877-999 7587

British Midland
www.iflybritishmidland.com
Spain: ☎ 95 204 82 94
UK: ☎ 0870 607 0555

Binter Mediterráneo
Spain: ☎ 902 40 05 00
UK: ☎ 020-7830 0011,
    0990 341341
US: ☎ 800 772 4642

British Airways
www.british-airways.com
Spain: ☎ 902 11 13 33
UK: ☎ 0345 22 21 11
US: ☎ 800-AIRWAYS
Gibraltar: ☎ 79300

Buzz
www.buzzaway.com
Spain: ☎ 91 749 66 33
UK: ☎ 0870 240 7070

CityJet
Ireland: ☎ 01-844 5566

Canada 3000
www.canada3000.com
Spain: ☎ 727-535 2004
UK: ☎ 01293-57 17 00
Canada: ☎ 888-CAN 300

easyJet
www.easyjet.com
Spain: ☎ 902 29 99 92
UK: ☎ 0870 600 00 00

GB Airways
www.british-airways.com
Spain: ☎ 902 11 13 33
UK: ☎ 0345 22 21 11
US: ☎ 800-AIRWAYS
Gibraltar: ☎ 79300

Go
www.go-fly.com
Spain: ☎ 901 33 35 00
UK: ☎ 0845 605 4321

Iberia
www.iberia.com
(France: www.iberia.fr)
Spain: ☎ 902 40 05 00

UK: ☎ 020-7830 0011,
    0990 34 13 41
US: ☎ 800 772 4642
Canada: ☎ 800 772 4642
France: ☎ 08 02 07 50 75
Morocco: ☎ 02-279600
Portugal: ☎ 21-355 8119

LTU International Airways
www.ltu.de
Spain: ☎ 95 238 30 77
US: ☎ 305-714 4701
Germany: ☎ 0180-5 20 65

Monarch Airlines
www.monarch-airlines.com
Spain: ☎ 95 204 83 47
UK: ☎ 08700 40 50 40
Gibraltar: ☎ 47477

Regional Air Lines
Gibraltar: ☎ 79300
Morocco: ☎ 02-538080

Royal Air Maroc
Spain: ☎ 902 21 00 10
UK: ☎ 020-7439 8854
US: ☎ 212-750 5115
Morocco: ☎ 02-31 41 41

Spanair
www.spanair.com
Spain: ☎ 902 13 14 15
UK: ☎ 01293-59 66 59
US: ☎ 888 545 5757

tickets from New Zealand can sometimes be cheaper than a return ticket.

Flights from Andalucía

For flights out of Andalucía, check the adverts in local foreign-language papers such as *Sur in English*. Servitour (☎ 95 256 60 00) and Flightline International (☎ 95 204 83 32) offer some of the best deals from Málaga, with occasional one-way winter fares to London, for instance, as cheap as 6500 ptas. During the summer a flight to London is likely to cost 15,000 ptas or more. You can always go along to Málaga airport early in the morning and ask around the offices for standby tickets. You may not get a flight that day – but if you do it will be cheap. For agencies selling flights out of Almería, see the Almería Province chapter.

LAND
If you're travelling overland to Spain, check whether you require visas for the countries that intend to pass through. An excellent Web site providing European train timetable information is operated by Deutsche Bahn (German Railways) at http://bahn.hafas.de.

The Rest of Spain
You could reach Andalucía in a day, if you wished, from almost any corner of Spain, by bus, train or your own vehicle. On some long-haul runs buses are cheaper and/or quicker than trains; on others it's the opposite.

Bus Daily buses to all main and many smaller Andalucian cities leave from Madrid's Estación Sur de Autobuses (% 91 468 42 00), Calle Méndez Álvaro (metro: Méndez Álvaro). In Barcelona, buses to Andalucía go from the Estació del Nord (☎ 93 265 65 08), Carrer d'Alí Bei 80. Buses also run to Sevilla from as far away as Extremadura, Galicia and Castilla y León.

Here are some sample journey times and one-way fares for bus travel within Spain:

from	to	fare (ptas)	duration (hrs)
Barcelona	Granada	7915	13–14
Cáceres	Sevilla	2200	4
Madrid	Málaga	2650	6

Train Most main-line trains of RENFE (Red Nacional de Ferrocarriles Españoles, Spanish National Railways) are reliable and quick. The quickest is the AVE (Alta Velocidad Española) train which covers the 471km from Madrid to Sevilla, via Córdoba, in just 2¼ to 2½ hours, reaching speeds of 280km/h. (If an AVE arrives more than five minutes late due to a delay attributable to RENFE, you get a refund – but don't get excited: this happens extremely rarely.)

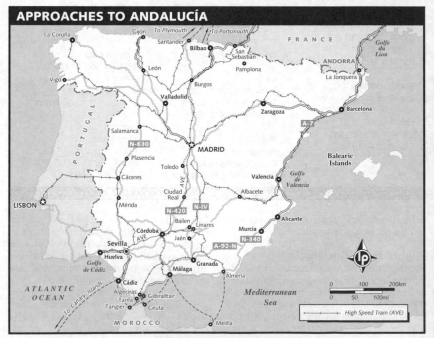

APPROACHES TO ANDALUCÍA

euro currency converter 1000 ptas = €6.01

For train information you can go to a station or RENFE's city centre ticket offices, call RENFE's national information and reservations number, ☎ 902 24 02 02, or visit RENFE's informative Web site at www.renfe.es, which gives all schedules and fares. The map 'Approaches to Andalucía' shows the rail routes into Andalucía from other parts of Spain.

Daytime Trains The terms *grandes líneas* and *largo recorrido* (long-distance) refer to trains travelling 400km or more. Most have 1st- and 2nd-class carriages and all except some night trains have some kind of catering. The basic long-distance daytime trains are *diurnos*. More comfortable trains with fewer stops are called InterCity – they are marginally more expensive than a diurno. Even more comfortable and expensive is a Talgo. A Talgo 200 is a Talgo that uses the high-speed AVE line for part of its trip between Madrid and destinations such as Málaga, Cádiz, Huelva and Algeciras.

The most expensive way to go is to take the AVE itself along the Madrid–Córdoba–Sevilla line. Even in the cheapest class *(turista)*, passengers have access to everything from videos and telephones to children's games and facilities for the disabled.

Regionales and *cercanías* are local, shorter-distance trains – see the Getting Around chapter.

Night Trains The basic type of overnight train, the *estrella*, usually has seats, couchettes and sleeping compartments. A *trenhotel* is a sleek, comfortable, expensive sleeping-car-only train. First class on these tends to be called *gran clase*, and 2nd class turista.

Couchettes, called *literas*, are fold-out bunk beds (generally six to a compartment). The standard price in addition to your 2nd-class ticket is 1500 ptas. More comfortable sleeping accommodation ranges from shared cabins to luxury singles. Prices depend on the distance you travel.

Reservations On most trains you don't need to book in advance, but if you want to be sure of a place, it may be wise to do so.

Bookings can be made at stations, RENFE offices, many travel agents and online (for AVE, Talgo 200 and TRD trains) on the RENFE Web site at www.renfe.es. Online booking was still only available in Spanish at the time of writing: you pick up your tickets on board the train or at the station of departure. However you book, there's usually no booking fee.

Costs The variety of possible fares from A to B is almost mind-boggling. A saving of a couple of hours on a faster train can mean a big hike in the fare. Fares quoted elsewhere in this guide are basic 2nd-class seat fares.

Your fare depends first on the type of train. On daytime trains you then generally have the easy choice of 2nd- or 1st-class seats (turista and *preferente* on the classier trains). AVEs also have a super-1st class called *club*. Night trains offer varied combinations of 1st and 2nd-class seats, couchettes and in some *camas* (sleeping compartments).

In some cases, especially on AVE and Talgo 200 trains, the fare also depends on the time you travel. The cheaper times are called *valle* and the more expensive *llano*.

The table below takes one route as an example, Madrid to Sevilla:

train	class	fare (ptas)	duration (hrs)
Trenhotel	1st	6600	3¾
Talgo	2nd/1st	7300/10,200	3¼
Talgo 200	2nd/1st	8300/12,000	3¼
AVE (valle)	2nd/1st	8400/12,200	2½
AVE (llano)	2nd/1st	9900/14,400	2½

Other one-way 2nd- or turista-class seat fares within Spain include:

from	to	fare (ptas)	duration (hrs)
Madrid	Málaga	4700–8200	4–11½
Barcelona	Granada	6100–6500	12½
Cáceres	Sevilla	2245	5¾

Car & Motorcycle Spain's main roads are good. You can drive from Barcelona to Málaga in eight hours (though at a sane pace it's more like 11 or 12).

euro currency converter €1 = 166 ptas

The main highway from Madrid to Andalucía is the N-IV to Córdoba, Sevilla and Cádiz. Branch off this at Bailén for Jaén, Granada, Almería or Málaga. Another road, N-401 becoming the N-420, heads from Madrid to Córdoba via Toledo and Ciudad Real.

From the ferry at Santander or Bilbao or the French border at Irún, the most direct route is to head for Burgos, from which it's a pretty straight 240km to Madrid. The main Irún–Bilbao and Bilbao–Burgos highways are each subject to tolls of about 2000 ptas.

The A-7 leads down the Mediterranean side of Spain from La Jonquera on the French border as far as Murcia. Tolls between La Jonquera and Alicante total about 7000 ptas, and toll-free alternative roads tend to be busy and slow. At Murcia the toll-free N-340 takes over as the main road and continues to Almería: branch off it along the A-92-N for Granada and Málaga.

The N-630 heads all the way down to Sevilla from Gijón on Spain's north coast, through Castilla y León and Extremadura.

See the Getting Around chapter for some general information on driving in Spain.

Hitching Hitchhiking is never entirely safe and we don't recommend it. Travellers who decide to hitch should understand that they are taking a small but potentially serious risk. Women should avoid hitching alone, and even men should consider hitching in pairs and letting someone know where they plan to go.

Hitching is illegal on the best Spanish roads – *autopistas* and *autovías* – and difficult on other major highways. You can try to pick up lifts before the tollbooths on tollways. Otherwise, you need to choose a spot where cars can safely stop prior to highway slipways, or use minor roads. The going can be slow on the latter.

One or two organisations, such as Compartecoche in Sevilla (see the Sevilla Getting There & Away section), organise car pooling – a kind of organised hitching service for which you pay a contribution to petrol and often a small fee.

Bicycle If you get tired of pedalling, it's often possible to take your bike on a bus (usually you'll just be asked to remove the front wheel). To take a bike on a train, you must comply with numerous conditions. On

Road Distances (km)

	Almería	Barcelona	Bilbao	Cádiz	Córdoba	Gibraltar	Granada	Huelva	Jaén	Madrid	Málaga	Sevilla
Almería	---											
Barcelona	809	---										
Bilbao	958	620	---									
Cádiz	484	1284	1058	---								
Córdoba	332	908	796	263	---							
Gibraltar	346	1124	1110	127	314	---						
Granada	166	868	829	355	166	256	---					
Huelva	516	1140	939	219	232	291	350	---				
Jaén	228	804	730	367	104	336	99	336	---			
Madrid	563	621	395	663	400	714	434	632	335	---		
Málaga	219	997	939	265	187	127	129	313	209	544	---	
Sevilla	422	1046	933	125	138	197	256	94	242	538	219	---

long-distance trains you have to be travelling overnight in a sleeper or couchette, and you have to remove the pedals and pack the bike in a container designed for the purpose.

The UK

Bus Buses from Britain to Andalucía cost more than the cheapest flights. Eurolines (☎ 0990 14 32 19), 52 Grosvenor Gardens, Victoria, London SW1 (the terminal is only a few blocks away), runs twice weekly to/from Granada (33 hours), Málaga, Torremolinos and Algeciras; and to/from Córdoba and Sevilla (41 hours) with a change of buses in Paris. One-way/return fares to all stops in Andalucía at the time of writing were, respectively, UK£77/139 (a little less for 13- to 25-year-olds and 60-or-overs, a little more during July and August). Euroline's Web site is at www.eurolines.co.uk.

In Málaga, Eurolines can be contacted by phone on ☎ 95 223 23 00.

Train The simplest and quickest route from London involves using the expensive Eurostar Channel Tunnel service from Waterloo to Paris, changing from Gare du Nord to Gare d'Austerlitz in Paris, taking the 'Francisco de Goya' sleeper-only train to Madrid's Chamartin station, and then taking a fast AVE or Talgo 200 train from Madrid to Andalucía. You will probably also have to change stations in Madrid. The best services to most of Andalucía use the expensive high-speed AVE line from Madrid's Atocha station.

Leaving Waterloo at about 2 pm, you can reach Sevilla at 12.30 pm the next day, or Málaga at 4.30 pm. Fares vary according to the time of year, day of the week, your age and the number of yellow cards waved at Real Madrid players the last time they played the team from your destination city, but you're looking in the region of UK£165/230 one way/return to Sevilla in 2nd-class, or UK£120/210 if you're under 26 (a little less to Málaga or Granada).

To cut costs – and add time – you can cross the English Channel by ferry or hovercraft, take a more economical Paris–Madrid service such as the 11.14 pm (changing at Irún on the France–Spain border), and catch a cheaper train from Madrid to Andalucía. London–Paris prices using trains from Charing Cross or Victoria and ferries or hovercrafts from Dover or Folkestone generally start at UK£20 to UK£25, one way or return.

For information on international rail travel from Britain, call Connex (☎ 0870 603 0405) or European Rail (☎ 020-7387 0444). Eurostar information is available on its Web site (www.eurostar.co.uk), from the Rail Europe Travel Centre (☎ 08705 84 88 48) or at Waterloo station.

For more on trains within Spain, see the Rest of Spain section earlier in this chapter.

Car & Motorcycle Two people should be able to get return flights from London to Málaga and two weeks' car hire for a total of UK£350 to UK£500, depending on the time of year. Driving your own car to Andalucía works out cheaper if you plan to stay there a few weeks and want a car most of the time.

The options for getting your vehicle from Britain to continental Europe are threefold: you can use Eurotunnel – the Channel Tunnel car train from Folkestone to Calais; put your vehicle on a cross-channel ferry or hovercraft to France; or use the direct vehicle ferries from England to Bilbao or Santander in northern Spain (from which it's possible to reach Andalucía in one long day).

Using Eurotunnel or a ferry to France, then driving hard to Andalucía, should cost between UK£275 and UK£500 for a return trip for two people, including petrol, food and one night's accommodation each way en route. To this, add about UK£60 each way for road tolls if you use the quickest routes.

Eurotunnel (☎ 08705 35 35 35) runs around the clock, with up to four crossings (35 minutes) an hour. You pay for the vehicle only. Economy return fares range from UK£260 to UK£360 for a car and UK£140 to UK£260 for a motorcycle, depending on the season, day of week and time of day. Eurotunnel's Web site is at www.eurotunnel.co.uk.

Train Passes & Discounts

Passes for unlimited train travel over varying periods are an attractive option for some, but assess carefully how much train travel you'll really be doing. Cards don't cover sleeping accommodation on trains, and cardholders have to pay 500 ptas each time they reserve a seat on a Spanish train – which is advisable on all long-distance trains, and compulsory on some.

Eurail & Europass These passes are for non-European residents. Eurail passes are similar to InterRail but valid in 17 countries. A Europass is more like Eurodomino, entitling you to between five and 15 days' travel within two months in various countries. A 15-day Europass for Spain, France, Italy, Germany and Switzerland costs US$513/728 for those under/over 26. With either Eurail or Europass you pay a 1500 ptas supplement on AVE or Talgo 200 trains.

Euro<26 & Explorer Rail The Euro<26, a European youth card for the under-26s, called the Carnet Joven in Spain, gives 20% off Spanish *largo recorrido* (long-distance) and regional train fares, and 25% to 40% off the fast AVE and Talgo 200 services.
   Euro<26 holders and ISIC holders under 30 can buy an Explorer Rail card, allowing unlimited travel on all trains in Spain except *cercanías*, international trains and the Barcelona–Alicante Euromed. It costs 19,000/23,000/30,000 ptas for 7/15/30 days, and is sold by authorised travel agencies, including usit Unlimited (☎ 902 32 52 75) which has offices in several Spanish cities including Granada and Sevilla (Web site at www.unlimited.es).

Freedom/Eurodomino Pass This pass for European residents, called the Freedom Pass in Britain and Eurodomino everywhere else, entitles you to between three and eight days' travel in a month, in any one of 29 countries. Eight days' 2nd-class travel in Spain costs UK£139/189 for those

Refer to the Rest of Spain section earlier in this chapter for a summary of routes through Spain, and to the later Sea section for more details of the ferry options.

Paperwork & Preparations Proof of ownership of a private vehicle (Vehicle Registration Document for UK-registered cars), roadworthiness certificate (MOT) and insurance certificate should always be carried when driving in Europe. See Visas & Documents in the Facts for the Visitor chapter for information on driving licences. Third-party motor insurance is a minimum requirement throughout Europe. It's advisable – and for travellers who are not citizens of EU countries, Switzerland or Norway, it is compulsory – to have a Green Card, an internationally recognised proof of insurance, which can be obtained from your insurer. Also ask your insurer for a European Accident Statement form, which can simplify matters in the event of an accident.
   A European breakdown assistance policy

such as the AA Five Star Service or the RAC European Motoring Assistance is a good investment.
   Every vehicle crossing an international border should display a nationality plate of its country of registration. Two warning triangles (to be used in the event of a breakdown) are compulsory in Spain. Recommended accessories are a first-aid kit, spare bulb kit and fire extinguisher. If the car is from the UK or Ireland, remember to adjust the headlights for driving in continental Europe (motor accessory shops sell stick-on strips which deflect the beams in the required direction).
   In the UK, further information is available from the RAC (☎ 0990 72 27 22) or the AA (☎ 0990 50 06 00). Their Web sites are www.rac.co.uk and www.theaa.co.uk, respectively.

Rental If you want to use one of the major international car rental companies, which will provide a reliable service and good

Train Passes & Discounts

under/over 26. Eurodomino gives you 25% off travel as far as the Spanish frontier. You must pay a 1500 ptas supplement on AVE or Talgo 200 trains.

InterRail Available to European residents, InterRail passes give unlimited 2nd-class train travel for 22 or 30 days. Twenty-two days in one InterRail zone (for example, Spain, Portugal and Morocco) costs UK£159/229 for those under/over 26. A 30-day ticket for two zones (which from the UK would get you across France too) is UK£209/279. The pass also gives you reduced-price train travel to/from your zone(s), and 30% off Trasmediterránea ferry fares between Andalucía and Tangier, Ceuta and Melilla, but is not valid on the Eurostar from London. You must pay a 1500 ptas supplement to ride AVE or Talgo 200 trains.

Rail Europe Senior This pass gives the over-60s roughly 30% off train trips that cross at least one border. UK citizens pay UK£5 for it, and must already have a Senior Citizens Rail Card (UK£18).

Return & Child Fares Return fares in Spain are generally 20% less than two one-ways if you're coming back within 60 days. Children aged under four years travel free on Spanish trains. Those aged from four to 11 get 40% off the cost of seats and couchettes.

Spain Flexipass This pass for non-European residents, also called the Tarjeta Turística, is valid for three to 10 days' travel in a two-month period on all Spanish trains. In 2nd class, a three/10-day pass costs US$155/365. A 1500 ptas supplement is payable on AVE and Talgo 200 trains, but there's a 20% discount on Algeciras–Tangier ferries. The Flexipass is sold by travel agents outside Europe and at a few main stations and RENFE offices in Spain, including Santa Justa station in Sevilla.

standard of vehicle, you'll almost always save a lot of money by booking the car before leaving home – or even calling home from Spain and making the booking in your home country, rather than from the same company in Spain. Major firms active in Andalucía include Avis, Budget, Europcar, Hertz and National.

Malaga Car Hire (UK ☎ 020-8398 2662) offers cars to be picked up at Málaga airport or Gibraltar from UK£84 a week, all-inclusive, in summer (from UK£64 November to February).

See Car & Motorcycle in the Getting Around chapter for general information on driving in Spain.

Bicycle People do make their way to Andalucía by bike – best in spring, early summer or autumn. Bicycles can also travel by air: usually you can check them in as a piece of baggage, but confirm this with the airline well in advance, preferably before you pay for your ticket.

France

Bus Eurolines (Paris ☎ 01 49 72 57 80) runs to several Andalucian cities from numerous points around France. Paris–Granada (24 hours) costs around 800/1300FF one way/return (700/1200FF if you're under 26 or over 60). Eurolines' Web site is at www.eurolines.fr.

Train Most routes enter Spain at Irún, on the Bay of Biscay, or Portbou on the Mediterranean, and all involve at least one change of train (usually in Madrid). The easiest and most expensive Paris–Madrid option is the overnight, sleeper-only 'Francisco de Goya' from Gare d'Austerlitz to Madrid Chamartin, costing around 700/1200FF one way/return in 2nd-class. Less expensive options will involve at least one change of train between Paris and Madrid.

Trains from Madrid (usually Atocha station) can get you to the main Andalucian cities in a few hours for between 3600 ptas and 9900 ptas.

euro currency converter €1 = 166 ptas

Car & Motorcycle See the UK section earlier for general information on taking a vehicle across Europe. The main highways from France into Spain run to Barcelona and San Sebastián at either end of the Pyrénées. There are good routes from both borders (see the earlier Rest of Spain section for a note on tolls).

Portugal

There are usually no customs or immigration presence at either of the main border crossings between Portugal and Andalucía – Vila Real de Santo António/Ayamonte and Ficalho/Rosal de la Frontera.

Bus Transportes Agobe (☎ 958 63 52 74), based at Almuñécar, Granada province, runs three buses a week from Lisbon to Granada (13 hours) via Albufeira, Huelva, Sevilla, Málaga, Almuñécar and Granada, with one in each direction continuing to/from Porto. One-way fares from Lisbon to Sevilla/Granada cost 5800$00/10,000$00 (4800/8300 ptas). Departure and ticket points in Portugal include:

Porto (☎ 22-208 47 07) Viagens Resende, Rua
  Carmelitas 7
Lisbon (☎ 21-796 61 48) Viagens Samar,
  Avenida do Brasil, corner of Avenida Roma
Albufeira (☎ 289-58 04 70) Rua 1° Dezembro
  32

In Spain, Agobe's departures are from main city bus stations. Check out its Web site at www.agobe.es.

Eurolines (Lisbon ☎ 21-357 17 45, or ☎ 21-315 26 44, Málaga ☎ 95 223 23 00) travels each way between Lisbon's Terminal Rodoviaria Arco do Cego and Málaga bus station (15 hours), via Elvas, Badajoz, Sevilla (Plaza de Armas), Cádiz (Viajes Rico, Glorieta Ingeniero La Cierva), Algeciras and the Costa del Sol, two to four times a week. Lisbon to Sevilla/Málaga, one way, costs 5870$00/9480$00 (4800/8150 ptas). The under-26s and over-60s pay 20% less. Eurolines' Web site is at www .eurolines.es.

From Sevilla (Plaza de Armas), the Casal

line goes twice daily via Aracena to the border at Rosal de la Frontera, where you can change onto Portuguese buses to Serpa and beyond.

Portugal's EVA Transportes and Spain's Damas run a joint service twice each way daily between Lagos (Terminal EVA, Rossio de São João, ☎ 282-76 29 44) and Sevilla (Plaza de Armas) via Albufeira and Huelva. Lagos–Sevilla takes 4½ hours and costs 2600$00 (2135 ptas). The same companies run twice daily year-round (except Sundays from October to March), between Faro (Avenida da República 5, ☎ 289-89 97 60) and Huelva via Tavira, Vila Real de Santo António and Ayamonte.

Alcotan/Intersul (Sevilla ☎ 95 490 11 60) runs from Lagos to Sevilla (Plaza de Armas) and vice versa, four to six times a week, taking six hours and costing 3170$00 (2600 ptas).

Train No railway line crosses from Portugal into Andalucía, but trains run along the Algarve to Vila Real de Santo António, where there's a ferry service across the Río Guadiana to Ayamonte in Andalucía (525 ptas for a car and driver, 250 ptas for a motorcycle and rider, and 135 ptas for other adult passengers and foot passengers), 50km from Huelva train station. You can get from Lagos to Vila Real at Tunes or Faro (five decent connections daily).

You can travel from Lisbon to Sevilla, or vice versa, in about 16 hours by changing trains (and waiting four hours at night) at Cáceres in Spain's Extremadura. Departure from Lisbon's Santa Apolónia station is around 10 pm daily. The 2nd-class Sevilla–Lisbon fare costs about 7000 ptas one-way.

Car & Motorcycle From Lisbon, head for Beja and Serpa and cross into Spain at Rosal de la Frontera, where the N-433 runs 160km to Sevilla via Aracena. From the Algarve a modern road bridge crosses the Río Guadiana just north of Vila Real de Santo António. See the UK section earlier in this chapter for general information about taking your own vehicle across Europe.

Elsewhere in Europe

Eurolines' buses run to Andalucía from Germany and Switzerland (call ☎ 069-790350 in Germany or visit Euroline's Web site at www.eurolines.es). Direct trains run at least three times a week from Geneva, Berne, Zürich, Turin and Milan to Barcelona, where you can transfer to an Andalucía-bound train.

Morocco

Eurolines (Málaga ☎ 95 223 23 00, Granada ☎ 958 15 75 57, Casablanca ☎ 02-44 81 08, Tangier ☎ 09-93 11 72) runs several weekly buses from Córdoba, Granada, Málaga and the Costa del Sol to Casablanca, Marrakesh, Fès and other places in Morocco, via Algeciras–Tangier ferries. Granada to Casablanca costs 10,200/17,300 ptas one way/return.

You can transport vehicles by ferry from several Andalucian ports (see the following section on travel by Sea for details).

SEA
Portsmouth–Bilbao

P&O Ferries (UK ☎ 0870 242 4999, Spain ☎ 94 423 44 77) operates a ferry from Portsmouth to Bilbao. As a rule, there are two sailings a week except for a few weeks in January. Voyage time varies between 29 and 35 hours. P&O Ferries' Web site is at www.poef.com.

Standard one-way/return fares for two people with a car are around UK£250/500 in the cheapest period (mid-September to mid-December, January to March) and UK£460/840 in the most expensive (mid-July to mid-August from Britain, late August from Spain). This includes the cheapest available form of cabin accommodation. Cabins are compulsory – all have a shower and toilet.

The ferries dock at Santurtzi, about 14km north-west of central Bilbao.

Plymouth–Santander

Brittany Ferries (UK ☎ 0870 901 2400, Spain ☎ 942 36 06 11) operates a twice-weekly car ferry from Plymouth to Santander (24 hours sailing time), between mid-March and mid-November. For two people with a car, they quoted return fares

of UK£462/560 in April with seat/cabin, and UK£692/822 in July. The Web site is at www.brittanyferries.co.uk.

To/From Britain via France

You can transport your vehicle by ferry or hovercraft to France and then drive to Spain. (For the Eurotunnel car train service through the Channel Tunnel, see under The UK in the Land section earlier in this chapter.)

The quickest and busiest cross-Channel sailing route, with around 60 crossings daily at peak times, is Dover–Calais, operated by ferries and catamarans of P&O Stena Line (☎ 0870 600 0600), SeaFrance (☎ 08705-71 17 11) and hovercraft of Hoverspeed (☎ 0870-240 8070). Their Web sites are at www.posl.com, www.seafrance.com and www.hoverspeed.co.uk, respectively.

Fares are volatile and you should research the latest options and offers. A typical August Dover–Calais return ticket for a car and two people will cost in the region of UK£170. Winter fares can be around UK£100 and it's generally cheaper to travel early in the morning or in the evening.

Other routes include Newhaven–Dieppe (Hoverspeed), Folkestone–Boulogne (Hoverspeed), Portsmouth–Caen (Brittany Ferries); and Portsmouth–Cherbourg (P&O Ferries).

Morocco

You can sail to Tangier or to Ceuta or Melilla (Spanish enclaves on the Moroccan coast) from one or more of Almería, Málaga, Algeciras, Gibraltar, Tarifa or Cádiz. All routes usually take vehicles as well as passengers. The cheapest sailings are from Algeciras, Tarifa and Cádiz, and by far the most frequent are from Algeciras. Usually at least 20 sailings a day go from Algeciras to Tangier (taking one to 2½ hours) and 40 or more to Ceuta (30 minutes to 1½ hours), with many more during the peak summer months when hundreds of thousands of Moroccans return home from Europe for holidays.

The most prominent ferry company, with sailings from Algeciras, Málaga and Almería, is Trasmediterránea (☎ 902 45 46 45) with a Web site at www.trasmediterranea.es. The other main operator from Algeciras is Euro-Ferrys (☎ 956 65 11 78). Its Web site is at www.euroferrys.com. One-way passenger fares cost 3500 ptas to 4400 ptas to Tangier and 1945 ptas to 3095 ptas to Ceuta. A car costs 10,750 ptas to Tangier and 8930 ptas to Ceuta. Euro>26 cardholders and EU citizens aged over 60 are entitled to about 20% off Trasmediterránea's Ceuta passenger fares. The superfast Buquebus service (☎ 902 41 42 42) to Ceuta takes just 30–35 minutes from Algeciras and 1½ hours from Málaga.

Anyone crossing from Morocco to Spain with a vehicle should be prepared for rigorous searches in Ceuta and Melilla and on disembarking on the mainland.

For more details see the Getting There & Away entries for Algeciras, Almería, Cádiz, Gibraltar, Málaga and Tarifa.

Canary Islands
A weekly car ferry sails from Cádiz – see the Cádiz section for details.

ORGANISED TOURS
Many companies offer tours to Andalucía, sometimes combining it with other parts of Spain. Special interest tours include horse riding, walking, bird-watching, cycling and wine trips. Spanish tourist offices can often provide long lists of tour firms, as can the Internet (check www.antor.com/Spain/uktourops.html for specialist tour operators in Britain). The following examples are just a tiny sample of tours available.

Short Breaks
Kirker Travel (☎ 020-7231 3333), 3 New Concordia Wharf, Mill St, London SE1 2BB, UK, offers short breaks from London in good hotels in Sevilla, Granada and Córdoba. As a rule, they will set you back around £250 per person for three nights, breakfast only included. Sovereign Cities (☎ 0900 76 83 73), based in Crawley, Sussex, UK, does Spanish city breaks with car hire included.

Walking Holidays
The popularity of Andalucía walking holidays is growing by leaps and bounds, and so is the number of companies offering them.

Headwater Holidays (☎ 01606-81 33 33), 146 London Rd, Northwich, Cheshire CW9 5HH, UK, offers one-week walking holidays in Las Alpujarras and the Sierra de Aracena from UK£700 including flights and meals (Web site www.headwater.com). Exodus (☎ 020-8675 5550) also does well-priced Aracena walking trips from Britain.

The Walking Safari Company (☎ 01572-82 38 20, fax 82 10 72), 54 High St East, Uppingham LE15 9PZ, UK, does gentle holidays in the Ronda and Arcos de la Frontera areas for around UK£1200 plus flights (Web site at www.walkeurope.com).

Explore Worldwide (☎ 01252-76 00 00), 1 Frederick St, Aldershot, Hants GU11 1LQ, UK, and with offices in several other countries around the world, runs small group Andalucía tours, which include walking in the Alpujarras and Sierra Nevada, or the Parque Natural de Cazorla. A two-week trip costs around UK£400 plus flights. Its Web site is at www.explore.co.uk.

Rustic Blue (☎ 958 76 33 81, fax 958 76 31 34), Barrio de la Ermita, 18412 Bubión, Granada, offers one-week walking holidays in Las Alpujarras and the Sierra Nevada for UK£430 plus flights (Web site at www.rusticblue.com).

Other British providers of Spanish walking holidays include Inntravel (☎ 01653-62 90 00, fax 62 87 41), Hovingham, York YO62 4JZ (Web site www.inntravel.co.uk); Alternative Travel (☎ 01865-51 33 33), 69–71 Banbury Rd, Oxford OX2 6PE; and Waymark Holidays (☎ 01753-51 64 77, fax 517016), 44 Windsor Road, Slough SL1 2EJ.

A leading Dutch operator is Sindbad Reizen (☎ 020-521 8484, fax 423 2517), Keizersgracht 181–1016 DR Amsterdam. Its Web site is at www.sindbad.nl.

Country Walkers (☎ 800 464 9255), PO Box 180, Waterbury, VT 05676, USA, offers a week of Alpujarras walking and Granada in the region of US$2000. Its Web site is at www.countrywalkers.com.

Golf Holidays
Longshot Golf Holidays (UK ☎ 01730-26 86 21,) includes some of Andalucía's best courses in its holidays. Prices start at

around UK£525 for a week in July and August, including car hire. Its Web site is at www.longshotgolf.co.uk.

Wine Tours

Arblaster & Clarke (UK ☎ 01730-89 33 44) runs occasional 'Sherry and Andalucía' trips at around UK£900 for one week, including flights from the UK. Its Web site is at www.arblasterandclarke.com.

Riding Tours

Andalucía Trails (UK ☎ 01672-54 11 60) offers a variety of one-week riding holidays from around UK£500 to UK£700 plus flights, based at Bolonia near Tarifa (Web site at www.andaluciatrails.com).

Rustic Blue (see Walking Holidays) offers one-week riding holidays in Las Alpujarras and the Sierra Nevada, for UK£830 plus flights. Inntravel (see Walking Holidays) is another operator. Forty-odd Andalucian riding holiday establishments are listed at www.ridingholidays.com.

Cycling Tours

Discover Adventure (☎ 01722-74 11 23, ✉ info@discoveradventure.com), 5 Nether-hampton Cottage, Netherhampton Rd, Netherhampton, Salisbury SP2 8PX, UK, offers one-week mountain-bike tours in Andalucía (Sierra Nevada, Alpujarras and Sierra de Cazorla) for UK£650 per person.

Inntravel (see Walking Holidays) also does Spanish cycling trips.

Language Tours

Caledonia Languages Abroad (☎ 0131-621 77 21, fax 0131-621 77 23), The Clockhouse, Bonnington Mill, 72 Newhaven Rd, Edinburgh EH6 5QG, UK organises trips with a language study and activities components in southern Spain. Its Web site is at www.caledonianlanguages.co.uk.

Nature & Bird-watching Tours

Country Connoisseurs (☎/fax 01428-72 79 29, ✉ mail@co-connoisseurs.demon.co. uk), 2 Wey Lodge Close, Liphook, Hants GU30 7DE, UK, offers one-week bird-watching holidays for around UK£835 plus flights. Naturetrek (☎ 01962-73 30 51) does a week of botany and gentle walking for around UK£900 from Britain including flights and meals. Another company to check out is Cox & Kings (☎ 020-7873 5010).

Getting Around

You will probably find that a combination of trains and buses best suits your needs if you're using public transport. Train services are good between some cities, nonexistent between others. Buses get to just about every town and village, but the frequency and convenience of services varies enormously.

Touring Andalucía on your own wheels has many advantages – roads are generally good (though country roads can be badly surfaced), you can get well off the beaten track and you have much more flexibility about where you go and when.

AIR
There are no direct flights between Andalucian cities.

BUS
Most larger towns and cities have one main *estación de autobuses* (bus station) where all out-of-town buses stop. In smaller places, buses tend to operate from a particular street or square, which is often unmarked. Ask around; everyone generally knows where to go and there's usually a specific bar that sells tickets and has schedule information. Services to small villages may run just once a day – or not at all on Saturday or Sunday.

During Semana Santa, July and August it's advisable to buy long-distance bus tickets in advance. Occasionally, a return ticket

is cheaper than two singles. People aged under 26 should always inquire about discounts.

TRAIN
Good or reasonable train services, with at least three direct trains each way daily (often many more), run on the following routes:

> Algeciras–Ronda–Bobadilla
> Córdoba–Málaga
> Málaga–Torremolinos–Fuengirola
> Sevilla–Jerez de la Frontera–El Puerto de Santa María–Cádiz
> Sevilla–Córdoba
> Sevilla–Huelva
> Sevilla–Málaga
> Sevilla–Antequera–Granada–Guadix–Almería

These routes apart, trains between Andalucía's main cities and towns tend to be infrequent and journeys often involve changing trains at the small junction station of Bobadilla, where lines from Sevilla, Córdoba, Granada, Málaga and Algeciras all meet. Except for the short Málaga–Fuengirola line, no trains run along any of Andalucía's coasts. But, with a little perseverance, you *can* reach a surprising number of places by train, including Jaén, the Sierra Norte de Sevilla province and the Sierra de Aracena.

On some routes – such as between Córdoba and Málaga, Cádiz, Algeciras, Ronda or Sevilla – you can use long-distance trains heading into or out of Andalucía (for information on long-distance trains, see The Rest of Spain under Land in the Getting There & Away chapter). But more often you'll use the cheaper *regional* or *cercanía* trains. Regionales run between Andalucian cities, stopping at towns en route. Most are classed as Tren Regional Diésel (TRD) or, slower and a bit cheaper, Andalucía Expres (AE). AEs are in turn a bit quicker and more expensive than regional (R) trains. Cercanías are commuter trains that link Sevilla,

Selected One-Way Bus Fares

from	to	fare (ptas)	duration (hrs)
Cádiz	Sevilla	1385	1
Granada	Almería	1300	2¼
Granada	Pampaneira	635	2
Granada	Sevilla	2400	3
Jaén	Cazorla	960	2
Málaga	Sevilla	1900	2½

Selected One-Way Train Fares

from	to	type of train	2nd-class fare (ptas)	duration (hrs)
Granada	Almería	Andalucía Expres (AE)	1610	2¾
		Tren Regional Diésel (TRD)	1775	2¼
Granada	Sevilla	AE	2415	3½
		TRD	2665	2¾ to three
Málaga	Córdoba	Estrella	2100	2½
		Diurno, InterCity	2300	2¼
		Talgo 200	2000–2300	two to 2¼
		Trenhotel	2800	2¼
Sevilla	Cádiz	Regional (R)	1125	two
		AE	1290	1¾
		Talgo 200	1600	1½
		Estrella	1800	2¼
		Talgo	2100	1¾

Málaga and Cádiz with their suburbs and nearby towns.

You can consult the schedule and fares of every train in Spain on the Web site of the national rail authority, RENFE (Red Nacional de Ferrocarriles Españoles, Spanish National Railways; www.renfe.es). On RENFE's national information and reservations line, ☎ 902 24 02 02, you can reserve tickets for all trains except cercanías and the few regionales for which advance bookings are not accepted.

For information on train passes and fare discounts, see the Train Passes & Discounts box in the Getting There & Away chapter.

CAR & MOTORCYCLE

The Land section in the Getting There & Away chapter covers ways of getting a vehicle to Andalucía from other countries and from other parts of Spain, and the paperwork needed to drive in Spain. It also contains a chart of road distances between cities in Andalucía and elsewhere in Spain. For information about Hitching see Land in the Getting There & Away chapter.

There are only two toll roads in Andalucía – the A-7 between Fuengirola and Estepona, west of Málaga (1070 ptas from June to September, 785 ptas in other months), and the A-4 from Sevilla to Cádiz (900 ptas).

Road Rules

As elsewhere in continental Europe, drive on the right, overtake on the left. The minimum driving age is 18. Rear seat belts, if fitted, must be worn. The blood-alcohol limit is 0.05% (0.03% for drivers with a licence that is less than two years old) and breath-testing is carried out on occasion. Non-resident foreigners may be fined on the spot for traffic offences. You can appeal in writing (in any language) to the Jefatura Provincial de Tráfico (Provincial Traffic Headquarters) and if your appeal is upheld, you'll get your money back – but don't hold your breath for a favourable result.

Motorcyclists must have their headlights on at all times. Crash helmets are obligatory – though you wouldn't guess it from observing the locals. A licence is required to ride any bike or scooter. The minimum age for a machine of 80cc or more is 16; for 50cc bikes the minimum age is 14.

The speed limit is 50km/h in built-up areas, rising to 100km/h on major roads and 120km/h on *autopistas* (toll highways) and *autovías* (toll-free dual carriageways).

Road Maps & Atlases

Mapmakers have a hard time keeping up with the new roads that are being built around Andalucía and with changes in the numbering of roads. However, Michelin's *Southern Spain* map (see Planning in the Facts for the Visitor chapter) is pretty good for finding your way round. Michelin also publishes the good *Michelin Motoring Atlas – Spain & Portugal* (called *Michelin Atlas de Carreteras España Portugal* in Spain). Both of these are widely available in and outside Spain. In Spain, the atlas costs about 2600 ptas and the map about 900 ptas. Several other good road atlases are available, including one produced by the Campsa petrol company and the government-published *Mapa Oficial de Carreteras* (2300 ptas). Petrol stations and bookshops are the places to look for all these publications.

Road Assistance

The Real Automóvil Club de España (RACE) operates a 24-hour, countrywide emergency breakdown assistance service. This is available to members of some foreign motoring organisations, such as Britain's RAC and AA – ask your national association for their special contact numbers.

Petrol

Gasolina prices vary slightly between service stations and fluctuate with oil prices and tax policy. Lead-free *(sin plomo)* petrol usually comes in two versions: 95 octane, sometimes called Eurosúper, at around 128 ptas/L, and 98 octane, with names like Súper Plus, at about 140 ptas/L. Leaded Super – due to be phased out by 1 January 2002 in accordance with EU policy – costs around 134 ptas/L and diesel (or *gasóleo*) about 110 ptas/L.

Rental

Major international car hire companies are well represented in Andalucía, and there are plenty of local operators too. At Málaga airport, in Nerja, along the Costa del Sol and in the Almería resorts you can hire a small car from a local firm for around 20,000 ptas a week (as little as 15,000 ptas in winter), including unlimited mileage, collision damage waiver, insurance and 16% IVA (value-added tax). Elsewhere, and from the international firms, rates are often double

that, and you would be better off organising your car before you come to Spain (see The UK in the Land section of the Getting There & Away chapter).

If you hire after arriving, shop around a little. One established local firm with good prices – 15,900 to 20,900 ptas a month all inclusive for the cheapest cars, depending on season – is Helle Hollis (☎ 95 224 55 44, fax 95 224 51 86), with offices at Málaga airport and in Fuengirola and Marbella. Visit their Web site at www.helleauto .com/hellehollis. Wherever you hire from, make sure you understand what is included in the price.

You need to be aged at least 21 (23 with some companies) and to have held a driving licence for a minimum of one year (often two years). It's much easier, and often obligatory, to pay with a credit card. See Visas & Documents in the Facts for the Visitor chapter for information on driving licences.

Rental outlets catering for motorcycles and mopeds are rare and tend to be expensive. Moto Mercado (☎ 95 247 25 51, @ motomerc@futurnet.es), Avenida Jesús Santos Rein 47, Los Boliches, Fuengirola, has 50/125/250/600cc machines for 3500/ 5000/7000/11,500 ptas a day (less if you rent for three days or more). It also has branches in Torremolinos and Marbella.

City Driving & Parking

Driving in the bigger cities can be a little nerve-racking at the start. Road rules and traffic lights are generally respected, but the pace and jostling take a little getting used to.

Parking in cities is sometimes a bit of a headache. If you park on the street, don't leave anything that even looks to be of any value visible inside your vehicle, and take care not to park in prohibited zones (you risk being towed, which will cost you 10,000 ptas or so). If you must leave things in the vehicle, use an underground or multistorey car park. These usually cost 100 to 150 ptas an hour, or 1000 to 1200 ptas overnight. Blue lines on the street usually mean you must pay at a nearby meter to park during certain hours – typically 9 am to 2 pm Monday to Saturday, plus about 5 to 8 pm Monday to Friday. Meters usually cost under 100 ptas an hour. Yellow lines mean no parking (these are often ignored at the risk of being towed).

In areas of cities where street parking space is particularly at a premium, you'll see self-appointed attendants trying to wave you into available spaces, 'supervising' parking on waste ground, and so on. It's standard practice to give them 100 ptas; they will probably keep some kind of an eye on your vehicle and they are usually in fairly obvious need of cash. Sometimes they'll give you a receipt showing that you've just made a donation to some charity or cooperative.

BICYCLE

Bicycles are increasingly available for hire in main cities, coastal resorts and inland towns and villages which attract tourism. They're often mountain bikes (*bicis todo terreno*). Prices range from 1500 to 3000 ptas a day. One-day rides and touring by bike are particularly enjoyable in spring and autumn. See Activities in the Facts for the Visitor chapter for one or two hints on mountain biking.

Some regional trains have space for bicycles, others don't. Ask before buying tickets. Bikes are permitted on most cercanías trains (but not on the Cádiz–Jerez line in July or August, or on the Málaga–Fuengirola line). Bikes can also be carried on most inter-city buses if the front wheel is removed.

LOCAL TRANSPORT

Cities and larger towns have efficient bus systems, but in most places accommodation, attractions and main-line bus and train stations are usually within fairly comfortable walking distance of each other. All Andalucía's airports except Jerez de la Frontera are linked to city centres by bus – and in Málaga's case also by train. Gibraltar airport is within walking distance of downtown Gibraltar.

Taxis are plentiful in larger places and even many villages have a taxi or two. Fares are reasonable – a typical 3km trip should cost about 400 ptas (airport runs cost a bit extra). Inter-city runs cost around 100 ptas/km. You don't have to tip taxi drivers but a little rounding up doesn't go amiss.

ORGANISED TOURS

Guided tours of the major cities are an option, but as a rule it's cheaper and not a great deal more trouble to do it under your own steam. Of more potential use are trips in national and natural parks (see those sections for details), some of which are hard to penetrate if you don't have your own vehicle. Guides' local knowledge can be illuminating. The only way the general public is permitted to enter the Parque Nacional de Doñana is by guided tour.

Sevilla Province

The wonderful city of Sevilla (Seville) is the highlight of the province, but country-side lovers will enjoy heading north to the Parque Natural Sierra Norte. In the east, you can visit interesting old towns such as Carmona, Écija, Osuna and Estepa.

Sevilla

postcode 41080 • pop 702,000

Sevilla is Andalucía's biggest and most exciting city. It takes a stony heart not to be captivated by the city's unique atmosphere – stylish, ancient, proud, yet also convivial, fun-loving and intimate. One of the first people recorded as falling in love with Sevilla was Al-Mutamid, an 11th century Muslim poet-king. The place is working its enchantment every bit as well today.

Except along the Río Guadalquivir – navigable to the Atlantic Ocean 100km away and source of Sevilla's greatness in times past – this is not a city of great long vistas. Its crowded centre unfolds more subtly as you wend your way through narrow streets and small squares, stopping for a drink or a bite in some of the wonderful bars and cafes. Similarly, the city's two great monuments – the Muslim Alcázar and the Christian cathedral – reveal most of their glories only once you're inside them.

A great city in Muslim times and again in the 16th and 17th centuries, Sevilla has known bad times too, so it knows how to enjoy the good ones when they come. The year 1992, when the eyes of the world turned on Sevilla's world Expo, was one of the best (see the following History section for details). Every April for more than a century, Sevilla has been throwing one of Spain's biggest parties, the Feria de Abril (see that section under Special Events later in this chapter for details). And a couple of weeks before the fair, the city's Semana Santa (Holy Week) processions are among the most magnificent in Spain.

Highlights

- Marvel at the cathedral and the Alcázar, the city's great monuments
- Visit the Museo de Bellas Artes, full of paintings from the golden age of Spanish art
- Tour tapas bars in Sevilla, Andalucía's tapas capital
- Imbibe the atmosphere of Sevilla's lively nightlife
- Witness the Semana Santa processions in Sevilla; probably the most emotive and spectacular in Spain
- Enjoy the rolling Sierra Morena hills of the Parque Natural Sierra Norte

Outside its fascinating inner city, Sevilla enjoys some good green parks on the fringes of the centre. It's also one of the homes of flamenco and bullfighting, and has great nightlife. But above all, Sevilla is an atmosphere. Being out among its happy, celebratory crowds on a warm night is a not-to-be-forgotten experience. To put it in one Spanish word, the city has *alegría*.

There are a couple of catches. Sevilla is expensive. You might pay 6000 ptas here for a room that would cost 3000 ptas elsewhere. And prices go even higher during the two big festivals. Another thing to bear in mind is that Sevilla gets *very* hot in July and August: locals, sensibly, leave the city then.

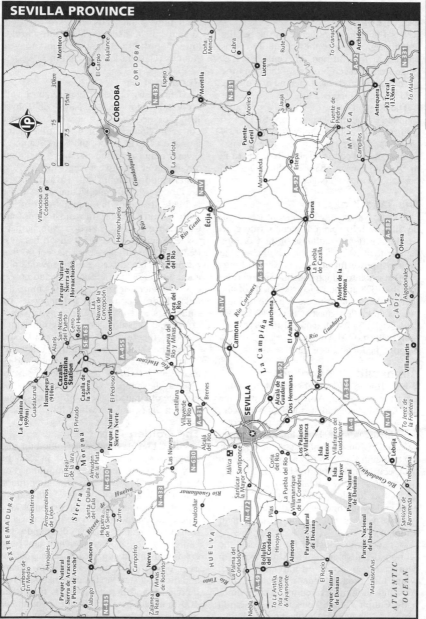

SEVILLA PROVINCE

HISTORY
Beginnings

It was Phoenician influence in the Sevilla area that gave rise to the ancient Tartessos culture in the 8th and 7th centuries BC, when iron replaced bronze for the first time in Andalucía, and a new method of working gold was developed.

The Roman town of Hispalis, probably founded in the mid-2nd century BC, was a significant river port, but overshadowed by Córdoba. Later, Hispalis became a Visigothic cultural centre, especially in the time of St Isidoro (AD 565–636), Spain's leading scholar of the Visigothic period.

The Taifa Kings

Under the Muslims, who called it Ishbiliya, Sevilla initially played second fiddle to Córdoba. After the collapse of the Córdoba Caliphate in 1031, however, Sevilla became the most powerful of the *taifa* (small kingdom) states into which Muslim Spain broke up. By 1078 it controlled the south of the Iberian Peninsula from the Algarve to Murcia. Its Abbadid dynasty rulers Al-Mutadid (1042–69) and Al-Mutamid (1069–91) were both poets too. Al-Mutamid presided over a languid, hedonistic court in the Alcázar.

Almoravids & Almohads

When Toledo in central Spain fell to the Christians in 1085, Al-Mutamid asked the Muslim fundamentalist rulers of Morocco, the Almoravids, for help against the growing Christian threat. The Almoravids came, defeated Alfonso VI of Castile at Sagrajas (Extremadura) in 1086, and went back to Morocco – but then returned in 1091 to help themselves to Al-Andalus too, ruling it harshly as a colony. But their hold slackened and by the middle of 12th century Al-Andalus was again breaking up into small kingdoms.

A new strict Muslim Berber sect, the Almohads, displaced the Almoravids in Morocco then moved on into Al-Andalus, which they brought under control by 1173. Arts and learning revived under the Almohads: Caliph Yacoub Yousouf made Sevilla capital of the whole Almohad realm, building a great mosque where the city's cathedral now stands. His successor Yousouf Yacoub al-Mansour added the Giralda tower and thrashed the Christian armies at Alarcos (Castilla-La Mancha) in 1195.

Reconquista

The Christians, however, bounced back with a pivotal victory at Las Navas de Tolosa, Jaén province (1212), after which Almohad power in Spain dwindled. Castilian King Fernando III (El Santo, the Saint) captured several major Andalucian cities – including Sevilla, after a two-year siege, in 1248.

Fernando brought 24,000 Castilian settlers to Sevilla. His intellectual son Alfonso X made it one of his capitals and by the 14th century it was the most important Castilian city. The monarch who perhaps loved Sevilla more than any other was Pedro I (1350–69), but his reign was plagued by bloody feuds in the royal family and conflict between monarchy and nobles (see the later Alcázar section for more details). Pedro's court included many Jewish financiers and tax collectors, which provoked racial jealousies. A pogrom which emptied the Jewish quarter in 1391 signalled the end of 'three cultures' tolerance.

The Catholic Monarchs, Fernando and Isabel, set up court in the Alcázar for several years as they prepared for the conquest of the Emirate of Granada, the last Muslim stronghold on the peninsula, which fell in 1492.

The Golden Age

Sevilla's biggest break was Columbus' discovery of the Americas in 1492. In 1503 the city was given an official monopoly on Spanish trade with the new continent. Galleons disgorged cargoes of gold and silver at El Arenal, a sandy riverbank area where the Plaza de Toros de la Real Maestranza now stands, and Sevilla rapidly became one of the biggest, richest and most cosmopolitan cities on earth, a magnet for everyone from beggars and *pícaros* (card and dice tricksters) to Dutch bankers, Italian merchants and the clergy of its more than 100 monasteries and religious institutions. Sevilla was labelled the *puerto y puerta de*

Indias (port and gateway of the Indies), the Babylon of Spain and even the New Rome. Its population jumped from about 40,000 in 1500 to 150,000 in 1600, lavish Renaissance and baroque buildings sprouted, and many figures of Spain's artistic golden age did the bulk of their work here.

The Not-so-Golden Age

A plague in 1649 killed half the city and, as the 17th century wore on, the Guadalquivir became more and more silted up and difficult for the increasingly big ships of the day, many of which foundered on a sandbar at its mouth near Sanlúcar de Barrameda. Cádiz began to take much of the American trade. By 1700 Sevilla's population was down to 60,000 and in 1717 the Casa de la Contratación, the government office which controlled the American commerce, was transferred to Cádiz. Another Sevilla plague in 1800 killed 13,000 people. The Napoleonic troops occupying the city from 1810 to 1812 stole, it's said, 999 works of art when they left.

A certain prosperity returned in the mid-19th century with the beginnings of industry. The first bridge across the Guadalquivir, the Puente de Triana (or Puente de Isabel II), was built in 1845 and the old Almohad walls were knocked down in 1869 to let the city expand. Romantic travellers were attracted by Sevilla's faded grandeur, but the majority in the city and countryside remained very poor.

The 20th Century

Middle-class optimism was expressed by Sevilla's first international fair, the Exposición Iberoamericana of 1929. The fair's architects tried to inspire a new future with buildings that looked back to the city's glorious past.

Sevilla fell very quickly to the Nationalists at the start of the Civil War despite resistance in working class areas (which brought savage reprisals). Urban development in Franco's time did little for the look of the city, with numerous historic buildings being demolished. Things looked up in the early 1980s when Sevilla was named capital of the new autonomous Andalucía and the PSOE (Socialist party), led by Sevillan Felipe González (see New Democracy in the History section of the Facts about Andalucía chapter for details), came to power in Madrid. The city received another big thrust forward from Expo 92, on the 500th anniversary of the discovery of America. As well as millions of extra visitors and a boost to its international image, Expo brought Sevilla eight new bridges across the Guadalquivir, the super-fast AVE rail link to Madrid, and thousands of new hotel rooms.

Almost inevitably, Expo was a source of controversy too. Costs escalated in the run-up to 1992, and no one seemed to know what to do with the site afterwards. In 1997, amid allegations that large sums had disappeared into private pockets and PSOE coffers, the national Accounts Tribunal reported that Expo had lost around 35 billion ptas.

The historic heart of the city retains plenty of the picturesque decay that attracted the 19th-century Romantics. Bureaucratic delay, political squabbling and lack of funds for renovation remain just as characteristic of Sevilla as do grand projects such as the new Olympic stadium built for the 1999 World Athletic Championships.

ORIENTATION

Sevilla straddles the Río Guadalquivir, with most places of interest on the east bank. The central area is mostly a tangle of narrow, twisting old streets and small squares, with the exceptions of Plaza Nueva and Avenida de la Constitución. The latter runs south from Plaza Nueva to the Puerta de Jerez, a busy intersection marking the southern edge of the central area. The area between Avenida de la Constitución and the river is called El Arenal. Just east of Avenida de la Constitución are the city's major monuments – the cathedral with its tower (the Giralda) and the fortress-palace, the Alcázar. The quaint Barrio de Santa Cruz, east of the cathedral and Alcázar, offers some budget accommodation. The true centre of Sevilla (El Centro) is a little farther north, around Plaza de San Francisco and Plaza Salvador.

SEVILLA

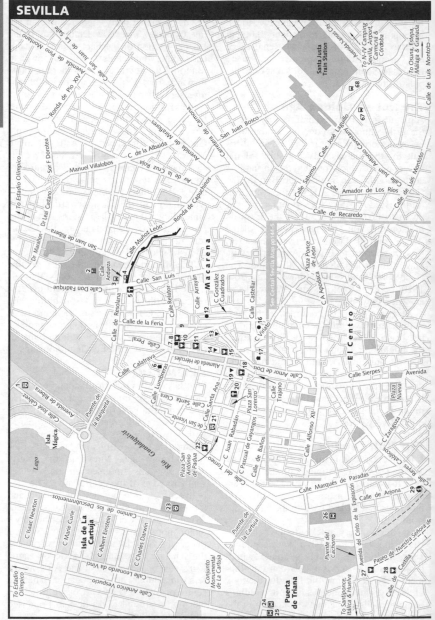

Santa Justa
Train Station

To N-IV Camping
Sevilla, Airport,
Carmona &
Córdoba

Avenida Kansas City

To Osuna, Estepa,
Málaga & Granada

68

67

Calle de Luis Montoto

Calle de Luis Montoto

Calle Juan Antonio Cavestany

Calle José Laguillo

Calle Saturno

Calle Amador de Los Ríos

Calle de Recaredo

Ronda de Pío XIX

Avenida de Pino Montano

Calle San Juan de La Salle

Carretera de Carmona

San Juan Bosco

Avenida de Miraflores

C de la Albaida

Av de la Cruz Roja

Manuel Villalobos

Ronda de Capuchinos

Sor F Durotea

Dr Leal Castaño

To Estadio Olímpico

Dr Marañón

San Juan de Ribera

Calle Muñoz León

M a c a r e n a

Plaza Ponce
de León

C A Apodaca

See Central Sevilla Map pp144-5

Plaza San
de León

E l C e n t r o

Calle
Andueza

2

3 4

Calle San Luis

Calle Don Fadrique

Calle de Resolana

Calle Relator

Calle Arrayán

C Gonzalez
Cuadrado

Calle Castellar

5

12

9

13

C Viriato

16

Calle de la Feria

Calle Peral

7 8

10

11

14

15

17

Calle Sierpes

Avenida

Alameda de Hércules

Calle Amor de Dios

18

Plaza
Nueva

Calle Calatrava

6

19

20

Calle Trajano

Calle Santa Ana

Plaza San
Lorenzo

Plaza
Zaragoza

C Zaragoza

Calle Lumbreras

Calle Santa Clara

Calle de San Vicente

21

C Juan Rabadán

Calle Alfonso XIII

C Reyes Católicos

Puente de
la Barqueta

Avenida de Ribera

Calle José Gálvez

Isla
Mágica

Lago

Plaza San
Antonio
de Padua

22

Calle del Torneo

C Pascual de Gayangos

Calle de Baños

Río Guadalquivir

Calle Marqués de Paradas

Calle de Arjona

29

Isla de La
Cartuja

Camino de los Descubrimientos

23

Puente del
Cachorro

26

Avenida del Cristo de la Expiración

27

C Isaac Newton

C Marie Curie

C Albert Einstein

C Charles Darwin

Calle Leonardo da Vinci

Calle Américo Vespucio

To Estadio
Olímpico

Conjunto
Monumental
de La Cartuja

Puente de
la Cartuja

Puerta
de Triana

24

25

28

Paseo de Nuestra Señora de la I

Calle de Castilla

To Santiponce,
Itálica & Huelva

SEVILLA

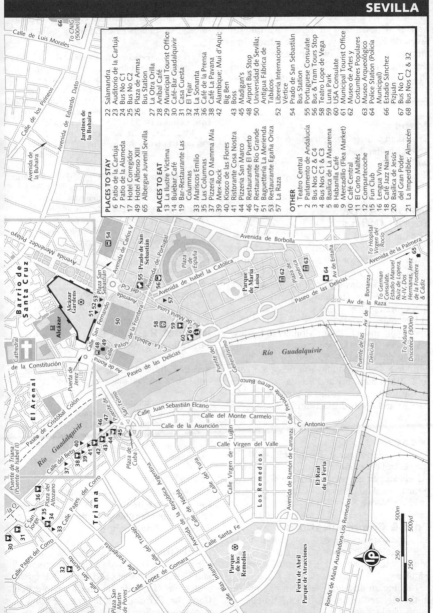

PLACES TO STAY
6 Patio de la Cartuja
7 Patio de la Alameda
17 Hotel Corregidor
49 Hotel Alfonso XIII
65 Albergue Juvenil Sevilla

PLACES TO EAT
13 La Ilustre Víctima
14 Bulebar Café
19 Bar-Restaurante Las Columnas
33 Mariscos Emilio
35 Las Columnas
37 Pizzería O Mamma Mia
39 Mex-Rock
40 Kiosco de las Flores
41 Ristorante Cosa Nostra
44 Pizzería San Marco
46 Restaurante El Puerto
47 Restaurante Río Grande
51 Baguetería La Merienda
53 Restaurante Egaña Oriza
57 La Raza

22 Salamandra
23 Auditorio de la Cartuja
24 Bus No C1
25 Bus No C2
26 Plaza de Armas Bus Station
27 La Otra Orilla
28 Aníbal Café
29 Municipal Tourist Office
30 Café-Bar Guadalquivir
31 Casa Cuesta
32 El Tejar
34 La Sonanta
36 Café de la Prensa
38 Café La Pavana
42 Alambique; Mui d'Aquí; Big Ben
43 Boss
45 Madigan's
48 Airport Bus Stop
50 Universidad de Sevilla; Antigua Fábrica de Tabacos
52 Librería Internacional Vértice
54 Prado de San Sebastián Bus Station
55 Portuguese Consulate
56 Bus & Tram Tours Stop
58 Teatro Lope de Vega
59 Luna Park
60 USA Consulate
61 Municipal Tourist Office
62 Museo de Artes y Costumbres Populares
63 Museo Arqueológico
64 Police Station (Policía Municipal)
66 Estadio Sánchez Pizjuán
67 Bus No C1
68 Bus Nos C2 & 32

OTHER
1 Teatro Central
2 Parlamento de Andalucía
3 Bus Nos C2 & C4
4 Bus Nos C1 & C3
5 Basílica de La Macarena
8 Habanilla Café
9 Mercadillo (Flea Market)
10 Café Central
11 El Corto Maltés
12 Compartecoche
15 Fun Club
16 Lengua Viva
18 Café Jazz Naima
20 Basílica de Jesús del Gran Poder
21 La Imperdible; Almacén

Transport terminals are on the periphery of the central area: Santa Justa train station is 1.5km north-east of the cathedral, on Avenida Kansas City; Plaza de Armas bus station is 1km north-west of the cathedral near the Puente del Cachorro bridge; and Prado de San Sebastián bus station is 750m south-east of the cathedral on Plaza San Sebastián.

Maps

The main tourist office hands out a reasonable city map but you can buy better ones, with street indexes, in bookshops. Compare their publication dates before parting with your money (around 700 ptas).

INFORMATION
Tourist Offices

The main tourist office (☎ 95 422 14 04) is at Avenida de la Constitución 21. Open 9 am to 7 pm Monday to Friday, 10 am to 2 pm and 3 to 7 pm on Saturday, and 10 am to 2 pm on Sunday (closed on holidays), it's often very busy. There are also two municipal tourist offices – one south of the centre at Paseo de las Delicias 9 (☎ 95 423 44 65), open 8.30 am to 2.45 pm Monday to Friday, the other at Calle de Arjona 28 by the Puente de Triana (☎ 95 450 56 00), open 8 am to 8.45 pm Monday to Friday, 8.30 am to 2.30 pm Saturday and Sunday. There are also tourist offices at the airport (☎ 95 444 91 28) and Santa Justa train station (☎ 95 453 76 26).

Money

There's no shortage of banks and ATMs in the central area. Santa Justa train station has ATMs and an exchange office which gives poor rates. The American Express office is at Plaza Nueva 8.

Post & Communications

The main post office, at Avenida de la Constitución 32, opens 8.30 am to 8.30 pm Monday to Friday, and 9.30 am to 2 pm on Saturday.

Finding an unvandalised coin pay phone in the city centre can take a long time, so a phonecard comes in handy.

Sevilla has heaps of cybercafes and other public Internet/email services. A typical rate is 300 ptas per hour. Places include:

Cibercafé Torredeoro.net (☎ 95 450 28 09) Calle Núñez de Balboa 3A, near the Torre del Oro – open 8.30 am to 1 am daily; 200 ptas an hour at off-peak 'happy hours'
Cibercenter (☎ 95 422 88 99) Calle Julio Cesar 8, near Plaza de Armas bus station
Inter@lfalfa (☎ 95 422 98 49) Calle Cabeza del Rey Don Pedro 22, El Centro
Puerta Centro, Calle San José 15, Barrio de Santa Cruz – open 8 am to 10 pm Monday to Friday; 400 ptas per hour
Sevilla Internet Center (☎ 95 450 02 75) Calle Almirantazgo 2, just off Avenida de la Constitución – open 9 am to 10 pm Monday to Friday, noon to 10 pm Saturday and Sunday; 10 ptas per minute; two-hour 'packages' cost 840 ptas; spacious premises with other communications and office services too
The E-m@il Place (☎ 95 421 85 92) Calle Sierpes 54, El Centro – open 8 am to 11 pm Monday to Friday, noon to 9 pm Saturday and Sunday
Undernet Ciber Café (☎ 95 450 21 75) Calle O'Donnell 19, El Centro – 5 ptas per minute

Internet Resources

The following Web sites are useful:

Sevilla Cultural This site tells you what's on and gives arts and music background; in Spanish.
www.sevillacultural.com
Sevilla Online This site provides information on sights, language schools, tours, entertainment, bars and nightlife, festivals, transport and so on; in English, Dutch and Spanish.
www.sol.com

Travel Agencies

The student/youth travel agency usit Unlimited has an office on Avenida de la Constitución and another at Calle Mateos Gago 2, Barrio de Santa Cruz.

Bookshops

Librería Beta at Avenida de la Constitución 9 and 27 has guidebooks and novels in English, and maps. Librería Internacional Vértice, Calle San Fernando 33, has a large range of books in English, French and German.

LTC, Avenida Menéndez Pelayo 42–44, near the Barrio de Santa Cruz, is with little doubt the best map shop in Andalucía (see Maps in the Facts for the Visitor chapter). It also sells Spanish-language guidebooks.

Laundry

Tintorería Roma (☎ 95 421 05 35), Calle Castelar 2C, will wash, dry and fold a load of washing in one hour for 1000 ptas. It opens 9.30 am to 1.30 pm and 5 to 8.30 pm Monday to Friday, 9 am to 2 pm Saturday.

Medical Services & Emergency

There's a Centro de Urgencias (Emergency Medical Post; ☎ 95 441 17 12) on the corner of Avenida Menéndez Pelayo and Avenida Málaga, near Prado de San Sebastián bus station. The main general hospital is the Hospital Virgen del Rocío (☎ 95 424 81 81) at Avenida de Manuel Siurot s/n, 1km south of the Parque de María Luisa. For an ambulance call ☎ 95 442 55 65.

The Policía Municipal station (☎ 95 461 54 50) is in the Pabellón de Brasil, Paseo de las Delicias 15, at the southern end of the Parque de María Luisa; the Policía Nacional station (☎ 95 422 88 40) is on Plaza Concordia, 900m north of the cathedral.

Dangers & Annoyances

Sevilla has a reputation for petty crime against tourists – pickpockets, bag snatchers and the like. We don't think the reputation is justified, but it pays to take care in any case.

CATHEDRAL & GIRALDA

Sevilla's immense cathedral (☎ 95 421 49 71) stands on the site of the main Almohad mosque. After Sevilla fell to the Christians in 1248 the mosque was used as a church until 1401. Then, in view of its decaying state, the church authorities decided to knock it down and start again. 'Let us create such a building that future generations will take us for lunatics,' they agreed (legend has it). They

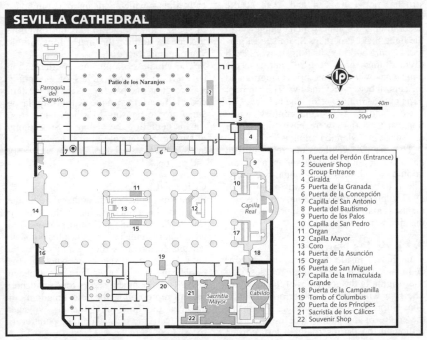

SEVILLA CATHEDRAL

Parroquia del Sagrario
Patio de los Naranjos

0   20   40m
0   10   20yd

1 Puerta del Perdón (Entrance)
2 Souvenir Shop
3 Group Entrance
4 Giralda
5 Puerta de la Granada
6 Puerta de la Concepción
7 Capilla de San Antonio
8 Puerta del Bautismo
9 Puerto de los Palos
10 Capilla de San Pedro
11 Organ
12 Capilla Mayor
13 Coro
14 Puerta de la Asunción
15 Organ
16 Puerta de San Miguel
17 Capilla de la Inmaculada Grande
18 Puerta de la Campanilla
19 Tomb of Columbus
20 Puerta de los Príncipes
21 Sacristía de los Cálices
22 Souvenir Shop

Capilla Real
Cabildo
Sacristía Mayor

certainly got themselves a big church. The main building (excluding the Patio de los Naranjos) is 126m long and 83m wide, one of the largest cathedrals in the world. It was completed by 1507 – all in Gothic style, though work done after its central dome collapsed in 1511 was mostly in Renaissance style. The architect is unknown.

Exterior

The bulky exterior of the cathedral gives few hints of the treasures within, apart from the **Puerta del Perdón** on Calle Alemanes (a survival from the Islamic building) and the one neo-Gothic and two Gothic **doorways** on Avenida de la Constitución. These last are sculpted with 15th-century terracotta reliefs and statues by Lorenzo Mercadante de Bretaña and Pedro Millán.

More impressive from outside is the **Giralda**, the 90m-high brick tower on the north-eastern side of the cathedral. The Giralda was the minaret of the mosque, constructed between 1184 and 1198 at the height of Almohad power. Its proportions, decoration and colour, which changes with the light, make it perhaps Spain's most perfect Islamic building. Its four sides are each divided into three vertical sections, the outer ones with delicate brick patterns and the central ones with windows. The topmost parts of the Giralda – from the bell level up – were added in the 16th century, when Spanish Christians were busy 'improving on' surviving Islamic buildings.

The bronze weathervane representing Faith, a symbol of Sevilla known as **El Giraldillo**, which tops the Giralda, is a copy. The 16th-century original was removed in 1997 to prevent further damage by the elements. It may eventually reappear in one of the city's museums.

Patio de los Naranjos

Immediately inside the Puerta del Perdón, and planted with over 60 orange trees, this was originally the courtyard of the mosque. The font where Muslims performed ablutions before entering the mosque remains in the centre of the patio. Hanging from the ceiling in the patio's south-eastern corner

are a stuffed crocodile – a gift to Alfonso X from the Sultan of Egypt – and an elephant's tusk, said to have been found in the Roman amphitheatre at nearby Itálica. You enter the cathedral proper by the impressive Puerta de la Concepción, a 20th-century addition to the cathedral's structure on the patio's southern side.

The Giralda

Turn left inside the cathedral for the climb up to the belfry of the Giralda. The ascent is quite easy as a series of ramps goes all the way up – built so that guards could ride up on horseback. The climb affords great views of the forest of buttresses and pinnacles that surround the cathedral, as well as of the city beyond.

Northern & Southern Chapels

The sheer size of the broad, five-naved cathedral is obscured by a welter of interior structures and decoration typical of Spanish cathedrals – which adds up to a storehouse of art and artisanry as rich as in any church in Spain. Don't forget to look up from time to time to admire the marvellous Gothic vaulting and tracery.

The chapels along the northern and southern sides hold riches of sculpture, stained glass and painting. Near the western end of the northern side is the **Capilla de San Antonio** housing Murillo's large 1666 canvas depicting the vision of St Anthony of Padua; thieves cut out the kneeling saint in 1874 but he was later found in New York and put back.

Columbus' Tomb

Inside the cathedral's southern door, the Puerta de los Príncipes, stands the tomb of Christopher Columbus (Cristóbal Colón). The great sailor's remains – or rather, his probable remains, for no one's 100% sure that the real ones didn't get mislaid somewhere in the Caribbean – were brought here from Cuba in 1899. The monument shows four sepulchrebearers representing the four kingdoms of Spain at the time of Columbus' voyage: Castile (carrying Granada on the point of its spear), León, Aragón and Navarra.

Coro

In the middle of the cathedral you will see the large choir *(coro)* with 117 carved Gothic-Mudéjar stalls. The lower ones have marquetry representations of the Giralda. Vices and sins are depicted on their misericords.

Capilla Mayor

East of the choir is the Capilla Mayor (Main Chapel). Its Gothic retable is the jewel of the cathedral and reckoned to be the biggest altarpiece in the world. Begun by Flemish sculptor Pieter Dancart in 1482 and finished by others in 1564, the sea of gilded and polychromed wood holds over 1000 carved biblical figures. At the centre of the lowest level is the 13th-century silver-plated cedar image of the Virgen de la Sede, patroness of the cathedral.

Eastern Chapels

East of the Capilla Mayor, against the eastern wall of the cathedral, are more chapels. They're usually roped off, which prevents you getting a close view. This is a pity because the central of these is the **Capilla Real** (Royal Chapel) containing the tombs of two great Castilian kings. The silver and bronze tomb of Fernando III stands in front of the altar (he's mummified inside); the tombs of his son, Alfonso X, and wife, Beatrice of Swabia, are at the sides.

Sacristía de los Cálices

South of the Capilla Mayor is the entrance to rooms containing some of the cathedral's main art treasures. The westernmost room is the Sacristía de los Cálices (Sacristy of the Chalices), built between 1509 and 1537. Goya's painting of the Sevilla martyrs *Santas Justa y Rufina* (1817) hangs above the altar. These two potters died at the hands of the Romans in AD 287: the Giralda and cathedral in the background are anachronistic. The other art is 16th and 17th century, including Juan Martínez Montañés' masterly sculpture *Cristo de la Clemencia* (Christ of Clemency; 1603) and Zurbarán's painting *San Juan Bautista* (1640).

Sacristía Mayor

This large domed room east of the Sacristía de los Cálices is a plateresque creation of 1528–47: the arch over its portal has carvings of 16th-century foods. Pedro de Campaña's 1547 *Descendimiento* (Descent from the Cross), above the central altar at the southern end, and Zurbarán's *Santa Teresa*, to its right, are two of the cathedral's masterpieces. Murillo's *San Isidoro* (reading) and *San Leandro* face each other across the room: the pair were leaders of the Visigothic church in Sevilla. This room also holds 17th-century images of San Fernando (Fernando III) and La Inmaculada (Mary, the Immaculate), and a huge 475kg silver *custodia* (monstrance) made in the 1580s by the celebrated Renaissance metalsmith Juan de Arfe, all of which are carried in Sevilla's Corpus Christi processions, and, in one of the glass cases, the city keys handed over to the conquering Fernando III in 1248.

Cabildo

The beautifully domed chapter house, in the south-eastern corner of the cathedral, was built between 1558 and 1592 for meetings of the cathedral hierarchy, to the designs of Hernán Ruiz, architect of the Giralda. At the base of the dome, above the archbishop's throne at the southern end, is a Murillo masterpiece, *La Inmaculada*. Eight Murillo saints adorn the dome at the same level.

Admission

The entry system and timetable for visiting the cathedral and Giralda change frequently. Current regulations are usually posted up fairly clearly. At our last check the entrance on Plaza Virgen de los Reyes, beside the Giralda, was for guided groups only, with independent visitors entering by the Puerta del Perdón on the northern side of the building. Opening hours for the cathedral and Giralda were 11 am to 5 pm Monday to Saturday, 2 to 7 pm Sunday. Admission costs 700 ptas (children aged under 12, students and seniors 200 ptas); admission is free on Sunday. The ticket office closes one hour before closing time.

ALCÁZAR

South of the cathedral across Plaza del Triunfo, the Alcázar (fortress; ☎ 95 450 23 23) is more palace than castle. It's an intriguing, beautiful place that shouldn't be missed, not least for its associations with the lives and loves of several famous rulers, above all the extraordinary Pedro I, who was known either as El Cruel or as El Justiciero (the Justice-Dispenser) depending which side you were on.

History

The Alcázar was founded as a fort for the Cordoban governors of Sevilla in 913. It has

SEVILLA ALCÁZAR

1 Patio de las Banderas (Exit)	18 Puerta del Palacio de los Duques de Arcos
2 Puerta del León (Entrance)	19 Entrance to Baños de Doña María de Padilla
3 Patio del León	20 Patio de las Doncellas
4 Sala de la Justicia	21 Patio de las Muñecas
5 Patio del Yeso	22 Cuarto del Techo de los Reyes Católicos
6 Apeadero	23 Jardín del Príncipe
7 Jardín de la Alcabilla	24 Salón del Techo de Felipe II
8 Patio del Crucero	
9 Patio de la Montería	25 Salón de Embajadores
10 Salón del Almirante	26 Sala de Infantes
11 Sala de Audiencias	27 Salón del Techo de Carlos V
12 Entrance to Cuarto Real Alto	28 Estanque de Mercurio
13 Cuarto del Príncipe	29 Jardín de las Danzas
14 Cámara Regia	30 Jardín de Troya
15 Salón de Tapices	31 Jardín de las Galeras
16 Sala de las Bóvedas	32 Jardín de las Flores
17 Jardín del Chorrón	33 Jardín de las Damas

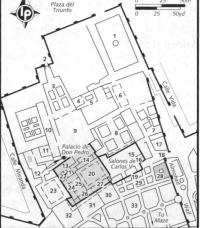

undergone many expansions and reconstructions in the 11 centuries since then, making it a complicated building to understand, but in the end only adding to its fascination.

Sevilla's prosperous 11th-century rulers built a palace called Al-Muwarak (The Blessed) in what's now the western part of the Alcázar. East of this, the 12th-century Almohad rulers added another palace around what's now the Patio del Crucero. Christian Fernando III moved into the Alcázar when he captured Sevilla in 1248, dying here four years later. Several later Christian monarchs also used the Alcázar as their main residence. Fernando's son Alfonso X replaced much of the Almohad palace with a Gothic one (which has now become the Salones de Carlos V). Between 1364 and 1366 Pedro I created the Alcázar's crown jewel, the sumptuous Mudéjar Palacio de Don Pedro, partly on the site of the old Al-Muwarak palace.

The whole complex was further adapted and expanded by later rulers, who also created the Alcázar's beautiful gardens.

Patio del León

This was the garrison yard of the original Al-Muwarak palace. Off its south-eastern corner is the **Sala de la Justicia**, with beautiful Mudéjar plasterwork and an artesonado ceiling – the room was built in the 1340s by the Christian king Alfonso XI, who disported here with his mistress Leonor de Guzmán, reputedly the most beautiful woman in Spain. Alfonso's sexual exploits left his heir Pedro I with five illegitimate half-brothers and a severe case of sibling rivalry. Pedro is said to have ordered a dozen relatives and friends murdered in his efforts to stay on the throne. Don Fadrique, one of the half-brothers, met his maker right here in the Sala de la Justicia.

The room gives on to the pretty **Patio del Yeso**, a 19th-century version of what was originally part of the 12th-century Almohad palace.

Patio de la Montería

The rooms on the western side of this courtyard were part of the Casa de la Contratación founded by the Catholic Monarchs in 1503 to control the American trade. The **Salón del Almirante** houses 19th- and 20th-century paintings showing historical events associated with Sevilla. The **Sala de Audiencias** is hung with the shields of admirals of the Spanish fleet and the *Virgen de los Mareantes* (Virgin of Sailors) by Alejo Fernández, painted in the 1530s and the earliest known painting on the subject of the discovery of the Americas. Columbus, Fernando El Católico, Carlos I, Amerigo Vespucci and native Americans can all be seen sheltered beneath the cloak of the Virgin in her role as protector of sailors. This room also contains a model of Columbus' ship, the *Santa María*.

Palacio de Don Pedro

Whatever else Pedro I may have done, posterity owes him a big thank you for creating this palace, which rivals Granada's Alhambra in its splendid design and decoration. The entrance is on the southern side of the Patio de la Montería.

Though unable to trust many of his fellow 'Christians' from closer to home, Pedro maintained a long-standing alliance with the Muslim emir of Granada, Mohammed V, the man responsible for much of the decoration of the Alhambra's magnificent Palacio Nazaries. So when, in 1364, Pedro decided to build himself a new palace within the Alcázar, Mohammed sent along many of his best artisans to help. These were joined by Jews and Muslims from Toledo, and others, mainly Muslim, from Sevilla. Their work, drawing on the earlier traditions of the Almohads and caliphal Córdoba, represented the best of contemporary architecture and design. It's a unique synthesis of Iberian Muslim art.

Inscriptions on the Palacio de Don Pedro's relatively austere **facade**, facing the Patio de la Montería, encapsulate the unusual nature of the enterprise. While one records that the building's creator was 'the very high, noble and conquering Don Pedro, by the grace of God king of Castile and León', another intones repeatedly that 'There is no conqueror but Allah'.

Cuarto Real Alto

The Alcázar is still a royal palace. As recently as 1995 it staged the wedding feast of the infanta Elena, daughter of King Juan Carlos I, after her marriage in Sevilla's cathedral. The Cuarto Real Alto, the rooms reserved for the Spanish royal family in and around the Palacio de Don Pedro, can now be visited on a guided tour. Tickets (400 ptas) are sold, and the tours start, in the south-western corner of the Patio de la Montería. Around 12 half-hour tours, for a maximum of 15 people, are given daily, alternately in Spanish and English. You can book in advance on ☎ 95 456 00 40. Highlights of the visit include a beautiful 1504 Italian Renaissance tile retable in the chapel, Pedro I's bedroom with marvellous Mudéjar tiles and plaster-work, and the 14th-century Salón de Audiencias, still the monarch's reception room.

Inside the entrance, the left-hand passage leads to the wonderful **Patio de las Doncellas**, surrounded by beautiful arches and with some exquisite plasterwork and tiling. The doors at the two ends are among the finest ever made by Toledo's carpenters. The upper galleries were added in 1540.

The **Cámara Regia**, on the northern side of the Patio de las Doncellas, has two rooms with stunningly beautiful ceilings and more wonderful plaster and tilework. The rear room was probably the monarch's summer bedroom.

From here you can move west into the small **Patio de las Muñecas**, the heart of the palace's private quarters, with delicate Granada-style decoration on its lowest level. The mezzanine and top gallery were added in the 19th century for Queen Isabel II, using plasterwork brought from the Alhambra. The **Cuarto del Príncipe** to the north has superb ceilings and was probably the queen's bedroom.

The spectacular **Salón de Embajadores** (Hall of Ambassadors), at the western end of the Patio de las Doncellas, was the throne room of Pedro I's palace – as it had been, in

JANE SMITH

Some of the palace's finest craftsmanship can be seen in the Patio de las Doncellas.

earlier form, of the Al-Muwarak palace (Al-Mutamid had held literary soirees here). Pedro retained the door arches, heavily reminiscent of the Medina Azahara palace near Córdoba, from Al-Muwarak. The room's fabulous wooden dome of multiple star patterns, symbolising the universe, was added in 1427. The dome's shape gives the room its alternative name, Sala de la Media Naranja (Hall of the Half Orange). The coloured plasterwork is equally magnificent. It was in this room that Pedro laid a trap for the so-called Red King, who had temporarily deposed Pedro's buddy Mohammed V in Granada. During a banquet, armed men suddenly leapt from hiding and seized the Red King and his retinue of 37, all of whom were executed outside Sevilla a few days later.

On the western side of the Salón de Embajadores the beautiful **Arco de Pavones** – named after its peacock motifs – leads into the **Salón del Techo de Felipe II**, with a Renaissance ceiling (1589–91). The **Salón del Techo de Carlos V**, along the southern side of the Patio de las Doncellas, has another fine ceiling (1540s) and used to be the palace chapel.

Salones de Carlos V

Reached by a staircase from the southeastern corner of Patio de las Doncellas, these are the much-remodelled rooms of the 13th-century Gothic palace built by Alfonso X. It was here that Alfonso's intellectual court gathered and, a century later, Pedro I installed the mistress he loved to distraction, María de Padilla (notwithstanding the fact that he was already married to a French princess). The **Sala de las Bóvedas** is now adorned with beautiful tiles made for Felipe II in the 1570s by Cristóbal de Augusta. In the **Salón de Tapices** hangs a collection of huge 18th-century tapestries showing Carlos I's 1535 conquest of Tunis from the Turkish-backed pirate Barbarossa.

Patio del Crucero

This patio outside the Salones de Carlos V's northern side was originally the upper level of the central patio of the 12th-century Almohad palace. At first it consisted only of walkways along the four sides and two cross-walkways which met in the middle. Below grew orange trees, whose fruit could be plucked at hand height by the lucky folk strolling along the upper walkways. María de Padilla must have liked strolling around picking oranges because the patio is also known as the Patio de María de Padilla.

The patio's whole lower level had to be built over in the 18th-century after earthquake damage.

Gardens & Exit

From the Salones de Carlos V you can go out into the Alcázar's large gardens, the perfect place to wind down a little after some intensive sightseeing. The gardens in front of the Salones de Carlos V and Palacio de Don Pedro go back to Muslim times, but were mostly brought to their present form in the 16th and 17th centuries. Immediately in front of the buildings is a series of small linked gardens, some with pools and fountains. From one, the Jardín de las Danzas, a passage runs beneath the Salones de Carlos V to the so-called **Baños de Doña María de Padilla**. Here you can see the vaults beneath the Patio del Crucero – originally that patio's lower level – and a grotto which replaced the patio's pool, in which, judging by the place's name, María de Padilla must have liked to bathe.

Farther out in the gardens is a **maze**. The gardens to the east, the other side of a long Almohad wall, are 20th-century creations. From them you can return to the corner of the Salones de Carlos V, where a passage leads north to the **Apeadero**, a 17th-century entrance hall now housing a collection of carriages. From here you leave the Alcázar via the **Patio de las Banderas**.

Admission
The entrance is the Puerta del León at the southern corner of Plaza del Triunfo. The Alcázar opens from 9.30 am to 7 pm (to 5 pm from October to March) Tuesday to Saturday, 9.30 am to 5 pm Sunday and holidays; it's closed on Monday. Admission costs 700 ptas (children under 12 years, students and seniors free).

ARCHIVO DE INDIAS
This building (☎ 95 421 12 34) on the western side of Plaza del Triunfo has been, since 1785, the main archive on Spain's American empire. Its 8km of shelves hold 80 million pages of documents dating from 1492 through to the end of the empire in the 19th century. Most of the archive can only be consulted with special permission but there are rotating displays of fascinating maps and documents, often including manuscripts written by Columbus or Cervantes or conquistadors such as Cortés or Pizarro. The 16th-century building, designed by Juan de Herrera, was originally Sevilla's Lonja (Exchange) for commerce with the Americas. It's open from 10 am to 1 pm Monday to Friday. Admission is free.

BARRIO DE SANTA CRUZ
This area east of the cathedral and Alcázar was Sevilla's medieval Jewish quarter (*judería*). Today it's a tangle of quaint, winding streets and lovely squares with flowers and orange trees. If you're not staying in the area, wander through it anyway: there are some good places to stop off for food or drink as you go.

The Judería, which extended to just east of Calle Santa María La Blanca, came into existence after the Reconquista (Reconquest) and was emptied by a pogrom in 1391. **Plaza Doña Elvira** is a very pretty spot, with tiled benches beneath the orange trees. On Plaza de los Venerables is the **Hospital de los Venerables Sacerdotes**. Used from its inception in the 17th century until the 1960s as a residence for aged priests, it is now open for guided visits (600 ptas) between 10 am and 2 pm and 4 to 8 pm daily, but you may find it closed in August. You can visit the lovely central courtyard, the old living quarters, several art exhibition rooms (one with an interesting collection of prints of Sevilla), and the church with murals by Juan de Valdés Leal and fine sculptures by Pedro Roldán. The *barrio's* (quarter's) most characteristic square is **Plaza de Santa Cruz**, whose central cross, made in 1692, is one of the finest examples of Sevilla wrought-iron work. A few steps away at Calle Santa Teresa 8 is the **Casa de Murillo**, where the famous painter lived. It opens 10.30 am to 1.30 pm and 5 to 9 pm daily except Monday. Admission is free. The permanent exhibits are minimal, but you might find an interesting temporary show. You may also find a good exhibition at the **Casa de la Memoria de Al-Andalus**, Calle Ximénez de Enciso 28, which is dedicated to Andalucía's Muslim era. The museum is open from 10 am to 2 pm and 5 to 9 pm daily. Admission costs 400 ptas (students and seniors 250 ptas).

EL CENTRO
The real centre of Sevilla is the densely packed zone of narrow, crooked streets north of the cathedral, broken up here and there by squares around which the city's life has revolved for aeons.

Plaza de San Francisco & Calle Sierpes
Site of a market in Muslim times, Plaza de San Francisco has been Sevilla's main public square since the 16th century. Once the scene of Inquisition burnings, today it's where the city's upper echelons sit on special viewing stands to watch the Semana Santa processions.

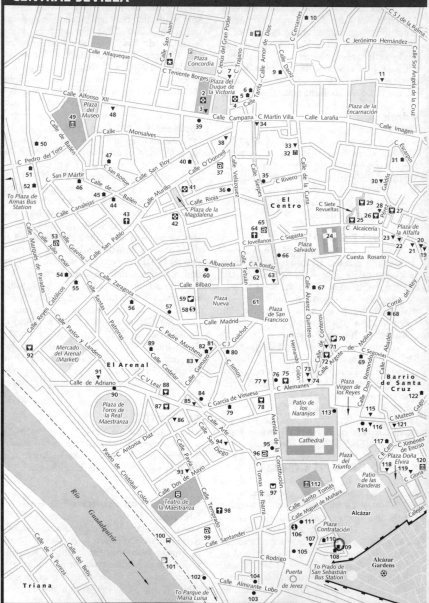

CENTRAL SEVILLA

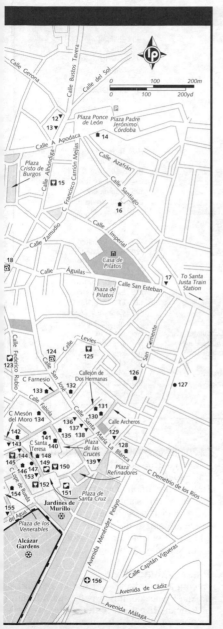

CENTRAL SEVILLA

PLACES TO STAY
5 Hostal Pino
6 Hostal Unión
9 Hotel Sevilla
10 Hotel Cervantes
14 Hotel Baco; Restaurante El Bacalao
16 Las Casas del Rey de Baeza
31 Hostal Lis
40 Hostal Lis II
44 Hotel Colón
45 Hotel Plaza Sevilla
46 Hostal Londres
47 Hotel Zaida
50 Hostal Romero
51 Hostal Gravina
52 Hostal Gala
54 Hotel Becquer
55 Hotel Puerta de Triana
56 Hostal Central
67 Las Casas de los Mercaderes
68 Hostal Sánchez Sabariego
69 Hotel Los Seises
79 Hotel Simón
80 Hotel Europa
82 Hotel Maestranza
89 Hotel La Rábida
108 Hostal Arias
109 Pensión Alcázar
110 Hostal Picasso
117 Hostal Monreal
122 Hostal Goya
126 Hostal La Montoreña
128 Huéspedes Dulces Sueños/Sweet Dreams
130 Hostal Bienvenido
131 Las Casas de la Judería
132 Hotel Fernando III
133 Hostal Córdoba
134 Pensión Fabiola
135 Pensión San Pancracio
140 Pensión Cruces
142 Pensión Vergara
146 Hotel Murillo
148 Hostal Toledo
154 Hostería del Laurel

PLACES TO EAT
3 Café Bar Duque
7 Horno del Duque
11 Mercado de la Encarnación (Market)
12 El Rinconcillo
13 La Giganta
17 Bodega Extremeña
19 La Trastienda
20 La Bodega Extremeña
21 La Bodega
22 Horno de San Buenaventura
23 Alfalfa 10
28 Habanita

CENTRAL SEVILLA

30 Sopa de Ganso	4 El Corte Inglés	90 Bullfighting Ticket Office
33 Restaurante San Marco	8 Itaca	92 Café Isbiliyya
34 Confitería La Campana	15 Café Lisboa	95 usit Unlimited
38 Patio San Eloy	18 Inter@lfalfa	96 Sevilla Internet Center
48 Bodegón Alfonso XII	24 Parroquia del Salvador	97 Post Office
63 Bar Laredo	25 Bar Europa	98 Hospital de la Caridad
71 Robles Placentines	26 Bare Nostrum; Cabo Loco; Nao	99 Cibercafé Torredeoro.net
73 Casa Robles	27 La Rebótica	100 Bus & Tram Tours Stop
74 Las Escobas	29 El Mundo	101 Jetty; Cruceros Turísticos Torre del Oro
77 Café de Indias	32 Palacio de Lebrija	102 Torre del Oro & Maritime Museum
81 Restaurante Enrique Becerra	35 Z Zulategui	103 Sevilla Car
83 Bodega Paco Góngora	36 La Teatral (Ticket Agency)	104 Triana Rent A Car
85 Mesón Cinco Jotas	37 Undernet Ciber Café	105 Librería Beta
86 Mesón Serranito	39 Sevilla Rock	106 Main Tourist Office
91 Casa Pepe-Hillo	41 El Corte Inglés	111 Sevilla Mágica
93 Mesón de la Infanta	42 El Corte Inglés	112 Archivo de Indias
94 La Infanta	43 Iglesia de la Magdalena	113 Giralda
107 Cafetería Las Lapas	49 Museo de Bellas Artes	114 usit Unlimited
115 Cervecería Giralda	53 Cibercenter	120 Hospital de los Venerables Sacerdotes
116 Café-Bar Campanario	57 RENFE Office	123 Australian Consulate
118 Restaurant La Cueva	58 American Express	124 Puerta Centro
119 El Rincón de Pepe	59 UK Consulate	125 La Carbonería
121 Bodega Santa Cruz	60 CLIC	127 LTC Map Shop
129 Restaurante La Judería	61 Ayuntamiento (City Hall)	141 Casa de la Memoria de Al-Andalus
136 Altaira Bar-Café; Carmela	62 Halcón Viajes	145 Bar Entrecalles
137 Bar Casa Fernando	64 Capilla de San José	147 Casa de Murillo
138 Restaurant El Cordobés	65 The E-m@il Place	149 French Consulate
139 Restaurante Modesto	66 Sport Zone	150 El Tamboril
143 Pizzeria San Marco	70 Netherlands Consulate	151 Irish Consulate
144 Café Bar Las Teresas	72 La Subasta; Antigüedades	152 Los Gallos
153 Restaurante La Albahaca	75 P Flaherty Irish Pub	156 Centro de Urgencias (Emergency Medical Post)
155 Corral del Agua	76 Librería Beta	
	78 Hijos de E Morales	
OTHER	84 Tintorería Roma	
1 Police Station (Policía Nacional)	87 A3	
2 El Corte Inglés	88 Arena	

The **City Hall** on the square's western side is a building of contrasting characters: its southern end is encrusted with lovely Renaissance carving from the 1520s and '30s, while its northern end, a 19th-century extension, is bare.

Pedestrianised Calle Sierpes, which heads north from the square, is Sevilla's fanciest shopping street. Take a few steps off Sierpes along Calle Jovellanos to the **Capilla de San José**. This small 18th-century chapel, created by the city's carpenters' guild, is a world unto itself of breath-catchingly intense baroque ornamentation. The altarpieces are absolute riots of gilded, curving, carved wood, with cherubim popping out all

over the place. The chapel is open 8 am to 12.30 pm and 6.30 to 8.30 pm daily.

The **Palacio de Lebrija**, a block east of Calle Sierpes at Calle de la Cuna 8, is a 16th-century noble mansion with a rich collection of art, statuary, furniture and artisanry, and a very beautiful Reniassance/ Mudéjar courtyard. It opens 11 am to 1 pm and 5 to 7 pm Monday to Friday, 10 am to 1 pm Saturday. Admission costs 500 ptas.

Plaza Salvador

A couple of blocks north-east of Plaza de San Francisco, this was the main forum of Roman Hispalis (see the earlier History section for details). It's dominated by the

Parroquia del Salvador, a big, red baroque church built between 1674 and 1712 on the site of Muslim Ishbiliya's main mosque. Inside are three huge, profuse baroque retables; on the northern side, the mosque's small patio remains, with orange trees, font, and a few half-buried Roman columns. The church is open 6.30 to 9 pm daily.

Plaza de la Alfalfa
Some 200m east of Plaza Salvador, this was the site of the Muslim silk exchange and a later medieval market. It's an animated place with many good bars nearby.

Casa de Pilatos
The finest of Sevilla's noble mansions, still occupied by the ducal Medinaceli family, stands 300m east of Plaza de la Alfalfa along Calle Águilas. The building is a mixture of Mudéjar, Gothic and Renaissance architecture and decoration, with some beautiful tilework and artesonado ceilings. The overall effect is similar to the Alcázar.

There are rival explanations for the building's name, which means Pilate's House. One is that its 16th-century creator, Don Fadrique Enríquez de Ribera, was trying to imitate Pontius Pilate's palace in Jerusalem, to which city he had made a pilgrimage. Another is that the house served as the first station – representing Christ's appearance before Pilate – of a *Via Crucis* (Way of the Cross) route, in which penitents symbolically retraced Christ's steps to the crucifixion.

The Casa de Pilatos (☎ 95 422 52 98) opens 9 am to 7 pm daily. Admission costs 500 ptas for each of the two floors – if time or money are short, skip the top floor.

A plan on your ticket helps you find your way round. From the **Apeadero**, a courtyard for boarding and alighting from carriages, you pass into the **Patio Principal** which has lots of wonderful 16th-century tiles, intricate Mudéjar plasterwork and a Renaissance fountain. The armless statue of Athene, on the far side from the entrance, is Greek, from around the 4th century BC; the statues in the other corners are Roman. Around the walls are busts of Roman historical and mythical figures plus King Carlos I of Spain.

The names of the rooms off the Patio Principal recall the supposed Pontius Pilate connection. The **Descanso de los Jueces** (Judges' Retiring Room), **Salón Pretorio** (Palace Hall) and **Gabinete de Pilatos** (Pilate's Study) all have fine artesonado ceilings. Beyond the Salón Pretorio are the **Zaquizami**, a corridor with Roman sculptures and inscriptions on display, and the **Jardín Chico** (Small Garden). The Gabinete de Pilatos leads into the leafy **Jardín Grande** (Big Garden), with Italian-style loggias on three of its sides.

The **staircase** leading from the Patio Principal to the upper floor has the most magnificent tiles in the building, and a great golden artesonado dome above. Visits to the **upper floor** itself, partly inhabited by the Medinacelis, are accompanied by a rather hurried guide. Of interest are the several centuries' worth of Medinaceli portraits and a small Goya bullfight painting, in the Salón Oviedo.

EL ARENAL
A short walk west from Avenida de la Constitución brings you to the bank of the Río Guadalquivir, a pleasant place for a stroll.

Torre del Oro
The 'Tower of Gold' is a 13th-century Almohad watchtower, on the riverbank just north of the Puente de San Telmo. It once crowned a corner of the city walls that stretched here from the Alcázar, and was supposedly covered in golden tiles. Inside is a small, crowded maritime museum, open 10 am to 2 pm Tuesday to Friday, 11 am to 2 pm Saturday and Sunday (closed August). Admission costs 100 ptas.

Hospital de la Caridad
A block east of the river at Calle Temprado 3, this hospice for the elderly was founded in the 17th century by Miguel de Mañara – by legend a notorious libertine who changed his ways after experiencing a vision of his own funeral procession. The interest lies in the hospital's church for which in the 1670s Mañara commissioned a collection of top-class Sevillan art and sculpture on the theme of death and redemption, by Murillo,

Juan de Valdés Leal and Pedro Roldán. The Hospital de la Caridad (☎ 95 422 32 32) opens 9 am to 1.30 pm and 3.30 to 6.30 pm Monday to Saturday, 9 am to 1 pm Sunday and holidays. Admission costs 400 ptas.

The two masterworks of Valdés Leal, chillingly illustrating the futility of worldly success in the face of death, are at the western end of the church. In *Finis Gloriae Mundi* (The End of Earthly Glory), above the door by which you enter, a bishop, a king and a knight of Calatrava are devoured in their coffins by worms and cockroaches, while Christ's hand weighs their virtues and their sins (represented by animals) in the balance. *In Ictu Oculi* (In the Blink of an Eye), on the opposite wall, shows a skeletal Death figure extinguishing the candle of life while trampling symbols of power, glory, wealth and knowledge. On this same side of the church are Murillo's *San Juan de Dios* (St John of God, caring for an invalid) and *Moises Haciendo Brotar el Agua de la Roca* (Moses Drawing Water from the Rock). These are two of eight large Murillo canvases painted for this church on themes of compassion and mercy – ways of transcending death. (Four of the eight were looted by Napoleonic troops.) To the left of the high altar there are steps that descend to the crypt where Miguel de Mañara is buried.

The sculpture on the high altar illustrates the ultimate act of compassion – the burial of the dead (in this case Christ). The tableau, with its strong sense of movement, is Pedro Roldán's masterpiece. It was polychromed (coloured) by Valdés Leal.

On the southern side of the church are the other two remaining Murillos: *La Multiplicación de Panes y Peces* (The Miracle of the Loaves and Fishes) and *Santa Isabel de Húngria* (St Isabel of Hungary, caring for the diseased and poor), plus another fine Roldán sculpture, of Christ praying before being nailed to the cross.

Plaza de Toros de la Real Maestranza

Sevilla's bullring (☎ 95 422 45 77) on Paseo de Cristóbal Colón is one of the most handsome and important in Spain, and probably the oldest (building began in 1758). It was in this ring and the one at Ronda in Málaga province that bullfighting on foot began in the 18th century. The site was originally a practice ground for Sevilla's Real Maestranza de Caballería (Royal Cavalry Masterhood) – hence its name today.

You can take a tour of the ring and its museum, and peep into its mini-hospital for bullfighters who have come off second best, from 9.30 am to 2 pm and 3 to 6 or 7 pm daily (bullfight days: 10 am to 3 pm). The interesting guided visits, in English and Spanish, happen about every 20 minutes (400 ptas). For more on bullfights in Sevilla, see Spectator Sports later in this chapter; for more general information, see Spectator Sports in the Facts for the Visitor chapter.

Iglesia de la Magdalena

This jewel among Sevilla's many baroque churches, on Calle San Pablo, was built between 1691 and 1709. Two paintings by Zurbarán hang in the Capilla Sacramental, and a fine 1612 crucifixion sculpture, *El Cristo del Calvario* (The Christ of Calvary) by Francisco de Ocampo, is in the chapel to the right of the main altar.

The church is the home of the Quinta Angustia brotherhood, whose 17th-century *Descendimiento* tableau, depicting the taking down of Jesus from the cross, is carried through Sevilla's streets during Semana Santa. This can usually be seen in the chapel on the left as you enter the church: the Christ is attributed to Pedro Roldán. The church is open at service times – normally 8 to 11 am and 6.30 to 9 pm daily.

Museo de Bellas Artes

As Spain's leading city during most of the 16th and 17th centuries, Sevilla played a major role in the country's artistic golden age, which ran from roughly the late 16th to the late 17th centuries. The Fine Arts Museum (☎ 95 422 07 90), housed in the beautiful former Convento de la Merced at Plaza del Museo 9, does full justice to this period, and a visit is a big help to understanding the context of much of the other art you see in Sevilla and Andalucía.

The 17th-century Sevillan masters Murillo, Zurbarán and Valdés Leal are particularly well represented. The museum also holds interesting Sevillan antecedents to the golden age, and some works by great artists who worked elsewhere such as El Greco and José de Ribera.

Room I exemplifies the 15th-century beginnings of the Sevillan school: the outstanding exhibits are Pedro Millán's terracotta sculptures, displaying a realism then rare in Spanish art.

Room II was the dining hall of the convent. Displayed here is Renaissance work from Sevilla and elsewhere, including El Greco's piercing portrait of his son Jorge Manuel and sculptures by Pedro Torrigiano, an Italian who came to Sevilla in 1522 and was the major artistic figure of the early Renaissance here. His life-size *San Jerónimo Penitente*, with its expressive head and finely studied anatomy, was very influential.

Room III exhibits Sevillan Renaissance retables and early 17th-century baroque Sevillan paintings – including Velázquez's portrait of Don Cristóbal Suárez de Ribera and Alonso Cano's *San Francisco de Borja*. Cano's striking *Las Ánimas del Purgatorio* (Souls in Purgatory) is in the corner between rooms III and IV.

In room IV, which is devoted mainly to Mannerism – a rather stiff transition between Renaissance and baroque art – Alonso Vázquez's large *Sagrada Cena* (Last Supper) stands out. From here you move through the beautiful cloister to room V, the convent church, which is hung with paintings by masters of Sevillan baroque. Zurbarán's masterpiece, the *Apoteosis de Santo Tomás de Aquinas* (Apotheosis of St Thomas Aquinas), is here, but the room is dominated by Murillo, whose *Inmaculada Concepción Grande*, depicting the Virgin borne aloft by cherubim, displays all the curving, twisting movement that is so central to baroque art. This painting hangs at the head of the church, along with other Murillo works which were, like it, originally painted for other churches.

Upstairs, highlights of room VI include Ribera's very Spanish-looking *Santiago Apóstol* (St James the Apostle) and Zurbarán's small *Cristo Crucificado, Expirante* (Christ Crucified, Expiring) – perhaps the most disturbing picture in the whole museum. Room VII is devoted to Murillo and his disciples, room VIII to Valdés Leal, and room IX to baroque art from elsewhere in Europe.

Room X is all Zurbarán: the *Cristo Crucificado* is one of his greatest achievements. He draws a masterly contrast between the worldly Pope Urban II and the ascetic St Bruno in *Visita de San Bruno a Urbano II*.

Room XI displays Sevillan and Spanish painting of the 18th century, a time when Spain had lost its creative verve. Rooms XII to XIV show 19th- and 20th-century painting, mainly Sevillan, with the works of Romantic Antonio María Esquivel and historical painter Eddo Cano among the most interesting.

The museum is open 3 to 8 pm Tuesday, 9 am to 8 pm Wednesday to Saturday, and 9 am to 2 pm Sunday. Admission is free for EU citizens with passport or identity card, 250 ptas for others.

SOUTH OF THE CENTRE
Antigua Fábrica de Tabacos

Sevilla's massive former tobacco factory on Calle San Fernando – workplace of Bizet's operatic heroine Carmen – was built in the 18th century and served its original purpose until the mid-20th century. For a long time a cornerstone of the city's economy, the factory had its own jail, stables for 400 mules, 21 fountains, 24 patios and even a nursery, since most of its workers were women. Measuring 250m by 180m, it covers a larger area than any building in Spain except El Escorial, the great palace-monastery near Madrid.

Neo-classical in style, it's an impressive, if rather gloomy building. The main portal sports carvings on the theme of the discovery of the Americas, the original source of tobacco – among them Christopher Columbus, Hernán Cortés (conqueror of the Aztecs) and two native Americans – one of them smoking a pipe. At the top of the portal is Fame blowing a trumpet.

The old tobacco factory is now part of the Universidad de Sevilla (Sevilla University) and you can wander round it between 8 am and 9.30 pm Monday to Friday, or 8 am to 2 pm Saturday.

Parque de María Luisa & Plaza de España

A large area south of the Antigua Fábrica de Tabacos was transformed for the 1929 Exposición Iberoamericana, when architects spattered it with all sorts of fancy and funny buildings, many of them harking back to Sevilla's eras of past glory. In their midst, the Parque de María Luisa is a beautiful respite from the hustle of the city, with its maze of paths, flowers, fountains, shaded lawns and 3500 magnificent trees. It opens 8 am to 10 pm daily.

Facing the north-eastern side of the park across Avenida de Isabel la Católica, Plaza de España is one of the city's favourite relaxation spots, with fountains and mini-canals. Curving round the square in a semicircle is the most grandiose of the 1929 buildings, a brick and tile confection featuring Sevilla tilework at its gaudiest, with a map and historical scene for each Spanish province.

On Plaza de América at the southern end of the park are a large flock of white pigeons (they'll clamber all over you if you buy a 200-ptas bag of seed from vendors), and two interesting museums. Highlights of the big **Museo Arqueológico** (☎ 95 423 24 01) include a room of gold jewellery from the mysterious Tartessos culture and fine collections of Iberian animal sculptures and beautiful Roman mosaics. Among large quantities of Roman sculpture are, in room XX, sculptures of the two emperors from Itálica near Sevilla, Hadrian (Adriano) and Trajan (Trajano, with the top half of his head missing). The Museo Arqueológico is open 3 to 8 pm Tuesday, 9 am to 8 pm Wednesday to Saturday, 9 am to 2.30 pm Sunday and holidays. Admission is free with an EU passport or identity card, 250 ptas otherwise.

Facing the Museo Arqueológico is the **Museo de Artes y Costumbres Populares**

(☎ 95 423 25 76), in the 1929 exhibition's Mudéjar pavilion, which appeared as an Arab palace in the film *Lawrence of Arabia*. Its collection includes mock-up workshops of local crafts such as guitar-making, ceramics and wrought iron, and some beautiful old bullfight and festival costumes. Hours and prices are the same as the Museo Arqueológico's.

NORTH OF THE CENTRE

The more working-class area north of Calle Alfonso XII and Plaza Ponce de León is an interesting contrast to the city centre. The city's best street markets (see under Things to Buy later in this chapter) are to be found up here.

Alameda de Hércules

This dusty 350m-long *paseo* (park-like strip) was created in the 1570s by draining a marsh. Two columns from a ruined Roman temple were erected at its southern end and topped with statues of Hercules and Julius Caesar by Diego de Pesquera.

Planted with avenues of *álamo* (poplar) trees – hence the name – the Alameda became a fashionable meeting place in the 17th century. By the 1980s, however, the area was little more than a red-light zone. But it has since come back up in the world and is now one of the city's liveliest nightlife areas – with a bohemian, alternative scene.

Basílica de Jesús del Gran Poder

This 1960s church, behind a large baroque portal in the corner of Plaza de San Lorenzo, houses, above its main altar, a famous and far older sculpture of a cross-bearing Christ (after which it is named). The almost wizened Christ image, sculpted in 1620 by Juan de Mesa, inspires much Sevillan devotion and takes a place of honour in the Semana Santa processions. On either side of the altar are a sculpture of St John the Evangelist, also by de Mesa, and an anonymous *Virgen del Mayor Dolor* (Virgin of the Deepest Grief) of the 18th century or earlier. The church is open 8 am to 1.45 pm and 6 to 9 pm daily.

Basílica de la Macarena & Around

If you're not in Sevilla for Semana Santa, you can get an inkling of what it's about at the Basílica de la Macarena (☎ 95 437 01 95) at Calle Bécquer 1, off Calle San Luis, open 9 am to 1 pm and 5 to 9 pm daily. This 1940s church contains the most adored religious image in Sevilla, the *Virgen de la Esperanza* (Hope), believed to have been created in the mid-17th century. The sculptor's identity is not certain but tradition says it was María Luisa Roldán, 'La Roldana'. Commonly known just as La Macarena, this Virgin is patron of bullfighters and Sevilla's supreme representation of the grieving, yet hoping, mother of Christ. She stands in appropriate splendour behind the main altarpiece, adorned with a golden crown, lavish vestments, and five diamond and emerald brooches donated by a famous early-20th-century matador, Joselito El Gallo.

In front of and below La Macarena stands a beautiful 1654 statue of *El Cristo de la Sentencia* (Christ of the Sentence) by Felipe Morales. Both statues are carried from the church at midnight at the start of every Good Friday: their journey through the city is the climax of Semana Santa in Sevilla. Their return to the church around 1.30 pm is attended by enormous crowds.

In the church's museum are displayed rich vestments of La Macarena and the lavish Semana Santa platforms *(pasos)* on which both images are carried. The paso of El Cristo de la Sentencia is in fact a tableau of the scene of Pontius Pilate washing his hands; that of La Macarena bears 90 silver candlesticks. The museum is open 9.30 am to 1 pm and 5 to 8 pm daily. Admission costs 400 ptas.

Bus Nos C1, C2, C3 and C4 (see Getting Around later in this chapter for details) stop near the Basílica de la Macarena, on Calle Andueza. East of the church extends the longest surviving stretch of Sevilla's 12th-century **Almohad walls**. On the far side of a small park across the road is the **Parlamento de Andalucía**, Andalucía's regional parliament (not generally open to visitors).

TRIANA

Across the Guadalquivir from the Torre del Oro and Plaza de Toros de la Real Maestranza is Triana, the barrio that used to be Sevilla's *gitano* (Roma people) quarter and was one of the birthplaces of flamenco. The gitanos were moved out to new suburban areas in the 1960s and '70s, and Triana is now rather trendified. The river-front streets Calle del Betis and Paseo de Nuestra Señora de la O make a very pleasant stroll, with views back across the river to the city centre, and some good restaurants and very popular bars and cafes.

ISLA DE LA CARTUJA

North of Triana, this northern part of an island formed by two branches of the Guadalquivir was the site of Expo 92. Since the big year, the area has had a chequered history and expanses of it now lie decaying, victims of political squabbles and lack of funds and purpose. But there's still a bit to see and do. Bus Nos C1 and C2 (see Getting Around later in this chapter for details) go to Isla Mágica and the Conjunto Monumental de La Cartuja.

Conjunto Monumental de La Cartuja

Columbus used to stay in La Cartuja monastery, and after his death his remains lay here from 1509 to 1536. In 1836 the monks were expelled during the Disamortisation (when church property was auctioned off by the state) and the monastery's many art treasures were moved elsewhere. Three years later the complex was bought by a Liverpudlian, Charles Pickman, who turned it into a porcelain factory. Pickman built the five tall bottle-shaped kilns which stand incongruously beside the monastery buildings, and the porcelain factory functioned till 1982.

The complex (☎ 95 448 06 11) was restored for Expo 92. Today you can visit the main monastery buildings which include the **Centro Andaluz de Arte Contemporáneo** (Andalucian Contemporary Art Centre), a set of exhibition rooms. The entrance is from the monastery's western side on

Calle Américo Vespucio, a 1km walk from the eastern side facing the Puente de la Cartuja footbridge. The monastery features a now rather bare 15th-century **church**, a pretty Mudéjar cloister from the same era, and a roomful of disarmingly realistic 16th-century funerary sculptures of members of the Ribera family. The **Capilla de Santa Ana**, off the church, was built as the Columbus family tomb. The complex is open 10 am to 8 pm Tuesday to Saturday, 10 am to 3 pm Sunday. Admission costs 300 ptas, free for EU citizens on Tuesday.

Exhibition Pavilions

Some of the exotic Expo pavilions north and south of the monastery are slowly being turned into a technology industries and trade park. Others are being used by the Universidad de Sevilla, and some are rotting away. Many can only be accessed from the western side (Calle Américo Vespucio), Monday to Friday.

Isla Mágica

The theme park Isla Mágica (☎ 902 16 17 16) opened in 1997 as a second attempt to get a post-Expo amusement/theme park going on a site around a lake on the eastern side of the island, near the Puente de la Barqueta. Like its predecessor, Isla Mágica has faced financial problems, and even though about 1.2 million visitors came in 1999, its private-enterprise operators had to be bailed out by the Junta de Andalucía so that it could open for the 2000 season.

The theme is the 16th-century Spanish colonial adventure. Highlight rides include a roller-coaster with high-speed 360° turns, and the Iguazú on which you descend a South American jungle waterfall. You may have to wait 45 minutes at busy times for the big attractions. There are also events such as pirate shows, movies, bird-of-prey displays and lots of entertaining street-theatre-type stuff.

Isla Mágica usually opens from 11 am to 11 pm daily from about April to September, and in some years also at weekends and holidays before and after those months. Admission costs around 3400 ptas (under-13s and over-60s 2300 ptas), or 2300 ptas (1700 ptas) after 6 pm. There are plenty of places to eat and drink inside the park.

COURSES
Language

For details of Spanish-language courses at the university, contact the Instituto de Idiomas, Universidad de Sevilla (☎ 95 455 11 56, fax 95 455 14 50, @ idijsec@cica.es), Avenida Reina Mercedes s/n, 41012 Sevilla. The main tourist office can give you a list of about a dozen private colleges. Two that we have heard good things about are CLIC (☎ 95 450 21 31) at Calle Albareda 19 just north of Plaza Nueva, and Lengua Viva (☎ 95 490 51 31), Calle Viriato 22, near the Alameda de Hércules. For further information on language courses in Andalucía see that section in the Facts for the Visitor chapter.

Dance & Guitar

The main tourist office has a list of several dance academies *(academias de baile)* which you can contact if you're looking for a course in flamenco or other Spanish dance, or guitar. You'll also find adverts in the magazines *El Giraldillo* (see Entertainment in the Facts for the Visitor chapter) and *Alma 100* (see Seeing Flamenco in the special section 'Flamenco: the Gitano's Lament').

ORGANISED TOURS

The open-topped double-decker buses and converted trams of Sevilla Tour (☎ 95 450 20 99) make several daily city tours of about one hour, with earphone commentary in a choice of several languages. You can board on Paseo de Cristóbal Colón (100m north of the Torre del Oro), or on Avenida de Portugal behind Plaza de España. Frequency of service depends on demand but buses typically leave every 30 minutes from 10 am to 8 pm. The adult fare is 1500 ptas. The ticket is valid for 24 hours and you can also get on or off on the Isla de La Cartuja. The route takes in the Puerta de Jerez, Antigua Fábrica de Tabacos, Parque de María Luisa, Plaza de España, Basílica de la Macarena and Plaza de Toros de la Real Maestranza.

Sevirama/Guide Friday (☎ 94 456 06 93) operates similar tours for a similar price from the same stops in open-top double-deckers.

One-hour river cruises by Cruceros Turísticos Torre del Oro go at least hourly from 11 am to 7 pm or later from the jetty *(embarcadero)* by the Torre del Oro. Cruises cost 1700 ptas.

From around May to September round-trip day cruises sail to Sanlúcar de Bar-rameda, 100km downriver at the river's mouth. Schedules vary from year to year: early and late in the season, cruises may only go at weekends. Several companies in-cluding Cruceros Turísticos Torre del Oro (☎ 95 456 16 92) make the trips, from the jetty by the Torre del Oro, for around 3500 ptas. It's 4½ hours each way, usually with 4½ hours in Sanlúcar in between.

The horse-drawn carriages that hang around near the cathedral and Plaza de Es-paña normally charge 4000 ptas for a one-hour trot around the Barrio de Santa Cruz and Parque de María Luisa areas (up to four people).

SPECIAL EVENTS
Sevilla's Holy Week processions (see the boxed text 'Semana Santa in Sevilla' on the next page) and its Feria de Abril, the fair which follows a week or two later, are two of Spain's most famous and exciting festivals.

Feria de Abril
The April Fair, in the second half of the month, is a kind of release after the solem-nity of Semana Santa. It takes place on a special site *(recinto)*, El Real de la Feria, in the Los Remedios area west of the Guadalquivir. The ceremonial lighting up of the fairgrounds on the opening Monday night is the starting gun for six nights of eating, drinking, talking, fabulous flouncy dresses, and music and dancing till dawn. Much of the site is taken up by private areas for clubs, associations, families and groups of friends. But there are public areas, too, where much the same fun goes on. There's also a huge fairground.

In the afternoons, from about 1 pm, those

who have horses and carriages *(enganches)* parade about the site – and the city at large – in their finery (many of the horses are dressed up too). Sevilla's major bullfight season also takes place during the fair.

Other Festivals
Other Sevilla events include:

Cabalgata de los Reyes Magos
Held on 5 January, this is a big evening parade of floats in which the Reyes Magos (Three Kings) and their retinues throw some 60,000kg of sweets to the crowds.
Corpus Christi
This is an important early morning procession of the Custodia de Juan de Arfe and accompa-nying images from the cathedral. It is held in late May or June.
Bienal de Flamenco
Most of the big names of the flamenco world participate in this major flamenco festival, with events most nights for about three weeks, in various Sevilla locations. It is held during Sep-tember of even-numbered years.

PLACES TO STAY
Just about every room in Sevilla costs more during Semana Santa and the Feria de Abril. The typical increase is about 50%, but a few places double or even triple their prices. This *temporada extra* ('extra sea-son') can last as long as two months at some hotels. You should book ahead for rooms in Sevilla at this time. Even at normal times accommodation is in demand, so it's always worth ringing ahead.

The summer prices given here can come down significantly between October and March. Some mid-range and top-end places cut prices during July and August. See Ac-commodation in the Facts for the Visitor chapter for more general information on places to stay.

PLACES TO STAY – BUDGET
Camping
Open year round, *Camping Sevilla* (☎ 95 451 43 79) is about 6km out on the N-IV to Córdoba – on the right, just before the air-port, if you're approaching from Sevilla. It costs 475 ptas per person and per car, and

Semana Santa in Sevilla

Every day of the week from Palm Sunday to Easter Sunday, large, richly bedecked images and life-size tableaux of scenes from the Easter story are carried from Sevilla's churches through the streets to the cathedral. They're accompanied by long processions, which may take more than an hour to pass, and watched by vast crowds. These rites go back to the 14th century but they took their present form in the 17th, when many of the images – some of them supreme works of art – were created.

Semana Santa (Holy Week) in Sevilla, with its combination of splendour and anguish, spectacle and solemnity, and overriding adoration of the Virgin, can give a special insight into the nature of Spanish Catholicism.

The processions are organised by over 50 different *hermandades* or *cofradías* (brotherhoods, some of which include women). Each brotherhood normally carries two *pasos*, as the lavishly decorated platforms bearing the images are called. The first paso supports a statue of Christ, crucified, bearing the cross, or in a tableau representing a scene from the Passion; the second carries an image of the Virgin. The pasos are carried by teams of about 40 bearers called *costaleros*, who work in relays. The pasos are heavy – each costalero normally carries about 50kg – and they move with a hypnotic swaying motion to the rhythm of their accompanying bands and the commands of their *capataz* (leader), who strikes a bell to start and stop the paso.

Each pair of pasos has up to 2500 costumed followers, known as *nazarenos*. Many of these wear tall Ku Klux Klan-like capes which cover their heads except for narrow eye slits. The most contrite go barefoot and carry crosses. Membership of a hermandad is an honour keenly sought, even by some who normally wouldn't dream of attending mass.

Each day from Palm Sunday to Good Friday, seven or eight hermandades leave their churches in the afternoon or early evening and arrive between 5 and 11 pm at Calle Campana at the northern end of Calle Sierpes in the city centre. This is the start of the *carrera oficial* along Calle Sierpes, through Plaza San Francisco and along Avenida de la Constitución to the cathedral. The processions enter the cathedral at its western end and leave at the eastern, emerging on Plaza Virgen de los Reyes. They get back to their churches some time between 10 pm and 3 am.

400 ptas or 450 ptas per tent, plus IVA. It runs a shuttle bus several times a day to/from Avenida de Portugal near Plaza de España in the city (200 ptas one-way). Slightly more expensive and impractical without your own wheels, *Camping Club de Campo* (☎ 95 472 02 50) and *Camping Villsom* (☎ 95 472 08 28) are in Dos Hermanas, 15km south of Sevilla on the N-IV towards Cádiz.

Hostels

Modernised a few years ago, the Inturjoven *Albergue Juvenil Sevilla* (☎ 95 461 31 50, *Calle Isaac Peral 2*) is south of the centre, just off Avenida de la Palmera. It has room for 277 people in twin or triple rooms, over half of which have a bathroom. The hostel is about 10 minutes by bus No 34 from opposite the main tourist office (ask for the *albergue juvenil*).

Hostales & Pensiones

The attractive Barrio de Santa Cruz, close to the cathedral and within walking distance of Prado de San Sebastián bus station, has lots of places, some of them reasonably good value. There are many more places north of Plaza Nueva, convenient to Plaza de Armas bus station and still pretty central. Even if every place we mention here turns out to be full, there are plenty more in the same areas of town.

Some places in this price range will give a discount if you stay a few days.

Barrio de Santa Cruz & Around The friendly *Huéspedes Dulces Sueños/Sweet Dreams* (☎ 95 441 93 93, *Calle Santa María La Blanca 21*) has eight nice, clean, air-con rooms. Singles/doubles cost 2000/4000 ptas, and singles with bathroom are 3500 ptas.

The climax of the week is the *madrugada* (early hours) of Good Friday, when some of the most respected and popular hermandades file through the city. The first to reach the carrera oficial, about 1.30 am, is the oldest hermandad, El Silencio, which goes in complete silence. At about 2 am comes Jesús del Gran Poder, whose 17th-century Christ is one of the masterpieces of Sevillan sculpture. This is followed at about 3 am by La Macarena, whose Virgin is the most passionately adored of all. Then come El Calvario from the Iglesia de la Magdalena, Esperanza de Triana, and finally, at about 6 am, Los Gitanos, the *gitano* (Roma people) hermandad.

On the Saturday evening just four hermandades make their way to the cathedral, and finally, on Easter Sunday morning, the Hermandad de la Resurrección. In contrast to their fascination with the Crucifixion and the events leading up to it, *sevillanos* show relatively little interest in the Resurrection.

The styles of the hermandades show marked differences. City centre hermandades, such as El Silencio, are traditionally linked with the bourgeoisie. They're austere, using little or no music, and wearing black tunics, usually without capes. Hermandades from the working-class *barrios* (quarters) outside the centre, such as La Macarena, have brass and drum bands accompanying more brightly bedecked pasos. Their nazarenos wear coloured, caped tunics, often of satin, velvet or wool. They also have to come from farther away, and some are on the streets for more than 12 hours.

Programs giving each hermandad's schedule and route are widely available before and during Semana Santa. *ABC* newspaper prints maps showing the churches, recommended viewing spots *(lugares recomendados)* and other details. It's not too hard to work out which procession will be where and when, so you can pick one up in its own barrio or as it leaves or re-enters its church, always an emotional moment.

Crowds along most of the carrera oficial make it hard to get much of a view there, unless you manage to get a seat. These are sold for anything from about 1000 ptas on Plaza Virgen de los Reyes behind the cathedral to 3000 ptas or more on Good Friday morning on Calle Sierpes. But if you arrive early in the evening, you can usually get close enough to the cathedral to see plenty for free.

Calle Archeros, a narrow street off Calle Santa María La Blanca, has four hostales. One, the friendly, 13-room **Hostal Bienvenido** (☎ 95 441 36 55, *Calle Archeros 14*), has singles costing 1900 ptas to 2200 ptas and doubles costing between 3700 ptas and 4200 ptas, with shared bathrooms. A little farther north-east, **Hostal La Montoreña** (☎ 95 441 24 07, *Calle San Clemente 12*) has 10 simple rooms with shared bathrooms at 2000/3000 ptas.

On a small square just west of Calle Santa María La Blanca, **Pensión San Pancracio** (☎ 95 441 31 04, *Plaza de las Cruces 9*) has poky singles costing 2000 ptas and bigger doubles for 3400 ptas, or 4000 ptas with bathroom. **Pensión Cruces** (☎ 95 422 60 41, *Plaza de las Cruces 10*), has a dorm room with beds costing 1500 ptas, singles from 2000 ptas to 2500 ptas, and doubles

from 4000 ptas to 6000 ptas. Some rooms have shower and toilet.

Pensión Fabiola (☎ 95 421 83 46, *Calle Fabiola 16*), with a plant-filled courtyard, has simple, well-kept singles/doubles for 3000/5000 ptas, and doubles with bathroom for 7000 ptas. The singles are small.

Pensión Vergara (☎ 95 421 56 68, *Calle Ximénez de Enciso 11*) consists of six brightly decorated rooms around the upper level of a 15th-century patio. Plants and skylights add to the cosy atmosphere. The rooms, with shared bathrooms, cost 2000/4000 ptas.

The friendly, well-kept **Hostal Toledo** (☎ 95 421 53 35, *Calle Santa Teresa 15*) has 10 clean rooms, all with bath or shower, for 3500/6000 ptas plus IVA. **Hostal Monreal** (☎ 95 421 41 66, *Calle Rodrigo Caro 7*) is bigger, with 20 varied rooms (a few with

* Difficult to find way in by car but worth it. Try for rooms on Top with terraces

5000 ptas plus ... 7000 ptas plus ... ... room.

... *Goya* (☎ 95 421 11 ... ...go 31) has pleasant, ...athroom costing 4300/ ...les with shower for 600... ...pleasant downstairs sitting area. A ... ther north, the friendly 11-room *Hosta...Sánchez Sabariego* (☎ 95 421 44 70, Corral del Rey 23), with an attractive little courtyard, has individually decorated rooms, most with bathroom, for around 3000/6000 ptas.

Pensión Alcázar (☎ 95 422 84 57, Calle Deán Miranda 12), on a peaceful little square just west of the Alcázar, has good doubles with bathroom for 5900 ptas to 7000 ptas plus IVA. There's a little terrace near the top with Giralda views. Round the corner, *Hostal Arias* (☎ 95 422 68 40, fax 95 421 83 89, @ reina@arrakis.es, Calle Mariana de Pineda 9) has 13 decent rooms with shower costing 5250/6900 ptas.

North & West of Plaza Nueva A three-minute walk west of Plaza Nueva, *Hostal Central* (☎ 95 421 76 60, Calle Zaragoza 18) has well-kept, decent-sized singles/doubles with bathroom for 4500/6500 ptas.

Hostal Lis II (☎ 95 456 02 28, @ lisII@sol.com, Calle Olavide 5), a pretty house on a narrow street off Calle San Eloy, charges 2300/4500 ptas for basic rooms with shared bathroom or 5000 ptas for doubles with bathroom. The singles are on the small side. You can use the Internet here (300 ptas per 30 minutes, 500 ptas per hour).

The good *Hotel Zaida* (☎ 95 421 11 38, fax 95 490 36 24, Calle San Roque 26) occupies an 18th-century house with a lovely Mudéjar-style arched patio. The 27 rooms are plain but decent, with air-con, TV and bathroom, at 4250/6300 ptas plus IVA. Ground-floor rooms open straight onto the lobby, with its TV, and might be noisy.

The 23-room *Hostal Londres* (☎ 95 421 28 96, Calle San Pedro Mártir 1) has a pleasant tiled lobby and plain but adequate air-con rooms with bath, TV and in some cases little balconies, for 4500/6500 ptas.

The small, friendly *Hostal Romero* (☎ 95 421 13 53, Calle Gravina 21) offers bare but clean rooms with shared baths for 2000/3500 ptas. *Hostal Gravina* (☎ 95 421 64 14, Calle Gravina 46), has adequate rooms costing 2000/3500 ptas or 2500/4000 ptas. The slightly bigger *Hostal Gala* (☎ 95 421 45 03, Calle Gravina 52) has singles for 2500 ptas and doubles with bathroom for 5000 ptas.

Near Plaza del Duque de la Victoria, a bustling square surrounded by classy big shops, friendly *Hostal Unión* (☎ 95 422 92 94 or 95 421 17 90, Calle Tarifa 4) has nine good, clean rooms that cost 2000/3500 ptas, or 3000/4500 ptas with bathroom. *Hostal Pino* (☎ 95 421 28 10, Calle Tarifa 6), next door in an old building with a small patio, charges 2000/3500 ptas (2500/5000 ptas with shower).

Hotel Sevilla (☎ 95 438 41 61, fax 95 490 21 60, Calle Daoíz 5) is past its prime but has 30 clean, plain, medium-sized rooms with bath for 4280/6420 ptas. Off its large lobby is a small greenery-filled patio.

PLACES TO STAY – MID-RANGE
Barrio de Santa Cruz & Around

Just west of the Alcázar, *Hostal Picasso* (☎/fax 95 421 08 64, @ hpicasso@arrakis.es, Calle San Gregorio 1) offers small but pretty rooms with comfortable beds. Rooms cost 7000 ptas with shared bathroom or 8500 ptas with private bathroom, single or double. *Hostal Córdoba* (☎ 95 422 74 98, Calle Farnesio 12) has a plant-draped atrium and 13 nice air-con singles/doubles with shared bathrooms for 5000/8000 ptas (7000/9500 ptas with a small shower room). *Hostería del Laurel* (☎ 95 422 02 95, fax 95 421 04 50, @ host-laurel@eintec.es, Plaza de los Venerables 5), above a characterful old bar in the heart of Santa Cruz, has 21 simple, attractive air-con rooms with TV and bath or shower. They cost 7000/9500 ptas plus IVA (but an excellent-value 5000/7500 ptas plus IVA in July and August). *Hotel Murillo* (☎ 95 421 60 95, fax 95 421 96 16, Calle Lope de Rueda 7), nearby, has a lobby like an antique showroom but its 57 rooms are a little tired, if clean. They cost 4800/8300 ptas (3900/6800 ptas from mid-June to early August) plus IVA.

El Arenal

This is a good, convenient location. *Hotel Simón* (☎ 95 422 66 60, fax 95 456 22 41, *Calle García de Vinuesa 19*), in a fine 18th-century house, has 29 very pleasant rooms with bathroom which cost 6500/9500 ptas plus IVA. It's extremely popular, so book ahead. Breakfast is available. *Hotel Europa* (☎ 95 421 43 05, fax 95 421 00 16, *Calle Jimios 5*) has 16 decent, quite sizeable rooms with TV from 7000/10,000 ptas to 7000/12,900 ptas plus IVA. The bigger *Hotel La Rábida* (☎ 95 422 09 60, fax 95 422 43 75, *Calle Castelar 24*) has an impressive lobby with a fountain, a restaurant, and good rooms with bathroom costing 6100/9300 ptas plus IVA. The 18 rooms at the *Hotel Maestranza* (☎ 95 456 10 70, fax 95 421 44 04, *Calle Gamazo 12*) come with TV, air-con and safes, for 6000/9300 ptas plus IVA.

North & West of Plaza Nueva

The pleasant 40-room *Hotel Plaza Sevilla* (☎ 95 421 71 49, *Calle Canalejas 2*) has well-kept if not huge rooms with bathroom and TV for 5000/8000 ptas plus IVA. *Hotel Puerta de Triana* (☎ 95 421 54 04, fax 95 421 54 01, *Calle Reyes Católicos 5*) is a good 65-room hotel in a well-modernised traditional-style house. Double rooms cost 11,600 ptas plus IVA. Breakfast is available.

Farther east, the recently upgraded seven-room *Hostal Lis* (☎ 95 421 30 88, *Calle Escarpín 10*) has a nice, tiled lobby, and singles/doubles with bathroom, TV and air-con for 4500/8500 ptas.

North towards the Alameda de Hércules, on a quiet little street, 77-room *Hotel Corregidor* (☎ 95 438 51 11, fax 95 438 42 38, *Calle Morgado 17*) has comfortable, clean, moderate-sized, air-con rooms with TV costing 9000/12,000 ptas plus IVA. Downstairs are spacious sitting areas, a bar and a little open-air patio. There's parking 200m away.

Patio de la Cartuja (☎ 95 490 02 00,

fax 95 490 20 56, @ patios@bbv.net, *Calle Lumbreras 8–10*), just off the northern end of the Alameda de Hércules, occupies a former *corral*, a three-storey community of apartments around a patio which was once the typical form of Sevillan lower-middle-class housing. Renovated into 30 cosy apartments with double bedroom, kitchen, bathroom, and sitting room with double sofa bed, it's a pleasant place to stay if you don't mind being this far north. Single/double occupancy costs 8800/11,000 ptas plus IVA (less in July and August). Garage parking costs 1200 ptas, and there's a cafe too. *Patio de la Alameda* (☎ 95 490 49 99, fax 95 490 02 26, @ patios@bbv.net, *Alameda de Hércules 56*), nearby, is similar, with the same ownership and prices.

PLACES TO STAY – TOP END

In the Barrio de Santa Cruz, *Hotel Fernando III* (☎ 95 421 73 07, *Calle San José 21*) has 156 comfortable if unimaginative rooms with TV and bathroom costing 13,600/17,000 ptas plus IVA. It also has a restaurant, bar, spacious lounge, garage and rooftop pool.

Nearby, *Las Casas de la Judería* (☎ 95 441 51 50, fax 95 442 21 70, *Callejón de Dos Hermanas 7*) consists of a group of charmingly restored old houses around several patios and fountains, with lots of pretty tiles and plants. Most of the 50-odd cosy rooms cost 12,500/18,000 ptas plus IVA (less during July and August). Breakfast is available, and there's a bar. Two other similarly-sized establishments in the same appealing small group of hotels are located in El Centro: *Las Casas de los Mercaderes* (☎ 95 422 58 58, fax 95 422 98 84, *Calle Álvarez Quintero 9–13*), centred on an 18th-century patio, with marginally lower rates; and the slightly more expensive *Las Casas del Rey de Baeza* (☎ 95 456 14 96, fax 95 456 14 41, *Plaza Cristo de la Redención 2*).

The luxurious *Hotel Los Seises* (☎ 95 422 94 95, fax 95 422 43 34, *Calle Segovias 6*) is set around the former rear patio of the 16th-century Archbishop's Palace, near the cathedral. The 43 rooms cost 20,000/27,000 ptas plus IVA (less during July and August). The hotel has a good restaurant.

Father north-west, *Hotel Becquer* (☎ 95 422 89 00, fax 95 421 44 00, ✉ hbecquer@ arrakis.es, Calle Reyes Católicos 4) has 118 comfortable, modern rooms that cost 13,000/ 15,000 ptas plus IVA. *Hotel Colón* (☎ 95 422 29 00, fax 95 422 09 38, ✉ dtoracol@ trypnet.com, Calle Canalejas 1) is one of the city's top hotels, a 200-room place modernised but with old-fashioned trimmings. Rooms cost 24,450/30,565 ptas plus IVA. In the east of El Centro, *Hotel Baco* (☎ 95 456 50 50, fax 95 456 36 54, Plaza Ponce de León 15) has 25 old-fashioned rooms costing 10,000/14,000 ptas plus IVA. You're probably best with an off-street room, because of the bus stop outside.

Hotel Cervantes (☎ 95 490 02 80, fax 95 490 05 36, Calle Cervantes 10) is a charming medium-sized hotel in modern style with 48 rooms at 11,000/15,750 ptas plus IVA (less in July and August). It's on a quiet street in a rather quaint old part of the city, up towards the Alameda de Hércules. Breakfast is available.

You can break the bank in style at the *Hotel Alfonso XIII* (☎ 95 422 28 50, fax 95 421 60 33, Calle San Fernando 2), just south of the centre, a magnificent 1920s confection of old Sevillan styles in mahogany, marble and tiles. Double rooms cost 51,000 ptas plus IVA.

PLACES TO EAT

Sevilla is one of Spain's tapas capitals, with scores and scores of bars serving all sorts of varied and tasty bites. To catch the atmosphere of the city, you should certainly do some of your eating in bars.

Meals

Breakfast is usually available until about 11 am; most restaurants serve lunch between about 1 and 3.30 pm and dinner from about 8.30 to 11 pm. If you fancy eating in tapas bars but need more than typical tapas quantity, you can always go for *raciones* (meal-sized servings of tapas) or *media-raciones* (half a *ración*) at some of the places recommended in the Tapas section.

Barrio de Santa Cruz & Around The narrow streets and squares immediately east of the Alcázar are dotted with numerous mainly tourist-oriented restaurants. *Restaurant La Cueva* (Calle Rodrigo Caro 18), a pleasant courtyard place, does a lunch *menú* (fixed-price meal) of *gazpacho* soup and the rice dish *paella*, plus salad and dessert for 1350 ptas plus IVA (minimum two people). *El Rincón de Pepe* (Calle Gloria 6), nearby, offers a slightly less obvious menú for the same price. Neither includes drinks. For something fancier, *Corral del Agua* (☎ 95 422 07 14, Callejón del Agua 6) has good, inventive food and its cool, green courtyard is great on a hot day, if you can get a table. Main courses cost between 1900 ptas and 2500 ptas and include some tasty fish choices, and varied dishes of the day. For starters, how about the avocado pudding on a coulis of fresh cheese (1000 ptas)? Perhaps the best meals in this part of town are at *Restaurante La Albahaca* (☎ 95 422 07 14, Plaza de Santa Cruz 12) which offers fare such as roast wild boar with fig jam and apple puree. Two courses a la carte will set you back at least 4500 ptas, but there's a three-course menú, including a drink, for 3500 ptas plus IVA.

Hostería del Laurel (Plaza de los Venerables 5) has an atmospheric old bar with herbs and hams dangling from the ceiling, and efficient, friendly waiters serving a wide range of good media-raciones (from 550 ptas to 1500 ptas) and raciones (from 950 ptas to 2450 ptas).

Cervecería Giralda (Calle Mateos Gago 1), in a former Muslim bathhouse, is a good spot for breakfast close to the cathedral and Alcázar. *Tostadas* (toasted rolls) cost from 100 ptas to 400 ptas depending what you have on them, or there's bacon and scrambled eggs for 525 ptas – all plus 20% at a table. Good tapas are also served here (see under Tapas later in this section). *Café de Indias* (Avenida de la Constitución 10), opposite the cathedral, is a bustling coffee stop with a large range of caffeine fixes starting at 150 ptas, plus pastries and cakes. *Cafetería Las Lapas* (Calle San Gregorio 6), just west of the Alcázar, bustles at morning-coffee time with office workers and students crowding in for the good *molletes* (soft bread rolls). It is closed Sunday.

Pizzeria San Marco (Calle Mesón del Moro 6), in another refurbished Muslim bathhouse, is extremely popular for its pizzas and pastas costing around 850 ptas. It opens 1.15 to 4.30 pm and 8.15 pm to 12.30 am daily except Monday (to 1 am on Friday and Saturday nights).

Calle Santa María La Blanca has several busy places where you can sit outdoors. At the *Carmela (Calle Santa María La Blanca 6)*, a media-ración of *tortilla Alta-Mira* (omelette with potatoes and vegetables) is almost a meal for 700 ptas. Next door at No 4, *Altamira Bar-Café* has similarly priced media-raciones, plus *platos combinados* (mixed platters) for around 1000 ptas. Busy little *Bar Casa Fernando* around the corner does good-value *platos del día* (dishes of the day) for 500 ptas, and a decent 1000-ptas lunch menú; *Restaurant El Cordobés* at No 20 offers breakfasts such as omelette, bacon, bread and coffee for 325 ptas. A couple of classier places nearby, both specialising in fish and seafood, are *Restaurante Modesto (Calle Cano y Cueto 5)* and *Restaurante La Judería (Calle Cano y Cueto 13A)*. Main dishes start at 1200 ptas at the Modesto and 1900 ptas at La Judería.

Among a clutch of somewhat touristy restaurants just north of the cathedral, *Las Escobas (Calle Álvarez Quintero 62)* has a reasonable menú of two courses, fruit, bread and wine for 975 ptas. The classier *Casa Robles (Calle Álvarez Quintero 58)* does raciones (1200 ptas to 1600 ptas) and media-raciones, and unusual *revuelto* (scrambled eggs) combinations such as *algas, erizos y gambas* (seaweed, sea urchins and prawns), at its bar. It also has a restaurant section with lots of lamb, beef, venison and fish costing around 1800 ptas to 2500 ptas.

El Arenal With a good selection of platos combinados (from 800 ptas), *Mesón Serranito (Calle Antonia Díaz 9)* also boasts interesting bullfight photos and some impressive bulls' heads. The busy *Bodega Paco Góngora (Calle Padre Marchena 1)* serves a huge range of good seafood at decent prices – media-raciones of fish *a la plancha* (grilled) are mostly 675 ptas. *Restaurante Enrique Becerra (Calle Gamazo 2)*, nearby, is a smarter place with good, varied Andalucian fare. Two courses with drinks will usually set you back 4000 ptas or more (closed Sunday).

El Centro On Calle Sierpes, *Bar Laredo* at the southern end is a popular breakfast stop, and *Confitería La Campana* at the northern end is the city's most famous bakery, in operation since 1885. It still turns out scrumptious cakes and pastries and has a small coffee shop.

Restaurante San Marco (Calle de la Cuna 6), in an 18th-century mansion one block east of Calle Sierpes, is the parent of Pizzeria San Marco in the Barrio de Santa Cruz, and it's a better and more expensive place, serving pizza and pasta amid classical surroundings for around 1000 ptas.

Alfalfa 10 and the *Horno de San Buenaventura* on Plaza de la Alfalfa 10 are bustling coffee stops – the San Buenaventura does good cakes too. *Habanita (Calle Golfo 3)*, off Calle Pérez Galdós, nearby, serves a winning variety of Cuban, andaluz and vegetarian food as raciones (700 ptas to 1500 ptas), media-raciones (350 ptas to 800 ptas) and tapas (see that section later in this chapter). Some Cuban specialities, such as *yuca can mojito* (cassava with an orange, oil and garlic sauce), will please vegetarians too. Pancakes and baked potatoes cost 250 ptas to 300 ptas. Habanita opens 12.30 to 4.30 pm and 8.30 pm to 12.30 am, daily except winter Sunday afternoons.

The handsomely blue-tiled *Restaurante El Bacalao (Plaza Ponce de León 15)* specialises in *bacalao* (salted cod), another Sevilla favourite. You can have your cod a dozen ways for 1200 ptas to 2150 ptas, or as a media-ración for 700 ptas to 950 ptas.

Bodegón Alfonso XII (Calle Alfonso XII 33), near the Museo de Bellas Artes, is excellent value with deals such as media-raciones of scrambled egg, cheese, ham and spinach for 550 ptas, or a breakfast of bacon, eggs and coffee for 400 ptas.

The *Horno del Duque* on Plaza del Duque de la Victoria is a good, busy cafe for breakfast, or for snacks or light meals later in the day, popular with shoppers from nearby El Corte Inglés. Platos combinados cost around 975 ptas to 1450 ptas (more expensive outside). On the opposite corner of the square, down-to-earth *Café Bar Duque* is a popular spot for *chocolate-y-churros* (deep-fried doughnuts to dip in hot chocolate), also doing a range of platos combinados for 800 ptas.

The *Mercado del Arenal*, on Calle Pastor y Landero, and the *Mercado de la Encarnación* on Plaza de la Encarnación are central Sevilla's two food markets. The Encarnación has been in its current temporary quarters, awaiting construction of a new permanent building, since 1973!

South of the Centre Several economical cafes face the entrance to the university on Calle San Fernando. *Baguettería La Merienda*, at No 27, serves a variety of snacks and meals including hot baguettes with various fillings for 275 ptas to 425 ptas.

La Raza (Avenida de Isabel la Católica 2) is a good stop in the Parque de María Luisa area. For breakfast, *café con leche* (coffee with hot milk) and a *mollete* (soft bread roll), butter and jam costs 300 ptas; later in the day it does a 2000-ptas menú. There are tables outside under the trees.

The Andalucian-Basque *Restaurante Egaña Oriza* (☎ 95 422 72 11, Calle San Fernando 41) has claims to be the best restaurant in Sevilla. It's certainly one of the smartest and most expensive. For two courses without drinks, you're looking at a bill of at least 4000 ptas. Main course specialities range from angler's hake with young garlic in parsley sauce to leg of lamb braised with aubergines and courgettes.

Triana Sevillans love their *pescaíto frito* (fried fish) and the city's favourite fried-fish eatery, the *Kiosco de las Flores*, was recently on the verge of moving from its 70-year-old corrugated-roof premises on Plaza del Altozano to new premises right on the Calle del Betis riverbank looking across

to the city centre. Raciones cost around 1200 ptas. *Restaurante Río Grande* at the southern end of Calle del Betis serves good food – 1800 ptas to 2500 ptas for most meat and fish main courses – in a great location looking across to the Torre del Oro. But *Restaurante El Puerto* next door also serves good food in just as good a location at about two-thirds of the price. Calle del Betis also boasts several popular pizzerias: at No 68, across the street from the Río Grande, is another *Pizzeria San Marco* (see Barrio de Santa Cruz & Around earlier in this section). Farther north are the good *Ristorante Cosa Nostra* (pizza 650 ptas to 1000 ptas, pasta 650 ptas to 1200 ptas) and the slightly more economical *Pizzeria O Mamma Mia* at No 33. Between these two, *Mex-Rock* at No 40–41 is another popular spot, serving tacos, quesadillas (folded tortillas with cheese fillings) and so on, for 400 ptas to 900 ptas, and the more substantial *solomillo azteca* (Aztec steak) for 1650 ptas.

Tapas

An evening of tapas-hopping round Sevilla's bars with a couple of friends is one of the most enjoyable experiences in the city. Most tapas bars are good at lunchtime too, but from about 4 to 8 pm often only cold tapas are available. Many Sevilla bars chalk your account on the counter in front of you as you order and add it up when you leave.

Favourite Tapas

Caña de lomo – pork loin
Cazón en adobo – dogfish marinated in vinegar, salt, lemon and spices, then deep fried (delicious)
Espinacas con garbanzos – spinach and chick peas
Papas aliñás – sliced potatoes and boiled eggs, with vegetable garnish and a vinegar-and-oil dressing
Pavía – battered fish or seafood
Puntillitas – baby squid, usually deep fried

All that glisters is not gold – the 13th-century Torre del Oro in Sevilla.

Sevilla's 16th-century Gothic and Renaissance cathedral is one of the largest in the world.

Casa de Pilatos, Sevilla

Patio de las Doncellas, Sevilla

Gaudy tiles represent Spain's provinces in Plaza de España, Sevilla.

The lush gardens of Sevilla's Alcázar provide welcome shade.

The Giralda, Sevilla Cathedral

Though many bars helpfully have a tapas menu – or at least a blackboard – you'll certainly find that you don't know what many things are. The boxed text on the previous page lists a few Sevilla tapas specialities.

Barrio de Santa Cruz Popular with visitors and locals, *Bodega Santa Cruz* on Calle Mateos Gago has a big choice of decent-sized tapas, most costing 175 ptas to 200 ptas. *Cervecería Giralda (Calle Mateos Gago 1)* does a wonderful variety of good tapas, some pretty exotic, costing 250 ptas to 300 ptas. Some are tiny, but the *pechuga bechamel* (chicken breast in bechamel sauce), *brocheta de mero* (halibut brochette) and *brocheta de solomillo* (steak brochette) are decent value. Good tapas at *Café-Bar Campanario*, across the street, include the *tortilla de patatas* (potato omelette) and *revuelto de espárragos* (scrambled eggs with asparagus).

Café Bar Las Teresas (Calle Santa Teresa 2) is an atmospheric old-style bar with lots of hanging hams; good tapas cost from 150 ptas to 275 ptas and media-raciones from 600 ptas to 1100 ptas. *Hostería del Laurel (Plaza de los Venerables 5)* does good tapas at its bar, mostly costing around 250 ptas. See Barrio de Santa Cruz & Around in the earlier Meals section for more details.

El Arenal The relaxed *Casa Pepe-Hillo (Calle de Adriano 24)* does some mouthwatering tapas costing from 275 ptas to 350 ptas – try mushroom-filled artichoke hearts. *Mesón Cinco Jotas (Calle Castelar 1)* specialises in succulent Jabugo ham – 400 ptas for tapas of the best, *cinco jotas*, and 250 ptas to 300 ptas for smoked salmon, sirloin, cheese and other tapas.

La Infanta (Calle Arfe 36), with sherry barrels for tables, is a smarter place serving exotic and delicious tapas from 250 ptas. The nearby *Mesón de la Infanta (Calle Dos de Mayo 26)*, with the same owners, has similarly delicious tapas *haute cuisine*, with some items composed of five or six separate but complementary elements (250 ptas to 400 ptas). *Bodega Paco Góngora* and

Restaurante Enrique Becerra (see under Meals, earlier in this section, for details) are good for tapas too.

El Centro In the south of El Centro, towards the Barrio de Santa Cruz, the excellent *Robles Placentines (Calle Placentines 2)* is a modern, uncluttered tapas bar, but still with traditional touches such as large sherry barrels. Temptations include duck slices in olive oil and three kinds of wild mushrooms from the Sierra de Aracena, costing around 250/700/1300 ptas a tapas/media-ración/ración.

Plaza de la Alfalfa is a hub of the tapas scene. Nearby *Sopa de Ganso (Calle Pérez Galdós 8)* offers innovative combinations like chicken and date brochette or sirloin with cheese and nuts, and usually has several vegetarian options among its daily specials. It has great cakes too, and plays good music for its youthful clientele. *Habanita (Calle Golfo 3)*, off Calle Pérez Galdós, does vegetarian and Cuban tapas (200 ptas to 350 ptas). Just off the eastern end of Plaza de la Alfalfa, on Calle Alfalfa, *La Trastienda*, with a smartish clientele, offers crabs and *La Bodega* deals in ham and sherry. Between these last two, on the corner of Calle Candilejo, tiny *La Bodega Extremeña* serves superb meat and cheese tapas and *montaditos* (small open sandwiches, often toasted) for 175 ptas to 275 ptas. The *solomillo beicon*, for instance, is medallions of pork steak wrapped in bacon, served with slices of boiled potato and marinated peppers. Or you might go for *huevos codorniz jamón* – two little fried quail eggs with ham, on bread. For great meat tapas *a la brasa* (grilled), head east along Calle Águilas to another *Bodega Extremeña (Calle San Esteban 17)*: try the *solomillo ibérico* (Iberian pork sirloin) or *chuletas de cordero* (lamb chops) for 275 ptas.

To the north, *El Rinconcillo (Calle Gerona 40)* is Sevilla's oldest bar, founded in 1670 and still going strong. The tapas are fairly straightforward but good, ranging in price from *espinacas con garbanzos* (spinach with chickpeas; 200 ptas) to *tortilla de jamón serrano* (omelette with serrano ham; 650 ptas). The newer ***La Giganta*** *(Calle Alhóndiga 6)*, round the corner, does good fish, meat and fried potato tapas costing around 250 ptas.

Westward is bright, busy ***Patio San Eloy*** *(Calle San Eloy 9)*. Good tapas of ham, cheese, smoked salmon, pork and more go for 175 ptas to 215 ptas. Also good are the *burguillos* (small home-made bread rolls with fillings) for 200 ptas. A group of people could enjoy a *turrada*, which is a plate of smoked salmon, anchovies and fine *pata negra* (black leg) ham. There's wine from 100 ptas a glass.

North of the Centre The Alameda de Hércules area has some good tapas stops. ***Bulebar Café*** *(Alameda de Hércules 83)* serves up unusual home-made tarts and sweet tapas: *pastel de verduras* – a type of vegetable flan – is good. It opens from 4 pm to the early hours daily. ***Bar-Restaurante Las Columnas***, on the western side of the Alameda, is a straightforward place serving a large variety of tapas (costing from 225 ptas to 300 ptas) and raciones.

A couple of minutes walk east of the Alameda, the cool ***La Ilustre Víctima*** *(Calle Doctor Letamendi 35)* serves some great *pinchos a la brasa* (small grilled-meat kebabs; 500 ptas) and vegetarian tapas such as *calabacines al roque* (courgettes with Roquefort cheese; 300 ptas).

Triana The bright ***Las Columnas*** *(Calle San Jacinto 29)* is brought to us by the inventors of the Patio San Eloy (see under El Centro earlier in this section) and purveys much the same excellent fare. ***Mariscos Emilio*** *(Calle San Jacinto 39)* is popular for its seafood tapas costing around 225 ptas.

ENTERTAINMENT

Sevilla's nightlife is among the liveliest in Spain. Bars begin to fill from 10 pm most nights but it really gets moving about midnight or 1 am on Friday and Saturday nights. You can find a range of live music any day except perhaps Monday. On warm nights, throngs of people block the streets

outside popular bars and crowd the banks of the Guadalquivir, while teenagers just bring their own *litronas* or *botellonas* (plastic litre bottles filled with something stronger than Coca-Cola) to mass open-air gathering spots such as the Mercado del Arenal. Sevilla also has some great music bars, often with space to dance.

To find out what's on in the way of music and the other arts, consult *Casco Antiguo*, a free fortnightly newspaper distributed around the central areas; *El Giraldillo*, a monthly what's-on magazine sometimes available free at tourist offices, hotels or museums; the free tourist magazines *Welcome & Olé* and *The Tourist* which you'll find in some hotels; and the *Sevilla Online* (www.sol.com) and *Sevilla Cultural* (www .sevillacultural.com) Web sites. None of these are comprehensive, but they'll give you a good start. There's also some information in the newspapers *El Correo*, *ABC* and *El País*.

Bars

Of course you can eat while you drink: for bars where the tapas are an attraction in themselves, see the preceding section.

Barrio de Santa Cruz & Around There are some hugely popular bars just north of the cathedral: ***P Flaherty Irish Pub*** *(Calle Alemanes 7)* gets packed with locals and visitors alike – you'll pay 600 ptas for your pint of Guinness or bitter. ***La Subasta*** and ***Antigüedades*** on Calle Argote de Molina are very popular with a slightly older, more conservative crowd.

In the heart of the Barrio de Santa Cruz, small bars such as ***Bodega Santa Cruz*** on Calle Mateos Gago, ***Bar Entrecalles*** on Calle Ximénez de Enciso and ***Café Bar Las Teresas*** *(Calle Santa Teresa 2)*, can all get pretty lively, usually with a mixed crowd of visitors and locals.

El Arenal Calle García de Vinuesa has a few bare, old-fashioned but popular *bodegas* (traditional-type wine bars) with wine and/or sherry from the barrel (and beer, of course). One of the best is ***Hijos de E***

Morales (Calle García de Vinuesa 11), with a large back room where old wine casks serve as tables. A little farther west, on Calle de Adriano, the scene changes again: the mostly young crowds here some nights have to be seen to be believed. This scene merges with the litrona mob around the nearby Mercado del Arenal. Busy music bars with inexpensive drinks on Adriano itself include *A3* and *Arena*. There are several more very lively bars on and just off nearby Calle Arfe. Just to the south, Calle Dos de Mayo has some more relaxed bars and bodegas, with an older crowd.

Café Isbiliyya (Paseo de Cristóbal Colón 2), near the Puente de Triana, is a bustling gay music bar – mostly men – overflowing onto the street on busy nights.

El Centro From mid-evening to around 1 am, Plaza Salvador is a very popular spot for an open-air drink, with a studenty crowd and a couple of little bars selling carry-out drinks. People stand around or sit on the steps of the Parroquia del Salvador, where hashish fumes may mingle incongruously with incense from the church. Just off the square at the corner of Calle Alcaicería and Calle Siete Revueltas, the long-established *Bar Europa* is a pleasant place for a sit-down drink, bright with colourful tiling.

Calle Pérez Galdós, off Plaza de la Alfalfa, has at least five throbbing music bars – *Bare Nostrum*, *Cabo Loco*, *Nao*, *La Rebótica* and *Sopa de Ganso*. If you're in a partyish mood, you should find at least one with a scene and music to your fancy.

Alameda de Hércules Several excellent bars and some live music attract an alternative, young-but-not-too-young crowd to this area. It used to be a red-light district and there are still a few seedy characters lurking around.

The *Bulebar Café (Alameda de Hércules 83)* is a relaxed place to go for a drink or some unusual tapas, with comfortable old-fashioned furniture and a good courtyard out front. Farther along this eastern side of the Alameda, *El Corto Maltés*, *Café Cen-*

tral and the especially bohemian *Habanilla Café* are all busy pub-like places that spill out onto the street.

A couple of blocks east of the Alameda, there's an international crowd and always a buzz in *La Ilustre Víctima (Calle Doctor Letamendi 35)*. The music and tapas are great (beer costs 150 ptas). It opens till 2 am daily (4 am Friday and Saturday nights).

A little south of the Alameda, *Itaca (Calle Amor de Dios 25)* is a big gay dance bar – mostly men.

Triana Calle del Betis, along the western bank of the Guadalquivir, has a string of bars from which you can carry your drink across the street and sit on the wall above the river. On the way to Calle del Betis, you could stop in at *Madigan's (Plaza de Cuba 2)*, another of Sevilla's popular Irish pubs – open daily from noon. *Alambique*, *Mui d'Aqui* and *Big Ben*, clustered side by side at Calle del Betis 54, and *Café La Pavana (Calle del Betis 41)* all play good music and attract an interesting mix of students and travellers. They open about 9 pm and some of them occasionally have live music. Bars towards the northern end of the street get a bit mellower, among them *Café de la Prensa (Calle del Betis 8)*.

North of Calle del Betis, Calle de Castilla has yet more good bars, overflowing with a mixed twenties-ish local crowd on weekend nights, including *Casa Cuesta*, No 2, *Café-Bar Guadalquivir*, No 17, and *Aníbal Café*, No 98. While you're here, have a look in at the great display of potted plants in the courtyard of Calle de Castilla 22. A couple of passages lead through to Paseo de Nuestra Señora de la O on the riverbank, where you'll find *La Otra Orilla*, a buzzing music bar blessed with a great outdoor terrace.

Summer Nights by the River

In summer, dozens of temporary open-air late-night bars *(terrazas de verano)*, many of them with live music and plenty of room to dance, spring up along both banks of the river. They change names and ambience from year to year.

Live Music

Tickets for some major events are sold at the Sevilla Rock music shop, Calle Alfonso XII 1. For information on flamenco in Sevilla, see the boxed text 'Flamenco Haunts of Sevilla'.

La Imperdible (*☎ 95 438 82 19, Plaza San Antonio de Padua 9*), a few blocks west of the Alameda de Hércules, is an epicentre of experimental arts in Sevilla. Its small theatre stages lots of contemporary dance and a bit of drama and music, usually at 9 pm and costing 800 ptas to 1000 ptas. Its

bar, the *Almacén* (*☎ 95 490 04 34*), stages varied free music events from around 11 pm Thursday to Saturday – from soul or blues bands to psychedelic punks to DJs purveying ambient or techno.

A little farther west, just across the road from the Guadalquivir, the *Salamandra* (*☎ 95 490 28 38, Calle del Torneo 43*) is one of Sevilla's top live music spots, with varied performers – Latin, ethnic, pop-rock, rap, blues – most often on Fridays and Saturdays, starting around 9 pm (usually 800 ptas to 1200 ptas).

Flamenco Haunts of Sevilla

Sevilla is one of Spain's flamenco capitals and its Triana *barrio* (district) on the western bank of the Guadalquivir, once the city's *gitano* (Roma people) quarter, was one of flamenco's birthplaces. Though impromptu flamenco in small, smoky bars in Triana or around the Alameda de Hércules is pretty much a thing of the past, there are plenty of spots in the city where you can catch live flamenco song, dance or guitar. Hotels and tourist offices tend to steer you towards *tablaos* (expensive, tourist-oriented flamenco venues) which put on nightly shows, sometimes including dinner. These can be inauthentic and lacking in atmosphere, but **Los Gallos** (*☎ 95 421 69 81, Plaza de Santa Cruz 11*) in the Barrio de Santa Cruz is a cut above the average. Some top-notch flamenco artists have trodden Los Gallos' boards in the early stages of their careers. There are two-hour shows at 9 and 11.30 pm nightly for 3500 ptas including one drink.

In general, you'll catch a more spontaneous atmosphere in one of the bars that stage regular nights of flamenco or *sevillanas*, usually with no entry charge. Quality is unpredictable. At the time of writing these bars include (see the Bars section for more details on some):

El Mundo (*Calle Siete Revueltas*) in El Centro – flamenco on Tuesdays starting at 11 pm (free admission)

El Tamboril (*Plaza de Santa Cruz*), Barrio de Santa Cruz – jolly crowds pack in to enjoy live sevillanas and rumba every night from 10 pm.

El Tejar (*☎ 95 434 33 40, Calle San Jacinto 68*) – Triana bar with flamenco every Friday night.

La Carbonería (*☎ 95 421 44 60, Calle Levíes 18*) – a converted coal-yard in the Barrio de Santa Cruz with two large rooms, each with a bar, that gets thronged nearly every night with locals and visitors alike who come to enjoy the social scene and hear live music – nearly always flamenco – from about 11 pm to 4 am (admission is free). A glass of wine costs around 250 ptas.

La Sonanta (*Calle San Jacinto 31*) – flamenco at 10 pm on Thursdays in this Triana bar.

Salamandra (*☎ 95 490 28 38, Calle del Torneo 43*), west of the Alameda de Hércules – flamenco nights on Thursday starting at 11 pm (admission costs 1500 ptas including a drink).

Big-name flamenco artists make fairly frequent appearances at some theatres (see Theatres later in this section), especially the Teatro Central, which runs flamenco seasons under the name Flamenco Viene del Sur. Sevilla also stages one of Spain's major flamenco festivals, the Bienal de Flamenco (see Special Events earlier in this chapter), and, if you're present for the Feria de Abril, you'll find plenty going on then.

The *Fun Club* (Alameda de Hércules 86) is a small dance warehouse with a long bar and a little stage, open Thursday to Sunday from around 11.30 pm (9.30 pm on live-band nights) till late. Live bands play Friday and/or Saturday (admission costs 500 ptas to 1000 ptas). Other nights admission is free and it usually gets pretty full (drinks start at 250 ptas). Just south of the Alameda, the mellow *Café Jazz Naima* (☎ 95 438 24 85, Calle Trajano 47) stages occasional live jazz or blues from around 10 pm (free admission).

In El Centro, *Café Lisboa* (Calle Al-hóndiga 43) offers DJ dance nights with varied electronic music from 10 pm Thursday to Saturday.

Discos (Clubs)

These come and go with amazing rapidity. They're places people might think of going to around 2, 3 or 4 am at the weekend. The big noise as we researched this edition was *Luna Park* (Avenida de María Luisa s/n), with three separate halls, including one each for salsa and *bacalao* (Spanish techno). *Boss* (Calle del Betis 67) is the most recent incarnation of a space that has been through many identities and seems to be attracting a less juvenile crowd than it used to. Another possibility, with an extremely mixed clientele, is *Aduana* (☎ 95 423 85 82, Avenida de la Raza s/n), 1km south of Parque de María Luisa.

Theatres

The *Teatro de la Maestranza* (☎ 95 422 65 73, Paseo de Cristóbal Colón 22), the *Teatro Lope de Vega* (☎ 95 459 08 53, Avenida de María Luisa s/n), and the *Teatro Central* (☎ 95 446 07 80) and *Auditorio de la Cartuja* (☎ 95 450 56 56), both on Isla de La Cartuja, all stage music, dance and drama. The Maestranza is big on opera and classical music.

Spectator Sports

The success of the 1999 World Athletics Championships, held in Sevilla's new 60,000-seat Estadio Olímpico, at the northern end of the Isla de La Cartuja, has en-couraged the city to bid for the 2008 Olympics. The decision on the 2008 host city will probably be taken in 2002.

La Teatral ticket agency (☎ 95 422 82 29) at Calle Velázquez 12 in El Centro sells ticket agency tickets for bullfights, soccer games and some concerts at a mark-up of a few hundred pesetas.

Bullfights Fights at Sevilla's Plaza de Toros de la Real Maestranza, on Paseo de Cristóbal Colón, are among the best in Spain. The ring, which holds 14,000 spectators, is one of the country's oldest and most elegant, and its crowds some of the most knowledge-able. The season runs from Easter Sunday to early October, with fights every Sunday, usually at 6.30 pm, and every day during the Feria de Abril and the week before it.

From the start of the season until late June/early July, nearly all the fights are by fully-fledged matadors (every big star in the bullfighting firmament appears at least once a year in the Maestranza). These are the sub-scription *(abono)* fights, for which locals buy up the best seats on season tickets. Often only *sol* seats (in the sun at the start of pro-ceedings) are available to non-subscribers at-tending these fights. They start at about 3000 ptas. The most expensive tickets, if available, cost around 13,000 ptas. Most of the rest of the season, the fights are novice bullfights *(novilleras)* with young bulls and junior bullfighters *(toreros)*. Tickets for these cost from 1500 ptas to 7000 ptas. Tickets are sold in advance at Calle de Adriano 37, and from 4.30 pm on fight days at the ticket win-dows *(taquillas)* at the bullring itself.

For more on the Plaza de Toros de la Real Maestranza, see the El Arenal section ear-lier in this chapter.

Football Sevilla has two professional clubs, Real Betis and Sevilla. Betis have had the upper hand in the past decade, usually occupying a modest First Division place, while Sevilla yo-yoed between the First and Second Divisions. But 1999–2000 was a miserable season, with both clubs being relegated to the Second Division, de-spite Betis having the Brazilian midfield player Denilson (who cost a world record transfer fee of US$35 million in 1997) and top Spanish striker Alfonso on their books.

Betis play at the Estadio Manuel Ruiz de Lopera, beside Avenida de Jerez (the Cádiz road) 1.5km south of Parque María Luisa (bus No 34 southbound from opposite the main tourist office). Sevilla's home is the Estadio Sánchez Pizjuán on Calle de Luis Morales, east of the centre.

Except for the biggest games – against Real Madrid or Barcelona, or when the Sevilla clubs meet each other – you can pay at the gate, from about 2500 ptas. For the big matches, prices may rise to a minimum of 6000 ptas or so, and it's advisable to get tickets in advance.

SHOPPING

Tourist-oriented craft shops are dotted all around the Barrio de Santa Cruz, east of the Alcázar. Many sell attractive local tiles and ceramics with colourful Islamic designs, scenes of old rural life, and so on, as well as a lot of particularly unimaginative T-shirts.

Pedestrianised Calle Sierpes, running north from Plaza de San Francisco in the city centre, is the fanciest shopping street. It's lined with smallish shops devoted to a wide range of everyday and luxury goods, from photo supplies or fashion clothes to antiques or polkadot flamenco dresses *(trajes de flamenca)*. Z Zulategui, No 41, and Sport Zone, No 81, have good stocks of sports and outdoor gear including backpacks. Streets near Sierpes such as Velázquez, Tetuán and Cuna have similar ranges of shops.

The large El Corte Inglés department store – the best single shop to look for almost anything – occupies four separate buildings a little to the west: two on Plaza de la Magdalena and two on Plaza del Duque de la Victoria. Sevilla Rock, just off the latter square at Calle Alfonso XII No 1, is a great music store.

To the north, you can have an interesting browse along Calle Amor de Dios and Calle Doctor Letamendi, near the hub of the city's alternative scene, the Alameda de Hércules. Shops along these two streets specialise in fabrics, jewellery and artefacts

from Africa or Asia, rare music recordings, second-hand clothes, and so on.

Street Markets The Sunday morning flea market at the Alameda de Hércules, with clothes, antiques, music, jewellery and so on, is a good browse, with inviting cafes and bars nearby. At the same time, Plaza de la Alfalfa stages a pet market. The large Thursday market on Calle de la Feria, east of the Alameda de Hércules, is a colourful event also well worth a visit. Plaza del Duque de la Victoria and Plaza de la Magdalena both stage markets of leather bags and belts, hippie-type necklaces and jewellery, and other clothes, Thursday to Saturday.

GETTING THERE & AWAY
Air

Sevilla's San Pablo airport (☎ 95 444 90 00) has a fair range of international and domestic flights. Iberia flies daily nonstop between Sevilla and Valencia/Bilbao/Madrid/ Barcelona with fares starting at 25,000/ 27,000/15,000/24,000 ptas one way or return. There are also Iberia flights between Sevilla and London. Spanair flies most days nonstop to/from Barcelona and Madrid, and Air Europa flies most days nonstop to/from Barcelona (flights cost from 16,500 ptas one way, from 18,500 ptas return) and Palma de Mallorca. All three airlines offer connections to other international and Spanish cities at Madrid and/or Barcelona. Airlines with nonstop international flights include British Airways (to/from London) and LTU (Dusseldorf).

The Iberia office (☎ 95 498 82 08) is east of the centre at Edificio Cecofar, Avenida de la Buhaira. At the airport, Iberia is on ☎ 95 467 29 81. Air Europa tickets are sold at Halcón Viajes (☎ 95 421 44 56), Calle Almirante Bonifaz 3, off Calle Sierpes. Spanair is at the airport, on ☎ 95 444 90 33.

Bus

Sevilla has two bus stations. Buses to/from the north of Sevilla province, Huelva province, Extremadura, Madrid and Portugal use the Plaza de Armas bus station

(☎ 95 490 80 40 or 95 490 77 37) just east of the Puente del Cachorro. Buses to/from most other places in Andalucía and places up the Mediterranean coast use the Prado de San Sebastián bus station (☎ 95 441 71 11) on Plaza San Sebastián, just south-east of the Barrio de Santa Cruz.

From Plaza de Armas there are frequent buses to Huelva (900 ptas, 1¼ hours); a few a day to other places in Huelva province such as La Antilla, Isla Cristina and Ayamonte, Aracena, Minas de Riotinto, El Rocío and Matalascañas; and 11 to Madrid (2745 ptas, six hours). For Extremadura and beyond, about 12 daily go to Mérida (1700 ptas, 3¼ hours), and five or more to Cáceres (2200 ptas, four hours) and Salamanca (3800 ptas), plus a few to Galicia. For information on buses to/from Portugal, see the introductory Getting There & Away chapter.

Plaza de Armas is also the station for frequent buses to Santiponce (for Itálica), and buses to the Parque Natural Sierra Norte.

From Prado de San Sebastián nine or more daily buses run to Cádiz (1385 ptas, 1¾ hours), Córdoba (1225 ptas, 1¾ hours), Granada (2400 ptas, three hours), Málaga (1900 ptas, 2½ hours), Jerez de la Frontera and Sanlúcar de Barrameda; and a few to Arcos de la Frontera and Ronda (1335 ptas, 2½ hours). This is also the station for frequent buses to Carmona, and a few daily to Osuna, Estepa and Écija in Sevilla province; Tarifa, Algeciras and La Línea in Cádiz province; Antequera and the Costa del Sol in Málaga province; and Jaén, Almería, Valencia and Barcelona.

Train

Sevilla's Santa Justa train station (☎ 95 454 02 02) is 1.5km north-east of the centre on Avenida Kansas City. There's also a city centre RENFE information and ticket office at Calle Zaragoza 31, open from 9 am to 1.15 pm and 4 to 7 pm Monday to Friday. Luggage lockers at the station cost 300 ptas to 600 ptas for 24 hours.

Four types of train run to/from Madrid. The best and costliest are the 14 daily super-fast AVEs, taking as little as 2¼ hours. (See The Rest of Spain section and the boxed text 'Train Passes & Discounts', under Land in the Getting There & Away chapter for fares and other information).

Other daily trains from Sevilla include about 20 that go to Córdoba (1090 ptas to 2800 ptas, 45 minutes to 1¼ hours,); up to 15 to Jerez de la Frontera and Cádiz (1125 ptas to 2100 ptas, 1½ to 2¼ hours); three or four to Granada (2415 ptas to 2665 ptas, three hours); five to Málaga (2130 ptas, 2¼ to 2½ hours); three to Huelva (995 ptas, 1½ hours); three or four north to Cazalla-Constantina (660 ptas, 1¾ hours); one to Mérida (1685 ptas, 4½ hours) and Cáceres; and one to Jaén (2255 ptas, three hours). For Ronda or Algeciras, you have to take a Málaga train and change at Bobadilla. Other destinations include Osuna, Antequera, El Chorro, Valencia and Barcelona. For Lisbon (7000 ptas in 2nd-class, 16 hours), you must change at Cáceres.

Car & Motorcycle

Good rental deals are hard to come by. Some of the cheaper firms are to be found along Calle Almirante Lobo off the Puerta de Jerez. Sevilla Car (☎ 95 422 25 87), Calle Almirante Lobo 1, quoted 6960 ptas a day including IVA and insurance for a small car such as a Renault Twingo. They will pick you up or drop you off at the train station for free. Triana Rent A Car (☎ 95 456 44 39), Calle Almirante Lobo 7, is also worth checking. Buizauto (☎ 95 421 18 58), Paseo de las Delicias 1, and Avis (☎ 95 421 65 49), Avenida de la Constitución 15, are also central. Agencies at the train station include Avis (☎ 95 453 78 61), National/Atesa (☎ 95 441 26 40) and Europcar (☎ 95 453 39 14). Several of them are at the airport too, as is Hertz (☎ 95 451 47 20).

Car Pooling Compartecoche (☎ 95 490 75 82), Calle González Cuadrado 49, is an intercity car-pooling service. Its service is free to drivers, while passengers pay an agreed transfer rate. Ring or visit them between 10 am and 1.30 pm or 5 and 8 pm for details.

GETTING AROUND
To/From the Airport

Sevilla airport is about 7km east of the centre on the N-IV Córdoba road. Buses of Amarillos Tour (☎ 902 21 03 17) make the trip between the airport and the Puerta de Jerez (½ hour), in front of the Hotel Alfonso XIII, at least nine times daily (350 ptas one way). A taxi costs about 2000 ptas.

Bus

Bus Nos C1, C2, C3 and C4 do useful circular routes linking the main transport terminals and the city centre. The C1, going east from in front of Santa Justa train station, follows a clockwise circular route via Avenida de Carlos V (close to Prado de San Sebastián bus station and the Barrio de Santa Cruz), Avenida de María Luisa, Triana, Isla Mágica and Calle de Resolana. The C2, heading west from in front of Santa Justa train station, follows the same route in reverse. Bus No 32, from the same stop as No C2, runs to/from Plaza de la Encarnación in the northern part of the city centre.

The clockwise No C3 will take you from Avenida Menéndez Pelayo (near Prado de San Sebastián bus station and the Barrio de Santa Cruz) to the Puerta de Jerez, Triana, Plaza de Armas bus station, Calle del Torneo, Calle de Resolana and Calle de Recaredo. The C4 does the same circuit anti-clockwise except that from Plaza de Armas bus station it heads south along Calle de Arjona and Paseo de Cristóbal Colón to the Puerta de Jerez, instead of crossing the river to Triana.

A single bus ride is 125 ptas. You can pick up a route map, the *Guía del Transporte Urbano de Sevilla*, from tourist offices or from information booths at major stops including Plaza Nueva, Plaza de la Encarnación, and the corner of Avenida de Carlos V and Avenida Menéndez Pelayo.

Car

Underground car parks are not very conveniently placed (one of the better locations is Plaza Concordia) and hotels with parking space usually charge as much as a car park, around 1500 ptas a day, for its use. If you park illegally on the street you risk having your vehicle towed away, which will cost you over 10,000 ptas. If you're staying in the Barrio Santa Cruz, you can usually find a parking place five minutes' walk away, east of Avenida Menéndez Pelayo in streets such as Avenida de Cádiz.

Bicycle

Pedalling your way around Sevilla can be a pleasant way of exploring the city. Sevilla Mágica (☎ 95 456 38 38), Calle Miguel de Mañara 11B, near the main tourist office, rents out decent bikes for 2000 ptas per day, Monday to Saturday.

Taxi

A taxi ride of up to 3km should cost 350 to 400 ptas. Add about 100 ptas per kilometre beyond 3km, and 25% from 10 pm to 6 am and on holidays.

AROUND SEVILLA
Itálica

Itálica, about 8km north-west of Sevilla on the north-western edge of the small town of Santiponce, was the first Roman town in Spain. It was founded in 206 BC for soldiers wounded in the Battle of Ilipa, nearby, in which Rome extinguished Carthaginian ambitions in the Iberian Peninsula. Itálica was also the birthplace of the 2nd-century-AD Roman emperor Trajan, and his adopted son and successor Hadrian (he of the wall across northern England) received some of his education here.

Most of the Romans' original *vetus urbs* (old town) now lies beneath Santiponce. The partly reconstructed ruins you visit are mainly in the *nova urbs* (new town), which was added by Hadrian. They include one of the biggest of all Roman amphitheatres, able to hold 25,000 spectators; a large public bathhouse, the Termas Mayores; and some excellent mosaics. To the west, in the old town, you can also visit a restored Roman theatre.

The site (☎ 95 599 73 76) is open 9 am to 8 pm Tuesday to Saturday, 10 am to 3 pm Sunday and holidays, from April to September; and 9 am to 5.30 pm Tuesday to Saturday, 10 am to 4 pm Sunday and holidays, from October to March. Admission is free for EU citizens with passport or identity card, 250 ptas otherwise. A tourist office (☎ 95 599 80 28) next to the Roman theatre opens 9 am to 4 pm daily except Monday and Saturday.

Frequent buses run to Santiponce from Sevilla's Plaza de Armas bus station.

La Campiña

This is the rolling area east of Sevilla and south of the Río Guadalquivir, crossed by the N-IV to Córdoba and the A-92 towards Granada and Málaga. La Campiña is still a land of huge agricultural estates belonging to a few landowners. Today's successors to the rural revolutionaries of the past are led by the communist villagers of Marinaleda, between Écija and Estepa, who stage periodic occupations of estates to draw attention to the need for land reform.

If you're not in a hurry there are four towns (two on the N-IV and two on the A-92) whose surprisingly grand architecture – though clear evidence of the area's long-standing wealth gap – makes them well worthy of a stop.

CARMONA
postcode 41410 • pop 24,000
• elevation 250m

Carmona stands on a low hill just off the N-IV, 38km east of Sevilla. Fortified as early as the 8th century BC, its strategic position was important to the Carthaginians as well as to the Romans. The latter laid out a street plan which survives to this day. Their Via Augusta, which ran from Rome to Cádiz, entered Carmona by the eastern Puerta de Córdoba and left by the western Puerta de Sevilla.

The Muslims built a strong defensive wall around the town but Carmona fell in 1247 to Fernando III (El Santo, the Saint). In the 14th century, Pedro I (El Cruel) turned Carmona's main fortress (alcázar) into a splendid residence. The town was later adorned

with churches, convents and mansions by Mudéjar and Christian artisans.

Orientation & Information
The old part of Carmona stands on the hill at the eastern end of the town: the Puerta de Sevilla marks its western end. Buses from Sevilla stop on Paseo del Estatuto, 300m west of the Puerta de Sevilla.

The helpful tourist office (☎ 95 419 09 55), in the Puerta de Sevilla, opens 10 am to 6 pm Monday to Saturday, 10 am to 3 pm Sunday and holidays. There are banks with ATMs on Paseo del Estatuto and Calle San Pedro, west of the Puerta de Sevilla, and on Plaza de San Fernando, the main square of the old town.

Roman Necropolis
The impressive Roman Necropolis (☎ 95 414 08 11) is just over 1km south-west of the Puerta de Sevilla, at Avenida de Jorge Bonsor 9. You can climb down into a dozen or more family tombs, hewn from the rock in the 1st and 2nd centuries AD, some of them elaborate and many-chambered. (A torch would be useful.) Most of the dead were cremated and you can see some of the cremation pits, also hewn from the rock. In the tombs are wall niches for the box-like stone urns containing the ashes.

Don't miss the Tumba de Servilia, as big as a temple (it was the tomb of a family of Hispano-Roman bigwigs), or the Tumba del Elefante, with a small elephant statue. The necropolis opens 10 am to 2 pm Tuesday to Saturday from 15 June to 15 September; the rest of the year, 9 am to 5 pm Tuesday to Friday, 10 am to 2 pm Saturday and Sunday (closed holidays). Admission is free to EU passport holders, 250 ptas for others.

Puerta de Sevilla & Around
This impressive main gate of the old town has been fortified for millennia. Today it also houses the tourist office, which sells tickets (200 ptas) for the interesting upper levels of the structure, the Alcázar de la Puerta de Sevilla (open the same hours as the tourist office, see under Orientation & Information for details). This affords fine

CARMONA

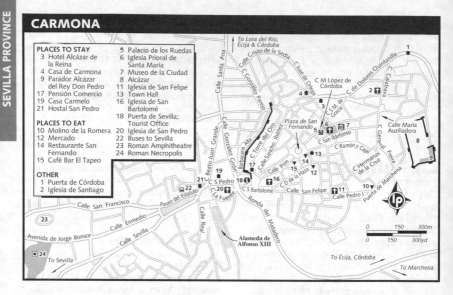

PLACES TO STAY
3 Hotel Alcázar de la Reina
4 Casa de Carmona
9 Parador Alcázar del Rey Don Pedro
17 Pensión Comercio
19 Casa Carmelo
21 Hostal San Pedro

PLACES TO EAT
10 Molino de la Romera
12 Mercado
14 Restaurante San Fernando
15 Café Bar El Tapeo

5 Palacio de los Ruedas
6 Iglesia Prioral de Santa María
7 Museo de la Ciudad
8 Alcázar
11 Iglesia de San Felipe
13 Town Hall
16 Iglesia de San Bartolomé
18 Puerta de Sevilla; Tourist Office
20 Iglesia de San Pedro
22 Buses to Sevilla
23 Roman Amphitheatre
24 Roman Necropolis

OTHER
1 Puerta de Córdoba
2 Iglesia de Santiago

views and includes an upstairs Almohad patio with traces of a Roman temple. An informative leaflet helps you identify the various Carthaginian, Roman, Muslim and Christian stages of the Alcázar's construction.

From the Puerta extend lengthy sections of Carmona's mainly Muslim **walls**. If the tower on the **Iglesia de San Pedro** on Calle San Pedro, west of the Puerta de Sevilla, looks familiar, that's because it's an imitation of Sevilla's Giralda.

Old Town Walking Tour

From the **Puerta de Sevilla**, Calle Prim leads up to Plaza de San Fernando (or Plaza Mayor), whose 16th-century buildings are painted a quaint variety of colours. Just off this square on Calle El Salvador, the patio of the 18th-century **Town Hall**, open 8 am to 3 pm Monday to Friday, contains a large, very fine Roman mosaic showing the Gorgon Medusa surrounded by four other heads.

Heading north-east off Plaza de San Fernando, Calle Martín López de Córdoba leads past the noble **Palacio de los Ruedas** to the **Iglesia Prioral de Santa María**, Carmona's most splendid church. Santa María was built,

mainly in the 15th and 16th centuries, in a typical Carmona combination of brick and stone on the site of the former main mosque. Especially to be admired inside are the fine Gothic pillars and ceiling tracery, the plateresque main retable, and the Patio de los Naranjos by which you enter (formerly the mosque's ablutions courtyard), with a 6th-century Visigothic calendar carved into one of its pillars. The church is open for tourist visits 10 am to 2 pm and 5 to 7.30 pm Tuesday to Saturday, 4.30 to 7.30 pm Sunday, with winter afternoon hours 30 minutes earlier. Admission costs 400 ptas.

Behind Santa María at Calle San Ildefonso 1 is the **Museo de la Ciudad** (City Museum) with archaeological and ethnographic displays, open 10.30 am to 2 pm and 6.30 to 9.30 pm daily except Tuesday afternoon, 1 June to 1 September; 11 am to 7 pm Wednesday to Monday and 11 am to 2 pm Tuesday at other times. Admission costs 300 ptas (free on Tuesday).

From the Iglesia de Santa María, Calle Santa María de Gracia and Calle de Dolores Quintanilla continue to the **Puerta de Córdoba**, an originally Roman gate, with good eastward panoramas.

Moving back uphill and turning southwest down Calle Calatrava you reach the **Iglesia de Santiago**, with a pretty Mudéjar tower tiered in red brick and blue tiles. South from here is the **Alcázar**, the Almohad fort that Pedro I turned into a country palace in a Mudéjar style similar to his parts of the Sevilla Alcázar. Ruined by an earthquake in 1504, the alcázar was in part restored as a parador in the 1970s. With excellent views and a lovely patio, this is a good place to stop for a drink or (if you can afford it) a meal.

From here, start back along Puerta de Marchena on the southern rim of the town, with more good views over the countryside around Carmona. Head into the tangle of streets to see the 14th-century **Iglesia de San Felipe**, with a pretty brick Mudéjar tower and Renaissance facade, and the 15th–18th-century **Iglesia de San Bartolomé**.

Places to Stay

In a lovely tiled old building with a Mudéjar-style entrance arch and brick-pillared patio, is *Pensión Comercio* (☎ 95 414 00 18, Calle Torre del Oro 56). The 14 well-kept, air-conditioned rooms cost 2500/5000 ptas for a single/double, or 6000 ptas for doubles with bathroom (rising to 3000/6000 ptas and 8000 ptas, respectively, from March to May). The restaurant here has very reasonable prices (400 ptas to 550 ptas for most main dishes). The restaurant is closed on Sunday. The smaller *Casa Curmelo* (☎ 95 414 05 72, Calle San Pedro 17) has doubles from 4000 ptas. *Hostal San Pedro* (☎ 95 414 16 06, Calle San Pedro 3) has comfortable if bare doubles with bathroom, TV and air-con for 6000 ptas (9000 ptas in spring).

From there, it's a big jump in price and quality to the historic *Parador Alcázar del Rey Don Pedro* (☎ 95 414 10 10, fax 95 414 17 12, ✉ carmona@parador.es), with 63 rooms costing 14,800/18,500 ptas plus IVA. The *Hotel Alcázar de la Reina* (☎ 95 419 62 00, fax 95 414 01 13, Plaza de Lasso 2) is another beautiful old-town hotel with 60 rooms costing 14,000/17,800 ptas plus IVA.

One of its two patios holds a pool. Yet more luxurious is the 30-room *Casa de Carmona* (☎ 95 419 10 00, fax 95 419 01 89, Plaza de Lasso 1) in a 17th-century mansion. Rooms here cost 23,000/25,000 ptas (34,000/39,000 ptas in spring) plus IVA. The hotel's Web site is at www.casadecarmona.com.

Places to Eat

The bars and cafes around Plaza de San Fernando do raciones and tapas; *Café Bar El Tapeo* has a menú for 1100 ptas. *Restaurante San Fernando*, accessed from Calle Sacramento, is a much classier place with a good 3500-ptas menú of several courses. It opens for lunch and from 9 pm for dinner (closed Sunday evening and all Monday). The three top-end hotels all have fine restaurants (see the preceding Places to Stay section). *Casa de Carmona* offers a choice of menús from 1800 ptas to 4800 ptas plus IVA. The Alcázar de la Reina's *Ristorante Ferrara* is Italian-based, with pasta dishes costing around 1000 ptas.

At *Molino de la Romera*, an interesting 15th-century oil mill building on Puerta de Marchena, you can choose between restaurant, cafe and bar sections; the three-course menú costs 1250 ptas including a drink.

Getting There & Away

Frequent buses run to Carmona from Sevilla (Prado de San Sebastián) for 270 ptas. Linesur (☎ 95 441 14 19) and Alsina Graells (☎ 95 441 88 11) run a few daily buses to/from Écija and Córdoba, stopping on Alameda de Alfonso XIII.

ÉCIJA

postcode 41400 • pop 37,000
• elevation 110m

Écija (**ess**-i-ha) stands on the Río Genil, 53km east along the N-IV from Carmona. It's known both as *la ciudad de las torres*, for its many fine baroque church towers studded with colourful tiles, and as *la sartén de Andalucía* (the frying-pan of Andalucía) for its summer temperatures, which have topped 50°C. The town, now quaintly dilapidated, owes its splendours to the 18th century, when the local gentry splashed out on large mansions, and the church towers were rebuilt following a 1757 earthquake.

The **Town Hall** on the central square, Plaza de España, boasts a Roman mosaic depicting the punishment of Queen Dirce, tied to the horns of a bull. It is open 8 am to 3 pm Monday to Friday. A block south along Calle Cintería is the **Palacio de Benamejí**, Calle Cánovas del Castillo 4, an impressive 18th-century mansion housing the tourist office (☎ 95 590 29 33), the town's archaeological museum (with another Roman mosaic) and an equestrian museum (Écija is a horse breeding centre). All are open 9 am to 2 pm daily except Monday from June to September, and in other month 9.30 am to 1.30 pm and 4.30 to 6.30 pm Tuesday to Friday, 9 am to 2 pm Saturday, Sunday and holidays. Admission is free. The tourist office gives out useful printed material to guide you round town.

Two of the most impressive church towers are on the **Iglesia de Santa María** just off Plaza de España, and the **Iglesia de San Juan Bautista** to the east on Plaza San Juan. Another highlight is the huge **Palacio de Peñaflor** at Calle Caballeros 26, south-east of the main square, with frescos on its curved facade. You can enter to see the grand staircase and the pretty two-storey patio, which houses the town library and two exhibition halls, from 10 am to 1 pm Monday to Friday, 11 am to 1 pm Saturday.

Places to Stay & Eat

The only places to stay in the centre, but both good value, are *Pensión Santa Cruz* (☎ 95 483 02 22, Calle Practicante Romero Gordillo 8), charging 3000 ptas to 3500 ptas for double rooms with shared bathrooms, and *Hotel Platería* (☎ 95 483 50 10, Calle Garcilópez 1A), where good doubles with bathroom cost 6500 ptas to 7500 ptas. Both are within two blocks east of Plaza de España. *Casa Herrera (Plaza de España 41)* serves good fried seafood at moderate prices.

Getting There & Away

Sevibús runs five buses a day to Écija from Sevilla (Prado de San Sebastián). There are three or more buses a day from Córdoba (500 ptas).

OSUNA

postcode 41640 • pop 17,000
• elevation 330m

Osuna, 91km south-east of Sevilla, does not look much from the A-92 but you'll find it a handsome old place with many lovely stone buildings from the 16th to 18th centuries. Several of the most impressive were created by the ducal family of Osuna, one of Spain's richest since the 16th century.

The tourist office (☎ 95 582 14 00), next to the town hall on the central Plaza Mayor, hands out useful little guides in various languages detailing the town's monuments. It opens 10 am to 2 pm and 4 to 7 pm Monday to Saturday (though you may find it opens shorter hours in winter).

Plaza Mayor

The leafy square has the partly modernised 16th-century town hall on one side, a large market building on the other, and the 16th-century church of the Convento de la Concepción at the end.

Baroque Mansions

You can't go inside Osuna's mansions but the facades of a few are particularly worth hunting out. One is the **Palacio de los Cepeda** on Calle de la Huerta behind the town hall, with rows of Churrigueresque columns topped by stone halberdiers holding the Cepeda family coat of arms. The 1737 portal of the **Palacio de Puente Hermoso**, Calle Sevilla 44, a couple of blocks west of Plaza Mayor, has twisted pillars encrusted with grapes and vine leaves.

Moving north from Plaza Mayor up Calle Caballos and its continuation Calle Carrera, you pass the **Iglesia de Santo Domingo** (1531) before you reach the corner of Calle San Pedro (marked by an El Monte bank). At Calle San Pedro 16 the **Palacio del Cabildo Colegial** bears a sculpted representation of Sevilla's Giralda, flanked by the Sevilla martyrs Santa Justa and Santa Rufina. Farther down this street, on the corner of Calle Jesús, the **Palacio de los Marque-**

ses de La Gomera has elaborate clustered pillars, and the family shield at the top of the facade.

Museo Arqueológico

The Torre del Agua, a 12th-century Almohad tower on Plaza de la Duquesa, just east of the Plaza Mayor, houses Osuna's Archaeological Museum. The mainly Iberian and Roman collection includes copies of local Iberian bronzes and reliefs whose originals are now in the Louvre in Paris and Spain's national archaeological museum in Madrid. The museum is open 11.30 am to 1.30 pm and 4 to 6 pm (May to September, 5 to 7 pm), daily except Monday. Admission costs 300 ptas.

Colegiata de Santa María & Around

Osuna's most impressive monuments overlook the centre from the hill above the Museo Arqueológico. Pre-eminent is the Colegiata de Santa María de la Asunción (☎ 95 481 04 44), a 16th-century church containing a wealth of fine art collected by the Duques de Osuna. It opens for guided tours (300 ptas) from approximately 10 am to 1.30 pm and 4 to 7 pm, daily except Monday.

In the main body of the church are José de Ribera's *Cristo de la Expiración*, a marvellous example of this 17th-century painter's use of light/dark contrast; an elaborate baroque main retable; a contrasting 14th-century retable in the Capilla de la Virgen de los Reyes; and, in the Capilla de la Inmaculada, a Crucifixion sculpture attributed to the 17th-century Sevillan Juan de Mesa. The church's sacristy contains, amid much more religious art, four more Riberas. The tour also includes the lugubrious underground Sepulcro Ducal, created in 1548 with its own chapel as the family vault of the Osunas, who are entombed in wall niches. Art down here includes work by the Sevilla sculptor Pedro Torrigiano and the painter Luis 'El Divino' Morales from Extremadura, two leading figures of the Renaissance in Spain.

Beside the Colegiata is the **Convento de la Encarnación**, now a museum with mainly religious art and artefacts, and beautiful old tiles in the cloister – open daily except Monday for the same hours as the Colegiata. Admission costs 250 ptas. Behind the Colegiata, the **Antigua Universidad** (Old University), a square building with pointed towers, was founded in 1549.

Places to Stay & Eat

Pensión-Residencia Esmeralda (☎ 95 582 10 73, Calle Tesorero 7), two minutes' walk south of Plaza Mayor, has respectable singles/doubles with toilet from 1500/3000 ptas to 2000/4000 ptas.

Hostal 5 Puertas (☎ 95 481 12 43, Calle Carrera 79), five minutes' walk north of Plaza Mayor, has smallish but decent rooms with shower and toilet for 2500/5000 ptas (more in April and May). *Hostal Caballo Blanco* (☎ 95 481 01 84, Calle Granada 1), an old coaching inn across the corner, is slightly more expensive at 3500/6000 ptas with bathroom, TV and courtyard parking. The Caballo Blanco has a restaurant too.

Restaurante Doña Guadalupe (Plaza Guadalupe 6), on a small square between Calle Quijada and Calle Gordillo off Calle Carrera, does a four-course menú for 1700 ptas. You can sit in green wicker chairs in the bar area, or in the restaurant behind.

Getting There & Away

The bus station (☎ 95 481 01 46) is on Plaza de San Agustín, a few minutes' walk southeast of Plaza Mayor. Half a dozen daily buses run to/from Sevilla (Prado de San Sebastián), four to/from Estepa and Antequera, and there's also service to/from Málaga.

Three or more trains a day run to/from Sevilla, Antequera, Granada and Málaga: the station (☎ 95 481 03 08) is on Avenida de la Estación in the south-west of town, about 15 minutes' walk from the centre.

ESTEPA

postcode 41560 • pop 11,000
• elevation 600m

Picturesque Estepa, climbing a hill above the highway 24km east of Osuna, was the scene of a mass suicide back in 207 BC when its inhabitants, who had picked the wrong (Carthaginian) side in the Second Punic War, decided not to throw themselves on the mercy of their Roman conquerors. The town has a tourist office (☎ 95 591 27 71) at Calle Saladillo 12.

The most impressive buildings in the lower part of town are baroque: the lavish **Iglesia del Carmen** by the central Plaza del Carmen, and the 18th-century **Palacio de los Cerverales**.

In the upper part of the town – still surrounded by walls and towers constructed by the medieval Knights of Santiago – are the **Torre del Homenaje**, the 14th-century castle keep; the fort-like Gothic **Iglesia de Santa María de la Asunción**, built in the 15th century on the site of a mosque; and, next door to the church, the 16th-century **Convento de Santa Clara** with a lovely patio. Also up here, the **Balcón de Andalucía** mirador has fine views over the countryside and town – including the 18th-century **Torre de la Victoria**, 50m high, which once adorned another convent.

Hostal Balcón de Andalucía (☎ 95 591 26 80, Avenida de Andalucía 11) has doubles costing 5000 ptas.

The buses mentioned for Osuna also serve Estepa.

Parque Natural Sierra Norte

This 1648 sq km natural park, stretching right across the north of Sevilla province, is rolling Sierra Morena country, with no great mountains, but it's attractive, remote and often wild. Much of it is covered in *dehesas*, woodlands of scattered evergreen oaks rising from scrub or pasture. The valleys tend to be more richly vegetated.

Many villages and towns bear a clear Muslim imprint, with forts or castles that go back to Muslim times, part-Mudéjar churches and narrow, zig-zagging white streets. The park is good walking territory, especially around Cazalla de la Sierra and

in the lovely valley of the Río Huéznar. Most visitors are Sevillans in search of fresh air and rural calm.

The heart of the park is around the two main towns, Cazalla de la Sierra and Constantina, which are 20km apart.

Getting There & Away
There's no public transport between the park and Carmona, or east or west into Córdoba or Huelva provinces.

Bus Linesur runs buses between Sevilla (Plaza de Armas) and Cazalla de la Sierra, Constantina (785 ptas, both 1¾ hours), El Pedroso, San Nicolás del Puerto, Alanís and Guadalcanal twice or more daily each way (but at the time of writing there was only one bus back from Cazalla, at 6.30 pm on Sunday and holidays). To/from Las Navas de la Concepción there's one bus daily except Sunday.

Train Cazalla-Constantina station is on the A-455 Cazalla-Constantina road, 7km from Cazalla, 12km from Constantina and 2km from Camping La Fundición (see Places to Stay under Sierra Norte Villages later in this section for details). There are three or four trains daily to/from Sevilla (660 ptas, 1¾ hours), all stopping at El Pedroso. Two a day go on to/from Guadalcanal, and one to/from Mérida and Cáceres in Extremadura.

Currently no bus service links the station with Cazalla or Constantina.

Getting Around
Buses between the small towns and villages have complicated, changing schedules. For up-to-date details contact Linesur in Sevilla (☎ 95 490 23 68) or Bar Gregorio (where the buses stop in Constantina), or try one of the tourist offices. Buses run Monday to Friday between Constantina and San Nicolás del Puerto, Alanís, Guadalcanal and Las Navas de la Concepción. Most buses between Sevilla and Cazalla de la Sierra or Constantina stop at El Pedroso. There's no direct service between Cazalla and Constantina.

CAZALLA DE LA SIERRA
postcode 41370 • pop 5000
• elevation 600m
This pretty little white town, 85km north-east of Sevilla, is the best geared up for visitors in the region. It has a tourist office (☎ 95 488 35 62), open 10.30 am to 2.30 pm daily except Sunday, at Paseo del Moro 2, on the road into town from the south.

Things to See
The most impressive building in Cazalla's tangle of old-fashioned streets is the enormous fortress-like **Iglesia de Nuestra Señora de la Consolación** on Plaza Mayor, a 14th-century Mudéjar and Gothic construction in the typical brick and stone of the region. It was badly damaged in the civil war but has been restored. If its main door on Plaza Mayor is not open, the one on the other side often is. **La Cartuja de Cazalla** is a large 15th-century monastery in a beautiful, secluded nook of the Sierra Morena, 4km from Cazalla (take the A-455 Constantina road for 2.5km, then turn along a signposted side road). Built on the site of a Muslim mill and mosque, the monastery fell into ruin in the 19th century. In 1977 it was bought by a redoubtable art lover called Carmen Ladrón de Guevara, who is devotedly restoring it, in part as an arts and cultural centre – there are a ceramics museum and workshop, an exhibition of work by past artists-in-residence, and a concert room – and has opened a guesthouse to help pay for the project (see under Places to Stay for details). La Cartuja is open for visits 10 am to 2 pm and 5 to 9 pm daily. Admission costs 500 ptas.

Walks
Two tracks lead from Cazalla down to the Huéznar valley and by combining them you can enjoy a round trip of 9km. They pass through typical Sierra Norte evergreen oak woodlands, olive groves and small cultivated plots, and the odd chestnut wood and vineyard. Overhead look for eagles, griffon vultures and the rare black vulture (sometimes the two types of vulture fly together).

One track is the Camino (or Sendero) de las Laderas (also called the Vereda del Valle) which starts at El Chorrillo fountain on the eastern edge of Cazalla at the foot of Calle Parras. The path leads down to the Puente de los Tres Ojos bridge on the Huéznar, from where you go up the west bank of the river a short way, then pass under the Puente del Castillejo railway bridge and head back towards Cazalla by the Camino Viejo de la Estación (Old Station Road).

You can also join this walk from Cazalla-Constantina station by following the 'Molino del Corcho' path down the Huéznar for approximately 1km to the Puente del Castillejo.

Places to Stay
On the main road heading north from the town centre, *Hospedaje La Milagrosa* (☎ 95 488 42 60, Calle Llana 29) has half a dozen small singles/doubles costing 2400/4200 ptas. Much nicer is *Posada del Moro* (☎ 95 488 43 26, fax 95 488 48 58, Paseo El Moro s/n), near the southern entrance to the town, where comfortable rooms with tiled floors, cork-topped furniture and bathroom cost 5000/8000 ptas. The rooms overlook a patio and garden with a pool.

Two kilometres south of Cazalla on the Sevilla road, then 1km east down a dirt road (signposted), *Las Navezuelas* (☎/fax 95 488 47 64) is a restored 17th-century olive oil mill with rooms for 7500 ptas to 8500 ptas a double including breakfast. There's a pool, and a good restaurant.

Hospedería La Cartuja (☎ 95 488 45 16, fax 95 488 47 07) is the guesthouse at La Cartuja de Cazalla (see Things to See). The eight rooms are simple and modern, hung with work by former resident artists. Rooms with bath cost 8500/12,000 ptas for one night including breakfast; the rate goes down if you stay longer. There are also four suites for up to four people. Dinner is 3500 ptas – much of the food is home grown and the dining rooms are in the monastery's old pilgrims' hostel. There's a nice pool too. Check out the Web site at www.skill.es/cartuja.

Places to Eat

For tapas and raciones, there are bars on and near the central pedestrian street La Plazuela. *Cafetería-Bar Gonzalo (Calle Caridad 3)*, a few steps off La Plazuela, does inexpensive meals. If you fancy Italian, head for *Pizzería Mediterránea (Calle Daoíz 30)*. The *Posada del Moro* (see Places to Stay) has a good restaurant with lunch or dinner for around 2500 ptas.

Shopping

Cazalla is known for its *anisados*, aniseed-based liqueurs. Two places you can sample and buy them are Anís Miura, Calle Virgen del Monte 54, and Anís del Clavel, Calle San Benito 8. Miura's *guinda* (wild cherry) anisado is a rich, tasty and heart-warming concoction.

CONSTANTINA

postcode 41450 • pop 7500
• elevation 555m

The likeable valley town of Constantina is the 'capital' of the Sierra Norte. Constantina has a tourist office (☎ 95 588 12 97) at Paseo de la Alameda 7, and the Parque Natural's visitor information centre, the Centro de Interpretación El Robledo (☎ 95 588 15 97), is 1km west along the A-452 El Pedroso road from the petrol station at the southern end of Constantina. Both open rather limited hours – at our last check, El Robledo opened 10 am to 2 pm and 4 to 6 pm Thursday, Saturday, Sunday and holidays, and 4 to 6 pm Friday.

Buses stop at the Bar Gregorio on Calle El Peso in the centre. There are several banks with ATMs on the pedestrianised main street Calle Mesones, just north of the bus stop.

Things to See & Do

The western side of Constantina is topped by a **Muslim fort** surrounded by shady gardens. Below are the medieval streets and 18th-century mansions of the **Barrio de la Morería**. The **Iglesia de Santa María de la Encarnación**, just off Calle El Peso, has a Mudéjar tower topped by a belfry, added in 1568 by Hernán Ruiz, who also did the one atop the Giralda in Sevilla.

The marked walk to **Los Castañares**, north-west from the town's bullring (by the Cazalla road in the north of town), takes you in about two hours up through thick chestnut woods to a hilltop viewpoint, then back down to Constantina's fort.

Places to Stay

The *Albergue Juvenil Constantina (☎ 95 588 15 89, Cuesta Blanca s/n)* has room for 93, all in single or twin rooms. Cuesta Blanca leads uphill behind the petrol station at the southern end of town. *Casa Mari Pepa (☎ 95 588 01 58, Calle José de la Bastida 25)* offers seven good rooms in a modernised old house at 6000 ptas a double with shared bathroom, or 7000 ptas with bathroom, including breakfast.

Places to Eat

Most options are on or near the pedestrianised main street Calle Mesones. *Restaurant Las Farolas (Calle Mesones 14)* serves up good food: the *tortilla espárragos silvestre* (wild asparagus omelette, 700 ptas) followed by the *solomillo de cerdo ibérico al roquefort* (Iberian pork sirloin in Roquefort sauce, 1500 ptas) make a pretty good meal, but there are cheaper options too, including pizzas for around 700 ptas. *Cafetería Mesones 39 (Calle Mesones 39)* is a decent spot for breakfast. The local sweet red wine, called *mosto*, is a good, inexpensive drop.

SIERRA NORTE VILLAGES

The other main settlements in the park are **El Pedroso**, 16km south of Cazalla de la Sierra; **Las Navas de la Concepción**, 22km north-east of Constantina; **San Nicolás del Puerto**, 17km north of Constantina; **Alanís**, 8km north-west of San Nicolás, with a Muslim castle; and **Guadalcanal**, a farther 11km north-west, an ancient mining centre with a castle, medieval walls and Mudéjar churches.

Walks

Fourteen walks of a few hours each are marked out in various areas of the park. They're shown on the IGN/Junta de Andalucía 1:100,000 map *Parque Natural Sierra Norte*, and described in Spanish in the booklet *Cuaderno de Itinerarios del Parque Natural Sierra Norte de Sevilla*. Tourist and information offices in the park should have these for sale, but if you come across them elsewhere, pick them up in case local supplies have run out.

Huéznar Valley It's about 1km up the valley from Cazalla-Constantina station to the Isla Margarita picnic area on an island in the Río Huéznar. From Isla Margarita a path (not included in the *Cuaderno de Itinerarios*) leads up the eastern side of the river all the way to San Nicolás del Puerto: after about 4km it meets the line of a disused railway running to San Nicolás and the old mines of Cerro del Hierro – you can walk along this instead of the path, if you like. Two kilometres before San Nicolás are the impressive Cascada Martinete waterfalls.

Cerro del Hierro The village of this name (meaning Hill of Iron) is a dilapidated ex-mining settlement a short distance east of the SE-163 Constantina-San Nicolás del Puerto road. One kilometre south of the village is a parking area which is the starting point of the marked Sendero de El Cerro del Hierro, a 6.5km loop walk through unusual karstic rock formations and old mining tunnels.

Sendero del Arroyo de las Cañas This 10km triangular marked route, around the country west of El Pedroso, is one of the prettiest in the park. The landscape is notable for its large, curiously shaped, granite rocks.

La Capitana The top of this highest hill in the park (959m) affords tremendous long-distance views over much of the Sierra Norte and north into Extremadura. The 5km walk north-westward to it from Guadalcanal (690m) takes you along the Sierra del Viento, one of the park's most abrupt ranges.

Places to Stay
Situated beside the Río Huéznar, 2km up the San Nicolás del Puerto road from Cazalla-Constantina station is *Camping La Fundición* (☎ 95 595 41 17). It costs around 300 ptas for each person and car, and 350 ptas per tent. The slightly more expensive *Camping Cortijo* (☎ 95 595 41 63), also called Camping Batán de las Monjas, about 5km farther up the same road, has just 20 sites.

In El Pedroso, *Hotel Casa Montehuéznar* (☎ 95 488 90 00, Avenida de la Estación 15), has attractive singles/doubles with bath for 4000/7500 ptas, and a good restaurant specialising in meat and game.

At Las Navas de la Concepción, *Hostal Los Monteros* (☎ 95 588 50 62) has rooms for 5000 ptas a double. San Nicolás del Puerto has a hostal, the *Venta La Salud* (☎ 95 488 52 53), on the Constantina road on the south-eastern edge of town.

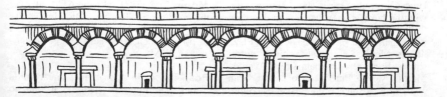

Huelva Province

Most travellers only pass through Andalucía's westernmost province on the way to or from Portugal. But Huelva (**wel**-vah) actually has something for everyone. It contains most of the Parque Nacional de Doñana, whose famous wetlands are a bird habitat of huge international importance. The *lugares colombinos* (Columbus sites), where Columbus planned his 1492 voyage and set sail, will fascinate anyone with a historical leaning. Also along Huelva's coast are around half of the excellent Atlantic beaches of the Costa de la Luz (Coast of Light). The Parque Natural Sierra de Aracena y Picos de Aroche, in the north, is a large area of beautiful, verdant hill country with many good walking routes (and the best *jamón serrano* – mountain ham – in Spain). On the way north, the age-old mining centre of Minas de Riotinto makes an unusual and fascinating stop.

Highlights

- Explore the Parque Nacional de Doñana – a wetland haven for huge numbers of birds and other wildlife
- Absorb the historical significance of the *lugares colombinos* – where Christopher Columbus planned his great voyage and set sail
- Walk in the hills and old-fashioned villages of northern Huelva
- Relax on the long sandy beaches of the Costa de la Luz

Huelva & Around

HUELVA
postcode 21080 • pop 140,000

The provincial capital is a port lying between the Odiel and Tinto estuaries. Industry dominates the approaches to the city, but central Huelva is a likeable and bustling place with an interesting mix of old and new architecture. It was probably founded by the Phoenicians as a trading settlement about 3000 years ago, but much of it was destroyed by the earthquake that devastated Lisbon in 1755.

Orientation

Huelva's central area is about 1km square, with the bus station at its western edge, on Calle Doctor Rubio, and the train station at its southern edge, on Avenida de Italia. Plaza de las Monjas is the unexciting central square. From here the main street, Avenida Martín Alonso Pinzón (also called Gran Vía), leads east and becomes Alameda Sundheim. Parallel to Avenida Pinzón, one block south, is a long, narrow, pedestrianised shopping street that runs through several names, from Calle Concepción to Calle Berdigón.

Information

Tourist Offices Huelva's tourist office (☎ 959 25 74 03) is at Avenida de Alemania 12, a few steps from the bus station. It opens 9 am to 7 pm Monday to Friday, 10 am to 2 pm Saturday.

Money There are banks and ATMs all over the town centre. The bus station has an exchange booth, where you can change cash or travellers cheques daily except Sunday, and an ATM.

Post The main post office, on Avenida Tomás Domínguez, opens 8.30 am to

178

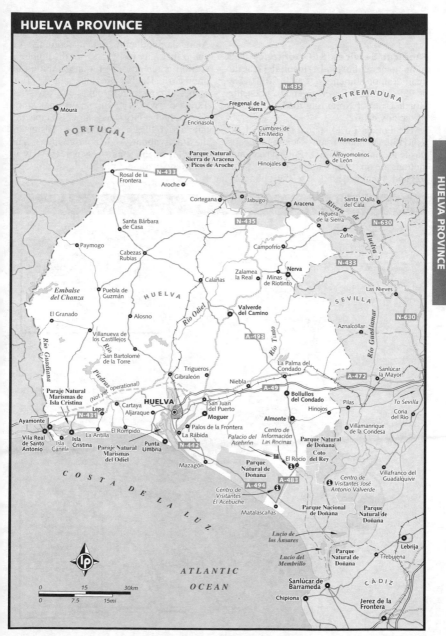

HUELVA PROVINCE

Moura

PORTUGAL

Fregenal de la Sierra

Encinasola

EXTREMADURA

Cumbres de En-Medio

Monesterio

Arroyomolinos de León

Parque Natural Sierra de Aracena y Picos de Aroche

Hinojales

Rosal de la Frontera

N-433

Aroche

Cortegana

Jabugo

Aracena

Santa Olalla del Cala

N-435

Higuera de la Sierra

N-630

Santa Bárbara de Casa

Zufre

Paymogo

Campofrío

Nerva

N-433

Cabezas Rubias

Calañas

Zalamea la Real

Minas de Riotinto

Las Nieves

Embalse del Chanza

Puebla de Guzmán

HUELVA

Río Odiel

Valverde del Camino

SEVILLA

El Granado

Alosno

Aznalcóllar

N-630

Villanueva de los Castillejos

Río Piedras (Not yet operational)

San Bartolomé de la Torre

A-493

Río Tinto

Río Guadiamar

Trigueros

La Palma del Condado

Sanlúcar la Mayor

Gibraleón

Niebla

A-472

Paraje Natural Marismas de Isla Cristina

A-49

Bollullos del Condado

Pilas

To Sevilla

Coria del Rio

Río Guadiana

Ayamonte

N-431

Lepe

Cartaya

Aljaraque

HUELVA

San Juan del Puerto

Moguer

Hinojos

Almonte

Villamanrique de la Condesa

Vila Real de Santo António

Isla Canela

La Antilla

Isla Cristina

El Rompido

Palos de la Frontera

La Rábida

Palacio del Acebrón

Centro de Información Las Rocinas

Parque Natural de Doñana

Paraje Natural Marismas del Odiel

Punta Umbría

N-442

Villafranco del Guadalquivir

Coto del Rey

El Rocío

COSTA DE LA LUZ

Mazagón

Parque Natural de Doñana

A-494

A-483

Centro de Visitantes José Antonio Valverde

Centro de Visitantes El Acebuche

Matalascañas

Parque Nacional de Doñana

Parque Natural de Doñana

Lucio de los Ansares

Lebrija

Lucio del Membrillo

Parque Natural de Doñana

Trebujena

ATLANTIC OCEAN

Sanlúcar de Barrameda

CÁDIZ

0 15 30km

0 7.5 15mi

Chipiona

Jerez de la Frontera

8.30 pm Monday to Friday, 9.30 am to 2 pm Saturday.

Medical Services & Emergency The main general hospital, Hospital General Juan Ramón Jiménez (☎ 959 20 10 88, ☎ 959 20 10 00 for emergency), is on the Ronda Exterior Norte ring road, 4km north of the city centre.

The Policía Local station (☎ 959 21 02 21) is on Avenida Tomás Domínguez, opposite the main post office. Policía Nacional stations are on Paseo Santa Fé (☎ 959 24 05 92) and Avenida de Italia (☎ 959 24 84 22).

Things to See

The **Museo de Huelva** (☎ 959 25 93 00), Alameda Sundheim 13, is undergoing a revamp that may last years, but the highlight section is already open – an exhibition on prehistoric Huelva province and the Tartessos culture which makes the case that Tartessos was a trading port that stood where Huelva city stands now (for more details about Tartessic culture, see History in the Facts about Andalucía chapter). The museum opens 9 am to 8 pm Tuesday to Saturday, 9 am to 3 pm Sunday. Admission is free.

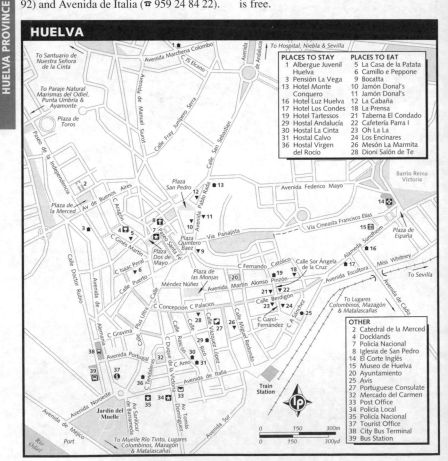

HUELVA PROVINCE

HUELVA

PLACES TO STAY
1 Albergue Juvenil Huelva
3 Pensión La Vega
13 Hotel Monte Conquero
16 Hotel Luz Huelva
17 Hotel Los Condes
19 Hotel Tartessos
29 Hostal Andalucía
30 Hostal La Cinta
31 Hostal Calvo
36 Hostal Virgen del Rocío

PLACES TO EAT
5 La Casa de la Patata
6 Camillo e Peppone
9 Bocatta
10 Jamón Donal's
11 Jamón Donal's
12 La Cabaña
18 La Prensa
21 Taberna El Condado
22 Cafetería Parra I
23 Oh La La
24 Los Encinares
26 Mesón La Marmita
28 Dioni Salón de Te

OTHER
2 Catedral de la Merced
4 Docklands
7 Policía Nacional
8 Iglesia de San Pedro
14 El Corte Inglés
15 Museo de Huelva
20 Ayuntamiento
25 Avis
27 Portuguese Consulate
32 Mercado del Carmen
33 Post Office
34 Policía Local
35 Policía Nacional
37 Tourist Office
38 City Bus Terminal
39 Bus Station

The **Barrio Reina Victoria** (Queen Victoria Quarter), just off the eastern end of Alameda Sundheim, was built in 1917 by the British mining firm Rio Tinto Company for its employees. Its straight streets of cute little cottages – in a kind of hybrid English-Spanish style – make for a curious stroll. Another stroll with Rio Tinto associations is along the **Muelle Río Tinto**, an impressive iron pier curving out into the Odiel estuary about 500m south of the port. It was built for the Rio Tinto Company in the 1870s by George Barclay Bruce, a British disciple of tower specialist Gustave Eiffel.

The **Santuario de Nuestra Señora de la Cinta**, a chapel 2km north of the city centre off Avenida de Manuel Siurot, was visited by Columbus – an event portrayed in tiles here by artist Daniel Zuloaga. Its hilltop position affords good views over the Odiel estuary and the wetlands to the west. Admission is free. City bus No 6 (100 ptas) from the terminal outside the main bus station will take you there.

Special Events
Columbus set off for the Americas on 3 August 1492. Each year, Huelva celebrates the occasion with its Fiestas Colombinas, a week of music, dancing, sport, cultural events and bullfighting (normally around 3–9 August).

Places to Stay
The modern *Albergue Juvenil Huelva* (☎ 959 25 37 93, Avenida Marchena Colombo 14) is 2km north of the bus station. The hostel has room for 128 in doubles and quads, all with private bathroom. City bus No 6 (100 ptas) from the terminal outside the main bus station stops just round the corner from the hostel, on Calle JS Elcano.

Pensión La Vega (☎ 959 24 15 63, Paseo de la Independencia 15), near the Catedral de la Merced, is friendly, with 15 fairly comfortable rooms, though some are rather airless and it can be noisy during weekend nights. Singles/doubles without bathroom cost 1750/3500 ptas; doubles with bathroom are 4000 ptas. Some rooms have TV.
Hostal Andalucía (☎ 959 24 56 67, Calle

Vázquez López 22) has singles/doubles for 2500/3500 ptas without bathroom or 3000/4500 ptas with. Rooms are clean and decent-sized but a bit gloomy.

Most other budget accommodation is in the streets near the Mercado del Carmen, the fish market. *Hostal Virgen del Rocío* (☎ 959 28 17 16, Calle Tendaleras 14) offers bare rooms for 2500/4500 ptas. The doubles have bathrooms. *Hostal Calvo* (☎ 959 24 90 16, Calle Rascón 35) has basic but clean rooms without bathroom for 1200/2400 ptas. *Hostal La Cinta* (☎ 959 24 85 82, Calle Rascón 31) is very similar.

Hotel Los Condes (☎ 959 28 24 00, Alameda Sundheim 14) has 54 air-con singles/doubles with bathroom and TV for 4500/7500 ptas plus IVA, and boasts an economical restaurant.

The three top places, each modern and with over 100 rooms, are: *Hotel Tartessos* (☎ 959 28 27 11, Avenida Martín Alonso Pinzón 13), where doubles cost 12,500 ptas plus IVA; *Hotel Monte Conquero* (☎ 959 28 55 00, Avenida Pablo Rada 10), with similar prices; and the cheaper *Hotel Luz Huelva* (☎ 959 25 00 11, Alameda Sundheim 26), charging 11,500/17,000 ptas plus IVA.

Places to Eat
In the evening, many restaurants and tapas places don't open till 8.30 or 9 pm.

Taberna El Condado (Calle Sor Ángela de la Cruz 3), just south of Avenida Martín Alonso Pinzón, is an atmospheric bar for tapas (from 250 ptas), while the straightforward *Cafetería Parra I* (Calle Sor Ángela de la Cruz 2) is popular for its *platos combinados* (mixed platters) costing 600 to 800 ptas, three-course set lunch (900 ptas), and meat and fish *raciones* (meal-sized servings of tapas) and tapas. *Oh La La* (Calle Berdigón 26), a few steps away, packs 'em in for baguettes and croissants (300 to 475 ptas), and pizza and pasta (500 to 850 ptas). It's one of the few places where you can find a Sunday morning breakfast. *Los Encinares* (Calle Garcí-Fernández 5), nearby, does excellent grills, such as *brocheta de solomillo ibérico con patatas* (brochette of Iberian pork sirloin with chips; 1700 ptas).

Mesón La Marmita (Calle Miguel Redondo 12) is smart but cosy, with red-checked tablecloths, and grills and fish costing 1200 to 1600 ptas. Its lunch *menú* (fixed-price meal) costs 900 ptas plus IVA. The shiny, almost English-style tearoom *Dioni Salón de Te (Calle Palacios 3)* is great to drop into for tea or coffee and a mouthwatering array of cakes and pastries.

La Prensa, near the eastern end of Avenida Martín Alonso Pinzón, is a pleasant cafe plastered with old newspaper pages.

Bocatta (Plaza Quintero Baez) serves excellent hot and cold baguettes for 350 to 680 ptas. North from here, Avenida Pablo Rada is lined with popular eateries, many of them with terraces, where you can eat snacks or sit down to something more substantial. Busy *Jamón Donal's* has branches on both sides of the street, turning out *montaditos* (small open sandwiches, often toasted) for 100 ptas. *La Cabaña* is a bit fancier, with montaditos for 350 ptas, *revueltos* from 900 to 1200 ptas and grills from 1400 ptas.

Camillo e Peppone (Calle Isaac Peral) serves up excellent pasta and pizza for 550 to 1000 ptas. It opens 1 to 4.30 pm and 9.30 pm to 1 am, Thursday to Tuesday; you may have to queue for a table in the evening at weekends. *La Casa de la Patata (Calle Ginés Martín)*, nearby, specialises in baked potatoes, with varied fillings assiduously mashed into the spud, for 150 to 500 ptas. It's closed on Monday.

Entertainment

From around 9 to 11 pm, some of the tapas bars off Avenida Martín Alonso Pinzón, such as *Los Encinares*, *Taberna El Condado* and *Cafetería Parra I* (see Places to Eat), get quite lively. Later, crowds flock to the bars and terraces lining Avenida Pablo Rada and, to a lesser extent, the bars around Plaza de la Merced and in the streets to its south, especially Calle Aragón, where among other spots you'll find the Irish pub *Docklands*.

Shopping

There's an El Corte Inglés department store on Plaza de España. Many smaller shops are strung along the pedestrianised street running from Calle Concepción to Calle Berdigón.

Getting There & Away

Bus Damas services (☎ 959 25 69 00) run frequently to and from Sevilla (900 ptas). For destinations in Huelva province, see those sections later in this chapter. Three or four buses run to Madrid daily, but for other major destinations outside Huelva province, you normally have to change in Sevilla. For services to Portugal, see the Getting There & Away chapter.

Train From the train station (☎ 959 24 56 14) three trains run daily to Sevilla (995 ptas, 1½ hours), an afternoon Talgo 200 goes to Córdoba (2400 ptas, two hours) and Madrid (8300 ptas, 4¼ hours), and two trains head north to Extremadura (see the West of Aracena section later in this chapter).

Car & Motorcycle For car hire, Avis (☎ 959 28 38 36) is at Avenida de Italia 107, and Europcar (☎ 959 28 53 35) and Hertz (☎ 959 26 04 60) are at the train station. Local firms include Auto Alquiler Huelva (☎ 959 28 31 38), in the bus station.

PARAJE NATURAL MARISMAS DEL ODIEL

This 72-sq-km wetland reserve lies across the Odiel estuary from Huelva. The Odiel wetlands are remarkably wild and peaceful, with a large, varied bird population. Some of these birds are easily viewed from a 20km-long road that runs the length of the marshes. In winter there are up to 1000 greater flamingoes, and 400 pairs of spoonbills – about one-third of the European population – are resident. Other birds you may see include the osprey, grey heron and purple heron.

For those with their own vehicle, access is much easier than to the more famous Parque Nacional de Doñana. Take the A-497 Punta Umbría road west from Huelva and, at the far end of the bridge over the Odiel, fork right for 'Ayamonte, Corrales, Dique Juan Carlos I' then immediately left for

HUELVA PROVINCE

Espigón. This curves you back towards Huelva, but instead of re-crossing the bridge take the right turn marked 'Dique Juan Carlos I'. This road leads to the Centro de Visitantes Calatilla (☎ 959 50 09 11), open 8 am to 2.30 pm Monday to Friday (except holidays). You can ask here which of the several paths that strike off from the road farther south are open. Ranging from 1km to 4.5km in length, the paths lead to bird-watching sites and to the excavations of the Almohad town of Shalthis (at the time of writing Shalthis was only open to guided groups – see the next paragraph). It's possible to drive several kilometres along the breakwater at the end of the reserve's southernmost island, Isla de Saltés, but signs warn you that high seas sometimes cover the road.

Erebea SL (☎ 959 50 05 12), at the Centro de Visitantes Calatilla, runs guided trips in the reserve by boat (1800 ptas per person for four hours), by 4WD (2500 ptas) or on foot (900 ptas). If you don't have transport, they may be able to pick you up in Huelva.

LUGARES COLOMBINOS
La Rábida, Palos de la Frontera and Moguer, three of the key sites in the Columbus story, lie along the eastern bank of the Tinto estuary and can all be visited in a fascinating 40km return trip from Huelva. There are accommodation options here too.

Getting There & Away
At least 10 Damas buses run daily from Huelva bus station to La Rábida and Palos de la Frontera; some then continue to Mazagón, but most terminate at Moguer. The last daily bus back to Huelva leaves Moguer at 8.15 pm.

La Rábida
La Rábida is 9km from central Huelva. Just off the main road is a tourist office, the Centro de Recepción (☎ 959 53 11 37), open from 10 am to 8 pm (to 7 pm from mid-September to mid-April), closed Monday.

Monasterio de La Rábida This 14th-century monastery (☎ 959 35 04 11), set in

pleasant park-like grounds a short walk from the Centro de Recepción, was visited several times by Columbus as he attempted to win royal patronage for his projected voyage. Absorbing monastery tours are given in simple Spanish by monks at 10, 10.45 and 11.30 am and 12.15, 1, 4, 4.45, 5.30 and 6.15 pm, Tuesday to Sunday. In August, extra tours may be given later if demand is sufficient. You pay by donation at the end of the tour.

Highlights of the tour include a room of 1930s murals portraying the Columbus story by Huelvan artist Daniel Vázquez Díaz; the monastery church, where Martín Alonso Pinzón is buried and which has a lovely *artesonado* ceiling (see the section on Mudéjar & Mozarabic architecture in the Facts about Andalucía chapter) and a chapel with a 13th-century alabaster Virgin before which Columbus prayed; the peaceful, 15th-century Mudéjar cloister, off which are a room where Columbus and Padre Marchena discussed the projected voyage and the refectory where Columbus ate; and the upstairs Sala Capitular (Chapter House), where Columbus, the Pinzóns and Abbot Pérez discussed final plans for their voyage.

Muelle de las Carabelas Down on the waterfront below the monastery is the Wharf of the Caravels (☎ 959 53 05 97), where you can board accurate replicas of Columbus' three ships and visit an exhibition on his life. From 20 April to 20 September it's open 10 am to 2 pm and 5 to 9 pm Tuesday to Friday, 11 am to 8 pm Saturday, Sunday and holidays. The rest of the year, the hours are 10 am to 7 pm daily except Monday. Admission costs 430 ptas.

Places to Stay Next to the monastery, *Hostería de La Rábida* (☎ 959 35 03 12) has just five rooms, with bathroom, costing 7500 ptas for a single or double. It's a nice place, but usually booked up well in advance. *Hotel Santamaría* (☎ 959 53 00 01), 1km north on the Palos road, has 18 rooms costing 6500 ptas plus IVA per double.

euro currency converter €1 = 166 ptas

The Four Voyages of Christopher Columbus

Christopher Columbus (Cristóbal Colón to Spaniards) was born in Genoa, Italy, in 1451, and gained his early sailing experience in the Mediterranean and on trips to Portugal, England, Iceland and Madeira. In 1484 Columbus presented to Portugal's King João II his idea of reaching the spice-rich Orient by sailing west. The notion that the world was round was already widespread, but Columbus' plan was turned down by João.

In 1485 Columbus travelled to the Franciscan monastery of La Rábida, near Huelva, where one of the monks, Antonio de Marchena, encouraged his ambition. Later, the abbot, Juan Pérez, who happened to be a former confessor of Queen Isabel, took up Columbus' cause. In April 1492 Columbus finally won Spanish royal support and was given a *cédula real* (royal document) ordering the port of Palos de la Frontera, near La Rábida, to put two armed caravels at his disposal. The crown also paid for the use of his flagship the *Santa María*.

Columbus sailed from Palos on 3 August 1492 with about 100 men. His three vessels – none more than 30m long – were the *Santa María*, a *nao* (ship for carrying merchandise) piloted by its owner, Juan de la Cosa from El Puerto de Santa María; the *Niña*, owned by Juan Niño from Moguer and captained by Vicente Yañez Pinzón from Palos; and the *Pinta*, captained by Pinzón's cousin, Martín Alonso Pinzón.

MICK WELDON

The Santa María

After a month in the Canary Islands, Columbus and his crew sailed west in early September. For 31 days they sighted no land and the rebellious crew gave Columbus just two more days. Then, on

Palos de la Frontera

The small town of Palos, 4km north-east of La Rábida, was the port from which Columbus set sail, and provided two of his ships and more than half his crew. Palos' access to the Tinto estuary is now silted up, but the town remains proud of its role in the discovery of the Americas – especially the part played by the Pinzón cousins.

Things to See The central square, where buses stop, boasts a statue of Martín Alonso Pinzón. Moving north-east up Calle Cristóbal Colón, you soon reach the **Casa Museo Martín Alonso Pinzón** at No 24 (between Nos 32 and 36!). Open 10.30 am to 1.30 pm and 5 to 7.30 pm Monday to Friday, this was the home of the captain of the *Pinta* and the place where, an inscription proudly claims, the discovery of America was organised. Admission is free.

Farther along Calle Cristóbal Colón (now heading downhill) is the 14th-century **Iglesia de San Jorge**, open 10.30 am to 1 pm

and 7 to 8 pm Monday to Friday. Columbus and his men took communion in this church before embarking on 3 August 1492 and left the building by the Mudéjar portal facing the small square. Ten weeks earlier, the royal document ordering Palos to help Columbus had been read out in the square. A monument in the square lists 35 Palos men who sailed with Columbus.

A little farther down the street, now within a small park, is **La Fontanilla**, a brick well where Columbus' crews drew water for their voyage. A viewing platform above has a plaque marking the site of the jetty from which the three ships sailed.

Places to Stay & Eat Just off Palos' central square, ***Pensión Rábida*** (☎ *959 35 01 63, Calle Rábida 9*) has singles/doubles without bathroom for 1500/3000 ptas and a cafeteria with platos combinados for 700 to 750 ptas. Farther along the same street is the better ***Hotel La Pinta*** (☎ *959 35 05 11, fax 959 53 01 64, Calle Rábida 79*), with rooms

HUELVA PROVINCE

The Four Voyages of Christopher Columbus

12 October, Columbus landed on the island of Guanahaní, Bahamas, which he named San Salvador. The expedition went on to discover Cuba and Hispaniola, where the *Santa María* sank and its timbers were used to build a fort, Fuerte Navidad.

In January 1493 the remaining two ships left for home, leaving 33 Spaniards at Fuerte Navidad. The *Niña* and the *Pinta* reached Palos on 15 March. Columbus, with animals, plants, gold ornaments and six Caribbean Indians, received a hero's welcome from the Catholic monarchs in Barcelona the following month. Everyone was under the impression he had reached the East Indies.

Late in 1493, Columbus sailed from Sevilla and Cádiz on his second voyage, this time with 17 ships and about 1200 men. The *Niña* was now his flagship. Still in search of Cathay and the Great Khan, he came across Jamaica and other Caribbean islands, but found Fuerte Navidad in ruins, its 33 Spaniards killed. He returned to Cádiz in June 1495.

Columbus sailed west for the third time, with six ships, from Sanlúcar de Barrameda in May 1498. This time he reached Trinidad and the mouth of the Orinoco, but his failings as a colonial administrator led to a revolt by settlers on Hispaniola. Before he could suppress the uprising he was arrested by a royal emissary from Spain in 1500 and sent home a prisoner (though he was released on arrival).

On Columbus' fourth and final voyage, from Sevilla and Cádiz in April 1502, he reached Honduras and Panama, returning to Sanlúcar de Barrameda in November 1503.

Columbus died in 1506 in Valladolid, northern Spain – poor and apparently still believing he had reached Asia. His remains lay at La Cartuja monastery in Sevilla before being moved to Hispaniola in 1536. They were later transported to Cuba, then in 1899 back again to Sevilla and their current resting place in the city's cathedral (unless, as some believe, they were mistakenly replaced with someone else's during their Caribbean wanderings).

costing 6000/10,000 ptas. *Mesón Frenazo*, a few doors farther down the street, serves good meat and fish main dishes from 1000 to 1500 ptas, plus montaditos and other tapas.

One kilometre south of the centre on the Mazagón road, *Hostal La Niña* (☎ 959 53 03 60, Calle Juan de la Cosa 37) and *Hostal Los Príncipes* (☎ 959 35 04 22, Calle Brasil 4), behind La Niña, both have doubles with bathroom for around 4000 ptas plus IVA.

Getting There & Away A Damas bus timetable is posted in the town hall window on the central square.

There are three turnings into central Palos from the La Rábida–Moguer road; the northernmost is right by La Fontanilla.

Moguer

Moguer, 7km north-east of Palos, provided much of Columbus' crew. This pleasant town was also the birthplace and long-time home of the 1956 Nobel literature laureate, Juan Ramón Jiménez (1881–1958). The streets are dotted with plaques that bear quotes from Jiménez' *Platero y Yo* (see Literature in the Facts about Andalucía chapter) and his old home is now a museum.

Orientation & Information Finding your way into town can be tricky, but once you have located the central Plaza del Cabildo, with its statue of Juan Ramón Jiménez, things are straightforward. There's a helpful tourist office (☎ 959 37 23 77), open 10 am to 3 pm Monday to Friday, in the Casa de la Cultura at Calle Andalucía 5, a few steps off the square. It has leaflets for those who wish to follow the Juan Ramón Jiménez trail in detail.

Things to See The pretty, arcaded, cream-and-brown town hall on Plaza del Cabildo is a classic western-Andalucian building.

The 14th-century **Monasterio de Santa Clara** (☎ 959 37 01 07), on Plaza de las Monjas – up the side street almost opposite the Calle Andalucía tourist office – is where

Columbus kept vigil the night after returning from his first voyage, having vowed to do so if he survived a particularly bad storm off the Azores. It's open for guided visits (300 ptas) at 11 am, noon, and 1, 5, 6 and 7 pm, Tuesday to Saturday (except holidays). You'll see a lovely Mudéjar cloister, some of the old nuns' quarters and a worthy collection of religious art.

The **Casa Museo Zenobia y Juan Ramón** (☎ 959 37 21 48) is at Calle Juan Ramón Jiménez 10, a five-minute walk from Plaza del Cabildo (start along Calle Burgos y Mazo and keep going). It's full of interesting memorabilia of the life and times of Juan Ramón Jiménez and his wife, Zenobia Camprubí, and is open for 45-minute guided visits (300 ptas) every hour from 10.15 am to 1.15 pm and 5.15 to 7.15 pm, daily except Sunday afternoon and holidays.

The large, baroque **Iglesia de Nuestra Señora de la Granada**, one block south-east of Plaza del Marqués (which is halfway from Plaza del Cabildo to the Casa Museo), has a tower in imitation of Sevilla's La Giralda.

Places to Stay & Eat Moguer has three solidly decent hostales. *Hostal Lis* (*☎ 959 37 03 78, Calle Andalucía 6*), a sturdy old house with a nice patio, opposite the tourist office, has doubles with bathroom for 2500 ptas plus IVA. *Hostal Pedro Alonso Niño* (*☎ 959 37 23 92, Calle Pedro Alonso Niño 13*), 1½ blocks straight on from the north-eastern end of Plaza de las Monjas, charges 2600 ptas for doubles with shower. The best is *Hostal Platero* (*☎ 959 37 21 59, Calle Aceña 4*) – turn left just before Hostal Pedro Alonso Niño coming from Plaza de las Monjas – where comfy little singles/doubles with bathroom and TV are 2400/3000 ptas plus IVA.

Mesón La Parrala on Calle Fray Andrés de Moguer, just off Plaza de las Monjas, serves up excellent grills and fish, many for under 1000 ptas.

NIEBLA

An interesting stop for travellers between Huelva and Sevilla is this small town on both the A-472 and the railway linking the two cities, 29km out of Huelva. Niebla's 2km ring of Muslim defensive walls remains complete, its 15th-century Castillo de los Guzmanes is one of Spain's biggest castles, and the Mezquita-Iglesia Santa María de la Granada combines the features of a mosque and a Gothic-Mudéjar church in one building.

The municipal tourist office (☎ 959 36 22 70) on Plaza Santa María, in the centre of the walled area, has information on these and other historic buildings. *Pensión Hidalgo* (*☎ 959 36 20 80, Calle Moro 3*) has doubles without bathroom for 2500 ptas.

South-East of Huelva

Running 60km south-east from the outskirts of Huelva to the mouth of the Río Guadalquivir, is a wide, sandy, dune-and-pine-backed beach. Apart from the seaside resorts of Mazagón and Matalascañas, it's almost uninhabited and the final 25km lie within the Parque Nacional de Doñana.

MAZAGÓN
postcode 21130 • pop 130

Of the two coastal resorts, the lower-key Mazagón is the more pleasant. It has a tourist office on Carretera de la Playa, the main street which runs 1km down from the main road, the N-442, to the beach, and a large marina to the right from the bottom of Carretera de la Playa. Mazagón stretches nearly 3km east from here along Avenida de los Conquistadores, but much of it is only two or three blocks deep behind the beach.

East of Mazagón, you can access the **beach** easily beside the Parador de Mazagón, 3km from the town, and at Cuesta de Maneli, 9km beyond, where a 1.2km boardwalk leads across 100m-high dunes. The Cuesta de Maneli beach has a nudist section.

Places to Stay & Eat
Camping Playa Mazagón (*☎ 959 37 62 08, Cuesta de la Barca s/n*) is a couple of min-

utes' walk up from the beach at the eastern end of Mazagón. Despite its 3000-person capacity it can get crowded. **Camping La Fontanilla** (☎ *959 53 62 37*) is just above the beach and accessible from the highway 700m east of Camping Playa Mazagón. Seven kilometres farther is the huge **Camping Doñana Playa** (☎ *959 53 62 81*), with room for 6000. All these camp sites are open year round and charge 500 to 600 ptas plus IVA for each adult, car and tent.

Mazagón has only a few hostales. A good one to try first is **Hostal Álvarez Quintero** (☎ *959 37 61 69, Calle Hernández de Soto 174*), just off Carretera de la Playa, a two-minute walk from the beach. It's plain but decent, with doubles for 2900 ptas without bathroom, or 4500 ptas with bathroom. *Hostal Hilaria* (☎ *959 37 62 06, Calle Buenos Aires 20*), just off Carretera de la Playa farther up the hill, has doubles for 5370 ptas plus IVA, and a restaurant. *Hostal Acuario* (☎ *959 37 72 86, Avenida Fuentepiña 17*), on a pedestrian street east off Carretera de la Playa a bit north of the Hilaria, is a cheap, basic option. Single/doubles cost 2500/5000 ptas.

The nice **Hotel Albaida** (☎ *959 37 60 29*), on the main road 600m east of the town centre, has 24 air-con rooms with bathroom, costing 9500 ptas plus IVA per double, and a restaurant. *Hotel Carabela Santa María* (☎ *959 53 60 18, fax 959 37 72 58*) at the top of Carretera de la Playa near the main road, is a shiny, modern 70-room hotel with air-con doubles at 12,100 ptas plus IVA. The luxurious 43-room **Parador de Mazagón** (☎ *959 53 63 00, fax 959 53 62 28,* ✉ *mazagon@parador.es*) is set in clifftop gardens 3km east of Mazagón, with easy access to the beach below. Singles/doubles cost 15,200/19,000 ptas plus IVA.

Places to eat are mainly on Carretera de la Playa and Avenida Fuentepiña.

Getting There & Away
Monday to Friday, six buses run daily from Huelva to Mazagón via La Rábida and Palos, and vice versa. At weekends and holidays there are three daily in each direction.

MATALASCAÑAS
postcode 21760 • pop 420
This modern resort, with a number of tall hotels, couldn't be in greater contrast to the wildernesses of the Doñana national park, which it adjoins, but it *is* set on an excellent beach.

Orientation & Information
Matalascañas extends 4km south-east from the junction of the A-494 with the A-483 from El Rocío. From this junction Avenida de las Adelfas heads south straight to the beach, passing the tourist office (☎ *959 43 00 86*), which opens 9 am to 2.30 pm Monday to Saturday. Buses stop by the roundabout at the beach end of Avenida de las Adelfas, a spot known as Torre Higuera.

Places to Stay & Eat
The huge **Camping Rocío Playa** (☎ *959 43 02 40*), open year-round and with room for 4000, is just above the beach 1km west of Avenida de las Adelfas. It charges 600 ptas plus IVA for each adult, car and tent. *Hostal Rocío* (☎ *959 43 01 41, Avenida El Greco 60*), just a minute's walk north of the tourist office, has doubles with bathroom for 3500 ptas plus IVA. *Hostal Los Tamarindos* (☎ *959 43 01 19, Avenida de las Adelfas 31*) and *Hostal El Duque* (☎ *959 43 00 58, Avenida de las Adelfas 34*) have doubles with bath for 7000 and 8000 ptas, respectively. *Hotel Flamero* (☎ *959 44 80 20*), on Ronda Maestro Alonso, 1km east along the beach, is one of the more appealing of the bigger hotels, with doubles costing 12,100 ptas.

Several restaurants line up just behind the beach near the end of Avenida de las Adelfas, among them *Restaurante El Pichi*, which offers a three-course menú for 1250 ptas, platos combinados for 800 ptas and good-value raciones.

Getting There & Away
Normally there's one bus daily to/from Huelva (470 ptas) via Mazagón, Monday to Friday, leaving Matalascañas at 7.10 am and Huelva at 2.45 pm. Extra services may run in summer. Buses also link Matalascañas

HUELVA PROVINCE

with El Rocío and Sevilla (see Getting There & Away in the following Parque Nacional de Doñana section).

PARQUE NACIONAL DE DOÑANA

The Doñana National Park, which contains some of Europe's most important wetlands, covers 507 sq km in the south-east of Huelva province and neighbouring Sevilla province. The park is a vital refuge for endangered species such as the pardel lynx and Spanish imperial eagle (with populations here of around 50 and 15, respectively), and a crucial habitat for millions of other birds.

Much of the national park's boundary is bordered by the separate Parque Natural de Doñana, which consists of four distinct zones totalling 540 sq km and forming a buffer for the national park.

Perhaps once the site of fabled Tartessos, and in latter centuries a favourite hunting ground of Spanish nobility and royalty, Doñana was made a national park in 1969, following concern over threats to its wetlands from rice-growing, road and tourism schemes. The World Wide Fund for Nature – then called the World Wildlife Fund – raised much of the cash for the initial land purchases. James Michener, in *Iberia*,

Parque Nacional de Doñana is home to imperial eagles, Europe's most endangered raptor.

writes how members of one Danish shooting club were persuaded to dig into their pockets: 'Gentlemen,' they were told, 'if the lakes of [Doñana] are allowed to disappear, within five years there will be no ducks in Denmark'.

Access to the national park itself is limited. Anyone may walk along the 28km stretch of Atlantic beach between Matalascañas and the mouth of the Guadalquivir (which can be crossed by boats from Sanlúcar de Barrameda), as long they do not stray inland off the beach. To visit the park's interior, you have to book ahead – and pay for – a guided tour. These go from the Centro de Visitantes El Acebuche, on the western side of the park (see the Centro de Visitantes El Acebuche entry later in this section), and from Sanlúcar de Barrameda (see the Cádiz Province chapter). There are, however, several interesting areas bordering the national park which you can visit independently, without paying or booking.

A good base is the village of El Rocío, at the north-western corner of the park. Another possibility is Matalascañas, 16km south-west of El Rocío (see the preceding Matalascañas section).

The Junta de Andalucía 1:75,000 map *Doñana* (1998) shows the national and natural parks and their surrounds in reasonable detail, and on our last visit was on sale at the Centro de Visitantes El Acebuche. The IGN's 1:50,000 *Parque Nacional de Doñana* (1992) covers a smaller area in greater detail.

Flora & Fauna

The national park is a refuge for 125 resident and 125 migratory bird species. Six million birds spend at least part of the year here.

Half the national park consists of wetlands, the marshes of the delta of the Guadalquivir, which enters the Atlantic Ocean at the south-eastern corner of the park. The park contains only about one-tenth of the Guadalquivir *marismas* (marshlands), but most of those outside it have been drained and/or channelled for agriculture.

The park's marshlands are almost dry from July to October. In autumn they start to

Aznalcóllar: The Aftermath

The Parque Nacional de Doñana has always had to battle agricultural and tourism schemes around its fringes that threaten to reduce the flow of water to its *marismas* (marshlands). But the biggest threat to the park's delicate balance came in April 1998, when a dam broke at the Los Frailes heavy-metals mine at Aznalcóllar, 50km north of the park. Nearly 7 million cubic metres of water and mud loaded with acids and heavy metals – left over from the mine's metal-separation processes – flooded into the Río Guadiamar, one of the chief waterways flowing into Doñana's wetlands. Hastily erected dikes prevented the poisonous tide from entering all but a small corner of the national park itself, but up to 100 sq km of wetlands to its north-east were contaminated, and agricultural land bordering about 70km of the river was devastated.

Most of the toxic mud deposited along the Guadiamar valley was removed by fleets of lorries within six months, but biologists and environmentalists feared the effects of the spill could be felt for decades to come, through poisons entering the Doñana area's water table and the food chain of its birds and animals. There was no dramatic increase in mortality, but chronic long-term effects, such as reductions in fertility, were feared.

The disaster provoked typical squabbling between Spain's right-of-centre national government and Andalucía's left-of-centre regional government, the Junta de Andalucía, over how to clean up the mess, who was to blame for it and who should control the park in future (in 1999 the Junta passed a law giving itself full management control, but the national government challenged this in the constitutional court).

At the same time, the disaster catalysed ambitious environmental improvement plans by both governments. The Junta's Corredor Verde del Guadiamar (Guadiamar Green Corridor) project is intended to decontaminate and reforest the 115km course of the Guadiamar all the way downstream from its source in the Sierra Morena. A major part of the decontamination is likely to be carried out by sowing plants of the brassica family, such as cabbage, which can extract metals such as lead, zinc, copper and cadmium from the soil. The heavy deposits of arsenic present a greater problem as no known organism is capable of extracting arsenic. The central government's Plan Doñana 2005, meanwhile, is designed to seal off the national park from the Guadiamar for several years, but ultimately to restore the park's original 19th-century water supplies, including the Guadiamar, to ensure the survival of the marshlands. The cost of these projects, plus that of the initial cleanup and associated work, add up to about US$300 million.

The Los Frailes mine reopened in 1999 amid a chorus of disapproval from ecologists. The mine's toxic waste is now being stored – together with the toxic mud removed from the Guadiamar valley in the initial cleanup – in an old opencast working at the mine, which environmentalists fear is far from safe. The mine, owned by Boliden-Apirsa (the Spanish subsidiary of Boliden Ltd, a Swedish-Canadian company with operations in several countries), employs 500 people and claims that 1800 other jobs depend on it, and is heavily subsidised by the Spanish and Andalucian governments.

fill with water, eventually leaving only a few islets of dry land. Over 500,000 water birds arrive from the north to winter here, including an estimated 80% of Western Europe's wild ducks. As the waters sink in spring, other birds – the greater flamingo, spoonbill, stork, heron, avocet, hoopoe, bee-eater, stilt – arrive for the summer, many of them to nest. Fledglings flock around shrinking ponds called *lucios* in summer. As the lucios dry up in July, herons, storks and kites move in to feast on trapped perch.

Between the marshlands and the park's 28km-long beach is a band of moving sand dunes, up to 5km wide. Winds move the dunes inland at a rate of up to 6m per year: in shallow valleys called *corrales*, between the dunes, grow pines and other trees

HUELVA PROVINCE

favoured as nesting sites by raptors. When dune sand eventually reaches the marshlands, rivers carry it back down to the sea, which washes it up on the beach where the cycle begins all over again. The beach and moving dunes together make up 102 sq km of the park.

In other parts of the park, stable sand supports 144 sq km of *coto*, the favoured habitat of an abundant mammal population – including red and fallow deer, wild boar, mongoose and a handful of *Homo sapiens*. Coto vegetation ranges from heather and scrub through dense wooded thickets to stands of umbrella pine and cork oak.

Centro de Visitantes El Acebuche

El Acebuche (☎ 959 44 87 11) is the national park's main visitor centre and the starting point for tours into the park. Head 12km south from El Rocío on the A-483, then 1.6km west along an approach road. Open daily from 8 am to 7, 8 or 9 pm depending on the season, it includes a cafe, shop and park exhibition, and can provide maps. Short paths lead to hides overlooking a lagoon with birds.

National Park Tours Trips from El Acebuche into the national park are run, in all-terrain vehicles holding about 20 people each, by the Cooperativa Marismas del Rocío (☎ 959 43 04 32). This is the only way for ordinary folk to get inside the park proper except for guided trips from Sanlúcar de Barrameda (see Sanlúcar de Barrameda in the Cádiz Province chapter). You need to book ahead by telephone – for spring, summer and all holiday times the tours can get booked up more than a month ahead, but otherwise a week, sometimes less, is usually adequate. Bring binoculars if you can and, except in winter, mosquito repellent. The trips go at 8.30 am year round, and 3 pm in winter and 5 pm in summer, daily except Monday. They last about four hours and cost 2750 ptas per person. Most guides speak Spanish only. The route normally begins with a drive along the beach to the mouth of the Guadalquivir, then loops

back through the south of the park, taking in moving dunes, marshlands and woods, where you can be pretty certain of seeing a good number of deer and boar. Serious ornithologists may be disappointed by the limited bird-watching opportunities.

Monday to Saturday, on current schedules, the first morning bus from El Rocío towards Matalascañas should get you to El Acebuche in good time for the morning tour.

Centro de Visitantes José Antonio Valverde

Some of the best bird-watching in the Doñana area is to be had at this visitor centre overlooking a year-round lucio on the northern fringe of the national park. Also called the Centro Cerrado Garrido, it's about 30km south of the town of Villamanrique de la Condesa by minor roads and driveable tracks (60km from El Rocío). The Centro de Visitantes El Acebuche has maps and directions.

El Rocío

postcode 21750 • pop 690

Overlooking the marshlands at the corner of the fenced-off national park, El Rocío has a touch of the Wild West about it. Its sandy streets bear almost as many hoofprints as tyre marks and are lined by rows of verandahed houses – far more than El Rocío's permanent population could ever need and most of them usually standing empty. But this is no ghost town, for the houses are in excellent repair: most of them belong to the 90-odd *hermandades* (brotherhoods) of pilgrim-revellers who converge on El Rocío every Pentecost (Whitsuntide) in the Romería del Rocío (see boxed text). Indeed, a fiesta atmosphere pervades the village most weekends of the year as hermandades arrive to carry out lesser rituals.

Information There's a tourist office (☎ 959 44 26 84) at Avenida de la Canaliega s/n, just south of the Hotel Puente del Rey, at the western end of the village. Its hours are 10 am to 2 pm daily (plus 4.30 to 6.30 pm Wednesday). When it's closed, the town

The Romería del Rocío

Like most of Spain's holiest images, Nuestra Señora del Rocío – aka La Blanca Paloma (White Dove) – has legendary origins. Back in the 13th century, the story goes, a hunter from the village of Almonte found her in a tree in the *marismas* (marshlands) and started to carry her home. But when he stopped for a rest, the Virgin made her way back to the tree.

Before long, a chapel was built where the tree had stood (El Rocío) and it became a place of pilgrimage. By the 17th century, *hermandades* (brotherhoods) were forming in nearby towns to make pilgrimages to El Rocío at Pentecost, the seventh weekend after Easter (2–4 June in 2001, 18–20 May in 2002, 7–9 June in 2003). Today, the Romería del Rocío (Pilgrimage to El Rocío) is a vast festive cult that draws people from all over Spain. There are over 90 hermandades, some with several thousand members, both men and women, and they still travel to El Rocío on foot, on horseback and in gaily decorated covered wagons pulled by cattle or horses along cross-country tracks.

Solemn is the last word you'd apply to this quintessentially Andalucian event. In an atmosphere similar to Sevilla's Feria de Abril, participants dress in fine Andalucian costume and sing, dance, drink, laugh and romance their way to El Rocío. The total number of people in the village on this special weekend can reach about a million.

The weekend comes to an ecstatic climax in the very early hours of Monday. Members of the hermandad of Almonte, which claims the Virgin for its own, barge into the church and bear her out on a float. Violent struggles ensue as others battle with the Almonte lads for the honour of carrying La Blanca Paloma. The crush and chaos is immense, but somehow good humour survives and the Virgin is carried round to each of the hermandad buildings, before finally being returned to the Ermita in the afternoon.

hall, on the other side of the hotel, can help with information. National park information is available at the Centro de Información Las Rocinas (see Things to See & Do).

An El Monte ATM on the northern side of the Ermita del Rocío takes major cards.

Things to See & Do The heart of the village is the **Ermita del Rocío**, a church built in its present form in 1964, which houses the celebrated Nuestra Señora del Rocío – a small wooden image, dressed in long, bejewelled robes, which normally stands above the main altar. The church is open from about 8 am to 9 pm daily, with people arriving to see the Virgin every day of the year.

The **marshlands** at El Rocío contain water all year, thanks to the Río Madre de las Marismas which flows through here, so it's nearly always a good place to spot birds and animals. Deer and horses graze in the shallows and you may be lucky enough to see a flock of flamingoes wheeling through the sky in a big pink cloud. The Spanish

Ornithological Society's observatory, the **Observatorio Madre del Rocío** (☎ 959 50 60 93), is by the waterside about 150m east of the Hotel Toruño (see Places to Stay & Eat). It has telescopes and is open to the public from 10 am to 2 pm and 4 to 7 pm Tuesday to Sunday. Admission is free.

The bridge over the river on the A-483 1km south of the village is another good viewing spot. Just past the bridge is the **Centro de Información Las Rocinas** (☎ 959 44 23 40), open 9 am to 3 pm and 4 to 7, 8 or 9 pm depending on the season, daily. From this national park information centre, short paths lead to bird-watching hides by a year-round creek. Though outside the park itself, this section of the creek is in a special *zona de protección* and has fairly abundant bird life.

Six kilometres west along a road from Las Rocinas, in the same zona de protección, is the **Palacio del Acebrón** (an old country lodge used for exhibitions on Doñana, but currently closed for restoration), with a 1.5km walking track through riverbank woodland.

HUELVA PROVINCE

For a longer walk from El Rocío, cross the Puente del Ajolí, at the north-eastern edge of the village, and head along the track into the woodland ahead. This is the **Coto del Rey**, a large woodland zone where you can wander freely for hours. It's crossed by numerous tracks which vehicles might manage in dry seasons. In early morning or late evening you may spot deer or boar.

Discovering Doñana (☎ 959 44 24 66) runs daily **bird-watching trips** in the Parque Natural de Doñana costing 3000 ptas per person, with binoculars, telescopes and field manuals provided. For more information, ask at Pensión Cristina.

You can hire **horses** at various places in El Rocío, including Calle Sanlúcar 75 (☎ 959 45 01 68), one block back from the waterfront at the eastern end of the village, and Doñana Ecuestre (☎ 959 44 24 74), at the Hotel Puente del Rey. Doñana Ecuestre charges 3000/4000 ptas for two/three hours or 12,000 ptas a day.

Places to Stay & Eat Don't bother even trying for a room at Romería time.

Pensión Cristina (☎ 959 44 24 13, Calle El Real 58), a short distance east of the church, has reasonable singles/doubles with bathroom for 3000/4000 ptas, and a decent restaurant where paella, or veal/lamb/venison and chips, costs 700 ptas. **Pensión Isidro** (☎ 959 44 22 42, Avenida de los Ánsares 59), 400m north of the church, also with a restaurant, is a little better, at 3000/6000 ptas.

Hotel Toruño (☎ 959 44 23 23, fax 959 44 23 38, Plaza Acebuchal 22), a short distance east of Pensión Cristina, is an attractive, modern place with 30 air-con rooms at 5850/8000 ptas plus IVA. All have bathroom and some have views of the marshlands. **Hotel Puente del Rey** (☎ 959 44 25 75, Avenida de la Canaliega s/n), by the main road, is bigger, with rooms at 6800/8600 ptas plus IVA (9000/11,300 ptas in August).

Many bars and cafes serve food. **Café Bar El Pocito**, on Calle Ermita just east of the church, does good tapas for 250 ptas, platos combinados and *media-raciones* (half a *ración*) for around 600 ptas, and raciones for around 1000 ptas. **Bar Cafetería El Real**, facing the northern side of the church, is marginally more expensive but offers a particularly wide choice. **Bar-Restaurante Toruño** on Plaza Acebuchal, overlooking the marshlands and with handsome tile-and-wood-beam decor, offers lots of meat and fish main dishes costing between 1300 and 2200 ptas.

Getting There & Away

Bus Damas runs three or more daily buses from Sevilla to El Rocío (660 ptas, 1½ hours), Matalascañas and back. Three to six Damas buses run daily each way along the A-483 between Almonte and Matalascañas, stopping at El Rocío. All these buses will stop outside the Las Rocinas and El Acebuche national park visitor centres (you may have to request this).

From Huelva, take a Damas bus to Almonte (450 ptas, six daily Monday to Friday, but few at weekends), then another from Almonte to El Rocío.

Car & Motorcycle For those wanting to drive between the eastern and western sides of the national park, the farthest point downstream where you can get a vehicle across the Guadalquivir is the ferry at Coria del Río (almost within sight of Sevilla's bridges). The seasonal Barca de la Mínima ferry, shown on some maps east of Villafranco del Guadalquivir, has been out of action for several years, we were told when we tried to cross the river there. Isla Menor, on the eastern bank of the river there, is, however, a very good area for bird spotting. We saw huge numbers of white storks and got close to many seemingly fearless eagles on a drive through the area during December.

West of Huelva

The coast between Huelva and the Portuguese border, 53km to the west, alternates between estuaries, wetlands, good sandy beaches, and small and medium-sized resorts and fishing ports.

They breed 'em big round here! A Toro de Osborne looms over the Cádiz–Tarifa road.

It took over 100 years to build the cathedral in Cádiz, resulting in a curious mix of styles.

Perching high above the Río Guadalete is the old town of Arcos de la Frontera, Cádiz province.

A splash of colour in the centre of Vejer de la Frontera, Cádiz province

Flat out – Gibraltar's tailless Barbary apes (really macaques), Europe's only wild primates

PUNTA UMBRÍA
postcode 21100 • pop 10,800

Punta Umbría, on a point of land between the Atlantic and the Marismas del Odiel, is Huelva's summer playground, 21km from the city by road. It's a modern and pleasant enough resort, though very busy in July and August.

Places to stay include two *camp sites* a few kilometres out of town, off the road from Huelva, and the *Albergue Juvenil Punta Umbría* (☎ 959 31 16 50, *Avenida Océano 13*), close to the Atlantic beach. *Hostal Playa* (☎ 959 31 01 12, *Avenida Océano 95*), *Hostal Emilio* (☎ 959 31 18 00, *Calle Ancha 21*) and *Hotel Ayamontino Ría* (☎ 959 31 14 58, *Paseo de la Ría 1*) have doubles with bathroom for between 7000 and 9000 ptas. The last two are near the estuary on the eastern side of town.

From Huelva, buses run to Punta Umbría every hour from 8 am to 9 pm. In summer, hourly ferries (255 ptas), known as *canoas*, sail from the Muelle de Levante at Huelva port.

EL ROMPIDO
El Rompido, 16km north-west of Punta Umbría, on the Río Piedras estuary, is a fishing and yachting village-cum-minor resort, with several seafood restaurants. The estuary is divided from the ocean by a long spit of land, both sides of which are lined by sandy beaches.

Camping Catapum (☎ 959 39 91 65), which can get crowded, is at the eastern end of the village.

Several buses run daily from Huelva to El Rompido Monday to Friday, but there are only a couple on Saturday, Sunday and holidays. Drivers continuing west along the coast must go inland to the N-431 and turn south again at Lepe.

LA ANTILLA
postcode 21449 • pop 520

La Antilla's holiday chalets and apartments now stretch 9km along the fine, wide, sandy beach that runs all the way from the Río Piedras to Isla Cristina, but the place only extends a few blocks inland. It's a likeable, low-key resort, and out of season almost empty. The more recent Islantilla development at its western end, with a 27-hole golf course, is less sympathetic.

Camping Luz (☎ 959 34 11 42), near the western end of town, charges 2400 ptas plus IVA for two adults with car and tent. There are two other *camp sites*, one at each end of town. At least six *hostales* are bunched near the beach, on Plaza La Parada, with doubles for between 5600 and 7500 ptas plus IVA in summer (but you'd be lucky to get a room in August). For an apartment, try asking at the Islantilla tourist office (☎ 959 64 60 13), 1km west of central La Antilla.

Monday to Friday, several Damas buses run daily to La Antilla from Huelva and Isla Cristina, and two from Sevilla. At weekends and on holidays there's at most one a day from each place.

ISLA CRISTINA
postcode 21410 • pop 17,000

As well as being a beach resort (packed in August), Isla Cristina is enlivened by a sizeable fishing fleet.

Orientation & Information
The main road running east to La Antilla and north to the N-431 passes through the north of town. The bus station – a large white garage with 'Damas SA' on it – is beside this road, just south of the bridge where the fishing fleet moors. The town centre, around Plaza de las Flores, is two minutes' walk from here. Gran Vía Román Pérez heads south for about 1km from Plaza de las Flores to the western end of Isla Cristina's beach. The Oficina Municipal de Turismo (☎ 959 33 26 94) is on Avenida Madrid – 150m east off Gran Vía Román Pérez from the southern end of the Hotel Pato Azul.

Things to See & Do
The **Puerto Pesquero** (fishing port), a couple of blocks west of Plaza de las Flores, is a lively scene in the morning and evening as fishing boats check in with their catches.

North of town, the road towards the N-431 crosses the **Paraje Natural Marismas de Isla Cristina**, which has a rich bird life, including

HUELVA PROVINCE

greater flamingo and spoonbill. Signs 2km from Isla Cristina indicate the **Sendero de Molino Mareal de Pozo del Camino**, a 1km walking track across the marshlands.

Places to Stay & Eat
Camping Giralda (☎ 959 34 33 18), among pines by the main road at the eastern edge of town, has room for 2200 people at around 650 ptas plus IVA for each adult, tent and car. Playa Central is a stone's throw away.

Hostal Gran Vía (☎ 959 33 07 94, *Gran Vía Román Pérez 10*), just south of Plaza de las Flores, about 1.5km from Playa Central, has singles/doubles with bathroom for 3800/6000 ptas plus IVA. The best hotels, all charging 9000 to 10,000 ptas plus IVA for a double with bathroom, are on or just off Camino de la Playa near Playa Central: *Hotel Paraíso Playa* (☎ 959 33 18 73), *Hotel Los Geranios* (☎ 959 33 18 00) and, right on the seafront, *Hotel Sol y Mar* (☎ 959 33 20 50).

Acosta Bar-Restaurante on Plaza de las Flores does good seafood (900 to 1800 ptas), or you could head over to the seafood bars and restaurants on the square outside the Puerto Pesquero, such as *Bar-Restaurante Hermanos Moreno*. There are eateries at Playa Central too.

Getting There & Away
Bus Damas buses (☎ 959 33 16 52) run at least six times daily to/from Huelva (450 ptas), three or more times daily to/from Ayamonte (165 ptas), and one to three times daily to/from Sevilla (1275 ptas).

Car & Motorcycle In your own vehicle, turn off the main road just west of Camping Giralda on the eastern edge of town. For Playa Central (the best beach) turn left almost immediately, at a roundabout. If you continue ahead at the roundabout, you'll approach the town centre along Avenida de España.

AYAMONTE
postcode 21400 • pop 16,000
Ayamonte stands beside the almost-1km-wide Río Guadiana, which divides Spain

from Portugal. A toll-free road bridge crosses the river 2km north of Ayamonte but, if you like doing things the old-fashioned way, the ferry across the Guadiana between Ayamonte and Vila Real de Santo António (Portugal) still runs.

There are no customs or immigration checks heading in either direction by road or ferry.

Orientation & Information
The bus station is on Avenida de Andalucía, 700m east of the central square, Paseo de la Ribera. The ferry dock (*muelle transbordador*) is on Avenida Muelle de Portugal, 300m north-west of Paseo de la Ribera.

The tourist office (☎ 959 47 09 88) is 300m south of Avenida de Andalucía, on Avenida Alcalde Narciso Martín Navarro. It opens 10.30 am to 1.30 pm and 5 to 8 pm Monday to Friday.

In the pedestrianised streets behind Paseo de la Ribera are several banks with ATMs, open for exchange during banking hours Monday to Friday. The souvenir shop at Calle Hermana Amparo 2, 30m behind Paseo de la Ribera, changes money during shop hours.

Beach
Ayamonte's beach is at **Isla Canela**, 6km to the south. It's wide, sandy and several kilometres long, with a small, quite tasteful development of holiday flats and one big, very expensive hotel. From June to September, buses run every half-hour from Ayamonte.

Places to Stay
Just west of the bus station, *Hostal Los Robles* (☎ 959 47 09 59, *Avenida de Andalucía 121*) has doubles for 3700 ptas, or 4800 ptas with bathroom.

Hotel Marqués de Ayamonte (☎ 959 32 01 25, *Calle Trajano 14*), half a block west of Paseo de la Ribera, has plain but decent singles/doubles with bathroom for 2500/5000 ptas plus IVA.

Parador de Ayamonte (☎ 959 32 07 00, ✉ ayamonte@parador.es) at El Castillito, on a hill 1.5km north of the town centre, is modern with rooms costing 12,000/15,000 ptas plus IVA.

Places to Eat
The restaurants on Paseo de la Ribera cater mainly to passing tourist trade. *Mesón La Casona (Calle Lusitania 2)*, a block north, is a better bet. It has a menú for 900 ptas and main dishes from 800 ptas. Many other cafes and bars in the pedestrianised streets behind the square also serve food.

Getting There & Away
Bus Several daily buses run to/from Isla Cristina, Huelva (525 ptas), Sevilla and Madrid. One goes to Málaga at 6.45 am. There are also a few buses along the Algarve and to Lisbon. The bus station (☎ 959 32 11 71) has details.

Boat The ferry to/from Vila Real de Santo António runs at least hourly from about 8 am to 8 pm, depending on demand. One-way fares are 525 ptas (650$00 from Portugal) for a car and driver, 250 ptas (350$00) for a motorcycle and rider, and 135 ptas (160$00) for other adult passengers. Fairly frequent buses and trains run through the Algarve from Vila Real.

The North

The verdant valleys and at times dramatic hills that form Huelva's portion of the Sierra Morena offer some beautiful walks between old-fashioned villages. These hills – relatively rainy and a little cooler than most of Andalucía in summer – form the 1840-sq-km Parque Natural Sierra de Aracena y Picos de Aroche, Andalucía's second-largest protected area.

MINAS DE RIOTINTO
postcode 21660 • pop 5000
• elevation 420m
The town of Minas de Riotinto, 68km north-east of Huelva at the heart of one of the world's oldest mining districts, makes a fascinating stop on the way north. You can ride an early-20th-century train, visit a huge opencast mine and take in an excellent mining museum.

The Río Tinto (Coloured River), which rises nearby, takes its name from the hue of the copper and iron oxides washed into it from the ores of the mining zone.

Copper may have been mined in this district as early as 3000 BC, silver was being extracted before the Phoenicians came here, in around 1000 BC, and iron was mined at least as early as Roman times. After the Romans, the lodes were largely neglected until 1725. In 1872 the mines were bought by the British-dominated Rio Tinto Company. The company turned the area into one of the world's great copper-mining centres, diverting rivers, digging away an entire metal-rich hill – Cerro Colorado – and founding the town of Minas de Riotinto to replace a village they demolished. The mines returned to Spanish control in 1954.

Orientation
Minas de Riotinto is 5km east along the A-461 off the N-435 Huelva–Jabugo road. The Barrio de Bella Vista (see later in this section) is on the left of the A-461, opposite the turning into the town centre. Entering the town, veer right at the first roundabout to reach the Museo Minero, about 400m uphill. Buses stop on Plaza de El Minero, a little beyond the same roundabout.

Museo Minero & Reception Centre
The museum, at Plaza del Museo s/n, is also the reception centre and main ticket office for visits to the Corta Atalaya opencast mine and rides on the old train, the Ferrocarril Turístico-Minero. All three are run by Aventura Minaparque (☎ 959 59 00 25). There are small discounts if you opt for more than one of the three. It's worth ringing ahead to confirm timetables, especially if you plan to ride the train.

Exhibits in the Museo Minero cover geology, the archaeology and history of the mines (including some very ancient tools), and jewellery and statuary of the peoples who lived here. Two rooms are devoted to the railways that the Rio Tinto Company built to serve the mines. At one time, 143 steam engines, mostly British-built, were puffing up and down these tracks. Pride of

HUELVA PROVINCE

place goes to the Vagón del Maharajah, a luxurious carriage built in 1892 for a tour of India by Britain's Queen Victoria. That trip never happened, but the carriage was later used for a visit to the mines by Spain's Alfonso XIII. The museum opens 10 am to 7 pm daily (to 4 pm in July, August and September). Admission costs 300 ptas.

Barrio de Bella Vista

Bella Vista was built in the late 19th century as an exclusive home-from-home for the Rio Tinto Company's mainly British management, with houses, cottages and a Protestant church, all in a kind of Hampstead Garden Suburb style. There's nothing to stop you wandering round the *barrio* (quarter), now inhabited by Spaniards.

Corta Atalaya

This terraced, oval basin, 1.2km long and 335m deep – one of the world's biggest opencast mines – lies 1km west of the town. In the past it yielded huge quantities of copper-bearing iron pyrites, but it sees little mining activity today. Guided visits (600 ptas) depart from the Museo Minero hourly from 11 am to 3 pm daily in July, August and September, and hourly from 11 am to 6 pm (except 3 pm) daily in other months.

Ferrocarril Turístico-Minero

The mine train takes visitors 24km through the scarred landscape of the Río Tinto valley in refurbished early-20th-century carriages pulled by a steam engine of similar vintage. Trips start at Talleres Mina, the old railway repair workshops 2.5km east of Minas de Riotinto, just off the road to Nerva. They depart at 1 pm daily, except Monday, in July, August and September; at 5 pm weekends and holidays from 16 April to 30 June; and at 4 pm weekends and holidays between 1 October and 15 April. Tickets cost 1200 ptas and are available from the Museo Minero.

Corta Cerro Colorado

About 1km north of Minas de Riotinto, the road towards Aracena passes the Corta Cerro Colorado, a vast opencast mine where nearly all the area's mining activity happens today. There's a viewing platform (the Mirador Cerro Colorado) across the road. A century ago Cerro Colorado was a hill.

Places to Stay & Eat

Hostal Galán (☎ 959 59 18 52, *Avenida La Esquila 10*), on the street outside the Museo Minero, has doubles with bathroom costing 4250 ptas plus IVA, and a restaurant and bar serving decent tapas (200 to 250 ptas) and raciones (750 to 1800 ptas). *Hotel Santa Bárbara* (☎ 959 59 11 88, *Cerro de los Embusteros s/n*), on a hilltop at the eastern end of town, offers air-con doubles with bathroom for 6875 ptas plus IVA, including breakfast. It has a pool.

In Nerva, 4km to the east, *Hostal El Goro* (☎ 959 58 04 37, *Calle Reina Victoria 2*) has doubles for 3000 to 3500 ptas plus IVA, and *Hotel Vázquez Díaz* (☎ 959 58 09 27, *Calle Cañadilla 51*) has doubles for 5000 ptas plus IVA.

Getting There & Away

Three or more Damas buses run daily from Huelva to Minas de Riotinto (680 ptas) and Nerva. The last one back leaves Nerva at 4 pm and Minas de Riotinto a few minutes later. Casal runs services from Aracena to Minas de Riotinto (300 ptas, 40 minutes) and Nerva at 9.55 am Monday to Friday and 5.15 pm Monday to Saturday, returning from Nerva at 6 am Monday to Saturday and 12.15 pm Monday to Friday, and from Minas de Riotinto a few minutes later.

From Sevilla (Plaza de Armas bus station) there are two or more Casal buses to Nerva and Minas de Riotinto daily.

ARACENA
postcode 21200 • pop 6700
• elevation 730m

Aracena, the 'capital' of hilly northern Huelva, spreads beneath a hill topped by a medieval church and a ruined castle. Although budget accommodation is limited, it's an obvious initial point to head for in the region.

HUELVA PROVINCE

Orientation & Information

The town lies between the castle hill, Cerro del Castillo, in the south, and the N-433 Sevilla–Portugal road round the east and north. The main square is Plaza del Marqués de Aracena, from which the main street, Avenida de los Infantes Don Carlos y Doña Luisa (more simply known as Gran Vía), runs west. The Casal and Damas bus office and stop is a few minutes' walk south-east of Plaza del Marqués de Aracena, on Avenida de Andalucía.

The Centro de Visitantes Cabildo Viejo (☎ 959 12 88 25), on Plaza Alta, is the main information centre of the Parque Natural Sierra de Aracena y Picos de Aroche, but also has information on Aracena town. Located in Aracena's 15th-century former town hall, it has informative displays in the building's handsome brick vaults. It opens 10 am to 2 pm and 6 to 8 pm (4 to 6 pm in winter) Friday to Sunday and holidays, and also on Wednesday and Thursday for much

of the year. The other tourist office is the Centro de Turismo Rural y Reservas (☎ 959 12 82 06), on Calle Pozo de la Nieve, facing the entrance to the Gruta de las Maravillas. It opens 9 am to 2 pm and 4 to 7 pm daily.

Gruta de las Maravillas

Aracena's 'Cave of Marvels' (☎ 959 12 83 55), carved out of the limestone beneath Cerro del Castillo by millennia of water action, ranks among the most spectacular caves in Spain and attracts 150,000 visitors each year. The 1.2km route open to visitors, featuring 12 chambers and six lakes, has all sorts of weird and beautiful stalactites, stalagmites and rock formations, culminating in the aptly named Sala de los Culos (Chamber of Bottoms). Coloured lighting and piped music heighten the romantic-cum-kitsch effect.

The cave entrance is on pedestrianised Calle Pozo de la Nieve, off Plaza San Pedro in the south-west of town. It's open from

HUELVA PROVINCE

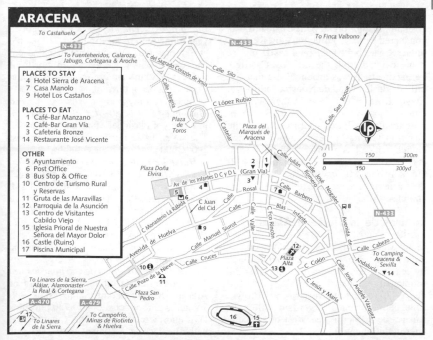

ARACENA

PLACES TO STAY
4 Hotel Sierra de Aracena
7 Casa Manolo
9 Hotel Los Castaños

PLACES TO EAT
1 Café-Bar Manzano
2 Café-Bar Gran Vía
3 Cafetería Bronze
14 Restaurante José Vicente

OTHER
5 Ayuntamiento
6 Post Office
8 Bus Stop & Office
10 Centro de Turismo Rural y Reservas
11 Gruta de las Maravillas
12 Parroquia de la Asunción
13 Centro de Visitantes Cabildo Viejo
15 Iglesia Prioral de Nuestra Señora del Mayor Dolor
16 Castle (Ruins)
17 Piscina Municipal

10.30 am to 1.30 pm and 2.30 to 6 pm daily, with visits – a 60-minute guided tour in Spanish (900 ptas) – about every half-hour weekends and holidays, about hourly on other days. The tours go when there are 25 people: this is no problem in summer, but on a wet Monday in November you might wait all day.

Plaza Alta

This handsome, cobbled square on the slopes of Cerro del Castillo was once the centre of town. On one side stands the 15th-century **Cabildo Viejo** (Old Town Hall – see Orientation & Information). The huge, Renaissance **Parroquia de la Asunción**, at the foot of the square, is built in stone with the brick bands typical of the area's churches. Building of the church began in 1528 and went on into the 17th century, but was never completed. It opens only for Mass, at noon on Sunday and 8.30 pm Monday to Friday (7.30 pm in winter).

Cerro del Castillo

A small Muslim fort atop the castle hill was conquered in the 13th century by the Portuguese, who built their own **castle** before being evicted from the area by Castile's Fernando III. It was around 1300 that the hilltop **Iglesia Prioral de Nuestra Señora del Mayor Dolor** was built, and the castle rebuilt – probably by the Knights of Santiago.

A road from Plaza Alta runs up to the beautiful Gothic-Mudéjar stone-and-brick church, which has a tower with brick tracery and, inside, three rib-vaulted naves. It normally opens 10 am to 7 pm. The ruins of the castle stretch along the hilltop beside the church.

Linares de la Sierra & Alájar Walk

Many walking routes start from Aracena. A good round trip of about 12km can be made by leaving Aracena between the Piscina Municipal (municipal swimming pool) and the A-470 road at the western end of town. This path descends a verdant valley to Linares de la Sierra (see West of Aracena later in this chapter).

To return by the more southerly PRA39 path, find a small stone bridge over the river below Linares, beyond which the path goes round Cerro de la Molinilla, passing old iron mines, and then crosses a stream for a stony ascent to Aracena, bringing you out on the A-479 in the south-west of town.

You could extend the walk by continuing 4km west along the PRA38 path from Linares to Alájar, via the hamlet of Los Madroñeros. There are fine views on this stretch. From Alájar you can walk back the way you came or catch the afternoon bus, daily except Sunday, to Aracena (see Getting There & Away under West of Aracena for bus information).

Special Events

Aracena's main summer fair, with fireworks, music, dancing, funfairs, bullfights and more, happens in the third week of August.

Places to Stay

Camping Aracena (☎ 959 50 10 05), open year round with room for about 270 people at 525 ptas plus IVA for each person, tent and car, is in a valley 500m north of the N-433, 2km east of Aracena. Take the Corteconcepción turning.

Aracena's only budget beds are at *Casa Manolo* (☎ 959 12 80 14, Calle Barbero 6), just south of Plaza del Marqués de Aracena. The seven basic but adequate rooms cost 2000/3400 ptas for singles/doubles.

Hotel Sierra de Aracena (☎ 959 12 61 75, Gran Vía 21) has 43 well-used but comfy rooms, with TV and bathroom, at 4400/6500 ptas plus IVA. There's a cosy lounge but no restaurant. The 33-room *Hotel Los Castaños* (☎ 959 12 63 00, Avenida de Huelva 5) charges 5000/8000 ptas.

Easily the most charming place in the area is *Finca Valbono* (☎ 959 12 77 11, fax 959 12 75 76, Carretera de Carboneras Km 1), a converted farmhouse 1km north of Aracena. Six nice, comfortable rooms with TV and bathroom cost 6000/8750 ptas plus IVA, and there are 14 *casitas* (apartments) with fireplace and kitchen at 10,000 ptas plus IVA for up to four people. Other facilities include a bar, a pool, riding stables and a good, medium-priced restaurant.

Places to Eat

Café-Bar Manzano on Plaza del Marqués de Aracena is a fine spot for varied tapas (150 to 300 ptas), raciones and platos combinados (900 to 1200 ptas). Steak, egg and chips will set you back 1000 ptas. Add 20% for table service.

On Gran Vía, the bustling *Café-Bar Gran Vía* has tons of tapas and raciones – it costs 600 ptas for a prawn salad. The trendier *Cafetería Bronze*, across the street, does pizzas for 800 ptas.

Several restaurants, many of them with platos combinados for 800 to 1000 ptas, line Plaza San Pedro and Calle Pozo de la Nieve near the Gruta de las Maravillas.

A good place to enjoy the area's famous ham and pork is *Restaurante José Vicente (Avenida de Andalucía 53)*. An excellent menú of three courses and a drink goes for 2500 ptas, or you could specialise in a ración of *jamón Jabugo* (Jabugo ham) at 2100 ptas. A la carte main dishes are around 1600 to 2000 ptas.

Getting There & Away

Casal (☎ 959 12 81 96) runs three daily buses to/from Sevilla's Plaza de Armas (770 ptas, 1¼ hours), plus buses to Minas de Riotinto (see that section earlier in this chapter), to villages around northern Huelva province (see the following West of Aracena section) and one daily bus at 10.30 am to Rosal de la Frontera, near the Portuguese border, where you can change to onward Portuguese buses. From the same Avenida de Andalucía stop, Damas runs daily buses to/from Huelva (1070 ptas).

WEST OF ARACENA

West of Aracena stretches one of Andalucía's most unexpectedly beautiful landscapes, a sometimes lush, sometimes severe hill-country region dotted with old stone villages where time seems to have proceeded very slowly. Many of the valleys are full of woodlands, while elsewhere are expanses of *dehesa* – evergreen oak groves where the region's famed black or dark-brown Iberian pigs, raw material of the best ham in Spain, forage for acorns.

Some of the villages date back a long, long time, but others owe their existence to a Castilian repopulation drive after Castile had pushed out Portugal (which had driven out the Muslims) in the 13th century. Most villages grew up around fortress-like churches, or hilltop castles, constructed to deter the Portuguese.

There's an extensive network of marked walking trails throughout the Parque Natural Sierra de Aracena y Picos de Aroche, and particularly between Aracena and Aroche. Most villages are served by buses and many have accommodation, so you can make day hikes or string together a route of several days. It's advisable to phone ahead for rooms.

The N-433 from Aracena to Aroche passes through Galaroza, and close to Cortegana, Fuenteheridos and Jabugo. A more scenic route as far as Cortegana is the A-470 through Santa Ana la Real and Almonaster la Real (passing close to Linares de la Sierra and Alájar). Several roads and paths cut across the hills to link these two roads.

Walking

Information Local availability of maps and leaflets on walking routes is erratic, but you should be able to pick up enough from tourist offices and town halls to find your way around.

The schematic map *Footpaths of the Sierra de Aracena and Picos de Aroche* (in Spanish *Senderos de la Sierra de Aracena y Picos de Aroche*) shows many marked paths in the area, and details their numbers and starting and finishing points. For more information on walks, the best maps we encountered are in a *Senderismo* leaflet (covering 13 routes within about 15km of Aracena) given out by the Centro de Turismo Rural y Reservas in Aracena, and in *Senderos de Pequeño Recorrido en el Entorno de Cortegana*, given out by the Cortegana town hall and covering walks from Cortegana as far as Almonaster la Real,

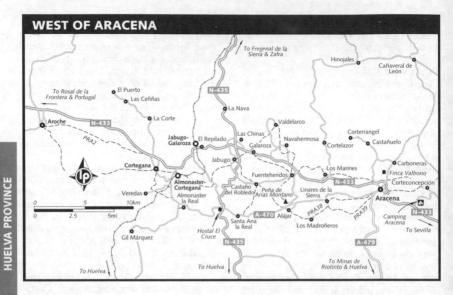

WEST OF ARACENA

Jabugo and Aroche. Also worth having are the SGE 1:50,000 sheets *Aracena*, *Aroche* and *Santa Olalla del Cala*, even though they date from the 1980s, and the *Parque Natural Sierra de Aracena y Picos de Aroche* (1:75,000), published by the Junta de Andalucía in 1998. The latter should be available locally, but the SGE maps aren't.

Routes The possible permutations along the area's paths are endless. In four or five days you could do a fairly easy circuit of about 100km from Aracena to Aroche and back. An obvious route, nearly all off-road, is: Aracena, Linares de la Sierra, Alájar, Castaño del Robledo, Santa Ana la Real, Almonaster la Real, Cortegana, Aroche, Cortegana, Jabugo, Galaroza, Fu-enteheridos, Los Marines, Aracena. See the Aracena section for more on the Aracena–Linares–Alájar stretch. One of the most attractive sections – with lots of varied woodland, streams and fine views – is be-tween Aracena and Castaño del Robledo. The more open country between Cortegana and Aroche provides a contrast. Good north–south trails include Alájar to Fuente-heridos and Castaño del Robledo to Jabugo.

Linares de la Sierra
Seven kilometres west of Aracena on the A-470, a 1km side-road leads down to this poor but pretty little village, surrounded by stone-walled fields in a verdant river valley. The street cobbles are set in patterns in front of many doors – rather like stone door mats. The *bar* on the square next to the church serves food.

Alájar
Five kilometres west of Linares and also off the A-470 in a river valley, Alájar is a big-ger cobblestoned village, clustered around a typical large sierra church.

Almost opposite the Alájar turning on the A-470, another side-road leads uphill towards Fuenteheridos. After 1km this reaches the **Peña de Arias Montano**, a spur of the hillside which supports a 16th-century chapel, the Ermita de Nuestra Señora Reina de los Ángeles. This church, with its 13th-century carving of the Virgin, is the focus of a hectic pilgrimage on 7 September, with Alájar villagers racing up here on horseback. The crag gets its name from Benito Arias Montano, a 16th-century poly-math who – having produced one of the first maps of the world, learned 11 languages and been confessor, adviser and librarian to Felipe II – late in life became parish priest to nearby Castaño del Robledo and made many visits to this spot for retreat and meditation. There are great views from up here, and steps down from the end of the car park lead to a cave where it's said Felipe II spent time in contemplation when visiting Arias Montano.

The cosy *La Posada* (☎ *959 12 57 12, Calle Médico Emilio González 2)*, near Alájar's church, has eight singles/doubles with bathroom costing 4000/5000 ptas plus IVA, and a restaurant with dishes from 700 ptas and a menú for 1500 ptas.

Horses (1000 ptas per hour) and bicycles (500/1500 ptas per hour/day) are available to hire at La Pasoda.

Santa Ana la Real

Santa Ana, 7km west of Alájar, is nothing special. A farther 1.5km west, at the junction of the A-470 and N-435, *Hostal El Cruce* (☎ *959 12 23 33)* has singles/doubles for 2500/5000 ptas, and a restaurant.

Almonaster la Real

This picturesque village, 7km west of Santa Ana la Real, is home to one of the most perfect little gems of Islamic architecture in Spain. The **mosque** *(mezquita)* stands on a hilltop five minutes' walk up from the main square. It's normally open from 9.30 am to 8 pm daily (to 6 or 7 pm in winter). If you find it shut, ask for the key at the town hall on the square (if the town hall is locked, knock on the window to the right of its door).

The mosque was built in the 10th century. In the 13th century the conquering Castilians turned it into a church, but left the Islamic structure largely intact. The building also incorporates bits of an earlier Visigothic church which had stood here, and even earlier stonework from Roman times.

At one side stands the original minaret, a square, three-level tower. You can climb up inside it and look down on Almonaster's 19th-century bullring, adjoining.

As you enter the mosque, you pass beneath an original Muslim horseshoe arch

and a Visigothic lintel carved with a cross and two fleurs-de-lis. The inside is like a miniature version of the great Mezquita in Córdoba, with rows of brick arches supported by varied columns. The capitals of the two columns at the far end of the first row to the left as you enter, and the one at the end of the second row, are Roman. Also at the eastern end is the semicircular *mihrab* (prayer niche), indicating the direction of Mecca. The Christians added a Romanesque apse on the northern side, where parts of a broken Visigothic altar, carved with a dove and angels' wings, have been reassembled.

In the village, the Mudéjar brick-and-stone **Iglesia de San Martín** on Placeta de San Cristóbal has a 16th-century portal in the Portuguese Manueline style, unique in the region.

Casa García (☎ *959 14 31 09, Avenida San Martín 4)*, at the entrance to the village from the A-470, has doubles without/with bathroom for 3000/5000 ptas plus IVA. *Hostal La Cruz* (☎ *959 14 31 35, Plaza El Llano 8)* has a few doubles costing 3000/3700 ptas plus IVA with shower/bathroom. Both places have restaurants.

Cortegana

With 5000 inhabitants, Cortegana, 6km north-west of Almonaster la Real, is one of the bigger places in the district.

The town hall on the central Plaza de la Constitución, open 10 am to 1.30 pm Monday to Friday, hands out a useful map leaflet on walks from Cortegana.

The road up to the town's hilltop 13th-century **castle** is driveable. Next to the castle, the **Capilla de Nuestra Señora de la Piedad**, which dates from the 16th century, has curious modern frescos of sweetly smiling angels. The castle normally opens 10 am to 2 pm and 5 to 7 pm daily except Monday, and contains an exhibition on medieval fortifications in northern Huelva, which was an important frontier zone between Sevilla and Portugal. The chapel is open 9 am to 1 pm and 3.30 to 6.30 pm Monday to Friday, 9.30 am to 1 pm and 4 to 6.30 pm at the weekend.

Also worth a look is the 16th-century

HUELVA PROVINCE

Gothic-Mudéjar **Iglesia del Divino Salvador** on Plaza del Divino Salvador, a brick-and-stone construction with a pointed tower.

Accommodation is limited to **Pensión Cervantes** (☎ *959 13 15 92, Calle Cervantes 27B)*, just off Plaza de la Constitución; doubles without bathroom cost 2700 ptas plus IVA.

Aroche

From Cortegana, the N-433 and the PRA2 footpath run 12km west along a broad, open valley to the friendly little town of Aroche, just 10km from the Portuguese border.

Aroche's **castle**, at the top of the village, was originally built by the Almoravids in the 12th century and has more recently been converted into a bullring. It's normally open 10 am to 2 pm and 5 to 7 pm Saturday, Sunday and holidays. At other times you can ask at the Casa Consistorial (town hall), on the central Plaza de Juan Carlos I, or the Cafetería Lalo, up the steps beside the Casa Consistorial, for a guide to take you up.

Just below the castle is the large **Iglesia de Nuestra Señora de la Asunción**. It is Gothic-Mudéjar in style, but has a 16th-century Renaissance portal. The **Museo del Santo Rosario**, just before the car park as you drive into the village from the N-433, has a collection of more than 1000 rosaries from around the world, some donated by the rich and famous.

At **Hostal Picos de Aroche** (☎ *959 14 04 75, Carretera de Aracena 12)*, on the road up into town from the N-433, doubles with bathroom cost 5000 ptas. **Pensión Romero** (☎ *959 14 00 22)*, on Calle Ordóñez Váldez, just off the same road but a little higher up, has singles/doubles with bathroom for just 1000/2000 ptas. **Centro Cultural Las Peñas**, on Calle Real, does excellent tapas for 125 to 200 ptas.

Jabugo

Just south of the N-433, 10km east of Cortegana, Jabugo (population 2600) is famous throughout Spain for its *jamón ibérico* (see the boxed text 'From Little Acorns, Great

Hams Grow' in the Food & Drink special section).

The village is the main processing centre for hams from the Huelva sierras, and a line of bars and restaurants along Carretera San Juan del Puerto, on the eastern side of the village, wait for you to sample what's acclaimed as the best jamón in the country. At **Mesón Cinco Jotas**, run by the biggest producer, Sánchez Romero Carvajal, a serving of the best ham, *cinco jotas* (5 Js), will set you back 1100 ptas, or you could really 'pig out' on cinco jotas and fried eggs for 1500 ptas. In the bars a *bocadillo* (sandwich) of fine jamón costs 700 or 800 ptas, while shops sell jamón to take away for between 3000 and 5000 ptas per kilogram. The best is *jamón ibérico de bellota* (ham from acorn-fed Iberian pigs). A typical whole ham weighs 7kg or 8kg.

Ham apart, Jabugo is unspectacular. **Pensión Aurora** (☎ *959 12 11 46, Calle Barca 9)* has six rooms with bathroom at 4000 ptas plus IVA for a double. It's between Carretera San Juan del Puerto and the central square, which is called, of course, Plaza del Jamón.

Galaroza

Galaroza is situated a little over 1km cross-country north-east of Jabugo. It is pretty but unexciting, except on 6 September, when villagers throw a great deal of water at each other in the Fiesta del Jarrito. There are three places to stay: **Hostal Toribio** (☎ *959 12 30 73, Calle Iglesia 1)*, in the centre, where rooms with bathroom cost 3600 ptas plus IVA a double; **Hostal Venecia** (☎ *959 12 30 98)*, marginally cheaper, on the N-433; and **Hotel Galaroza Sierra** (☎ *959 12 32 37)*, on the N-433 at the western end of the village, with a pool, garden and doubles for 8000 ptas plus IVA.

Fuenteheridos

Fuenteheridos (population 700), just south of the N-433, is one of the quainter villages in the district. It's reasonably lively down around the wide Plaza del Coso, with its Fuente de los Doce Caños (Fountain of the 12 Spouts), but up around the 18th-century church, where grass grows on the narrow streets, you could be in another age.

Camping-Cortijo El Madroñal (☎ 959 50 12 01), 1km west on the Castaño del Robledo road, is set in ancient chestnut woods and has room for just 60 people at 500 ptas plus IVA for each adult, tent and car. It opens from about 1 July to 15 November. *Pensión Carballos (☎ 959 12 51 08, Calle Fuente 16)*, between Plaza del Coso and the church, has doubles without bathroom for 2800 ptas. Just off the N-433, the *Villa Turística Fuenteheridos (☎ 959 12 52 02)* is a tasteful development of self-catering chalets costing 11,000 ptas plus IVA for two people or 15,000 ptas plus IVA for four. It also has a pool, a restaurant and a cafe.

Several restaurants and bars surround Plaza del Coso.

Castaño del Robledo

This small, impoverished village, on a minor road between Fuenteheridos and the N-435, has a positively medieval feel, with two large churches in states of advanced disrepair and the tiled roofs of houses bending under the weight of the years.

You'll find a couple of bars on Plaza del Álamo, behind the Iglesia de Santiago el Mayor (the church with the pointier tower).

Getting There & Away

Bus Casal (☎ 959 12 81 96) runs buses from Sevilla (Plaza de Armas) and Aracena to many of the villages. At the time of writing there were two buses daily, except Sunday, from Aracena to Cortegana (340 ptas), and two back, via Linares de la Sierra, Alájar, Santa Ana la Real and Almonaster la Real, with one of them continuing to/from Aroche and the other to/from Sevilla. Four buses run daily each way between Aracena and Cortegana, via Fuenteheridos, Galaroza and Jabugo, with two or three continuing to/from Aroche and Rosal de la Frontera and two to/from Sevilla.

Damas buses run each way between Huelva and Almonaster la Real, Cortegana and Aroche (1000 ptas), twice a day Monday to Friday and once on Saturday.

Train Two trains run daily each way between Huelva and Almonaster-Cortegana (760 ptas) and Jabugo-Galaroza (835 ptas) stations, and vice versa, taking about two hours. Both trains from Huelva terminate in Extremadura – one at Fregenal de la Sierra, the other at Zafra. Almonaster-Cortegana station is 1km off the Almonaster–Cortegana road, about halfway between the two villages. Jabugo-Galaroza station is in El Repilado, on the N-433, 4km west of Jabugo.

Cádiz Province

The province of Cádiz (**cad**-i, or even just **ca**-i) stretches from the mouth of the Río Guadalquivir to the Strait of Gibraltar and inland to the rainy Sierra de Grazalema. Its attractions include the historic port of Cádiz, the triangle of sherry-making towns (Jerez de la Frontera, Sanlúcar de Barrameda and El Puerto de Santa María), the long, sandy and little-developed Atlantic beaches along the Costa de la Luz (Coast of Light) and the beautiful, green Sierra de Grazalema with its remote white towns and villages.

The proliferation of 'de la Frontera' place names here dates from the days of the Reconquista (Reconquest). Castile took most of what's now Cádiz province from the Muslims in the 13th century, but the south was then raided repeatedly by the Merenids of Morocco, while to the east lay the Emirate of Granada. Hence for over 200 years this region was one of the frontiers of Christian territory. In the mid-14th century King Alfonso XI offered a free pardon to murderers and criminals who would come here and serve a year and a day in his army. The region still feels untamed today, with windy coasts, large tracts of sparsely inhabited mountain range and big lowland ranches that breed the famous fighting bulls.

CÁDIZ
postcode 11080 • pop 155,000

Few people remember Cádiz when they list the great cities of Andalucía, yet this port is as famous and historic as almost any of them. It's just that it's out on a limb, almost as intimate with the oceans and distant continents as with its own land, and with no Muslim or Reconquista heritage whatsoever.

Once past the desolate coastal marshes and industrial sprawl around Cádiz, you emerge into a largely 18th-century city of decayed grandeur, crammed onto the head of a long peninsula like some huge, over-crowded, ocean-going ship. The people of Cádiz, called *gaditanos*, are mostly an unassuming and tolerant lot whose main concern

Highlights

- Make the trip to Tarifa, an old Muslim town on Spain's southern tip, one of Europe's top windsurfing spots
- Explore the fun-loving, historic port city of Cádiz
- Visit Jerez de la Frontera, famous for its sherry, horses and flamenco
- Enjoy a succulent seafood dinner watching the sun go down over the Río Guadalquivir at Sanlúcar de Barrameda
- Roam the tranquil cork oak forests of the Parque Natural Los Alcornocales
- Unwind on the Atlantic coast – long, sandy beaches and laid back villages

is to make the best of life – whether staying out late to enjoy the after-dark cool in the sweltering summer months, or indulging in Spain's most riotous *carnaval* (carnival; for more details see the Facts for the Visitor chapter) in spring. Cádiz has 36% to 40% unemployment, the highest in Spain, partly due to the decline of the shipbuilding and fishing industries.

History

Cádiz may be the oldest city in Europe. It was founded, tradition says, in 1100 BC by the Phoenicians, who called it Gadir and traded Baltic amber and British tin as well as Spanish silver here. Later, it became a

CÁDIZ PROVINCE

naval base for the Romans, who heaped praise on its culinary, sexual and musical delights. It then faded into obscurity until 1262 when it was taken from the Muslims by Alfonso X.

Cádiz began to boom with the discovery of America. Christopher Columbus sailed from this port on his second and fourth voyages. It attracted Spain's enemies too: in 1587 England's Sir Francis Drake 'singed the king of Spain's beard' with a raid on the harbour, delaying the imminent Spanish Armada. Then, in 1596, Anglo-Dutch attackers burnt almost the entire city.

Cádiz's golden age was during the 18th century when it enjoyed 75% of Spanish trade with the Americas. It grew into the richest and most cosmopolitan city in Spain and gave birth to the country's first middle class of progressive, liberal inclinations. Most of the city's fine buildings date from this era.

The Napoleonic Wars brought British warships back to blockade and bombard the city and shatter the Spanish fleet at the Battle of Trafalgar, nearby, in 1805. After Spain turned against Napoleon in 1808, Cádiz was one of the few cities not to fall to the French, withstanding a two-year siege from 1810.

During this time a national parliament convened here. It was a lopsidedly liberal gathering which adopted Spain's 1812 constitution, proclaiming sovereignty of the people and setting the scene for a century of struggle between liberals and conservatives.

The loss of the American colonies in the 19th century plunged Cádiz into a decline from which it is still recovering.

Orientation

Breathing space between the huddled streets of the old city is provided by numerous squares. From Plaza de San Juan de Dios, towards the eastern end of the old city, Calle Nueva, which becomes Calle San Francisco, leads north-west towards another important square, Plaza de Mina. The train station is in the east of the old city just off Plaza de Sevilla, with the main bus station, of the Comes line, 800m to the north on Plaza de la Hispanidad. The main harbour lies between the two.

The 18th-century Puertas de Tierra (Land Gates) mark the eastern boundary of the old city. Modern Cádiz extends the only way it can – back along the peninsula.

Information

The municipal tourist office (☎ 956 24 10 01), at Plaza de San Juan de Dios 11, opens 9 am to 2 pm, and 5 to 8 pm Monday to Friday. A kiosk opens on the square from 10 am to 1.30 pm and 4 to 6.30 pm (5 to 7.30 pm in summer) at weekends. The well-stocked regional tourist office (☎ 956 21 13 13), at Calle Calderón de la Barca 1, opens 9 am to 7 pm Tuesday to Friday, and 9 am to 2 pm Saturday and Monday.

You'll find banks with ATMs on Avenida Ramón de Carranza and Calle San Francisco, north-west of Plaza de San Juan de Dios. The main post office is on Plaza de Topete. The Policía Local station (☎ 092 in emergency) is at Campo del Sur s/n. The main hospital is the Residencia Sanitaria (☎ 956 27 90 11), 2.25km south-east of the Puertas de Tierra, at Avenida Ana de Viya 21.

Torre Tavira

This highest and most important of the city's old watchtowers, at Calle Marqués del Real Tesoro 10, is a fine place to get your bearings and a dramatic panorama of Cádiz. Its camera obscura projects moving images of the city onto a screen (shown at half-hourly intervals). Back in the 18th century Cádiz had no less than 160 towers to watch over its harbours. The Torre Tavira (☎ 956 21 29 10) opens from 10 am to 8 pm (to 6 pm mid-September to mid-June), daily. Admission costs 500 ptas.

Plaza de Topete

A couple of blocks south-east of the Torre Tavira, this square is one of Cádiz's liveliest, bright with flower stalls and adjoining the large covered Mercado Central (central market). It's still commonly known by its old name, Plaza de las Flores (Square of the Flowers).

Hospital de Mujeres

The real attraction of this 18th-century former women's hospital on Calle Hospital de Mujeres is its chapel (capilla). One of the many profusely decorated churches from Cádiz's golden century, this contains El Greco's *Extasis de San Francisco* (Ecstasy of St Francis), depicting the grey-cloaked saint experiencing a mystical vision. Admission costs 100 ptas. The chapel is open from 10 am to 1 pm Monday to Friday.

Museo Histórico Municipal

The City History Museum (☎ 956 22 17 88), Calle Santa Inés 9, contains a large and detailed 18th-century model of the city, made in mahogany and marble for Carlos III, which would merit a visit even if there were nothing else here. The museum opens 9 am to 1 pm and 4 to 7 pm Tuesday to Friday (5 to 8 pm June to September), and 9 am to 1 pm Saturday and Sunday. Admission is free.

Oratorio de San Felipe Neri

Also on Calle Santa Inés, this is one of Cádiz's finest baroque churches and was also the meeting place of the 1812 parliament.

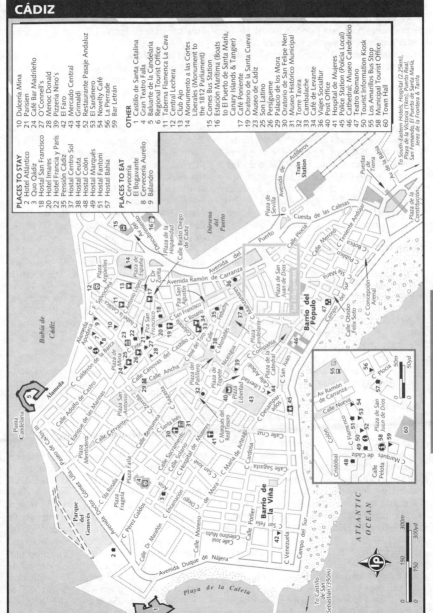

CÁDIZ

PLACES TO STAY
2 Hotel Atlántico
3 Quo Qádiz
18 Hostal San Francisco
20 Hotel Imares
22 Hotel Francia y París
35 Pensión Cádiz
37 Hostal Centro Sol
38 Hostal Ceuta
48 Hostal Colón
49 Hostal Marqués
51 Hostal Fantoni
57 Hostal Bahia

PLACES TO EAT
7 Cervecería
    El Bogavante
8 Cervecería Aurelio
9 Balandro

10 Dulcería Mina
21 Parisién
24 Café Bar Madrileño
27 O'Connell's
28 Menoc Donald
39 Pizzeria Nino's
42 El Faro
43 Mercado Central
44 Grimaldi
52 Restaurante Pasaje Andaluz
53 El Sardinero
54 Novelty Café
56 La Pierrade
59 Bar Letrán

OTHER
1 Castillo de Santa Catalina
4 Gran Teatro Falla
5 Baluarte de la Candelaria
6 Regional Tourist Office
11 Taberna Flamenca La Cava
12 Central Lechera
13 Club Ajo
14 Monumento a las Cortes
    Liberales (Monument to
    the 1812 Parliament)
15 Estación Marítima (Boats
    to El Puerto de Santa María,
    Canary Islands & Tangier)
16 Comes Bus Station
17 Oratorio de la Santa Cueva
19 Oratorio de San Felipe Neri
23 Museo de Cádiz
25 Son Latino
26 Persígueme
29 Palacio de los Mora
30 Oratorio de San Felipe Neri
31 Museo Histórico Municipal
32 Torre Tavira
33 Cambalache
34 Café de Levante
36 Viajes Socialtur
40 Post Office
41 Hospital de Mujeres
45 Police Station (Policía Local)
46 Cathedral; Museo Catedralicio
47 Teatro Romano
50 Tourist Information Kiosk
55 Los Amarillos Bus Stop
58 Municipal Tourist Office
60 Town Hall

CÁDIZ PROVINCE

euro currency converter €1 = 166 ptas

The interior has an unusual oval shape and a beautiful dome. One of Murillo's masterpieces, an Inmaculada Concepción of 1680, has a place of honour in the main retable. The church opens 10 am to 1.30 pm Monday to Saturday. Admission costs 150 ptas.

Calle Ancha

A couple of blocks east of the Oratorio de San Felipe Neri is Calle Ancha, the main street of late-18th- and early-19th-century Cádiz. Its cafes and bars were the unofficial gathering and debating places for members of the 1812 parliament. The **Palacio de los Mora** at No 28–30 is one of the most sumptuous of Cádiz's urban mansions, built in the eclectic Isabelline style of the mid-19th century. At the time of writing it was closed for reconstruction.

Oratorio de la Santa Cueva

This 1780's neo-classical church, attached to the Iglesia del Rosario on Calle Rosario, is a two-in-one affair, with the austere underground Capilla Baja contrasting sharply with the richly decorated oval-shaped upper Capilla Alta. Framed by three of the Capilla Alta's eight arches are paintings by Goya depicting the Miracle of the Loaves and Fishes, the Guest at the Wedding, and the Last Supper. The church opens 10 am to 1 pm Monday to Friday. Admission is free.

Museo de Cádiz

The city's major museum (☎ 956 21 22 81) is on one of its most attractive squares, Plaza de Mina. Pride of the ground-floor archaeology section is a pair of Phoenician white-stone sarcophagi carved in human likeness. There's also some beautiful Phoenician jewellery and Roman glassware, and lots of headless Roman statues – plus Emperor Trajan, with head, from Baelo Claudia (see the Bolonia section later in this chapter).

A highlight of the 2nd-floor fine arts collection is a group of 21 superb canvases of saints, angels and monks by Zurbarán. The museum also has a room of beautiful old puppets used in satirical puppet theatre in Cádiz. It opens 2.30 to 8 pm Tuesday, 9 am to 8 pm Wednesday to Saturday and 9.30 am to 2.30 pm Sunday. Admission is free for EU residents (250 ptas for others).

Coastal Walk

Head one block north of Plaza de Mina to emerge on the city's northern seafront, with views across the Bahía de Cádiz to El Puerto de Santa María. From here you could head west along the **Alameda** garden to the **Baluarte de la Candelaria** bastion, then south-west beside the sea wall to the **Parque del Genovés**, which was laid out, like the Alameda, in the 19th century. From the park, Avenida Duque de Nájera leads south to **Playa de la Caleta** (very crowded in the summer), on a bay between two forts. The star-shaped **Castillo de Santa Catalina**, built in 1598, at the northern end of the beach, was for a long time Cádiz's main citadel. It opens 10 am to 6 pm Monday to Friday, and 10 am to 1 pm at the weekend. Admission is free. The **Castillo de San Sebastián**, far out on the southern side of the bay, is in military use and usually closed to the public. From Playa de la Caleta you can follow the coast eastwards to the cathedral.

Cathedral & Around

The story of Cádiz's yellow-domed cathedral on Plaza de la Catedral reflects that of the whole city in the 18th and 19th centuries. The decision to build it was taken in 1716 on the strength of the imminent transfer from Sevilla to Cádiz of the Casa de la Contratación, which controlled Spanish trade with the Americas. But the cathedral wasn't finished till 1838, by which time not only had neo-classical elements diluted Vicente Arturo's original baroque design, but funds had dried up, forcing cutbacks in size and quality. It's still a large and impressive construction, with little ornamentation to distract from the grandeur of the marble and stone interior, lit from the 50m-high main dome. The Cádiz-born composer Manuel de Falla is buried in the crypt. The cathedral opens to visitors 10 am to 1 pm and 5.30 to 7 pm Monday to Saturday. The attached **Museo Catedralicio**, open 10 am to 1 pm

Tuesday to Saturday, contains some very large and lavish monstrances. Admission costs 500 ptas.

A short distance east along Campo del Sur are the excavated remains of a Roman theatre, the **Teatro Romano**, open 11 am to 1.30 pm Tuesday to Sunday. Admission is free.

Plaza de San Juan de Dios & Around

The shabby **Barrio del Pópulo** district between the Teatro Romano and Plaza de San Juan de Dios was the kernel of medieval Cádiz, a fortified enclosure wrecked in 1596. Its three 13th-century gates, the Arco de los Blancos, Arco de la Rosa and Arco del Pópulo, however, remain. Plaza de San Juan de Dios is dominated by the imposing neoclassical town hall built around 1800.

If by now you're in need of a cool, quiet and leafy resting spot, the bougainvillea-shaded benches in **Plaza Candelaria**, 250m north-west of Plaza de San Juan de Dios, fit the bill very nicely.

Playa de la Victoria

This wide beach stretches many kilometres back down the ocean side of the peninsula, beginning about 1km beyond the Puertas de Tierra. On hot summer weekends almost the whole city seems to be out here. Bus No 1 'Plaza España-Cortadura' from Plaza de España runs along the peninsula one or two blocks inland from the beach.

La Ruta de Camarón

A handful of sites associated with the legendary flamenco singer El Camarón de la Isla (died 1992) in his home town of San Fernando, 13km south-east of Cádiz, are linked together in the self-guided Ruta de Camarón. You can pick up a leaflet with a description and map of the route at Cádiz's regional tourist office.

Language Courses

Cádiz's most popular language school is Gadir Escuela Internacional de Español (☎/fax 956 26 05 57, ✆ gadir@arrakis .es), Calle Pérgolas 5. Two weeks' intensive

classes (five hours daily) in a small group cost 46,250 ptas in summer. The postal address is Apartado de Correos 31, Cádiz 11007.

Special Events

No other Spanish city celebrates Carnaval with the verve of Cádiz, where it turns into a 10-day singing, dancing and drinking fancy-dress party that continues until the weekend after the normal Shrove Tuesday close. Everyone – locals and visitors – dresses up, and the fun, abetted by enormous quantities of alcohol, is infectious. Costumed groups called *murgas* tour the city on foot or on floats, singing witty satirical ditties, dancing or performing sketches. In addition to the 300 or so officially recognised murgas, judged by a panel in the Gran Teatro Falla, there are also the *ilegales* – any group that fancies taking to the streets and trying to play or sing.

Some of the liveliest scenes are in the working-class Barrio de la Viña, between the Mercado Central and Playa de la Caleta, and on Calle Ancha and Calle Columela where ilegales tend to congregate.

Rooms in Cádiz for Carnaval get booked up months in advance. Assuming you haven't managed this, you could just go for the night from Sevilla or anywhere else within striking distance. Plenty of people do this – many in fancy dress.

Places to Stay – Budget

Hostels Cádiz's excellent independent youth hostel, *Quo Qádiz* (☎/fax 956 22 19 39, Calle Diego Arias 1), is in a revamped old house just a block south of the Gran Teatro Falla (see under Entertainment later in this chapter). Cheerful dorms and private singles and doubles occupy several floors topped by an extensive roof terrace. A dorm bed costs 1000 ptas, singles/doubles 2100/3200 ptas, though 2000 ptas per person is the rate at peak times. Prices include a decent breakfast. Vegetarian food is served for dinner (costing 550 ptas). The energetic owners organise trips to beaches up and down the coast, the mountain ranges of Cádiz province, and even Morocco.

Hostales & Pensiones Cheaper places cluster just north-west of Plaza de San Juan de Dios. A good choice is the friendly family-run *Hostal Fantoni* (☎ *956 28 27 04, Calle Flamenco 5*) in an old house. With a roof terrace catching a breeze in summer, it has very clean, renovated singles/doubles costing 2000/3700 ptas, and doubles with bathroom for 5500 ptas. *Hostal Marqués* (☎ *956 28 58 54, Calle Marqués de Cádiz 1*) has slightly ageing but clean rooms, all with balcony, for 2000/3500 ptas, or doubles with bathroom for 4500 ptas. *Hostal Colón* (☎ *956 28 53 51, Calle Marqués de Cádiz 6*) is more modern and has doubles for 4000 ptas.

A bit farther north-west, *Pensión Cádiz* (☎ *956 28 58 01, Calle Feduchy 20*) is a popular little place with rooms costing 2000/4000 ptas with shared bathroom. Close by, *Hostal Ceuta* (☎ *956 22 16 54, Calle Montañés 7*) has clean doubles with bathroom costing 3500 ptas.

A good choice farther into the old city is the clean but basic *Hostal San Francisco* (☎/fax *956 22 18 42, Calle San Francisco 12*). Rooms cost 2500/4250 ptas; doubles with shower are 5850 ptas. Rooms at the friendly *Hotel Imares* (☎ *956 21 22 57, Calle San Francisco 9*), across the street, range from some airless and odorous interior ones to bright and breezy ones overlooking the street. Rooms with bathroom cost 3600/5800 ptas.

Places to Stay – Mid-Range

Just off Plaza de San Juan de Dios, *Hostal Bahía* (☎ *956 25 90 61, fax 956 25 42 08, Calle Plocia 5*) has comfortable air-con singles/doubles with TV costing 6400/8300 ptas. Three short blocks north, the efficient, clean and friendly *Hostal Centro Sol* (☎ *956 28 62 41, fax 956 28 31 03, Calle Manzanares 7*) has smallish rooms with bathroom at 4500/6500 ptas. The owners speak French. *Hotel Francia y París* (☎ *956 21 23 18, fax 956 22 23 48, Plaza San Francisco 2*) is bigger (with 57 rooms) and more luxurious, with rooms for 8080/10,100 ptas plus IVA.

Other mid-range options are mostly out-side the old city. *Hotel Regio II* (☎ *956 25 30 08, fax 956 25 30 09, Avenida de Andalucía 79*) and *Hotel Regio* (☎ *956 27 93 31, fax 956 27 91 13, Avenida Ana de Viya 11*) are both on the main road down the peninsula, 1.5km and 2km, respectively, from the Puertas de Tierra. Doubles cost 9500 ptas plus IVA at both.

Places to Stay – Top End

The modern parador *Hotel Atlántico* (☎ *956 22 69 05, fax 956 21 45 82, Avenida Duque de Nájera 9*) is on the seafront by Parque del Genovés. Rooms cost 12,500/15,000 ptas plus IVA.

Outside the old city, the large, stylish *Hotel Puertatierra* (☎ *956 27 21 11, fax 956 25 03 11, Avenida de Andalucía 34*), 750m south-east of the Puertas de Tierra, has doubles costing 17,500 ptas plus IVA. *Hotel Meliá Caleta* (☎ *956 27 94 11, fax 956 25 93 22, Avenida Amilcar Barca s/n*) is on the beachfront 1.5km farther south-east with doubles costing 17,000 ptas plus IVA. The biggest and best is the 188-room *Hotel Playa Victoria* (☎ *956 27 54 11, fax 956 26 33 00, Glorieta Ingeniero La Cierva 4*) on the beachfront a farther 400m along, with doubles costing 19,000 ptas plus IVA.

Places to Eat

Barrio de la Viña In the old fishermen's district, around 600m west of the cathedral, is Cádiz's most famous seafood restaurant *El Faro* (*Calle San Felix 15*) with a fancy menu and prices to match. However, its attached bar has exquisite seafood tapas. Choose from an extensive list costing from 190 ptas to 225 ptas. We enjoyed the *frituritas de bechamel con espinacas y gambas* (fried pastries with a filling of prawns and spinach in a bechamel sauce). *Raciones* (meal-sized servings of tapas) of fried fish cost around 1100 ptas. El Faro opens noon to 4.30 pm and 8 pm to midnight, daily.

Another good seafood place to try is *Grimaldi* (*Calle Libertad 9*), between the market and the seafront, where most main dishes are in the 1000 ptas range. It's decorated with old photos of Cádiz.

Plaza de San Juan de Dios This central square offers plenty of choice. *Bar Letrán* does *platos combinados* (mixed platters) for 550 ptas to 1000 ptas; *menús* (fixed-price meals) start at 1000 ptas. *Restaurante Pasaje Andaluz* has menús from 950 ptas and main dishes from 550 ptas. Popular *El Sardinero* does similar fare better, but for almost twice the price – main dishes cost from 1000 ptas; the menú is 1450 ptas.

A few doors east, the *Novelty Café* is a fine place to go for a light breakfast, cakes or snacks. French-speaking *La Pierrade (Calle Plocia 2)*, one block off the square, is a touch adventurous. The three-course menú (1200 ptas) might offer *mejillones* (mussels) *al roquefort*, or *brocheta de cordero* (lamb kebab), and includes wine and bread.

Plaza de Mina For a wide choice of food at a reasonable price try *Café Bar Madrileño*, with tapas costing around 200 ptas, salads from 350 ptas, vegetable raciones from 600 ptas, fish and seafood raciones from 800 ptas, and a menú costing 900 ptas. *Dulcería Mina (Calle Antonio López 2)* has good pastries and excellent filled baguettes, and is a good spot for breakfast (tea/coffee, juice and *tostada* – toasted roll or slice of bread) for 300 ptas, or a bacon and eggs option for 450 ptas.

Off the northern side of the square, it's hard to pass by the mouthwatering fresh seafood tapas at *Cervecería Aurelio (Calle Zorrilla 1)*. Try the *cazón en adobo* (marinated, deep-fried dogfish; 175 ptas). Down at the end of this street, enjoy the bay views at *Cervecería El Bogavante* with good scrambled eggs, prawns and asparagus for 900 ptas, big salads for 600 ptas, and fish and meat main courses from 900 ptas to 1200 ptas.

Balandro (Alameda Apodaca 22), a few doors east, has sea views from its terrace and an upstairs dining room; it is popular year-round for its good food, cheap prices and attractive old crockery. Try the pizza-like *pan horneado* with a smoked salmon, anchovies and cream cheese topping (900 ptas and enough for two with a salad).

Meat and fish raciones start at 975 ptas. The desserts look scrumptious. It's closed Sunday evening and Monday.

Plaza de Topete Just off the square on Calle Columela, *Pizzeria Nino's* does tasty pizzas costing from 740 ptas, pasta from 625 ptas, and Tex-Mex fare and burgers in the same range. The nearby *Mercado Central* sells, among other things, *churros* (long, deep-fried doughnuts), which you can take to nearby cafes to enjoy with a hot chocolate for breakfast.

Plaza San Francisco With tables on the square opposite the church, *Parisien* is good for a drink at any time of day and has breakfast deals from 250 ptas. *O'Connell's*, the Irish pub adjacent on Calle Tinte, has Irish beers and food, including baked potatoes with fillings. Around the corner on Calle Sagasta, *Menoc Donald* is *the* place in this part of town for pizzas and burgers.

Entertainment

There's a great atmosphere in some of the old city's squares on hot summer nights, with bars and cafes busy till well after midnight, and kids playing football or cruising on bikes or skates – everyone out enjoying the relative cool.

From midnight or so in summer the real scene migrates to the Paseo Marítimo along Playa de la Victoria – about 3km down the peninsula from the Puertas de Tierra. Here, some 300m past the big Hotel Playa Victoria, you'll find lively music bars; 350m farther on is Calle Villa de Paradas where throngs of people stand in the street with *macetas* (large plastic mugs) of beer from the bars here. A lot of people simply mess around on the beach until dawn. A taxi from the old city (try Plaza de España) to this area costs around 600 ptas. Up to about 1.30 am you can use bus No 1 to get there (see the Playa de la Victoria section earlier in this chapter).

In winter, the bars in the streets west of Plaza de España, such as Calle Dr Zurita, are among the liveliest, and the square itself is the setting for the Saturday night scene.

CÁDIZ PROVINCE

Club Ajo (Plaza de España 5) is a popular hangout open late from Thursday (when it has live music) to Sunday. *Café Poniente (Calle Beato Diego de Cádiz 18)* is a good gay bar.

In the centre *Persígueme*, on the corner of Calle Tinte and Calle Sagasta, has live music on Thursdays. Nearby on Plaza de la Mina, **Son Latino** often has excellent live music from 11 pm. The hip bar/pub *Cambalache (Calle José del Toro 20)* is the place to hear good jazz. Or, stop by at the laid-back *Café de Levante (Calle Rosario 35)*.

Taberna Flamenca La Cava (☎ 956 21 18 66, Calle Antonio López 16), between Plaza de la Mina and Plaza de España, has a flamenco show at 10.30 pm on Thursdays and 1.30 pm on Sundays.

Gran Teatro Falla, in the north-west of the old town, is the main venue for cultural events, including music, dance (sometimes flamenco), film and theatre. The ageing *Central Lechera (Plaza de Argüelles s/n)* also hosts theatre and concerts.

Getting There & Away

Bus Most buses are run by Comes (☎ 956 21 17 63) from Plaza de la Hispanidad. These include at least 10 daily each to Sevilla (1385 ptas, 1¾ hours), El Puerto de Santa María, Jerez de la Frontera, Tarifa and Algeciras (1270 ptas, two hours), three or more to Arcos de la Frontera, Ronda and Málaga, and buses at least daily to Zahara de los Atunes, Córdoba and Granada.

Los Amarillos (call Viajes Socialtur on ☎ 956 28 58 52 for information) runs up to 10 buses daily to El Puerto de Santa María (180 ptas) and Sanlúcar de Barrameda (390 ptas), and two or three daily to Arcos de la Frontera (380 ptas), El Bosque (915 ptas) and Ubrique (1080 ptas), from its stop by the southern end of Avenida Ramón de Carranza. Tickets can be bought at Viajes Socialtur, Avenida Ramón de Carranza 31.

Buses to Madrid (3105 ptas, six hours) are run up to six times daily by Secorbus (☎ 956 25 74 15) from Plaza Elios by the Estadio Ramón de Carranza football ground, about 2km south-east of the old city.

Train The station (☎ 956 25 43 01) is just off Plaza de Sevilla, near the port. Up to 20 suburban trains *(cercanías)* run daily to/from El Puerto de Santa María and Jerez de la Frontera (380 ptas and 475 ptas, 40 minutes), and up to 12 regional trains *(regionales)* to/from Sevilla (1290 ptas, two hours) via the same places.

There are four trains daily to/from Córdoba (2415 ptas to 3900 ptas, three hours) and two each for Madrid (8000 ptas) and Barcelona.

Car & Motorcycle The A-4 motorway from Sevilla to Puerto Real on the eastern side of the Bahía de Cádiz carries a toll of 900 ptas. The toll-free alternative, the N-IV, is a lot busier and slower. From Puerto Real the N-443 crosses a bridge over the narrowest part of the bay to join the southern road into Cádiz about 4km short of the old city.

Boat See the El Puerto de Santa María section later in this chapter for details of services from Cádiz to that town.

Vapores Suardiaz (☎ 956 28 21 11) operates two ferries daily between Cádiz and Tangier. The journey takes three hours and costs 3900 ptas for adults, 3000 ptas for motorbikes and bicycles and 9900 ptas for cars. The return passenger fare is 5440 ptas. Trasmediterránea (☎ 902 45 46 45) at the Estación Marítima operates a passenger and vehicle ferry to the Canary Islands, leaving Cádiz on Saturday and arriving in Santa Cruz de Tenerife, Las Palmas (Gran Canaria) and Santa Cruz de la Palma (La Palma) respectively 1½, two and three days later. The one-way passenger fare costs from 30,515 ptas to 55,430 ptas. It's an often bumpy ride.

The Sherry Triangle

North of Cádiz, the towns of Jerez de la Frontera, Sanlúcar de Barrameda and El Puerto de Santa María are best known for being the homes of sherry. But there's a wealth of other good reasons to visit them – beaches, music, horses, history and access to the Parque Nacional de Doñana.

EL PUERTO DE SANTA MARÍA
postcode 11500 • pop 69,000

El Puerto, 10km north-west of Cádiz across the Bahía de Cádiz (22km by road), is easily and enjoyably reached on the ferry *Motonave Adriano III*, better known as *El Vapor*. Columbus visited El Puerto in the 1480s and received some encouragement from the local Duke of Medinaceli for his travel plans. It was also here that Columbus met the owner of his 1492 flagship, the *Santa María*, Juan de la Cosa, who acted as his pilot on the great voyage and, in 1500, issued the first world map showing America. Later, El Puerto was heavily involved in trade with the Americas and from the 16th to 18th centuries it was the base of the Spanish royal galleys.

Orientation & Information
The heart of the town is on the north-west bank of the Río Guadalete, just upstream from its mouth, though development spreads along the beaches to the east and west. *El Vapor* arrives dead centre at the Muelle del Vapor jetty, on Plaza de las Galeras Reales. Calle Luna, one of the main streets, runs straight ahead inland. The excellent tourist office (☎ 956 54 24 13), 2½

blocks along at Calle Luna 22, opens 10 am to 2 pm and 6 to 8 pm (5.30 to 7.30 pm from October to May) daily. Immediately inland of the tourist office, another main street, Calle Larga (also called Calle Virgen de los Milagros), crosses Calle Luna. Calle Palacios, parallel to Calle Luna one block southwest, runs up to Plaza de España, seven blocks inland.

The train station is a 10-minute walk north-east of the centre, beside the Cádiz–Jerez road. Some buses stop at the train station, others at the Plaza de Toros (bullring), three blocks south-west of Plaza de España.

Walking Tour
Most of the sights are between the river and Plaza de España. The four-spouted **Fuente de las Galeras Reales** (Fountain of the Royal Galleys), by the Muelle del Vapor, supplied water to America-bound ships leaving from here. The **Castillo San Marcos**, three blocks south-west along Avenida Aramburu de Mora from Plaza de las Galeras Reales, then a block inland, was built by Alfonso X after he took the town in 1260. Free guided tours are given on Saturday between 11 am and 1 pm. Two and a half blocks inland from the castle at Calle

Sacred Bulls

Roaming the highways of Spain, every now and then you catch sight of the silhouette of a truly gigantic black bull on the horizon. When you get closer to the creature you'll realise it's made of metal and held up by bits of scaffolding. But what's it for?

It's not a silent homage to bullfighting erected by the local folk, nor a sign that you're entering a notable bull-breeding area. It's a sherry and brandy advert for the Osborne company of El Puerto de Santa María. At the last count there were 93 *toros de Osborne*, each weighing 50 tonnes, looming beside roads all over the country. And over the years they have raised as much dust as a champion bull trying to stay alive on a hot Sunday afternoon.

Why doesn't Osborne put its name on the bulls if it's trying to advertise, you might ask? From 1957, when the first bull was erected on the Madrid–Burgos road, until 1988, it did. Then a new law banned advertising hoardings beside main roads, to prevent drivers being distracted. Osborne left the bulls standing but removed its name, which seemed to pacify the authorities, until 1994 when word got about that the law was going to be enforced strictly, meaning no more bulls. This provoked an enormous furore, with intellectuals writing to newspapers about the national heritage, the Junta de Andalucía declaring the 21 bulls in Andalucía protected monuments, and Osborne taking the fight to the courts. In 1997 Spain's supreme court decided that the bulls had transcended their original advertising purpose and were now part of the landscape. They still are.

Andalucian sherry-wine is made and drunk by the barrel-load.

Santo Domingo 25 is the **Fundación Rafael Alberti**, with interesting exhibits on El Puerto native Rafael Alberti (1902–99), a painter, poet and communist politician of the Generation of '27 (for further details about the Generation of '27 see the Facts About Andalucía chapter). The foundation opens 10.30 am to 2.30 pm Monday to Friday, mid-June to mid-September, and 11 am to 2.30 pm Tuesday to Sunday at other times. Admission costs 300 ptas.

Between there and Plaza de España, the little **Museo Municipal**, Calle Pagador 1, has interesting archaeological and fine arts sections. It opens 10 am to 2 pm Monday to Saturday. Admission is free. The impressive **Iglesia Mayor Prioral**, built between the 15th and 18th centuries, dominates Plaza de España. It's open 10 am to noon and 7 to 8.30 pm daily. From here it's three blocks west to El Puerto's **Plaza de Toros**, completed in 1880 and with room for 15,000 spectators. You can visit from 11 am to 1.30 pm and 6 to 7.30 pm Tuesday to Sunday, except on days before and after bullfights. Admission is free.

Sherry Bodegas
Phone ahead if you want to visit either of the best known *bodegas* (cellars). **Osborne** (☎ 956 85 52 11), at Calle Fernán Caballero 3, offers tours in English at 10.30 am and Spanish at 11 am and noon, Monday to Friday. Visits to **Terry** (☎ 956 54 36 90, 956 85 77 00) at Calle Toneleros s/n, are at 9.30 and 11 am, and 12.30 pm, Monday to Friday. On Saturday **Gutiérrez Colosía**, Avenida de la Bajamar 40, offers a 1.30 pm visit for which you don't need to ring ahead. These tours cost 300 ptas, 325 ptas and 350 ptas, respectively.

Beaches
Pine-flanked **Playa de la Puntilla** is a half-hour walk south-west of the town centre, or you can get there by bus No 26 (90 ptas) heading south-west on Avenida Aramburu de Mora. **Playa Fuentebravía**, farther out west, is reachable by bus No 35 (90 ptas) from the same stop. Between the two beaches is a swish marina development called, of course, **Puerto Sherry**.

Boat Trips
La Niña (☎ 956 85 57 28), a replica of one of Columbus' ships, makes daily cruises from the Muelle Pesquero (fishing pier) for 1000 ptas a person.

From about mid-July to early September *El Vapor* (☎ 956 87 02 70, ☎ 956 85 59 06) does 1½-hour night cruises around the bay at 9.45 pm on Tuesday and Saturday. It costs 600 ptas.

Organised Tours
Free guided tours of the town set off at 11 am on Tuesday and Saturday from the tourist office on Calle Luna.

Special Events
El Puerto's Feria de la Primavera (spring fair) early in May is in large measure dedicated to sherry, with around 180,000 half-bottles being drunk in a week.

Places to Stay
Just behind Playa de la Puntilla is *Camping Las Dunas* (☎ 956 87 22 10). It has shade

CÁDIZ PROVINCE

and is open year round. It costs 565 ptas for each adult and tent, plus 485 ptas per car, all plus IVA.

Hostal Santamaría (☎ *956 85 36 31, Calle Pedro Muñoz Seca 38*), off Calle Palacios five blocks inland, has good, clean singles/doubles costing 1750/3500 ptas, or 2000/4000 ptas with a private bathroom. Its signs don't display the name of the hotel, they just say 'CH' and 'Camas'. Friendly *Hostal Manolo* (☎ *956 85 75 25, Calle Jesús de los Milagros 18*), a block inland from Plaza de las Galeras Reales, is a bit better, with rooms costing 2500/4000 ptas to 2900/4800 ptas with private shower room. *Hostal Loreto* (☎/*fax 956 54 24 10, Calle Ganado 17*), off Calle Larga one block north-east of Calle Luna, set around a leafy courtyard, charges 3000/6000 ptas (2500/5000 ptas with shared bathroom).

The 39-room *Hotel Los Cántaros* (☎ *956 54 02 40,* @ *los_cantaros@raini-computer .net, Calle Curva 6*), a couple of short streets behind the Romerijo restaurants (see Places to Eat), is a big step up in quality. Doubles cost 12,840 ptas in the first half of May and from mid-July to mid-September, but 8560 ptas or less at other times. *Hostal Chaikana* (☎ *956 54 29 01, fax 956 54 29 22, Calle Javier de Burgos 17*), a block behind Hotel Los Cántaros, has comfortable rooms at 6500/9500 ptas plus IVA, and a cafe.

At the luxurious *Hotel Monasterio San Miguel* (☎ *956 54 04 40, fax 956 54 26 04, Calle Larga 27*), a converted 18th-century monastery, singles/doubles start at 15,550/ 19,425 ptas plus IVA.

Places to Eat

El Puerto is an excellent place to sample seafood. Crowds flock to the *Romerijo*, with two buildings a block north-east from the Muelle del Vapor along Ribera del Marisco. Here you can buy portions of seafood in paper cones to take away or eat at the many tables outside. One building specialises in boiled fresh seafood while the other fries it. Everything's on display and you just take your pick and buy by the quarter-kilogram: it costs 800 ptas to

1200 ptas for boiled prawns or fried *puntillitas* (mini-ature squid), for example. Just behind here on Plaza de la Herrería, *La Herrería* has good food and good prices with a nice little salad at 300 ptas and *pinchitos morunos* (Morrocan-style kebab) for 500 ptas a *media-ración* (half a *ración*).

Near the castle, *Restaurante El Resbaladero*, in the handsome old fish exchange on Avenida Aramburu de Mora, offers air-conditioned comfort and a medium-to-expensive menu with lots of seafood and fish choices.

Cafetería las Capuchinas (*Calle Larga 27*), in the Hotel Monasterio San Miguel, provides welcome air-conditioning on a hot day. Enjoy a drink or a sandwich from 400 ptas to 900 ptas or platos combinados from 750 ptas to 1400 ptas.

Entertainment

El Puerto is a lively place with plenty of bars and quite a lot more going on, especially during the summer. There's flamenco at 10.30 pm, Thursday to Saturday at *El Rengue Mesón Rociero* (*Calle Jesús de los Milagros 27*) – admission is free. The tourist office can tell you about other upcoming music events. There's more action – bars and discos (clubs) – on the eastern side of town at Playa Valdelagrana.

Getting There & Away

Bus Monday to Friday, buses to Cádiz (380 ptas) go almost half-hourly, 6.30 am to 9.30 pm, from Plaza de Toros, and hourly, 8.30 am to 9.30 pm, from the train station. Weekend services are less frequent. For Jerez de la Frontera (185 ptas) there are seven to 14 buses daily from the train station and four to six from Plaza de Toros. For Sanlúcar de Barrameda (210 ptas), four to 10 buses daily go from Plaza de Toros. For Algeciras and La Línea de la Concepción (1400 ptas), two buses go from the train station.

Train From El Puerto station (☎ 956 54 25 85) up to 35 trains daily travel to/from Jerez (from 175 ptas, 10 minutes) and Cádiz (from 330 ptas, 30 minutes), and up to 15 to/from Sevilla (from 925 ptas).

CÁDIZ PROVINCE

Boat *El Vapor* (☎ 956 87 02 70, ☎ 956 85 59 06) sails from the Estación Maritima in Cádiz at 10 am, noon and 2 and 6.30 pm daily (except non-holiday Mondays) from February to November, with an extra trip at 4.30 pm on Sunday and at 8.30 pm daily in the summer. Trips back from El Puerto are at 9 and 11 am, and 1 and 3.30 pm, plus 5.30 pm Sunday and 7.30 pm daily in summer. The crossing takes 45 minutes and costs 275 ptas one way.

SANLÚCAR DE BARRAMEDA
postcode 11540 • pop 60,000

The northern tip of the sherry triangle and a flourishing summer resort, Sanlúcar is 23km north-west of El Puerto de Santa María. It has a likeable atmosphere and a fine location on the Guadalquivir estuary looking across to the Parque Nacional de Doñana.

Fears for Doñana have provoked strong environmentalist opposition to a plan by Alfonso von Hohenlohe, the man who brought the jetset to Marbella, to build a 2-sq-km country club near Sanlúcar with luxury hotels, a golf course, river marina and hundreds of apartments.

Orientation & Information

Sanlúcar stretches along the south-east side of the Guadalquivir estuary. Calzada del Ejército, running 600m inland from the seafront Paseo Marítimo, is the main avenue. A block beyond its inland end is Plaza del Cabildo, the central square. The Los Amarillos bus station is on Plaza La Salle, 500m south-west of Plaza del Cabildo along Calle San Juan.

The old fishing quarter, Bajo de Guía, site of Sanlúcar's best restaurants and Doñana boat departures, is 750m north-east along the riverfront from Calzada del Ejército.

The tourist office (☎ 956 36 61 10) is towards the inland end of Calzada del Ejército. It opens 10 am to 2 pm and 6 to 8 pm (5 to 7 pm in winter) Monday to Friday, 10 am to 1 pm Saturday and summer Sundays.

The Centro de Visitantes Fábrica de Hielo (☎ 956 38 16 35) at Bajo de Guía has displays and information on the Parque Nacional de Doñana and related topics. It opens 9 am to 7 pm daily.

Walking Tour

A stroll around the monuments doesn't take long as you can't usually go inside most of them. From Plaza del Cabildo, cross Calle Ancha to Plaza San Roque and head up Calle Bretones to **Las Covachas**, a set of 15th-century wine cellars. Here, the street turns right and becomes Calle Cuesta de Belén, where you'll probably be able to look into the **Palacio de Orleans y Borbon**, now the town hall. The creation of this 19th-century neo-Mudéjar fantasy as a summer home for the aristocratic Montpensier family was what started Sanlúcar's growth as a resort.

From the top of Calle Cuesta de Belén, a block to the left along Calle Caballeros is the 15th-century **Iglesia de Nuestra Señora de la O**, with a Mudéjar facade and ceiling

Sanlúcar to Sanlúcar via Tierra del Fuego

Columbus, on his third voyage to the Caribbean, set sail from Sanlúcar in 1498. So, on 20 September 1519, did another foreigner sailing under the Castilian flag – the Portuguese Ferdinand Magellan, who set off with five ships and a crew of 265 seeking, like Columbus, a westerly route to the spice islands of Indonesia.

Magellan made the first known voyage through the strait between Tierra del Fuego and the South American mainland (now the Magellan Strait), but was killed in a battle in the Philippines. By the time Magellan's Basque pilot Juan Sebastián Elcano completed the first circumnavigation of the globe by returning to Sanlúcar via the Cape of Good Hope in 1522, just 17 crew members and one ship, the *Victoria*, were left.

(for more information about Mudéjar architecture see the Facts about Andalucía chapter). Adjoining is the **Palacio de los Duques de Medina Sidonia**, home of the aristocratic family that once owned more of Spain than anyone else. Some 200m farther along the street is the 15th-century **Castillo de Santiago**, amid buildings of Barbadillo, Sanlúcar's biggest sherry company. From the castle you can return directly downhill to the town centre.

Beach
Sanlúcar's sandy beach runs along the riverfront and several kilometres beyond to the south-west.

Sherry
Sanlúcar produces a distinctive sherry, manzanilla. Three bodegas give tours for which you don't need to book ahead. All start at 12.30 pm and cost 300 ptas:

Monday, Tuesday
  La Cigarrera, Plaza Madre de Dios
Wednesday, Thursday
  Bodegas Barbadillo, Calle Luis de Eguilaz 11, near the castle
Friday, Saturday
  Pedro Romero, Calle Trasbolsa 60

Parque Nacional de Doñana
Viajes Doñana (☎ 956 36 25 40), Calle San Juan 20, operates 3½-hour guided tours (costing 4700 ptas per person) into Doñana at 8.30 am and 4.30 pm Tuesday and Friday, leaving from Bajo de Guía. After the river crossing, the trip is by 4WD vehicle holding about 20 people, visiting much the same spots as the tours from El Acebuche (see Parque Nacional de Doñana in the Huelva Province chapter). Book as far ahead as you can.

Once or twice daily except Monday, the boat *Real Fernando* makes 3½-hour trips on the Guadalquivir from Bajo de Guía. Despite brief stops in the national park and the Parque Natural de Doñana, these trips are not designed for serious nature enthusiasts. Tickets are sold at the Centro de Visitantes Fábrica de Hielo; they cost 2200 ptas

Horsing Around with the Tides

Sanlúcar's *carreras de caballos*, held every year since 1845 (bar a couple of interruptions for war), may be the only sporting event in the world where police crowd control involves gently persuading the spectators to take off their shoes and stand in the sea. It's an exciting spectacle in which genuine racehorses, many of them Irish, French or British-bred thoroughbreds, thunder along Sanlúcar beach watched by large crowds.

Two meetings of three or four days each are held every August, one in the first half or middle of the month, the other in the second half, usually with four races each day. Exact starting times depend on the tides, but the first race normally begins around 6 pm. Most races start at Bajo de Guía and the finish is about 1km south-west of Calzada del Ejército. Prize money for the two meetings totals around 15 million ptas.

Serious racegoers make for the area with spectator stands, bookmakers, paddock and winner's enclosure, up by the finishing post. The rest of the crowd strings itself back along the course. Here the only bookies, it seems, are children who set up little cardboard-box booths and scrape a line across the track in front, then take money on which horse will cross their 'finish' first!

(1100 ptas for children aged five to 12). In summer and during holiday periods, book a week ahead (☎ 956 36 38 13, fax 956 36 21 96).

On any of these trips, take mosquito repellent or wear clothes that cover your skin.

Special Events
The Sanlúcar summer gets going with a sherry festival, the Feria de la Manzanilla, in late May or early June, and blossoms in July and August with happenings such as the Noches de Bajo de Guía flamenco season (late July), jazz and classical music festivals, one-off concerts by good visiting bands and Sanlúcar's unique horse races (see the boxed text 'Horsing Around with the Tides').

Places to Stay

Book well ahead for a room at holiday times. Budget accommodation is scarce. *Hostal La Blanca Paloma (☎ 956 36 36 44, Plaza San Roque 9)* has eight adequate singles/doubles costing 3000/4500 ptas. *Hostal La Bohemia (☎ 956 36 95 99, Calle Don Claudio 1)*, off Calle Ancha, 300m north-east of Plaza del Cabildo, has better rooms with bathroom at 5500 ptas a double.

Hotel Los Helechos (☎ 956 36 13 49, Plaza Madre de Dios 9), off Calle San Juan 200m from Plaza del Cabildo, has two pretty courtyards and a cosy bar. Singles/doubles with bathroom cost 6000/8000 ptas plus IVA. However, rooms on the courtyards can be noisy. *Hotel Posada de Palacio (☎ 956 36 48 40, fax 956 36 50 60, Calle Caballeros 11)*, in the upper part of town, is a charming 18th-century mansion with 10 good-sized rooms costing just 6000/8000 ptas (year-round), and its own good restaurant. It closes for a couple of months in winter. *Hotel Tartaneros (☎ 956 36 20 44, Calle Tartaneros 8)*, at the inland end of Calzada del Ejército, is a century-old industrialist's mansion with solidly comfortable singles/doubles costing 6500/10,000 ptas plus IVA. The much bigger, modern *Hotel Guadalquivir (☎ 956 36 07 42, Calzada del Ejército 10)*, nearby, has doubles costing 12,000 ptas plus IVA.

Places to Eat

The line of seafood restaurants facing the riverfront at Bajo de Guía are a reason in themselves for visiting Sanlúcar. It's an idyllic experience to watch the sun go down over the Guadalquivir while tucking into the succulent fresh fare here and washing it down with a drop of manzanilla. Just wander along and pick a restaurant that suits your pocket. The most popular include *Casa Bigote*, *Restaurante Poma*, *Restaurante Virgen del Carmen*, *Casa Juan* and *Bar Joselito Huerta*. At the Virgen del Carmen most fish mains, *plancha* (grilled) or *frito* (fried), cost from 1000 ptas to 1400 ptas. Don't skip the starters: *langostinos* (king prawns) and the juicy *coquines al ajillo* (clams in garlic), both 1000 ptas, are

specialities. A half-bottle of manzanilla costs 600 ptas.

Lots of cafes and bars, many serving manzanilla from the barrel, surround Plaza del Cabildo. *Casa Balbino (Plaza del Cabildo 14)* has wonderful seafood tapas – try the *patatas rellenas*, potatoes stuffed with meat or fish, in a delicious tomato *salsa*. Two blocks south-west, *Da Francesco (Calle Bolsa 22)* doesn't look overly inviting, but it serves good pizzas and pastas for under 800 ptas. *Bar El Cura (Calle Amargura 2)*, in an alley between Calle San Juan and Plaza San Roque, does very economical platos combinados. At *Café Tartaneros (Calle Tartaneros 8)*, in Hotel Tartaneros (see Places to Stay), you can sink into a comfortable chair and enjoy a pot of tea and chocolate cake for 500 ptas.

Entertainment

There are some lively music bars and discos on and around Calzada del Ejército and Plaza del Cabildo.

Getting There & Away

Bus Los Amarillos (☎ 956 36 04 66) runs up to six buses daily to/from El Puerto de Santa María and Cádiz and up to nine to/from Sevilla (920 ptas). Linesur (☎ 956 34 10 63), whose stop is at Bar La Jaula behind the tourist office, runs at least seven buses daily to/from Jerez de la Frontera.

Boat Though you can visit Sanlúcar on day-trip boats from Sevilla (see the Sevilla Province chapter), you can't take a one-way ride upriver from Sanlúcar to Sevilla.

CHIPIONA
postcode 11550 • pop 15,000

Chipiona, 9km west of Sanlúcar, has long sandy beaches, about 30 hostales and hotels, and Spain's tallest lighthouse (69m). The tourist office (☎ 956 37 28 28) is on Plaza de Andalucía in the older part of town. *Hotel La Española (☎ 956 37 37 71, Calle Isaac Peral 4)*, a few steps back from Chipiona's northern seafront, has good singles/doubles starting at 4000/7000 ptas plus IVA in high season, and a reasonable restaurant.

CÁDIZ PROVINCE

JEREZ DE LA FRONTERA
postcode 11480 • pop 182,000
• elevation 55m

The large town of Jerez, 36km north-east of Cádiz, is world famous for its wine – sherry – made from grapes grown on the chalky soil surrounding the town. Many people come here to visit its bodegas, but Jerez (heh-**reth** or, in Andalucian, just heh-**reh**) is also Andalucía's horse capital and, alongside its affluent uppercrust society, supports a *gitano* (Roma) community which is one of the hotbeds of flamenco.

The British have for many centuries had a special taste for sherry, and British money was largely responsible for the development of the wineries from around the 1830s. Today, Jerez high society is a mixture of Andalucian and British due to intermarriage among families of wine traders over the past 150 years. Since the 1980s most of the wineries, previously owned by about 15 families, have been bought out by multinational companies. Jerez reeks of money. It has loads of fancy shops, well-heeled residents, wide, spacious streets and old mansions and beautiful churches in its interesting old quarter. It puts on fantastic fiestas with sleek horses, beautiful people and flamenco, though ordinary life goes on in its backstreets and suburbs. The town hopes for a million visitors in 2002 when it will host the World Equestrian Games.

History
The Muslims called the town 'Scheris', from which 'Jerez' and 'sherry' are derived. The drink was already famed in England in Shakespeare's time. Jerez had its share of strife during the late 19th century when anarchism gained ground in Andalucía – one day in 1891 thousands of peasants armed with scythes and sticks marched in and occupied the town for a few hours, succeeding only in bringing about further repression. The sherry industry has provided greater prosperity in more recent times. Jerez brandy, consumed widely in Spain, is also a profitable product.

Orientation & Information
The centre of Jerez is between the Alameda Cristina and Plaza del Arenal, connected by the north–south Calle Larga and its continuation Calle Lancería (both pedestrianised). Budget accommodation clusters around two streets east of Calle Larga – Avenida de Arcos and Calle Medina. West of Calle Larga is the old quarter. North-east from Alameda Cristina runs Calle Sevilla, becoming Avenida Álvaro Domecq, which has some of the upmarket hotels. Several of the sherry bodegas are north-east and south-west of the centre.

The tourist office (☎ 956 33 11 50), Calle Larga 39, has energetic multi-lingual staff with mountains of information. Basic hours are 9 am to 3 pm and 4 to 7 pm Monday to Friday, 10 am to 2 pm and 5 to 7 pm Saturday.

There are plenty of banks and ATMs on and around Calle Larga. The post office is on the corner of Calle Cerrón and Calle Medina, just east of Calle Larga.

Jerez Undernet on Calle Santa María, near the corner with Calle Doña Blanca, offers internet access for 5 ptas a minute. It opens 11 am to 2 pm and 5 to 9 pm daily.

Old Quarter
The obvious place to start a tour of the old town, parts of whose walls survive, is the **Alcázar**, the 12th-century Almohad fortress south-west of Plaza del Arenal. Inside the Alcázar are the **Capilla Santa María la Real**, a chapel converted from a mosque by Alfonso X in 1264, the **Baños Arabes** (Arab Baths; recently restored) and the also-recently-restored 18th-century **Palacio Villavicencio**. The pretty chapel retains most of the mosque's features including the mihrab. The impressively spacious Palacio Villavicencio has fantastic city views from its tower which contains a camera obscura (see the Torre Tavira section under Cádiz for information about camera obscura). It provides a picturesque panorama of Jerez accompanied by an interesting 15-minute commentary (Spanish and English). Camera obscura sessions begin every half-hour, 11 am to 8 pm May to mid-September,

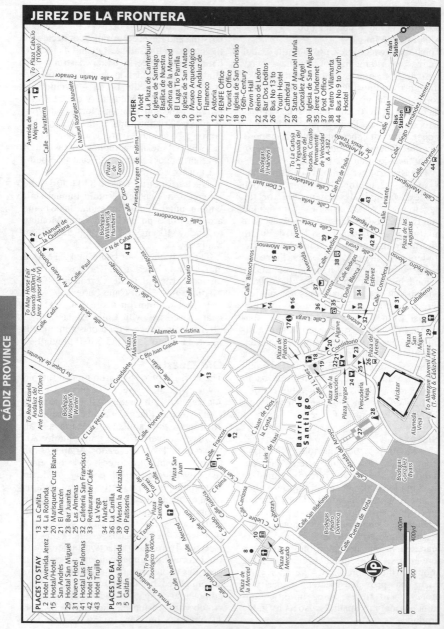

JEREZ DE LA FRONTERA

OTHER
1 Moët
4 La Plaza de Canterbury
6 Iglesia de Santiago
7 Basílica de Nuestra
    Señora de la Merced
8 El Laga Tío Parrilla
9 Iglesia de San Mateo
10 Museo Arqueológico
11 Centro Andaluz de
    Flamenco
12 Astoria
16 RENFE Office
17 Tourist Office
18 Iglesia de San Dionisio
19 16th-Century
    Town Hall
22 Reino de León
24 Bar Dos Deditos
26 Bus No 13 to
    Youth Hostel
27 Cathedral
28 Statue of Manuel María
    González Ángel
30 Iglesia de San Miguel
35 Post Office
37 Jerez Undernet
38 Teatro Villamarta
44 Bus No 9 to Youth
    Hostel

PLACES TO STAY
2 Hotel Avenida Jerez
15 Hostal/Hotel
    San Andrés
29 Hostal San Miguel
31 Nuevo Hotel
41 Hostal Las Palomas
42 Hotel Serit
43 Hotel Trujillo

PLACES TO EAT
3 La Mesa Redonda
5 Gaitán
13 La Cañita
14 La Rotonda
20 Marisquería Cruz Blanca
21 El Almacén
23 Bar Juanita
25 Las Almenas
32 Cafetería San Francisco
33 Restaurante/Café
    La Vega
34 Market
36 La Canilla
39 Mesón la Alcazaba
40 Patisseria

CÁDIZ PROVINCE

10 am to 5.30 pm at other times of year, daily. Admission to the sessions costs 500 ptas. The Alcázar opens from 10 am to 8 pm (to 6 pm from October to April), daily. Admission costs 200 ptas.

The orange-tree-lined square outside the Alcázar's entrance has good vistas to the west. In the foreground is the mainly 18th-century **cathedral** which has Gothic, baroque and neo-classical features, and was built on the site of the Muslim town's main mosque. Note the 15th-century Mudéjar belfry, set slightly apart. Behind the cathedral is a large statue of Manuel María González Ángel (1812–87), the founder of Bodegas González Byass.

A couple of blocks north-east of the cathedral is Plaza de la Asunción with a splendid 16th-century **town hall** and the lovely 15th-century Mudéjar **Iglesia de San Dionisio**, named after the town's patron saint.

North and west of here is the **Barrio de Santiago**, a quarter with a sizeable gitano population and one of the centres of flamenco. The barrio has churches dedicated to all four evangelists: the Gothic **Iglesia de San Mateo**, with Mudéjar chapels, is on Plaza del Mercado, where you'll also find the excellent **Museo Arqueológico** (☎ 956 34 13 50). The pride of the museum's collection is a 7th-century BC Greek helmet, found in the Río Guadalete. The museum opens 10 am to 2.30 pm daily except Monday, 15 June to 31 August; at other times of year 10 am to 2 pm and 4 to 7 pm Tuesday to Friday, and 10 am to 2.30 pm at weekends. Admission costs 250 ptas.

Also in this area is the **Centro Andaluz de Flamenco** (Andalucian Flamenco Centre, ☎ 956 34 92 65, fax 956 32 11 27), in the 18th-century Palacio de Pemartín on Plaza de San Juan. Jerez is at the heart of the Sevilla–Cádiz axis where flamenco began and which remains its heartland today (see the Flamenco special section). The centre is a kind of museum and school dedicated to the preservation and promotion of flamenco. It has a library with 4000 works on flamenco and other subjects, a music library and a video library. Opening hours are from 9 am to 2 pm Monday to Friday. In the main tourist seasons a free audio-visual introduction to Andalucía and flamenco is screened hourly from 9.30 am to 1.30 pm.

Just south-east of Plaza del Arenal is one of Jerez's loveliest churches, the 16th-century **Iglesia de San Miguel** built in Isabelline Gothic style and featuring superb stained glass windows and a retable by Juan Martínez Montañés.

Sherry Bodegas

For most of the bodegas, you need to phone ahead to book your visit. Some bodegas, such as Williams & Humbert (makers of the well known Dry Sack, a blend of *oloroso* and *amontillado* sherries and sweet wine), are closed from late July through much of August. The two biggest companies, both handily located west of the Alcázar, are González Byass (☎ 956 35 70 00), Calle Manuel González s/n, and Pedro Domecq (☎ 956 15 15 00/16), Calle San Ildefonso 3. González Byass, maker of Tio Pepe, the world's best-selling dry sherry, opens for visits at least from 9.30 am to 2 pm and 4.30 to 6 pm Monday to Friday (500 ptas), and 10 am to 2 pm at weekends (600 ptas). Domecq, maker of the famous dry sherry La Ina, has several tours Monday to Friday from 9 am to 1 pm costing 400 ptas. The tourist office has a complete list of bodegas that welcome visitors.

Other Things to See

One of Jerez's big attractions is the **Real Escuela Andaluz del Arte Ecuestre** (Royal Andalucian School of Equestrian Art; ☎ 956 31 80 08), on Avenida Duque de Abrantes in the north of town. The school trains horses and riders in dressage and you can watch them being put through their paces in training sessions from 11 am to 1 pm Monday, Wednesday and Friday. Admission to this costs 1000 ptas. At noon on Thursday year-round, noon on Tuesday from March to October, and 10 am Thursday from April to June, there's an official show where the handsome white horses perform to classical music. Admission costs from 2000 ptas to 3000 ptas.

The Solera Process

Once sherry grapes have been harvested, they are pressed and the resulting must is left to ferment. Within a few months a frothy veil of yeast called *flor* appears on the surface. The wine is then transferred to the bodegas in big barrels of American oak.

Wine enters the solera process when it is a year old. The barrels, about five-sixths full, are lined up in rows, called *escalas*, at least three barrels high. The barrels on the bottom layer, called the *solera* (from *'suelo'*, meaning 'floor'), contain the oldest wine. From these, around three times a year, 10% of the wine is drawn off. This is replaced with the same amount from the barrels in the layer above, which is in turn replaced from the next layer. The wines are left to age for between three and seven years. A small amount of brandy is added to stabilise the wine before bottling, bringing the alcohol content to 16–18%, which stops fermentation. (This constitutes the 'fortification' of the wine.)

Sherry houses are often beautiful buildings in attractive gardens. A tour will take you through the bodegas where the wine is stored and aged, inform you about the process and the history of the sherry producers, and allow you a tasting. You'll also be shown the use of a *venencia*, a long-handled cup for sampling sherry from the barrel. The venencia is expertly manipulated, with the sherry cascading from head height into a glass held at waist level.

See the special section 'Food & Drink' for more on the subject of sherry.

A couple of kilometres west of the centre is the **Parque Zoológico** or Zoo Jerez with lovely gardens and a wild animal recuperation centre. It's open 10 am to 6 pm (to 8 pm in summer) Tuesday to Sunday. Admission costs 600 ptas (children 400 ptas).

Special Events

Jerez's Feria del Caballo (horse fair) in May is one of Andalucía's biggest festivals, with music and dance as well as all kinds of horse competitions. Colourful parades of horses pass through the Parque González Hontoria fairgrounds in the north of town, the aristocratic-looking male riders decked out in flat-topped hats, frilly white shirts, black trousers and leather chaps, their female *crupera* (sideways pillion) partners in traditional long, frilly, spotted dresses. Female riders, sporting flat-topped hats, white blouses and cropped woollen jackets with matching longish, full skirts, look as smart as their male counterparts.

Preceding the horse fair is the Festival de Jerez, a two-week event dedicated to music and dance, particularly flamenco. This is a good opportunity to see big flamenco names perform, especially dancers. The Teatro Villamarta (☎ 956 34 47 50) on Calle Medina, near Calle Bodegas, is the main venue.

In early or mid-September Jerez stages a one-day festival of flamenco song and dance, the Fiesta de la Bulería. The Fiestas de Otoño (autumn festivals) from mid-September to mid-October, celebrating the grape harvest, range from flamenco and the traditional treading of the first grapes outside the cathedral, to horse races on Plaza del Arenal and dressage contests. It concludes with a massive parade of horses and riders and horse-drawn carriages.

In April, Jerez hosts one of Spain's major alternative music festivals, Espárrago Rock, over a weekend out at the Circuito Permanente de Velocidad – see Spectator Sports later in the Jerez section.

Places to Stay

Room rates go sky-high during the Feria del Caballo. Book well ahead. You can also expect to pay more when there's a competition on at the Circuito Permanente de Velocidad – see Spectator Sports later in the Jerez section.

Places to Stay – Budget

The modern *Albergue Juvenil Jerez* (☎ 956 26 97 88, fax 950 27 17 44, Avenida Carrero Blanco 30), 1.5km south of the centre, has 16 singles, 12 doubles and

CÁDIZ PROVINCE

16 triples/quadruples, with shared bathrooms. Bus No 13 from Plaza del Arenal in the centre, or bus No 9 with a stop on Calle Porvenir (one block south of the bus station) will take you there. Get off at the Campo Juventud stop. (Local buses are painted an eye-catching fluorescent lilac.)

Other budget choices are more conveniently located around Calle Medina, Avenida de Arcos and on Calle Caballeros, which runs south-east off Plaza del Arenal. The friendly *Hostal/Hotel San Andres* (☎ 956 34 09 83, fax 956 34 31 96, Calle Morenos 12), with two pretty plant-filled patios and a sun terrace, is a good choice. Singles/doubles with bathroom, TV and winter heating cost 2500/4500 ptas; rooms with shared bathroom are 2000/3000 ptas. *Hostal Las Palomas* (☎ 956 34 37 73, Calle Higueras 17) is another good bet. Spacious, nicely furnished rooms with shared bathroom cost 2000/3500 ptas, doubles with bathroom 4000 ptas.

Nuevo Hotel (☎ 956 33 16 00, fax 956 33 16 04, @ nuevohotel1927@teleline.es, Calle Caballeros 23), in an old mansion has spacious rooms with bathroom, TV and winter heating from 2500/4000 ptas. *Hostal San Miguel* (☎ 956 34 85 62, Plaza San Miguel 4), costs 1800/3800 ptas with shared bathroom, 2500/5000 ptas with attached bathroom. The owner is pleasant, the rooms are fine and there's a roof terrace where you can go and relax.

Places to Stay – Mid-Range & Top End

Add IVA to all the following prices. *Hotel Trujillo* (☎/fax 956 34 24 38, Calle Medina 3), has singles/doubles with all mod-cons costing 5900/9800 ptas (but only 3500/5500 ptas from November to Easter). Nearby, *Hotel Serit* (☎ 956 34 07 00, Calle Higueras 7) has similar rooms costing 7000/10,000 ptas. There are a couple of rooms especially adapted for wheelchair users. At *Hotel Avenida Jerez* (☎ 956 34 74 11, Avenida Álvaro Domecq 10) doubles cost 14,000 ptas (28,000 ptas in April, May and October). There are more top-end places on the same road.

Places to Eat

Not surprisingly, sherry is used to flavour many local dishes, such as *riñones al jerez* (kidneys in gravy), and *rabo de toro* (oxtail or bull's tail stew). Jerez food combines its Muslim heritage and proximity to the sea with English and French touches. A good place to try Jerez specialities if you're not on a tight budget is the small *La Mesa Redonda* (Calle Manuel de la Quintana 3), north-east of the centre. Many Jerez restaurants are closed on Sunday night.

The restaurants on Pescadería Vieja, a little alley on the western side of Plaza del Arenal which catches a refreshing breeze on a hot day, are moderate to expensive. *Las Almenas* has menús costing 950 ptas and 1550 ptas with two courses, bread and dessert. Tapas start at 250 ptas, fish raciones at 950 ptas. *Bar Juanita*, and *El Almacén*, (Calle Ferros 8), round the corner, are local tapas haunts (shellfish are the thing) and good places to sample a dry sherry too.

A short walk north-west, *Marisquería Cruz Blanca* (Calle Consistorio 16) has tables outside on pretty Plaza de la Yerba under tall jacaranda trees. Try the seafood tapas (175 ptas to 300 ptas) and raciones – the sushi-style *bacalao* (salted cod) is sensational!

La Canilla (Calle Larga 8) is fine for simple breakfasts, under big canvas sunshades in summer. Or, for a tostada and coffee after 10 am, try *La Rotonda* at the northern end of Calle Larga (150 ptas). Later in the day, it serves tapas, raciones, ice creams and cakes.

The *produce market* (mercado) is on Calle Doña Blanca, a stone's throw east of Calle Larga, past Plaza Estévez, which has a couple of good places for teas, coffees, pastries, breakfasts, reasonably priced meals and cheap menús, including *Cafetería San Francisco* at No 2, and *Restaurante/Café La Vega*, right by the market. La Vega does churros.

Méson la Alcazaba (Calle Medina 19), with a covered patio, has cheap, filling food; menús (costing 800 ptas and 1000 ptas) offer plenty of choice and include two courses, a drink and fruit. Breakfasts of

CÁDIZ PROVINCE

coffee, a *mollete* (a tasty soft roll) and fresh juice cost 200 ptas. The ***Patissería*** on the corner of Calles Medina and Higueras, has delicious cakes, pastries, baguettes and ice creams.

For a splash-out meal at ***Gaitán*** *(Calle Gaitán 3)*, two blocks west of the Alameda Cristina, you can expect to pay 675 ptas for soup, 1500 ptas for a seafood cocktail starter, and 1875 ptas to 2475 ptas for fancy main courses. *La Cañita*, nearby on Calle Porvera, is another tapas haunt.

Entertainment

Check at the tourist office and watch out for posters advertising upcoming events. *Diario de Jerez* newspaper has some what's-on information and the Teatro Villamarta puts out a monthly program. The *Astoria*, an outdoor concert area on Calle Francos, has live music from blues to flamenco; there are sometimes concerts in the bullring too. ***Bar Dos Deditos*** *(Plaza Vargas 1)*, behind Pescadería Vieja, has live music some nights, including blues – if there's something on, the crowd spills out onto the pavement.

North-east of the centre just before the bullring, *La Plaza de Canterbury*, with lots of bars around a central courtyard, attracts a young crowd. Between the bullring and Plaza Caballo is a small nightlife area centred on Calle Salvatierra, with bars and a couple of clubs for dancing until late on weekend nights and festivals, including *Moët* on Avenida de Méjico. Another bar and restaurant area worth investigating centres on Calle Cádiz and Calle Divina Pastora, close to the Real Escuela Andaluz de Arte Ecuestre.

For flamenco, there are several clubs in the Barrio de Santiago; the tourist office keeps a complete list. ***El Laga Tío Parrilla*** *(☎/fax 956 33 83 34)* on Plaza del Mercado has more tourist-oriented flamenco performances, at 10.30 pm and 12.30 am Monday to Saturday nights, but you never know what you might strike there out of the main tourist seasons. We stopped by and were included in a family party of 20 where everyone either sang, danced, played guitar or a combination of all three – an outstanding

display of gutsy flamenco lasting well into the early hours. The youngest dancer (brilliant) was a rotund seven-year old wearing a tracksuit! *Reino de León* on Calle Ferros, next to Bar Almacén, has flamenco from 10 pm to 3 am on Thursday night.

Spectator Sports

Jerez has a motorcycle and car racing track, the Circuito Permanente de Velocidad (☎ 956 15 11 00) on the A-382, 10km east of town. Motorcycle races are held here throughout the year including – in April or May – one of the Grand Prix races of the World Motorcycle Championship, one of Spain's biggest sporting events with around 150,000 spectators. There are three or four car races annually: occasionally one of them is a Formula One Grand Prix.

Getting There & Away

Air The airport (☎ 956 15 00 00), the only one serving Cádiz province, is 7km north-east of Jerez on the N-IV. Iberia (☎ 956 18 43 94/5) has several direct flights daily to/from Madrid and one daily to/from Barcelona. Air Europa also flies to/from Madrid daily. The budget airline Buzz (☎ 91 749 66 33) began flights to/from London Stansted on Saturdays in 2000 with fares from UK£49 one way (including tax).

Bus The bus station (☎ 956 34 52 07) is on Calle Cartuja, the extension of Calle Medina, about 1km south-east of the centre. Comes (☎ 956 34 21 74) has buses for Cádiz (370 ptas, up to 19 daily), El Puerto de Santa María (up to five daily), Vejer de la Frontera and Barbate (810 ptas and 950 ptas, one daily), Ronda (1320 ptas, four daily) with one continuing to Málaga (2540 ptas), and Córdoba (1950 ptas, one daily). There are plenty of buses to Sevilla (890 ptas) by Linesur-Valenciana (☎ 956 34 78 44) and Comes. Linesur-Valenciana also runs to Sanlúcar de Barrameda hourly from 7 am to 9 pm. Los Amarillos (☎ 956 34 78 44) handles buses to towns inland and has plenty to Arcos de la Frontera and up to seven daily to El Bosque and Ubrique.

CÁDIZ PROVINCE

Train The train station (☎ 956 34 23 19) is a couple of blocks south-east of the bus station at the end of Calle Cartuja. A taxi from the town centre costs between 400 ptas and 500 ptas. Jerez is on the Cádiz–Sevilla line with plenty of trains in both directions. The central RENFE office (☎ 956 33 48 13), Calle Larga 34, opens 9 am to 2 pm and 5 to 8.30 pm Monday to Friday, 9.30 am to 1.30 pm Saturday.

AROUND JEREZ
La Cartuja
The monastery of La Cartuja (☎ 956 15 64 65), founded in the 15th century and with an impressive 17th-century baroque facade, is set in attractive gardens on the road to Medina Sidonia, 4km from Jerez. The early Carthusian monks are credited with breeding the much-prized Spanish thoroughbred horse, also called the Andaluz or the Cartujano. Around 1950 the former monastery was returned to the Carthusian monks, a closed religious order. Its gardens are open to all (9.30 am to 6 pm daily) but only men are allowed to visit the monastery's interior (5 to 6 pm Wednesday and Saturday, by appointment). Women are soon to be given permission to view inside.

La Yeguada del Hierro del Bocado
Most of the world's horse breeds are found in Andalucía, though the major breeding stocks here are the Arab and the Spanish Thoroughbred (Cartujano). The Cartujano is particularly admired for its grace and gentle temperament. La Yeguada del Hierro del Bocado (☎ 956 16 28 09) at Finca Fuente del Suero, off the A-381 to Medina Sidonia, 6.5km from Jerez, a stud farm dedicated to promoting the Cartujano, is open for visits. Turn up on any Saturday at 11 am for their two-hour tour. Admission costs 1500 ptas (800 ptas for children aged under 12).

Arcos & the Sierra

The mountainous Parque Natural Sierra de Grazalema in the north-east of Cádiz province is one of Andalucía's most beautiful and green areas. Between it and Jerez is the picturesque old town of Arcos de la Frontera.

ARCOS DE LA FRONTERA
postcode 11630 • pop 28,000
• elevation 185m
Arcos is 30km east of Jerez de la Frontera along the A-382 across pretty wheat and sunflower fields, vineyards and fruit orchards. The castle and old town atop a ridge, with the Río Guadalete meandering below, make a striking sight. Arcos is said to have a dark, sinister side; there are tales of madness, interbreeding, covens and witchcraft. Whatever the truth of that, Arcos is well worth visiting to explore its old town whose street plan has changed little since medieval times. There are some lovely post-Reconquista buildings including Renaissance palaces and two splendid churches.

History
Arcos has always been prized for its strategic location. It was taken from the Visigoths by the Muslims in 711. In the 11th century it was, for a time, an independent kingdom until being absorbed by Sevilla. In 1255 Alfonso X took the town and repopulated it with Castilians and Leonese. Some Muslims stayed but rebelled in 1261 and were evicted by 1264. In 1440 the town passed to the Ponce de León family, known as the Duques de Arcos, who were active in the conquest of Granada. When the last Duque de Arcos died heirless in 1780, his cousin, the Duquesa de Benavente, took over his land. She was partly responsible for replacing sheep farming with cereals, olives, vines and horse breeding as the dominant economic activities around Arcos. During the period of liberal rule from 1820 to '23, the so-called *señorío* system of land ownership by noble families was abolished, but the rural poverty that was part and parcel of the system continued well into the 20th century.

Orientation & Information
From the bus station, on Calle Corregidores in the new town (see the inset on the Arcos map), it's a 1km uphill walk to the old town.

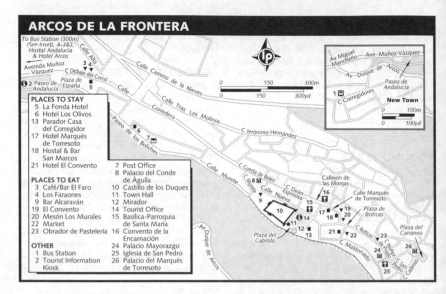

ARCOS DE LA FRONTERA

PLACES TO STAY
5   La Fonda Hotel
6   Hotel Los Olivos
13 Parador Casa
    del Corregidor
17 Hotel Marqués
    de Torresoto
18 Hostal & Bar
    San Marcos
21 Hotel El Convento

PLACES TO EAT
3   Café/Bar El Faro
4   Los Faraones
9   Bar Alcaraván
19 El Convento
20 Mesón Los Murales
22 Market
23 Obrador de Pastelería

OTHER
1   Bus Station
2   Tourist Information
    Kiosk
7   Post Office
8   Palacio del Conde
    de Águila
10 Castillo de los Duques
11 Town Hall
12 Mirador
14 Tourist Office
15 Basílica-Parroquia
    de Santa María
16 Convento de la
    Encarnación
24 Palacio Mayorazgo
25 Iglesia de San Pedro
26 Palacio del Marqués
    de Torresoto

About halfway up is the leafy Paseo de Andalucía. From Plaza España (occupied by
a roundabout) at the top of Paseo de Andalucía, Paseo de los Boliches and Calle
Debajo del Corral (becoming Calle Corredera) both head east up to the old town's
main square, Plaza del Cabildo. Parking is
available around Paseo de Andalucía and on
Plaza del Cabildo.

The tourist office (☎ 956 70 22 64), on
Plaza del Cabildo, opens 10 am to 2 pm and
5 to 7 pm Monday to Friday (to 6.30 pm
Saturday) and 10.30 am to 12.30 pm Sunday, and has lively staff. There's a tourist
information kiosk on Paseo de Andalucía,
open 10.30 am to 1.30 pm Monday to
Saturday.

Banks and ATMs, on Calle Debajo del
Corral and Calle Corredera, and the post office on Paseo de los Boliches, near Hotel
Los Olivos, are down to the west of the old
town. There are telephones by the church
on Plaza del Cabildo.

Things to See & Do
The best thing to do in Arcos is simply to
wander around the old town with its narrow
cobbled streets, Renaissance buildings and

whitewashed houses. **Plaza del Cabildo** is
surrounded by fine old buildings and has a
mirador with panoramic views over the
river and countryside. On the western side
of the square, Arcos' crowning glory, the
Castillo de los Duques, dating from the
11th century, is privately owned and not
open to the public. On the northern side,
take a look at the **Basílica-Parroquia de
Santa María**, begun on the site of a mosque
in the 13th century but not completed until
the 18th century. On the eastern side, the
parador, with striking views from its restaurant and terrace, is a 1960s reconstruction
of a 16th-century magistrate's house, the
Casa del Corregidor. The **town hall** at the
south-western corner of the square has a
Mudéjar panelled ceiling and a portrait of
Carlos IV attributed to Goya. Ask at the
tourist office for the key.

Explore the streets east of here, passing
by some lovely buildings such as the 16th-
century **Convento de la Encarnación**, on
Calle Marqués de Torresoto, which has a
Gothic facade. On Calle Núñez de Prado is
the **Iglesia de San Pedro**, in 15th-century
Gothic style but with an impressive baroque
facade and bell tower (the latter currently

CÁDIZ PROVINCE

closed). Inside is a large collection of religious paintings. Nearby, the 17th-century **Palacio Mayorazgo**, with a Renaissance facade, is now a senior citizens' centre.

The 15th-century Gothic/Mudéjar **Palacio del Conde de Águila**, on Calle Cuesta de Belén, has the town's oldest facade.

Organised Tours

The tourist office organises hour-long guided tours (400 ptas) of the old town and its fine patios. Times are posted at the tourist kiosk on Paseo de Andalucía.

Special Events

Easter processions through the town's narrow streets are dramatic. At the beginning of August the three-day Fiesta de la Virgen de las Nieves includes late-night music in Plaza del Cabildo, especially flamenco on the night of the 5th. On 29 September, during the fair dedicated to Arcos' patron saint San Miguel in the last few days of the month, there's a hair-raising running of the bulls.

Places to Stay – Budget

Open year round, **Camping Lago de Arcos** (☎ 956 70 05 14, ☎ 956 70 83 33) is in El Santiscal near the Lago de Arcos reservoir north-east of the old town. The easiest route from the old town is by the A-382 and the Carretera El Bosque y Ubrique. Turn left after the bridge across the dam. A local bus runs out here from Arcos. The cost for two people with a tent and a car is 1785 ptas. There's a good swimming pool.

There's little budget accommodation in the old town. **Hostal San Marcos** (☎ 956 70 07 21, Calle Marqués de Torresoto 6), above the bar/restaurant of the same name a short walk east of Plaza del Cabildo, has a handful of good, simple rooms with hand-painted furniture and attached bathroom. There's a roof terrace. Single/double rooms cost 2500/4500 ptas.

Hostal Andalucía (☎ 956 70 07 14, Polígono Industrial El Retiro), on the A-382 about 300m south-west of the bus station, offers the best deal in town, but it's above a car yard and backed by workshops. Large

rooms with attached bathroom, fan and TV cost 1605/3210 ptas, which is excellent value for singles.

Two kilometres from Arcos towards Jerez, **Hotel Arcos** (☎ 956 70 16 05, A-382 Km 24) has 20 comfy rooms from 4500/6500 ptas.

Places to Stay – Mid-Range & Top End

Arcos has some charming places to stay in these ranges. Add IVA to all prices. **La Fonda Hotel** (☎ 956 70 00 57, Calle Debajo del Corral), in a listed 19th-century building near Plaza España, has newly-renovated singles/doubles with bathroom, heating, air-con and TV costing 5000/7500 ptas. **Hotel El Convento** (☎ 956 70 23 33, fax 956 70 41 28, Calle Maldonado 2), in a 17th-century convent just east of Plaza del Cabildo, has similar views to the parador's. Tasteful rooms cost 8000/10,000 ptas, or 12,000 ptas with a terrace.

In the same part of town, **Hotel Marqués de Torresoto** (☎ 956 70 07 17, fax 956 70 42 03, Calle Marqués de Torresoto 4), a converted mansion, has singles/doubles for 7820/10,465 ptas. Down the hill towards Plaza España, the attractive **Hotel Los Olivos** (☎ 956 70 08 11, fax 956 70 08 11, Paseo de los Boliches 30) has rooms costing 5000/9000 ptas.

Parador Casa del Corregidor (☎ 956 70 05 00, fax 956 70 11 16, Plaza del Cabildo) offers typical parador luxury at 14,000/17,500 ptas.

Elegant **Hacienda El Santiscal** (☎ 956 70 83 13, fax 956 70 82 68, ✉ santiscal@estancias.es, Avenida El Santiscal 129), at the Lago de Arcos (see Camping Lago de Arcos for directions), costs 7000/12,000 ptas. It has a pool and riding stables.

Places to Eat

In the old town the homely **Bar San Marcos** (Calle Marqués de Torresoto 6) does platos combinados from 500 ptas to 900 ptas, tapas for around 200 ptas and a menú costing 900 ptas. Opposite, **El Convento**, in a 16th-century palace, is a classy restaurant (some say overpriced) turning

CÁDIZ PROVINCE

out interesting fare – the three-course menú costs 3000 ptas plus IVA. *Mesón Los Murales* (*Plaza de Boticas 1*), near the Hotel El Convento, has a cheaper menú costing 1000 ptas and main dishes from 600 ptas to 1400 ptas. The *market* (mercado) is opposite. A little east of here on Calle Núñez de Prado is the good bakery *Obrador de Pastelería*. The cave-like *Bar Alcaraván* (*Calle Nueva 1*), with tables outside under the castle walls, is good for tapas.

In the new town, there are a couple of options on Calle Debajo del Corral near Plaza España. *Café/Bar El Faro* at No 14 has breakfasts costing 225 ptas, main dishes from 500 ptas to 1500 ptas and a menú costing 900 ptas. *Los Faraones* at No 8 does cheap breakfasts (150 ptas), platos combinados (600 ptas) and a menú (800 ptas), plus excellent but pricier Arabic food with some tasty vegetarian choices.

There are more eateries down by the river, below the castle.

Entertainment

In July and August flamenco happens at 10.30 pm on Thursdays at the small but atmospheric Plaza del Cananeo, in the old town at the bottom of Calle Cadenas, opposite the Palacio del Marqués de Torresoto. In summer, the flat ground below the castle and near the river is lively with bars, restaurants and music.

Getting There & Away

Daily buses from Calle Corregidores (in the new town) from Monday to Friday include 19 to Jerez, six to El Bosque and a few each to Cádiz, Sevilla and Ronda with Los Amarillos. There are additional buses with Comes. Fewer buses run at the weekend.

PARQUE NATURAL SIERRA DE GRAZALEMA

The Cordillera Bética, the band of rugged mountain ranges that stretches across much of Andalucía, has beautiful beginnings in the Sierra de Grazalema – actually a group name for several small ranges – in northeast Cádiz province. This area, dotted with white mountain villages, contains a great

variety of marvellous landscapes, from pastoral river valleys to precipitous gorges and rocky summits. It's one of the greenest parts of Andalucía and Grazalema town has the highest measured rainfall in Spain at an average 2153mm a year. Snow is common on the mountains in late January or February.

This is excellent walking country (the best months are May, June, September and October) and there are opportunities for a range of other activities from rock climbing and caving to paragliding and trout fishing.

A fairly good map of the 517 sq km Parque Natural Sierra de Grazalema, which with luck you'll find in shops and tourist offices locally, is the IGN/Junta de Andalucía *Sierra de Grazalema*, at 1:50,000. The park extends into north-western Málaga province, where it includes the Cueva de la Pileta near Ronda.

Flora & Fauna

Much of the area is covered in beautiful Mediterranean woodland of evergreen oaks, wild olive (*acebuche*) and carob (*algarrobo*). In autumn, broom adds splashes of yellow. The northern flank of the Sierra del Pinar between Grazalema and Benamahoma supports a famous 3 sq km *pinsapar*, the best preserved woodland of the rare Spanish fir (*pinsapo* in Spanish). Over 500 ibex live in the park: you may see some if you climb El Torreón. You *will* see a lot of domesticated animals grazing in semi-liberty – among them plenty of Iberian pigs. Around 100 pairs of griffon vultures live in the Garganta Verde and Garganta Seca gorges.

Getting There & Away

Bus schedules are subject to change. To confirm Los Amarillos times, ring their offices in Cádiz or Jerez (see those city sections) or Ubrique (☎ 956 46 80 11), Màlaga (☎ 95 235 00 61), Ronda (☎ 95 218 70 61) or Sevilla (☎ 95 441 71 11).

Los Amarillos runs up to seven buses a day to El Bosque and Ubrique from Jerez and Arcos de la Frontera, and two or three from Cádiz and Sevilla (Prado de San Sebastián bus station). Fares to El Bosque are 915 ptas from Cádiz, 800 ptas from Jerez,

Walks in the Grazalema Área de Reserva

Much of the Grazalema natural park's most spectacular scenery, and its three major highlight walks, are within a 30 sq km *área de reserva* between Grazalema, Benamahoma and Zahara de la Sierra.

Rules for entering the área de reserva have changed from time to time in the past. At the time of writing, you need a free permit from the El Bosque park office (see the El Bosque section), which is attended 10 am to 2 pm Monday and Tuesday, as well as during its normal opening hours, for issuing permits. You can call in advance to request permits for specific days and/or to arrange to collect your permit at Zahara or Grazalema instead of El Bosque. Booking ahead is recommended as there are limits on the numbers of people per day on the main routes – 60 for the *pinsapar* (woodland of Spanish fur) walk and 30 each for Torreón and the Garganta Verde. A further rule is that from January to June (the vulture nesting season) the Garganta Verde can only be visited with an authorised guide from Horizon or Pinzapo (see the Grazalema section).

Ascent of El Torreón

The usual route up El Torreón (1654m), the highest peak in Cádiz province, is from the southern side, starting about 8km from Grazalema, 100m east of the Km 40 marker on the Grazalema–Benamahoma road. From this point (about 850m high), it takes about 2½ hours of walking to reach the summit and 1½ hours to get back down. From the summit on a very clear day you can see Gibraltar, the Sierra Nevada and the Rif Mountains of Morocco.

Grazalema–Benamahoma via the Pinsapar

This 14km walk takes around six hours. Going from east to west, after a couple of steepish ascents in the first third of the walk, it's downhill most of the way.

Walk up from Grazalema to a point about 700m along the Zahara road from the A-372 (this takes about 40 minutes). Here turn onto the footpath that will lead across the northern slopes of the Sierra del Pinar. After an initial ascent of some 300m, you stick close to the 1300m contour passing below Pico San Cristóbal, whose pointed summit has long provided the first glimpse of home for Spanish sailors crossing the Atlantic.

The thickest part of the pinsapar comes in the middle third of the walk, below the range's precipitous upper slopes. The dark green *pinsapo* (Spanish fir) survives in significant numbers only in isolated pockets in south-west Andalucía and northern Morocco. Growing up to 30m high, it's a relic of the extensive Mediterranean fir forests of the Tertiary Period (which ended about 2.5 million years ago).

Garganta Verde

The path into the 'green gorge' – a lushly vegetated ravine, 100m and more deep – starts 3.5km from Zahara de la Sierra on the Grazalema road. It passes a viewpoint overlooking a colony of griffon vultures (around 100 pairs of these huge birds nest here and in the Garganta Seca, 2km west) before the 300m descent to the bottom of the gorge. It's a beautiful walk. Allow three to four hours if you drive to the start, five or six if you walk from Zahara.

370 ptas from Arcos and 960 ptas from Sevilla. From El Bosque, except on Sunday, there's a 3.15 pm Los Amarillos bus to Grazalema (275 ptas). The Grazalema–El Bosque bus departs at 5.30 am Monday to Friday, with an additional service at 7 pm on Friday.

Los Amarillos also runs from Málaga to Ubrique via Ronda, Grazalema and Benaocaz. At the time of writing buses leave Málaga at 10.30 am and 4 pm Monday to Friday, 10.30 am and 3 pm at weekends and holidays. They leave Ronda two to 2½ hours later. The return buses leave Ubrique at 7.30 am and 3.30 pm Monday to Friday, 8.30 am and 3.30 pm Saturday, Sunday and holidays, stopping in Benaocaz after about five minutes and Grazalema after half an hour. Fares to Grazalema are 310 ptas from Ronda and 1380 ptas from Málaga.

Comes (☎ 95 287 19 92) operates two buses each way Monday to Friday between Ronda and Zahara de la Sierra (475 ptas), via Algodonales. Departures from Ronda are at 7 am and 1 pm, and from Zahara at 8.15 am and 2 pm. To travel between Zahara and Sevilla, Arcos, Jerez or Cádiz, you need to change buses at Algodonales. There's no bus service between Zahara and Grazalema.

El Bosque
postcode 11670 • pop 1800
• elevation 385m

El Bosque, 33km east of Arcos de la Frontera across rolling countryside, is prettily situated below the wooded Sierra de Albarracín to the south-east. There's a take-off point for hang-gliders and paragliders in the Sierra de Albarracín, and plenty of trout to be fished in local streams. A pleasant 5km path up the Río El Bosque to Benamahoma starts beside El Bosque's youth hostel.

The natural park's main information centre (☎ 956 72 70 29) is at Avenida de la Diputación s/n, down a short lane off the A-372 at the western end of the village, opposite Hotel Las Truchas. It opens 10 am to 2 pm and 4 to 6 pm Wednesday to Sunday. El Bosque's large public swimming pool, with shade, is next door. Admission costs 350 ptas.

Camping La Torrecilla (☎/fax 956 71 60 95) is 1km south of the village centre on the old road to Ubrique (it is closed from 16 December to 31 January). It costs 1750 ptas for two adults with one tent and a car. The youth hostel, *Albergue Campamento Juvenil El Bosque* (☎ 956 71 62 12, Molino de Enmedio s/n) is pleasantly sited 800m up a side-road from beside Hotel Las Truchas. It has bungalows and a shady camping area as well as double and triple rooms, most with bathroom. It costs 900 ptas per person including breakfast. There's a swimming pool too.

Hostal Enrique Calvillo (☎ 956 71 61 05, Avenida Diputación 5), near the park information office, has doubles with bathroom for 4500 ptas. *Hotel Las Truchas* (☎ 956 71 60 61, Avenida Diputación 1) has comfy singles/doubles with bathroom for 4600/7500 ptas plus IVA, and a restaurant terrace overlooking the village and countryside. Try the trout, the local speciality.

Benamahoma
postcode 11679 • elevation 450m

The small village of Benamahoma, 4km east of El Bosque on the A-372 to Grazalema, is known for its market gardens, trout farm and a cottage industry of rush-backed chairs. You can walk to Zahara de la Sierra from here on dirt roads via the Puerto de Albarranes, Laguna del Perezoso and Puerto de Breña – a beautiful trip of 16km (five hours plus stops). Benamahoma remembers its past in its Fiestas de Moros y Cristianos (Festival of Moors and Christians), on the first Sunday of August.

Camping Los Linares (☎ 956 71 62 75), 600m up Camino del Nacimiento at the back of the village, has cabins with bedding that cost around 4500 ptas for two or 7000 ptas for four, as well as camping costing 475 ptas plus IVA for each adult and tent, and 375 ptas plus IVA per car. In winter it normally opens at weekends and holidays only.

Grazalema
postcode 11610 • pop 2300
• elevation 825m

From Benamahoma the A-372 winds east over the Puerto del Boyar (1103m) to Grazalema. Take care driving on this road when the mist comes down.

A haunt of nature lovers and artists (with a drug rehabilitation centre too), Grazalema is a neat, pretty, picture-postcard village, especially when dusted with snow. Its steep cobbled streets, lined by white houses with flowery window boxes, nestle into a corner of some beautiful mountain country beneath the rock climbers' crag Peñon Grande. Local products include pure wool blankets and rugs – a centuries-old tradition here.

CÁDIZ PROVINCE

The village centre is Plaza de España where you'll find the tourist office (☎ 956 13 22 25) doubling as a crafts and produce saleroom. It opens 10 am to 2 pm and 4 to 6 pm (6 to 8 pm in summer), Tuesday to Sunday. Unicaja bank, right by Plaza de España, has an ATM.

Things To See & Do Grazalema has a couple of lovely 17th-century churches, **Iglesia de la Aurora** on Plaza de España and the nearby **Iglesia de la Encarnación**.

Horizon (☎ 956 13 23 63), Calle Agua 5, offers a range of **guided activities** such as climbing, bridge-jumping, bird-watching and walking, with a minimum group size of four to six. Prices per person range from around 1700 ptas for a half-day walk to over 4000 ptas for some caving or canyoning trips. The office opens 11 am to 1 pm (to 2 pm at weekends) daily except Tuesday. Pinzapo (☎ 956 13 21 66), Calle Las Piedras 11, offers some similar activities.

Grazalema's large public swimming pool, with good views, is by the El Bosque road up at the eastern end of the village.

Camping Tajo Rodillo (see Places to Stay) rents out mountain bikes for 1400 ptas a day (1200 ptas if you're staying there).

Special Events Grazalema's Fiestas del Carmen, with plenty of late-night music and dance performances, fill a week in mid-July, ending on a Monday with a bull-running through the streets.

Places to Stay & Eat At the top of the village beside the A-372 to El Bosque, *Camping Tajo Rodillo (☎ 956 13 20 63)* charges 1575 ptas for two adults, a tent and car. In winter you may only find it open at weekends and holidays. In the village centre, *Casa de las Piedras (☎ 956 13 20 14, Calle Las Piedras 32)* is a good-value hostal with a couple of patios and a lounge with a log fire in winter. Singles/doubles cost 1500/3000 ptas, or 3600/4800 ptas with attached bathroom. Its restaurant, when open, serves hearty medium-priced breakfasts and meals.

The comfortable *Villa Turística (☎ 956 13 21 62, fax 956 13 22 13, El Olivar s/n)*,

above the village to the north, has manicured lawns with a swimming pool, a restaurant and great views. Its 24 rooms with all mod cons cost 4600/7500 ptas plus IVA; the 38 apartments cost from 6400 ptas plus IVA for one person to 16,900 ptas plus IVA for four.

There are plenty of places to eat and drink on Calle Agua, off Plaza de España, among them *Bar La Posadilla* with very acceptable platos combinados for only 300 ptas to 500 ptas.

Restaurante Cadiz El Chico (Plaza de España 8) is good for a more expensive meal, with venison, lamb or pork costing from 1200 ptas to 1600 ptas, and *carnes a la plancha* (grilled meat), fish and seafood starting at 600 ptas to 800 ptas. *Restaurante El Tajo*, with panoramic views above the swimming pool at the eastern end of the village, has classy airs. The buffet lunch, in summer, costs around 1200 ptas, salads cost from 250 ptas to 500 ptas, and trout stuffed with ham costs 1350 ptas.

Zahara de la Sierra
postcode 11688 • pop 1550
• elevation 550m

Topped by a crag with a ruined castle, Zahara de la Sierra is the most northerly and most dramatically sited of the natural park's villages. It feels quite otherworldly if you've driven the 18km from Grazalema through heavy mist via the vertiginous 1331m Puerto de los Palomas (Doves' Pass, but with more vultures than doves). There's a reservoir below the village, to the north and the east.

Founded by Muslims in the 8th century, Zahara fell in 1407 to the Castilian prince Fernando de Antequera. Its recapture by Abu al-Hasan of Granada in a daring night raid in 1481 sparked the last phase of the Reconquista, which ended in the fall of Granada. In the late-19th century Zahara was a noted hotbed of anarchism.

The village centres on Calle San Juan, a cobblestone street with a church at each end. At one end of this, at Plaza del Rey 3, is a natural park information office (☎ 956 12 31 14), open from at least 9 am to 2 pm daily.

CÁDIZ PROVINCE

Things to See & Do There's a **mirador** at one end of Calle San Juan, in front of the 18th-century baroque **Iglesia de Santa María de la Mesa**. You can climb to the 12th-century **castle**, of which one tower survives, by a road behind this church – or by a path with steps from the main road below the village. Zahara's steep streets invite investigation, with vistas framed by tall palms or hot-pink bougainvillea in summer, fruited orange trees in winter.

Places to Stay & Eat Three kilometres south-east of Zahara near the reservoir, *Camping Arroyomolinos* (☎ 956 23 40 79), charges 1000 ptas for two adults with a tent and a car. *Pensión Los Tadeos* (956 12 30 86, Paseo de la Fuente s/n) has a few basic rooms costing 3000 ptas a double. *Hostal Marqués de Zahara* (☎ 956 12 30 61, Calle San Juan 3), a converted mansion, has 10 comfy singles/doubles with bathroom and winter heating, costing 3750/5650 ptas. Its restaurant, with a 1500-ptas menú, is for guests only, but there are other places to eat on this street, including *Bar Nuevo* with homely, cheap food. The new *Hotel Arco de la Villa* (☎ 956 12 32 30, fax 956 12 32 44, Camino Nazarí s/n) has 17 air-con rooms with TV and good views, costing 4600/7500 ptas plus IVA, and a restaurant.

Benaocaz
postcode 11612 • pop 575
• elevation 790m
The pretty village of Benaocaz, on the A-374 Ubrique–Grazalema road amid limestone country in the south of the park, has a couple of reasonable accommodation options and is the start or end of some good walks. It has a historical museum and a Barrio Nazarí, the ruins of a Nasrid settlement (see the History section in the Facts About Andalucía chapter for more information about the Nasrids).

Walks It's about 1¼ hours' walk north to the **Salto del Cabrero**, a dramatic fissure in the earth's surface 500m long, 100m wide and 100m deep; or 1½ hours north-east to the **Casa del Dornajo**, a ruined farmstead high in a beautiful valley. From either of

these you can continue to Grazalema in about two hours via the Puerto del Boyar pass on the A-372. A 6km stretch of **Roman road** heads south-west down from Benaocaz to the town of Ubrique.

Places to Stay & Eat Up at the northern end of Benaocaz, *Refugio de Montaña El Parral* (☎/fax 956 12 55 65, ☎ 608 32 25 73) has clean six-bunk dormitories costing 900 ptas plus IVA per person (bring your own sleeping bag), and a dining room and bar. Just below El Parral, *Hostal San Antón* (☎ 956 12 55 77, Plaza de San Antón s/n) offers singles/doubles with bathroom costing 5000/9000 ptas plus IVA. A good place to eat in the centre of Benaocaz is *La Palmera*, with a nice terrace.

Costa de la Luz

The 90km coast between Cádiz and Tarifa can be windy, and its Atlantic waters are a shade cooler than those of the Mediterranean. But these are small prices to pay for an unspoiled, often wild shore, strung with long, clean, white-sand beaches and just a few small towns and villages. Andalucians are well aware of its attractions and flock down here in their thousands during July and August, bringing a vibrant fiesta atmosphere to the normally quiet coastal settlements. It's advisable to ring ahead for rooms in these months.

From before Roman times until the advent of 20th-century tourism, this coast was mainly devoted to tuna fishing. Shoals of big tuna, some weighing 300kg, are still intercepted by walls of net several kilometres long as the fish head in from the Atlantic towards their Mediterranean spawning grounds in spring, and again as they head out in July and August. Barbate has the main tuna fleet today.

VEJER DE LA FRONTERA
postcode 11150 • pop 12,900
• elevation 190m
This old-fashioned white town looms mysteriously atop a rocky hill above the busy

CÁDIZ PROVINCE

N-340, 50km from Cádiz and 10km inland. It's well worth a wander.

Orientation & Information

The oldest area of town, still partly walled and with narrow winding streets clearly signifying its Muslim origins, spreads over the highest part of the hill. Just below is the small Plazuela, more or less the heart of town, with the Hotel Convento de San Francisco and, close by, the tourist office (☎ 956 45 01 91), Calle Marqués de Tamarón 10, open 8 am to 2 pm and 4 to 7 pm Monday to Friday, 11 am to 2 pm at weekends. When the tourist office is closed you can pick up a town map from the Hotel Convento de San Francisco. Buses stop on Avenida Remedios, the road up from the N-340, about 500m below the Plazuela.

Things to See

Within the walled area, seek out the **Iglesia del Divino Salvador** whose interior is Mudéjar at the altar end and Gothic at the other; and the much-reworked **castle**, open during Easter and summer only, with great views from its battlements and a small museum that preserves one of the black cloaks, covering everything but the eyes, that Vejer women wore until just a couple of decades ago.

Places to Stay & Eat

Across town from the old walled area, *Hostal La Janda* (☎ 956 45 01 42, Calle Machado 16) has doubles with bathroom costing 6000 ptas. Down a side-street nearby, *Hostal Buena Vista* (☎ 956 45 09 69, Calle Manuel Machado 20), has good-value, spotless doubles with bathroom costing 5000 ptas plus IVA, some with fine views across to the old part of town. The *Hotel Convento de San Francisco* (☎ 956 45 10 01, Plazuela s/n), in a restored 17th-century convent, has singles/doubles costing 6800/9100 ptas plus IVA. *La Bodeguita* (Calle Marqués de Tamarón 9), near the tourist office, has excellent tapas and meals. Across the street, *Bar Joplin* is a laid-back place for a drink, especially late at weekends.

Getting There & Away

The small Comes office (☎ 956 44 71 46) on Plazuela has bus information. Buses run to/from Cádiz (550 ptas) and Barbate (140 ptas) up to nine times a day. More buses for the same places, plus Tarifa and Algeciras (about 10 daily), La Línea, Málaga and Sevilla (three daily) stop at La Barca de Vejer, on the N-340 at the bottom of the hill. By road it's 4km uphill from La Barca to the town; on foot, there's a shortcut – follow the locals up the path!

BARBATE

postcode 11160 • pop 18,000

A fishing and canning town with a long sandy beach and a big harbour, Barbate becomes a fairly lively resort in summer, but it's mostly a drab place. You might need to use Barbate as a staging post if you're travelling by bus. The Comes bus station (☎ 956 43 05 94) is more than 1km back from the beach at the northern end of the long main street, Avenida del Generalísimo. The only tourist office (☎ 956 43 39 62) for the Los Caños de Meca–Zahara de los Atunes–Barbate area is at Plaza Onésimo Redondo s/n. Coming from the bus station, turn left off Avenida del Generalísimo at Calle Agustín Varo (opposite Avenida de Andalucía with the market) and follow it for nine blocks to Plaza Onésimo Redondo. Basic opening hours are 8 am to 8 pm Monday to Friday.

Hotel Mediterráneo (☎ 956 43 02 43, Calle Albufera 1), near the market, has doubles with bathroom costing 4800 ptas, but only opens at Easter and from July to mid-September. The better *Hotel Galia* (☎ 956 43 04 82, Calle Doctor Valencia 5), a few blocks back towards the sea from the bus station, has singles/doubles costing from 3500/5000 ptas to 5000/8000 ptas. You'll find plenty of seafood eateries with lots of local specialities on Paseo Marítimo.

Buses run to/from La Barca de Vejer (see the earlier Vejer de la Frontera section) and Cádiz up to 12 times daily, Vejer de la Frontera up to nine times daily, Sevilla twice (once on Saturday and Sunday) and Tarifa and Algeciras once. Three buses run daily

CÁDIZ PROVINCE

Monday to Friday (two on Saturday and Sunday) to/from Zahara de los Atunes.

LOS CAÑOS DE MECA
postcode 11159

Los Caños, once a hippy hideaway, straggles untidily along a series of sandy coves beneath a pine-clad hill 12km west of Barbate. It maintains its laid-back, off-the-beaten-track air even during the height of summer.

The coast between Barbate and Los Caños is mostly cliffs up to 100m high. The road between the two places runs inland through the Breña umbrella pine forest. These cliffs and forest, along with wetlands east and north of Barbate, form the **Parque Natural de la Breña y Marismas de Barbate**. A couple of walking paths start from the road: one goes to Playa de la Hierbabuena beach just west of Barbate, the other to the Torre del Tajo, a 16th-century clifftop lookout tower. Another tower, the Torre de Meca on the hill behind Los Caños, can be reached from this road.

The road emerges towards the eastern end of Los Caños' single street, which is mostly called Avenida Trafalgar. The main beach is straight in front of you. Those who want to swim nude do so around the small headland at its eastern end. At the western end of the village a side-road leads out to a lighthouse on a low spit of land with a famous name – Cabo de Trafalgar. It was off this cape that Spanish naval power was terminated in a few hours one day in 1805 by a British fleet under Admiral Nelson. Further decent beaches stretch either side of Cabo de Trafalgar.

Places to Stay

Three medium-sized camp sites open from April to September and get pretty crowded in high summer. Nearest the centre is *Camping Camaleón* (☎ *956 43 71 54, Avenida Trafalgar s/n*), about 1km west from the corner of Barbate road, with a shady site costing about 2385 ptas for two people with a car and tent. *Camping Faro de Trafalgar* (☎ *956 43 70 17*) is another 700m west, and *Camping Caños de Meca* (☎ *956 43 71 20*),

1km farther on in the separate settlement of Zahora, are slightly cheaper.

About 10 hostales are strung along Avenida Trafalgar in Los Caños, and there are more at Zahora. Most are pretty similar and have decent rooms with bathroom.

The quieter end of the village is east from the Barbate road corner. *Hostal Fortuna* (☎ *956 43 70 75*), a couple of hundred metres along, has excellent singles/doubles costing 4000/6000 ptas (6000/8000 ptas in August). A bit farther on, the laid-back *Hostal Los Castillejos* (☎ *956 43 70 19*) is a quaint turreted little place with lingering hippy vibes. It's open at least in the summer when doubles with bathroom cost from 5500 ptas to 7500 ptas.

Immediately west of the Barbate road corner, *Hostal Villa de Guadalupe* (☎ *956 43 72 29, Avenida Trafalgar 56*) is a bit classier with doubles costing 10,000 ptas, but it only opens in the summer. Farther in the same direction, *Hostal Mar y Sol* (☎ *956 43 72 55, Avenida Trafalgar 102*), open from June to September, has doubles costing 5500 ptas or 6500 ptas plus IVA. *Hostal Miramar* (☎ *956 43 70 24*), a few doors farther on, boasts a pool and restaurant and opens from Easter to the end of September. High season rates for doubles with bathroom are 6000 ptas. Past the Camping Camaleón turning, *Hostal El Ancla* (☎ *956 43 71 00*) has doubles or triples with bathroom, fridge and TV which cost from 5000 ptas to 7000 ptas. It's closed in winter.

Just past El Ancla, an 'Apartamentos y Bungalows' sign points to *Casas Karen*, also called *Fuente del Madroño* (☎ *956 43 70 67, fax 956 43 72 33, ✆ karen@jet.es, Fuente del Madroño 6*). Follow the sign then take the second turning to the right, and you'll reach the accommodation about 500m from the road, on a large, pretty acacia-covered plot. Run by a warm and dynamic young Englishwoman, the eclectic buildings, all with kitchen, bathroom, lounge and outdoor sitting areas, range from a converted farmhouse to an exotic thatch-roofed hut *(choza)*, a traditional dwelling built of local materials. Decoration is simple with Spanish and Moroccan touches. Individuals, and short stays, are welcome but the place caters more for weekly rentals. One-night prices for doubles start at 6000 ptas to 9000 ptas depending on season. A week in the hut, for two people, costs 36,000 ptas to 54,000 ptas.

At Zahara, *Hostal Alhambra* (☎ 956 43 72 16), opposite Camping Caños de Meca, has Alhambra-esque trimmings, a restaurant and nice rooms with little verandas costing 6000 ptas plus IVA for doubles.

Places to Eat

A short distance east from the Barbate road corner, but only open in season, *Bar-Restaurante El Caña* has a fine position atop the small cliff above the beach. Most seafood costs around 1300 ptas, but there are cheaper dishes of chicken, meatballs and so on. You may wait a long time for a waiter, though.

El Pirata, overlooking the beach a couple of hundred metres west, is a good bet during the day in season, with salads costing from 300 ptas and seafood mediaraciones at 600 ptas. The excellent *revueltos de gambas y ortigas* (scrambled eggs with shrimps and sea anemones) are around 1000 ptas. This place is a hip little bar on winter weekend nights with an open fire and good music.

In winter, when no eatery is open in the village, try *Las Acacias* on the road to Zahora near the Trafalgar turning, or *Restaurante El Capi*, attached to the hostal of the same name on the main road at Zahora, which serves decent tapas and good fish dishes and has a welcoming open fire.

Entertainment

In the main tourist season good bars include the cool *Bonano*, next to Hostal Los Castillejos (see Places to Stay), *Café-Bar Ketama* across the street from El Pirata and a couple of livelier places with music on the road out to Cabo de Trafalgar – *Las Dunas* here opens year round. *La Jaima*, in a Moroccan tent *(carpa)* with plush red seats, overlooking the beach just east of the Barbate road corner, has belly dancing shows.

The *Sajoramí* restaurant/bar on Playa Zahora often has live rock, blues or flamenco on summer nights. Turn left by Camping Caños de Meca, then first right along a sandy road and keep going for 600m.

Getting There & Away

Monday to Friday, two buses each run to/from Barbate and Cádiz and one each to/from Sevilla (Prado de San Sebastián) and Zahara de los Atunes daily. From mid-June to early September, there's usually a daily bus leaving Sevilla for Los Caños (1900 ptas), Barbate and Zahara at 9 am, and returning from Los Caños to Sevilla at 7 pm.

ZAHARA DE LOS ATUNES
postcode 11393

Plonked in the middle of nothing except a broad, 12km-long, west-facing sandy beach, Zahara is an elemental sort of place. At the heart of the village stand the crumbling walls of the old Almadraba, once a depot and refuge for the local tuna fishers, who were an infamously rugged lot. Cervantes, in *La Ilustre Fregona*, wrote that no one deserved the name *pícaro* (low-life scoundrel) unless they had spent two seasons at Zahara fishing for tuna. The pícaros were evidently good at their job for records state that in 1541 no fewer than 140,000 tuna were brought into Zahara's Almadraba. Today the tuna industry has dwindled out of sight but Zahara is an increasingly popular, almost fashionable, Spanish summer resort. With a little old-fashioned core of narrow streets, it's altogether a fine spot to let the sun, sea, wind – and, in summer, a spot of lively nightlife – batter your senses.

Unicaja bank on Calle María Luisa has an ATM.

Places to Stay

The good *Camping Bahía de la Plata* (☎ 956 43 90 40), open year round, is near the beach at the southern end of Zahara on Carretera de Atlanterra. It costs 2490 ptas for two people with a car and a tent.

Otherwise the cheapest place, and the most likely to have a room when everywhere else is full in July/August, is *Hostal*

euro currency converter €1 = 166 ptas

Monte Mar (☎ *956 43 90 47, Calle Peñón 12),* at the northern tip of the village. The rooms are fine at 6500 ptas a double with bathroom. The small *Hotel Nicolás* (☎ *956 43 92 74, Calle María Luisa 13)* has simple but attractive singles/doubles with TV and bathroom costing 5000/7000 ptas plus IVA, and a restaurant. Next door is the *Hotel Almadraba* (☎ *956 43 93 32, Calle María Luisa 15)* with doubles costing 8500 ptas plus IVA.

The prime beach position is occupied by the *Hotel Gran Sol* (☎ *956 43 93 01, Calle Sánchez Rodríguez s/n),* right by the sands and facing the old Almadraba walls, with large, comfortable doubles costing 12,500 ptas plus IVA. It has a beachfront pool. *Hotel Doña Lola* (☎ *956 43 90 09, Plaza Thompson 1),* near the entrance to Zahara, is a modern place in an attractive old-fashioned style, with good doubles costing 10,000 ptas plus IVA.

Places to Eat

Most restaurants are on or near Plaza de Tamarón near the Hotel Doña Lola, and most offer similar lists of fish, seafood, salads, meat and sometimes pizzas. *Patio la Plazoleta* on Plaza de Tamarón is a good one, open to the air: a media-ración of *pez limón a la plancha* (grilled tuna with vegetables and lemon) costs 800 ptas, and it does good pizzas for around 1000 ptas. *Café-Bar Casa Juanita*, off the square on Calle Sagasta, is another pleasant place, with similar fare a little cheaper. It's not a bad spot for your morning coffee and tostada, either.

Entertainment

In July and August a line of tents and makeshift shacks along the beach south of the Almadraba serve as bars, discos and *teterías* (Islamic-style tearooms). They get busy from about midnight, and some have live flamenco or other music.

Getting There & Away

The Comes line runs three buses daily Monday to Friday (two on Saturday and Sunday) to/from Cádiz (850 ptas) via Bar-

bate, and one each Monday to Friday to/from Sevilla via Los Caños de Meca (1950 ptas) and to/from Tarifa (410 ptas). There are more buses from mid-June to September.

BOLONIA
postcode 11391

This tiny village, 10km down the coast from Zahara and about 20km from Tarifa, has a fine white sand beach good for windsurfing, several restaurants and small hostales, lots of cockerels, and the ruins of the Roman town of **Baelo Claudia**. The ruins include substantial remains of a theatre, a paved forum surrounded by remains of temples and other buildings, and the remains of the workshops that turned out the products which made Baelo Claudia famous in the Roman world: salted fish and *garum* paste (a spicy seasoning derived from fish). The site (☎ 956 68 85 30) opens 10 am to 6 pm Tuesday to Saturday (to 7 pm in spring, 8 pm in summer) and 10 am to 2 pm on Sunday. Admission is free for EU citizens (250 ptas for others).

Bolonia is destined to be the Spanish end of a tunnel under the Strait of Gibraltar to Tangier, Morocco. The 38km tunnel, for vehicle-carrying trains, is projected by the Spanish and Moroccan governments but won't happen until sufficient funds are found. It will actually begin a couple of kilometres inland and cross under the coastline between Bolonia and Punta Paloma.

Places to Stay

In the centre of the village, *Hostal Bellavista* (☎ 956 68 85 53) has singles/doubles with bathroom costing 4000/6500 ptas (2000/4000 ptas in winter). *Hostal Miramar* (☎ 956 68 85 61), open from Easter until September, has doubles with bathroom costing from 4000 ptas to 5500 ptas, and apartments. *Hostal Lola* (☎ 956 68 85 36), with a pretty garden, has basic rooms with bathroom costing from 4000 ptas to 6000 ptas. Follow the signs on giant surfboards to beyond and behind Hostal Miramar.

Places to Eat

There are three or four *open-air restaurants* on the beach at the eastern end of the village. (Windsurfers' camper vans park nearby.) In the village, the *Hostal Bella-vista* restaurant does straightforward Spanish fare very nicely. The friendly, relaxed *El Rincón de Loli* near Hostal Lola prepares a tasty *entrecot* (sirloin steak) *al roquefort* (1400 ptas) and *croquetas* (croquettes; 1000 ptas). Nearby, try the seafood at *Restaurante Marisma* with tables outside.

Getting There & Away

The only road to Bolonia heads west off the N-340, 15km from Tarifa. Without wheels it's a 7km hilly walk from the main road as there's no regular bus service. You can also walk 8km along the coast from Ensenada de Valdevaqueros via Punta Paloma (see Windsurfing in the Tarifa section).

TARIFA

postcode 11380 • pop 14,000

Even at peak times Tarifa is an attractive, laid-back town. Until 15 years or so ago it was relatively unknown, but it has since become a mecca for windsurfers. It's strange to see the international surf scene transported to this European setting with a strong Arabic feel, but if you're Australian, Californian or Hawaiian you'll feel right at home: the beaches have clean, white sand and good waves, and inland the country is green and rolling, though it can be chilly and wet in winter. Then there's the old town to explore with its pretty, narrow streets, whitewashed houses and flowers cascading from balconies and window boxes. Tarifa's castle is striking too. The only negative – though not for windsurfers or the hundreds of modern windmills on the hilltops inland – is the wind on which Tarifa's new prosperity is based. For much of the year, either the *levante* (easterly) or *poniente* (westerly) is blowing, ruinous for a relaxed sit on the beach and tiring if you're simply wandering around. August can be blessedly still, hot but not too hot, crowded but not overly so. The windmills, incidentally, are a mainly EU-funded experiment feeding power into Spain's national grid.

History

Tarifa may be as old as Phoenician Cádiz and was definitely a Roman settlement, but it takes its name from Tarik ibn Malik who led a Muslim raid in 710, the year before the main Islamic invasion of the peninsula. Muslims built the castle in the 10th century as fortification against Norse and African raids. (Pirates in the area at this time are said to have extracted a fee from ships wishing to pass safely from the Atlantic through the Strait of Gibraltar to the Mediterranean. This may be the origin of the Spanish word *tarifa* and its English equivalent, tariff.) Christians took Tarifa in 1292 but it was not secure until Algeciras was won in 1344. Later, Tarifa was active in the colonisation of the Americas: many of its people left for Peru in the 16th and 17th centuries.

Orientation & Information

Two roads lead into Tarifa from the N-340. The one from the north-west becomes Calle Batalla del Salado, which ends at east–west Avenida de Andalucía, where the Puerta de Jerez leads through the walls into the old town. The one from the east becomes Calle Amador de los Ríos, which also meets Avenida de Andalucía at the Puerta de Jerez.

The main street of the old town is Calle Sancho IV El Bravo, with the Iglesia de San Mateo at its eastern end. The castle overlooks the port on the southern side of the old town. To the south-west protrudes the Punta de Tarifa, a military-occupied promontory that is the southernmost point of continental Europe, with the Strait of Gibraltar to the south and east and the Atlantic Ocean to the west.

The tourist office (☎ 956 68 09 93) is near the top end of the palm-lined Paseo de la Alameda, which stretches down the western side of the old town. It opens 10.30 am to 2 pm and 5 to 7 pm (6 to 8 pm in summer) Monday to Friday, and summer Saturdays.

There are banks and ATMs on Calle Sancho IV El Bravo and Calle Batalla del Salado. The post office is at Calle Coronel Moscardó 9, south from the Iglesia de San

CÁDIZ PROVINCE

Mateo. The Policía Local station (☎ 956 61 41 86) is in the town hall. The Cruz Roja (Red Cross; ☎ 956 64 48 96) is at Calle Alcalde Juan Núñez 5, a short distance west of the bottom of the Paseo de la Alameda. Tarifa's hospital (☎ 956 68 15 15/35) is on Calle Amador de los Ríos.

International newspapers are sold at the News Stand on Calle Batalla del Salado, opposite the Puerta de Jerez. Internet access is available from 9 am to 1.30 pm and 5 to 8.30 pm at Pandora's Papelería, opposite Café Central on Calle Sancho IV El Bravo.

Things to See

Tarifa is best enjoyed by strolling through the tangled streets of the old town to the castle walls, checking out the castle, stopping in at the busy port and sampling the beaches.

The Mudéjar **Puerta de Jerez** was built after the Reconquista. Look in at the bustling, neo-Mudéjar **market** on Calle Colón before winding your way to the heart of the old town and the mainly 15th-century **Iglesia de San Mateo**. The streets south of the church are little changed since Islamic times. Climb the stairs at the end of Calle Coronel Moscardó and go left on Calle Al-

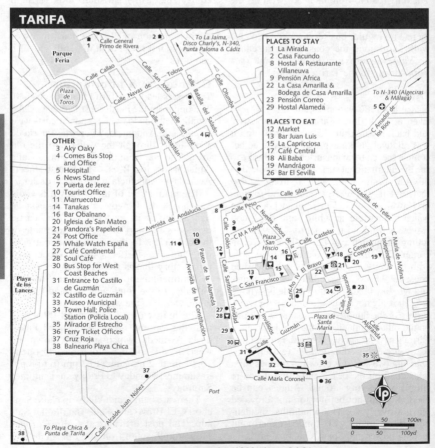

TARIFA

PLACES TO STAY
1 La Mirada
2 Casa Facundo
8 Hostal & Restaurante Villaneuva
9 Pensión Africa
22 La Casa Amarilla & Bodega de Casa Amarilla
23 Pensión Correo
29 Hostal Alameda

PLACES TO EAT
12 Market
13 Bar Juan Luis
15 La Capricciosa
17 Café Central
18 Ali Baba
22 Mandrágora
26 Bar El Sevilla

OTHER
3 Aky Oaky
4 Comes Bus Stop and Office
5 Hospital
6 News Stand
7 Puerta de Jerez
10 Tourist Office
11 Marruecotur
14 Tanakas
16 Bar Obaïnano
20 Iglesia de San Mateo
21 Pandora's Papelería
24 Post Office
25 Whale Watch España
27 Café Continental
28 Soul Café
30 Bus Stop for West Coast Beaches
31 Entrance to Castillo de Guzmán
32 Castillo de Guzmán
33 Museo Municipal
34 Town Hall; Police Station (Policía Local)
35 Mirador El Estrecho
36 Ferry Ticket Offices
37 Cruz Roja
38 Balneario Playa Chica

CÁDIZ PROVINCE

jaranda to reach the **Mirador El Estrecho** atop part of the castle walls, with spectacular views across to Africa. Nearby is Plaza de Santa María, where the small **Museo Municipal** may be open from 10 am to 2 pm Monday to Friday. Admission is free.

The **Castillo de Guzmán**, extending west from here (but entered at its far end on Calle Guzmán), is named after the Reconquista hero Guzmán El Bueno who, when Islamic attackers threatened to kill his kidnapped son unless he relinquished the castle to them, threw down his dagger for his son to be killed. (This happened in 1294 when the Christians were defending Tarifa against the Merenids of Morocco. Tarifa's Calle Batalla del Salado is named after a battle north of Vejer de la Frontera in 1340, in which Alfonso XI finally dealt the Merenids a conclusive defeat.)

Guzmán's descendants became the Duques de Medina Sidonia, who ran much of Cádiz province as a private fiefdom for a long time and remained Spain's largest landowners well into the 20th century. The imposing fortress was originally built in 960 under the orders of the Cordoban Caliph, Abd ar-Rahman III. You can walk along the parapets and stand atop the 13th-century Torre de Guzmán El Bueno for 360° views out to sea and Africa and back across the town to the windmills on the hills behind. The castle opens 10 am to 2 pm and 4 to 8 pm daily. Tickets can be bought in the stationery shop across the street from the castle entrance and cost 200 ptas.

Beaches

The popular town beach is the sheltered but very small **Playa Chica**, on the isthmus leading out to the Punta de Tarifa. From here **Playa de los Lances** stretches 10km north-west to the huge sand dune at Punta Paloma.

Outdoor Activities

Aky Oaky (☎ 956 68 53 56), Calle Batalla del Salado 37, offers a range of organised activities (costing from 2500 to 7000 ptas) including diving, walking, caving, mountain biking through a natural park, horse riding and visiting fighting bull farms.

Windsurfing

Conditions are often right for windsurfing on Tarifa's town beaches but most of the action occurs along the coast between Tarifa and Punta Paloma, 10km north-west. The best spots, of course, depend on wind and tide conditions. El Porro, on Ensenada de Valdevaqueros, the bay formed by Punta Paloma, is one of the most popular as it has easy parking and plenty of space to set up. The Río Jara, about 3km from Tarifa, is another popular take-off point.

You can buy new and second-hand gear in Tarifa at the windsurf shops along Calle Batalla del Salado. For board rental and classes you need to try places up the coast such as Club Mistral at the Hurricane Hotel (see Places to Stay), or Spin Out on the beach in front of Camping Torre de la Peña II, near El Porro. At Club Mistral board rental costs 2800 ptas an hour or 7500 ptas a day, and a six-hour beginner's course costs 19,500 ptas.

Competitions are held year round with two big events in summer – the World Speed Cup in July and the World Cup (Formula 42) in July or August.

Horse Riding

On Playa de los Lances, both the Hotel Dos Mares (☎ 956 68 40 35), about 4km from Tarifa, and the Hurricane Hotel (☎ 956 68 49 19), 6km out, rent out horses with guides. An hour's ride along the beach costs about 3000 ptas.

Whale Watching

Three-hour boat trips to track and watch dolphins and whales are run by Whale Watch España (☎ 956 62 70 13, ☎ 639 47 65 44). They have an office next to the Unicaja bank on Calle Sancho IV El Bravo, open daily. Trips cost 4500 ptas for adults (3000 ptas for children under 12).

Bird-Watching

The Tarifa area is one of the best places in Andalucía for bird-watching (see the boxed text 'High-Fliers over the Strait of Gibraltar' in the South-East section later in this chapter).

CÁDIZ PROVINCE

Places to Stay

Camping There are six year-round *camp sites*, with room for more than 4000 campers, on or near the beach between Tarifa and Punta Paloma, 10km north-west along the N-340. All charge about 2200 ptas for two people with a tent and a car. The two Torre de la Peña sites are among the more modern, with good restaurants and bars.

Hostales & Hotels There are several options in the old town and plenty of choice on and around Calle Batalla del Salado. At least nine more places are dotted along the beach and the inland side of the N-340 within 10km north-west from Tarifa, but none are cheap. Rooms can be tight in summer and when there are windsurfing competitions. It's best to phone ahead in August. Prices given here are for this peak month: you can expect reductions of 25% to 40% at most places for much of the rest of the year.

In Town Located in the old post office, *Pensión Correo* (☎ *956 68 02 06, Calle Coronel Moscardó 9*) is a good choice. Brightly painted rooms, some with bathroom, cost from 2000 ptas per person. The best double (with gorgeous views and its own terrace) costs 7000 ptas. The Italian owner is lively and helpful. *La Casa Amarilla* (☎ *956 65 19 93, fax 956 68 05 90,* @ lacasaamarilla@via.goya.es, *Calle Sancho IV El Bravo 9*) is in an imaginatively restored and beautifully decorated 19th-century building. Most of the rooms have a kitchenette with a small cooker and fridge: all have a private bathroom, heating and cable TV. Doubles cost 8000 ptas plus IVA.

The friendly, French-speaking *Hostal Villanueva* (☎ *956 68 41 49, Avenida de Andalucía 11*) is built into the old city walls a few doors west of the Puerta de Jerez. Good clean singles/doubles, all with bathroom and some with views to the castle, cost 4000/8000 ptas.

Pensión Africa (☎ *956 68 02 20, Calle María Antonia Toledo 12*), close to the market, has lively, well-travelled owners who have revamped an old house to make bright, comfortable rooms. There's a large roof terrace. Rooms cost 2500/4000 ptas with shared bathroom, 3500/5000 ptas with private bathroom.

On the edge of the old town, *Hostal Alameda* (☎ *956 68 11 81, Paseo de la Alameda 4*) has doubles with attached bathroom and air-con costing 9000 ptas.

Popular *Casa Facundo* (☎ *956 68 42 98, Calle Batalla del Salado 47*) is geared to windsurfers and even has a storage place for boards. Doubles with private bathroom and TV cost 6000 ptas; other singles/doubles cost 3000/4000 ptas. If you're after sea views, *La Mirada* (☎ *956 68 06 26, Calle San Sebastián 48*) has rooms costing from 6000/8000 ptas plus IVA.

Along the Coast All these places have rooms with a private bathroom.

Hostal Millón (☎ *956 68 52 46*), 5km from the town centre, has a nice little garden going onto the beach, its own small restaurant, and reasonable doubles costing 12,000 ptas.

Hurricane Hotel (☎ *956 68 49 19, fax 956 68 03 29*), 6km out, is the place to go if money is no object. Set in beachside semitropical gardens, it has 33 large, comfy rooms, two pools (one heated), a health club and a windsurfing school with board rental next door. Doubles cost 18,000 ptas plus IVA on the ocean side and 16,000 ptas plus IVA on the land side – including an excellent buffet breakfast.

Hostal Oasis (☎ *956 68 50 65*) and *Hotel La Ensenada* (☎ *956 68 06 37*), both about 8km out, are two of the less pricey places along here, with doubles costing up to 10,000 ptas depending on the season. Hostal Oasis also has 11 apartments with equipped kitchen costing up to 12,500 ptas for two people. La Ensenada closes for winter. *Cortijo Las Piñas* (☎ *956 68 51 36*), 10km out, is the closest hotel to Punta Paloma, with doubles costing 9800 ptas. Across the N-340, almost on the beach, the attractive *Cortijo Valdevaqueros* (same owners as the Hurricane Hotel), open from Easter to mid-September, has rooms costing around 10,000 ptas. There's a metallic sign above the beginning of a long, bumpy driveway.

CÁDIZ PROVINCE

Bridging Ronda's turbulent past with a peaceful present – Puente Nuevo, Málaga province

El Torcal, in Málaga province, was sculpted by millions of years of wind and water.

When in Ronda, it becomes hard to believe that Málaga province is the most populous in Andalucía.

Time for tee – one of Costa del Sol's 40 golf clubs at Marbella, Málaga province

A colourful past and present, Málaga province

Taking the rocky route, Los Cotos, El Chorro

Puerto Banús in Málaga province, known as the golden mile, is the marina to see and be seen in.

Places to Eat

Thanks to Tarifa's high number of international visitors, you're guaranteed some variation from regular Spanish fare.

In Town Calle Sancho IV El Bravo has all manner of takeaway options. Popular *Ali Baba*, with benches and stand-up tables outside, has cheap, filling and tasty Arabic food made with lovely fresh ingredients. Vegetarians can enjoy excellent falafel for 375 ptas; carnivores pay 450 ptas for the kebabs. A few doors away *Café Central* has delicious *churros y chocolate* (deep-fried doughnuts to dip in hot chocolate) and a large range of breakfasts costing from 300 ptas to 650 ptas. Main dishes on the long menu are 975 ptas.

There's excellent food nearby at the intimate *Mandrágora (Calle Independencia 3)*, behind Iglesia San Mateo. Delicious options include peppers stuffed with bacalao (1300 ptas) and chicken breasts stuffed with cheese (1000 ptas). The *boquerones* (anchovies, 1100 ptas) are sensational!

The best-value seafood in town is at *Bar El Sevilla*, the *marisquería* (seafood place) on Calle Inválidos west of the town centre. There's no name outside – some locals call it El Gallego. Mixed fish and seafood fry-ups cost 200 ptas for a generous tapa or 950 ptas for a ración – excellent washed down with a beer!

Bar Juan Luis (Calle San Francisco) does fantastic *lomo* (pork loin) sandwiches (300 ptas) while the Italian *La Capricciosa*, nearer the town centre on the same street, does very good pizzas (500 ptas to 1000 ptas).

Restaurante Villanueva (Avenida de Andalucía 11), attached to the hostal, does a brisk trade with its 850-ptas lunch menú.

Along the Coast Most hotels and hostales up here have their own restaurants. Hostal Millon's restaurant does good standard fare and has lovely ocean and Morocco views. The Hurricane Hotel's *Terrace Restaurant*, with the same views, is good for a medium-priced lunch (various salads, chicken, local fish and seafood) or drinks. In the evenings the hotel's interior restaurant does a wonderful beef fillet and very good roast lamb (each costing around 2000 ptas). Terrace Restaurant's fare is replicated at *Cortijo Valdevaqueros* near Punta Paloma (see Places to Stay), a hunk of chicken with good salads, bread and various condiments costs around 1200 ptas. Try the cakes!

Entertainment

The convivial *Bodega de Casa Amarilla*, on Calle Sancho IV El Bravo, opens from 7.30 pm, plus weekends from 1 to 4.30 pm for lunch and live flamenco. Close by, *Bar Obaïnano* serves fresh juices and exotic cocktails to cheerful background music. On Paseo de la Alameda, *Café Continental* has live music on summer weekend nights; it's also a good tapas, drinking or coffee stop at any time. *Soul Café*, nearby on Calle Santísima Trinidad, next to Café Continental's back entrance, is a popular disco/bar in the tourist season. *Tanakas* on Plaza San Hiscio is the biggest disco in town, open Friday and Saturday until 5 am.

In July and August the open-air disco at Balneario Playa Chica, with two dance floors, is fun. Also in summer, a big Moroccan tent known as *La Jaima* pops up on Playa de los Lances near the edge of town; from 7 to 10 pm it's an Islamic-style tearoom (try the mint tea at sunset!) but, come midnight, it's a proper disco. *Disco Charly's*, just out of town on the N-340, is a huge barn with a couple of bars, pool table, indoor swimming pool and a couple of raised platforms for dancers. On weekend nights, and nightly in summer, the whole place jumps; on other nights a small section opens as a disco.

Getting There & Away

Bus The Comes bus stop and office (☎ 956 68 40 38) is on Calle Batalla del Salado, 1½ blocks north of Avenida de Andalucía. Comes runs seven or more buses daily to Cádiz and Algeciras; a few each to La Línea, Jerez de la Frontera, Sevilla and Málaga; two to Facinas (except Sunday), and two to Barbate and Zahara de los Atunes (except Saturday and Sunday).

CÁDIZ PROVINCE

Car & Motorcycle Stop at the Mirador del Estrecho, about 7km out of Tarifa on the N-340 towards Algeciras, to take in magnificent views of the Strait of Gibraltar, the Mediterranean, the Atlantic and two continents. Beware of the frequent police speed trap in the 50km/h zone at Pelayo, a few kilometres farther east.

Boat A ferry between Tarifa and Tangier (one hour) had just begun services at the time of writing, departing Tarifa at 9 am and Tangier at 5 pm (3pm Moroccan time). Additional sailings are planned. Check at the harbour, or at Marruecotur (☎ 956 68 47 51), Avenida de la Constitución 5/6, opposite Paseo de la Alameda. Fares cost 3200 ptas for passengers, 9900 ptas for a driver and car, and 3000 ptas for a motorcycle.

Getting Around

Local buses run from Tarifa up the coast to just beyond Punta Paloma. There's a stop at the bottom of the Paseo de la Alameda. Taxis line up on Avenida de Andalucía near the Puerta de Jerez. You can hire bicycles from the Hurricane Hotel for 3000 ptas a day.

The South-East

PARQUE NATURAL LOS ALCORNOCALES

This large (1700 sq km) natural park stretches 75km north from the Strait of Gibraltar to the southern boundary of the Parque Natural Sierra de Grazalema. It's a jumble of sometimes rolling, sometimes rugged mountain ranges of medium height, and much of it is covered in Spain's most extensive cork oak woodlands *(alcornocales)*.

There are plenty of walks and possibilities for other activities in the park, but you need your own wheels to make the most of it, as it's sparsely populated and public transport runs mostly along its fringes. The park office (☎ 956 42 02 77) is at Plaza San Jorge 1 in the sleepy white town of Alcalá de los Gazules on the park's western fringe. Another information office, the Centro de Visitantes Huerta Grande (☎ 956 67 91 61),

with accommodation (☎ 956 67 97 00), is beside the N-340 Tarifa–Algeciras road at Pelayo, about 12km from Tarifa and 750m east of the modern *Albergue Juvenil Algeciras* (☎ 956 67 90 60). There's a bus stop on the N-340 in front of the hostel, which has a few singles, 17 doubles and 15 three/four-person rooms, with a bathroom for each two rooms and a swimming pool.

One road into the south of the park goes through the village of Facinas, off the N-340, 20km north of Tarifa. Facinas Natural (☎/fax 956 68 74 29), Calle Divina Pastora 6, offers a wide range of activities in the park including 15 routes for guided walks and cycling trips (each costing 2500 ptas), horse riding and donkey trips (5000 ptas each). Bicycle hire costs 1300 ptas a day.

The small town of **Jimena de la Frontera**, on the A-369 on the park's eastern boundary, is a good base for the generally higher and more rugged northern part of the park. Jimena is crowned by a fine **Muslim castle**, has a couple of *hostales*, and is served by train and bus from Algeciras and Ronda, and bus from La Línea. The CA-3331 heading north-west from here, a paved but rough road, will take you to La Sauceda, an abandoned village that's now the site of a camping area and cabins (☎ 902 23 73 30).

The La Sauceda area, which is actually a finger of Málaga province jutting into Cádiz province, is beautiful country covered in cork and gall oaks, laurel, wild olives, rhododendrons and ferns. It's a fairly remote area, once a den of bandits, smugglers and even guerrillas during the Spanish Civil War (during which the village was bombed by Franco's planes). Walking possibilities include the ascent of Aljibe (1092m), the park's highest peak, and nearby El Picacho (883m).

ALGECIRAS

postcode 11280 • pop 102,000

Algeciras, the major port linking Spain with Africa, is an unattractive, polluted place with little to hold you for longer than it takes to organise your crossing to Tangier or

CÁDIZ PROVINCE

High-Fliers over the Strait of Gibraltar

Most keen bird-watchers in Andalucía will want to head at some point for the Strait of Gibraltar, a key point of passage for raptors, storks and other migrators between Africa and Europe. In general, northward migrations occur between mid-February and early June, and southbound flights happen between late July and early November. When a westerly wind is blowing, Gibraltar itself is usually a good spot for seeing the birds. When the wind is calm or easterly, the Tarifa area (including the Mirador del Estrecho 7km east of the town) is usually better.

Soaring birds such as raptors, storks and vultures cross at the Strait of Gibraltar because they rely on thermals and updrafts, which don't happen over wider expanses of water. White storks sometimes congregate in flocks of up to 3000 to cross the strait (January and February northbound, July and August southbound).

From mid-July to mid-September every year, the Sociedad Española de Ornitología (SEO/BirdLife) organises a watch of migrating soarers over the strait. If you're interested in volunteering, send your name, address and passport number, a brief resumé of your ornithological experience and your preferred dates, to the Programa Migres (☎/fax 956 67 91 58), Centro Ornitológico del Estrecho de Gibraltar, Parque Natural Los Alcornocales, Carretera Nacional N-340 Km 96, 11390 Algeciras, Cádiz, Spain. The centre is in the same building as the Centro de Visitantes Huerta Grande of the Parque Natural Los Alcornocales.

Ceuta, though the town centre has at least been prettified. During the summer the port is hectic with hundreds of thousands of Moroccans working in Europe who return home for summer holidays. Algeciras is also an industrial town, a big fishing port and a centre for drug smuggling.

History

Algeciras was an important Roman port. In 711 it fell to the Islamic invaders. Alfonso XI of Castile wrested it from the Merenids of Morocco in 1344 but later Mohammed V of Granada razed it to the ground. In 1704, Algeciras was repopulated by many of those who left Gibraltar after the British took it. During the Franco era, industry was developed.

Orientation

Algeciras is on the western side of the Bahía de Algeciras, opposite Gibraltar. Avenida Virgen del Carmen runs north to south along the seafront, becoming Avenida de la Marina around the entrance to the port. From here Calle Juan de la Cierva (becoming Calle San Bernardo) runs inland beside a disued rail track to the Comes bus station (about 350m) and the train station (400m).

The central square, Plaza Alta, is a couple of blocks inland from Avenida Virgen del Carmen. Plaza Palma, with a bustling daily market (except Sunday), is one block west of Avenida de la Marina.

Information
Tourist Offices The English-speaking main tourist office (☎ 956 57 26 36) at Calle Juan de la Cierva s/n, a block inland from Avenida de la Marina, opens 9 am to 2 pm Monday to Friday. Inside there's a useful message board – helpful if you're trying to meet up with someone for the ferry.

Money Ignore money-changing touts around the port – they're a rip-off for pesetas and you'll get a better deal buying dirham if you wait until you reach Morocco. However, if you reach Morocco late at night you should have some dirham with you. Exchange rates are better at the banks than at travel agencies. There are banks and ATMs on Avenida Virgen del Carmen and around Plaza Alta, plus a couple of ATMs inside the port.

Post & Communications The post office is on Calle José Antonio just south of Plaza

CÁDIZ PROVINCE

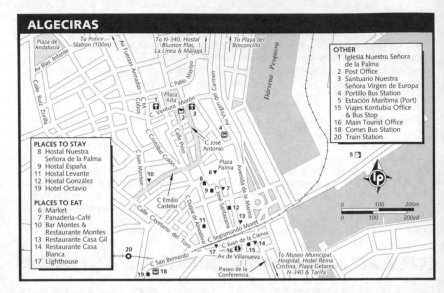

ALGECIRAS

OTHER
1 Iglesia Nuestra Señora de la Palma
2 Post Office
3 Santuario Nuestra Señora Virgen de Europa
4 Portillo Bus Station
5 Estación Marítima (Port)
15 Viajes Kontubia Office & Bus Stop
16 Main Tourist Office
18 Comes Bus Station
20 Train Station

PLACES TO STAY
8 Hostal Nuestra Señora de la Palma
9 Hostal España
11 Hostal Levante
12 Hostal González
19 Hotel Octavio

PLACES TO EAT
6 Market
7 Panadería-Café
10 Bar Montes & Restaurante Montes
13 Restaurante Casa Gil
14 Restaurante Casa Blanca
17 Lighthouse

Alta. There are telephones in the port, on Avenida de la Marina, near the market and at the train station.

Left Luggage In the port, luggage storage is available from 7.30 am to 9.30 pm costing 150 ptas for a small bag and 200 ptas for a large bag; bags need to be secured. If you have valuables there are lockers nearby (400 ptas).

Medical Services & Emergency The Hospital Cruz Roja (☎ 956 60 31 44) is central at Paseo de la Conferencia s/n, on the southern extension of Avenida de la Marina. The Policía Nacional station (☎ 956 66 04 00) is at Avenida de las Fuerzas Armadas 6 next to Parque de María Cristina. For an ambulance dial ☎ 956 65 15 55.

Dangers & Annoyances Keep your wits about you in the port, bus terminal and market, and ignore offers from the legions of money-changers, drug-pushers and ticket-hawkers who approach you. (It's nowhere near as bad as in Tangier!) Walk purposefully when moving between the Comes and Portillo bus stations in the evening.

Things to See & Do
Wander up to palm-fringed **Plaza Alta**, which has a lovely tiled fountain. On its western side is the 18th-century **Iglesia Nuestra Señora de la Palma** and on its eastern side the 17th-century **Santuario Nuestra Señora Virgen de Europa**, both worth a look. Some of the houses on the streets around here are delightfully tumbledown.

Leafy **Parque de María Cristina**, a few blocks to the north, also provides a change from the hustle and bustle of the port. The **Museo Municipal**, on Calle Nicaragua just south of the main tourist office, is reasonably interesting. If you've got your own wheels, check out the town's two beaches – **Playa Getares** (to the south) and **Playa del Rinconcillo** (north).

Special Events
The fair happens in the last week of June. On 15 August the town honours its patroness in the Fiesta del Virgen de la Palma.

Places to Stay
There's loads of budget accommodation in the streets behind Avenida de la Marina, but market traffic in the small hours makes

sleep difficult. If it's not too hot, try for an interior room.

The friendly **Hostal González** (☎ 956 65 28 43, Calle José Santacana 7) has good, clean singles/doubles with private bathroom costing 2000/4000 ptas in summer. **Hostal España** (☎ 956 66 82 62, Calle José Santacana 4) has large, clean rooms costing 1200 ptas per person, but it's right by the market.

Also near the market, **Hostal Nuestra Señora de la Palma** (☎ 956 63 24 81, Plaza Palma 12) has comfortable rooms with bathroom and TV costing 2000/4000 ptas. **Hostal Levante** (☎ 956 65 15 05, Calle Duque de Almodóvar 21) is a little removed from the thick of things; reasonable rooms with a shower cost 1500/3000 ptas, though the corridors are a bit musty. The cheerful **Hostal Blumen Plas** (☎ 956 63 16 75, N-340 Km 108), north of the town, with doubles costing 5500 ptas (6500 ptas in August), is a good choice if you want to stay out of the town centre.

Hotel Octavio (☎ 956 65 27 00, Calle San Bernardo 1), with doubles costing 20,000 ptas (15,000 ptas from January to April) plus IVA, is a big step up in price despite being unsalubriously located above the Comes bus station. **Hotel Reina Cristina** (☎ 956 60 26 22, Paseo de la Conferencia s/n), a brisk five-minute walk south of the port, is an old colonial-style hotel set amid tropical gardens. Doubles cost 22,000 ptas (16,000 ptas in winter) plus IVA. This hotel, a suitable place to observe sea traffic in the Strait of Gibraltar, was a haunt of spies in WWII.

Places to Eat

The city **market** has a wonderful array of fresh fruit, vegetables, hams and cheese – perfect for packing a picnic lunch. The excellent **Panadería-Café** at the market end of Calle José Santacana is good for breakfast. Plaza Alta is dotted with sidewalk cafes and restaurants. English-speaking Christians run the friendly little **Lighthouse**, 200m east of the railway station on Calle Juan de la Cierva, with decent breakfasts and generally helpful tourist advice.

Restaurante Casa Blanca (Calle Juan de la Cierva 1), near the tourist office, is popular for its 900-ptas menú of two courses, bread, soft drink and dessert; other options, including Arabic food, are moderately priced. **Restaurante Casa Gil** on Calle Segismundo Moret – the street on the northern side of the rail track facing the main tourist office – is bright and clean and has menús costing from 900 ptas to 1200 ptas.

In the evening you can sample tasty tapas from 7 pm at **Bar Montes** (Calle Emilio Castelar 36) several blocks north-west of the main tourist office. There are tables out front. The attached **Restaurante Montes** and another slightly flashier-looking **Restaurante Montes** (Calle Juan Morrison 27), around the corner, have a 1100-ptas menú of two courses, bread, wine and dessert, and an a la carte seafood list from 1500 ptas. Tea on the terrace at the Hotel Reina Cristina is pleasant.

Entertainment

In the summer, flamenco, rock and other concerts happen at some of the more attractive spots in town – the Plaza de Toros, Parque de María Cristina, Plaza de Andalucía and Playa Rinconcillo. The tourist office has a list of events.

Getting There & Away

The daily paper Europa Sur has up-to-date transport arrival and departure details.

Bus The Comes bus station (☎ 956 65 34 56) is on Calle San Bernardo. To Tarifa there are at least seven buses daily. Buses run to La Línea every 45 minutes from 7 am to 9.15 pm. Other daily buses include 10 to Cádiz (1260 ptas), five to Sevilla (2100 ptas), three to Jimena de la Frontera (two on Saturday, none on Sunday), and three to Madrid (3375 ptas). There's one bus daily (except Sunday) to Zahara de los Atunes and Barbate (615 ptas), and a bus to Ronda at 8.30 am Monday to Friday.

Portillo (☎ 956 65 10 55), at Avenida Virgen del Carmen 15, operates six direct buses daily to Málaga (1990 ptas, 1¾ hours), four to Granada (2595 ptas, 3¾ hours) and two to

Jaén (3460 ptas). Several more buses daily to Málaga (1390 ptas, three hours) stop at Estepona, Marbella, Fuengirola and Torremolinos.

Bacoma (☎ 956 66 50 67), inside the port, runs up to four services daily to Alicante, Valencia and Barcelona. There are also buses to France, Germany and Holland with Bacoma and Viajes Kontubia.

Train From the station (☎ 956 63 02 02), adjacent to Calle San Bernardo, two direct trains run daily to/from Madrid (9300 ptas or 5200 ptas, six or 11 hours) and one to/from Granada (2665 ptas, four hours). All trains pass through Ronda and Bobadilla (1395 ptas, 2½ hours) taking in some dramatic scenery en route. At Bobadilla you can change for Málaga, Córdoba and Sevilla plus more trains to Granada and Madrid. There are further trains to Granada from Antequera in Málaga province.

Boat Trasmediterránea (☎ 956 65 17 55, ☎ 902 45 46 45), EuroFerrys (☎ 956 65 11 78) and other companies operate frequent daily passenger and vehicle ferries to/from Tangier and Ceuta, the Spanish enclave on the Moroccan coast. Usually at least 20 sailings a day go to Tangier and 40 or more to Ceuta. From late June to September there are ferries almost round the clock to cater for the Moroccan migration – you may have to queue for up to three hours. Buy your ticket in the port or at the agencies on Avenida de la Marina: prices are the same everywhere.

To Tangier one adult passenger pays 3500 ptas (children 1750 ptas) one way on a ferry taking 2½ hours, or 4440 ptas on a hydrofoil (one hour). A motorcycle over 500cc costs 3000 ptas and a car costs 10,750 ptas.

To Ceuta, it costs 1945 ptas (children 975 ptas) on an ordinary ferry, taking 1½ hours, and 3095 ptas (children 1548 ptas) on a 'fast ferry' *(rapido)*, taking 40 minutes. Cars cost 8930 ptas and motorcycles cost 3000 ptas. The Buquebus service (☎ 902 41 42 42) does Algeciras–Ceuta in 30 to 35 minutes, at least nine times daily, and costs

2945 ptas for passengers, 8223 ptas for a car.

LA LÍNEA DE LA CONCEPCIÓN
postcode 11300 • pop 61,000

La Línea, 20km east of Algeciras, round the bay, is the unavoidable stepping stone to Gibraltar. A left turn as you exit La Línea's bus station will bring you out on Avenida 20 de Abril, which runs the 300m or so between the town's main square, Plaza de la Constitución, and the Gibraltar border. There's a regional tourist office (☎ 956 76 99 50) on the corner of the square. At the opposite end of Avenida 20 de Abril facing the border is the slick new municipal tourist office (☎ 956 17 19 98).

Places to Stay & Eat
Pensión La Perla (☎ 956 76 95 13, *Calle Clavel 10)*, two blocks north of Plaza de la Constitución, has clean, spacious pink-trimmed singles/doubles, with shared bathrooms, costing 1500/3000 ptas. *Hostal La Campana* (☎ 956 17 30 59, *Calle Carboneros 3)*, just off the western side of Plaza de la Constitución, has decent rooms with bathroom and TV costing 5200 ptas a double. Its restaurant has a three-course menú for 850 ptas. *Hostal La Estepanera* (☎ 956 17 66 68, *Calle Carteya 10)*, several blocks west of La Perla, has doubles with shared bathroom costing 2200 ptas, or with a private bathroom for 3200 ptas.

La Crema on Calle Real just off the north-western corner of Plaza de la Constitución is a good place to head to for breakfast.

Getting There & Away
Bus Buses run about every 30 minutes to/from Algeciras (235 ptas, 40 minutes). There are four buses daily to Málaga (1270 ptas, 2½ hours), stopping in Estepona, Marbella, Fuengirola and Torremolinos; five to Tarifa (455 ptas) and Cádiz (1500 ptas, 2½ hours); three to Sevilla (2640 ptas, four hours); and two to Granada (2475 ptas). A bus at 3.30 pm Monday to Friday runs to Jimena de la Frontera (515 ptas).

Car & Motorcycle Owing to the usually long vehicle queues at the Gibraltar border, many visitors to Gibraltar opt to park in La Línea then walk across the border. Parking meters in La Línea cost 165 ptas an hour, or 710 ptas for 10 hours; they're free from 10.30 pm to 9.30 am. The underground Parking Fo Cona, just off Avenida 20 de Abril, charges 150 ptas per hour or 1000 ptas per day; another underground car park on Plaza de la Constitución is a little cheaper.

Gibraltar

Looming like some great ship off almost the southernmost tip of Spain, the British colony of Gibraltar is such a compound of curiosities that a visit can hardly fail to tweak the interest buds.

The mere sight of the thing is impressive. Gibraltar is 5km long and 1.6km at its widest. Most of it is one huge lump of limestone, rising to 426m and almost sheer at its northern end and along its eastern side. To the ancient Greeks and Romans, Gibraltar was one of the two Pillars of Hercules, set up by the mythical hero to mark the edge of the known world. (The other pillar is the coastal mountain Jebel Musa in Morocco, 25km south across the storm-prone Strait of Gibraltar.)

History

About 50,000 years ago Gibraltar was home to Neanderthal humans, as skulls found there in 1848 and 1928 testify. The former was actually discovered eight years before the skull in Germany's Neander valley, which gave these people their modern name.

Phoenicians and ancient Greeks left traces here, but Gibraltar really entered the history books in AD 711 when Tariq ibn Ziyad, the Muslim governor of Tangier, made it the initial bridgehead for the Islamic invasion of the Iberian Peninsula, landing with an army of some 10,000 men. The name Gibraltar is derived from Jebel Tariq (Tariq's Mountain).

The Almohad Muslims founded a town here in 1159 and Muslims held it most of the time until Castile wrested it from them in 1462. Then in 1704 an Anglo-Dutch fleet captured Gibraltar during the War of the Spanish Succession. Spain ceded the Rock of Gibraltar to Britain by the Treaty of Utrecht in 1713, but didn't finally give up military attempts to regain it until the failure of the Great Siege of 1779–83. Britain developed it into an important naval base and in WWII, when the local population was evacuated to Britain, Madeira and

Jamaica, Gibraltar became a base for allied landings in North Africa. The British garrison was withdrawn in the early 1990s but the British navy continues to use Gibraltar.

Spain still wants Gibraltar back. During the Franco period Gibraltar was an extremely sore point between Spain and Britain: Franco closed the Spain–Gibraltar border in 1967 and it was not re-opened until 1985, 10 years after his death. In a 1969 referendum, Gibraltarians voted by 12,138 to 44 in favour of British rather than Spanish sovereignty. That year a new constitution committed Britain to respecting Gibraltarians' wishes over sovereignty, and gave Gibraltar domestic self-government and its own parliament, the House of Assembly.

Gibraltar Today Gibraltar's last two elections (1996 and 2000) have been won by the centre-right Gibraltar Social Democrat Party, led by Peter Caruana. The main opposition is the Gibraltar Socialist Labour Party led by Joe Bossano. Caruana has shown himself willing to talk with Spain over Gibraltar's future but fiercely opposes any concessions over sovereignty.

When Spain wants to exert pressure on Gibraltar, it uses arcane diplomatic quarrels and such methods as extra-thorough customs and immigration procedures, which cause hours-long delays at the border. Spain has proposed a period of joint British–Spanish sovereignty leading to Gibraltar eventually becoming the 18th Spanish region, with greater autonomy than any of the others. Britain continues to refuse any compromise over sovereignty.

Tourism, the port and financial services are the mainstays of Gibraltar's economy. Spanish police complain that Gibraltar, with more than 70,000 domiciled companies, is a centre for the laundering of illicit money from organised crime and tax evasion elsewhere in Europe. Much of this money, it's said, is invested in property in southern Spain. Caruana does not deny that Gibraltar is a tax haven but says it is a well supervised one. Another problem, cigarette smuggling from Gibraltar into Spain, seems to have diminished under the Caruana government.

Population & People Of Gibraltar's 29,000 people, about 75% are classed as Gibraltarians, 14% British and 7% Moroccan. The Gibraltarians are of mixed Genoese, Jewish, Spanish and British ancestry, the Genoese element coming from Genoese ship repairers brought here by the British in the 18th century. The Moroccans are mostly short-term workers.

Language Gibraltarians speak both English, Spanish and a curiously accented, singsong mix of the two, slipping back and forth from one to the other – often in mid-sentence. Signs are in English.

Orientation & Information

To reach Gibraltar by land you must pass through the Spanish border town of La Línea de la Concepción (see the Cádiz Province chapter). Just south of the border, the road crosses the runway of Gibraltar airport, which stretches east to west across the neck of the peninsula. The town and harbours of Gibraltar lie along the Rock's less steep western side, facing the Bahía de Algeciras (or, as Gibraltarians call it, the Bay of Gibraltar).

Tourist Offices The Gibraltar Tourist Board has several very helpful information offices with plenty of good give-away material. One (☎ 50762) is in the customs and immigration building at the border, open 9 am to 4.30 pm Monday to Friday. The main office (☎ 45000) is in Duke of Kent House on Cathedral Square and is open 9 am to 5.30 pm Monday to Friday; others are at The Piazza on Main St (☎ 74982), open 9 am to 5.30 pm Monday to Friday, and from 10 am to 4 pm Saturday, Sunday and bank holidays; and at the airport (☎ 47227) and cruise ship terminal (☎ 47671), open when flights and ships arrive.

Foreign Consulates Twelve countries, mostly European, have consulates in Gibraltar. Tourist offices have lists.

Visas & Documents To enter Gibraltar you need a passport or, for those EU nationalities that possess them, an identity card. Australia, Canada, EU, Israel, New Zealand, Singapore, South Africa and USA passport-holders are among those who do not need visas for Gibraltar. For further information you can contact Gibraltar's Immigration Department (☎ 46411).

Those who need visas for Spain should have at least a double-entry Spanish visa so that they can return to Spain from Gibraltar. Passports are not always checked when you enter Spain from Gibraltar but you certainly can't count on it.

Money The currencies in Gibraltar are the Gibraltar pound and the pound sterling, which are interchangeable. You can buy things with pesetas (except in pay phones and post offices) but you'll get a better exchange rate if you convert them into

GIBRALTAR

pounds. Exchange rates for buying pesetas are, however, a bit better than in Spain. You can't use Gibraltar money outside Gibraltar, so it's worth requesting change in British coins and changing any unspent Gibraltar pounds before you leave.

Banks are generally open between 9 am and 3.30 pm Monday to Friday. There are several on Main St. There are also exchange offices which are open longer hours. American Express is represented by Bland Travel (☎ 77012), 81 Irish Town.

Post & Communications The main post office (☎ 75714), at 104 Main St, is open from 9 am to 4.30 pm (to 2.15 pm during the summer) Monday to Friday, and from 10 am to 1 pm Saturday.

To phone Gibraltar from Spain, precede the five-digit local number with the code ☎ 9567; from other countries dial the international access code, then ☎ 350 (the Gibraltar country code) and the local number.

In Gibraltar you can make international as well as local calls from street pay phones. To phone Spain, just dial the nine-digit number. To phone other countries dial the international access code (☎ 00), then the country code, area code and number.

Bookshops Bell Books, 11 Bell Lane, and Gibraltar Bookshop, 300 Main St, are both good places to stock up on English-language reading material.

Medical Services & Emergency St Bernard's Hospital (☎ 79700) on Hospital Hill has 24-hour emergency facilities. There's also a health centre (☎ 72355/77003) on Grand Casemates Square. The police station (☎ 72500) is in the south of the town at New Mole House on Rosia Rd, but there's a more central station at 120 Irish Town. The police wear British uniforms. In an emergency you can call ☎ 199 for the police or an ambulance.

Electricity Electric current is the same as in Britain, 220V or 240V, with plugs of three flat pins.

Public Holidays Gibraltar observes the following public holidays: 1 January, Commonwealth Day (second Monday of March), Good Friday, Easter Monday, 1 May, Spring Bank Holiday (last Monday in May), Queen's Birthday (Monday after the second Saturday in June), Late Summer Bank Holiday (last Monday in August), Gibraltar National Day (10 September), 25 and 26 December.

Work Gibraltar is no longer an easy place to find paid work but it's better than anywhere in Spain, except Palma de Mallorca, for finding an unpaid yacht crew place. During the summer places come up on yachts cruising the Mediterranean, and from November to January there's a chance of working your passage to the Caribbean. Ask around at Marina Bay harbour.

The Town

Gibraltar's town centre, with its British shops, British pubs and British shoppers, is far from exotic but it has been spruced up in recent years. Most Spanish and Islamic buildings were destroyed in 18th-century sieges but British fortifications, gates and gun emplacements are all over the place; the *Guided Tour of Gibraltar* booklet by TJ Finlayson is good if you want to delve into details of the British heritage.

The **Gibraltar Museum**, on Bomb House Lane, contains very worthwhile historical, architectural and military displays and goes back to prehistoric times. Highlights include a well preserved Muslim bathhouse, and a detailed model of the Rock made in the 1860s by British officers. The museum is open 10 am to 6 pm Monday to Friday, and 10 am to 2 pm Saturday. Admission costs £2.

The nearby Anglican **Cathedral of the Holy Trinity** was built in the 1820s and 1830s. The Catholic **Cathedral of St Mary the Crowned** on Main St stands on the site of Muslim Gibraltar's chief mosque. The **King's Chapel**, also on Main St, is part of a 16th-century Franciscan convent which is now the governor's residence. Inside are buried the wife of the Spanish governor of 1648 and two 19th-century British governors.

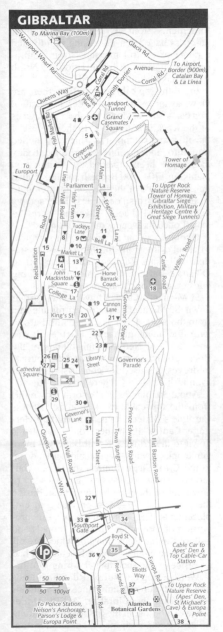

GIBRALTAR

PLACES TO STAY
- 4 Emile Youth Hostel
- 6 Continental Hotel
- 19 Cannon Hotel
- 23 Eliott Hotel
- 25 Bristol Hotel
- 33 Toc H Hostel
- 35 Queen's Hotel
- 38 Rock Hotel

PLACES TO EAT
- 7 House of Sacarello
- 8 The Clipper
- 12 Viceroy of India
- 13 The English Tea Room
- 16 The Piazza
- 21 Three Roses Bar
- 22 Cannon Bar
- 24 Maxi Manger
- 32 Minister's Restaurant
- 36 Piccadilly Gardens

OTHER
- 1 Watergardens Quay
- 2 Bus No 9
- 3 Health Centre
- 5 Tourafrica
- 9 Main Post Office
- 10 Bland Travel
- 11 Bell Books
- 14 Police Station
- 15 Bus No 10
- 17 Tourist Office
- 18 St Bernard's Hospital
- 20 Cathedral of St Mary the Crowned
- 26 Gibraltar Museum
- 27 Bus No 3
- 28 Cathedral of the Holy Trinity
- 29 Main Tourist Office
- 30 Gibraltar Bookshop
- 31 King's Chapel
- 34 Trafalgar Cemetery
- 37 Lower Cable-Car Station

Many of the graves in the **Trafalgar Cemetery**, just south of Southport Gate, are of British sailors who died at Gibraltar after the Battle of Trafalgar (1805). A short distance south of here are the **Alameda Botanical Gardens**, entered from Europa Rd and open daily from 8 am to sunset. Admission is free. Just over 1km farther south, **Nelson's Anchorage** on Rosia Rd contains a 100-ton Victorian supergun, made in Britain in 1870, and overlooks Rosia Bay,

GIBRALTAR

where Nelson's body was brought ashore from *HMS Victory* – in a rum barrel, legend has it – after the Battle of Trafalgar. Nelson's Anchorage is open 9.30 am to 5 pm daily except Sunday. Admission is free. A little farther south on Rosia Rd, the **Parson's Lodge** gun battery, atop a 40m cliff, is open 10 am to 6 pm Monday to Friday (£1). Beneath the gun emplacements is a labyrinth of tunnels with former ammunition stores and living quarters.

Down at **Europa Point**, the southern tip of Gibraltar, are a lighthouse, the Christian Shrine of Our Lady of Europe and the Mosque of the Custodian of the Two Holy Mosques. This last, with a tall minaret, is claimed to be the largest mosque in a non-Islamic country. It was opened in 1997, cost £5 million and was paid for by King Fahd of Saudi Arabia. It's intended to be a focal point for Arabs travelling in southern Europe. Call ☎ 47693 for information on current opening hours.

Upper Rock Nature Reserve

Most of the upper parts of the Rock, starting just above the town, are a nature reserve with spectacular views, a web of quiet roads and pathways, and several interesting spots to visit. Once covered in trees, the Rock was virtually stripped of vegetation by the British garrison and grazing goats in the 18th and 19th centuries. Since then it has recovered to some extent and is home to 600 plant species. It's often a fine spot for observing the migrations of birds between Europe and Africa (see the boxed text 'High-Fliers over the Strait of Gibraltar' in the Cádiz Province chapter).

The upper rock's most famous inhabitants are Gibraltar's colony of **Barbary macaques**, the only wild primates (apart from *Homo sapiens*) in Europe. Some of these hang around the **Apes' Den** near the middle cable-car station; others can often be seen at the top cable car station and Great Siege Tunnels. Legend has it that when the monkeys (which may have been introduced from North Africa in the 18th century) disappear from Gibraltar, so will the British. When numbers were at a low ebb during WWII, the British brought in simian reinforcements from Africa. Recently their numbers have been increasing rapidly and a range of control measures from contraceptive implants to 'repatriation' to North Africa have been considered.

From the **top cable-car station**, there are views as far as Morocco in decent weather. You can also look down the sheer precipices of the Rock's eastern side to the biggest of the old **water catchments** which channelled rain into underground reservoirs. Today these have been replaced by desalination plants. In 1704, 500 Spanish soldiers scaled the eastern side of the Rock in an attempt to surprise the British occupiers. They spent a night in St Michael's Cave but were defeated once they came out of hiding.

About 15 minutes walk south down St Michael's Rd from the top cable-car station, O'Hara's Rd leads up to the left to **O'Hara's Battery**, an emplacement of big guns on the Rock's summit.

St Michael's Cave, a few minutes farther down St Michael's Rd (or 20 minutes up from the Apes' Den), is a big natural grotto with fine stalagmites and stalactites. It was once home to Neolithic inhabitants of the Rock. Today, apart from attracting tourists in droves, it's used for concerts, plays and even fashion shows. There's a cafe outside.

About 30 minutes' walk north (downhill) from the top cable-car station is Princess Caroline's Battery, housing a **Military Heritage Centre**. From here one road leads down to the Princess Royal Battery – more gun emplacements – while another leads up to the **Great Siege Tunnels** (or Upper Galleries). These impressive galleries were hewn out of the rock by the British during the siege of 1779–83 to provide gun emplacements. They constitute only a tiny proportion of more than 70km of tunnels and galleries in the Rock, most of which are off limits to the public. General Eisenhower had an office in one such tunnel during WWII.

Worth a stop on Willis's Rd, which leads down to the town from Princess Caroline's Battery, are the **Gibraltar, A City Under Siege** exhibition, in the first British building on the Rock (originally an ammunition

GIBRALTAR

store), and the **Tower of Homage**, the remains of Gibraltar's Muslim castle built in 1333.

The Upper Rock Nature Reserve is officially open 9.30 am to 7 pm daily. From late afternoon you may find its entrance gates unstaffed and left open, which means you can enter free but must pay individually to visit any sights that are still open. Most stay open to 6.15 or 6.30 pm. Admission by road, costing £5 an adult, £2.50 a child and £1.50 a vehicle, includes all the sights mentioned in this section. Cable-car tickets (see Getting Around) include admission to the reserve, the Apes' Den and St Michael's Cave.

Dolphins

The Bahía de Algeciras has a sizeable year-round population of dolphins and at least six boats run dolphin-spotting trips. From about April to September most boats make two or more daily trips; at other times of year there's usually at least one in daily operation. Most of the boats go from Watergardens Quay or the adjacent Marina Bay, north-west of the town centre. Trips last about 2½ hours and the cost per adult ranges from £12 to £15. Children can go for about half price. You'll be unlucky if you don't get plenty of close-up dolphin contact, and you may even come across whales. Tourist offices have full details of the boats.

Organised Tours

Taxi drivers will take you on a 1½ hour 'Official Rock Tour' of Gibraltar's main sights for £7 per person (minimum four people) plus the cost of admission to the Upper Rock Nature Reserve. Most drivers are knowledgeable. Many travel agents run tours of the same sights for £11.50. Bland Travel (see Money under Information for details) offers guided day trips (not Monday) to Tangier for £45, including lunch.

Places to Stay

The independent *Emile Youth Hostel* (☎ *51106/75020, Montagu Bastion, Line Wall Rd*) has 43 places in two- to eight-person rooms, for £12 including continental breakfast. There are showers, a TV/sitting

room and an outside patio. *Toc H Hostel* (☎ *73431*), a ramshackle old place tucked into the city walls at the southern end of Line Wall Rd, is the cheapest place with beds at £6 a night or £25 a week and cold showers.

Queen's Hotel (☎ *74000, fax 40030, 1 Boyd St*) has a restaurant, bar, games room, and singles/doubles costing £20/30, or £36/40 with private bath or shower. Reduced rates of £14/20 and £16/24 are offered for students and young travellers. All rates include English breakfast. *Cannon Hotel* (☎/*fax 51711, 9 Cannon Lane*) also has decent rooms, each sharing a bathroom with one other room, for £22.50/34.50 including English breakfast.

Rooms at the *Bristol Hotel* (☎ *76800, fax 77613, 10 Cathedral Square*) are pleasant enough and a decent size, with TV and bathroom, but nothing special for the price of £47/61 interior or £51/66 exterior. The *Continental Hotel* (☎ *76900, fax 41702, 1 Engineer Lane*) is cosier, with air-con rooms costing £42/55 including continental breakfast.

Gibraltar has two luxury hotels with over 100 rooms each. The centrally-placed *Eliott Hotel* (☎ *70500, fax 70243, 2 Governor's Parade*) charges £165 to £220 per room. Up the hill a bit, *Rock Hotel* (☎ *73000, fax 73513, 3 Europa Rd*), has a bit more colonial history – past guests include Winston Churchill and Noel Coward – and rooms (all with sea view) costing £160 for both singles and doubles, and £165 with a balcony; English breakfast is included. Both hotels have good restaurants and pools.

If Gibraltar prices don't grab you, there are some economical options in the Spanish border town of La Línea (see the Cádiz Province chapter for details).

Places to Eat

Most of the many pubs in town do typical British pub meals. One of the best, with an eclectic menu, is *The Clipper* (*78B Irish Town*), where a generous serving of fish and chips will set you back £5.25. The lasagne is pretty good (£4.50). Live music happens here on weekend nights. *Three Roses Bar* *(60 Governor's St)* does an all-day breakfast of two eggs, sausage, bacon, fried bread, beans, tomato and mushrooms for £3.50. *Cannon Bar (27 Cannon Lane)* does some of the best fish and chips in town, with big portions for £4.75. At the popular *Piccadilly Gardens* pub on Rosia Rd you can sit out in the garden and have a three-course dinner for £9.95. Lunch is a la carte with main dishes at around £8. They do tapas too!

Maxi Manger on Main St is a good sandwich bar with filled baguettes from £1.25 to £2.20. Baked potatoes with the same fillings are available. For a restaurant meal, the chic *House of Sacarello (57 Irish Town)*, is a good bet, with good soups around £2 and some excellent daily specials from £5.50 to £6.10. You can linger over a £7.65 afternoon tea for two between 3 and 7.30 pm. The Indian food at the *Viceroy of India (9/11 Horse Barrack Court)* is usually pretty good: it has a three-course lunch special for £6.75. A la carte, there are vegetarian dishes for £2 to £3.25 and main courses from £6 to £11. *The Piazza (156 Main St)* does decent burgers and pizzas for £3.95 to £6, and fish and meat main courses from £5.50 to £8. On Friday and Saturday nights it has live music (blues and country when we last checked). *Minister's Restaurant (310 Main St)* does good servings of fish and seafood for £7.50 to £9, or fish, meat or pasta with either chips or salad from £7.50.

The English Tea Room (9 Market Lane), open 9 am to 7 pm, isn't much to look at but the scones, jam and cream are great. It does lunchtime specials too.

A little out of the centre, there's a line of pleasant waterside cafes and restaurants at Marina Bay.

Things to Buy

British expats from the Costa del Sol come to Gibraltar to stock up on British goods at cheaper prices than in Spain. Gibraltar has lots of British high street chain stores, such as Marks & Spencer, Mothercare and The Body Shop (all on Main St) and Safeway (in the Europort development at the north-

ern end of the main harbour). There are even a few Indian corner shops on streets such as Irish Town. Shops are normally open 9 am to 7.30 pm Monday to Friday and until 1 pm Saturday.

Getting There & Away

The border is open 24 hours daily.

Air GB Airways (☎ 79300) flies daily to/from London. Return fares from London range from around UK£175 to UK£275, depending on season and offers. Morocco's Regional Air Lines flies Gibraltar to Casablanca most days for around UK£100 return.

Monarch Airlines (☎ 47477) flies daily to/from Luton. Return fares range from UK£100 to UK£250.

In Gibraltar the airline offices are at the airport; alternatively, book through travel agents.

Bus There are no regular buses to Gibraltar itself. However, the bus station in La Línea (see the *Cádiz Province* chapter) is only a five-minute walk from the border, from where there are ample buses into Gibraltar town centre (see Getting Around).

Car & Motorcycle Vehicle queues at the border often make it less time-consuming to park in La Línea, then walk across the border. To take a car into Gibraltar you need an insurance certificate, registration document, nationality plate and driving licence. You do not have to pay any fee: some people driving into Gibraltar have been cheated of a few thousand pesetas by con artists claiming you need to pay to take a vehicle across the border. In Gibraltar, driving is on the right, as in Spain. At the time of writing petrol in Gibraltar was around 10% cheaper than in Spain.

Boat The ferry between Gibraltar and Tangier takes two hours, and normally runs twice a week each way. The one-way/return fare is £18/30 per person and £40/80 per car. The passenger catamaran *Mons Calpe II* sails daily except Monday and Saturday to/from Tangier (75 minutes) for £18/33 one way/return. In Gibraltar, you can buy tickets for the catamaran at Bland Travel (☎ 77012, 81 Irish Town) and for the ferry at Tourafrica (☎ 77666, ICC Building, Main St). Ferries from Algeciras are more frequent.

Getting Around

The 1.5km walk from the border to the town centre is quite fun as it crosses the airport runway. A left turn (south) off Corral Rd will take you through the pedestrian-only Landport Tunnel (once the only land entry through Gibraltar's walls) into Grand Casemates Square. Alternatively, bus Nos 3 and 9 go from the border into town about every 15 minutes. No 9 goes to Market Place and runs between 8.30 am and 8.30 pm. No 3 runs between 7.30 am and 11.30 pm, stops at Cathedral Square and the lower cable-car station, then goes up Europa Rd and on to Europa Point at the southern end of the Rock. Bus No 10 runs from the border to Europort (with a stop at the Safeway supermarket), then via Queens Way to Reclamation Rd near the town centre. There are fewer buses after 2 pm on Saturday and none on Sunday, except for No 4 which connects Catalan Bay on the rock's eastern side with the centre and Europort. All buses cost 40p or 100 ptas a ride.

All of Gibraltar can be covered on foot and much of it (including the upper rock) by car or motorcycle, but there are other options worth considering. Most obvious is the cable car which, weather permitting, leaves its lower station on Red Sands Rd every few minutes between 9.30 am and 5.15 pm from Monday to Saturday. Fares cost £3.65/4.90 one way/return (children aged under-10 £1.80/2.45), including admission to the Upper Rock Nature Reserve, Apes' Den and St Michael's Cave. For the Apes' Den, disembark at the middle station. You can get back on to go up to the top station.

Málaga Province

This southern province – many people's point of entry into Andalucía – is much more than the Costa del Sol, Spain's most densely packed holiday coast. Málaga city is Andalucía's second biggest and one of its most vibrant, with a spectacularly festive August fair. Inland, intriguing old towns such as Ronda and Antequera invite exploration, and there are lots of rugged hill country and old-fashioned white villages, with good walking in areas such as the Serranía de Ronda.

Málaga

postcode 29080 • pop 528,000

Málaga is a completely different kettle of fish from the nearby Costa del Sol. It's a lively, historic and very Spanish city, with a real southern port atmosphere. The city centre, with the backdrop of a sparkling blue Mediterranean, combines wide, leafy boulevards, beautiful gardens, some impressive monuments and some charmingly dilapidated old streets. Málaga has come a little late to the notion of sprucing itself up to attract tourists, but things are changing with the impetus provided by a major new museum devoted to Málaga-born Pablo Picasso, due to open in late 2002. Málaga stays open very late – there are bars with happy hours that don't start until midnight – and inspires fierce devotion among its citizens.

HISTORY

Early Phoenician traders are credited with planting the area's first vineyards. In Muslim times, Málaga flourished under the 11th-century Granada kingdom and the later Emirate of Granada. Its fall to the Christians in 1487 was a big nail in the emirate's coffin.

The expulsion of the Moriscos, who had been active in agriculture, contributed to famine in the 17th century, but some prosperity arrived in the 19th century with a dynamic middle class led by the Larios and Heredia families who founded textile factor-

Highlights

- Check out Málaga's exuberant August fair and splendid Semana Santa (Holy Week) processions
- Wander through the fascinating hill town of Ronda
- Explore the spectacular and historic El Chorro gorge area
- Discover the white villages of La Axarquía
- Walk in the Sierra de las Nieves
- Relax on the cliff-foot beaches east of Nerja

ies, sugar mills, shipyards and steel mills. Málaga dessert wine, popular in Victorian England, was profitable until a bug devastated the vineyards around the city. Early tourism helped compensate: the city had been popularised by the Romantic movement and in the 1920s it became the favourite winter resort of rich people from Madrid.

In the civil war, Málaga was initially a Republican stronghold. Hundreds of Nationalist sympathisers were killed and churches and convents burnt. The city was then bombed by Italian planes before falling to the Nationalists in February 1937. Particularly vicious reprisals followed.

Málaga's economy has enjoyed plenty of spin-offs from tourism on the Costa del Sol since the 1960s, but youth unemployment is high.

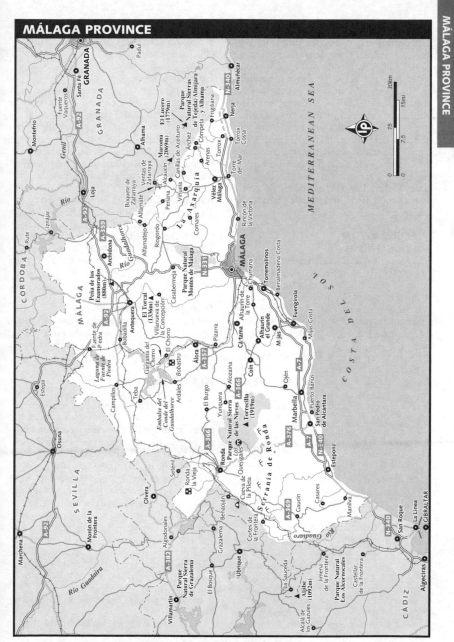

ORIENTATION

The central axis comprises Paseo del Parque, Alameda Principal and Avenida de Andalucía. The city is dominated by the Gibralfaro, the hill rising above the eastern half of Paseo del Parque and supporting the Alcazaba and Castillo de Gibralfaro. The old heart of the city, with narrow, winding streets, spreads north from the western half of Paseo del Parque and the Alameda Principal. The main streets leading north into the old town are Calle Marqués de Larios, ending at Plaza de la Constitución, and Calle Molina Lario. The modern shopping district stretches between Calle Marqués de Larios and Calle Puerta del Mar.

INFORMATION
Tourist Offices

The Junta de Andalucía's helpful tourist office (☎ 95 221 34 45) is at Pasaje de Chinitas 4, an alley off Plaza de la Constitución. It opens 9 am to 7 pm Monday to Friday, and 10 am to 2 pm Saturday and Sunday. The main municipal tourist office (☎ 95 260 44 10), also helpful, is at Avenida de Cervantes 1, just off Paseo del Parque – open 8.15 am to 2 pm and 4.30 to 7 pm Monday to Friday, and 9.30 am to 1.30 pm Saturday. There are smaller tourist offices at the airport and bus station, and information kiosks on Plaza de la Merced and outside the post office.

Money

There are plenty of banks with ATMs on Calle Puerta del Mar and Calle Marqués de Larios. The airport arrivals hall has ATMs giving cash pesetas on a wide variety of cards.

Post & Communications

The main post office, at Avenida de Andalucía 1, opens 8 am to 8.30 pm Monday to Friday, and 9.30 am to 2 pm Saturday. Public Internet services, all with plenty of computers, include Spider.es on the corner of Calle Méndez Núñez and Calle Juan de Padilla, Ciberw@y at Calle Gómez Pallete 9, and Pasatiempos on Plaza de la Merced. All charge 100 ptas per 15 minutes and

open long hours – Spider.es stays open till 5 am on Thursday to Saturday nights (1.30 am other nights).

Bookshops

Librería Alameda, Alameda Principal 16, is a big Spanish bookshop which stocks some English and French titles. Atlante Mapas (☎/fax 95 260 27 65), Calle Echegaray 7, is an excellent source of maps of all kinds and Spanish-language guidebooks for most parts of Andalucía; it also sells a wide range of Lonely Planet titles.

Medical Services & Emergency

The main general hospital is Hospital Carlos Haya (☎ 95 239 04 00) on Avenida de Carlos Haya, 2km west of the city centre. The Policía Nacional (☎ 95 204 62 00) has an office at Plaza de la Aduana 1. The Policía Local (☎ 95 212 65 00) is at Avenida de la Rosaleda 19.

Dangers & Annoyances

Take care of your valuables in the dark corners of the city centre and at the bus station, where pickpockets and bag-snatchers have been known to operate.

ALCAZABA

The Alcazaba, at the lower, western end of the Gibralfaro, was the palace-fortress of Málaga's Muslim governors. It looks splendid in spring when the jacaranda trees at its base are in full purple bloom. Begun in 1057 by the fearsome Granada kingdom ruler Badis, the Alcazaba has two rings of walls, a large number of defensive towers, and staggered entrance passages to impede attackers. It was heavily reconstructed in 1930, but the first of its three patios contains an original arch. With luck, by the time you visit, several years of works on the site will have been completed and the whole Alcazaba will be open, with explanatory displays. At the time of writing only half of it was visitable (9.30 am to 7 pm daily except Tuesday). Admission is free.

Below the Alcazaba, a **Roman theatre** is being excavated.

MÁLAGA

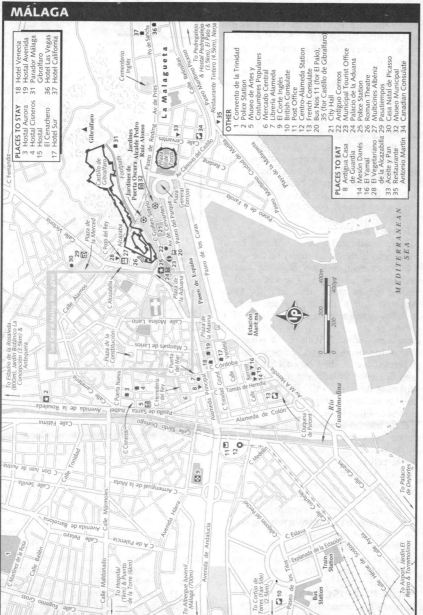

PLACES TO STAY
3 Hostal Aurora
4 Hostal Cisneros
15 Hostal
   Gibralfaro
17 Hotel Sur
18 Hotel Venecia
19 Hostal Avenida
31 Parador Málaga
   Gibralfaro
36 Hotel Las Vegas
37 Hotel California
15 El Cenachero

OTHER
1 Convento de la Trinidad
2 Police Station
5 Museo de Artes y
   Costumbres Populares
6 Mercado Central
7 Librería Alameda
9 El Corte Inglés
10 British Consulate
11 Post Office
12 Centro-Alameda Station
13 French Consulate
20 Bus Nos 11 (for El Palo),
   35 (for Castillo de Gibralfaro)
21 City Hall
22 Antigua Correos
23 Municipal Tourist Office
24 Palacio de la Aduana
25 Police Station
26 Roman Theatre
27 Multicines Albéniz
29 Pasatiempos
30 Casa Natal de Picasso
32 Museo Municipal
34 Canadian Consulate

PLACES TO EAT
8 Antigua Casa
   de Guardia
14 Mesón Danés
16 El Yamal
28 El Vegetariano
   de la Alcazabilla
33 Aceite y Pan
35 Restaurante
   Antonio Martín

CASTILLO DE GIBRALFARO

Above the Alcazaba rises the older Castillo de Gibralfaro, built by Abd ar-Rahman I, the 8th-century Cordoban emir. It was rebuilt in the 14th and 15th centuries, when Málaga was the Emirate of Granada's main port. The views from up here are great. Open 9 am to 6 pm daily, the fortress includes a good walkway round the top of its walls and an interesting museum that demonstrates its and the city's development over the centuries. Admission is free.

The Alcazaba and fortress are connected by a curtain wall called La Coracha. You can walk up by a path beside this to the fortress, or take bus No 35 from Avenida de Cervantes (roughly every 45 minutes).

CATHEDRAL

Málaga's cathedral on Calle Molina Lario was begun in the 16th century on the site of the former main mosque. Building continued for two centuries. The cathedral is known locally as La Manquita (the One-Armed) owing to the fact that the southern tower was never completed (money allocated for it was diverted to the Spanish campaign against Britain in the American War of Independence, and a few years ago, in belated thanks, the Costa del Sol's American Society handed over money towards repairs at the cathedral). The cathedral has an 18th-century baroque facade but the inside is chiefly Gothic and Renaissance. Of special interest are the finely carved 17th-century wooden choir stalls by Pedro de Mena (see Painting, Sculpture & Metalwork section in the Facts about Andalucía chapter for further details). The cathedral and attached museum open 9 am to 6.45 pm daily except Sunday and holidays. Enter from Calle Císter. Explanatory panels in English, French and Spanish tell you what's what inside. Admission costs 300 ptas.

On the cathedral's northern side, the Iglesia del Sagrario has a splendid late-Gothic portal and a gilded Renaissance retable.

PALACIO EPISCOPAL

Opposite the cathedral on Plaza del Obispo is the 18th-century bishop's palace, now an

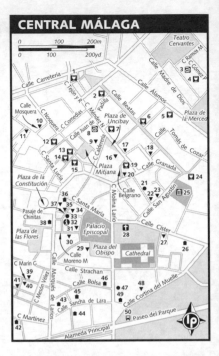

exhibition hall, with one of the most impressive facades in the city and a beautiful patio with an imperial-type staircase. Admission is free.

MUSEO PICASSO & MUSEO DE MÁLAGA

The 16th-century Palacio de los Condes de Buenavista on Calle San Agustín, in what was Málaga's Judería (Jewish Quarter) in Muslim times, is being converted into a major new Picasso museum, centred on 186 Picasso works donated or lent by his daughter-in-law Christine Ruiz-Picasso and grandson Bernard Ruiz-Picasso. The museum is due to open in late 2002.

The Picasso donation means that the Museo de Málaga, a fine arts and archaeological museum which occupied the Buenavista palace from 1961, has had to move out. Debate about where it should reopen has raged in the city: the Palacio de la Aduana (see the Alameda Principal &

CENTRAL MÁLAGA

PLACES TO STAY
26   Hotel Carlos V
36   Hostal Lampérez
38   Hotel Larios
42   Pensión Rosa, Pensión
      Ramos
43   Hostal Victoria
44   Hostal Derby
45   Hotel Don Curro
46   Pensión Córdoba
49   Hotel AC Málaga Palacio

PLACES TO EAT
 9   Bocatta
10   Mesón Las Bigas
11   Tetería El Harén
16   Mesón Ajoblanco
17   Cervecería Uncibay
18   El Vegetariano de San
      Bernardo

20   La Posada
22   Café de l'Abuela
23   La Tetería
27   El Jardín
29   Cafes
30   Mesón El Chinitas
31   Bar Orellana
34   Rincón Chinitas
35   Málaga Siempre
37   Café Central
39   Bar Lo Güeno
40   La Alegría
41   Mesón La Aldea
48   La Fragata Bar

OTHER
 1   ZZ Pub
 2   Sodoma
 3   Ciberw@y
 4   Onda Pasadena

 5   La Botellita
 6   Café Liceo
 7   Discoteca Anden
 8   Spider.es
12   Siempre Asi
13   O'Neill's
14   Saloma
15   La Cervecería
19   Salsa
21   Atlante Mapas
24   Bodegas El Pimpi
25   Museo Picasso (due to open
      2001)
28   Iglesia del Sagrario
32   Junta de Andalucía Tourist
      Office
33   Romero de la Cruz (former
      Café de Chinitas)
47   Iberia; Binter Mediterráneo
50   Bus No 19 to Airport

Paseo del Parque section below), close to the Buenavista palace, is a popular choice but at the time of writing it looked as if only the archaeological section may end up there, with the art going to the Convento de la Trinidad, west of the Río Guadalmedina, which won't be ready to open till at least late 2002. Meanwhile, selections from the art collection are usually on temporary display in the Palacio de la Aduana (admission is free) – well worth a look as there's some excellent art in the collection including works by Zurbarán, Murillo, Ribera, Pedro de Mena and many artists originating from Málaga (including Picasso!).

CASA NATAL DE PICASSO

The house where Picasso was born in 1881, at Plaza de la Merced 15, is a centre of exhibitions and research on Picasso and contemporary art – some good shows are held. It opens 11 am to 2 pm and 5 to 8 pm Monday to Saturday, and 11 am to 2 pm Sunday. Admission is free.

ALAMEDA PRINCIPAL & PASEO DEL PARQUE

The Alameda Principal, now a busy thoroughfare, was created in the late 18th century as a boulevard on what were then the sands of the Guadalmedina estuary. It's adorned with old trees from the Americas and lined with 18th- and 19th-century buildings.

In the 1890s the palm-lined Paseo del Parque, an extension of the Alameda, was built on land reclaimed from the sea. The garden along its southern side, Paseo de España, is full of exotic tropical plants, making a pleasant refuge from the bustle of the city. Along the garden's northern side are several notable buildings: the elegant 18th-century **Palacio de la Aduana** (Customs House), fronted by rows of tall palms, which originally had the sea lapping at its doors (it's now government offices, but see the earlier Museo Picasso & Museo de Málaga section); the former **Casita del Jardinero**, the gardener's cottage (now a tourist office); the early 20th-century **Antiguo Correos** (Old Post Office), now a branch of the national bank; and the striking 20th-century neo-baroque **City Hall**, flanked and backed by further attractive gardens.

PASAJE DE CHINITAS

In the late 19th century the bars in this passage off the eastern side of Plaza de la Constitución were popular after-work meeting places for Málaga's businessmen, who would often end up at the Café de Chinitas, one of the most famous of the flamenco *cafés cantante* (see the Flamenco special section). In the 1920s and 1930s, the still-going-strong Café de Chinitas attracted bullfighters, stage performers, artists and writers, including Federico García Lorca, whose friend Juan Breva, a famous singer of malagueñas (a local type of flamenco song), sang there frequently. Today, the Café de Chinitas is a fabric shop, Romero de la Cruz, with a plaque above the door verifying its past.

MUSEO DE ARTES Y COSTUMBRES POPULARES

The Museum of Popular Arts & Customs, housed in a 17th-century inn at Pasillo de Santa Isabel 10, is a fun place to visit, especially for children. The collection focuses on everyday life and includes items connected with farming and fishing. Note the glass cabinets containing painted clay figures *(barros)* of the highwayman, the couple dancing, the rider from Ronda and other characters from local folklore. Figures of this type, particularly the jasmine seller *(biznagero)* and fish seller *(cenachero)*, fascinated 19th-century travellers influenced by the Romantic movement. The museum opens 10 am to 1 pm (to 1.30 pm, 1 October to 15 June) and 5 to 8 pm (4 to 7 pm, 1 October to 15 June) Monday to Saturday, except Saturday afternoons. Admission costs 200 ptas (children under 16 free).

MUSEO MUNICIPAL

This modern exhibition space, opened in 1999 at Paseo de Reding 1, houses varied visiting exhibitions and will eventually have a permanent art collection of its own. It opens 10 am to 8 pm daily; admission is free.

PLAZA DE TOROS & CEMENTERIO INGLÉS

You can visit the bullring, on Paseo de Reding, from 8 am to 3 pm (9 am to 2 pm in winter), Monday to Friday. Just beyond, across the street, is the leafy English cemetery, founded in 1829. (Before then, non-Catholic bodies were buried at night upright in the sand at the foot of the beach. Corpses were liable to be ravaged by dogs, or washed out to sea or back to shore.) Some of the graves and monuments have fascinating inscriptions. A variety of people of many nationalities, from poets to consuls to children, are buried here. The original walled inner cemetery, in the far corner, contains many graves covered in cockle shells. St George's Anglican church here has regular Sunday services. The cemetery opens 9 am to 1 pm and 3 to 5 pm Monday to Friday, and 9 am to noon on Saturday.

JARDÍN EL RETIRO

A few kilometres south-west of the city in Churriana, on the C-344 to Alhaurín de la Torre, are the lovely El Retiro gardens and bird park (☎ 95 262 16 00). The gardens were developed and landscaped by the Condes de Buenavista and other owners in the 18th century. They retain much of their original design which incorporated English, Italian baroque and French styles. There are marble classical statues, lovely fountains and buildings and an impressive collection of exotic birds, some in aviaries, some roaming freely. The gardens open 9 am to 6 pm daily. Admission is a steep 1250 ptas (children 600 ptas, pensioners 750 ptas). To get there take one of the hourly buses bound for Alhaurín de la Torre from Málaga bus station (Paseo de los Tilos).

JARDÍN BOTÁNICO LA CONCEPCIÓN

Four kilometres north of the city centre, the largely tropical La Concepción gardens (☎ 95 225 21 48) have a more modest admission fee of 435 ptas (children 215 ptas). In the 1850s, Englishwoman Amalia Livermore and her Spanish husband, Jorge Loring Oyarzábal, began collecting plants from all over the world to establish the gardens. La Concepción features towering trees (including hundreds of palms) and spectacular colours provided by seasonal blooms: in spring, purple wisteria flowers creep up the trunks of exotic palms. It opens at 10 am daily except Monday and 25 December and 1 January. Visits are by 1¼-hour guided tour, with the last starting at 7.30 pm from

21 June to 10 September, at 4 pm from 11 December to 31 March, and at varying intermediate hours in other seasons.

By car, take the N-331 Antequera road north from the Málaga ring road (N-340) to Km 166 and follow signs. On Saturday, Sunday and holidays there are buses to La Concepción leaving Málaga's Alameda Principal hourly from 11 am.

BEACHES

Sandy beaches line most of the waterfront for several kilometres in each direction from the port. As city beaches go, they're not bad. Playa de la Malagueta is handy for the centre, with several places to eat and drink close by.

LANGUAGE COURSES

Foreigners' courses run by the Universidad de Málaga (☎ 95 227 82 11, fax 95 227 97 12) are very popular. Four-week intensive Spanish language courses cost 83,000 ptas, and accommodation with a family or in apartments or university residences can be arranged. For information, you can write to Universidad de Málaga Cursos de Español para Extranjeros, Inés Carrasco Cantos (Directora), Avenida de Andalucía 24, 29007 Málaga.

There are at least 20 private language schools in Málaga; the main tourist offices have contact lists.

SPECIAL EVENTS

Málaga's big annual festivals are as follows:

Semana Santa

Holy Week (the week before Easter) in Málaga is second only to Sevilla in splendour and solemnity. Each night from Palm Sunday to Good Friday, six or seven ley brotherhoods (cofradías) bear their holy images for several hours through the city, watched by big crowds. Málaga's floats (tronos) are large and heavy and are borne on long poles by teams of up to 150 carriers. On the Monday, the procession of Jesús Cautivo (Christ taken prisoner) is joined by as many as 25,000 people, some barefooted or hooded or with their ankles in chains. Events climax on Good Friday. A good place to watch is the Alameda Principal, where the processions pass through between about 7 pm and midnight.

World Dance Costa del Sol

The port area becomes a massive dance venue for one Saturday night in May, with as many as 200,000 people enjoying top international DJs and live bands.

Feria de Málaga

Málaga's nine-day mid-August Fair, launched by a huge midnight firework display on the opening Friday, is the biggest and most ebullient of Andalucía's summer fairs. During daytime, especially on the two Saturdays, celebrations overwhelm the city centre, with music and dancing in the packed streets and bars, and horses and riders in their finery parading round a circuit of streets. Head for Plaza Uncibay, Plaza de la Constitución, Plaza Mitjana or Calle Marqués de Larios to be in the thick of it. At night the fun switches to the large fairgrounds at Cortijo de Torres, 4km south-west of the city centre, with fairground rides and lots more music and dancing, including nightly concerts by rock, flamenco and other performers. Special buses run from all over the city. Málaga also stages its main bullfight season during the fair. Tourist offices have programs of fair events.

Fiesta Mayor de Verdiales

On 28 December thousands congregate at Puerto de la Torre on the Almogía road on the north-western outskirts of the city, for a grand gathering of verdiales groups, who perform an exhilarating type of folk music and dance unique to the Málaga area – a kind of Celtic/gitano mix, with lots of high-pitched fiddle and tambourine-type percussion. It accompanies intricate, flag-waving dances and participants wear colourful, flowery hats. Bus No 21 from the Alameda Principal goes to Puerto de la Torre.

PLACES TO STAY

Outside the July-to-September peak season, many places, especially in the mid-range and top end, reduce prices significantly, and some places which don't have single-occupancy rates in the peak season introduce them.

PLACES TO STAY – BUDGET
Hostels

One and a half kilometres west of the centre and a couple of blocks north of Avenida de Andalucía, *Albergue Juvenil Málaga* (☎ 95 230 85 00, Plaza Pío XII No 6) has 110 places, most in double rooms and many with bathroom. Bus No 18 along Avenida de Andalucía from the Alameda Principal goes most of the way.

Hostales & Pensiones

True budget rooms are, on the whole, not particularly attractive.

North of the Alameda The homey *Pensión Córdoba* (☎ 95 221 44 69, *Calle Bolsa 9*) has singles/doubles with shared bathroom costing 1500/3000 ptas. *Hostal Lampérez* (☎ 95 221 94 84, *Calle Santa María 6*), also called Hostal Santa María, off Plaza de la Constitución, charges 2000/ 3000 ptas. The bathroom is a bit grim.

Friendly *Hostal Derby* (☎ 95 222 13 01, *Calle San Juan de Dios 1*) has spacious rooms with big windows and bathroom costing 4500/6000 ptas. Find its bell beside the big studded street door.

South-west of Plaza de la Constitución, neighbours *Pensión Rosa* (☎ 95 221 27 16, *Calle Martínez 10*) and *Pensión Ramos* (☎ 95 222 72 68, *Calle Martínez 8*) have adequate rooms with shared bathrooms costing 5000 ptas a double. You can't miss their flowery balconies. *Hostal Aurora* (☎ 95 222 40 04, *Calle Muro de Puerta Nueva 1*), off Calle Puerta Nueva, has six clean, attractive rooms costing 2600/5000 ptas, despite the dingy entrance. *Hostal Cisneros* (☎ 95 221 26 33, *Calle Cisneros 7*) is spotless and friendly. Rooms cost 2800/ 4800 ptas, or 5800 ptas for doubles with bathroom, all plus IVA.

South of the Alameda Clean, basic rooms with shared bathroom at *Hostal Avenida* (☎ 95 221 77 28, *Alameda Principal 5*) cost 1820/3100 ptas; doubles with private bathroom cost 4100 ptas. *Hostal El Cenachero* (☎ 95 222 40 88, *Calle Barroso 5*) is a fair bet at 3900/5900 ptas for rooms with bathroom, or doubles for 5100 ptas with shared bathroom.

PLACES TO STAY – MID-RANGE

In this range, bathroom, TV (often cable) and air-con are standard.

Just east of the cathedral, *Hotel Carlos V* (☎ 95 221 51 20, *fax 95 221 51 29, Calle Císter 10*) has comfortable doubles costing 8300 ptas. The popular, recently remodelled *Hostal Victoria* (☎ 95 222 42 24, *fax 95 222*

42 23, Calle Sancha de Lara 3) has 16 rooms costing 8500 ptas. On the southern side of the Alameda, *Hotel Venecia* (☎ 95 221 36 36, *Alameda Principal 9*), also recently modernised, has 40 agreeable rooms costing 10,500 ptas. *Hotel Sur* (☎ 95 222 48 03, *fax 95 221 24 16, Calle Trinidad Grund 13*) charges 9100 ptas.

One kilometre east of the city centre and close to the beach, *Hotel California* (☎ 95 221 51 65, **❷** *hcalifornia@spa.es, Paseo de Sancha 17*) has 28 comfy, good-sized rooms costing 9645 ptas a double. Breakfast is available. The larger *Hotel Las Vegas* (☎ 95 221 77 12, *fax 95 222 48 89, Paseo de Sancha 22*) has singles/doubles costing around 7500/10,700 ptas all year, and a pool. About 4km east of the city centre and again near the beach, *Hostal Pedregalejo* (☎ 95 229 32 18, **❷** *hosped@spa.es, Calle Conde de las Navas 9*) has attractive rooms costing 4600/6740 ptas.

PLACES TO STAY – TOP END

With an unbeatable location up on the Gibralfaro, *Parador Málaga Gibralfaro* (☎ 95 222 19 02, **❷** *gibralfaro@parador.es*) was refurbished not long ago and has a pool and a good restaurant. Singles/doubles cost 14,000/17,500 ptas plus IVA.

In the city centre, *Hotel Don Curro* (☎ 95 222 72 00, *fax 95 221 59 46, Calle Sancha de Lara 7*) has rooms costing 9800/13,850 ptas (a bit more in August). Also central, 40-room *Hotel Larios* (☎ 95 222 22 00, **❷** *info@hotel-larios.com, Calle Marqués de Larios 2*) has polished doubles costing 22,470 ptas (rising to 47,080 ptas during Semana Santa). The larger *Hotel AC Málaga Palacio* (☎ 95 221 51 85, **❷** *malaga @ac-hoteles.com, Calle Cortina del Muelle 1*) charges 26,750 ptas.

PLACES TO EAT

A speciality of Málaga is fish fried quickly in olive oil. *Fritura malagueño* consists of fried fish, anchovies and squid. Cold soups are popular: as well as gazpacho, in the tomato season, and *sopa de ajo* (garlic soup), try *sopa de almendra con uvas* (almond soup with grapes).

Seafood

At **Rincón Chinitas** *(Pasaje de Chinitas)* *raciones* (meal-sized servings of tapas) of fried fish cost around 750 ptas and a serving of *tortillitas* (shrimp fritters) costs 350 ptas. In the well-heeled La Malagueta area, the more up-market **Aceite y Pan** *(Calle Cervantes 5)*, and **Restaurante Antonio Martín** *(Plaza de la Malagueta)* facing the beach, do a wide range of fish and seafood dishes.

The seafront eateries at Pedregalejo, 4.5km east of the city centre, serve plenty more fish, or you could continue a farther 1km east to the seafront **Restaurante Tintero** in El Palo, where plates of fish and seafood (around 600 ptas) are brought out by the waiters and you shout for what you want. The food is not exquisite (get it hot) but the place is fun.

Near Plaza de la Constitución

On the busy eastern side of Plaza de la Constitución, **Café Central** is a noisy local favourite; its coffee will satisfy even hardened caffeine addicts. Prices for food are reasonable and there's plenty of choice. It closes mid-evening. Round the corner, the popular bar **Málaga Siempre** *(Pasaje de Chinitas 7)* serves a good range of tapas (150 ptas including a glass of beer) and coffee. Nearby, **Mesón El Chinitas** *(Calle de Moreno Monroy 4)* is a fancy place with prices to match, serving many typical Andalucian dishes from 1400 ptas to 2500 ptas, and a *menú* (fixed-price meal) costing 2200 ptas. Tiny **Bar Orellana** *(Calle de Moreno Monroy 5)* has excellent, varied tapas – if you can get near enough to the bar to order them.

For a reasonably priced sit-down meal at a pavement table, head for pedestrian Calle Marín García and Calle Esparteros, just west of Calle Marqués de Larios. **La Alegría**, **Bar Lo Güeno** and **Mesón La Aldea** serve plenty of fish and other dishes costing under 1000 ptas.

A short walk north-east from Plaza de la Constitución, the barn-like **La Posada** *(Calle Granada 33)* is great for *carnes a la brasa* (grilled meat), and for tapas such as *montadito de lomo* (hot bread roll with a slice of pork; 200 ptas) and *chuletillas de cordero* (lamb chops; 1600 ptas). Just north, **Mesón Ajoblanco** *(Plaza de Uncibay 2)*, with tables outside and in, offers a wide range of tasty fare from baguettes (425 ptas to 500 ptas) to meat-and-potato mini-brochettes (650 ptas) or boards of cheese, meats or *ahumados* (smoked fish) for 1200 ptas to 1800 ptas.

Cervecería Uncibay *(Plaza de Uncibay 5)* has *embutidos* (sausages), cheeses, patés and *pulpo a la gallega* (Galician-style octopus). **Bocatta** *(Calle Calderería 11)* serves hot and cold baguettes (365 ptas to 565 ptas) – pay at the counter and carry your food to a table.

To the north-west, **Mesón las Bigas** *(Calle Mosquera 7)*, a traditional-style restaurant-bar, does *carnes a la brasa* (grilled meats) from 1200 ptas, *revueltos* (scrambled egg dishes) for 800 ptas to 900 ptas, and tempting mushrooms and artichokes *a la plancha* (grilled) for 500 ptas a *media-ración* (half a *ración* – a meal-sized serving of tapas). It is closed on Monday.

Tetería El Harén *(Calle Andrés Pérez 3)* is a tea house with a real caravanserai atmosphere – wooden balcony and beams, a small patio open to the sky, candlelit tables in several nooks and rooms. Heaps of aromatic and classic teas, herbal infusions, coffees, juices, liqueurs and crepes are on offer for 250 ptas to 350 ptas. It's very popular with a young clientele, and open from 5 pm to late, some nights with live music, card or tea-leaf readings or story telling.

Near the Cathedral

The *cafes* on Plaza del Obispo have a great view of the cathedral facade. **El Jardín** *(Calle Cañón)*, with open air tables by the garden behind the cathedral, has a fancy interior and *platos combinados* (mixed platters) at 700 ptas to 1250 ptas. It's also a pleasant spot for morning coffee and *tostada* (toasted roll). The unassuming **La Fragata Bar** *(Calle Cortina del Muelle)*, open 7 am to 4 pm daily, serves up scrumptious *pitufos* (small filled rolls) with fillings such as spinach omelette or *jamón serrano* (cured ham) and tomato, for 150 ptas to 200 ptas. **Café de l'Abuela** *(Calle San*

Agustín) offers a coffee-juice-croissant/ toasted roll breakfast for 350/400 ptas, and later in the day serves crepes (275 ptas to 500 ptas) and a myriad of teas and coffees. A couple of doors along this pleasant pedestrian street (leading to the future Museo Picasso), the soothing *La Tetería (Calle San Agustín 9)* offers an even greater range of teas (200 ptas to 300 ptas, including an *'antidepresivo'*), plus crepes, pastries and sorbets (250 ptas to 400 ptas).

Near the Market

The colourful *Mercado Central*, north of the Alameda Principal, built in the 19th century in a Mudéjar-influenced style and retaining a 14th-century arch, has terrific fresh produce. Nearby are plenty of *cafes* on pedestrian Calle Herrería del Rey. These open early and pack up promptly at 1 pm. A particularly atmospheric bar in this area is the *Antigua Casa de Guardia (Alameda Central 18)*, going since 1840. Málaga wine from the barrel starts at 110 ptas a glass, and it serves good seafood tapas, closing about 10 pm.

South of the Alameda

Relaxed *El Yamal (Calle Blasco de Garay 3)* cooks up excellent Moroccan food in the traditional *tajines*, earthenware dishes with pointed lids: fish or chicken, or couscous with vegetables, costs 1225 ptas to 1500 ptas; a tasty salad with hummus and flat bread costs 675 ptas. It's closed Sunday evening. *Mesón Danés (Calle Barroso 5)* offers Danish and Spanish food, with a menú for 1995 ptas (closed Sunday).

Vegetarian

The good *El Vegetariano de la Alcazabilla (Calle Pozo del Rey 5)*, on the eastern edge of the central district, has a fair range of dishes, including a nice Greek salad for two, wholemeal pasta and *empanadillas de espinacas* (spinach pies), all costing between 950 ptas and 1100 ptas. It opens 1.30 to 4 and 9 to 11 pm Monday to Saturday. Its more central sibling, *El Vegetariano de San Bernardo (Calle Niño de Guevara)*, has a similar menu and the same hours.

ENTERTAINMENT

The weekly *Informaciones de Málaga*, available free from tourist offices, is a good source of what's-on information. The back pages of *Sur* newspaper, and its Friday *Evasión* section, are also useful.

Bars & Music

The narrow old streets north of Plaza de la Constitución heave with people having a good time from midnight or so on fine weekend nights – and there's some action almost any day of the week. The action reaches as far as Plaza de la Merced in the north-east and nearly to Calle Carretería in the north-west. Bars playing great music for a predominantly 20s and late teens crowd are to be found on virtually every street, especially near Plaza Mitjana (officially called Plaza del Marqués Vado Maestre) and Plaza de Uncibay.

Near Plaza de Uncibay, there's space to dance (salsa of course) at *Salsa*, on the corner of Calle Belgrano, open from 11 pm, sometimes with live bands. *Discoteca Anden* on Plaza de Uncibay rages till dawn Thursday to Saturday. *Bodegas El Pimpi (Calle Granada 62)*, a minor warren of rooms and mini-patios, has traditional decor of casks and bullfight posters but attracts a young, fun-loving crowd with its sweet wine and thumping music. *Café Liceo (Calle Beatas 21)*, an old mansion turned young music bar, buzzes after midnight with a clientele at the younger end of their 20s in the second half of the week. *La Botellita (Calle Álamos 36)*, just off Plaza de la Merced, playing Spanish music, is popular with a similar crowd.

Onda Pasadena (Calle Gómez Pallete 9) is a good live music bar, usually with jazz on Saturday from 11.30 pm and flamenco and/or other styles midweek. *ZZ Pub (Calle Tejón y Rodríguez 6)* usually has rock or blues bands starting about midnight on Monday and Thursday.

La Cervecería, a large beer bar, the Irish pub *O'Neill's* and *Saloma*, with space to dance (but expensive drinks), are all on Calle Luis de Velázquez, just south off Plaza Mitjana. The alleys just to the west harbour another couple of dozen lively bars ranging from **Siempre Asi** *(Calle Convale-cientes 5)*, playing flamenco and rumbas to a 25-to-40 year old crowd from 9.30 pm Thursday to Saturday, to **Sodoma** *(Calle Juan de Padilla 15)*, with house music from 11 pm the same nights.

Pedregalejo, a beach suburb 4.5km east of the city centre, buzzes until late during the summer.

Other
The **Teatro Cervantes** *(Calle Ramos Marín s/n)* has a good regular program of music, dance and theatre.

Posters and *Sur* newspaper list the current movies at Málaga's cinemas. **Multicines Albéniz** *(Calle Alcazabilla 4)* is the home of the Cinemateca Municipal, showing international films with Spanish subtitles at 10 pm most nights.

SPECTATOR SPORTS
Málaga football club went bankrupt and out of existence around 1990, but was reborn and, in 1999, won its way back into Spain's First Division. The club plays at the Estadio de la Rosaleda, beside the Río Guadalmedina, 2km north of the city centre. Málaga's Unicaja basketball team does quite well in the national league and was due to move into a brand new stadium, the Palacio de los Deportes, in the west of the city out towards the airport, in autumn 2000.

GETTING THERE & AWAY
Air
Málaga's busy airport (☎ 95 204 88 04), the main international gateway to Andalucía, is 9km south-west of the city centre. See the introductory Getting There & Away chapter for information on international and domestic flights. Iberia's and Binter Mediterráneo's Málaga office (☎ 902 40 05 00) is at Calle Molina Lario 13. Most airline offices are at the airport.

Bus
The bus station (☎ 95 235 00 61) is on Paseo de los Tilos, 1km west of the centre. Frequent buses run along the coast and sev-

eral daily go to inland towns including Antequera (475 ptas) and Ronda (around 1100 ptas). Other destinations include Sevilla (1900 ptas, 2½ hours, 10 buses daily), Córdoba (1570 ptas, 2½ hours, five daily), Granada (1185 ptas, 1½ to two hours, 16 daily), Cádiz, Jaén, Valencia, Barcelona (8495 ptas, 15 hours), and Madrid (2650 ptas, six hours, seven or more daily). There are also buses to Germany, England, Portugal, France, Belgium, the Netherlands and Morocco.

Train
The train station (☎ 95 236 02 02) is on Explanada de la Estación, round the corner from the bus station.

Nine or more trains run daily to/from Córdoba (2100 ptas to 2800 ptas, two to 2½ hours). To/from Sevilla (2130 ptas, 2½ hours) there are five regional Tren Regional Diésels (TRDs) daily. For Granada there are no direct trains, but you can get there in 2¼ hours for 1800 ptas with a transfer at Bobadilla. For Ronda, too, you usually change at Bobadilla: the best connections give a 1¾-hour journey (1250 ptas).

Four or more daily Talgo 200s go to/from Madrid (7000 ptas to 8200 ptas, four to 4½ hours). Three other Madrid trains cost 4700 ptas to 5500 ptas, taking up to 13 hours. For Valencia and Barcelona (6400 ptas to 8400 ptas, 13 to 14 hours) there are three trains daily, two of them overnight.

Car
Numerous international and local agencies have desks at the airport. You'll find them down a ramp in the luggage-carousel hall, and out the side of the arrivals hall.

Boat
Trasmediterránea (☎ 95 206 12 18, 902 45 46 45), Estación Marítima, Local E1, operates ferries daily (except Sunday from mid-September to mid-June) to/from Melilla. The trip takes about 7½ hours, with passenger fares starting at 4020 ptas one way; a car costs 16,125 ptas. Also from the Estación Marítima (port), the high-speed

Buquebus (☎ 95 222 79 05, 902 41 42 42) has fast sailings to/from Ceuta (1½ hours) at least twice daily (passenger 4995 ptas, car 8995 ptas).

GETTING AROUND
To/From the Airport
A taxi from the airport to city centre costs around 1300 ptas.

Bus No 19 to the city centre (135 ptas) leaves from the 'City Bus' stop outside the arrivals hall, about every half-hour from 7 am to midnight, stopping at Málaga's main train and bus stations en route. Going out to the airport, you can catch it at the western end of Paseo del Parque, and outside the stations, about every half-hour from 6.30 am to 11.30 pm. The journey takes around 20 minutes.

The Aeropuerto train station, on the Málaga-Fuengirola line, is a five-minute walk from the airport terminal: follow signs from the departures hall. Trains run about every half-hour from 7 am to 11.45 pm to Málaga's main station (135 ptas, 11 minutes) and the Centro-Alameda station beside the Río Guadalmedina. Departures from the city to the airport and beyond are about every half-hour from 5.45 am to 10.30 pm. Fares are slightly higher at the weekend and holidays.

Bus
Useful buses around town (120 ptas) include No 11 to Pedregalejo and El Palo from Avenida de Cervantes.

Taxi
Fares within the city centre, including to the train and bus stations, are around 550 ptas. Expect to pay 750 ptas to the Castillo de Gibralfaro.

Parking
Convenient car parks such as on Plaza de la Marina tend to be expensive (260 ptas an hour). Vacant lots are much cheaper (just give 100 ptas to the attendant) – there have been large ones behind El Corte Inglés and Museo de Artes y Costumbres Populares for several years.

Costa del Sol

The Costa del Sol, a string of resorts along the coast from Málaga to Gibraltar, might best be described as an international strip stuck on the bottom of Spain. The Costa's recipe for success is sunshine, beaches (although, with mostly grey-brown sand, these are not Andalucía's best), warm Mediterranean water, cheap package deals and plenty of nightlife and entertainment.

The resorts were fishing villages until the 1950s or '60s, but there's little evidence of that left now. Launched as a Francoist development drive for impoverished Andalucía, the Costa del Sol is now a series of townscapes from one end to the other – arguably Europe's finest example of how overdevelopment can ruin a spectacular landscape.

Activites
The Costa del Sol is good for sport lovers, with nearly 40 golf clubs, several busy marinas, tennis and squash courts, riding schools, swimming pools and gyms. Many of the beaches have facilities for water sports such as windsurfing, water-skiing and parasailing.

Places to Stay
The Costa del Sol has huge numbers of rooms at almost every price, but even so, to avoid a weary trudge from one *completo* (full) sign to another, it's highly advisable to book ahead during the high season of July, August and, in some places, September. Outside these peak months, room rates in many places come down sharply.

The Costa has about 15 camp sites.

Getting There & Around
A convenient train service links Málaga and its airport with Torremolinos, Arroyo de la Miel (Benalmádena) and Fuengirola, and plenty of buses link the coastal towns.

The recently opened A-7 Autopista del Sol, bypassing Fuengirola, Marbella, San Pedro de Alcántara and Estepona, makes moving along the Costa del Sol a lot easier for those willing to pay its tolls

(470 ptas Marbella–Estepona, 600 ptas Mijas–Marbella, coming down to 290 ptas and 495 ptas, respectively, from October to May). Horrible tailbacks continue on the N-340 south-west of Estepona, beyond the end of the new highway, but otherwise the N-340, formerly the Costa's main trunk road, is now considerably less overpopulated. The N-340 remains a key to orientation as many places use Km numbers on it to pinpoint their location. These numbers rise from west to east: Estepona is at Km 155 and central Marbella at Km 181. Km markers aside, undoubtedly the most useful sign on the N-340 is 'Cambio de Sentido', indicating that you can change direction to get back to a turning you have missed. Meanwhile, beware of other motorists and watch out for cats, dogs and inebriated pedestrians.

Bargain rental cars (14,000 ptas to 20,000 ptas a week, all inclusive) are available from local firms in all the resorts.

TORREMOLINOS & BENALMÁDENA

(Torremolinos) postcode 29620
• pop 32,000

If they had built Blackpool in the 1960s in a place with sunshine, it would have looked like Torremolinos. This concrete high-rise jungle, beginning 5km south-west of Málaga airport, is designed to squeeze as many paying customers as possible into the smallest possible space. Even in winter, traffic jams of pedestrians can block the narrow lanes behind the main beach. Rose Macaulay, in *Fabled Shore*, the account of her travels along Spain's Mediterranean coast in the late 1940s, wrote that in Torremolinos, 'a pretty country place' of 'incredible beauty', she saw three young Englishmen, 'the first English tourists I had seen since I entered Spain'.

One of the few legacies of Torremolinos' past is an Islamic watchtower at the foot of Calle San Miguel, once known as the Torre de los Molinos (Tower of the Mills). After leading the Costa del Sol's mass tourist boom of the 1950s and '60s, 'Torrie' lost ground to other resorts but spruced up in the

'90s. A pleasant seafront walk, the Paseo Marítimo, now extends for nearly 7km.

Beach excepted, many of Torremolinos' attractions are actually in Benalmádena, its neighbour to the south-west.

Orientation

The main road through Torremolinos from the north-east (the direction of the airport and Málaga) is called Calle Hoyo, becoming Avenida Palma de Mallorca after it passes through Plaza Costa del Sol. Calle San Miguel, running most of the 500m from Plaza Costa del Sol down to the central beach, Playa del Bajondillo, is the main pedestrian artery. The bus station is on Calle Hoyo and the train station is on Avenida Jesús Santos Rein, a pedestrian street intersecting Calle San Miguel 200m from Plaza Costa del Sol. South-west of Playa del Bajondillo, around a small point, is Playa de la Carihuela, once the fishing quarter, backed by generally lower-rise buildings.

The south-western end of Torremolinos merges with Benalmádena Costa, the coastal bit of Benalmádena. About 2km uphill from here is the part of Benalmádena called Arroyo de la Miel, with the original, surprisingly unspoiled village, Benalmádena Pueblo, to its west.

Information

Torremolinos has tourist offices on Playa del Bajondillo (☎ 95 237 19 09); Calle Borbollón Bajo (☎ 95 237 29 56), La Carihuela; Plaza de la Independencia (☎ 95 237 42 31), a block inland from Plaza Costa del Sol; and in the town hall (☎ 95 237 95 11), farther inland on Plaza de Blas Infante. The first two open 10 am to 2 pm Monday to Friday from October to May, and 10 am to 2 pm and 5 to 8 pm daily from June to September. The others open 9.30 am to 1.30 pm Monday to Friday.

Benalmádena's main tourist office (☎ 95 244 24 94) is at Avenida Antonio Machado 10, on the main road from Torremolinos. Benalmádena's population numbers 25,000; Benalmádena Costa's postcode is 29630, whilst Benalmádena Pueblo's postcode is 29639.

euro currency converter €1 = 166 ptas

Beaches

Torremolinos' beaches are wider, longer and a paler shade of grey-brown than most on the Costa del Sol – which is why they pull in so many people.

Aquapark

Aquapark (☎ 95 238 88 88), Calle Cuba 10, has varied water slides and a wave pool in the typical water-fun-park mould. It usually opens 10 am to 6 or 7 pm daily, from about late May to late September. A day ticket costs 1995 ptas (children 1295 ptas).

Sea Life

In Benalmádena Costa's swish Puerto Deportivo (marina), Sea Life (☎ 95 256 01 50) is a good modernistic aquarium of mainly Mediterranean marine creatures. Highlights include the walk-through shark and stingray tunnel and a recreation of Atlantis. It opens 10 am to 6 pm or later; admission costs 995 ptas (children aged four to 12 years 695 ptas).

Tivoli World

The Costa's biggest amusement park, at Arroyo de la Miel, is visited by about a million people a year. As well as multifarious rides and slides, Tivoli World (☎ 95 257 70 16) stages daily dance, musical and children's events. It's five minutes walk from Benalmádena-Arroyo de la Miel train station. Hours vary but expect it to be open from 4 or 5 pm to about 1 am in April, May, June, October and the second half of September; 6 pm to 3 am daily from July to mid-September; and noon to 9 pm on Saturday and Sunday from November to March. Admission costs 600 ptas, then you pay for your rides; for children, look into the 'Supertivolino' ticket.

Museo Arqueológico

The Archaeological Museum (☎ 95 244 85 93), on Plaza de Thomson in Benalmádena Pueblo, exhibits an interesting collection of pre-Columbian sculpture and ceramics from Mexico and Central America. It opens 10 am to 2 pm and 4 to 7 pm (5 to 7 pm in July and August), Monday to Friday. Admission is free.

Places to Stay

Torremolinos has more than 50,000 hotel and apartment beds. The pleasant, 17-room *Hostal Micaela* (☎ 95 238 33 10, fax 95 237 68 42, Calle Bajondillo 4) is close to Playa del Bajondillo and has doubles with bathroom costing 4650 ptas plus IVA. *Hostal Guillot* (☎ 95 238 01 44, Pasaje Río Mundo 4), off Pasaje de Pizarro near Plaza Costa del Sol, is nowhere near as pleasant, but has doubles costing 4000 ptas. Just across the Paseo Marítimo from Playa del Bajondillo, the small *Hostal Guadalupe* (☎ 95 238 19 37, Calle del Peligro 15) charges 5000/6000 ptas for singles/doubles with bathroom. The 28-room *Hotel El Pozo* (☎ 95 238 06 22, Calle Casablanca 2) in central Torremolinos boasts a 'family atmosphere' with doubles costing 7500 ptas plus IVA.

In La Carihuela, about 1.5km southwest of central Torremolinos, *Hostal Flor Blanco* (☎ 95 238 20 71, Pasaje de la Carihuela 4) is almost on the beach and several of its 12 rooms (with bathroom) have sea views. Doubles are 5900 ptas plus IVA. *Hotel Miami* (☎ 95 238 52 55, Calle Aladino 14), a few blocks back from La Carihuela beach, is a quaint 1940s villa turned into a small hotel with nice gardens, a pool and doubles costing 7500 ptas.

The charming *La Fonda* (☎/fax 95 256 82 73, Calle Santo Domingo 7), in Benalmádena Pueblo, has large rooms built around patios with fountains, and a restaurant that forms part of a catering school and serves excellent food at excellent prices. Singles/doubles cost 8000/10,800 ptas.

Places to Eat

One of the best things about Torremolinos is the plentiful good seafood. On Playa del Bajondillo, *Restaurante Los Pescadores Playa* does a large variety of grilled fish and meat from 750 ptas. *Bodega Quitapeñas* on Cuesta del Tajo, near the tower, and *Bar La Bodega* (Calle San Miguel 40) are popular with Spaniards for their seafood raciones (550 ptas to 950 ptas) and tapas. *Restaurante Miramar* at the bottom of Calle San Miguel will serve you a Chinese menú for 695 ptas (795 ptas at night).

More eateries, many specialising in seafood, line the Paseo Marítimo in La Carihuela. At the north-eastern end, *Restaurante La Marina* is popular for its 950 ptas menú. *Restaurante Juan*, *Restaurante El Roqueo* and *Restaurante Gauquín* are particularly good, with fish and seafood main courses costing between 750 ptas and 2500 ptas.

There's no shortage of British bars with British beer, British breakfasts for 500 ptas or so, roast beef lunches for 900 ptas, and British football on TV.

Entertainment
The weekend nightlife at Benalmádena Costa's Puerto Deportivo attracts Spaniards from Málaga and all along the coast as well as holidaymakers. The bars really start to throb after midnight on Friday and Saturday. Buses run there right through Saturday night/Sunday morning. Torremolinos itself has a big gay and transvestite scene – most of the gay bars are on Calle Nogalera off Avenida Jesús Santos Rein.

Getting There & Away
From a stop on Avenida Palma de Mallorca at the corner of Calle Antonio Girón, 200m south-west of Plaza Costa del Sol, buses run to/from Benalmádena Costa and Málaga (140 ptas, 30 minutes, about every 15 minutes from 7 am to 1.30 am); Benalmádena Pueblo and Fuengirola (every 20 or 30 minutes from 7 am to 10 pm); and Mijas (hourly from 7 am to 10 pm).

From the bus station (☎ 95 238 24 19) on Calle Hoyo, buses run to Marbella (455 ptas, one hour, 14 or more times daily) and to Ronda, Estepona, La Línea, Algeciras, Tarifa, Cádiz and Granada a few times a day.

Trains run to Torremolinos, about every half-hour, 5.30 am to 10.30 pm, from Málaga city (160 ptas, 20 minutes) and the airport (140 ptas, 10 minutes), then continue to Benalmádena-Arroyo de la Miel and Fuengirola (160 ptas, 20 minutes).

FUENGIROLA
postcode 29640 • pop 43,000
Fuengirola, another beach resort 18km down the coast from Torremolinos, has more of a family holiday scene but is even more densely packed with buildings and even more dedicated to British breakfasts, beer and football.

Orientation & Information
The narrow streets in the few blocks between the beach and Avenida Matías Sáenz de Tejada (the street the bus station is on) constitute what's left of the old town, with Plaza de la Constitución at its heart. The train station is a block inland from the bus station, on Avenida Jesús Santos Rein.

The tourist office (☎ 95 246 74 57) at Avenida Jesús Santos Rein 6, just along from the train station, opens 9.30 am to 2 pm and 4.30 to 7 pm Monday to Friday, and 10 am to 1 pm Saturday.

Things to See & Do
The **Parque Acuático Mijas** (☎ 95 246 04 09), beside the N-340 Fuengirola bypass, is like Torremolinos' Aquapark but slightly cheaper, and usually open from May to September. Admission costs 1800 ptas (children aged four to 12 years 1150 ptas). The **Castillo de Sohail** at the south-western end of Fuengirola beach dates from the 10th century. Recently restored, with an auditorium in its central courtyard, it opens 10 am to 2.30 pm and 4 to 6 pm, Tuesday to Sunday. Admission costs 200 ptas.

The **Hipódromo Costa del Sol** (☎ 95 259 27 00), Andalucía's only horse race track, opened in 2000 at Urbanización El Chaparral, off the N-340 at the south-western end of Fuengirola. The summer race meetings were run between 11 pm and 2 am every Saturday night. A switch to Sunday morning meetings was envisaged for winter. A large **street market** is held every Tuesday on Avenida Jesús Santos Rein.

Special Events
The 16 July Virgen del Carmen celebrations in Los Boliches, a former fishing village that's now an eastern suburb of Fuengirola, are famous. In a two-hour procession 120 bearers carry a heavy platform, supporting the image of the virgin, from Los Boliches church into the sea.

Places to Stay

The friendly, 35-room *Hostal Italia* (☎ *95 247 41 93, Calle de la Cruz 1)* is in the heart of things a couple of blocks from the beach and has singles/doubles with bathroom, air-con and TV costing around 6400/ 8000 ptas. *Hostal Cuevas* (☎ *95 246 06 06, Calle Capitán 7)*, along the street, is a decent smaller place with doubles costing 4950 ptas. Swedish-owned *Hostal Marbella* (☎/fax *95 266 45 03, Calle Marbella 34)*, just south-west of Plaza de la Constitución, is friendly and clean, with rooms costing 6500/8000 ptas.

Places to Eat

On Calle Moncayo – a block back from the beachfront Paseo Marítimo – and Calle de la Cruz (which intersects Moncayo) you can choose from a host of British bars and Italian, Belgian, Cypriot, Chinese, Indonesian and even Spanish restaurants, several with menús for 800 ptas or 900 ptas.

On the Paseo Marítimo itself and in the Puerto Deportivo (Marina) off the Paseo Marítimo are further strings of bargain eateries, some with menús under 700 ptas. Among the classier places, *Restaurante Portofino (Paseo Marítimo 29)*, near the end of Calle de la Cruz, has main courses costing from 1275 ptas (fish dishes cost from 1725 ptas), and *Pastelería Costa del Sol (Calle Marbella)*, just off Plaza de la Constitución, is excellent for breakfast, cakes, toasted sandwiches and the like.

Entertainment

Lively *Pub Route 66* (☎ *95 246 32 05, Calle Medina 16)*, a couple of blocks southwest of Plaza de la Constitución, stages blues or jazz groups from 9.30 pm to 12.30 am Thursday to Sunday (admission costs 700 ptas Thursday to Saturday, free on Sunday). Music bars and discos cluster opposite the Puerto Deportivo. The *Irish Times* and *Cafetería La Plaza* bars at opposite ends of Plaza de la Constitución fill up with lively, mainly Spanish crowds in the evening. The Irish Times' patio is great on a hot night.

Getting There & Away

From the bus station (☎ 95 247 50 66) frequent buses run to Torremolinos (155 ptas), Málaga (310 ptas) and Marbella (310 ptas), plus a few a day to Ronda, Sevilla, Granada and elsewhere.

Fuengirola is served by the same trains as Torremolinos, costing 325 ptas from Málaga and 240 ptas from the airport.

MIJAS

postcode 29650 • pop (estimated) 12,000 • elevation 428m

Mijas, a village of Muslim origin looking down on Fuengirola from the hillside 8km north, was where foreign artist and writer types settled in the 1950s and '60s when their package-tour compatriots were pouring into the beach towns below. Since then villas and suburbs have spread wide over the surrounding hills. Mijas remains a pretty place but it's full of souvenir and craft shops and busloads up from the Costa. It has a few *hostales* and *hotels* and a gamut of *restaurants* and *cafes*, if the mood takes you. Frequent buses run from Fuengirola (110 ptas).

MARBELLA

postcode 29600 • pop 86,000

Marbella, 28km west of Fuengirola and overlooked by the dramatic Sierra Blanca, is the most interesting town on the Costa de Sol.

It was the building in the 1950s of the exclusive Marbella Club Hotel, just west of town, by Alfonso von Hohenlohe, a part-Mexican, part-Austrian aristocrat with strong Spanish connections, that turned Marbella into a playground of the international jet set. For three decades oil-rich Arabs and other glitterati flocked to build luxury pieds-a-terre and be seen here.

In the 1980s, an economic slump and the rapid growth of suburbs with their own bars and restaurants sent Marbella into decline, but in 1991 Jesús Gil y Gil, a flamboyant right-wing businessman, won a landslide victory to become mayor. Gil, who has expressed the view that Spain was 'better off under Franco', set about restoring Marbella's image by laying marble pavements,

The distinctive design of the Mezquita, Córdoba

A palmy summer's day, Córdoba

Knocking about the Mezquita

Walking in the footsteps of kings – Patio de los Naranjos, entrance to the Mezquita, Córdoba

An exquisite celebration of faith, the building of the Moorish Mezquita was begun in 756.

A door for the Moors – the eastern entrance to the Mezquita, Córdoba

planting palms, building underground car parks and – with notoriously heavy-handed police methods – ridding the streets of petty criminals, prostitutes and drug addicts. The beaches are clean, and the tourists have returned to Marbella.

Gil also encouraged property development and courted the wealthy and famous, including the Costa's recent wave of nouveau-riche Russians. He was re-elected mayor in 1995 and 1999, but has had to face a growing mountain of lawsuits in which he has been accused of a welter of misdeeds ranging from town-planning irregularities to illegally diverting 450 million ptas of Marbella council money to the Atlético Madrid football team (of which he was president). Gil spent a brief spell in jail in the Atlético case in 1999. His critics also argue that a lot of serious organised crime, related to drug trafficking and money laundering, goes on unchecked in Marbella.

Orientation

The N-340 through town goes by the names Avenida Ramón y Cajal and, farther west, Avenida Ricardo Soriano. The old town is centred on Plaza de los Naranjos, north of Avenida Ramón y Cajal. The bus station is on the northern side of the Marbella bypass, about 1.2km north of Plaza de los Naranjos.

Information

The helpful tourist offices on Glorieta de la Fontanilla (☎ 95 277 14 42) and at Plaza de los Naranjos 1 (☎ 95 282 35 50) open 9 am to 8 or 9 pm daily except holidays. Another office (☎ 95 282 28 18), in the 'Marbella' arch over the N-340 at the eastern entrance to the town, opens 10 am to midnight daily except 1 January.

The main post office is on Calle de Jacinto Benavente. Two establishments called Cibercafé, at Avenida Miguel Cano 6 and in Edificio Alameda on nearby Calle Carlos Mackintosh, offer Internet access.

Emergency medical attention is available at the Centro de Salud Leganitos (☎ 95 277 21 84) on Plaza Leganitos, 8 am to 5 pm Monday to Friday, 9 am to 5 pm Saturday. Hospital Europa (☎ 95 277 42 00) is 1km

east of the centre on Avenida de Severo Ochoa. The Policía Nacional (☎ 091) station is on Avenida Doctor Viñals north of the town.

Things to See & Do

The central **Playa de Venus**, immediately east of the Puerto Deportivo, is a reasonable piece of beach, but for a longer, broader and usually less crowded stretch of sand walk to the 800m-long **Playa de la Fontanilla**, west of Glorieta de la Fontanilla, or even better, the 2km **Playa de Casablanca** beyond Playa de la Fontanilla.

Marbella's picturesque, largely pedestrianised old town has Muslim origins. At its heart is pretty **Plaza de los Naranjos**, with the 16th-century town hall on its northern side and a 17th-century fountain on the southern side. Nearby, on Plaza de la Iglesia is the **Iglesia de la Encarnación**, begun in the 16th century and later redone in baroque style.

A little farther east, the **Museo del Grabado Español Contemporáneo** (Museum of Contemporary Spanish Prints), in a 16th-century hospital on Calle Hospital Bazán, exhibits work by Picasso, Miró and Dalí, among others. It opens 10 am to 2 pm and 5.30 to 8.30 pm Monday to Friday, and 10 am to 2 pm Sunday. Admission costs 300 ptas. Just to the north, along streets such as Calle Arte and Calle Portada, are remains of Marbella's old **Muslim walls**.

North-east of the old town, in the watery Parque de la Represa, is the charming **Museo Bonsai** (☎ 95 286 29 26), devoted to Japanese miniature-tree art; it opens 10 am to 1.30 pm and 4.30 to 8 pm daily. Admission costs 500 ptas.

There are good walks in the **Sierra Blanca** starting from the Refugio de Juanar, a 17km drive from Marbella.

Special Events

Marbella's big week-long fair happens around 11 June. The Castillo de Cante flamenco song festival on the first or second Saturday of August (starting about 11 pm) in Ojén village, 10km north of Marbella, always features some of the big names.

MÁLAGA PROVINCE

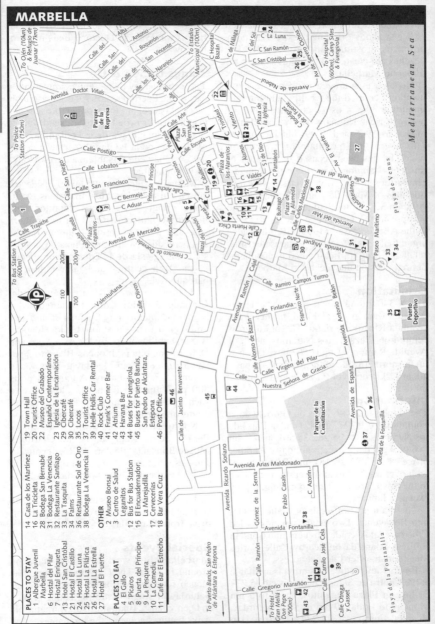

MARBELLA

PLACES TO STAY
1 Albergue Juvenil Marbella
6 Hostal del Pilar
7 Hostal Enriqueta
13 Hotel San Cristóbal
21 Hostal El Castillo
24 Hostal La Luna
25 Hostal La Pilárica
26 Hostal La Estrella
27 Hotel El Fuerte

PLACES TO EAT
4 El Gallo
5 Picaros
8 Puerta del Príncipe
9 La Pesquera
10 La Comedia
11 Café Bar El Estrecho

14 Casa de los Martínez
16 La Tricicleta
28 Bodega San Bernabé
31 Bodega La Venencia
32 Restaurante Santiago
33 La Tasquita
34 Palms
36 Restaurante Sol de Oro
38 Bodega La Venencia II

OTHER
2 Museo Bonsai
3 Centro de Salud Leganitos
12 Bus for Bus Station
15 El Encuadernador; La Marejadilla
17 Cervecerías
18 Bar Vera Cruz

19 Town Hall
20 Tourist Office
22 Museo del Grabado Español Contemporáneo
23 Iglesia de la Encarnación
29 Cibercafé
30 Cibercafé
35 Locos
37 Tourist Office
39 Helle Hollis Car Rental
40 Rock Club
41 Frank's Corner Bar
42 Atrium
43 Havana Bar
44 Buses for Fuengirola
45 Buses for Puerto Banús, San Pedro de Alcántara, Estepona
46 Post Office

euro currency converter 1000 ptas = €6.01

Places to Stay – Budget

On the beach 3km east, *Camping Marbella 191* (☎ *95 277 83 91, N-340 Km 184.5)* has a limited opening season and charges around 3000 ptas a site in the high season. Three bigger and less expensive year-round sites are in the next 10km of the N-340 heading east, all within walking distance of the beach.

The modern *Albergue Juvenil Marbella* (☎ *95 277 14 91, fax 95 286 32 27, Calle Trapiche 2)*, near the Islamic walls, has plain, old-fashioned but comfy enough singles/doubles with bathroom costing 3200/5600 ptas. Check the aerial photo of 1950s Marbella on the staircase! *Hostal Enriqueta* (☎ *95 282 75 52, Calle Los Caballeros 18)* has nice doubles/triples with bathroom and fan costing 7000/9000 ptas.

British-run *Hostal del Pilar* (☎ *95 282 99 36,* @ *hostal@marbella-scene.com, Calle Mesoncillo 4)*, off Calle Peral, is deservedly popular with backpackers. Singles, doubles and triples with shared bathroom cost 1500 ptas to 2000 ptas a person, depending on the season, and there's a bar with a pool table (and a log fire in the cooler months). Big English breakfasts are served for 700 ptas.

Just south-east of the old town, small hostales cluster on narrow Calle San Cristóbal and nearby streets. Three of the better ones, all charging 5000 ptas to 6000 ptas for doubles with bathroom, are *Hostal La Luna* (☎ *95 282 57 78, Calle La Luna 7)*, *Hostal La Estrella* (☎ *95 277 94 72, Calle San Cristóbal 36)* and *Hostal La Pilárica* (☎ *95 277 42 52, Calle San Cristóbal 31)*.

Places to Stay – Mid-Range & Top End

Above the hostal bracket you'll normally pay 10,000 ptas or more for a double in summer. One of the more economical hotels

is *Hotel San Cristóbal* (☎ *95 277 12 50, fax 95 286 20 44, Avenida Ramón y Cajal 3)*, with doubles costing 11,600 ptas plus IVA; you'll probably be better off with a room at the back or side, away from the noisy avenue. The 263-room *Hotel El Fuerte* (☎ *95 286 15 00, fax 95 282 44 11, Avenida El Fuerte s/n)*, close to Playa de Venus, has doubles costing 16,400 ptas plus IVA.

The ritziest hotels are mostly along the coast to the east or west, but the five-star *Hotel Gran Meliá Don Pepe* (☎ *95 277 03 00, fax 95 277 99 54, Calle José Meliá s/n)* is just over 1km west of the town centre, with doubles costing 48,000 ptas plus IVA.

Places to Eat

Old Town The restaurants around Plaza de los Naranjos are popular with visitors but not cheap. For a local adventure head for the bar *El Gallo* (*Calle Lobatos 44)* – egg and chips cost 300 ptas and it has the cheapest *langostinos pil pil* (prawns in a chilli-spiked garlic sauce) in town at 550 ptas (closed Tuesday). Popular with locals is *Casa de los Martínez* (*Avenida Ramón y Cajal 7)*, where tapas cost around 150 ptas and a decent-value menú is served for 1000 ptas. *Café Bar El Estrecho* (*Calle San Lázaro 12)* is another good spot for varied tapas (175 ptas to 200 ptas), raciones and media-raciones.

For something more up-market book a patio table at *Pícaros* (☎ *95 282 86 50, Calle Aduar 1)*. The open-air terrace is beautiful. You could start with a walnut and Stilton salad (750 ptas) then choose from an eclectic list of main courses costing from 1200 ptas to 1975 ptas (all plus IVA). It opens from 7.30 pm, but in winter you may find it closed from Sunday to Tuesday. *La Comedia*, on narrow Calle San Lázaro, offers interesting international fare such as Ethiopian chicken stew with barley cakes. Main courses cost 1300 ptas to 2400 ptas. *La Tricicleta*, also on Calle San Lázaro, open for dinner only, Monday to Saturday, has a pleasant setting, with meat and fish mains costing around 1900 ptas to 2400 ptas. On Calle Huerta Chica, the *Puerta del Príncipe* does good grilled meat and fish from around 950 ptas to 2000 ptas; *La Pesquera* next door concentrates on seafood, at similar prices.

Elsewhere On Calle Carlos Mackintosh, facing the leafy Plaza de la Alameda, *Bodega San Bernabé* is wonderfully traditional, with tapas of ham and cheese only. On Playa de Venus beside the Puerto Deportivo, *Palms* specialises in interesting salads costing from 950 ptas and *La Tasquita* serves good fried and grilled fresh fish and seafood for 600 ptas to 1200 ptas.

The seafront Paseo Marítimo is lined with restaurants all the way from Hotel El Fuerte to Glorieta de la Fontanilla. One of the best is *Restaurante Santiago* (☎ 95 277 00 78, Paseo Marítimo 5), a seafood specialist with big windows looking on to Playa de Venus. Two courses would cost you around 4000 ptas. *Restaurante Sol de Oro* near Glorieta de la Fontanilla, does a good-value lunch menú, including a glass of wine, for 1200 ptas.

Bodega La Venencia (Avenida Miguel Cano 15), just behind Playa de Venus, and *Bodega La Venencia II* (Avenida Fontanilla 4) serve great ham tapas and *montaditos* (small sandwiches, often toasted) from 175 ptas, plus raciones and media-raciones.

Entertainment
On little Calle San Lázaro, the bars *El Encuadernador* and *La Marejadilla* stay lively late, even in the low season when the rest of the old town has gone home. The Canadian-run *Bar Vera Cruz* (Calle Buitrago 7), one street east, opens 7.30 pm to 3 am (except Sunday) and has a cosy open fire in winter. The next street east, Calle Pantaleón, has a string of beer bars buzzing late into weekend nights with a young crowd. A line of music bars and discos at the marina throbs till dawn in summer: check out *Locos*, run by the vocalist of leading Marbella rock/Latin/reggae band Hyperbórea.

An older crowd gravitates to the streets around Calle Camilo José Cela, where *Frank's Corner Bar*, the *Rock Club*, the *Atrium* and *Havana Bar* are among the main hang-outs.

The free bimonthly publication *Marbella Día y Noche* contains useful information on concerts and exhibitions. It's on the Internet (in Spanish) at www.guiamarbella.com.

Shopping
The old town is full of enticing craft, clothes, jewellery and antique shops. A lively street market takes place on Monday mornings around the Estadio Municipal football ground, east of the old town.

Getting There & Away
Bus Buses to Fuengirola, Puerto Banús (130 ptas), San Pedro de Alcántara and Estepona leave about every 30 minutes from Avenida Ricardo Soriano. Services from the bus station (☎ 95 276 44 00) in the north of town include frequent buses to Benalmádena Costa, Torremolinos and Málaga (635 ptas), and a few a day to Ronda (610 ptas), Sevilla (1895 ptas), Granada (1785 ptas), La Línea, Algeciras and Cádiz.

Getting Around
From the bus station, bus No 7 (135 ptas) runs to the Fuengirola/Estepona bus stop on Avenida Ricardo Soriano near the town centre. Returning from the centre to the bus station, take No 2 from Avenida Ramón y Cajal (corner of Calle Huerta Chica). To walk from the bus station to the centre, cross the bridge over the bypass and carry straight on down Calle La Florida, which leads down to the Albergue Juvenil Marbella.

PUERTO BANÚS
The coastal strip between Marbella and Puerto Banús, 5km west, is known as *La Milla de Oro* (the golden mile) because of its number of super-luxury properties – including the Marbella Club Hotel and King Fahd of Saudi Arabia's Mar Mar estate. Puerto Banús is the flashiest marina on the Costa del Sol, often a port of call for gin palaces that moor in Monte Carlo at other times of year. A few travellers get work on the yachts – if they're not already working as time-share touts elsewhere. Puerto Banús is also a nightlife centre, though its prices are high.

The marina's main entrance has security gates to prevent access by unauthorised cars. By the control tower at the western end of the harbour – where the swankiest boats tie up – is the **Aquarium de Puerto Banús** (☎ 95 281 87 67), similar to Sea Life at Benalmádena Costa (see the earlier Torremolinos & Benalmádena section for details). It opens 11 am to 6 pm daily most of the year, but may shut Monday to Friday in winter. Admission costs 750 ptas (children 550 ptas). As an optional extra, you can take a dive in the aquarium's tanks with rays, lobsters and small sharks.

Places to Eat & Drink

The marina is surrounded by glittery shops and restaurants that get less expensive as you move east. Towards the western end you'll find *Salduba Pub* and *Sinatra Bar*, two of the most popular bars. Just east is *The Red Pepper*, with good Greek dishes, seafood and grilled meats all starting from around 1900 ptas. Farther east, *Don Leone* is a good Italian restaurant with salads and homemade pasta costing between 1000 ptas and 2000 ptas. A little farther along, *Pizzeria Picasso* does a brisk trade in sizeable but rather dull pizzas costing 900 ptas to 1000 ptas.

At night, *Old Joy's Pub*, just east of Pizzeria Picasso, and behind it, the *Navy*, are popular haunts, both with live music. For the liveliest disco try *La Comedia* on Calle de Ribera behind The Red Pepper. *El Boss/Moskito Disco*, just inland of the N-340, stages some of the best local bands.

Getting There & Away

Several boats a day usually go from Marbella's Puerto Deportivo (look for signs there advertising the trip) for around 700 ptas one-way or 1100 ptas return. For bus information, see the Marbella Getting There & Away section.

ESTEPONA

postcode 29680 • pop 36,000

Estepona has controlled its development relatively carefully and remains a fairly agreeable seaside town. The oldish town centre around leafy, traffic-free Plaza Las

Flores is quite pleasant. A sizeable fishing fleet shares the port beyond the lighthouse at the western end of town with a large marina.

The tourist office (☎ 95 280 09 13) at Avenida San Lorenzo 1 in the town centre opens 9 am to 6 pm Monday to Friday, and 9 am to 2 pm Saturday. The bus station (☎ 95 280 02 49) is 400m west, on the seafront Avenida de España.

Selwo Costa del Sol (☎ 95 279 21 50), opened in 1999 at Las Lomas del Monte, 2km off the N-340 6km east of Estepona, is a 1-sq-km safari park with 200 exotic animal species from around the globe. Some you see on foot, others from 4WD vehicles. One feature is the walk-through Cañón de las Aves, a 300m-long natural canyon filled with birds. Selwo's opening hours are 10 am to 6.30 pm daily except winter Mondays. Admission costs 2500 ptas (children 1750 ptas). To get there from Estepona, a taxi is best. A direct daily bus runs from Málaga via Torremolinos, Fuengirola and Marbella (phone Selwo for information).

Centrally located accommodation in Estepona is limited. The old-fashioned *Hostal Pilar* (☎ 95 280 00 18, Plaza Las Flores 22) has rooms with shared or private bathroom costing 4700 ptas and 5300 ptas a double, respectively. *Pensión Malagueña* (☎ 95 280 00 11, Calle Castillo 1), just off Plaza Las Flores, has doubles with bathroom costing 6000 ptas. Friendly *Pensión San Antonio* (☎ 95 280 14 76, Calle Adolfo Suárez 9), a block east of the square, offers basic singles/doubles costing 2200/3900 ptas. On the seafront, *Hotel Buenavista* (☎ 95 280 01 37, fax 95 280 55 93, Paseo Marítimo 180) has doubles with bathroom costing 6500 ptas.

Plaza Las Flores is home to a few *tapas bars* and *restaurants*, and you'll encounter a dozen or two more places within a couple of blocks. Nightlife focuses on the marina.

CASARES

postcode 29690 • pop 3200
• elevation 435m

Casares, clinging to steep hillsides below the well-preserved remains of a Muslim castle, 18km from Estepona (10km inland), offers wonderful views and is well worth an outing. The Sierra Crestellina to its north-west offers good walking opportunities.

Pensión Plaza (☎ 95 289 40 88, Plaza de España 6) on the main square, has adequate rooms with bathroom costing around 2800 ptas a double.

Buses leave Estepona for Casares at 11 am, 1.30 pm and 7 pm daily except Sunday. The last one back leaves Casares at 4 pm.

Inland

Málaga province's interior is a far cry from the touristy coasts. Here you'll find spectacular gorges and remote mountainous areas with good walking; intriguing towns and villages of Muslim origin with winding streets and ancient castles; and traces of even earlier humanity in the form of impressive cave paintings and megalithic tombs.

EL CHORRO, ARDALES & AROUND

Fifty kilometres north-west of Málaga the Río Guadalhorce carves its way through the awesome Garganta del Chorro (El Chorro Gorge). Also called the Desfiladero de los Gaitanes, the gorge is about 4km long, as much as 400m deep, and sometimes just 10m wide. Its often sheer walls and other rock faces nearby are the biggest magnet for rock climbers in Andalucía. Along the gorge run the main railway into Málaga (with the aid of 12 tunnels and six bridges) and a path called the Camino (or Caminito) del Rey, which for long stretches becomes a concrete catwalk clinging to the gorge walls up to 100m above the river. The Camino del Rey is in a dangerously decayed state and unless long-discussed repairs are actually made, you should not attempt to walk along it. But you *can* view much of the gorge and path by walking along the railway.

This craggy north-western area of the province is full of other places of historic and natural interest. The pleasant town of Ardales is the main centre.

El Chorro

postcode 29552 • pop (estimated) 100
• elevation 200m

El Chorro village is a tiny settlement above a dam on the Guadalhorce, just south of the gorge.

The Swiss-run Finca La Campana (see Places to Stay & Eat) offers climbing courses and climbing, caving, walking and mountain bike trips, and rents out mountain bikes for 1500 ptas a day. Aventur El Chorro (☎ 649 24 94 44), near the station, rents out mountain bikes for 250 ptas an hour or 2500 ptas a day and offers a similar range of guided activities. Camping El Chorro (see Places to Stay) rents out bikes for 300 ptas an hour.

Camino del Rey The Camino del Rey (King's Path) is so named because Alfonso XIII reputedly walked it in 1921, when he opened the reservoirs above the gorge which supply much of Málaga province's water. It has been officially closed since 1992 and, by 2000, gaping holes in its concrete floor had made it impassable for all but mountaineers.

To view the gorge and camino, follow the road up the eastern side of the reservoir from El Chorro village for 900m to a point below a railway viaduct (where you can park vehicles). Walk up to the railway and go about 2.25km north along it, through tunnels Nos 10, 9, 8 and 7 (No 9 has three separate sections). The tunnels have plenty of space at the side should a train come. The Camino del Rey begins along the cliff face to the left between tunnels Nos 10 and 9 and after a short distance crosses to the western side of the gorge. After tunnel No 7 a narrow concrete footbridge crosses the gorge from the railway to the camino – but within a short distance in either direction from here you reach impassable gaps in the camino.

Places to Stay & Eat Amid eucalyptus trees 350m towards the gorge from the village, *Camping El Chorro (☎ 95 211 26 96)* has room for 150 people. It costs 500 ptas per adult, 275 ptas to 475 ptas per tent and 125 ptas per car. At El Chorro station, *Pen-*

sión Estación (☎ *95 249 50 04*) has four clean little singles/doubles costing 2000/3500 ptas, and *Restaurante Estación*, also called *Bar Isabel*, a renowned climbers' gathering spot, serves platos combinados from 375 ptas to 550 ptas.

Apartamentos La Garganta (☎ *95 249 51 19, fax 95 249 52 98,* ✆ *elchorro@vnet.es*), a converted flour mill just south of the station, has small apartments for up to five people costing 6000 ptas to 10,000 ptas, plus a pool and a good restaurant. It also runs *Refugio de Escalada La Garganta*, just below the station, which has bunks costing 600 ptas (bring a sleeping bag) and a kitchen.

Finca La Campana (☎*/fax 95 211 20 19*), 2km from the station (signposted), offers bunks for 1500 ptas, a double room for 3000 ptas and apartments for up to four people costing 4000 ptas to 8000 ptas. It has a pool and guest kitchen; prepared breakfasts are available too. Its Web site is at www.el-chorro.com.

Bobastro

Back in the 9th century, the rugged El Chorro area was the redoubt of a kind of Robin Hood of Andalucía, Omar ibn Hafsun, who resisted the armies of Córdoba for nearly 40 years from the hill fortress of Bobastro. Ibn Hafsun came from a landed family of Muwallads (converts from Christianity to Islam) but turned to banditry after killing a neighbour. Quickly gaining popular support – partly, it's said, because he defended the peasants against taxes and forced labour – he at one stage controlled territory all the way from Cartagena to the Strait of Gibraltar.

To reach Bobastro from El Chorro village, follow the road up the valley from the western side of the dam, and after 3km take the signposted Bobastro turning. Nearly 3km up from the turning, an 'Iglesia Mozárabe' sign indicates the 500m footpath to the remains of a Mozarabic church cut out of the rock. Legend, supported by some historical sources, says that Ibn Hafsun converted to Christianity (thus becoming a Mozarab) before his death in 917, and was buried in this church. Mozarabs certainly

played an important part in his uprising. When Bobastro was finally conquered by Córdoba in 927, Ibn Hafsun's remains were taken away for posthumous crucifixion outside Córdoba's Mezquita.

Faint traces of Ibn Hafsun's rectangular fortress remain on the highest point of the hill, a farther 2.5km up the road. The views are magnificent and you can take refreshments at *Bar La Mesa*.

Ardales
postcode 29550 • pop 3200
• elevation 450m

If you continue westward past the Bobastro turn-off on the MA-444 from El Chorro, after 2.5km you reach a T-junction. A left turn here will take you south to Ardales (6km); a right turn leads to the Parque Ardales camp site (600m), the Restaurante El Mirador (2km) and other restaurants near the picturesque Embalse del Conde del Guadalhorce.

Things to See & Do The Museo de la Historia y las Tradiciones (☎ 95 245 80 46), at the entry to Ardales from the A-357, provides tourist information. The **Museo Municipal Cueva de Ardales**, on Plaza Ayuntamiento adjoining Ardales' central Plaza de San Isidro, is devoted to the Cueva de Ardales, 3.5km south-east of the town, with copies of its prehistoric rock paintings and carvings. The museum opens 10.30 am to 2 pm and 5 to 7 pm (4 to 6 pm in winter), daily except Monday. Admission costs 100 ptas. Up near the top of the village, the **Iglesia de la Nuestra Señora de los Remedios** was originally a mosque and has a good Mudéjar *artesonado* ceiling (wooden ceiling with interlaced beams). If it's closed ask at Plaza de la Iglesia 1, opposite, for the key. Above the church is **La Peña**, a crag with the remains of a 10th-century fort probably built by Omar ibn Hafsun. For two-hour guided visits costing 700 ptas to the **Cueva de Ardales** itself, possible between May and October, contact Ardales town hall (☎ 95 245 80 87) a week or two in advance. The caves contain 60 Palaeolithic paintings and carvings of animals, done between about 18,000 and 14,000 BC, and traces of later occupation and burials from about 8000 to after 3000 BC

A track leaving the road opposite the steps up to Restaurante El Mirador leads 600m to the start of a walking track on the right, which leads down to the northern end of **El Chorro** gorge in 1.5km.

You can hire mountain bikes or canoes at Parque Ardales camp site.

Places to Stay Seven kilometres north of Ardales on the banks of the Embalse del Conde del Guadalhorce, *Parque Ardales (☎ 95 211 24 01)* has a large, shady camp site costing 1275 ptas plus IVA for two people with a car and small tent, and apartments for up to four people costing 8500 ptas plus IVA in the high season.

The friendly *Pensión Bobastro (☎ 95 245 91 50, Plaza de San Isidro 13)*, in the centre of Ardales, has singles/doubles costing 2000/4000 ptas. Prices are similar at *Pensión El Cruce (☎ 95 245 90 12)* near the A-357, 500m from the centre.

Places to Eat The best food in Ardales town – tapas and raciones – is at *Bar El Casino* on Plaza de San Isidro. Try the delicious *huevos con bechamel* (hard-boiled eggs in bechamel sauce) or *pimientos rellenos de ternera* (veal-stuffed peppers): both are rolled in breadcrumbs then deep fried.

Several restaurants along the road beyond Parque Ardales are very popular at the weekend and holidays. *Restaurante El Mirador*, overlooking the reservoir, serves economical salads and omelettes as well as more expensive meaty options. One kilometre farther on, across a dam, *Mesón El Oasis* offers varied grilled meats (650 ptas to 1450 ptas), but the star item on its menu is *paletillas de cordero en miel* (shoulder of lamb in honey) costing 2500 ptas.

Getting There & Away

Los Amarillos buses run from Málaga to Ronda and vice-versa, via Ardales, four times daily, but there's no bus service to El Chorro.

A lot of trains pass through El Chorro station but few stop there. At the time of writing you could reach El Chorro from Málaga (475 ptas, 45 minutes), Ronda (760 ptas, 80 minutes) or Sevilla by one direct train daily in each case (except Sunday and holidays from Málaga and Ronda). Only from Ronda (except Friday, Sunday and holidays) did schedules allow a round trip in one day. Timetables change from time to time, however.

Drivers from Málaga should branch off the A-357 near Pizarra to reach El Chorro, passing through Álora. From Ardales a partly unpaved road leads 20km south-west along the remote Turón valley to El Burgo (see Around Ronda later in this chapter).

RONDA
postcode 29400 • pop 34,500
• elevation 725m

Though just an hour or so up from the Costa del Sol, Ronda is a world away from the coastal hustle. It's a historic town with a spectacular cliff-top setting, astride the 100m-deep El Tajo gorge amid the beautiful Serranía de Ronda. It attracts its quota of visitors but many come from the coast just for the day.

Capital of a small Berber kingdom after the collapse of the Córdoba caliphate, Ronda came under Sevillan rule in the mid-11th century but regained a large measure of independence after Sevilla's fall in 1248. With a near-impregnable site, it fell to Fernando El Católico in 1485 only because its governor and army had left to defend Málaga, thinking that city was about to come under Christian attack.

Orientation & Information

The old Muslim part of town, known as La Ciudad, stands on the southern side of El Tajo gorge, with the newer town, called El Mercadillo, to the north. Three bridges cross the gorge, the main one being the Puente Nuevo linking Plaza de España with Calle de Armiñán. Both parts of town come to an abrupt end on their western sides with cliffs plunging away to the valley of the Río Guadalevín far below. Places of interest are

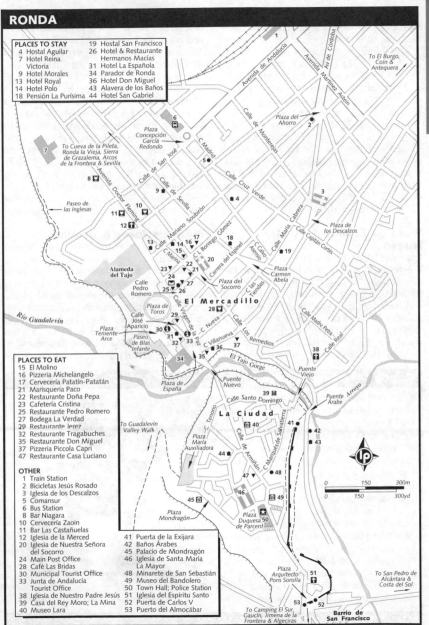

RONDA

PLACES TO STAY
4   Hostal Aguilar
7   Hotel Reina
    Victoria
9   Hotel Morales
13 Hotel Royal
14 Hotel Polo
18 Pensión La Purísima
19 Hostal San Francisco
26 Hotel & Restaurante
    Hermanos Macías
31 Hotel La Española
34 Parador de Ronda
36 Hotel Don Miguel
43 Alavera de los Baños
44 Hotel San Gabriel

PLACES TO EAT
15 El Molino
16 Pizzeria Michelangelo
17 Cervecería Patatín-Patatán
21 Marisquería Paco
22 Restaurante Doña Pepa
23 Cafetería Cristina
25 Restaurante Pedro Romero
27 Bodega La Verdad
29 Restaurante Jerez
32 Restaurante Tragabuches
35 Restaurante Don Miguel
37 Pizzeria Piccola Capri
47 Restaurante Casa Luciano

OTHER
1   Train Station
2   Bicicletas Jesús Rosado
3   Iglesia de los Descalzos
5   Comansur
6   Bus Station
8   Bar Niagara
10 Cervecería Zaoin
11 Bar Las Castañuelas
12 Iglesia de la Merced
20 Iglesia de Nuestra Señora
    del Socorro
24 Main Post Office
28 Café Las Bridas
30 Municipal Tourist Office
33 Junta de Andalucía
    Tourist Office
38 Iglesia de Nuestro Padre Jesús
39 Casa del Rey Moro; La Mina
40 Museo Lara
41 Puerta de la Exijara
42 Baños Árabes
45 Palacio de Mondragón
46 Iglesia de Santa María
    La Mayor
48 Minarete de San Sebastián
49 Museo del Bandolero
50 Town Hall; Police Station
51 Iglesia del Espíritu Santo
52 Puerta de Carlos V
53 Puerto del Almocábar

mainly concentrated in La Ciudad while most places to stay and eat, along with the bus and train stations, are in the new town.

The Junta de Andalucía tourist office (☎ 95 287 12 72), Plaza de España 1, opens 9 am to 7 pm Monday to Friday, and 10 am to 2 pm Saturday. A new municipal tourist office on Plaza Teniente Arce will probably also be open by the time you visit.

Banks and ATMs are mainly on Calle Virgen de la Paz (opposite the bullring) and Plaza Carmen Abela. The main post office is at Calle Virgen de la Paz 18–20. The Comansur shop on Calle Madrid sells 1:50,000 SGE maps of the region. The Policía Local (☎ 95 287 13 69) station is in the town hall on Plaza Duquesa de Parcent.

Plaza de España & Puente Nuevo

Chapter 10 of Ernest Hemingway's *For Whom the Bell Tolls* tells how early in the civil war the 'fascists' of a small town were rounded up in the town hall, then clubbed and flailed as they were made to walk the gauntlet between two lines of townspeople 'in the plaza on the top of the cliff above the river'. At the end of the line the victims, dead or still alive, were thrown over the cliff. The episode was based on real events in Ronda, though the real perpetrators were, according to Hugh Thomas' authoritative *The Spanish Civil War*, a gang from Málaga. Ronda's Parador, on Plaza de España, was, before it became a hotel, the town hall.

The majestic Puente Nuevo (New Bridge) spanning El Tajo from Plaza de España is two centuries old. A Ronda tradition relates that its architect, Martín de Aldehuela, fell to his death in 1793 while trying to engrave the bridge's date on its side – a legend no doubt encouraged by the incomplete hieroglyphics accompanying the word *año* (year) beside the shield on the side of the bridge. Historians, however, insist that Aldehuela died in 1802, nine years after the bridge was opened.

Plaza de Toros & Around

Ronda's elegant bullring on Calle Virgen de la Paz is a Mecca for aficionados. Opened in 1785, it's one of the oldest bullrings in Spain, has one of the biggest arenas, and has been the site of some of the most important events in bullfighting history (see the boxed text 'Ronda's Fighting Romeros'). Open for visits 10 am to 6 pm daily, it contains a **Museo Taurino** with memorabilia such as costumes worn by

---

Ronda's Fighting Romeros

Ronda can justly claim to be the home of bullfighting. In the 18th and 19th centuries three generations of the Romero family from Ronda established most of the basics of modern bullfighting on foot (previously it was on horseback as a kind of cavalry training-cum-sport for the nobility). Francisco Romero, born in 1698, invented the use of the cape to attract the bull, and the *muleta*, its cloth replacement, in the kill. His son Juan introduced the matador's supporting team, the *cuadrilla*; and grandson Pedro (1754–1839) perfected a serious, elegant and classical style, still known as the Escuela Rondeña (Ronda School) – in which matadors work very close to the bulls – before becoming director of the country's first bullfighting college (in Sevilla) at the age of 77. Pedro killed 5500 bulls in his career, without being gored once. His skill was such, it's said, that outlaws from the bandit-ridden mountains around Ronda would risk capture to see him in action.

MICHAEL WELDON

The *picador*, part of Romero's *cuadrilla*.

Pedro Romero and 1990s star Jesulín de Ubrique, and photos of famous fans including Ernest Hemingway and Orson Welles. Admission costs 400 ptas.

Vertiginous clifftop views open out from **Paseo de Blas Infante**, behind the Plaza de Toros, and the shady **Alameda del Tajo** park nearby.

La Ciudad

Though most of its Muslim buildings have been heavily modified over the centuries, La Ciudad retains the character of a typical old Muslim town.

Casa del Rey Moro & La Mina From the Puente Nuevo, head along La Ciudad's main street, Calle de Armiñán, then take the first street to the left to visit the Casa del Rey Moro (House of the Moorish King) at Calle Santo Domingo 17. The house itself – built in the 18th century, supposedly over remains of a Muslim palace – is closed. But for 600 ptas, from 10 am to 7 pm daily, you can visit its terraced, gorge-side gardens and climb down La Mina, a Muslim-era stairway cut inside the rock all the way to the river in the bottom of the gorge. These 200 steps enabled Ronda to maintain water supplies when under attack, and provided a hidden entry/exit into the old city – but were also one of the points where Christian troops forced entry when they finally took Ronda in 1485.

Museo Lara This recently opened art and antiques museum, in a handsome old mansion at Calle de Armiñán 29, exhibits over 2000 diverse items. It opens 10 am to 8 pm daily. Admission costs 400 ptas.

Palacio de Mondragón The Mondragón Palace, on Plaza Mondragón, is thought to have been built for Abomelic, ruler of Ronda, in 1314. It was altered soon after the Christian conquest, and Fernando and Isabel lodged here at some point. Of the ground floor's three courtyards, the only one to preserve Islamic character is the Patio Mudéjar, from which a horseshoe arch leads into a clifftop garden. Some rooms house a museum on prehistoric life in the

Ronda area. The palace opens 10 am to 6 pm (to 3 pm at the weekend and holidays); admission costs 250 ptas. Nearby **Plaza María Auxiliadora** offers fine views.

Iglesia de Santa María La Mayor A minute's walk south-east from the Palacio de Mondragón is Plaza Duquesa de Parcent where this fine church stands on the site of Muslim Ronda's main mosque. Its tower betrays Islamic origins and the galleries beside it, built for viewing festivities in the square, also date from Muslim times. Just inside the church entrance is an arch covered with Arabic inscriptions, which was part of the mosque's *mihrab* (prayer niche indicating the direction of Mecca). The church was begun in Gothic style but, as building went on over the centuries, tastes changed to the Renaissance style and finally to the baroque of the northern end. It opens 10 am to 8 pm daily (to 6 pm in winter); admission costs 200 ptas.

Barrio de San Francisco In this southern quarter of La Ciudad you'll find the imposing late 15th-century **Iglesia del Espíritu Santo**, and a stretch of the old city walls pierced by two gates, the 16th-century **Puerta de Carlos V** and the 13th-century **Puerta del Almocábar**.

Museo del Bandolero This interesting museum at Calle de Armiñán 65 is dedicated to the banditry for which central Andalucía, including the Ronda area, was once renowned (see the boxed text 'Bandoleros, Guerrilleros & Treachery in the High Sierras' on the next page). It opens 10 am to 8 pm daily (to 6 pm in winter); admission costs 350 ptas.

Just off the same street, to the north, the little **Minarete de San Sebastián** was built in Granada style, as part of a mosque, in the 14th century.

Walls, Baths & More Bridges Beside the Museo del Bandolero, steps lead down to an impressive stretch of Ronda's old walls along the eastern side of La Ciudad. Following them down, you pass through the

Bandoleros, Guerrilleros & Treachery in the High Sierras

Andalucía's complicated mountain ranges, full of ravines, caves and hidden valleys, for centuries offered refuge to those who didn't get on with the authorities. As long ago as the 9th century the El Chorro area was the epicentre of prolonged, widespread opposition to Cordoban rule led by a sort of Islamic Robin Hood, Omar ibn Hafsun (see Bobastro in the El Chorro, Ardales & Around section).

In the 19th century some of the bandits *(bandoleros)* who preyed on the rich also became folk heroes. The most famous was José María Hinojosa, known as El Tempranillo (the Early One), born around 1800 at Jauja, near Lucena in Córdoba province. By the 1820s he claimed: 'The king may reign in Spain, but in the sierra I do.' El Tempranillo reputedly demanded an ounce of gold for each vehicle which crossed his domain.

The activities of the 19th-century bandits, and of the smugglers who carried contraband through the Ronda hills from Gibraltar, led the government to set up the Guardia Civil, Spain's rural police force, in 1844. Many bandoleros were then forced into the service of the local landowners and political bosses, or of the Guardia Civil itself. El Tempranillo met his end this way, murdered by an old comrade who was still on the wrong side of the law.

The last of the bandolero breed was Juan José Mingolla, alias Pasos Largos (Big Steps, 1873–1934), an orphan from the El Burgo area, east of Ronda, who turned to poaching and murdered a game warden who had reported him to the police. He was killed in 1934 in a cave shootout with the Guardia Civil.

After the civil war Andalucía's mountain ranges became the refuge of a new kind of fugitive: communist *guerrilleros* waging the last resistance to Franco. The Sierra Bermeja, north of Estepona, and the mountains of La Axarquía, east of Málaga, were among their hideouts. This little known chapter of Spanish history closed in the 1950s.

Puerta de la Exijara, which was the entry to Islamic Ronda's Jewish quarter, outside the walls. A path continues down to the beautiful, almost intact, 13th- and 14th-century **Baños Árabes** (Arab Baths), open 9.30 am to 1.30 pm and 4 to 6 pm Tuesday, and 9.30 am to 3.30 pm Wednesday to Saturday. Admission is free.

From the northern side of the nearby Puente Viejo, you can make your way back up to Plaza de España via a small park along the gorge's edge.

Guadalevín Valley Walk

This walk of 1½ to two hours offers fine views of Ronda from the rural valley below the gorge. A path down from Plaza María Auxiliadora in La Ciudad passes two Islamic arches before meeting a cobbled road descending from the Barrio de San Francisco. Turn right down the cobbled road and after about 400m you have a fine view up to the Puente Nuevo to your right. A farther 300m or so downhill, beside an old mill, fork left onto a track that winds down over the Río Guadalevín then up through a small farm. It continues roughly north-west along the valley then crests the cliff line 1.5km from the river. Here turn right and walk along the clifftop back to the northern end of Ronda.

Special Events

Ronda's famous old bullring stages relatively few fights, but in early September it holds some of the most celebrated and unusual in Spain; the Corridas Goyescas, in which top matadors fight in early 19th-century-style costumes as in Goya's depictions of Ronda bullfights. The *goyescas* are the culmination of a general fiesta starting in late August, the Feria de Pedro Romero, which includes an important flamenco event, the Festival de Cante Grande.

Places to Stay – Budget

A good small camp site in a pleasant setting 2km south-west of Ronda on the A-369 Algeciras road, *Camping El Sur* (☎ 95 287 59

39) charges 1860 ptas plus IVA for two adults with a car and tent.

Budget rooms in Ronda generally don't offer great value. Better than most is the clean and friendly *Pensión La Purísima* (☎ 95 287 10 50, Calle de Sevilla 10) with 10 rooms costing 2000/4000 ptas for singles/doubles. The owner speaks French. *Hostal Aguilar* (☎ 95 287 19 94, Calle Naranja 28), handy for the bus station, offers small but adequate rooms costing 2800 ptas a double (5000 ptas with bathroom). The 16-room *Hostal San Francisco* (☎ 95 287 32 99, Calle María Cabrera 18) has rooms with bathroom costing 2000/4000 ptas.

A bit more money can buy you considerably better accommodation. *Hotel Royal* (☎ 95 287 11 41, fax 95 287 81 32, Calle Virgen de la Paz 42) has 29 plain but decent rooms with bathroom and TV costing 3500/5700 ptas plus IVA. *Hotel Hermanos Macías* (☎ 95 287 42 38, Calle Pedro Romero 3) charges 5000 ptas a double. *Hotel Morales* (☎/fax 95 287 15 38, Calle de Sevilla 51) has 18 pleasant rooms with bathroom costing 3500/6000 ptas. Its walls are decked with maps of the area, it has a room for bicycles, and the friendly staff are full of information on the town and nearby natural parks. They can help you rent bicycles, hire guides and so on.

Places to Stay – Mid-Range

The only hotel in La Ciudad is the exceptional *Hotel San Gabriel* (☎ 95 219 03 92, fax 95 219 01 17, @ sangabriel@ronda.net, Calle José M Holgado 19), owned and run by a charming family. Opened in 1998, it's a converted 18th-century mansion, with 16 stylish and comfy rooms, all different, and a cafe. Singles/doubles cost 9000/11,000 ptas plus IVA.

Alavera de los Baños (☎/fax 95 287 91 43, Hoyo San Miguel s/n), owned by a friendly Spanish/German couple, is another small and individual new hotel, in a converted tannery next door to the Baños Árabes. The attractive rooms cost 7000 ptas a single and 9000 ptas or 10,000 ptas a double, including breakfast. The hotel restau-

rant sports vegetarian options and, like the decor, it has some interesting Moroccan touches. Its Web site is at www.andalucia.com/alavera.

Hotel Polo (☎ 95 287 24 47, fax 95 287 24 49, Calle Mariano Soubirón 8), another good family-run hotel, offers 33 spacious rooms costing 6300/9500 ptas plus IVA. It also has a busy restaurant.

The least expensive option overlooking the gorge is *Hotel Don Miguel* (☎ 95 287 77 22, fax 95 287 83 77, Calle Villanueva 8), where doubles cost 9500 ptas plus IVA.

get in emergency !

Places to Stay – Top End

On the narrow pedestrian street between Plaza de España and the bullring, *Hotel La Española* (☎ 95 287 10 52, fax 95 287 80 01, Calle José Aparicio 3) charges 12,600 ptas plus IVA for comfortable doubles.

The 90-room *Hotel Reina Victoria* (☎ 95 287 12 40, fax 95 287 12 40, Avenida Doctor Fleming 25) was built by a British company in the 1900s when Ronda was a popular outing from Gibraltar by the recently constructed railway from Algeciras. The old-fashioned comfort recalls far-flung parts of the British empire. Rooms cost from 9900/15,600 ptas to 12,200/18,500 ptas plus IVA. The hotel has fine clifftop gardens.

The stylish *Parador de Ronda* (☎ 95 287 75 00, @ ronda@parador.es, Plaza de España s/n) is right on the edge of the gorge with an almost-clifftop pool. Bright singles/doubles cost from 14,800/18,500 ptas plus IVA.

Places to Eat

Typical Ronda food is hearty mountain fare, with a strong emphasis on stews (called *cocido, estofado* or *cazuela*), trout (*trucha*), game such as rabbit (*conejo*), partridge (*perdiz*), quail (*codorniz*) and oxtail (*rabo de toro*).

On Plaza del Socorro, a block northeast of the bullring, *Marisquería Paco* does good seafood and *jamón* (cured ham) tapas and *El Molino* is popular for its pizzas and pasta costing 550 ptas to 775 ptas, platos combinados from 650 ptas and varied breakfasts from a good *tostada* and *café con leche* (coffee with hot milk) at 350 ptas to *desayuno americano* (American breakfast) at 1000 ptas. **Cafetería Cristina** in Pasaje del Correos, an arcade running between Plaza del Socorro and Calle Virgen de la Paz, does platos combinados from 675 ptas, and good pastries. **Restaurante Doña Pepa** (*Plaza del Socorro 10*), solid and old-fashioned in food and decor, has menús costing 1800 ptas and 2100 ptas and lots of a la carte choices including vegetarian options.

Restaurante Hermanos Macías (*Calle Pedro Romero 3*), on a pedestrian street between Plaza del Socorro and Calle Virgen de la Paz, is a friendly mid-range eatery with decent if unspectacular food – meat and fish main dishes cost from 800 ptas to 1600 ptas. The tapas bar **Bodega La Verdad**, next door, is popular with locals.

The bright **Cervecería Patatín-Patatán** (*Calle Lorenzo Borrego Gómez 7*), off the other side of Plaza del Socorro, serves sherry and wine costing 125 ptas to 150 ptas a glass, and a range of tasty tapas. Don't hesitate to ask for the *carta de tapas* (tapas menu): most bites are 100 ptas, but it's hard to resist an *orejitas*, which is a small slice of steak with ham, melted cheese, tomato, capsicum, a quail egg and sauce of your choice, for 250 ptas. Busy **Pizzería Michelangelo** (*Calle Lorenzo Borrego Gómez 5*), next door, serves economical pizza and pasta for 425 ptas to 650 ptas.

Restaurants in the bullring/Plaza de España area tend to be touristy but several are good. **Restaurante Pedro Romero** (☎ 95 287 11 10, Calle Virgen de la Paz 18), opposite the bullring, is a celebrated eatery dedicated to bullfighting, with blood-red tablecloths and decor of bulls' heads and fight photos. The food is classic *rondeño*, with a la carte mains costing between 1400 ptas and 2700 ptas plus IVA and a set lunch for 1650 ptas plus IVA (plus drinks). **Restaurante Jerez** (*Plaza Teniente Arce 2*), on the corner of Calle José Aparicio, serves soups and salads costing 500 ptas to 900 ptas, oxtail at 1850 ptas and partridge for 2275 ptas.

The recently opened **Restaurante Tragabuches** (☎ 95 219 02 91, Calle José Aparicio 1) has quickly gained a high reputation. For your main course here you might go for venison and sweet potatoes or pork trotters with squid and sunflower seeds. Two courses will cost you between 3000 ptas and 5000 ptas plus IVA. It opens 1 to 4 pm and 5.30 to 11 pm, except Monday.

Restaurante Don Miguel (*Calle Villanueva 4*), off Plaza de España, has tables overlooking El Tajo and serves huntin' and shootin' fare such as partridge stew or roast stag leg for 1600 ptas to 2200 ptas.

Pizzería Piccola Capri (*Calle Villanueva 18*) has some tables overlooking the gorge and serves reasonable-value tortillas, pizzas and pasta for 500 ptas to 700 ptas.

In La Ciudad, the pleasant little **Restaurante Casa Luciano** (*Calle de Armiñán 42*) serves breakfasts and a menú of three courses and a drink for 1200 ptas.

Entertainment

A modest nightlife zone centres around the foot of Avenida Doctor Fleming, with **Bar Niagara**, **Bar Las Castañuelas** and the youthful **Cervecería Zaoin**, with a pool table, among the more interesting spots. **Café Las Bridas** (*Calle Los Remedios 18*) sometimes puts on live flamenco or rock.

Getting There & Away

Bus The bus station is at Plaza Concepción García Redondo 2. Comes (☎ 95 287 19 92) has buses to Arcos de la Frontera, Jerez de la Frontera and Cádiz five times daily; Gaucín, Jimena de la Frontera and Algeciras (1010 ptas) at 4 pm Monday to Friday; and Zahara de la Sierra. Los Amarillos (☎ 95 218 70 61) goes to/from Sevilla (1285 ptas, 2½ hours) via Algodonales three to five times daily; Grazalema (200 ptas), Benaocaz and Ubrique twice daily; and Málaga (1075 ptas, two hours) via Ardales four times daily. Portillo (☎ 95 287 22 62) runs to/from Málaga (1110 ptas) via San Pedro de Alcántara and Marbella three or four times daily. Further services run to other hill towns and villages.

Train Ronda station (☎ 95 287 16 73), on Avenida de Andalucía, is on the scenic line between Bobadilla and Algeciras. Five or more trains run daily to/from Algeciras (910 ptas to 1500 ptas, 1½ to two hours) via Gaucín and Jimena de la Frontera; one runs daily to/from Granada (1775 ptas, 2¼ hours) via Antequera; one runs daily except Sunday to/from Málaga (1175 ptas, two hours); two run daily to/from Córdoba (2100 ptas to 2300 ptas, 2½ hours) and Madrid (by day 8200 ptas, 4½ hours; overnight 4700 ptas, nine hours). For Sevilla, and other trains to/from Granada, Málaga, Córdoba and Madrid, change at Bobadilla or Antequera.

Getting Around
It's less than 1km from the train station to most accommodation. Occasional town buses run to Plaza de España from Avenida Martínez Astein, across the road from the station.

Bicycle Bicicletas Jesús Rosado (☎ 95 287 02 21), Plaza del Ahorro 1, rents out well-equipped mountain bikes for 1500 ptas a day or 3000 ptas for three days.

AROUND RONDA
Fine hill country, with plenty of walking and biking possibilities and dotted with picturesque mountain towns and villages, stretches in every direction from Ronda. These green, misty hills (including the Sierra de Grazalema and Los Alcornocales natural parks to the west and south-west – see the Cádiz Province chapter for details) are the western end of the Cordillera Bética.

Ronda la Vieja
This ruined hilltop Roman town about 16km north-west of Ronda, also called Acinipo, has a partly reconstructed theatre. A site plan you'll be given will help you decipher other buildings. It opens 10 am to 5 or 6 pm daily except Monday; admission is free. You'll need your own wheels: the turning north off the A-376 is about 6km from Ronda.

Serranía de Ronda
The mountains and valleys south and east of Ronda that go by this name are not Andalucía's highest or deepest, but are certainly among the greenest and prettiest. Any of the roads through them makes a picturesque route between Ronda and southern Cádiz province, Gibraltar or the Costa del Sol, and many of the white villages here have accommodation. **Cortés de la Frontera**, overlooking the Guadiaro valley, and **Gaucín**, looking across the Genal valley to the Sierra Crestellina, are among the most beautiful spots to halt.

Cueva de la Pileta & Benaoján Palaeolithic paintings of horses, goats, fish and even a seal, dating from 20,000 to 25,000 years ago, are preserved in the Cueva de la Pileta, an impressive cave 19km south-west of Ronda. Beautiful stalactites and stalagmites add to the effect, and you'll be guided by kerosene lamp by one of the knowledgeable Bullón family from the farm in the valley below. A member of the family discovered the paintings in 1905 when searching for bat dung to use as fertiliser.

The Cueva de la Pileta (☎ 95 216 73 43) is 4km south of Benaoján village, about 250m off the Benaoján–Cortes de la Frontera road. The turnoff is signposted. Visits are by one-hour guided tour at 10 and 11 am, noon and 1, 4 and 5 pm daily, plus 6 pm from 16 April to 31 October. They cost 800 ptas or 900 ptas per person, depending how many turn up. Guides speak at least some English and German. The maximum group size is 25, so if you come on a busy day you may have to wait for a place. At peak seasons it's worth ringing ahead to try to book a particular time.

Molino del Santo (☎ 95 216 71 51, Barriada Estación s/n) in Benaoján is an attractive 17-room British-run hotel and restaurant in a converted water mill. Bed and breakfast costs 12,325/14,650 ptas to 14,375/18,750 ptas a single/double, depending on the room. From 15 April to 3 June and in September, half-board (with breakfast, afternoon tea and dinner) is obligatory, from 23,840 ptas a double. It's

MÁLAGA PROVI

advisable to book ahead. The Molino closes from mid-November to mid-February. Its Web site is at www.andalucia.com/molino.

Benaoján is the nearest you can get to the Cueva de la Pileta by public transport. It's served by two Los Amarillos buses (Monday to Friday) and up to four daily trains to/from Ronda. Walking trails link Benaoján with Ronda and villages in the Guadiaro valley.

Parque Natural Sierra de las Nieves
This 180 sq km park south-east of Ronda, the highest portion of the Serranía de Ronda, is noted for its stands of the rare Spanish fir and fauna including some 1000 ibex and various species of eagle. The snow (*nieve*) after which the mountains are named usually falls between January and March.

El Burgo, a remote but attractive village 10km north of Yunquera on the A-366, makes a good base for visiting the east and north-east of the park. A park information centre is being constructed on the A-366 in Yunquera on the eastern side of the park. Meanwhile, information is available from Yunquera's tourist office (☎ 95 248 25 01) at Calle del Pozo 17, or the town hall in El Burgo (☎ 95 216 00 02).

Torrecilla If you have wheels the obvious starting point for climbing Torrecilla (1919m), the highest peak in the western half of Andalucía, is the Área Recreativa Los Quejigales, 10km east by unpaved road from the A-376 Ronda–San Pedro de Alcántara road. The turnoff, 12km from Ronda, is marked by 'Parque Natural Sierra de las Nieves' signs. Walking from Los Quejigales you have a steepish 470m ascent by the Cañada de los Cuernos gully, with its Spanish fir wood, to the Puerto de los Pilones pass. Then there's a fairly level section followed by the final steep 230m to the summit – rewarded by marvellous views in decent weather. The walk up and down takes about five hours in total.

An alternative approach, slightly longer, is from the Puerto del Saucillo (c.1200m), 6km west of Yunquera by dirt road. En route you can take in another landmark peak, Peñón de los Enamorados (1777m).

These walks *can* be done any time of year by the properly equipped, but the heat of July and August demands extra stamina, and in winter be prepared for temperatures close to freezing. Avoid cloud, mist, heavy rain or snow and high winds. Carry water to get you as far as Cerro del Pilar, at the foot of the final ascent, where there's a freshwater spring. The IGN/Junta de Andalucía *Parque Natural Sierra de las Nieves* map (1:50,000) shows the relevant paths.

Places to Stay & Eat Eight hundred metres off the A-376 on the road to Los Quejigales, *Camping Conejeras* (☎ 619 18 00 12) charges 350 ptas for each person, tent and car. It closes for July, August and September.

At Km 135 on the A-376, just over 1km north of the Los Quejigales turn-off, *Pension Restaurante Navasillo* (☎ 95 211 42 35) has a few singles/doubles with bathroom costing 2000/4500 ptas and serves typical hill-country food, such as raciones of rabbit or wild boar for 800 ptas.

At Yunquera, *Camping Pinsapo Azul* (☎ 95 248 27 54), open April to October, charges around 450 ptas for each person, tent and car, and *Hostal Asencio* (☎ 95 248 27 16, Calle Mesones 1), with a restaurant, has rooms costing 2500/5000 ptas.

In El Burgo, *Posada del Canónigo* (☎ 95 216 01 85, Calle Mesones 24) is a really charming small hotel in a restored mansion, with rooms with bathroom costing 4000/6000 ptas and a good, moderately priced restaurant. The friendly management has information on walking routes and can organise horse riding. *Hostal Sierra de las Nieves* (☎ 95 216 01 17, Calle Real 26) has doubles with bathroom for 4000 ptas. *Bar Isla de las Palomas*, next door, has tapas for just 25 ptas!

Getting There & Away Buses between Málaga and Ronda (around 1100 ptas) through Yunquera and El Burgo are run by the Sierra de las Nieves line (☎ 95 287 54 35). Two or three daily run each way.

ANTEQUERA

postcode 29200 • pop 40,000
• elevation 575m

Antequera, 50km north of Málaga, is an attractive town with a well preserved old heart and two outstanding natural sites within 25km. It's set on the edge of a fertile plain, with mountainous country to the south and east, and its crossroads location in the middle of Andalucía has always made it a commercial centre.

The area's inhabitants around 2500 to 1800 BC erected some of Europe's largest dolmens (tombs built with huge boulders). Later Antequera was a significant Roman town. In Muslim times it was a favourite spot of the Granada emirs, before it became their first town to fall to Castile in 1410. Its 'golden age' came in the following couple of centuries, when dozens of churches and mansions were built.

Orientation & Information

The hilltop Muslim castle, the Alcazaba, dominates the town. Down to the north-west is Plaza de San Sebastián, from which the main street, Calle Infante Don Fernando, runs north-west. The bus and train stations are north of the centre: the bus station on Calle Sagrado Corazón de Jesús, about 1km from Plaza de San Sebastián; the train station about 1.5km out, at the end of Avenida de la Estación.

The tourist office (☎ 95 270 25 05), at Plaza de San Sebastián 7, opens 10 am to 2 pm and 5 to 8 pm (9.30 am to 1.30 pm and 4 to 7 pm from 1 October to 15 June) Monday to Saturday, and 10 am to 2 pm Sunday and holidays.

Things to See

The main approach to the hilltop Alcazaba is through an impressive archway, the **Arco de los Gigantes**, built in 1585 incorporating stones with Roman inscriptions. Not a huge amount remains of the **Alcazaba** itself, but it affords great views and you can visit the Torre del Homenaje (Keep) from 10 am to 2 pm daily except Monday. Admission is free. Just below the Alcazaba, on Plaza Santa María, is the large 16th-century

Colegiata de Santa María la Mayor. This church-cum-college played an important part in Andalucía's 16th-century humanist movement, and boasts a beautiful Renaissance facade, lovely fluted stone columns inside, and a Mudéjar artesonado ceiling. It's no longer in use (Antequera has 32 other churches to serve its needs) but is open to visitors the same hours as the Torre del Homenaje. Admission is free. Beside the church is the excavated site of some Roman baths.

In the town below, the pride of the **Museo Municipal** on Plaza Coso Viejo is a beautiful 1.4m bronze statue of a boy, 'Efebo', which is perhaps the finest piece of Roman sculpture found in Spain. Unearthed on a local farm in the 1950s, Efebo represents a Roman patrician's teenage 'toy boy'. The museum also displays some finds from a Roman villa in Antequera (not yet open to the public) where a superb group of mosaics was discovered in 1998. Museum visits are by guided tour (200 ptas) about every 30 minutes from 10 am to 1.30 pm and 4 to 6 pm Tuesday to Friday, 10 am to 1.30 pm Saturday, 11 am to 1.30 pm Sunday.

The **Museo Conventual de las Descalzas**, in the 17th-century convent of the Carmelitas Descalzas (Barefoot Carmelites) on Plaza de las Descalzas, 150m east of the Museo Municipal, displays highlights of Antequera's rich religious art heritage. Outstanding works include a painting by Lucas Giordano of St Teresa of Ávila (the 16th-century founder of the Carmelitas Descalzas), a bust of the Dolorosa by Pedro de Mena and a *Virgen de Belén* sculpture by La Roldana. The museum is open for guided visits only costing 300 ptas. They go every 30 minutes from 10 am to 12.30 pm and 4.30 to 6.30 pm Tuesday to Friday, 10 am to 12.30 pm Saturday, and 11 am to 12.30 pm Sunday.

Even those who are normally unexcited by church art and architecture will probably be impressed by the **Iglesia del Carmen**, on Plaza del Carmen about 400m farther southeast. The 18th-century Churrigueresque retable is a real marvel – one of the high points of Andalucian sculpture. Carved in red pine (unpainted) by *antequerano* Antonio Primo, it's spangled with statues of angels by Diego Márquez y Vega and saints, popes and bishops by José de Medina. The church is open 11.30 am to 2 pm Monday, 10 am to 2 pm Tuesday to Friday, 10 am to 2 pm and 4 to 7 pm Saturday, and 10 am to 2 pm Sunday. Admission costs 200 ptas.

The **Dólmen de Menga** (c. 2500 BC) and **Dólmen de Viera** (c. 2000 BC) are 1km from the town centre beside the road leading north-east to the N-331. Prehistoric inhabitants transported dozens of huge boulders from nearby hills to construct these tombs for their chieftains, which are covered by earth mounds. Menga, the larger, is 25m long, 4m high and composed of 32 slabs, the largest of which weighs 180 tonnes. At midsummer the sun rising behind the landmark Peña de los Enamorados mountain to the north-east shines directly into its mouth. Menga and Viera are open 9 am to 3.30 pm Sunday and Tuesday, 9 am to 6 pm Wednesday to Saturday. Admission is free. A third big tomb, the **Dólmen del Romeral** (c. 1800 BC), is farther out of town. Continue 2.5km past Menga and Viera through an industrial estate, then turn left following 'Córdoba, Sevilla' signs. After 500m, turn left at a roundabout and follow 'Dólmen El Romeral' signs for 200m. Its recent opening hours were 9 am to 3.30 pm Wednesday to Sunday. Admission is free.

Special Events
Antequera is a fairly sober place but lets its hair down for its Real Feria de Agosto in mid-August.

Places to Stay
The friendly *Camas El Gallo* (☎ 95 284 21 04, Calle Nueva 2), just off Plaza de San Sebastián, has clean, small, no-frills singles/doubles costing 1400/2400 ptas. Another friendly place, *Pensión Madrona* (☎ 95 284 00 14, Calle Calzada 25), 400m north-east of Plaza de San Sebastián, near the market, has comfy rooms with bathroom costing 2750/3850 ptas (plus a couple of small singles with shared bathroom for

1750 ptas). The rambling *Hotel Colón* (☎ 95 284 00 10, Calle Infante Don Fernando 31) has good, varied rooms with bathroom and TV costing 2600/4000 ptas plus IVA (more in August and at Easter and Christmas). *Hostal Manzanito* (☎ 95 284 10 23, Plaza de San Sebastián 5) could hardly be more central and charges from 2500/4000 ptas to 3000/5000 ptas, plus IVA, for rooms with bathroom.

Hotel Castilla (☎/fax 95 284 30 90, Calle Infante Don Fernando 40) offers brand new, comfy rooms with TV and bathroom for 4500/6500 ptas. *Parador de Antequera* (☎ 95 284 02 61, ✉ antequera@parador.es, Paseo García del Olmo s/n), in a quiet area north of the bullring, has nice gardens and rooms costing 10,800/13,500 ptas plus IVA.

Places to Eat
Local specialities you'll encounter on almost every Antequera menu include *porra antequerana*, a cold dip similar to gazpacho before the water is added; *bienmesabe* (literally 'tastes good to me'), a sponge dessert; and *angelorum*, another dessert incorporating meringue, sponge and egg yolk. Antequera is also one of the world capitals of the breakfast *mollete* (soft bread roll).

The restaurant of the *Hotel Castilla* (Calle Infante Don Fernando 40) is a good-value place to head for any meal. The fare is satisfying: ham, eggs and chips or chicken or pork with chips and veggies all cost 550 ptas to 650 ptas; tortillas with a bit of salad cost 300 ptas to 500 ptas. *Pensión Madrona* (Calle Calzada 25) has another good, economical restaurant. *Café-Bar Chicón* (Calle Infante Don Fernando 1), next door to Hostal Manzanito, is OK for any meal: its platos combinados cost from 600 ptas to 800 ptas.

For something a bit classier, *Restaurante La Espuela* (Calle San Agustín 1), off Calle Infante Don Fernando, offers traditional dishes such as wild boar, venison and oxtail for 1000 ptas to 2400 ptas, as well as pizzas and pasta from 700 ptas to 900 ptas, all plus IVA. It also serves a *menú del día* (fixed-price meal of the day) for 1000 ptas plus IVA and a *menú típico* of Antequera specialities for 2100 ptas plus IVA (closed Monday). The original, long-established *Restaurante La Espuela Plaza*, open daily in the bullring at the north-western end of Calle Infante Don Fernando, offers similar fare but without the pizza or pasta.

Restaurante El Angelote, in an 18th-century mansion on the lovely old Plaza Coso Viejo, offers a three-course menú for 1200 ptas plus IVA, and meat and fish main dishes from 950 ptas to 2100 ptas plus IVA.

Entertainment

Antequera's livelier, more interesting bars include *Le Bistrot* on Calle San Agustín off Calle Infante Don Fernando, and *La Guagua* and *La Calle* on Calle Diego Ponce near Pensión Madrona.

Getting There & Away

Several daily buses run to/from Málaga, and three to five each to/from Estepa, Osuna, Sevilla (Prado de San Sebastián), Granada and Córdoba. Most services are by Alsina Graells (☎ 95 284 13 65).

Two to four trains a day run to/from Granada, Sevilla, Ronda, Algeciras and Almería. For Málaga or Córdoba, change at Bobadilla. Antequera station is on ☎ 95 284 32 26.

AROUND ANTEQUERA
El Torcal

Millions of years of wind and water action have sculpted this 1336m mountain south of Antequera into some of the weirdest, most wonderful rock formations you'll see anywhere. A 12- sq-km area of gnarled, serrated and pillared limestone, formed as seabed 150 million years ago, constitute the protected Paraje Natural Torcal de Antequera. There are some deep ravines, and cliffs on most sides. The El Torcal visitor centre (☎ 95 203 13 89) opens 10 am to 2 pm and 4 to 6 pm (3 to 5 pm in winter).

Casual visitors are only allowed to follow a single marked walking trail, the 1.4km 'Ruta Verde', which starts and ends near the visitor centre. To see any more of El Torcal, you are supposed to go with a guide from the visitor centre: recently, two-hour

trips (600 ptas) were going at 10.30 am (and 12.30 and 3.30 pm if there is the demand) on Sunday. For other times you should ring the visitor centre in advance.

Getting There & Away You need a vehicle. Buses from Antequera will get you there, or back, but not both in the same day. Drivers should head south down Calle Picadero near the western end of Calle Infante Don Fernando, then follow the C-3310 towards Villanueva de la Concepción. Twelve kilometres from the town a turn uphill to the right leads 4km to the visitor centre.

Laguna de Fuente de Piedra

When it's not dried up by drought, this lake just south of the A-92, 20km north-west of Antequera, is the biggest natural lake in Andalucía and one of Europe's two main breeding grounds for the spectacular greater flamingo (the other is the Camargue in France). After a wet winter as many as 16,000 pairs of flamingo will breed at the lake. The birds arrive in January or February, with the chicks hatching in April and May. The flamingos stay till about August, when the lake, which rarely is more than 1m deep, no longer contains enough water to support them. They share the lake with thousands of other birds of some 170 species.

The Centro de Información Fuente de Piedra (☎ 95 211 10 50) at the lake, on the edge of Fuente de Piedra village, opens 10 am to 2 pm and 6 to 8 pm (4 to 6 pm from the last Sunday in October to the last Saturday in March), Wednesday to Sunday. It can advise on the best spots for viewing the birds. A vehicle and binoculars are very advantageous, as you may find that most of the flamingos are clustered towards the far side of the lake – a 6km or 7km drive away – and tend to fly away if you try to get *too* close.

Camping La Laguna (☎ 95 273 52 94), on the edge of Fuente de Piedra village with lake views, is inexpensive. *Hostal La Laguna* (☎ 95 273 52 92), just off the A-92 in Fuente de Piedra, has doubles costing 5000 ptas and a good-value restaurant.

Getting There & Away Buses run between Antequera bus station and Fuente de Piedra village nine times a day Monday to Friday, four times on Saturday and three times on Sunday and holidays.

Fuente de Piedra train station, about 500m from the lake, is on the Málaga–Córdoba line, with two trains each way daily. Schedules don't permit a day-trip from Málaga or Antequera.

East of Málaga

The coast east of Málaga, sometimes described as the Costa del Sol Oriental, is less developed than the coast west of the city. Along the grey-sand beaches is a string of medium-sized resort towns: Rincón de la Victoria, Torre del Mar, Torrox Costa and Nerja. The first two are mainly popular with Spaniards while Torrox is favoured by Germans and Nerja by the British. Sea water quality along this coast still leaves much to be desired – only Torrox has proper treatment facilities for sewage before it enters the sea (usually by outlets about 1.5km from the shore).

All the towns have hostales, hotels and holiday apartments – Nerja has the most – and there are several camp sites too.

Behind the coast the attractive La Axarquía region climbs to the rugged mountains straddling the border of Granada province. A 406 sq km area of these mountains was declared the Parque Natural Sierras de Tejeda, Almijara y Alhama, Andalucía's 23rd natural park, in 1999.

A series of crumbling old coastal watchtowers, many built after the Reconquista (Reconquest) to watch for Muslim raiders from North Africa, adds a romantic touch to the landscape.

RINCÓN DE LA VICTORIA
postcode 29730 • pop 16,000
Rincón's **Cueva del Tesoro** (Treasure Cave – gold was supposedly hidden here by Muslim emirs) is worth a stop. The series of underground caverns has stalagmites, stalactites, underground pools and some

Palaeolithic wall paintings, though these last are off-limits to visitors. Opening hours are 10 am to 2 pm and 3 to 6 pm Monday to Friday, and 10 am to 6 pm at the weekend and holidays. Admission costs 500 ptas.

TORRE DEL MAR
postcode 29740 • pop 6600
Despite the ugly line of apartments facing its seafront, Torre del Mar is a likeable place with more local flavour than the towns farther east. Its pleasant beachfront promenade continues a couple of kilometres east to Playa La Caleta, which has a marina. Torre fills up with Spanish holiday-makers in July and August. There's a tourist office (☎ 95 254 11 04) at Avenida Andalucía 119, a few blocks west of the central boulevard, Paseo de Larios.

La Cueva on Paseo de Larios does excellent seafood tapas and raciones. At the seafront end of Paseo de Larios is a line of *bars* and *discos* known as El Copo, which kick on all night on Friday and Saturday and attract crowds from far afield.

NERJA
postcode 29780 • pop 14,000
Nerja, 56km east of Málaga with the Sierra de Almijara rising close behind it, is older, whiter and more charming than the preceding towns, though it's inundated by tourism, which has pushed it far beyond its old confines since the 1960s.

There are good coastal views from the Balcón de Europa lookout point in the centre. The tourist office (☎ 95 252 15 31), nearby at Puerta del Mar 4, has pamphlets on some nice walks in the area. The best beach is Playa Burriana on the eastern side of town. Nerja Book Centre, Calle Granada 30, with second-hand books in English and other languages, is worth a browse. Nerja's annual fair (around 10 October) is one of the last of the year.

Places to Stay
The pleasant *Nerja Camping* (☎ 95 252 97 14), about 4km east of town on the N-340, charges 2200 ptas for two people, a tent and a car.

In August, try to arrive early in the day to ensure a room. A good choice among the couple of dozen hostales and pensiones is *Hostal Mena* (☎ 95 252 05 41, *Calle El Barrio 15*), a short distance west of the tourist office. Singles/doubles with bathroom cost 2250/4500 ptas (more in August, less from October to June). Prices are similar at *Hostal Atenbeni* (☎ 95 252 13 41, *Calle Diputación Provincial 12*), one block north of Calle El Barrio; *Hostal Alhambra* (☎ 95 252 21 74, *Calle Antonio Millón 12*), on the corner of Calle Chaparil, a block west of Calle El Barrio; and *Hostal Nerjasol* (☎ 95 252 22 21, *Calle Arropieros 4*), four blocks north of the tourist office.

Hotel Cala Bella (☎ 95 252 07 00, *Puerta del Mar 10*) and *Hotel Portofino* (☎ 95 252 01 50, *Puerta del Mar 2*), both close to the tourist office, have some rooms with good beach views. In the high season, doubles cost 6500 ptas at the Cala Bella and 9000 ptas at the Portofino, both plus IVA. The English-owned *Hotel Carabeo* (☎ 95 252 54 44, ✆ hcarabeo@arrakis.es, *Calle Carabeo 34*), close by, is a classy, small, family-run hotel with gardens and a pool overlooking the sea, and just six rooms and suites costing from 11,000 ptas to 20,500 ptas plus IVA, breakfast included.

Other top-end places include *Hotel Balcón de Europa* (☎ 95 252 08 00, *fax 95 252 44 90*), by the Balcón itself and with its own little beach (doubles 17,100 ptas plus IVA in the high season), and *Parador de Nerja* (☎ 95 252 00 50, ✆ nerja@parador.es, *Calle Almuñécar 8*) above Playa Burriana (19,000 ptas plus IVA).

Nerja has a lot of apartments to let – inquire at the tourist office.

Places to Eat
There are dozens of places to eat in town, but one of the best feeds to be had is at the open-air *Merendero Ayo*, towards the eastern end of Playa Burriana, where a plate of paella, cooked on the spot in great sizzling pans, costs 675 ptas. It does reasonably priced salads too, and more expensive meat and fish.

In town, *Havelí* (*Calle Cristo 44*), north off Puerta del Mar, is a good, medium-priced Indian restaurant with a roof terrace in summer. It has over 85 dishes to choose from (open evenings only). *Ostería di Mamma Rosa* (*Edificio Corona, Calle Chaparil*), about a 10-minute walk west of Puerta del Mar, is another good medium-priced option (closed Sunday). The more expensive *Carabeo 34* (*Calle Carabeo 34*), east off Puerta del Mar, has stunning Mediterranean views and serves excellent meals and tapas (closed Monday). Classy *Casa Luque* (*Plaza Cavana 2*), behind the Iglesia del Salvador (the church near the Balcón), does pricey Spanish and Basque food.

Getting There & Away
Alsina Graells (☎ 95 252 15 04), on the N-340 near the top of Calle Pintada which runs up from near the tourist office, has around 14 daily buses to/from Málaga (500 ptas), eight to/from Almuñécar, several to/from Almería and two to/from Granada.

AROUND NERJA
The area's really big tourist attraction is the **Cueva de Nerja**, 3km east of Nerja, just off the N-340. This enormous cavern, like some vast underground cathedral, remains impressive despite the crowds that continually traipse through it. Hollowed out by water around 5 million years ago, it was inhabited by Stone Age hunters around 15,000 BC. Their rock paintings are off-limits to visitors, but there are still lots of impressive stalactites, stalagmites and rock formations to admire. Every July, Spanish and international ballet and music stars perform in the cave as part of the Festival Cueva de Nerja. The cave is open 10 am to 2 pm and 4 to 6.30 pm daily and costs 750 ptas (children six to 12 years 400 ptas). About 14 buses a day run from Málaga and Nerja. Others even run from Marbella.

Farther east the coast becomes more rugged and scenic and with your own wheels you can head out to some good **beaches** reached by tracks down from the N-340, around 8 to 10km from Nerja. **Playa del Cañuelo**, immediately before the border with Granada province, is one of the best, with a couple of simple summer-only restaurants.

Seven kilometres north of Nerja and linked to it by several buses daily (except Sunday) is the pretty village of **Frigiliana**. El Fuerte, the hill that climbs above the village, was the scene of the final bloody defeat of the Moriscos of La Axarquía in their 1569 rebellion (see the following La Axarquía section). Some of the Moriscos reputedly threw themselves from the hilltop rather than be killed or captured by the Spanish. It's said that bones and rusted weapons from this encounter still lie among the scrub on El Fuerte (we found a bone but it probably belonged to a goat!).

LA AXARQUÍA

La Axarquía was one of Andalucía's forgotten areas until a decade or so ago, when northern-European expatriates became interested in it. Since then, rural tourism has taken off. The chief attractions include hill and mountain scenery; pretty white villages; strong, sweet, local wine made from sun-dried grapes; and good walking (best in April and May and from mid-September to late October).

La Axarquía is riven by deep valleys lined with terraces and irrigation channels that go back to Muslim times. Nearly all the villages dotted around the olive, almond and vine-planted hillsides are of Muslim origin, with narrow, higgledy-piggledy streets. La Axarquía joined the 1569 Morisco rebellion (see Las Alpujarras in the Granada Province chapter) and afterwards its inhabitants were replaced with Christians from farther north.

You can pick up information on La Axarquía at the tourist offices in Málaga, Nerja or Torre del Mar. Prospective walkers should ask for the leaflet on walks in the Parque Natural Sierras de Tejeda, Almijara y Alhama. Rural Andalus (☎ 95 227 62 29, see Accommodation in Facts for the Visitor chapter) and Axartur (☎ 95 254 20 58) have numerous *self-catering houses* and *apartments* in La Axarquía, typically costing around 2000 ptas a person per night.

The best maps for walkers are the SGE's 1:50,000 *Zafarraya* and *Vélez-Málaga*. Useful guides include *25 Walks in and around Cómpeta & Canillas de Albaida* by Albert & Dini Kraaijenzank. You should be able to find the maps and guide at Marco Polo in Cómpeta (see the Cómpeta section later in this chapter). Papelería Ariza, Avenida Constitución 57, Cómpeta, may have the Spanish walking guides *Sendas y Caminos por los Campos de la Axarquía* (Interguías Clave) and *Andar por La Axarquía* (El Búho Viajero).

Western Axarquía

The 'capital' of La Axarquía, **Vélez Málaga**, 4km north of Torre del Mar, is busy but unspectacular. Its restored hilltop Muslim castle is worth a look though. From Vélez the A-335 heads north past the Embalse de la Viñuela reservoir and up through the **Boquete de Zafarraya**, a dramatic cleft in the mountains, towards Granada. One bus a day each way between Torre del Mar and Granada makes its way over this road.

Westward, **Comares** sits like a snowdrift atop a conical hill. It has a history of rebellion against Muslim and Christian rulers, having been a stronghold of Omar ibn Hafsun (see El Chorro, Ardales & Around section earlier in this chapter). Some of the most dramatic Axarquía scenery is up around the highest villages, **Alfarnate** (925m) and **Alfarnatejo** (858m), with high, rugged crags such as Tajo de Gomer and Tajo de Doña Ana rising to their south.

Places to Stay & Eat On the western bank of the Embalse de la Viñuela, *Camping Presa La Viñuela* (☎ 95 203 01 27) charges 1775 ptas plus IVA for two people with a car and tent. *Camping El Mirador de la Axarquía* (☎ 95 250 92 09) at Comares charges only 1100 ptas plus IVA.

The modern *Hotel Atalaya* (☎ 95 250 92 08, Calle Encinilla s/n) in Comares has singles/doubles with bathroom costing 3000/6000 ptas, and a restaurant. *Hotel de La Viñuela* (☎ 95 251 91 93) has a fine position on the eastern bank of the Embalse de la Viñuela and very comfortable rooms costing

7170/9845 ptas and a restaurant. Near Periana, a few kilometres north, *Villa Turística de la Axarquía* (*☎/fax 95 253 62 22, Carril del Cortijo Blanco s/n*) has apartments and small villas costing 6420/10,035 ptas including breakfast, plus a pool; horse riding can be arranged. Both places have restaurants and raise prices in August.

Venta de Alfarnate (*☎ 95 275 93 88*), on the Loja road just outside Alfarnate, is probably the oldest inn in Andalucía, dating from 1690. It displays mementoes of past visitors including some of the bandits who used to roam these hills and, on occasions, took it over. It opens 11 am to 7 pm (to midnight on Friday and Saturday), daily except Monday. Foodwise it's renowned for *huevos a la bestia*, a kind of hill country mixed grill of fried eggs and assorted pork products (1450 ptas). Other items, mostly meaty, cost between 600 ptas and 2400 ptas.

Cómpeta
postcode 29754 • pop 2700
• elevation 625m
The highest mountains in the area stretch east from the Boquete de Zafarraya. The village of Cómpeta, currently attracting a growing wave of Spanish and foreign tourism and an increasing expat population, is one of the best bases for a stay in La Axarquía. It has some of La Axarquía's best local wine and quite a range of places to stay and eat. Its popular Noche del Vino (Night of the Wine), 15 August, features a program of flamenco and sevillana music and dance in the central Plaza Almijara, and limitless free wine. Marco Polo, Calle José Antonio 3, just off Plaza Almijara, sells books in English and several other languages, and maps.

Places to Stay The attractive stone-built *Hostal Alberdini* (*☎ 95 251 62 41*), on a hilltop at La Lomilla, 1km south-east of Cómpeta (turn right at the Venta de Palma bar on the Torrox road), has spectacular views and a garden of quirky sculpture. Singles/doubles with bathroom cost 3000/5000 ptas (discounts for more than one night); it also has a reasonably priced restaurant.

Rooms are available in several homes: bed and breakfast, with bathroom, costs 3600/6000 ptas at *Las Tres Abejas* (*☎ 95 255 33 75, ✉ bart333@teleline.es, Calle Panaderos 43*), about 150m uphill from Plaza Almijara, and 3500/6000 ptas at the beautifully renovated *Casa Azahara* (*☎/fax 95 251 61 53, Calle Carretería 9*), just off the square.

Hotel Balcón de Cómpeta (*☎ 95 255 35 35, Calle San Antonio 75*) has air-con rooms with balcony costing 6350/8700 ptas plus IVA, and a restaurant, bar, tennis court and good pool.

Places to Eat There's cheap and cheerful fare at *Bar Marcos* at the foot of the village, opposite the bus stop. *Café Bar Perico* on Plaza Almijara does decent standard fare with omelettes and *revueltos* (scrambled-egg dishes) at 400 ptas to 750 ptas and fish and meat mains from 675 ptas to 1950 ptas. *El Pilón* on nearby Calle Laberinto does very good Spanish and international food including prawn and avocado salad (750 ptas), *solomillo a la pimienta verde* (pork sirloin in green pepper sauce; 1300 ptas) and fish main dishes costing around 1400 ptas. The *Museo del Vino* (*Avenida Constitución 6*) serves ham, cheese and sausage raciones and wine from the barrel – plus good regional crafts. Next door, *Restaurante Asador Museo del Vino* specialises in excellent grilled meats, such as pork/lamb chops at 650/1275 ptas. The *Cortijo Paco* (*Avenida Canillas 6*), above the hotel, is another excellent restaurant, with a fine terrace and typical mains in the 1200 ptas region.

Getting There & Away Three buses a day (two on Saturday, Sunday and holidays) run from Málaga to Cómpeta and Canillas de Albaida, via Torre del Mar.

Around Cómpeta
A few kilometres down the valley, **Árchez**, has a beautifully decorated Almohad-style minaret next to its church. A scenic road winding west from Árchez through Salares, Sedella and Canillas de Aceituno eventually links up with the A-335 north of Vélez

Málaga. Another road leads south-west from Árchez to **Arenas** where a steep but driveable track climbs to the ruined Muslim **Castillo de Bentomiz**, crowning a hilltop with fine panoramas. Keep your eyes open for chameleons, which are more abundant around Arenas than anywhere else in Spain. In early October Arenas stages the Feria de la Mula, dedicated to that rapidly disappearing beast of burden, the mule.

Walks See the introductory paragraphs for La Axarquía for information on maps and walking guidebooks.

Perhaps the most exhilarating walk in the area is up the dramatically peaked **El Lucero** (1779m). From its summit on a clear day, there are stupendous views as far as Granada in one direction and Morocco in the other. This is a full, demanding day's walking with an ascent of 1150m from Cómpeta: start by climbing left along the track above Cómpeta football pitch. About 1¾ hours from Cómpeta you pass below and west of a fire observation hut on the hill La Mina. Turn right through a gap in the rock 400m past the turning to the hut. This path leads in one hour to Puerto Blanquillo (1200m), from which a path climbs 200m to the Puerto de Cómpeta.

One kilometre down from the latter pass, past a quarry, the summit path (1½ hours) diverges to the right across a stream bed, marked by a small cairn (mound of stones) and a green-and-white paint blob on the far bank. El Lucero is topped by the ruins of a Guardia Civil post built to watch for anti-Franco rebels after the civil war. It's possible to drive as far up as Puerto Blanquillo on a rough mountain track from Canillas de Albaida, a village 2km north-west of Cómpeta, in 40 minutes or so.

The highest peak hereabouts, **Maroma** (2069m), can be climbed from Canillas de Albaida, Salares, Sedella, Canillas de Aceituno or the El Alcázar picnic area, a 5km drive up from Alcaucín. In each case it's a demanding eight to 10 hours walk, with an ascent and descent of 1200 to 1400m. A couple of pleasant, less demanding outings are to the **Fábrica de Luz de Canillas de Albaida** and the **Fábrica de Luz de Cómpeta**, each 6 or 7km from Cómpeta. These buildings are tiny, ruined hydroelectric installations set in deep, luxuriantly vegetated river valleys among the hills. From the Fábrica de Luz de Cómpeta you can walk on to the abandoned hamlet of **Acebuchal**.

Córdoba Province

Córdoba city, in the fertile valley of the Río Guadalquivir which runs across the middle of the province, has a fascinating history and was capital of Al-Andalus (the Muslim-ruled parts of medieval Spain) when it was at its peak. Its former mosque *(mezquita)* is one of the most magnificent Islamic buildings in the world. The rest of Córdoba province contains many appealing country areas where remote, ancient villages and hilly terrain combine with a rare beauty.

CÓRDOBA

postcode 14080 • pop 310,000
• elevation 110m

Lying on a curve of the Guadalquivir with countryside stretching far in every direction around it, Córdoba is by far the biggest place in a rural province, and feels at once provincial and sophisticated. The labyrinthine medieval quarter, focused on the Mezquita, is what fascinates most visitors, but the modern heart of the city is farther north. To get an idea of what being *cordobés* is about, you should try to experience both parts.

Córdoba is a sleepy place for much of the year, but bursts into life from mid-April to mid-June. At this time the skies are blue but the heat is tolerable, the city's many trees and lovely patios drip with foliage and blooms, and Córdoba stages most of its major fiestas. September and October are climatically pleasant too.

History

The Roman colony of Corduba, founded in 152 BC, became the capital of Baetica province, covering most of today's Andalucía. This major Roman cultural centre was the birthplace of the writers Seneca and Lucan.

Córdoba fell to the Islamic invaders in AD 711 and soon became the Muslim capital on the Iberian Peninsula. It was here that in 756 Abd ar-Rahman I set himself up as the independent emir of Al-Andalus, founding the Omayyad dynasty. Córdoba's

Highlights

- Be mesmerised by the Mezquita, one of the greatest of all Islamic buildings
- Enjoy the spring flowers and greenery in Córdoba's patios, the Alcázar gardens, and in the countryside almost everywhere
- Wander the labyrinthine Jewish and Muslim quarters of old Córdoba
- Visit Medina Azahara, Andalucía's most impressive archaeological site
- Explore the mountainous south-east, with its dramatically sited villages and the architectural treasures of Priego de Córdoba

– and Al-Andalus' – heyday came under Abd ar-Rahman III (912–61), who in 929 named himself caliph, setting the seal on Al-Andalus' long-standing de facto independence of the Abbasid caliphs in Baghdad. Córdoba was by now the biggest city in western Europe, with a population somewhere between 100,000 and 500,000. Its economy flourished on the agriculture of its irrigated hinterland and the products of its skilled artisans – leather and metalwork, textiles, glazed tiles and more. It had dazzling mosques, patios, gardens and fountains, plus aqueducts and public baths. Abd ar-Rahman III's court was frequented by Jewish, Arab and Christian scholars, and Córdoba's university, library, observatories

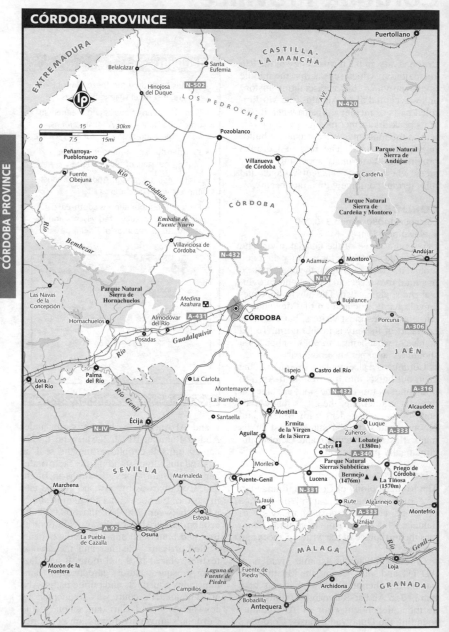

CÓRDOBA PROVINCE

and other institutions made it a centre of learning whose impact was still being felt in Christian Europe many centuries later. Abulcasis (936–1013), author of a 30-volume medical encyclopaedia and considered the father of surgery, was the most remarkable scholar of this age.

One of Mohammed's arm bones, kept in the Mezquita, became a psychological weapon against the Christians and was partly responsible for the development of the opposing cult of Santiago (St James). Córdoba became a place of pilgrimage for Muslims who could not get to Mecca or Jerusalem.

Towards the end of the 10th century, Al-Mansour (Almanzor), a ruthless general whose northward raids struck terror into Christian Spain, took the reins of power from the caliphs. When he destroyed the cathedral at Santiago de Compostela, home of the Santiago cult, he had its bells carried to Córdoba by Christian slaves and hung upside-down as gigantic oil lamps in the Mezquita. After the death of Al-Mansour's son Abd al-Malik in 1008, the caliphate descended into anarchy. Rival claimants to the title, Berber troops and Christian armies from Castile and Catalunya all fought over the spoils. The Berbers terrorised and looted the city and, in 1031, Omayyad rule ended.

Al-Andalus collapsed into dozens of petty kingdoms (taifas). Córdoba became part of the Sevilla kingdom in 1069 and has been overshadowed by that city ever since. But Córdoba's intellectual traditions lived on. The 11th-century philosopher-poets Ibn Hazm (who wrote in Arabic) and Judah Ha-Levi (Hebrew) both spent important parts of their lives here. Twelfth-century Córdoba produced the two most celebrated of all Al-Andalus' scholars – the Muslim Averroës (1126–98; see Literature in the Facts about Andalucía chapter) and the Jewish Maimonides (1135–1204). Both were men of multifarious talents, best remembered for their philosophical efforts to harmonise religious faith with Aristotelian reason. But while Averroës held high office under the Almohads in Córdoba and Sevilla, Maimonides fled Almohad intolerance and spent most of his career in Egypt.

When Córdoba was taken by Castile's Fernando III in 1236, much of its population fled. Fernando returned the bells to Santiago de Compostela and Córdoba became a provincial city of shrinking importance. Its decline was only reversed by the arrival of industry in the late 19th century – though Christian Córdoba had managed to produce one of the greatest Spanish poets, Luis de Góngora (1561–1627).

Orientation

The medieval city is immediately north of the Guadalquivir, a warren of narrow streets homing in on the Mezquita just a block from the river. Within the medieval city, the area north-west of the Mezquita was the *judería* (Jewish quarter), the Muslim quarter was north and east of the Mezquita, and the Mozarabic (Christian) quarter was farther to the north-east.

The main square of modern Córdoba is Plaza de las Tendillas, 500m north of the Mezquita, with the main shopping streets to its north and west. The train and bus stations are 1km north-west of Plaza de las Tendillas.

Maps Librería Luque, Calle Conde de Gondomar 13, sells city and Michelin maps at about half the price of the tourist shops near the Mezquita. It also sells some CNIG maps.

Information

Tourist Offices The helpful, multilingual Junta de Andalucía tourist office (☎ 957 47 12 35) at Calle de Torrijos 10, in a 16th-century chapel facing the western side of the Mezquita, opens 9.30 am to 8 pm Monday to Friday, 10 am to 8 pm Saturday, and 10 am to 2 pm Sunday and holidays, closing at 7 pm from Monday to Saturday in March, October and sometimes August and September, and at 6 pm from November to February. The municipal tourist office (☎ 957 20 05 22), on Plaza de Judá Leví, a block farther west, is also helpful but only opens 8.30 am to 2.30 pm Monday to Friday, sometimes longer in summer.

A tourist information kiosk at the train station opens 10 am to 2 pm and 4.15 to 8 pm Monday to Friday.

CÓRDOBA

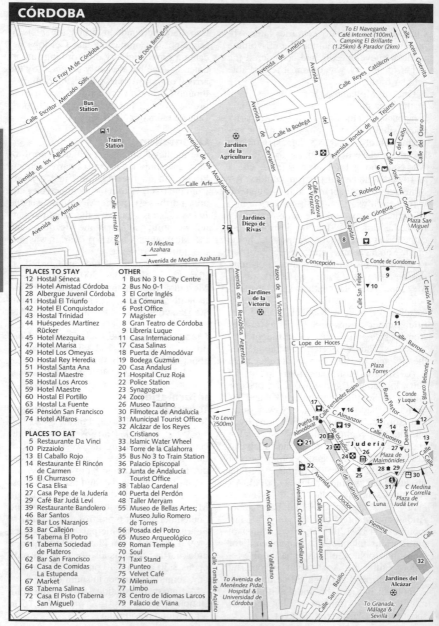

PLACES TO STAY
12 Hostal Séneca
25 Hotel Amistad Córdoba
28 Albergue Juvenil Córdoba
41 Hostal El Triunfo
42 Hotel El Conquistador
43 Hostal Trinidad
44 Huéspedes Martínez Rücker
45 Hotel Mezquita
47 Hotel Marisa
49 Hotel Los Omeyas
50 Hostal Rey Heredia
51 Hostal Santa Ana
57 Hostal Maestre
58 Hostal Los Arcos
59 Hotel Maestre
60 Hostal El Portillo
63 Hostal La Fuente
66 Pensión San Francisco
74 Hotel Alfaros

PLACES TO EAT
5 Restaurante Da Vinci
10 Pizzaiolo
13 El Caballo Rojo
14 Restaurante El Rincón de Carmen
15 El Churrasco
16 Casa Elisa
27 Casa Pepe de la Judería
29 Café Bar Judá Leví
31 Restaurante Bandolero
46 Bar Santos
52 Bar Los Naranjos
53 Bar Callejón
54 Taberna El Potro
61 Taberna Sociedad de Plateros
62 Bar San Francisco
64 Casa de Comidas La Estupenda
67 Market
68 Taberna Salinas
72 Casa El Pisto (Taberna San Miguel)

OTHER
1 Bus No 3 to City Centre
2 Bus No 0-1
3 El Corte Inglés
4 La Comuna
6 Post Office
7 Magister
8 Gran Teatro de Córdoba
9 Librería Luque
11 Casa Internacional
17 Casa Salinas
18 Puerta de Almodóvar
19 Bodega Guzmán
20 Casa Andalusí
21 Hospital Cruz Roja
22 Police Station
23 Synagogue
24 Zoco
26 Museo Taurino
30 Filmoteca de Andalucía
31 Municipal Tourist Office
32 Alcázar de los Reyes Cristianos
33 Islamic Water Wheel
34 Torre de la Calahorra
35 Bus No 3 to Train Station
36 Palacio Episcopal
37 Junta de Andalucía Tourist Office
38 Tablao Cardenal
40 Puerta del Perdón
48 Taller Meryam
55 Museo de Bellas Artes; Museo Julio Romero de Torres
56 Posada del Potro
65 Museo Arqueológico
69 Roman Temple
70 Soul
71 Taxi Stand
73 Punteo
75 Velvet Café
76 Milenium
77 Limbo
78 Centro de Idiomas Larcos
79 Palacio de Viana

CÓRDOBA PROVINCE

CÓRDOBA

Plaza de Colón

Plaza de Don Gome

79

Calle Juan Rufo

77

76

75

C Carbonell y Morand

Calle Alfaros

Calle Santa Marta

C Conde de Arenales

78

74

73 Calle de San Pablo

Villalones

72

Calle de Alfonso XIII

Plaza de las Tendillas

71

70

69

Calle Tundidores

Calle Pedro López

C Claudio Marcelo

C Conde Cárdenas

Calle Ambrosio Morales

Diario de Córdoba

R Marín

68

Plaza de la Corredera

67

66

Calle Maese Luis

Calle Tarnillo

C Juan Valera

Pompeyos

Calle Marqués del Villar

65

Calle de San Fernando

64

63

62

Plaza del Potro

Calle de Lineros

Plaza de Jerónimo Páez

61

San Francisco

C R Barros

55

Calle de Lucano

54

53

Calle de Rey Heredia

60

59

58

57

56

52

C E R Torres

C Céspedes

48

49

47

46

50

51

To Recinto Ferial (800m) & N-IV (east)

Cárdenal Herrero

45

44

C Magistral G Francés

43

42

Paseo de la Rivera

40

Patio de los Naranjos

Mezquita

C Corregidor Luis de la Cerda

41

Río Guadalquivir

de Torrijos

39

38

37

36

Amador de los Ríos

35

Ronda de Isasa

Acera Mira al Río

Calle del Santo Cristo

33

34

Puente Romano

Plaza Santa Teresa

0   100   200m
0   100   200yd

Money Most banks and ATMs are in the newer part of the centre, around Plaza de las Tendillas and Avenida del Gran Capitán. The bus and train stations have ATMs.

Post & Communications The main post office, Calle José Cruz Conde 15, opens 8.30 am to 8.30 pm Monday to Friday, and 9.30 am to 2 pm Saturday. El Navegante Café Internet (☎ 957 49 75 36), Llanos del Pretorio 1, opens 9 am to 1 am daily and offers 15/30/60 minutes on-line for 250/350/600 ptas.

Medical Services & Emergency The main general hospital, Hospital Reina Sofía (☎ 957 21 70 00), is 1.5km south-west of the Mezquita at Avenida de Menéndez Pidal s/n. The Hospital Cruz Roja (Red Cross Hospital; ☎ 957 42 06 66) is more central at Avenida Doctor Fleming s/n. For an ambulance you can call ☎ 957 21 79 03 or ☎ 957 29 55 70.

The Policía Nacional (☎ 957 47 75 00) station is at Avenida Doctor Fleming 2.

Mezquita

This superb building can seem a little bewildering to begin with. Because of major Christian alterations to the original Islamic structure, and the darkness they impose, you need a bit of imagination to picture the Mezquita as it was, an architectural unity open to and in harmony with its surroundings.

The Mezquita has some truly beautiful architectural features, among them the famous rows of two-tier arches assembled in mesmerising stripes of red brick and white stone, and the more elaborate arches, domes and decoration in and around the splendid prayer niche (*mihrab*).

From the outside the building looks like a fortress, with thick stone walls punctuated by decorated portals; it's low-slung except for the protruding roofs of the cathedral within and the lower domes along the southern wall.

The Mezquita (☎ 957 47 05 12) is open for tourist visits 10 am to 7.30 pm Monday to Saturday and 3.30 to 7.30 pm Sunday from April to September; and 10 am to 5.30 pm Monday to Saturday and 2 to 5.30 pm Sunday and holidays in other months. Admission costs 800 ptas.

History Abd ar-Rahman I founded the Mezquita in 785 on the site of a church which had been partitioned between Muslims and Christians, reputedly purchasing the Christian half from the Christian community. Abd ar-Rahman II (821–52) and Al-Hakim II in the 960s extended the Mezquita southwards to cater for Córdoba's expanding population. Al-Hakim II also added the existing mihrab and, for extra light, built a number of domes with skylights over the area in front of it. Under Al-Mansour, eastward extensions were made and the mihrab lost its central position in the south wall.

What you see today is the building's final Islamic form with one major alteration – a 16th-century cathedral right in the middle (hence the often-used description 'Mezquita-Catedral'). For this the extensions made under Abd ar-Rahman II and Al-Mansour were partly dismantled.

Orientation The main entrance is the Puerta del Perdón, a 14th-century Mudéjar gateway on Calle Cardenal Herrero, with the ticket office immediately inside.

Beside the Puerta del Perdón is a 16th- and 17th-century tower built around the remains of the original minaret. Inside the gateway is the pretty **Patio de los Naranjos** (Courtyard of Orange Trees), from which a door leads inside the building itself.

A leaflet given free to visitors contains a map clearly outlining the stages of the

Opening Hours

Opening hours for Córdoba's sights change frequently, so check with the tourist offices for the latest times. Most places except the Mezquita close on Monday. Closing times are generally an hour or two earlier in winter than summer.

building's construction. The first 12 east-to-west aisles inside the building, a forest of pillars and arches, comprise Abd ar-Rahman I's original 8th-century mosque, completed by his son Hisham I and extending a little over halfway across the building from west to east. The mihrab is visible straight ahead from the entrance door, in the far (southern) wall. In the centre of the building is the Christian cathedral, aligned east to west and surrounded by more Islamic aisles, pillars and arches. Just past the right-hand (western) end of the cathedral, heavier, more elaborate arches mark the approach to the mihrab.

Abd ar-Rahman I's Mezquita This original section incorporated columns and capitals – of various coloured marbles, granite and alabaster – from the site's previous Visigothic church, from Roman buildings in Córdoba and elsewhere, and even from ancient Carthage. The columns were of differing heights so the tall ones had to be sunk into the floor. They support two tiers of arches, giving an effect reminiscent of Roman aqueducts and/or date palms. The use of bicoloured materials for the arches was inspired. Most of the columns for other parts of the building were made by Córdoban artisans.

Mihrab & Maksura The bay immediately in front of the mihrab and the bay to each side form the *maksura*, the area where the caliphs and their retinues would have prayed (today enclosed by railings). The maksura and mihrab are the artistic pinnacle of the building. Each of the maksura's three bays has a skylit dome with star-pattern stone vaulting. Because these domes were made of stone, rather than the wood used for the rest of the Mezquita's roofs, they rested on stronger, more elaborate arches. The mosaic decoration on the dome over the central bay is particularly beautiful. In the central bay is the horseshoe-arched entrance to the mihrab itself. This arch and its rectangular frame *(alfiz)* were superbly decorated with mosaic flower motifs and inscriptions from the Qur'an, all in gold, purple, green, blue and red, and rich stucco work. The mihrab itself, which you cannot enter, is octagonal with a shell-shaped dome. The mihrab served both to amplify the voice of the prayer leader and to indicate the direction of Mecca.

Cathedral The Mezquita, as was, was used as a cathedral after Fernando III took Córdoba. Early modifications, such as the Mudéjar tiling added in the 1370s to the Mozarabic and Almohad Capilla Real (nine bays north and one east of the mihrab), were carried out with restraint. But in the 16th century the centre of the Mezquita was ripped out to allow construction of the Capilla Mayor (the altar area) and choir *(coro)* designed by Hernán Ruiz the Elder. The Capilla Mayor has a rich 17th-century jasper and marble retable; the choir's fine mahogany stalls were carved in the 18th century by Pedro, Duque Cornejo.

If you think of the whole building as a cathedral, the forests of Islamic arches and pillars provide a superb setting for the central structures. If you see it as a mosque, the Christian additions wreck its whole conception. King Carlos I overrode the wishes of Córdoba's city council in permitting the church authorities to build the Capilla Mayor and choir. Legend has it that when he saw the results he was horrified, exclaiming: 'You have destroyed something that was unique in the world.'

Other Sections The Mezquita contains many further chapels: one next to the mihrab and others lining the eastern and western walls. Wandering around the rest of the Mezquita, it's possible to lose yourself in the aisles with views of only the incredible columns and arches, uninterrupted by the Christian alterations. The final Islamic building had 1300 columns, of which 850 remain. In Muslim times the Mezquita would have been better lit, with doors open along its sides.

Palacio Episcopal
The Bishops' Palace, on Calle de Torrijos, houses the **Palacio de Congresos y Exposi-**

JANE SMITH

An architectural masterpiece – brick and stone arches top a forest of pillars in the Mezquita.

ciones, which stages some interesting exhibitions, and the **Museo Diocesano** with a collection of religious art including some outstanding medieval woodcarving.

Judería
The old Jewish quarter extends west and north-west from the Mezquita, almost to the beginning of Avenida del Gran Capitán. It's a maze of narrow streets and small squares, of whitewashed buildings with flowers dripping from window boxes and of wrought-iron doorways giving glimpses of plant-filled patios (see the boxed text 'Córdoba's Hidden Heart' on the next page for details). The tourist shops and restaurants around the Mezquita thin out quickly within one or two blocks.

The **Museo Taurino** (Bullfighting Museum), in a 16th-century mansion on Plaza de Maimónides, celebrates Córdoba's legendary *toreros*, with rooms dedicated to El Cordobés and Manolete, and the skin, tail and ear of Islero, the bull that fatally gored Manolete at Linares in 1947. The museum opens 10 am to 2 pm and 6 to 8 pm (4.30 to 6.30 pm from October to April) Tuesday to Saturday, and 9.30 am to 3 pm Sunday and holidays. Admission costs 450 ptas (free on Friday).

Just up Calle de los Judíos from the Museo Taurino is the **Zoco**, a group of craft workshops/showrooms around an old patio (see Shopping later in this chapter). At Calle de los Judíos 20 is the 14th-century **synagogue**, one of the very few medieval Spanish synagogues that survives reasonably intact. It's a beautiful little building, retaining its upstairs women's gallery and stucco work that includes Hebrew inscriptions and intricate Mudéjar star and plant patterns. Opening hours are 10 am to 2 pm and 3.30 to 5.30 pm Tuesday to Saturday,

Córdoba's Hidden Heart

Concealed behind heavy wooden doors or partly hidden by wrought-iron gates are many examples of a beautiful Cordoban tradition.

For centuries, the patios of Córdoba have provided shade during the searing heat of summer, a haven of peace and quiet, and a place to talk and entertain. In Roman times they were meeting places. In Islamic times they were used for rest and recreation.

In the first half of May, you'll notice 'patio' signs in the streets and alleyways, which means that you're invited to enter and view what is for the rest of the year closed to the outside world. At this time of year the patios are at their prettiest as new blooms proliferate, though not all displays are on a grand scale. Many patios will have been entered in the annual competition, the Concurso de Patios Cordobeses. You can get a map of patios open for viewing from the tourist office but, if you don't have a lot of time, the patios on and around Calle San Basilio, about 400m west of the mosque, are some of the best.

During the competition, the patios are generally open 5 pm to midnight Monday to Friday and noon to midnight Saturday and Sunday. Admission is usually free but sometimes there's a container for donations.

and 10 am to 1.30 pm Sunday and holidays (free for EU citizens, 50 ptas for others). The **Casa Andalusí** at Calle de los Judíos 12 is a 12th-century house prettily decked out with a tinkling fountain in the patio and a variety of exhibits, mainly relating to Córdoba's medieval Muslim culture, but also including a Roman mosaic in the cellar. It opens 10.30 am to 8 pm (7 pm in winter); admission costs 300 ptas.

Just to the left at the top of Calle de los Judíos is the **Puerta de Almodóvar**, an Islamic gate in a restored stretch of the old city walls.

Alcázar de los Reyes Cristianos

The Castle of the Christian Monarchs, south-west of the Mezquita, began as a palace and fort for Alfonso X in the 13th century. From 1490 to 1821 the Inquisition operated from here. Its large gardens, full of fish ponds, fountains, orange trees, flowers and topiary, are among the most beautiful in Andalucía. The building itself, much altered, houses an old royal bathhouse and a museum, with some interesting Roman mosaics.

It opens 10 am to 2 pm and 6 to 8 pm (4.30 to 6.30 pm from October to April) Tuesday to Saturday, and 9.30 am to 3 pm Sunday and holidays. Admission costs 300 ptas (free on Friday).

Río Guadalquivir & Torre de la Calahorra

The Guadalquivir here is not particularly impressive, except when it's swollen by winter rains. Just south of the Mezquita, it's crossed by the much-restored **Puente Romano** (Roman Bridge). Slightly downstream, near the northern bank, is a restored **Islamic water wheel**, which raised water to the caliphs' palace on the site of the Palacio Episcopal.

At the southern end of the Puente Romano is the **Torre de la Calahorra**, a 14th-century tower with a curious museum highlighting the intellectual achievements of Islamic Córdoba and focusing rather rose-tintedly on its reputation for religious tolerance. A 55-minute earphone commentary, available in several languages, guides you through the displays while preaching an 'all religions are one' message. In one room, lifesized models of Averroës, Maimonides, the Andalucian Muslim mystic Ibn al-Arabi (c. 1169–1240) and the Castilian King Alfonso X expound on themes of tolerance and understanding of other religions. The museum also contains excellent models of the Mezquita and Granada's Alhambra. Oddly, its founder, French Muslim Roger Garaudy, was fined in a Paris court in 1998 for racial libel, questioning the Holocaust and provoking racial hatred, as a result of his book *The Founding Myths of Israeli Politics*, which questioned the existence of the Nazi gas chambers and argued that Nazi killing of the Jews did not amount to genocide. The Torre de la Calahorra opens 10 am to 2 pm and 4.30 to 8.30 pm daily (10 am to 6 pm from October to April). Admission costs 500 ptas.

Museo Arqueológico

Córdoba's archaeological museum is in a Renaissance mansion with a large patio at Plaza de Jerónimo Páez 7. A reclining stone lion takes pride of place in the Iberian section. The Roman period is well represented with large mosaics, elegant ceramics and tinted glass bowls. The upstairs is devoted to medieval Córdoba, including bronze animals from Medina Azahara. It opens 3 to 8 pm Tuesday, 9 am to 8 pm Wednesday to Saturday, and 9 am to 3 pm Sunday and holidays. Admission is free with an EU passport or identity card, 250 ptas otherwise.

Plaza del Potro

This attractive square 400m north-east of the Mezquita is mentioned in *Don Quijote*, whose author, Miguel Cervantes, lived for a spell in a nearby street. The square's heyday was the 16th and 17th centuries when it was a hangout for traders and adventurers. In the centre is a lovely 16th-century stone fountain topped by a rearing colt *(potro)*. On the western side of the square is **Posada del Potro**, formerly an inn but now an art gallery. Opposite, the former Hospital de la Caridad houses the **Museo de Bellas Artes**,

with a collection by mainly Cordoban artists, and the **Museo Julio Romero de Torres**, devoted to local painter Julio Romero de Torres (1880–1930), who specialised in dark, sensual portraits of Cordoban women. The Museo de Bellas Artes has the same hours and prices as the Museo Arqueológico. The Romero de Torres museum opens 10 am to 2 pm and 6 to 8 pm (4.30 to 6.30 pm from October to April) Tuesday to Saturday, and 9.30 am to 2.30 pm Sunday and holidays. Admission costs 450 ptas (free on Friday).

Plaza de la Corredera

This once handsome square 200m north of Plaza del Potro always seems to be under some kind of reconstruction. Córdoba's Roman amphitheatre stood here; later, Inquisition burnings and bullfights happened in the square. Today it's the site of a small food market and, when building work permits, a lively Saturday flea market.

Palacio de Viana

This Renaissance palace at Plaza de Don Gome 2, 500m north of Plaza de la Corredera, has 12 patios and a formal garden, which are lovely to visit in spring though unspectacular in midwinter. The palace was occupied by the Marqueses de Viana until a couple of decades ago. Opening hours are 9 am to 2 pm Monday to Saturday from June to September; 10 am to 1 pm and 4 to 6 pm Monday to Friday and 10 am to 1 pm Saturday in other months. The 500 ptas charge covers a one-hour guided tour of the rooms (packed with art and antiques) and access to the patios and garden (which take about half an hour to stroll round).

Plaza de las Tendillas & Around

Córdoba's main square features a clock with flamenco chimes and an equestrian statue – much loved by pigeons – of local lad Gonzalo Fernández de Córdoba, who rose to become the Catholic Monarchs' military right-hand man and earn the name El Gran Capitán. A ruined **Roman temple** has been partly restored, with 11 columns standing, nearby on Calle Claudio Marcelo.

Language Courses

For information on monthly courses at the university from October to June (60,000 ptas), contact the Universidad de Córdoba, Servicio de Lenguas Modernas y Traducción Técnica (☎ 957 21 81 33, fax 957 21 89 96, **@** si3goluj@uco.es), Edificio E U Enfermería, Avenida de Menéndez Pidal, 5° Planta, 14071 Córdoba.

Private language schools include Centro de Idiomas Larcos (☎ 957 47 11 03), Calle Manchado 9, and Casa Internacional (☎ 957 48 06 42), Calle Rodríguez Sánchez 15. Both offer a range of Spanish courses lasting from one or two weeks upwards, and varied accommodation options. Their respective Web sites are www.larcos.net and www .cybercordoba.es/casa_internacional. A typical two-week course costs 40,000 ptas, and two weeks in a shared apartment costs between 17,000 and 25,000 ptas.

Special Events

Spring and early summer is the chief festival time for Córdoba. The major events are:

Semana Santa
Every evening during Holy Week (from Palm Sunday to Good Friday) up to 12 *pasos* (religious images carried on platforms) and their processions file through the city, passing along the *carrera oficial* (official course) – Calle Claudio Marcelo, Plaza de las Tendillas, Calle José Cruz Conde – between about 8 pm and midnight. The climax is the *madrugada* of Good Friday, when six pasos pass along the carrera oficial between 4 and 6 am.

Cruces de Mayo
During the first few days of May squares and patios are decked with flower crosses, which become a focus for wine and tapas stalls, music and merrymaking.

Concurso & Festival de Patios Cordobeses
During the first half of May, at the same time as the patio competition (see the boxed text 'Córdoba's Hidden Heart'), there's a busy cultural program which, every three years (next in 2001 and 2004), includes the Concurso Nacional de Arte Flamenco, an important flamenco competition, with performances by many stars.

Feria de Mayo
During the last week of May and first days of June there are 10 days of partying with concerts, a big fairground in the El Arenal area south-east

of the city centre, the main bullfight season in the Los Califas ring on Gran Via Parque, and a general celebratory atmosphere.

Festival Internacional de Guitarra
A two-week celebration of the guitar with live performances of classical, flamenco, rock, blues and more; top names play in the Alcázar gardens at night. Held during late June and the first half of July.

Places to Stay

Many Córdoba lodgings are built around the charming patios for which the city is famous. There are plenty of places near the Mezquita, with the cheaper ones chiefly in the streets to the east. Those mentioned here are just a selection. Try to book ahead during the main festivals. Single rooms for a decent price are in short supply. Prices are generally reduced from November to mid-March; some places also cut their rates in hot July and August.

Places to Stay – Budget

Camping About 1.25km north of Plaza de Colón is *Camping El Brillante* (☎ 957 27 84 81, Avenida del Brillante 50). Open year round, it charges 570 ptas for each adult and car, and 450 to 570 ptas per tent, all plus IVA. Bus Nos 10 and 11 run to/from the train and bus stations and Plaza de Colón.

Hostels The excellent, modern *Albergue Juvenil Córdoba* (☎ 957 29 01 66, fax 957 29 05 00, Plaza de Judá Leví s/n), perfectly positioned in the Judería, accommodates 167 people in double, triple, quadruple and quintuple rooms, all with air-con, heating and private bathroom. One wing is in a converted 16th-century convent.

Hostales Friendly *Huéspedes Martínez Rücker* (☎ 957 47 25 62, **@** hmrucker@ alcavia.net, Calle Martínez Rücker 14) has a pretty patio and 12 small, very clean singles/doubles costing 2000/3500 ptas. Prices rise a few hundred pesetas during Semana Santa and for a couple of weeks in August. *Hostal Rey Heredia* (☎ 957 47 41 82, Calle de Rey Heredia 26) is simple, old-fashioned and friendly, with a plant-filled

patio. The nine decent rooms cost 1500/
3000 ptas, or 2000/4000 ptas with bathroom. Little *Hostal Trinidad* (☎ 957 48 79
05, Calle Corregidor Luis de la Cerda 58)
charges 1500/3200 ptas. *Hostal Santa Ana*
(☎ 957 48 58 37, Calle Corregidor Luis
de la Cerda 25) has one single costing
1800 ptas and doubles costing 4000 ptas,
or 5000 ptas with bathroom; the rooms
upstairs are more appealing. Parking is
available.

A short distance north of the Mezquita,
the 12-room *Hostal Séneca* (☎/fax 957 47
32 34, Calle Conde y Luque 7) is charming,
with friendly management, a *típico* patio
and a breakfast room. Rooms cost 2550/
4700 ptas with shared bathroom or 4750/
5900 ptas with private bathroom – all
including breakfast. It's worth phoning
ahead.

The following hostales are around Calle
de San Fernando, away from the Mequita
and the main tourist crowds. *Hostal La
Fuente* (☎ 957 48 78 27, Calle de San Fernando 51) offers 40 decent rooms all with
private bath, TV, air-con and heating. Com-
pact singles cost 3500 ptas; doubles cost
6000 ptas. It has courtyards for sitting out
and serves a decent breakfast. Friendly
Hostal Los Arcos (☎ 957 48 56 43, fax 957
48 60 11, Calle Romero Barros 14) is fairly
modern and centred on a pretty courtyard.
Rooms cost 2500/4000 ptas; doubles with
attached bathroom cost 5000 ptas.

Pleasant *Hostal Maestre* (☎ 957 47 24
10, fax 957 47 53 95, Calle Romero Barros
16) has 20 clean, spacious rooms with bathroom costing 3000/5000 ptas. *Hostal El
Portillo* (☎ 957 47 20 91, Calle Cabezas 2)
is simple, old-fashioned and friendly with
seven rooms costing 1500/3000 ptas. Tiny
Pensión San Francisco (☎ 957 47 27 16,
Calle de San Fernando 24) has rooms costing 5000 ptas single or double, or 6000 ptas
with private bathroom; English and Dutch
are spoken.

Places to Stay – Mid-Range
Half a block from the Mezquita, *Hotel Los
Omeyas* (☎ 957 49 22 67, fax 957 49 16 59,
Calle Encarnación 17) is only a few years

old but in ve... Comfortable, ... cost 5000/8500... patio and cafe. ... 42, fax 957 4... Herrero 6), faci... Mezquita, offers... rooms costing 5... *Hostal El Triunfo* ... Corregidor Luis de ... /9), facing the
southern side of the Mezquita, has 70 rooms
with air-con and TV costing 5000/8000 ptas
plus IVA, and a restaurant. *Hotel Mezquita*
(☎ 957 47 55 85, fax 957 47 62 19, Plaza
Santa Catalina 1), across the street from
the eastern side of the Mez-quita, offers 21
good rooms at 5150/9850 ptas plus IVA.
It's advisable to book ahead. Farther east,
Hotel Maestre (☎ 957 47 24 10, fax 957 47
53 95, Calle Romero Barros 4) has plain but
bright rooms with attached bathroom for
3800/6500 ptas plus IVA, and garage parking costing 850 ptas a night.

Places to Stay – Top End
The elegant 102-room *Hotel El Conquistador* (☎ 957 48 11 02, fax 957 47 46 77,
Calle Magistral González Francés 15), facing the eastern side of the Mezquita,
has comfortable rooms costing 18,000/
22,000 ptas plus IVA. In the Judería the attractive *Hotel Amistad Córdoba* (☎ 957 42
03 35, Plaza de Maimónides 3), occupying
two modernised mansions, has doubles
costing 18,000 ptas plus IVA (12,500 ptas
plus IVA on some off-peak weekends). The
133-room *Hotel Alfaros* (☎ 957 49 19 20,
Calle Alfaros 18), north of the city centre,
is a good larger place, with doubles costing
17,500 ptas plus IVA.

Córdoba's modern *Parador* (☎ 957 27 59
00, fax 957 28 04 09, @ cordoba@parador
.es, Avenida de la Arruzafa s/n) is 3km
north of the city centre on the site of Abd ar-
Rahman I's summer palace, where Europe's
first palm trees were planted. Rooms cost
14,000/17,500 ptas plus IVA.

Places to Eat
Salmorejo, found on almost every Cordoban menu, is a very thick tomato-based

bits of hard-boiled egg on
e toro (oxtail stew) is another
. Some of the top restaurants fea-
ecipes from Al-Andalus such as garlic
up with raisins, honeyed lamb, fried
aubergine and meats stuffed with dates and
pine nuts. The local wine from nearby Montilla and Moriles is similar to sherry and
made by the same process but without being
fortified. Like sherry, it comes *fino*, *amontillado* or *oloroso* (see Sherry & Manzanilla
in the special section 'Food & Drink' for
details on the different types) and there's
also the sweet Pedro Ximénez variety made
from raisins.

Córdoba prides itself on its *tabernas*,
busy bars where you can usually also sit
down to eat.

There are loads of places to eat right
by the Mezquita, some expensive, some
mediocre and some awful. A few better-
value places are a short walk west into the
Judería. A longer walk east or north will
produce even better options for the budget-
conscious or inquisitive.

Around the Mezquita Tiny *Bar Santos
(Calle Magistral González Francés 3)* is a
fine stop for *bocadillos* (long bread rolls
with fillings; 200 to 300 ptas), tapas
(150 ptas) and *raciones* (meal-sized servings of tapas; 500 ptas). You can have the
excellent *tortilla española* (potato
omelette) in any of the three forms, and
wash it down with inexpensive *sangría* by
the glass. *El Caballo Rojo (Calle Cardenal
Herrero 28)* specialises in Mozarabic food
from caliphal times. The *menú* (fixed-
priced meal) costs 2950 ptas plus IVA and
mains cost from 1300 to 2750 ptas plus
IVA, but you're guaranteed something out
of the ordinary. There's good food too at
*Restaurante Bandolero (Calle de Torrijos
6)*, facing the western side of the Mezquita.
It has *media-raciones* (half-*racións*) from
250 to 1000 ptas and small *platos combinados* (mixed platters) from 975 to
1100 ptas. A la carte, expect to pay 3000 to
4000 ptas for three courses with drinks.
You can sit in the bar, the patio or the
restaurant at the back.

Judería Tasty tapas and raciones are served
by *Casa Pepe de la Judería (Calle Romero
1)* in its bar and in rooms around its
little patio. *Puntillitas* (fried young squid;
700 ptas a media-ración) and *croquetas
caseras* (home-made croquettes; 500 ptas)
are fine choices. The patio and upper floor
comprise a good restaurant with most main
dishes in the 1600 to 2400 ptas range – and
a complimentary glass of Montilla to start
you off. A few doors up the street, comfy
*Restaurante El Rincón de Carmen (Calle
Romero 4)* has a patio with a menú costing
1600 ptas and an attached cafe that does
good snacks and breakfasts. *El Churrasco*
(☎ 957 29 08 19, Calle Romero 16) is one
of Córdoba's top restaurants. The food is
rich, the portions generous and the service
attentive, with prices to match. The menú
costs 3500 ptas; most mains cost 2000 ptas-
plus, though *churrasco* (barbecued) pork
fillet is 1600 ptas and some fish dishes cost
1200 ptas – all plus IVA.

Café Bar Judá Leví on Plaza de Judá
Leví is a pleasant spot for an ice cream, and
does platos combinados from 700 ptas.
Hole-in-the-wall *Casa Elisa (Calle Almanzor 34)* does excellent take-away hot bread
rolls with all sorts of fillings for 150 to
275 ptas.

East of the Mezquita A popular tavern
serving reasonably priced breakfast and
tapas is *Taberna Sociedad de Plateros
(Calle San Francisco 6)*. It is closed Monday. On Calle de San Fernando, a coffee and
tostada (toasted roll) costs 200 ptas at *Bar
Los Naranjos*, platos combinados cost
750 ptas at *Bar San Francisco*, and *Casa
de Comidas La Estupenda* does an 1100-
ptas menú. On pedestrian Calle Enrique
Romero de Torres (a nice place to sit at sunset), with tables outside looking up to Plaza
del Potro, *Bar Callejón* has omelettes, meat
and fish dishes and platos combinados for
500 to 900 ptas, and a three-course menú
with a drink for 1200 ptas. *Taberna El
Potro* next door is a bit more expensive.

The convivial *Taberna Salinas (Calle
Tundidores 3)*, a little farther north, serves
good, inexpensive Cordoban fare – *bacalao*

(salted cod) with bitter oranges makes an interesting change. Other good options include *revuelto de ajetes, gambas y jamón* (scrambled eggs with garlic shoots, prawns and ham) and *chuletas de cordero* (lamb chops). All cost between 675 and 775 ptas. It opens Monday to Saturday for lunch and dinner.

City Centre One of Córdoba's most popular and atmospheric tabernas, going since 1880, is Casa El Pisto, officially *Taberna San Miguel (Plaza San Miguel 1)*. You'll find a good range of tapas (250 to 275 ptas), media-raciones (500 to 1000 ptas) and raciones, and inexpensive Moriles wine ready in jugs on the bar. You can stand at the bar or eat at tables in the back. It opens noon to 4 pm and 8 pm to midnight, Monday to Saturday. A little farther north, *Restaurante Da Vinci (Plaza de Chirinos 6)* does reasonable pizzas and pasta from 600 to 950 ptas, plus more expensive *carnes a la brasa* (grilled meat) and fish. *Pizzaiolo (Calle San Felipe 5)* made the *Guinness Book of Records* for having the world's longest menu (more than 360 dishes always available). It's bright and popular without reaching any great culinary heights – pizza and pasta cost from 600 to 1100 ptas plus IVA.

Entertainment

The magazine *¿Qué hacer en Córdoba?*, given out by the tourist offices, has some what's-on information, as does the daily newspaper *Córdoba*. Posters for live bands appear in music bars, the Albergue Juvenil Córdoba (see Places to Stay) and Punteo music shop on Calle Alfaros. Bands usually start around 10 pm and there's rarely a cover charge.

Most bars in the medieval city close around midnight. *Bodega Guzmán (Calle de los Judíos 7)* is an atmospheric local favourite, with wines from the barrel and bullfight/festival decor. *Casa Salinas*, round the corner on Calle Fernández Ruano, is a cosier alternative. East of the Mezquita, *Taberna Sociedad de Plateros (Calle San Francisco 6)* is popular with

locals and visitors alike (see Places to Eat). There's a fairly good and authentic flamenco show most nights at *Tablao Cardenal (☎ 957 48 33 20, Calle de Torrijos 10)*, opposite the western side of the Mezquita. It starts at 10.30 pm (2800 ptas including one drink).

Córdoba's liveliest bars are mostly scattered around the newer parts of town. *Casa El Pisto* (see City Centre in Places to Eat) is a classic, very popular, traditional taberna. More youthful places start to get going around 11 pm or midnight, but there's little action early in the week. *Soul (Calle Alfonso XIII 3)* attracts a studenty/arty crowd with its good, vanguard music (occasionally live) and stays open to 3 am every night. It's worth passing by nearby bars such as *Velvet Café (Calle Alfaros 29)*, *Milenium (Calle Alfaros 33)* and *Limbo (Calle Juan Rufo 2)* to see what's cooking. Some of them have live bands a couple of nights a week. *La Comuna (Calle del Caño 1)* is another youthful bar worth checking out.

A slightly more mature crowd gathers at *Magister (Calle Morería)*, which brews its own beer on the spot. Five tasty varieties are on offer, at around 250 ptas a glass: the blond *rubia* and *tostada*, the dark *caramelizada* and *morenita*, and the *especial*, which varies from season to season.

After midnight on Friday and Saturday, the happening place to head for is *Surfer Rosa*, a riverbank warehouse in the Recinto Ferial El Arenal (the May fairgrounds). Live bands play frequently, the recorded music is infectious, and admission is often free.

Another busy live band venue is *Level (Calle Antonio Maura 10)* in Ciudad Jardín suburb, west of the city centre. Several lively bars dot nearby Camino de los Sastres.

The *Gran Teatro de Córdoba (☎ 957 48 02 37, Avenida del Gran Capitán 3)*, has a busy program ranging from varied concerts and theatre to dance and film festivals. The *Filmoteca de Andalucía (☎ 957 47 20 18, Calle Medina y Corella 5)*, just west of the Mezquita, regularly shows subtitled foreign films for 150 ptas.

CÓRDOBA PROVINCE

Shopping

Córdoba is known for its embossed leather (*cuero repujado*) products, silver jewellery (particularly filigree) and attractive pottery. Shops selling these and other crafts concentrate around the Mezquita. The best place for embossed leather is Taller Meryam on Calleja de las Flores, a pretty alley just north of the Mezquita. You should be able to find a wallet or pair of slippers for 1500 to 2000 ptas. Attractive boxes start around 2500 ptas. The Zoco on Calle de los Judíos is a group of workshops/showrooms with good but rather pricey crafts on sale.

Plaza de la Corredera has just a few shops selling boots, music and bric-a-brac, but when the square is not covered in building debris it becomes a lively flea market (*mercadillo*) on Saturday morning.

Calle José Cruz Conde is the smartest central shopping street. The excellent El Corte Inglés department store is on Avenida del Gran Capitán.

Getting There & Away

Bus The bus station (☎ 957 40 40 40) is on Plaza de las Tres Culturas behind the train station. Minimum daily services by Alsina Graells (☎ 957 27 81 00) include 10 buses to/from Sevilla (1225 ptas, 1¾ hours), eight to/from Granada (1515 ptas, three hours) and five to/from Málaga (1570 ptas, 2½ hours). Alsina Graells also serves Écija, Carmona, Antequera, Cádiz, Nerja and Almería. Bacoma (☎ 957 27 98 60) runs to Baeza, Úbeda, Valencia and Barcelona. Transportes Ureña (☎ 957 40 45 58) serves Jaén five or more times daily. Secorbus (☎ 902 22 92 92) operates six buses to/from Madrid daily (1600 ptas, 4½ hours).

Autotransportes López y Lisetur (☎ 957 76 70 77) runs to Extremadura and north-western Córdoba province. Autotransportes Ureña (☎ 957 27 81 00) serves central north Córdoba province, Autotransportes San Sebastián (☎ 957 27 67 71) and Autocares Pérez Cubero (☎ 957 68 40 23) go to western Córdoba province, and Empresa Carrera (☎ 957 40 44 14) heads south, with several daily buses to Priego de Córdoba and Cabra, and at least two a day to Zuheros, Rute and Iznájar.

Train Córdoba's modern train station (☎ 957 40 02 02) is on Avenida de América, 1km north-west of Plaza de las Tendillas.

About 20 trains a day run to/from Sevilla, ranging from Andalucía Exprés regional trains (1090 ptas, 1¼ hours) to AVEs (2400 to 2800 ptas in the cheapest class, *turista*, 45 minutes). Options to/from Madrid range from several daily AVEs (6100 to 7200 ptas in turista, 1¾ hours) to a middle-of-the-night Estrella (3700 ptas in a seat, 6¼ hours).

Several trains head to Málaga daily (2000 to 2800 ptas, two to three hours), Cádiz and Barcelona, and one or two each to Jaén, Huelva and Fuengirola. For Granada (1900 ptas, four hours), you need to change at Bobadilla.

Car Rental firms include Avis (☎ 957 47 68 62) at Plaza de Colón 32, and Europcar (☎ 957 40 34 80) and Hertz (☎ 957 40 20 60) at the train station.

Getting Around

Bus City buses cost 115 ptas. Bus No 3 from the street between the train and bus stations runs to Plaza de las Tendillas and down Calle de San Fernando, 300m east of the Mezquita. For the return trip, pick it up on Ronda de Isasa, just south of the Mezquita, or Avenida Doctor Fleming.

Car & Motorcycle Córdoba's one-way system is nightmarish, and parking in the old city can be tough. But the routes to many hotels and hostales are fairly well signposted, and the signs display a 'P' if the establishment has parking.

Taxi In the city centre, cabs congregate at the north-eastern corner of Plaza de las Tendillas. The fare from the train or bus station to the Mezquita is around 600 ptas.

AROUND CÓRDOBA
Medina Azahara

In 936 Abd ar-Rahman III decided his new caliphate needed a new capital, and duly had one built 8km west of Córdoba at the foot of the Sierra Morena. Records state that 10,000 labourers worked on its construction, setting 6000 stone blocks a day, and by 945 the caliph was able to install himself and his retinue. Stretching 1.5km from east to west and 700m from north to south, the new city was called Medina Azahara, or Madinat al-Zahra, after Abd ar-Rahman's wife Azahara. It was undoubtedly a magnificent place, though the chronicler who wrote that the fish in its ponds ate 12,000 loaves of bread a day should no doubt be taken with a pinch of salt.

Medina Azahara's glory was short-lived. Al-Mansour transferred the seat of government to a new palace-complex of his own, east of the city, in 981. Then, between 1010 and 1013, Medina Azahara was wrecked by Berber soldiers who occupied it during the anarchic collapse of the caliphate. Over succeeding centuries its ruins were plundered repeatedly for building material.

Though less than one-tenth of the city has been excavated, and what's open to visitors is only about a quarter of that, Medina Azahara (☎ 957 32 91 30) is still intriguing and its country location adds to the appeal.

The visitor route takes you down through the city's original northern gate to the **Dar al-Wuzara** (House of the Viziers), a partly-restored building which would have been used by the caliphs' administrative advisers. It has several horseshoe arches and is fronted by a square garden. Down to the east from here is a **portico**, a row of arches in red and white stripes similar to the Córdoba Mezquita, which fronted a military parade ground. From here your path leads downhill, with views over Medina Azahara's ruined caliphal **mosque**, to the most impressive building on the site, the much-restored **Salón de Abd ar-Rahman III**, facing a large garden. This was the caliphs' throne hall, a three-aisled affair with beautiful horseshoe arching. Its floral, geometric and calligraphic stone carving (still being pieced back together) was of a lavishness unprecedented in the Islamic world. Richard Fletcher writes in *Moorish Spain* that in the centre of the hall stood a bowl containing mercury: when the caliph wished to impress visitors, he would have a

slave rock the bowl so that reflected light flashed around the hall like lightning.

Medina Azahara opens 10 am to 2 pm and 6 to 8.30 pm (4 to 6.30 pm from October to April) Tuesday to Saturday, and 10 am to 2 pm (1.30 pm from mid-June to end-September) Sunday. Admission is free with an EU passport, 250 ptas otherwise.

Getting There & Away The nearest you can get by bus is the Cruce de Medina Azahara, the turnoff from the A-431, from which it's a 3km slightly uphill walk to the site. City bus No 0-1 will drop you at the *cruce*. At the time of writing this departed the northern end of Avenida de la República Argentina at 9.40 and 11.20 am and 1, 2, 3.20 and 6 pm daily.

A taxi costs 3900 ptas for the return trip, with one hour's waiting.

Córdoba Vision runs tours to Medina Azahara twice daily, except Sunday afternoon and Monday, for 2500 ptas – you can book at many hotels and agencies around town or by calling ☎ 957 23 17 34.

If you're driving, take Avenida de Medina Azahara west from the city centre, leading out onto the A-431. The Medina Azahara turnoff is signposted 5km from the city centre.

NORTH OF CÓRDOBA
The Sierra Morena rises sharply just north of Córdoba city then rolls fairly gently over most of the north of the province.

Los Pedroches
You can have an interesting day or two poking around Los Pedroches, the province's northernmost district, between Belalcázar in the north-west and Cardeña in the north-east. Buses reach most of its villages from Córdoba, but to tour freely you need your own wheels.

Los Pedroches is especially appealing in spring. As close in atmosphere to neighbouring Castilla-La Mancha as to Andalucía, it's a sparsely populated area of scattered granite-built settlements, occasional rocky outcrops and large expanses of woodland pasture *(dehesa)*. (The AVE train

CÓRDOBA PROVINCE

line passes through some of the finest dehesas, near Villanueva de Córdoba.) White storks nest precariously on church towers, castles and many other upward protuberances around the district.

Two essential places to head for are the castles at Belalcázar and Santa Eufemia. Both villages have simple, inexpensive hostales. The Castillo de los Sotomayor looming over remote **Belalcázar** is one of the spookiest fortifications in Andalucía. It was built in the 15th century on the site of an old Muslim fort by Gutierre de Sotomayor, master of the Knights of Calatrava, a Reconquista (Reconquest) crusading order which controlled a huge swath of territory from Córdoba to Toledo and Badajoz. Even the Renaissance palace that one of Gutierre's descendants tacked onto the castle later is dwarfed by the huge, top-heavy keep which dominates the edifice.

To reach the castle from the village you must go down a cobbled lane, past a grandiose 16th-century water trough and a shack labelled 'Disco Pub Nomada', across an old stone bridge, and past a gate enclosing viciously snarling dogs and a sign announcing that the olive grove around the castle has been treated with poison. When you finally reach the castle (by a path avoiding the olive grove), you find that all its entrances are concreted up – but this only adds to the Romantic effect, and makes it all the more secure for the storks, rooks and pigeons that call it home.

Santa Eufemia, 26km east of Belalcázar across empty countryside, is Andalucía's northernmost village. The Castillo de Miramontes, originally Muslim, on a crag above it to the north, is a tumbled ruin but the 360° views from it are stupendous. To reach the castle turn west off the N-502 main road at Hostal La Paloma in the village, and after 1km turn right at the 'Camino Servicio RTVE' sign, from which it's a 1.5km uphill drive to the castle.

The eastern end of Los Pedroches is occupied by the **Parque Natural Sierra de Cardeña y Montoro**, a hilly, wooded area that is one of the last Andalucian redoubts of the wolf and lynx. There's a tourist office

(☎ 957 17 43 70) at Calle Miguel Gallo 33 in Cardeña village, and cottage accommodation and camping space at Aldea Cerezo (☎ 957 17 43 70), 7km east, where a number of walking routes converge.

Montoro

This old town, off the N-IV south of Cardeña, is one of the prettiest in the province, rising above a bend of the Río Guadalquivir. It's well worth a wander if you're not in a hurry: the tourist office (☎ 957 16 00 89) on the central Plaza de España will point you in the right directions.

WEST OF CÓRDOBA

Twenty-five kilometres down the Guadalquivir valley from Córdoba, **Almodóvar del Río** is crowned by an impressive eight-towered castle (☎ 957 63 51 16), visible from far away. The castle was founded in 740 but owes most of its present appearance to post-Reconquista rebuilding. Pedro I (the Cruel) used it as a treasure store. It has never been taken by force of arms. It opens 11 am to 6 pm daily (donation).

North-west of Almodóvar, the **Parque Natural Sierra de Hornachuelos** is 672-sq-km of hilly, wooded Sierra Morena country with some pretty river valleys. It's renowned for its populations of vultures, eagles and other raptors, and for large numbers of red deer and wild boar, which attract many hunters. The Centro de Visitantes Huerta del Rey (☎ 957 64 11 40), 1.5km north-west of Hornachuelos town on the road to San Calixto, is the focus of a network of walking trails of varied lengths. Hornachuelos town has two hostales.

TOWARDS MÁLAGA

The N-331 to Antequera and Málaga crosses mainly unspectacular, rolling agricultural country known as La Campiña. **Montilla**, 45km from Córdoba, is the main production centre for Córdoba's sherry-like wines. You can visit Bodegas Alvear (☎ 957 65 01 00) at Avenida María Auxiliadora 1, but you should call first to book. Montilla has several hotels and hostales.

Farther south, **Lucena** is an industrial

town with many furniture, wrought iron and lighting showrooms lining the N-331.

LA SUBBÉTICA

The south of Córdoba province straddled the Muslim-Christian frontier from the 13th to 15th centuries and many towns and villages are crowned by castles. The beautiful, mountainous south-east is known as La Subbética after the Sistema Subbético range which crosses this corner of the province. The mountains, canyons and wooded valleys of the 316 sq km Parque Natural Sierras Subbéticas offer some enjoyable walks (the CNIG 1:50,000 map *Parque Natural Sierras Subbéticas* is useful). The park's **Centro de Visitantes Santa Rita** (☎ 957 33 40 34) is located, not very conveniently, 10km east of Cabra on the A-340.

Zuheros & Around

postcode 14870 • pop 950
• elevation 625m

Rising above a sea of olive trees south of the N-432, Zuheros is a beautiful base for exploring the region. Tourist information is available from Turismo Zuheros (☎ 957 69 47 75), or from an occasionally open park information point (☎ 957 33 52 55) a few hundred metres up the road towards the Cueva de los Murciélagos.

Zuheros' **castle**, of Muslim origin, sits perched at one end of the village against a background of surreally picturesque crags. Near the castle are a church that was once a mosque, and an archaeological museum. The castle and museum can be visited by guided tour hourly from 12.30 to 2.30 pm and 6.30 to 8.30 pm (4.30 to 6.30 pm from 15 September to 15 April) on Saturday, Sunday and holidays except in July (215 ptas). A 4km drive up the mountain behind the village is the **Cueva de los Murciélagos** (Cave of the Bats), which was inhabited by Neanderthals more than 35,000 years ago. It's renowned for its rock paintings of goats and people from Neolithic times (6000–2000 BC). Guided visits take place at 11 am and 12.30, 2, 6 and 7.30 pm on Saturday, Sunday and holidays (550 ptas), up to a maximum of 150 people

a day. In July visits are only at noon and 7 pm, and from 15 September to 15 April the last two visits are at 4.30 and 6 pm.

The good *Hotel Zuhayra* (☎ 957 69 46 93, Calle Mirador 10) has singles/ doubles with private bathroom for 4600/ 6200 ptas plus IVA and can provide information on walking routes. You can eat at the hotel restaurant or at the medium-priced *Mesón Los Palancos*, which has a superbly situated terrace just below the castle.

Ermita de la Virgen de la Sierra

This hilltop chapel atop El Picacho (1217m), a 15km drive east of the humdrum town of Cabra, offers great panoramas and attracts numerous festive pilgrimages *(romerías)* including the celebrated Romería de los Gitanos on a Sunday in mid-June, when *gitanos* (Roma people) and others from around Spain gather to honour the Virgen de la Sierra – and sing, play and dance a great deal of flamenco. In Cabra, *Fonda Guerrero* (☎ 957 52 05 07, Calle Pepita Jiménez 7) has simple doubles with bathroom for 3900 ptas.

Priego de Córdoba

postcode 14800 • pop 22,000
• elevation 650m

This sizeable town is another possible base for exploring the mountain range. Two of the province's highest peaks, 1570m La Tiñosa and 1476m Bermejo, rise to the south-west. Priego is blessed with a series of outstanding baroque churches, built in the 18th century when the town enjoyed a textiles boom. The very helpful tourist office (☎ 957 90 06 25) at Calle del Río 33, a short walk south of the central Plaza de la Constitución, opens 9 am to 1 pm Tuesday to Sunday. Outside those hours you can call at Calle Real 46, the house of the office's energetic chief, José Mateo Aguilera, for information.

Priego's churches are normally open 10 am to 1 pm daily.

Things to See The highlight church is the 16th-century **Parroquia de la Asunción** on Plaza de Abad Palomino, 200m north-east of Plaza de la Constitución. The main part

CÓRDOBA PROVINCE

of the church is ornate enough but the Sagrario chapel is one of the supreme works of Andalucian baroque, an amazingly lavish confection of white stucco and sculpture with a beautiful windowed dome. Behind La Asunción are the winding streets of the old Muslim quarter, the **Barrio de La Villa**, where Andalucía's love affair with potted geraniums reaches its ultimate expression on beautiful Calle Real.

Other sumptuous baroque churches include the **Iglesia de San Pedro** on Plaza San Pedro, the **Ermita de la Aurora** on Carrera de Álvarez, and the **Iglesia de San Francisco** on Calle Buen Suceso.

Don't miss the **Fuente del Rey** at the end of Calle del Río, a wonderfully elegant 1780s fountain which would be more at home in the gardens of Versailles than a small town in provincial Andalucía. Water flows from 139 spouts – the upper ones in the form of grotesque stone faces – into three curvaceous pools adorned with classical sculpture.

Also worth a visit is the **Museo Histórico** at Carrera de las Monjas 16, just west of Plaza de la Constitución – open 10 am to 2 pm and 5 to 9 pm Tuesday to Friday, and 11 am to 3 pm Saturday and Sunday.

Places to Stay & Eat Just east of Plaza de la Constitución, *Hostal Rafi* (☎ 957 54 07 49, Calle Isabel La Católica 4) has good doubles with bathroom costing 4300 ptas plus IVA. *Hostal Andalucía* (☎ 957 54 01

74, Calle del Río 13), also central, has basic doubles with bathroom for 3500 ptas or with a shared bathroom for 2800 ptas. The *Río Piscina* (☎ 957 70 01 86, Carretera Monturque-Alcalá La Real Km 44) is down on the eastern edge of town, with doubles costing 6200 ptas plus IVA, and a pool. The modern but Muslim-style *Villa Turística de Priego* (☎ 957 70 35 03), 7km north on the road to Zagrilla, offers self-catering apartments, costing around 9000 ptas for two people. It has a pool and a restaurant.

There are cafes around Plaza de la Constitución and the streets to its east, or you could try *El Aljibe* restaurant by the Parroquia de la Asunción.

Getting There & Away Priego's bus station is about 1km west of Plaza de la Constitución on Calle Nuestra Señora de los Remedios, off Calle San Marcos. Up to 12 buses run to/from Córdoba daily, two or more to Granada and others to Cabra and elsewhere.

South of Priego
The A-333 winds south from Priego – take the road signed 'Lagunillas, Rute' off the Loja road leaving the town centre – towards the A-92 Granada–Sevilla highway, through handsome olive-growing hill country. Iznájar, 26km from Priego, overlooks the Embalse de Iznájar reservoir from an imposing crag topped by a Muslim castle and a 16th-century church.

Granada Province

As well as the world-famous city of Granada, this eastern province includes Andalucía's highest mountains (in the Sierra Nevada) and the beautiful Las Alpujarras valleys to their south.

GRANADA
postcode 18080 • pop 241,000
• elevation 685m

At first, modern Granada, with its traffic fumes and high-rise apartment blocks, seems a disappointing world away from its Muslim past. However, the Alhambra, dominating the skyline from its hilltop perch, and the fascinating Albayzín, the old Islamic quarter which also rises above the modern city, are highlights of a visit to Andalucía.

The city has more to offer. Its setting, with the backdrop of the often snow-clad Sierra Nevada, is magnificent; its greenness is a delight in often-parched Andalucía, and its climate pleasant, especially in spring and autumn. Granada also has some impressive and historic post-Reconquista (Reconquest) buildings and, thanks to its university, a vibrant youthful population, a buzzing cultural life, some excellent bars and a hopping nightlife.

Granada is a wealthy city with an international feel. In tandem with this wealth subsists an underclass: you'll see quite a few beggars.

History

An Iberian tribe, the Túrdulos, settled here in the 5th century BC. The Romans arrived late in the 3rd century BC, settled in the vicinity of the Alcazaba (part of the Alhambra) and Albayzín, and called their town Illiberis. The Visigoths built city walls and laid the foundations of the Alcazaba. Muslim forces, with the help of the city's Jews, took the city in 711. It was ruled from Córdoba until 1031 and later from Sevilla by the Almoravids and then the Almohads. The Islamic city came to be called Karnattah, from which 'Granada' is derived (*granada* also

Highlights

- Admire the Alhambra and Generalife, the beautiful, legendary palace and gardens of Spain's last Muslim dynasty
- Explore the Albayzín, Granada's warren-like old Islamic quarter, with sunset views of the Alhambra
- Head for Granada's Capilla Real, burial place of the Catholic Monarchs
- Sample Granada's nightlife
- Walk in the beautiful, mysterious Las Alpujarras valleys and the snow-capped Sierra Nevada

JAÉN

CÓRDOBA

Granada pp318-19
Central Granada p320
Alhambra p323

ALMERÍA

MÁLAGA

happens to be the Spanish for pomegranate, the fruit which is on the city's coat of arms)

After the fall of Córdoba (1236) and Sevilla (1248) to Christian Castile, Muslims sought refuge in Granada, where the founder of the Nasrid dynasty, Mohammed ibn Yousouf ibn Nasr (also called Mohammed al-Ahmar), had recently established an independent emirate. Stretching from the Strait of Gibraltar to east of Almería, this emirate became the final remnant of Al-Andalus (the Muslim-controlled parts of the Iberian Peninsula), ruled by the Nasrids from the lavish Alhambra palace for 250 years. The Nasrids actually helped Fernando III take Sevilla and paid tribute to Castile from this time until 1476. Throughout their rule they played Castile and Aragón (the peninsula's

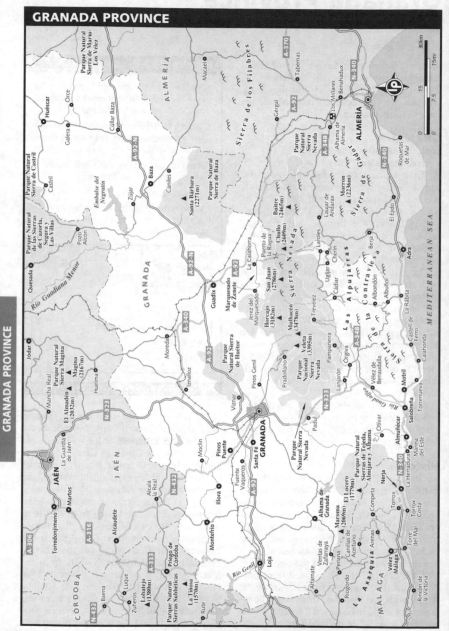

GRANADA PROVINCE

other main Christian state) off against each other, at times also seeking assistance from the Merenid rulers of Morocco.

Granada became one of the richest and most populous cities in medieval Europe, flourishing on the talents of its big population of traders and artisans. Two centuries of artistic and scientific splendour peaked under Yousouf I and Mohammed V in the 14th century.

But by the late 15th century the economy had stagnated, the rulers led a life of hedonism inside the Alhambra and violent rivalry developed over the succession. One faction supported the emir, Abu al-Hasan, and his harem favourite, Zoraya (actually a Christian from the north). The other faction backed Boabdil, Abu al-Hasan's son by his wife Aixa. In 1482 Boabdil rebelled, setting off a confused civil war. The Christian armies which invaded the Granada emirate that year took full advantage. The scene had been set for war by Abu al-Hasan's refusal to pay tribute to Castile from 1476, and the unification of Castile and Aragón through the marriage of Isabel and Fernando.

Capturing Boabdil in 1483, the Catholic Monarchs extracted from him a promise to surrender much of the emirate if they would help him regain Granada. Following Abu al-Hasan's death in 1485, Boabdil won control of the city. The Christians pushed across the rest of the emirate, besieging towns and devastating the countryside, and in 1491 they finally laid siege to Granada from the newly built town of Santa Fé.

After eight months Boabdil agreed to surrender the city in return for the Alpujarras valleys, 30,000 gold coins plus political and religious freedom for his subjects. To forestall trouble from hawkish factions in the city he allowed Castilian troops into the Alhambra on the night of 1–2 January 1492. The next day Isabel and Fernando entered the city ceremonially in Muslim dress. They set up court in the Alhambra for several years.

Under Isabel and Fernando, Granada became a dynamic Castilian city, but religious persecution soured the scene. Jews were expelled from Spain soon after the city's conquest and persecution of Muslims led to

revolts across the former emirate and finally their expulsion in the early 17th century.

By the early 17th century, Granada, having lost much of its talented populace, had fallen into a decline that was only arrested by the interest drummed up by the Romantic movement in the 1830s. This set the stage for the restoration of Granada's Islamic heritage and the arrival of tourism. Many historic buildings were, however, torn down to make way for wide thoroughfares.

Early 20th-century Granada frowned on liberalism, leading to the horrors unleashed after the Nationalists took the city at the start of the civil war in 1936. An estimated 4000 *granadinos* with left or liberal connections were killed, among them Federico García Lorca, Granada's and Andalucía's most famous writer. Granada still has a reputation for conservatism.

Orientation

The city's two main streets, Gran Vía de Colón and Calle Reyes Católicos, meet at Plaza Isabel La Católica. North-east of here, Calle Reyes Católicos passes through Plaza Nueva to Plaza Santa Ana, from where Carrera del Darro leads up to the Albayzín. To the south, Calle Reyes Católicos extends to Puerta Real, Granada's main square. From here, Acera del Darro heads south-east across the Río Genil.

The Alhambra, atop the hill north-east of the centre, overlooks Carrera del Darro and the Albayzín. Cuesta de Gomérez leads up to the Alhambra from Plaza Nueva.

Most major sights are within walking distance of the city centre though there are buses if you get fed up with walking uphill. The bus station (north-west) and train station (west) are out of the city centre but linked to it by plenty of buses.

Information

Tourist Offices Granada's provincial tourist office (☎ 958 22 66 88) is on Plaza de Mariana Pineda, east of Puerta Real. The helpful staff have free information on Granada and the province. It opens 9.30 am to 7 pm Monday to Friday, 10 am to 2 pm Saturday. The Junta de Andalucía has a more central tourist

GRANADA PROVINCE

office (☎ 958 22 59 90) in the Corral del Carbón on Calle Mariana Pineda. City maps cost 100 ptas. Bus and train information is posted in an adjacent room. Hours are 9 am to 7 pm Monday to Saturday, 10 am to 2 pm Sunday. There are also two tourist offices in the Alhambra complex that open 9 am to 4 pm Monday to Friday and 10 am to 2 pm on Saturday; they are not open during night visits to the Alhambra or on Sunday.

Money   There are several banks with ATMs on Gran Vía de Colón, Plaza Isabel La Católica and Calle Reyes Católicos. American Express (☎ 958 22 45 12) is at Calle Reyes Católicos 31.

Post & Communications   The main post office is at Puerta Real s/n.

Net (☎ 958 22 69 19), Calle Santa Escolástica 13, is one of many places offering public Internet access. It costs 200 ptas an hour. Hours are 9 am to 11 pm Monday to Saturday, 4 pm to 11 pm Sunday.

Internet Resources   Two Web sites worth checking out are:

Guía de Granada
www.moebius.es/ggranada
Granada en la Red
This site provides links to several good Granada sites, in English and Spanish; includes on-line bookshop with Granada-related titles.
http://granadainfo.com

Travel Agencies   The student/youth travel agency usit Unlimited is at Calle Las Navas 29.

Bookshops   Some books in English are available from Librería Urbano at Calle Tablas 6, south-west off Plaza de la Trinidad, and Librería Continental on Puerta Real. A good map and guidebook shop is Cartográfica del Sur (☎ 958 20 49 01), Calle Valle Inclán 2, just off Camino de Ronda.

Laundry   Lavandería Duquesa, Calle Duquesa 24, is a friendly place charging around 1100 ptas to wash and dry a bag of clothes.

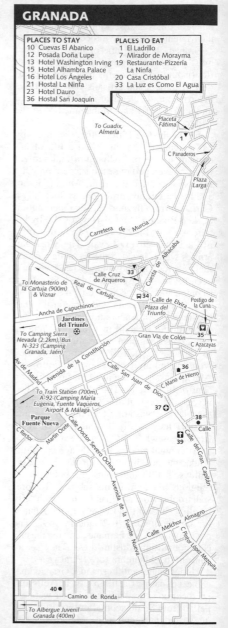

GRANADA

PLACES TO STAY
10 Cuevas El Abanico
12 Posada Doña Lupe
13 Hotel Washington Irving
15 Hotel Alhambra Palace
16 Hotel Los Ángeles
21 Hostal La Ninfa
23 Hotel Dauro
36 Hostal San Joaquín

PLACES TO EAT
1 El Ladrillo
7 Mirador de Morayma
19 Restaurante-Pizzería La Ninfa
20 Casa Cristóbal
33 La Luz es Como El Agua

GRANADA PROVINCE

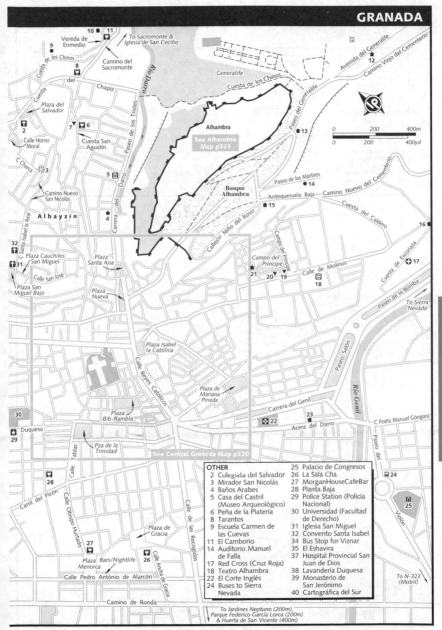

GRANADA

10 11
Vereda de Enmedio
9 To Sacromonte &
Iglesia de San Cecilio
Cuesta de los Chinos
Camino del Sacromonte
8
del
Chapiz
Río Darro
Generalife
Cuesta de los Chinos
Avenida del Generalife
Camino Viejo del Cementerio
12

Cuesta
Plaza del Salvador
Paseo de los Tristes
Alhambra
Paseo del Generalife

2
Calle Horno Moral
7 6
Cuesta San Agustín
See Alhambra Map p323
13

0   200   400m
0   200   400yd

C Charca 3
Darro
5
Paseo de los Mártires
14

Camino Nuevo San Nicolás
del
Bosque Alhambra
Paseo de los Mártires
Camino Nuevo del Cementerio

Albayzín
4
Carrera
Antequeruela Baja
15
Cuesta del Caldero

Calle Santa Isabel la Real
32
31
Plaza Cauchiles San Miguel
Plaza Santa Ana
Callejón Niño del Rollo
Campo del Príncipe
16

Calle San José
Plaza San Miguel Bajo
Plaza Nueva
21
20 19
Calle de Molinos
18
Cuesta de Escoriaza
17
Paseo de la Bomba
To Sierra Nevada

Plaza Isabel la Católica
Calle Reyes Católicos
Plaza de Mariana Pineda
Paseo Salón
Río Genil
GRANADA PROVINCE

30
Duquesa
29
Plaza Bib-Rambla
Plaza de la Trinidad
Tablas
Plaza de Gracia
Carrera del Genil
23
22
Acera del Darro
C Poeta Manuel Góngora
Paseo del

See Central Granada Map p320

28
Carril del Picón
Calle Obispo Hurtado
Calle de los Recogidas
Plaza de Gracia
24
25
Violón

27
Plaza de Menorca
Bars/Nightlife
26
Calle Ancha de Gracia
To N-323 (Motril)
Calle Pedro António de Alarcón
Camino de Ronda

To Jardines Neptuno (200m),
Parque Federico García Lorca (200m)
& Huerta de San Vicente (400m)

OTHER	
2 Colegiata del Salvador	25 Palacio de Congresos
3 Mirador San Nicolás	26 La Sala Cha
4 Baños Arabes	27 MorganHouseCafeBar
5 Casa del Castril (Museo Arqueológico)	28 Planta Baja
	29 Police Station (Policía Nacional)
6 Peña de la Platería	30 Universidad (Facultad de Derecho)
8 Tarantos	
9 Escuela Carmen de las Cuevas	31 Iglesia San Miguel
11 El Camborio	32 Convento Santa Isabel
14 Auditorio Manuel de Falla	34 Bus Stop for Viznar
	35 El Eshavira
17 Red Cross (Cruz Roja)	37 Hospital Provincial San Juan de Dios
18 Teatro Alhambra	38 Lavandería Duquesa
22 El Corte Inglés	39 Monasterio de San Jerónimo
24 Buses to Sierra Nevada	40 Cartográfica del Sur

CENTRAL GRANADA

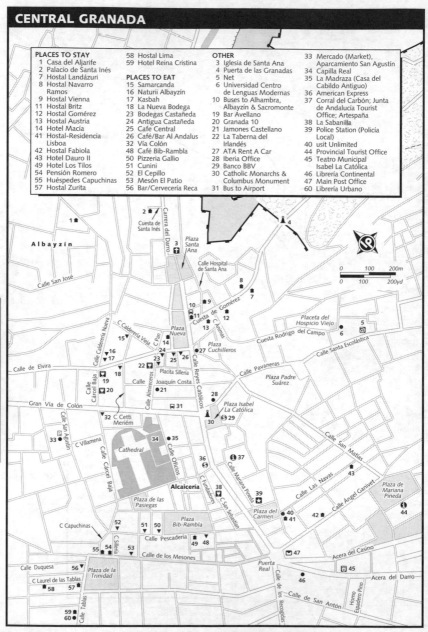

PLACES TO STAY
1 Casa del Aljarife
2 Palacio de Santa Inés
7 Hostal Landázuri
8 Hostal Navarro Ramos
9 Hostal Vienna
11 Hostal Britz
12 Hostal Gomérez
13 Hostal Austria
14 Hotel Macía
41 Hostal-Residencia Lisboa
42 Hostal Fabiola
43 Hotel Dauro II
49 Hotel Los Tilos
54 Pensión Romero
55 Huéspedes Capuchinas
57 Hostal Zurita
58 Hostal Lima
59 Hotel Reina Cristina

PLACES TO EAT
15 Samarcanda
16 Naturii Albayzín
17 Kasbah
18 La Nueva Bodega
23 Bodegas Castañeda
24 Antigua Castañeda
25 Cafe Central
26 Café/Bar Al Andalus
32 Vía Colón
48 Café Bib-Rambla
50 Pizzeria Gallio
51 Cunini
52 El Cepillo
53 Mesón El Patio
56 Bar/Cervecería Reca

OTHER
3 Iglesia de Santa Ana
4 Puerta de las Granadas
5 Net
6 Universidad Centro de Lenguas Modernas
10 Buses to Alhambra, Albayzín & Sacromonte
19 Bar Avellano
20 Granada 10
21 Jamones Castellano
22 La Taberna del Irlandés
27 ATA Rent A Car
28 Iberia Office
29 Banco BBV
30 Catholic Monarchs & Columbus Monument
31 Bus to Airport
33 Mercado (Market), Aparcamiento San Agustín
34 Capilla Real
35 La Madraza (Casa del Cabildo Antiguo)
36 American Express
37 Corral del Carbón; Junta de Andalucía Tourist Office; Artespaña
38 La Sabanilla
39 Police Station (Policía Local)
40 usit Unlimited
44 Provincial Tourist Office
45 Teatro Municipal Isabel La Católica
46 Librería Continental
47 Main Post Office
60 Librería Urbano

Medical Services & Emergency For urgent medical help, the Cruz Roja (Red Cross; ☎ 958 22 22 22) is at Cuesta de Escoriaza 8, near Paseo de la Bomba and the Río Genil. The Hospital Provincial San Juan de Dios (☎ 958 24 17 24) is fairly central at Calle San Juan de Dios 15.

The Policía Local (☎ 958 29 35 01) station is at Plaza del Carmen 5. The Policía Nacional (☎ 958 27 83 00) station is at Calle Duquesa 15.

Alhambra & Generalife

Nothing can prepare you for the delights of the Alhambra. Perched on top of the hill known as La Sabika, this monument is the stuff of fairy-tales. It may initially disappoint with its simple, unadorned red fortress towers and walls, though its Sierra Nevada backdrop and the cypress and elms among which it nestles are undeniably magnificent. Inside the marvellously decorated Palacio Nazaries (Nasrid Palace) and the Generalife (the Alhambra's gardens), you're in for a treat. Water is an art form in both places and even around the exterior of the Alhambra the sound of running water and the greenness contribute to a sense of calm – a world away from the bustle of the city and the general dryness of much of Spain.

This tranquillity can be completely shattered by the hordes of tourists who traipse through (an average of 6000 a day), so it's a good idea to visit first thing in the morning, late in the afternoon or – a magical experience – at night. (Note that only the major rooms of the Palacio Nazaries are open for night visits.)

The Alhambra proper has two main parts, the Alcazaba (Fortress) and the Palacio Nazaries. Also within it is the Palacio de Carlos V, the Iglesia de Santa María de la Alhambra, two hotels and a few restaurants (see under Places to Stay/Eat for details), souvenir shops and refreshment stalls. The Generalife is a short walk to the east.

History The Alhambra, from the Arabic *al-qala' at al-hamra* (red castle), began life as a fortress as early as the 9th century. The Nasrids of the 13th and 14th centuries turned it into a fortress-palace complex adjoined by a small city *(medina)*, of which nothing remains. The founder of the Nasrid dynasty, Mohammed ibn Yousouf ibn Nasr, set up home on the hill top, restoring and expanding the Alcazaba. His 14th-century successors, Yousouf I and Mohammed V, built the Palacio Nazaries: Mohammed V was responsible for much of the palace's decoration.

In 1492 the Catholic Monarchs moved into the Palacio Nazaries after their conquest of Granada. They appointed a Muslim to restore the decoration of the Palacio Nazaries and in time the palace mosque was replaced with a church and the Convento de San Francisco was built (now the Parador San Francisco; see under Places to Stay for details). Carlos I, grandson of the Catholic Monarchs, had a wing of the Palacio Nazaries destroyed to make space for a huge Renaissance palace, the Palacio de Carlos V (using Carlos' title as Holy Roman Emperor).

In the 18th century the Alhambra was abandoned to thieves and beggars and during the Napoleonic occupation it was used as a barracks and narrowly escaped being blown up. In 1870 it was declared a national monument as a result of the huge interest taken in it by Romantic writers such as Washington Irving, who wrote his wonderful *Tales of the Alhambra*, a great book to read while you're in Granada, in his study in some palace rooms during his stay in the 1820s. Since then it has been salvaged and heavily restored.

Admission To avoid queuing to visit the Alhambra and possible disappointment (the 8000 tickets allotted for each day can go quickly), it's advisable to book ahead, especially for visits between May and October. This you can do by calling ☎ 902 22 44 60 between 9 am and 6 pm (from outside Spain, precede the number with your international access code and Spain's country code, 34); or at any branch of Banco BBV, which has branches in Granada and many Spanish cities. In addition to the regular ticket price (1000 ptas for adults), you must pay a 125 ptas booking fee, and if you book

euro currency converter €1 = 166 ptas

by phone you must pay by Visa or Master-Card. Tickets booked by phone can be picked up at a Banco BBV branch or at the Alhambra ticket office. Any tickets available for same-day visits are sold at the Alhambra ticket office and, from 9 am to 2 pm Monday to Friday, at Banco BBV on Plaza Isabel la Católica in central Granada – but you face the prospect of queues and cannot rely on any tickets being available, especially from May to October.

Tickets are stamped with a half-hour time slot and you must enter the Palacio Nazaries within this time, though you can spend as long as you like once there. If you buy your ticket on the day of your visit, the time slot may be several hours after the time of your purchase (though in mid-winter it will probably be almost immediately). Waiting is little hardship, however, as you can visit the other parts of the complex beforehand.

The Alhambra and Generalife are open 8.30 am to 8 pm daily (to 6 pm, October to March). The Palacio Nazaries is also open 10 to 11.30 pm Tuesday to Saturday (8 to 9.30 pm Friday and Saturday, October to March). Admission costs 1000 ptas (free for disabled people and children under eight).

Ticketing arrangements change from time to time as the authorities strive to cope with the huge numbers of visitors. You may soon be able to book on-line.

Getting There & Around The Alhambra Bus from Plaza Nueva (120 ptas, every 10 minutes from 7.45 am to 10 pm) heads up Cuesta de Gomérez to the Alhambra ticket office at the eastern end of the complex, and returns to Plaza Nueva where there are also buses for the Albayzín and Sacromonte. Bus No 32 runs between the Alhambra ticket office and the Albayzín.

Walking up Cuesta de Gomérez from Plaza Nueva you soon reach the **Puerta de las Granadas** (Gate of the Pomegranates), a solid gateway with three carved stone pomegranates, built by Carlos I. Above the gate is the Bosque Alhambra (woods). If you already have your ticket, you can take a path up to the left, passing a beautiful Renaissance fountain, and enter the Alhambra

by the austere **Puerta de la Justicia** (Gate of Justice), constructed by Yousouf I in 1348 as the Alhambra's main entrance. From the gate, a passage leads to Plaza de los Aljibes, where there is a tourist office.

The ticket office (and another tourist office) are at the far (eastern) end of the complex, adjacent to the Alhambra car parks, 1km from the Puerta de las Granadas. To reach them, ignore the path up to the Puerta de la Justicia and continue ahead outside the Alhambra walls.

Audio guides in at least English, Spanish, French and Italian can be hired (500 ptas) at either of the two tourist offices in the complex.

Alcazaba What remains of the Alcazaba are the ramparts and several towers, the most important and tallest being the Torre de la Vela (watchtower). Here, a narrow, winding staircase leads to the top terrace which has splendid views of the city and surrounds. The cross and banners of the Reconquista were raised here in January 1492. The tower's bell rings on festive occasions only, but in the past it tolled to control the irrigation system of the Vega, the plain on which Granada stands.

Palacio Nazaries This is what all the fuss is about. The Nasrid Palace (also called the Casa Real or Royal House), with its fine knotted wooden ceilings, elaborate honeycomb vaulting, intricately carved stucco walls and beautifully proportioned rooms and courtyards, stands in marked contrast to the austere walls and towers of the Alcazaba. Arab inscriptions recur in the stucco work. Routes through the palace sometimes change from what follows, depending on restoration work.

Mexuar These rooms, through which you normally enter the palace, date from the 14th century and were used for bureaucratic and judicial purposes. The general public would not have been allowed beyond them. The first room, the council chamber, has been much altered and contains both Muslim and Christian motifs. At its far end is a

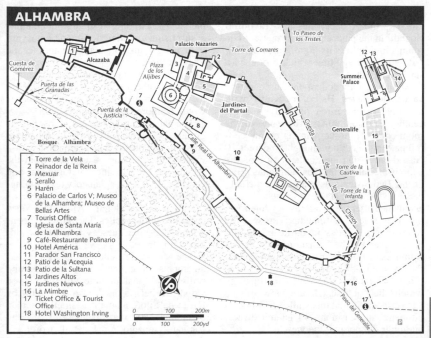

ALHAMBRA

1 Torre de la Vela
2 Peinador de la Reina
3 Mexuar
4 Serallo
5 Harén
6 Palacio de Carlos V; Museo de la Alhambra; Museo de Bellas Artes
7 Tourist Office
8 Iglesia de Santa María de la Alhambra
9 Café-Restaurante Polinario
10 Hotel América
11 Parador San Francisco
12 Patio de la Acequia
13 Patio de la Sultana
14 Jardines Altos
15 Jardines Nuevos
16 La Mimbre
17 Ticket Office & Tourist Office
18 Hotel Washington Irving

small, lavishly decorated room (originally a prayer room) that overlooks the Río Darro. From here you pass into the Patio del Mexuar or Patio del Cuarto Dorado, with a small fountain and the Mudéjar Cuarto Dorado (Golden Room) on the left. Opposite the Cuarto Dorado is the entrance to the Serallo through a beautiful façade of glazed tiles, stucco work and carved wood.

Serallo This was the official residence of the emir or sultan. Its rooms surround the Patio de los Arrayanes (Patio of the Myrtles), named after the hedges that flank its rectangular pool and fountains. It has the alternative name of Patio de la Alberca (Patio of the Pool). Finely carved arches sit atop marble pillars to form porticos at the northern and southern ends of the patio. Through the northern portico, inside the Torre de Comares (Comares Tower), is the Sala de la Barca (Hall of the Boat) with a beautiful inverted boat-shaped wooden ceiling. This

room leads into the impressive, square Salón de Embajadores (Hall of the Ambassadors), where the emirs would have conducted their negotiations with Christian emissaries. Its domed cedar ceiling is remarkable and the repeating patterns of the stuccoed and tiled walls mesmerising. The southern end of the patio is marred by the gloomy grey walls of the Palacio de Carlos V.

Harén The harem was built during Mohammed V's reign and surrounds the celebrated Patio de los Leones with its fountain feeding water through the mouths of 12 stone lions. The patio's gallery, including the beautiful structures protruding at its eastern and western ends, is supported by 124 slender marble columns.

Of the four halls bordering the patio, the **Sala de los Abencerrajes** on the southern side is legendary for the murders of the noble Abencerraj family, whose leader, the story goes, dared to dally with Zoraya,

Abu al-Hasan's harem favourite. (Historians say the Abencerrajes also favoured Boabdil in the palace power struggle.) The room's highlight is its high-domed ceiling with stalactite vaulting which produces a star-like effect.

At the eastern end of the patio is the **Sala de los Reyes** (Hall of the Kings) with a leather-lined ceiling painted by 14th-century Christian artists. The name of the room comes from the painting on the central part of the ceiling, thought to depict 10 Nasrid emirs. On the northern side of the patio is the **Sala de las Dos Hermanas** (Hall of the Two Sisters), as beautiful and richly decorated as the Sala de los Abencerrajes, and named after the two slabs of white marble either side of its fountain. This was the room of the sultan's favourite paramour. At its far end is the enchanting **Sala de los Ajimeces** or **Mirador de Lindaraja/Daraxa**, the favoured lady's dressing room and bedroom, with low-slung windows through which she could catch the view of the Albayzín and mountains while reclining on ottomans and cushions. In Islamic times, buildings did not mar the view.

Other Sections From the Sala de las Dos Hermanas a passageway leads through deserted rooms which were decorated by Carlos I and later used by Washington Irving. The Peinador de la Reina (Queen's Dressing Room), the last of these, was a dressing room for Isabel, wife of Carlos I. From here you descend to the Patio de los Cipreses (Patio of the Cypresses), off which are the richly decorated, but closed, Baños Reales (Royal Baths).

Outside the palace is a group of recent gardens, the **Partal**, graded in terraces and bordered by the palace towers and ramparts. From here there is an exit to the Palacio de Carlos V, or you can continue along a path to the Generalife.

Palacio de Carlos V This huge Renaissance palace, also called the Casa Real Nueva, is the dominant Christian building in the Alhambra. Begun in 1527 by Pedro Machuca, a Toledo architect who studied

under Michelangelo, it was never completed. The building is square but contains a surprising two-tiered circular courtyard with 32 columns. The main, western facade features three porticos divided by pairs of fluted columns and carvings of horsemen, angels and other mythological figures. Were the palace in a different setting its merits would be more readily appreciated.

The palace houses two museums. On the ground floor, the **Museo de la Alhambra** concentrates on the Muslim period with a wonderful collection of artefacts from the Alhambra, the province of Granada, and Córdoba. Detailed explanatory texts in English and Spanish fill out the picture. Its highlight is the elegant Alhambra Vase, decorated with gazelles. The museum opens 9 am to 2.30 pm Tuesday to Saturday (admission is free).

The **Museo de Bellas Artes** upstairs has an impressive collection of paintings and sculptures. Most notable are the carved wooden relief of the Virgin and child by Diego de Siloé; a small, enamelled screen of around 1500 that belonged to El Gran Capitán (Gonzalo Fernández de Córdoba), the military right-hand man of Isabel and Fernando; and various pieces by Alonso Cano. The museum is open from 2.30 pm to 6 pm Tuesday (to 8 pm April to September), 9 am to 6 pm Wednesday to Saturday (to 8 pm April to September), and 9 am to 2.30 pm Sunday. Admission is free for EU residents (250 ptas for others).

Other Christian Buildings The **Iglesia de Santa María de la Alhambra** was built between 1581 and 1617 on the site of the former palace mosque. The **Convento de San Francisco**, now the Parador San Francisco, was erected upon an Islamic palace. Isabel and Fernando were laid to rest in a sepulchre in what's now the parador's patio before being transferred to the Capilla Real.

Generalife The name means 'Garden of the Architect'. These palace gardens on the hillside facing the Palacio Nazaries have a beautiful, soothing composition of walkways, terraces, patios, fountains, trimmed

euro currency converter 1000 ptas = €6.01

hedges, tall, long-established trees (especially cypresses, poplars and chestnuts) and, in season, flowers of every imaginable hue. The Muslim rulers' summer palace is in the farthest corner. Within the palace, the Patio de la Acequia (Court of the Long Pond) has a long pool framed by flower beds and fountains whose shapes sensuously echo the arched porticos at each end. Off the Patio de la Acequia is the Patio de la Sultana, almost as lovely and with the trunk of a 700-year-old cypress tree, where Abu al-Hasan supposedly caught his lover, Zoraya, with the head of the Abencerraj clan, leading to the murders in the Sala de los Abencerrajes of the Palacio Nazaries. Above here are the modern Jardines Altos (Upper Gardens), and a stairway with cascading waterfalls. Back towards the entrance are the Jardines Nuevos (New Gardens). A pleasant alternative route back to town is along Cuesta de los Chinos which runs down a gully between the Generalife and Alhambra to the Río Darro.

Capilla Real

The Royal Chapel (☎ 958 22 92 39) on Calle Oficios, adjoining the cathedral, is Granada's outstanding Christian building.

It was built in elaborate Isabelline Gothic style, commissioned by the Catholic Monarchs as their mausoleum, but was not finished until 1521 so they were temporarily interred in the Convento de San Francisco. The monarchs lie with three relatives in simple lead coffins in the crypt beneath their marble monuments in the chancel, which is enclosed by a stunning gilded wrought iron screen made in 1520 by Maestro Bartolomé of Jaén. The coffins, from left to right, belong to Felipe El Hermoso (the Handsome; husband of the monarchs' daughter Juana la Loca), Fernando, Isabel, Juana la Loca (the Mad) and Miguel, the eldest grandchild of Isabel and Fernando. The carved effigies reclining above the crypt were a tribute by Carlos I to his parents and grandparents. The slightly lower of the two monuments, representing Isabel and Fernando, is the work of a Tuscan, Domenico Fancelli. The other monument, to Felipe and Juana, is higher, apparently because Felipe was the son of the Holy Roman Emperor, Maximilian. This is the work (1520) of Bartolomé Ordóñez from Burgos. The chancel's densely decorated plateresque retable (1522) is by Felipe de Vigarni. Note its kneeling figures of Isabel and Fernando,

How to Handle Unwanted Gifts

Many visitors to Andalucía feel uncomfortable and/or intimidated when *gitanas* (Roma women) step across their paths and thrust a sprig of rosemary or some other herb into their hands. (It used to be flowers.) In Granada, this happens throughout the day on Calle Oficios outside the Capilla Real, and on the pedestrian approaches to the Alhambra. The best thing to do if you don't want to hand over any money is to *resolutely* ignore any advance. The minute you allow the sprig to be pressed into your hand, you will be expected to pay something. Before you know it, your palm will have been read and payment demanded. I got caught, allowing a youngish woman to tell my fortune. She spoke rapidly in a soothing tone for about 20 seconds before putting out her hand for money. I handed over 200 ptas. The wily woman's tone changed to displeasure. She hissed that coins are bad luck and that she wanted paper money. I insisted that coins are part of the economy (how could they be bad luck?) and refused to hand over a note. With that, the woman took off angrily, but held on to the 200 ptas.

Several readers have commented on similar incidents both in Sevilla and Granada and their embarrassment about them. When first approached, you don't know who is accosting you.

Shoe shiners hang out in the same places and may demand outrageous fees for feeble efforts; they can be particularly mean with the shoe polish.

Susan Forsyth

attributed to Diego de Siloé, and the paintings below depicting the defeat of the Muslims and subsequent conversions to Christianity. Cardinal Cisneros is there too.

In the sacristy is a museum with an impressive collection including Isabel's sceptre and silver crown and Fernando's sword. Isabel's personal art collection, mainly Flemish, occupies one room; there is also Botticelli's *Prayer in the Garden of Olives* and two fine statues of the kneeling monarchs by Vigarni.

The Capilla Real is open 10.30 am (11 am Sunday) to 1 pm and 4 to 7 pm (3.30 to 6.30 pm in winter) daily. Admission costs 300 ptas.

Cathedral

Adjoining the Capilla Real is a chunky Gothic/Renaissance cathedral (☎ 958 22 29 59) with a cavernous interior. Building began in 1521 and was directed by Diego de Siloé from 1528 to 1563, but was not finished until the 18th century. The main facade on Plaza de las Pasiegas, with four heavy buttresses and an arched doorway, was designed by Alonso Cano (whose statue stands to the south-east). The lavish Puerta del Perdón on the north-western facade has statues carved by de Siloé. Much of the interior is also his work, including the gilded and painted Capilla Mayor. The Catholic Monarchs at prayer (each side of the main altar, above the lovely carved and painted pulpits) were carved by Pedro de Mena in the 17th century, and the busts of Adam and Eve are by Cano.

The cathedral is open for tourist visits 10.30 am (10.45 am in winter) to 1.30 pm and 4 to 7 pm Monday to Saturday, 4 to 7 pm Sunday. Admission costs 300 ptas. Enter from Gran Vía de Colón.

La Madraza

Opposite the Capilla Real remains part of the old Muslim university, La Madraza, also called the Casa del Cabildo Antiguo, as it was later used as a town hall. Now with a painted baroque facade, the much-altered building retains an octagonal domed prayer room with stucco lacework and pretty tiles.

The building is part of the modern university but you can take a look inside whenever it's open.

Corral del Carbón

This place's name (Coal Yard) disguises its original function as a 14th-century inn for merchants. The building has since had a chequered history, being used as an inn for coal dealers (hence its modern name) and later a theatre. It houses a tourist office, and Artespaña, a government-run crafts shop. To find it, cross Calle Reyes Católicos from the Capilla Real and look for the sign pointing down an alley. You can't miss the lovely Islamic facade with its elaborate horseshoe arch.

Alcaicería

The Alcaicería was the Muslim silk exchange but what you see now is a restoration, after a 19th-century fire, filled with tourist shops. It's charming in the early morning light and quiet. Its buildings, separated by narrow alleys, are just south-east of the Capilla Real.

Albayzín

A wander around the hilly streets and narrow, aged alleys of Granada's old Muslim quarter is a must. The Albayzín covers much of the hill that faces the Alhambra across the Darro valley. Its name derives from 1227, when Muslims from Baeza populated the district after their city was conquered by the Christians. It became a densely populated residential area and for a few decades after the Reconquista it survived as the Muslim quarter. Muslim ramparts, cisterns, gates, fountains and houses remain and many of the Albayzín's churches and *cármenes* (large walled villas with gardens) stand on the sites of, or incorporate the remains of, Islamic buildings. Bus Nos 31 and 32 from Plaza Nueva go to the upper Albayzín.

Carrera del Darro & Paseo de los Tristes

One way to approach the Albayzín is up Carrera del Darro from Plaza Nueva. On Plaza Santa Ana is the **Iglesia de Santa**

Ana, which incorporates a former mosque's minaret in its bell-tower, as do several churches in the Albayzín. Stop at Carrera del Darro 31 to see the remains of the 11th-century **Baños Árabes** (Muslim Baths), open 10 am to 2 pm Tuesday to Saturday. Admission is free.

At Carrera del Darro 41 is the Renaissance Casa del Castril, home to the **Museo Arqueológico** (☎ 958 22 56 40) which has some interesting finds from the province. The Islamic room on the upper floor displays some lovely tiles (azulejos), carved wood and fine ceramics. It opens 3 pm to 8 pm on Tuesday, 9 am to 8 pm Wednesday to Saturday and 9 am to 2.30 pm Sunday. Opening hours may be shorter in the winter. Admission costs 250 ptas (free with EU passport or national identity card).

Shortly after the museum, Carrera del Darro becomes Paseo de los Tristes (also called Paseo del Padre Manjón), with a number of cafes and restaurants with outdoor tables. This is a good spot to take in the view of the Alhambra's fortifications directly above.

Upper Albayzín From the north-eastern end of Paseo de los Tristes, Cuesta del Chapiz heads north and uphill, then curves west into Plaza del Salvador, where the **Colegiata del Salvador**, a 16th-century church, still contains the Islamic courtyard of the mosque it replaced; it opens 10.30 am to 1 pm and 4.30 to 6.30 pm daily. Admission costs 100 ptas. From here Calle Panaderos leads to **Plaza Larga** where there are lively bars offering cheap menús (fixed-price meals). On the far side of the square, at the top end of the Albayzín's surviving ramparts, is an impressive Islamic gateway. Back on Calle Panaderos, follow Calle Horno Moral and Calle Charca which lead to the **Mirador San Nicolás** with fantastic views of the Alhambra and the Sierra Nevada – you can't miss the trail at sunset!

Descent from Mirador San Nicolás
Descending from the view-point along Camino Nuevo San Nicolás, which becomes Calle Santa Isabel la Real, you pass

the **Convento Santa Isabel**, a former Islamic palace. Its church, supposedly open 10 am to 6 pm daily, has a Mudéjar ceiling. Nearby is Plaza San Miguel Bajo where the **Iglesia San Miguel** occupies the site of a former mosque. To wend your way back to the centre, follow Plaza Cauchiles San Miguel and then Calle San José. Calle San José meets the top of picturesque **Calle Calderería Nueva** with its teterías (Arabic-style tea rooms). Alternatively, enjoy getting lost – but not too late at night.

Sacromonte
Camino del Sacromonte leads from Cuesta del Chapiz up Sacromonte hill to the **Iglesia de San Cecilio**, passing by caves dug into the hillside; these caves have been occupied by gitanos (Roma people) since the 18th century. For more information, see the later Entertainment section and the boxed text 'Where to Find Authentic Flamenco'. Around six buses daily, between 7.50 am to 7.20 pm, head up here from the Alhambra bus stop on Plaza Nueva and return via the Albayzín. There are more buses between 10 pm and 2 am on Thursday, Friday and Saturday.

Plaza Bib-Rambla & Around
Just south-west of the Alcaicería is the large, pleasant Plaza Bib-Rambla with restaurants, flower stalls, and a central fountain with statues of giants. This square was the scene of Inquisition lashings and burnings, jousting and bullfights. Today buskers, mime artists and street sellers provide gentler entertainment.

A block south-west is pedestrianised Calle de los Mesones, with modern shops. At its north-western end is leafy Plaza de la Trinidad from which Calle Duquesa leads past the university founded by Carlos I (now the Law Faculty, with the main modern campus north of the city centre) to the 16th-century **Monasterio de San Jerónimo** on Calle del Gran Capitán. This features more work by the talented Diego de Siloé, including the larger of the monastery's two cloisters and much of the attached church. Either side of the church's altar are statues of El Gran Capitán and his wife María; El Gran Capitán is reputedly buried beneath the altar. The monastery is open 10 am to 1 pm and 4 to 7 pm (3 to 6.30 pm in winter) daily. Admission costs 300 ptas.

Monasterio de La Cartuja

The impressive, ornate La Cartuja Monastery is a 20-minute walk north of the Monasterio de San Jerónimo (or take bus No 8 from Gran Vía de Colón). The monastery, with an imposing, sand-coloured stone exterior, was built between the 16th and 18th centuries. Its baroque interior oozes wealth, especially the astonishingly lavish sacristy decorated in brown and white marble and stucco, and the adjacent sanctuary, a riot of colour and patterns with its twisted marble columns, abundant statues, paintings, gilt, and beautiful frescoed cupola. The monastery opens 10 am to 1 pm (to noon on Sunday) and 4 to 8 pm (3.30 to 6 pm in winter) daily. Admission costs 300 ptas.

Huerta de San Vicente

This house, where Federico García Lorca spent summers and wrote some of his best known works, is a 15-minute walk from the centre and was once surrounded by orchards. Today the new Parque Federico García Lorca separates it from whizzing traffic in an attempt to recreate the tranquil environment that inspired him.

The house contains some original furnishings, including Lorca's desk and piano, some of his drawings and other memorabilia, and exhibitions connected with his life and work. To find it head down Calle de las Recogidas from Puerta Real to Calle del Arabial; the park is to the right. Huerta de San Vicente (☎ 958 25 84 66) is open 10 am to 1 pm and 5 to 8 pm (4 to 7 pm in winter) Tuesday to Sunday, with guided tours in Spanish on the hour. Admission costs 300 ptas (free on Wednesday). See Around Granada later in this chapter for details of more Lorca sites.

Language and Flamenco Courses

With its many attractions and youthful population, Granada is a good city in which to study Spanish. The university offers a variety of intensive programs. A four-week 80-hour course will cost 62,000 ptas. For more information contact Universidad de Granada (☎ 958 22 07 90, fax 958 22 08 44), Centro de Lenguas Modernas, Cursos Para Extranjeros, Placeta del Hospicio Viejo s/n (Realejo), 18071 Granada.

The Escuela Carmen de las Cuevas (☎ 958 22 10 62, fax 958 22 04 76) in the Albayzín is another good choice; it offers Spanish language classes at all levels plus courses in history, literature, art, and flamenco dance, guitar and song. A four-week intensive language course costs 73,000 ptas. The postal address is Cuesta de los Chinos 15, 18010 Granada. Check out the Web site at www.carmencuevas.com.

Organised Tours

Granavisión (☎ 958 13 58 04) offers guided tours of the Alhambra and Generalife (4250 ptas), Granada Histórica tours (4400 ptas), flamenco shows (3900 ptas) and excursions farther afield. Phone direct or book through any travel agent.

Special Events

Semana Santa (Holy Week) and the Corpus Christi fair nine weeks later are the big two. Benches are set up in Plaza del Carmen to view the Semana Santa processions. Fairgrounds, drinking, *sevillana* (a traditional dance with similarities to flamenco) and bullfights are major features of Corpus Christi. Other festivals include:

Día de la Cruz (Day of the Cross)
Held on 3 May – squares, patios and balconies are adorned with floral crosses (the Cruces de Mayo), while horse riders, polka-dot dresses and sevillana dancing add to the colour.

Festival Internacional de Música y Danza
This international music and dance festival, with performances (some free) held in the Generalife, Palacio de Carlos V and other historical sites, is held in late June/early July. For information and tickets call the festival ticket office (☎ 958 22 18 44) or visit the Junta de Andalucía tourist office in the Corral de Carbón (tickets are also sold at El Corte Inglés).

Places to Stay

There should be no problem finding a room except during Semana Santa, and prices are no higher than elsewhere in Andalucía.

Places to Stay – Budget

Granada has some good budget options. At peak times rooms tend to fill up before noon, especially around Plaza Nueva.

Camping Within about 5km of Granada are several camp sites all accessible by bus. They cost 450 to 600 ptas per adult, 500 ptas per tent, and around 600 ptas per vehicle. The closest and biggest, though closed from November to February and now less tranquil with the bus station close by, is *Camping Sierra Nevada (☎ 958 15 00 62, Avenida de Madrid 107)*, 3km north-west of the centre. It has big clean bathrooms, a pool and a laundrette. Bus No 3 runs between here and Gran Vía de Colón in the city centre.

Year-round camp sites include *Camping Granada (☎ 958 34 05 48, Cerro de la Cruz s/n, Peligros)*, 4km north of Granada (take exit 123 from the N-323), and *Camping María Eugenia (☎ 958 20 06 06, Carretera A-92 Km 286)*, in the Vega en route to Santa Fé.

Hostels Just off Camino de Ronda, *Albergue Juvenil Granada (☎ 958 27 26 38, Calle Ramón y Cajal 2)* is 1.7km west of the centre and a 600m walk south-west of the train station. It's a large, modern, white building with nine singles, 37 doubles and 47 triples/quadruples, all with bathroom. There's a swimming pool. Bus No 3 from the bus station will get you fairly close – get off at the Constitución 4 bus stop and walk 400m west along Avenida de la Constitución and Avenida del Sur, then about the same distance south along Camino de Ronda. Alternatively you can continue on bus No 3 to the cathedral stop in the centre of town and pick up bus No 11: it runs a circular route and will drop you in front of the hostel.

Hostales & Pensiones Cheap *hostales* (budget guesthouses) are mainly located near Plaza Nueva, around Plaza de la Trinidad and near Plaza del Carmen.

One exception, handy for the Alhambra, is *Posada Doña Lupe (☎ 958 22 14 73, fax 958 22 14 74, Avenida del Generalife s/n)* with more than 40 rooms. Management does not like to show you the rooms. You can count on paying from 1500 ptas per person for what we have found to be clean rooms with showers: the rooms at the lower end of the scale are interior rooms with windows onto corridors. Better doubles cost from 3950 to 7500 ptas plus IVA. There is a cafe, a small rooftop pool, and a list of house rules. The Alhambra Bus from Plaza Nueva stops nearby.

Near Plaza Nueva There's plenty of choice on and just off Cuesta de Gomérez, which runs from Plaza Nueva towards the Alhambra. Most places have parking (1000 ptas a day). The friendly *Hostal Britz (☎/fax 958 22 36 52, Cuesta de Gomérez 1)* has 22 clean, adequate singles/doubles costing 2340/3900 ptas, or 4000/5400 ptas with bathroom. *Hostal Gomérez (☎ 958 22 44 37, Cuesta de Gomérez 10)* has a lively, helpful owner who speaks English, French and Italian. The nine well-kept rooms cost 1600/2700/3700 ptas for singles/doubles/triples.

Hostal Vienna (☎ 958 22 18 59, fax 958 22 18 54, Calle Hospital de Santa Ana 2) is a popular choice, although the new bar on the ground floor has made it less peaceful. Singles/doubles/triples with shared baths cost 3000/4000/5500 ptas. Management is obliging and English and German are spoken. The same people run *Hostal Austria (☎ 958 22 70 75, Cuesta de Gomérez 4)* where all rooms have bathrooms and heating. Singles/doubles cost 3500/5500 ptas.

Hostal Landázuri (☎ 958 22 14 06, Cuesta de Gomérez 24) is a good bet. Singles/doubles are nothing special and cost 2200/3200 ptas, 3100/4075 ptas with bathroom (all plus IVA), but the triples at 6000 ptas are excellent. The owner is cheerful, there's a pretty enclosed garden, and a terrace with views of the Alcazaba. There's an attached cafeteria too. Across the road,

Hostal Navarro Ramos (☎ *958 25 05 55, Cuesta de Gomérez 21)* lacks outdoor sitting areas but has better and cheaper singles/doubles with bathroom costing 2500/3900 ptas (1575/2500 ptas without).

Near Plaza del Carmen The family-run *Hostal Fabiola* (☎ *958 22 35 72, Calle Ángel Ganivet 5, 3rd floor)* has 19 good rooms, some with balcony and all with bathroom costing 1800/4000/5000 ptas for singles/doubles/triples. Two blocks north, the friendly *Hostal-Residencia Lisboa* (☎ *958 22 14 13, fax 958 22 14 87, Plaza del Carmen 27)* has singles/doubles that cost 3900/5600 ptas with bathroom (2600/ 3900 ptas without).

Near Plaza de la Trinidad & Around Some of the many hostales in this area fill up with university students in term-time. The following should have rooms year round. The good, family-run *Pensión Romero* (☎ *958 26 60 79, Calle Sillería 1)* on the corner of Calle de los Mesones, has singles/ doubles that cost 1700/2900 ptas, some with balconies. *Hostal Zurita* (☎ *958 27 50 20, Plaza de la Trinidad 7)* has good-value rooms costing 2000/4000 ptas, and doubles with bathroom costing 5000 ptas. The same friendly family runs *Hostal Lima* (☎ *958 29 50 29, Calle Laurel de las Tablas 17)* just around the corner: here the pleasant rooms with bath and TV cost 3000/5000 ptas. Also welcoming, *Huéspedes Capuchinas* (☎ *958 26 53 94, Calle Capuchinas 2, 2° Piso)*, has five clean rooms with shared bathrooms costing 2500/4000 ptas. *Hostal San Joaquín* (☎ *958 28 28 79, Calle Mano de Hierro 14)*, between the centre of town and the train station, is a rambling place set around a couple of leafy patios. The spacious, clean rooms, all with bath, cost 2500 ptas per person.

Places to Stay – Mid-Range

Add IVA to all of these year-round prices.

The following four hotels are standard city-centre-type places. *Hotel Los Tilos* (☎ *958 26 67 12, fax 958 26 68 01, Plaza Bib-Rambla 4)* charges 5000/7600 ptas for singles/doubles. Up the scale a bit, *Hotel*

Dauro (☎ *958 22 21 56, fax 958 22 85 19, Acera del Darro 19)* and *Hotel Dauro II* (☎ *958 22 15 81, fax 958 22 27 32, Calle Las Navas 5)* both charge 9150/11,750 ptas. *Hotel Macía* (☎ *958 22 75 36, fax 958 22 75 33, Plaza Nueva 4)* is good value with 44 comfortable rooms at 6375/9600 ptas.

Hotel Reina Cristina (☎ *958 25 32 11,* ✉ *clientes@hotelreinacristina.com, Calle Tablas 4)*, just off Plaza de la Trinidad, is in a renovated old building which once belonged to the Rosales family who were friends of Lorca. The writer spent his last days here before being arrested by the Nationalists. Rooms cost 8200/12,300 ptas.

Hotel América (☎ *958 22 74 71, fax 958 22 74 70, Calle Real de Alhambra 53)* is within the Alhambra grounds but as it has only 13 rooms (12,500 ptas for a double), and only opens from March to October, reservations are essential. *Hotel Washington Irving* (☎ *958 22 75 50, fax 958 22 75 59, Paseo del Generalife 2)* has been around since the last century and, according to readers, feels like it. However, renovations are under way. Rooms cost 8975/11,250 ptas.

Hostal La Ninfa (☎ *958 22 79 85, fax 958 22 26 61, Campo del Principe s/n)* has 12 attractive rooms, all with bathroom, TV and heating at 7000/8000 ptas. In the same vicinity, *Hotel Los Ángeles* (☎ *958 22 14 24, fax 958 22 12 25, Cuesta de Escoriaza 17)* has good doubles that cost 11,500 ptas, and a swimming pool.

Casa del Aljarife (☎/fax *958 22 24 25,* ✉ *most@mx3.redestb.es, Placeta de la Cruz Verde 2)* in the Albayzín, just a few steps uphill from the tea rooms on Calderería Nueva, occupies a beautifully restored 17th-century house but has only three rooms. Single/double/triple occupancy of the rooms costs 6420/9095/12,305 ptas.

Another possibility is the cave lodgings at *Cuevas El Abanico* (☎/fax *958 22 61 99, Vereda de Enmedio 89, Sacromonte)* where comfortable one- and two-bedroom caves with winter heating and equipped kitchens cost 8700 ptas and 11,700 ptas, respectively. The Web site is at www .granadainfo.com/abanico.

Places to Stay – Top End

Again, add IVA to these prices. *Parador San Francisco* (☎ *958 22 14 40, fax 958 22 22 64, Calle Real de Alhambra s/n)* is the top hotel in Granada and the most expensive parador in the whole country. But the converted monastery can't be beat for its location within the Alhambra, and historical connections. Singles/doubles cost 26,400/33,000 ptas, slightly less in winter; book well ahead. The distinctive and large neo-Islamic *Hotel Alhambra Palace* (☎ *958 22 14 68, fax 958 22 64 04, Peña Partida 2)* close to the Bosque Alhambra, has wonderful views over the city. Standard rooms cost 17,000/22,500 ptas, suites cost 33,000 ptas. *Palacio de Santa Inés* (☎ *958 22 23 62, fax 958 22 24 65, ☺ sinespal@ teleline.es, Cuesta de Santa Inés 9)*, in the Albayzín, is in a restored early 16th-century building. Standard rooms cost 12,000/15,000 ptas and suites (with fully equipped kitchens) cost 20,000 to 35,000 ptas. Some rooms have Alhambra views.

Places to Eat

Granadino cuisine uses the seafood and tropical fruits from the nearby coast, the meats and sausages of the interior (particularly from Las Alpujarras) and the excellent fresh vegetables from the Vega's market gardens (the broad beans are considered especially tasty and the asparagus is excellent). A hint of the Muslim past is evident in desserts, pastries such as syrup cakes, aniseed doughnuts, almond meringues and avocado ice cream, and in sorbets *(granizados)* – Muslim rulers liked their ices to be made with snow from the mountains.

Granadinos enjoy hearty soups and stews flavoured with herbs such as fennel. *Rabo de toro* (oxtail stew) and *habas con jamón* (broad beans with ham) are typical dishes. Granada's most famous dish, *tortilla Sacromonte*, is an omelette combining *jamón* (cured ham), prawns or oysters, greens and offal (traditionally, calf brains and bull testicles).

Bar flies will be pleased to find that tapas are often free at night, though at many places (especially around Plaza Nueva) you need to be drinking up at the bar from 8 pm to qualify for these titbits. Food and drink prices are higher in choice locations such as in and around the Alhambra, Plaza Bib-Rambla, Plaza Nueva and some of the tea rooms on Calle Calderería Nueva.

Near Plaza Nueva The popular *Cafe Central*, on Calle de Elvira facing Plaza Nueva, offers everything from good breakfasts through to snacks, menús (from 1100 ptas), and fancy teas and coffees. A few doors away, with tables on Plaza Nueva in good weather, *Café/Bar Al Andalus* has good cheap Arabic food to eat in or take away. Tasty falafel in pitta bread costs 300 ptas, kebabs or houmus 475 ptas, and spicy meat mains around 1000 ptas.

Two blocks west of Plaza Nueva along Calle de Elvira, *La Nueva Bodega (Calle Cetti Meriém 3)* has reliably good and economic food, if a little oily. Menús start at 950 ptas. Classier food in a more typical setting can be had at *Bodegas Castañeda* (an institution among locals and tourists alike) and *Antigua Castañeda*, back to back on Calle Almireceros and Calle de Elvira. Both places have barrels of potent coastal *(costa)* wine from the Sierra de la Contraviesa and offer delicious, beautifully presented food. Try the *montaditos* (325 ptas), slices of bread with toppings such as smoked salmon with avocado and caviar. More elaborate meals cost around 1700 ptas.

Vía Colón (Gran Vía de Colón 13) is a smart, popular cafe-bar serving up fancy *bocadillos* (long white bread rolls filled with cheese, ham, salad or tortilla; from 450 ptas), other snacks and typical granadino meals (from 1400 ptas). The menú costs 975 ptas.

Basic groceries, hams and cheeses can be bought at *Jamones Castellano* on the corner of Calle Almireceros and Calle Joaquín Costa.

For fresh fruit and veggies, the large covered *market* is on Calle San Agustín, a block west of the cathedral. There are more stalls.

Alhambra On the corner of Paseo del Generalife and Cuesta de los Chinos, *La Mimbre* has outdoor tables in a leafy garden

GRANADA PROVINCE

under the walls of the Alhambra. It specialises in medium-priced granadino fare.

Café/Restaurante Polinario has bocadillos to go; its buffet lunch costs 1350 ptas plus IVA. *Parador San Francisco* has a pricey restaurant and a terrace bar out the back with a lovely view, open 11 am to 11 pm daily, where teas and coffees cost 260 ptas; bocadillos cost from 825 ptas.

Albayzín Three blocks north-west of Plaza Nueva, atmospheric Calle Calderería Nueva has restaurants, tea shops, health food shops and takeaway food places. *Kasbah*, one of the more popular tea shops, makes a relaxed stop for time out from sightseeing: try a pot of one of the numerous teas on offer (300 ptas) or a glass of wine with a slice of fancy cake.

The excellent *Naturii Albayzín (Calle Calderería Nueva 10)* has an interesting vegetarian menu with an Arabic twist. No alcohol is served. Hunks of delicious wholemeal bread accompany the menús (available for lunch and dinner, 950 ptas or 1250 ptas, plus IVA). Or try the piping hot couscous with vegetables.

Lebanese *Samarcanda* on Calle Calderería Vieja has excellent Arabic food with hummus and falafel each at 500 ptas and mains such as fish tagines at 900 ptas. Portions are small and drinks expensive.

Near the top of the Albayzín, Plaza Larga and nearby Calle Panaderos have lively cafes and bars with cheap menús (850 ptas). A couple of blocks farther north, the tables at *El Ladrillo* on Placeta Fátima spill into the street in fine weather. It's a popular, fun, seafood place open for both lunch and dinner. Big platters of seafood called *barcos* go for 1200 ptas.

For a splash-out, try the *Mirador de Morayma (☎ 958 22 82 90, Calle Pianista Carrillo 2)*, off Cuesta San Agustín on the western side of Cuesta del Chapiz. It occupies a lovely walled villa *(carmen)*. You can expect to pay around 1500 ptas for a main course (closed Sunday).

On the western edge of the Albayzín, Plaza San Miguel Bajo has a couple of lively bars serving meals and tapas, popular with students. Down from here, close to Plaza del Triunfo, *La Luz es Como el Agua (☎ 958 20 13 68, Calle Cruz de Arqueros 3)* is a relaxed, alternative sort of place run by a multilingual Belgian who usually dishes up food from 8 pm Wednesday to Saturday, 2 to 5.30 pm Sunday (menú 1550 ptas). Phone before making a special trip, to check that it's open!

Plaza Bib-Rambla & Around With tables on the square, *Café Bib-Rambla* is a great place for breakfast. You can choose from seven types of bread and seven toppings. Coffee and toast with butter and excellent marmalade cost 400 ptas (less at the bar inside). *Pizzeria Gallio (Plaza Bib-Rambla 10)* does tasty Italian food. Try *pizza florentina*, with spinach and béchamel sauce (840 ptas plus IVA). Drinks are expensive.

A little to the west on Calle Pescadería is *Cunini*, an expensive seafood restaurant with tables outside – again, prices are lower at the bar. The menú costs 2400 ptas. A few doors away, *El Cepillo* is a popular, cheaper seafood restaurant with menús at 800 ptas – it gets packed at lunchtime (closed Sunday).

Bar/Cervecería Reca on the Plaza de la Trinidad is full to overflowing at lunch time. *Mesón El Patio (Calle de los Mesones 50)* is mid-priced with the usual Spanish/granadino mix of food, and a pleasant patio. A breakfast of coffee, juice, eggs, bacon and bread costs 500 ptas, but you can't have it before 10 am.

Campo del Príncipe South of the Alhambra, Campo del Príncipe is another area that buzzes at night. *Restaurante-Pizzería La Ninfa (Campo del Principe 14)* is a bright, cheerful place on two floors. Strings of red peppers hang from its terraces. Good pizzas come from a wood-fired oven and the excellent pasta is home-made. A few doors west, *Casa Cristóbal* has menús from 950 ptas and does wonderful sangría.

Entertainment

Available at kiosks at the beginning of each month, the excellent *Guía de Granada* (100 ptas) lists entertainment and places to eat including tapas bars.

Where to Find Authentic Flamenco

It's difficult to see flamenco that's not geared to tourists but some shows are more authentic than others and attract Spaniards as well as foreigners. Try the Friday or Saturday midnight shows at *Tarantos* (☎ 958 22 45 25 day, ☎ 958 22 24 92 night, Camino del Sacromonte 9), in a cave (3900 ptas). Tarantos' 10 pm shows attract more foreigners. *Jardines Neptuno* (☎ 958 52 25 33, Calle del Arabial), south-west of the centre, has a tourist-oriented flamenco performance at 10.15 pm daily (3900 ptas, with dinner 7900 ptas).

For these shows, you can pre-book tickets at the venues or through hotels and travel agents. Some will pick you up. The quality of the show depends on who is performing. If some of Granada's top professionals are dancing, you're in for a good evening. If not, you may be disappointed!

Flamenco dancers and singers also perform in some of Granada's more highbrow venues – see under Other Entertainment for details.

El Eshavira (see Bars, Music & Dancing) has live flamenco some nights. *Peña de la Platería* (☎ 958 21 06 50, Placeta de Toqueros), in the Albayzín, advertises flamenco from 10 pm Thursday and Saturday.

Some travellers go to the Sacromonte caves to see impromptu flamenco but it is extremely touristy and a bit of a rip-off. Watch your back if you go up there alone at night!

Bars, Music & Dancing You can easily dance the night away in Granada, just as elsewhere in Spain. Its large, youthful university population includes plenty of aspiring musicians and there are lots of gigs. Keep your eyes open for posters and leaflets advertising live music and non-touristy flamenco. The bi-weekly flyer *YOUthING* lists and describes many live music venues, some of which are also dance clubs where DJs do their thing.

Around Plaza Nueva The streets just west of Plaza Nueva are lively on weekend nights. *Bodegas Castañeda* and *Antigua Castañeda* (see the earlier Places to Eat section for details), with free tapas, make a good start to the evening. Nearby, there are popular bars with good music on Placita Sillería and Calle Joaquín Costa, while *La Taberna del Irlandés* on Calle Almireceros offers Tetley's Bitter, Guinness and Fosters as well as Spanish tipples.

Bar Avellano on the corner of Calle de Elvira and Calle Cárcel Baja has great music – African, blues, pop classics – best after midnight at weekends. *Granada 10*, the *discoteca* inside the plush cinema on Calle Cárcel Baja, has varied dance music. It opens about midnight and gets going

about 2 am. Don't look too scruffy! The 1000 ptas cover charge includes a drink. You can take in a movie beforehand!

Several of the bars on Carrera del Darro and its continuation Paseo de los Tristes get lively with a studenty crowd after midnight.

La Sabanilla (Calle San Sebastían 14), near the Alcaicería, is Granada's oldest bar: though showing its age, it's still worth a visit.

Elsewhere Don't miss *El Eshavira* (Postigo de la Cuna 2), a roomy jazz and flamenco club down a dark alley off Calle Azacayas, towards the northern end of Calle de Elvira. The bar is open from 10 pm nightly with live music some nights.

Planta Baja (Calle Horno de Abad 11), near Plaza de la Trinidad, features dance, tribal, house and deep house music from 1 to 6 am at weekends. It's also a live-music venue.

From about 11 pm at the weekend, crowds head for Calle Pedro António de Alarcón, a kilometre or so south-west of the centre, where a string of music bars offers cheap deals on drinks with free tapas.

Between Plaza de la Trinidad and Calle Pedro Antonio de Alarcón, *La Sala Cha* (Calle Ancha de Gracia 4) opens at least

GRANADA PROVINCE

Friday and Saturday nights and has live music and DJ evenings. Four blocks north, *MorganHouseCafeBar (Calle Obispo Hurtado 15)*, open from 4 pm to 4 am daily except Monday, has house DJs.

Some of the Sacromonte caves turn into lively clubs during university terms. The popular *El Camborio*, open year round at weekends from 11 pm, has two dance floors (one at cave level), with mixed music. Admission costs 600 ptas.

Other Entertainment The notice board in the foyer of La Madraza on Calle Oficios, opposite the Capilla Real, has large posters which list forthcoming cultural events.

Auditorio Manuel de Falla (☎ 958 22 00 22, Paseo de los Mártires s/n), near the Alhambra, is a venue for weekly orchestral concerts.

The *Teatro Alhambra (☎ 958 22 04 47, Calle de Molinos 56)* and the more central *Teatro Municipal Isabel La Católica (☎ 958 22 15 14, Puerta Real s/n)* have ongoing programs of theatre and concerts (sometimes flamenco).

Winter cultural programs include Música En Los Monumentos which features several concerts a month in historic buildings such as the Baños Arabes.

Things to Buy

A distinctive local craft is marquetry *(taracea)*, used on boxes, tables, chess sets and more – the best have shell, silver or mother-of-pearl inlays. Other granadino crafts include embossed leather, guitars, wrought iron, brass and copperwork, basket weaving, textiles and, of course, pottery. Places to look include the Alcaicería, the Albayzín and Cuesta de Gomérez.

You can watch marquetry experts at work in the shop opposite the Iglesia de Santa María in the Alhambra, and in a shop on Cuesta de Gomérez. There are at least two guitar makers on Cuesta de Gomérez. The government-run Artespaña in the Corral del Carbón has a good range of Spanish handicrafts.

Granada is also a good place to buy ethnic clothes and jewellery, especially around

Plaza Nueva. For general shopping, pedestrianised Calle de los Mesones has countless shops. El Corte Inglés department store is on Acera del Darro.

Getting There & Away

Air Iberia (☎ 958 22 75 92), Plaza Isabel La Católica 2, has daily flights to/from Madrid and Barcelona. See the following Getting Around section for details of getting to and from the airport.

Bus Granada's bus station, on Carretera de Jaén, is 3km north-west of the centre. All services operate from here except those to nearby destinations such as Fuente Vaqueros, Viznar and the Estación de Esquí Sierra Nevada (see those sections later in this chapter for details). Alsina Graells (☎ 958 18 54 80) runs to Córdoba (1515 ptas, three hours direct, eight times daily), Sevilla (2400 ptas three hours direct, nine daily), Málaga (1185 ptas, 1½ hours direct, 15 daily), Las Alpujarras (see that section later in this chapter for details), Jaén, Baeza, Úbeda, Cazorla, Almería, Almuñécar, Nerja and Torre del Mar.

At least nine daily buses go to Madrid (1950 ptas, five to six hours).

Bacoma (☎ 958 15 75 57) has daily services to Alicante, Valencia and Barcelona (7915 ptas, 14 hours). Buses to Guadix (550 ptas, 1½ hours) and Mojácar are run by Autedia (☎ 958 15 36 36).

Train The station (☎ 958 27 12 72) is 1.5km west of the centre on Avenida de Andaluces, off Avenida de la Constitución. Three to four trains run daily to/from Sevilla (2415 to 2665 ptas, 2¾ to 3½ hours), Antequera (1000 ptas, 1¼ hours), and Almería (1610 to 1775 ptas, 2¼ to 2¾ hours) via Guadix. For Málaga (1795 ptas) and Córdoba (2290 ptas) change trains at Bobadilla. One daily train goes direct to Ronda (1775 ptas, 2¼ hours,) and Algeciras (2665 ptas, four hours), with at least one more with a change at Antequera. For Cadiz (5½ hours) there are two daily trains but you need to change at Dos Hermanas, south of Sevilla. Four trains daily go to Linares/Baeza.

To Madrid there's a Talgo at 3.40 pm (4.35 pm on Saturday; 3800 ptas, six hours) and a night train (3600 ptas, 9½ hours). One train daily goes to Valencia and Barcelona (6100 ptas, 12½ hours).

Car Car rental is expensive. ATA Rent a Car (☎ 958 22 40 04), Plaza Cuchilleros 1, has weekly rentals from 37,300 ptas plus IVA, including insurance.

Getting Around
To/From the Airport The airport (☎ 958 24 52 23) is 17km west of the city on the A-92. At least four airport buses daily (725 ptas) leave from the Palacio de Congresos, stopping on Gran Vía de Colón just beyond Plaza Isabel La Católica. Call ☎ 958 13 13 09 for information. A taxi costs 2700 ptas.

Bus City buses cost 120 ptas. The tourist offices have a handy booklet showing routes. Bus No 3 runs from outside the bus station to the centre. You may have to wait up to 20 minutes. Get off at the cathedral stop. To reach the centre from the train station, walk straight ahead to Avenida de la Constitución and pick up bus No 3 or 11 going to the right (east). For details of buses to the Alhambra, the Albayzín and Sacromonte, see those sections.

Taxi Taxis line up on Plaza Nueva. Most fares within the city cost between 400 and 700 ptas.

AROUND GRANADA
Granada is surrounded by a fertile plain known as La Vega, planted with poplar groves and crops ranging from potatoes and maize to melons and tobacco. The Vega has always been vital to the city and was an inspiration to Federico García Lorca, who was born and also killed here.

Fuente Vaqueros
The house where Lorca was born in 1898, in this village 17km west of Granada, is now the **Casa Museo Federico García Lorca**. The place makes his spirit come alive, with numerous charming photos, posters and costumes for plays that he wrote and directed, and paintings illustrating some of his poems. A short video captures him in action with the touring Teatro Barraca.

The museum is open for guided tours in Spanish (300 ptas) on the hour from 10 am to 1 pm and 4 to 6 pm (5 to 7 pm, April to June; 6 to 8 pm, July to September) daily except Tuesday. To get there take a Ureña company bus (☎ 958 45 41 54) from outside Granada train station. On summer weekdays this service runs almost hourly from 9 am to 9 pm in both directions; at weekends it's every two hours. There are fewer buses in winter. There's a timetable at the roundabout in the village centre.

Viznar
To follow the Lorca trail to the bitter end you have to make your way out to this

GRANADA PROVINCE

Be Warned! – Driving in Granada
Access to some of Granada's main central streets is restricted by a little black post (*pilote*) with a red light, which pops up in the middle of certain roads at certain times. Some people have special cards which, when slotted into a box by the side of the road, cause the post to slide down into a hole thereby allowing the vehicle to pass. There is not time for two cars to pass through before the post pops up again! You'll see the warning sign 'Obstáculos en calzada a 20 metros' and will have to detour.

Tourists can drive into the centre south-eastwards along Gran Vía de Colón as far as the Aparcamiento San Agustín car park, a block before the cathedral. Police rather than posts restrict entry around here. For other parts of the centre, you'll need to phone your accommodation to find out what is the current best access and where to park. You can avoid it all by using the *circunvalacíon* (ring road) to get to the Alhambra car park and leaving your vehicle there.

village 8km north-east of the city. When the Spanish Civil War broke out in 1936 and Granada city was taken over by the Nationalists, Lorca took refuge in a friend's house. He was soon discovered, arrested and taken with hundreds of others to Víznar to be shot.

Outside the village, on the road to Alfacar, is the **Parque Lorca**, with a granite block marking the spot where the writer is believed to have been killed. His body has never been found.

The ***Albergue Juvenil Víznar*** *(☎ 958 54 33 07, Camino de la Fuente Grande s/n)* is a good, modern youth hostel, with its own swimming pool.

Buses to Víznar leave from Plaza del Triunfo in Granada at 12.30, 2.45 and 8 pm Monday to Friday, returning from Víznar at 7.45 am, 12.30 pm and 4 pm. There's one bus on Saturday, at 1.30 pm from Granada and 8.30 am from Víznar, and none on Sunday. Call Martín Perez (☎ 958 15 12 49) to check the schedule.

East of Granada

The A-92 heading north-east from Granada crosses the forested, hilly Parque Natural Sierra de Huétor before entering an increasingly arid landscape. Outside Guadix the A-92 veers south-east towards Almería, crossing the Marquesado de Zenete district at the northern foot of the Sierra Nevada, while the A-92-N heads north-east across the Altiplano, Granada's rather desolate 'high plain', which breaks out into mountains here and there and affords superb long-distance views on the way to northern Almería province.

GUADIX
postcode 18500 • pop 20,000
• elevation 915m
Guadix (gwah-**deeks**), 55km from Granada, is famous for its cave dwellings – not prehistoric remnants but the homes of about 3000 modern-day townsfolk. Cave living is fairly widespread in eastern Granada but Guadix has the biggest concentration of underground homes. The town dates back to

Iberian times and was the seat of an important Visigothic bishopric. There's a tourist office (☎ 958 66 26 65) at Carretera de Granada s/n, on the Granada road leaving the town centre.

Things to See
At the centre of Guadix is a fine sandstone **cathedral**, built in the 16th to 18th centuries on the site of the town's former main mosque. It is open 11 am to 1 pm and 4 to 6 or 7 pm Monday to Saturday. Gothic pointed arches and ceiling tracery predominate in part of the interior, while the rest of the inside and much of the exterior, constructed later to plans by Diego de Siloé, exhibit the round arches and flourishes of Renaissance and baroque. The arch at the end of the central choir, inside, even manages to be pointed on one side and round on the other. **Plaza de las Palomas** nearby is beautiful when floodlit at night.

A short distance south, on Calle Barradas, is the entrance to the 15th-century Muslim castle, the **Alcazaba** (open 9 am to 2 pm Monday to Saturday and a few afternoon hours Monday to Friday). From the Alcazaba there are views over the main cave quarter, the Barriada de las Cuevas, some 700m south.

The typical 21st-century cave has a whitewashed wall across the entrance, and a chimney and TV aerial sticking out of the top. Some have many rooms and all mod cons. The caves maintain a comfortable temperature around 18°C year round. A **Cueva Museo** on Plaza de Padre Poveda in the Barriada de las Cuevas recreates typical cave life and opens 10 am to 2 pm and 4 to 6 pm Monday to Friday, and 10 am to 2 pm on Saturday. Admission costs 200 ptas.

Places to Stay & Eat
On the Murcia road 600m from the town centre, ***Hotel Mulhacén*** *(☎ 958 66 07 50, Avenida Buenos Aires 41)* has doubles with bathroom costing 5395 ptas plus IVA. ***Cuevas Pedro Antonio de Alarcón*** *(☎ 958 66 49 86, Barriada San Torcuato)*, a modern cave hotel 2.5km farther out along the same road towards the A-92

Granada's Capilla Real

Puerta del Vino, Alhambra

The terraced gardens of the Partal, Alhambra, Granada

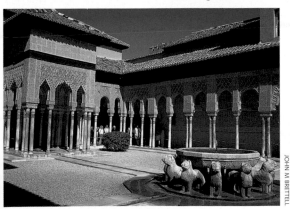

Water is an integral part of the design of the Alhambra.

Cool and calm – Generalife

Granada and the Alhambra boast one of the most dramatic settings in Spain.

The hill-town of Bubión is framed by the snow-capped peaks of Las Alpujarras, Granada province.

The Hombre de Orce

The remote Altiplano village of Orce, on a back road to María in the north of Almería province, styles itself the 'Cradle of European Humankind'. The claim rests on a fossilised bone fragment probably between one and two million years old, found in 1976 at nearby Venta Micena. The bone is widely accepted to be part of the skull of an infant *Homo erectus* that had probably been eaten by a giant hyena. *Homo erectus* was an ancestor of *Homo sapiens*, and the bit of bone would therefore be the oldest known human remnant in Europe. Many palaeontologists have taken this 'Hombre de Orce' as evidence that humans reached Europe much earlier than was previously believed, and direct from Africa, instead of via Asia as had been thought. Others dispute both the humanity and the age of the fragment, saying it was more likely horse or deer and could be under one million years old.

What's not disputed is that for most of the last four million years, much of the Hoya de Baza, the now arid basin in which the Baza-Orce area lies, was a lake. Wildlife drinking at the edge of the lake was vulnerable to attack by larger animals, and the fossilised bones of dozens of species, including mammoth, rhinoceros, sabre-tooth tiger, hippopotamus, giant hyena, wolf, bear, elephant and buffalo, resulting from such encounters between one and two million years ago, have been found at Venta Micena and nearby sites.

It's a bit of a thrill to know that the landscape you're crossing was once roamed by such creatures.

A good selection of the finds – including enormous mammoths' teeth and a replica of the 'Hombre de Orce' fragment (the original is in Orce town hall) – are on show in Orce's interesting Museo de Prehistoria y Paleontología (☎ 958 74 61 83), housed in a Muslim-era castle just off the village's central square. It's open 11 am to 2 pm and 6 to 8 pm daily (4 to 6 pm from October to May). Admission costs 200 ptas.

If you need accommodation in the area, the **Casas-Cueva** (☎ 958 73 90 68) in Galera, on the A-330 8km west, are comfortable cave-apartments starting at 5350 ptas for two people, with a restaurant and pool. Fans of the distant past could also seek out Galera's Bronze Age sites, El Castellón Alto and El Cerro de Real.

GRANADA PROVINCE

(look for '*Alojamiento en Cuevas*' signs), offers some comfortable cave apartments at 5000/6900/9900 ptas plus IVA for singles/doubles/quadruples (a bit more during Semana Santa and August). It has a pool and restaurant too. Good singles/doubles with bathroom cost 5500/7500 ptas plus IVA in the central **Hotel Comercio** (☎ 958 66 05 00, *Calle Mira de Amezcua 3*).

Getting There & Away
Guadix is about one hour from Granada and 1½ hours from Almería and accessible by around 10 daily buses or four daily trains in each direction. At least two daily buses head to Baza, Murcia, Madrid, Jaén and Mojácar. The bus station is at the end of Calle Concepción Arenal, off Avenida Medina Olmos about 700m south-east of the centre. The train station is off the Murcia road about 2km north-east of the town centre.

MARQUESADO DE ZENETE
This rather bleak area between Guadix and the Sierra Nevada was a prosperous agricultural district in Muslim times. After the Reconquista it was awarded to Cardinal de Mendoza, chief adviser to the Catholic Monarchs during the war against Granada. His illegitimate son Rodrigo de Mendoza became its first marquis (*marqués*).

The main town, **Jerez del Marquesado**, is a starting point for ascents of the high Sierra Nevada, including the tough **Ruta Integral de los Tresmil**, a four-day crossing of the range to Lanjarón in Las Alpujarras, which takes in all the mountain range's 3000m-plus peaks. Jerez is served by daily buses from Granada and Guadix.

Thirteen kilometres east of Jerez, the imposing **Castillo de la Calahorra**, with its domed corner towers, looms above the village of La Calahorra. The castle was built between 1509 and 1512 by Rodrigo de Mendoza, whose tempestuous life included a spell in Italy unsuccessfully wooing the infamous Lucrezia Borgia. The building's blank exterior encloses an amazingly elegant Italian Renaissance courtyard with a staircase of Carrara marble. The castle is open 10 am to 1 pm and 4 to 6 pm, on Wednesday only. There are two *hostales* in La Calahorra village.

From La Calahorra, the A-337 heads south over the **Puerto de la Ragua** pass (see East of Trevélez in the Las Alpujarras section).

PARQUE NATURAL SIERRA DE BAZA

This 523 sq km protected area lies between the A-92-N and A-92, south of Baza. It's a mountainous westward extension of Almería province's Sierra de los Filabres, with some precipitous drops, but crossed by several roads (mostly unpaved). The Centro de Visitantes Narvaez (☎ 958 86 10 13), open 10 am to 2 pm and 4 to 6 pm Wednesday to Sunday, is 5km off the A-92-N from a turning marked 'Parque Natural Sierra de Baza' about 15km from Baza. One road from the centre passes within half an hour's walk of the park's highest peak, Santa Bárbara (2271m).

BAZA

postcode 18800 • pop 21,000
• elevation 850m

The market town of Baza, 44km north-east of Guadix, dates back to Iberian times. Its attractive Plaza Mayor is dominated by the 16th-century **Iglesia Concatedral de la Encarnación**. Also on the square is the **Museo Municipal** with an archaeological collection that includes a copy of the *Dama de Baza*, a person-size Iberian goddess statue unearthed locally in 1971, which is one of the outstanding pieces of Iberian art (the original is in Madrid's Museo Arqueológico Nacional). The museum opens 10 am to 1 pm and 6 to 8 pm (4 to 6 pm in winter), Monday to Friday.

Hostal Avenida (☎ 958 70 03 77, *Avenida José de la Mora 26*), about 500m

south of Plaza Mayor, charges 4300 ptas with private bathroom or 3300 ptas with shared bathrooms. *Hotel Anabel* (☎ 958 86 09 98, *Calle María de Luna s/n*), nearby, has doubles that cost 6000 ptas plus IVA. *La Solana* on Calle Serrano is one of the best of a handful of beer and tapas bars close to Plaza Mayor.

The bus station (☎ 958 70 21 03) is on Calle Reyes Católicos 200m north of Plaza Mayor. There are about 15 buses a day to/from Guadix and Granada in one direction and Vélez Rubio and Murcia in the other.

Sierra Nevada & Las Alpujarras

The Sierra Nevada mountain range, which includes mainland Spain's highest peak, Mulhacén (3478m), forms an almost year-round snowy, south-eastern backdrop to Granada. The range extends about 75km from west to east, crossing from Granada into Almería province.

Along its southern side lies one of the oddest and most picturesque crannies of Andalucía, the 70km-long jumble of valleys known as Las Alpujarras or La Alpujarra. Here arid hillsides split by deep ravines alternate with oasis-like white villages set by rapid streams amid gardens, orchards and woodlands. It's a particularly delightful area to explore on foot.

All the Sierra Nevada's highest peaks (3000m or more) are towards its western (Granada) end, and it's here, on the northern flank of the range, that Europe's most southerly ski resort stands. The best overall maps of this area are Editorial Alpina's *Sierra Nevada, La Alpujarra* (1:40,000) and the CNIG's *Sierra Nevada* (1:50,000). Alpina's map is more up to date (1999) and comes with a booklet, in Spanish or English, describing 32 walking, mountain bike and cross-country skiing routes. The CNIG map, however, covers a bigger area. The best places to try for these maps locally are the El Dornajo and Pampaneira

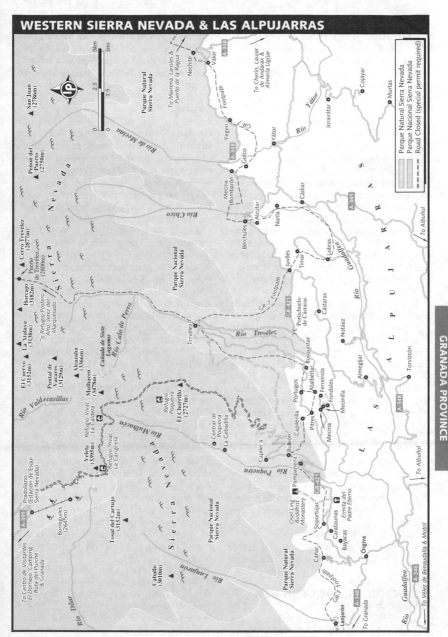

WESTERN SIERRA NEVADA & LAS ALPUJARRAS

Parque Natural Sierra Nevada
Parque Nacional Sierra Nevada
Road Closed (special permit required)

GRANADA PROVINCE

information offices (see later in this chapter for details). Pampaneira usually has some CNIG 1:25,000 sheets too.

The best times for walking in the high mountains (early July to early September) don't coincide with the most comfortable months down in Las Alpujarras (April to mid-June and mid-September to early November, when the temperatures are just right and the vegetation is at its most colourful). Late June/early July and the first half of September are the best compromise periods. In the Sierra Nevada – which are serious mountains – always be prepared for cloud or rain and come well equipped. The temperature on the mountain tops averages 14°C less than in the highest Alpujarras villages. At the high altitudes, only from early July to early September is the ground reliably snow-free and the weather relatively settled. Even under clear summer skies the heights of the mountains can be blasted by strong, very cold winds.

Lonely Planet's *Walking in Spain* details eight days of good walking in Las Alpujarras and the high Sierra Nevada. Andy Walmsley's *Walking in the Sierra Nevada of Spain* is a useful little book for those who fancy getting to know the range better.

Nearly all the upper reaches of the Sierra Nevada are included in the 862 sq km Parque Nacional Sierra Nevada, the biggest of Spain's dozen national parks. This rare high-altitude environment is home to about 2000 of Spain's 7000 plant species including 66 endemic species and subspecies, among them unique types of crocus, narcissus, thistle, clover, poppy and gentian. Andalucía's largest ibex population (about 5000) is here too – in summer, walkers may come across ibex anywhere above about 2800m.

Surrounding the national park, at lower altitudes, is the 848 sq km Parque Natural Sierra Nevada, which has a lesser degree of protection.

ESTACIÓN DE ESQUÍ SIERRA NEVADA

The A-395 leads from Granada to the Estación de Esquí Sierra Nevada (Sierra Nevada Ski Station), with high peaks rising behind it. About 10km before the ski station is the Centro de Visitantes El Dornajo (☎ 958 34 06 25), with plenty of information on Sierra Nevada possibilities and facilities.

Skiing

The ski station, at Pradollano, 33km from Granada, is an unattractive modern construction and very crowded at weekends in the season, but it's good enough to have hosted the world alpine skiing championships in 1996.

The season normally lasts from December to April or early May, though conditions are unpredictable. Prices of accommodation and ski passes (*forfaits*; 3200 to 3900 ptas for one day) are generally lowest in the 'promotional seasons' (the first half of December and from some time in April) and highest from Christmas to early January, during Semana Santa and the week-long Andalucian school vacation around 28 February. Details are on the ski station's Web site at www.sierranevadaski.com. There are also an interactive information telephone line, ☎ 958 24 91 19, and an information office (☎ 958 24 91 11) on Plaza de Andalucía at the resort.

The resort has 45 marked downhill runs totalling 61km – five graded black (very difficult), 18 red (difficult), 18 blue (easy) and four green (very easy). The highest start almost at the top of 3395m Veleta, the second highest peak in the Sierra Nevada. Cable cars (1075 ptas return for nonskiers) run up from Pradollano (2100m) to Borreguiles (2645m); other lifts go higher. There are cross-country routes too, and a snowboard area above Borreguiles. Nonskiers can try tobogganing, ice skating or snowmobile or dog-sled rides. During the ski season the resort has a thriving nightlife.

Rental of skis, boots and sticks costs 2600 ptas for one day. The resort has at least three ski schools, with a 15-hour Monday to Friday course costing 12,500 to 15,500 ptas. Private classes cost 3700 ptas an hour for one person and 6000 ptas for four people.

MARTIN HARRIS

Resorts in the Sierra Nevada boast nursery slopes as well as world-class runs.

For short-duration group classes, contact the Escuela Internacional de Esquí (☎ 958 48 01 42). Snowboard rental and classes are available too.

Walking

From the ski station in July and August you can walk up Veleta in three or four hours – a paved road actually runs right up there but it's closed at the Borreguiles turn-off about a quarter of the way up from Pradollano. From Veleta to the top of Mulhacén is about another five hours' walk and you would need to sleep in a *refugio* (basic mountain accommodation; see Mulhacén in the Las Alpujarras section for details). A variety of other walks are possible from the ski station.

Other Activities

In summer, you can rent mountain bikes at the resort for around 850 ptas a day. Guided walks, horse riding and paragliding are offered too.

Places to Stay & Eat

Room reservations are highly advisable in the ski season. Outside the ski season only a few hotels stay open.

The youth hostel *Albergue Juvenil Sierra Nevada* (☎ 958 48 03 05), near the top of the ski station, has 214 places in rooms holding two or four people and is open year round. Its low season, price-wise, is May to November and its high season periods are similar to other accommodation at the resort. The resort has around 15 hotels, hostales and apartment-hotels, with doubles costing

between about 8000 and 12,000 p... less expensive such as *Hotel Tele...* (☎ 958 24 91 20), *Hostal El Ciervo* (☎ ... 48 04 09) and *Hostal El Duende Blanco* (☎ 958 48 11 10). The best deals are ski packages which you should try to book at least two weeks ahead through the resort's central booking service (☎ 958 24 91 11, fax 958 24 91 46, ✆ agencia@cetursa.es). Per person, a two-night half-board package with two days' ski passes costs from 17,225 to 20,600 ptas at the youth hostel (also including six hours' ski classes and equipment rental), and from 15,000 to 40,000 ptas at hotels.

Getting There & Away

Autobús Viajes Bonal (☎ 958 27 31 00) runs three daily buses (four at weekends) to the ski resort from Bar Ventorrillo on Paseo del Violón near the Palacio de Congresos in Granada. The one-way/return fare is 425/800 ptas. A taxi from Granada costs about 6000 ptas.

The road over the top of the Sierra Nevada, from the ski station to Capileira in Las Alpujarras, is now closed to vehicles without a special permit above the Borreguiles turn-off, some 4km up from the top of Pradollano.

LAS ALPUJARRAS

Despite a burst of tourism in the last decade or two, Las Alpujarras remains a world apart, with a rare sense of timelessness and mystery. Its bizarre history saw a flourishing Muslim community replaced en masse by Christian settlers in the 16th century. Reminders of the Muslim past are ubiquitous in the form of the Alpujarras' Berber-style villages and the terracing and irrigation of the land.

History

The Alpujarras rose to prominence in the 10th and 11th centuries by supplying the silk workshops of Almería with silk thread – spun from the unravelled cocoons of the mulberry-leaf-eating caterpillars of the silk moth. This activity had arisen hand in hand with a wave of Berber migrants to the area.

GRANADA PROVINCE

Later, silk made from Alpujarras thread was an economic mainstay of Nasrid Granada. Together with successful irrigation and agriculture, silk production supported a population of probably over 150,000 in at least 400 villages and hamlets by the late 15th century.

On his surrender to Fernando and Isabel in 1492, Boabdil, the last Granada emir, was awarded the Alpujarras as a personal fiefdom. He settled at Laujar de Andarax in the Almerían Alpujarras but left for Africa the next year. Christian promises of tolerance gave way to forced mass conversions and land expropriations; in 1500, Muslims across the former emirate rebelled, with the Alpujarras in the thick of things. When the revolt failed, Muslims were given the choice of exile or conversion. Most converted – to become known as Moriscos – but the change was barely skin deep. A new repressive decree by Felipe II in 1567 forbade the use of Arabic names and dress and even of the Arabic language, leading to a new revolt in the Alpujarras in 1568, led by a Morisco named Aben Humeya and aided by North African Muslims. The rebellion spread across southern Andalucía. In the Alpujarras, two years of vicious guerrilla war ended only after Don Juan of Austria, Felipe's half-brother, was brought in to quash the insurrection and Aben Humeya was assassinated by his cousin Aben Aboo.

Almost the whole Alpujarras population was deported as land labour to western Andalucía and parts of Castile, and some 270 villages and hamlets were re-peopled with settlers from northern Spain. The other villages were abandoned. Over the following centuries, the silk industry fell by the wayside and swaths of the Alpujarras' woodlands were lost to mining and cereal growing. The region returned to the footnotes of history.

Books

In the 1920s literary Englishman Gerald Brenan settled in the Alpujarras village of Yegen with 'a good many books and a little money', aiming to educate himself unimpeded by British traditions. His *South From Granada* is a fascinating picture of what was then a very isolated and superstitious corner of Spain, leavened by visits from Virginia Woolf and other literati. Another Englishman, Chris Stewart, settled in Las Alpujarras somewhat more recently, as a sheep farmer near Órgiva: his successful *Driving over Lemons* tells entertainingly of life in Las Alpujarras in the 1990s.

Walking

There's a wealth of good walks linking valley villages or heading up into the Sierra Nevada. Some are mentioned in the following sections. The Alpujarras section of the GR-7 long-distance footpath, which crosses Europe from Greece to Algeciras, is marked by posts with red and white rings and the letters 'E4 GR7', and by signposts in villages. You can walk the GR-7 from Laroles at the foot of the Puerto de la Ragua pass to Lanjarón in the western Alpujarras in one week; the Spanish guide *GR-7: Senda Granadina: Tramo Alpujarreño* by Mariano Cruz, Jesús Espinosa and Natalio Carmona covers it in detail.

Accommodation

It's worth trying to book ahead for rooms in Las Alpujarras during Semana Santa and from June to September. In addition to hotels and hostales, many villages have apartments and houses for short-term rental – ask in information offices, look for signs or ask around. Organisations with a number of houses and apartments in different villages include Rural Andalus and RAAR (see Accommodation in the introductory Facts for the Visitor chapter for details) and Rustic Blue (☎ 958 76 33 81, fax 958 76 31 34), Barrio de la Ermita, 18412 Bubión. Prices for four people start around 10,000 ptas a night or 60,000 ptas a week. You can check out Rustic Blue's Web site at www.rusticblue.com.

Food & Drink

Most Alpujarras food is straightforward, hearty country fare, with lots of good meat and local trout. Trevélez is famous for its *jamón serrano*, but many other villages produce good hams too. A *plato alpujarreño* consists of fried potatoes, fried eggs, sausage, ham and maybe a black pudding, usually costing around 700 ptas.

Alpujarras or Costa wine comes mainly from the Sierra de la Contraviesa, between Las Alpujarras and the sea, and tends to be strong and fairly raw.

Getting There & Away

Bus Buses to the Alpujarras are run by Alsina Graells (☎ 958 18 54 80 in Granada). From Granada, buses run three times daily to Lanjarón, Órgiva (520 ptas, 1½ hours), Pampaneira, Bubión, Capileira and Pitres (2¾ hours). At the time of writing these left Granada at 10.30 am, noon and 5.15 pm), with the last two continuing to Trevélez (830 ptas, 3¼ hours) and Bérchules (3¾ hours). The return buses depart from Bér-chules at 5 am and 5 pm and from Pitres at 3.30 pm. There is also a twice-daily Granada–Ugíjar service via Lanjarón, Órgiva, Torvizcón, Cádiar (910 ptas, 3¼ hours), Yegen and Válor. Alsina runs a Málaga Lanjarón service via Órgiva, an Almería–Ugíjar bus via Berja, and an Almería–Bérchules service via Adra, daily except Sunday and holidays.

Car & Motorcycle The main road into the Alpujarras from the west is the A-348 (marked C-333 on some signs). The GR-421 turns north off the A-348 just west of Órgiva to wind along the northern slopes of the Alpujarras, rejoining it a few kilometres north of Cádiar. There's a petrol station on the GR-421 between Pampaneira and Pitres. From the Motril direction, turn east off the N-323 just north of Vélez de Benaudalla.

Lanjarón

postcode 18420 • pop 4000
• elevation 660m

Las Alpujarras' westernmost town, a spa, has a good setting on the southern slopes of the Sierra Nevada but what most people see is a straggly place along the A-348 (Avenida Andalucía). Numerous hostales and hotels,

with doubles costing between 3000 and 8000 ptas, are strung along Avenida Andalucía, but only a few stay open during winter. The cheaper ones tend to be towards the eastern end of town.

Órgiva

postcode 18400 • pop 6100
• elevation 725m

The main town of the western Alpujarras, Órgiva (sometimes spelt Órjiva) is a scruffy but bustling place, at its most interesting on Thursday mornings when both locals and the Alpujarras' sizeable international community (which has a strong alternative/New Age presence) gather to buy and sell everything from vegetables and wholefoods to hippie art at a colourful market in the upper part of town, the Barrio Alto.

From the Alsina Graells bus stop and office on Avenida González Robles, walk up the street and round the corner to the right and you'll come to Órgiva's central traffic lights. There are banks, some with ATMs, on and near Calle Doctor Fleming which heads uphill here.

The landmark 16th-century twin-towered **Iglesia de Nuestra Señora de la Expectación** stands at the foot of Calle Doctor Fleming.

Places to Stay & Eat Two kilometres south of the centre on the A-348, between the town and the Río Guadalfeo, *Camping Órgiva* (☎ 958 78 43 07) has a pool and restaurant but only a small area for camping. Two adults with a car and tent pay around 2000 ptas.

Pensión Alma Alpujarreña (☎ 958 78 40 85, Avenida González Robles 49), just below the central traffic lights, has singles/doubles for 2000/4000 ptas (doubles with bath 5000 ptas) and serves varied, reasonably priced food, including some vegetarian dishes, indoors and outdoors.

Hostal Mirasol (☎ 958 78 51 59, Avenida González Robles 3), near the A-348's bridge over the Río Chico towards the western end of town, has adequate rooms with bathroom for 2000/4000 ptas plus IVA. The adjacent *Hotel Mirasol* (☎ 958 78 51 08,

GRANADA PROVINCE

Avenida González Robles 5) has newer, more comfortable rooms with TV costing 7000/8000 ptas plus IVA. The two share a decent restaurant where a three-course dinner costs around 1700 ptas. *Hotel Taray* (☎ *958 78 45 25*), 1.5km south of the centre on the A-348, has rooms that cost 6180/8370 ptas plus IVA.

La Zahona bakery on Calle Doctor Fleming does good cakes and pastries which go well with a drink at the pavement tables of *Café Galindo Plaza*, which shares the same premises. The Galindo serves pizzas for 1000 ptas. You can get wholemeal bread *(pan integral)* in the daily market at the top of Calle Doctor Fleming.

Pampaneira, Bubión & Capileira

Pampaneira: postcode 18411, pop 350, elevation 1050m; Bubión: postcode 18412, pop 370, elevation 1300m; Capileira: postcode 18413, pop 580, elevation 1440m

These villages, clinging to the side of the deep Barranco de Poqueira ravine 14 to 20km north-east of Órgiva, are among the prettiest, most dramatically sited, and most touristed, in Las Alpujarras. Their whitewashed stone houses seem to clamber over each other in an effort not to slide into the gorge, while streets decked with flowery balconies climb haphazardly between.

Capileira, the highest of the three, is the best base for walks if you don't have your own vehicle.

Information The Centro de Visitantes de Pampaneira (☎ 958 76 31 27) on Pampaneira's square, Plaza de la Libertad, has a wealth of information on the Alpujarras and Sierra Nevada, including maps for sale, and can inform you about walks and mountain refuges. It opens 10 am to 2 pm and 4 to 6 pm (5 to 7 pm from about May to mid-October) Tuesday to Saturday, 10 am to 3 pm Sunday and Monday, and English is spoken. An information kiosk by the main road in Capileira gives out a useful village map.

There are ATMs just outside the car park entrance in Pampaneira and at La General bank on Calle Doctor Castilla in Capileira. All three villages have supermarkets.

The Houses of Las Alpujarras

Travellers who have been to Morocco may notice a resemblance between villages in the Alpujarras and those in the Atlas Mountains. The typical Alpujarras building style was introduced by Berber settlers during Muslim times.

Most houses have two storeys, with the lower one still often used for storage and animals. The characteristic flat roofs *(terraos)*, with their protruding chimney pots, consist of a layer of *launa* (a type of clay) packed onto flat stones which are laid on beams of chestnut, ash or pine. Nowadays there's often a layer of plastic between the stones and the launa for extra waterproofing. Whitewash is a fairly modern introduction too: the villages used to be stone-coloured.

Things to See These villages – like many others in Las Alpujarras – have solid 16th-century **Mudéjar churches** (open at mass times, which are posted on the doors). They also have small **weaving workshops** which you can poke your head into, and plentiful craft shops selling, among other things, colourful homespun Alpujarras cotton rugs.

Given the somewhat Himalayan character of the Poqueira landscape, it is not entirely surprising that a small Tibetan Buddhist monastery, **Osel Ling** (Place of Clear Light), stands about 1550m up on the far side of the valley from Pampaneira. The monastery welcomes visitors at certain times (call ☎ 958 34 31 34 for hours). You can walk to it from any of the villages or drive up from the turn-off marked 'Ruta Pintoresca' opposite the Ermita del Padre Eterno, a wayside chapel on the GR-421, 5km below Pampaneira.

Walking Eight trails ranging from four to 23km (two to eight hours) are marked out in the beautiful Barranco de Poqueira with little colour-coded posts. Their outlines are shown on rather rough maps posted in the villages, and they are marked and described on Editorial Alpina's *Sierra Nevada, La Alpujarra* map. Most routes start from

GRANADA PROVINCE

Capileira, though No 1 (6km) is a circuit from Pampaneira and No 6 (23km) is a circuit from Bubión.

Route No 4 from Capileira (8km, 3½ hours) takes you up to the hamlet of La Cebadilla, then down the western side of the valley and back up to Capileira. To find its start, walk down to the end of Calle Cubo at the northern end of Capileira, turn right at Apartamentos Vista Veleta and keep going. Route Nos 7 and 8 both continue up the valley from La Cebadilla. Nos 2 and 5 start at the end of Calle Cerezo in Capileira.

You can walk from Capileira to Trevélez in about five hours using a broad track heading to the right 4km up the Mulhacén road from Capileira, a couple of hundred metres after the 8km marker. This track is driveable too.

Nevadensis (☎ 958 76 31 27, fax 958 76 33 01, 🅔 nevadensis@arrakis.es), a group of mountain guides who also run the visitor centre at Pampaneira, offers guided hikes and treks, with a minimum of five people usually needed. A five-hour outing in the Barranco de Poqueira costs 2300 ptas per person; a combined 4WD and foot ascent of Mulhacén is 4000 ptas per person. Four or five-day treks are available too. Check www.nevadensis.com for further information.

Other Activities Depending on the season, Nevadensis (see the preceding Walking section for details) can organise horse riding (around 4000 ptas per person for two hours or 8500 ptas for a day), ski touring, mountain biking, climbing, paragliding and 4WD trips. For horse riding you could also contact Rafael Belmonte (☎ 958 75 31 35) or Dallas Love (☎ 958 76 30 38, fax 958 76 30 34). Both are Bubión-based, speak English and offer guided rides lasting anywhere from two hours to a week or so.

Places to Stay & Eat There are options in all three villages.

Pampaneira Two good hostales face each other across Calle José Antonio at the entrance to the village. *Hostal Pampaneira*

(☎ 958 76 30 02) has singles/doubles with bathroom that cost up to 3000/4000 ptas and the cheapest restaurant in the village (trout or pork chops 650 ptas). *Hostal Ruta del Mulhacén* (☎ 958 76 30 10, fax 958 76 34 46) has rooms with bathroom for 3100/4250 ptas and uninterrupted valley views from some rooms. Of the three restaurants just along the street on Plaza de la Libertad, *Restaurante Casa Diego*, with a pleasant upstairs terrace, is a good choice. Most main dishes cost between 600 to 1200 ptas (trout with ham, and local ham and eggs, are among the cheaper options). *Bar Belezmín* has a few vegetarian dishes.

Bubión Just off the main road at the top of the village, *Villa Turística de Bubión* (☎ 958 76 31 11, fax 958 76 31 36, Barrio Alto s/n) has comfortable self-catering apartments with fireplaces for two to six people (12,000 ptas plus IVA for two or three). There's a restaurant too. *Hostal Las Terrazas* (☎ 958 76 30 34, fax 958 76 32 52, Plaza del Sol 7), below the main road, has pleasant though smallish singles/doubles with bathroom costing 2750/3900 ptas, and apartments in nearby buildings for around 6000 to 12,000 ptas for two to six people. Both these establishments have mountain bikes to rent for clients.

Restaurante Teide, by the main road, is good, with a three-course menú, including a drink, for 1100 ptas plus IVA. Several a la carte main dishes come in under 800 ptas, including trout with ham and vegetarian options such as fennel-stuffed aubergines. Up the street is the convivial, pub-like *Café-Bar Fuenfria*, with a terrace across the road.

Capileira Just off the main road, *Mesón Hostal Poqueira* (☎/fax 958 76 30 48, Calle Doctor Castilla 6) has good singles/doubles with bathroom that cost 2400/4000 ptas. *Hostal Atalaya* (☎ 958 76 30 25, Calle Perchel 3), 100m down the main road, has similar prices but is smaller and less appealing. *Hostal Paco López* (☎ 958 76 30 11, Carretera de la Sierra 5), just up the main road, has rooms with bath from 2000/3000 ptas. A short distance farther up

GRANADA PROVINCE

the street, round a right-hand bend, *Restaurante Ruta de la Nieves* (☎ 958 76 31 06, *Carretera de la Sierra s/n*) has eight decent rooms with bathroom costing 2000/4000 ptas. *Finca Los Llanos* (☎ 958 76 30 71, fax 958 76 32 06), at the top of the village, has classier apartments at 12,000 ptas plus IVA for two people.

Most places to stay have restaurants but there are alternatives. *Bar El Tilo* on Plaza Calvario, just down from the far end of Calle Doctor Castilla, serves good-value *raciones* (meal-sized servings of tapas) such as *patatas a lo pobre* (poor man's potatoes: a potato dish with peppers and garlic, 400 ptas) or *chuletas de cerdo* (pork chops, 550 ptas). *Casa Íbero* below the church (follow signs) makes original international food ranging from vegetarian croquettes (850 ptas) or several couscous dishes (875 to 1300 ptas) to lamb with ginger sauce (1300 ptas). It opens for lunch and dinner except Sunday night and one whole day (recently Wednesday).

Mulhacén

The Sierra Nevada's two highest peaks – Mulhacén (3478m) and Veleta (3395m) – rise above the head of the Poqueira valley. Mulhacén, the highest peak in mainland Spain, is named after Moulay Abu al-Hasan, father of the ill-fated Boabdil. Its summit supports a small shrine, a roofless chapel and a broken metal cross. Immediately behind the summit is a near-perpendicular 500m drop to the Hoya de Mulhacén basin. The views, on a good day, take in such distant ranges as the Sierra de Cazorla and the Rif Mountains of Morocco.

A road climbs over the Sierra Nevada from Capileira to the Estación de Esquí Sierra Nevada but it is now closed to vehicles without a special permit some 7 or 8km up from Capileira.

There are many ways to approach the high peaks on foot. By virtually any route it's six or more hours walking (plus time for halts) to the top of Mulhacén, so it's advisable to spend a night in one of three mountain refuges, or camping.

The modern, 87-bunk *Refugio Poqueira*

(☎ 958 34 33 49, 608 55 42 24) is towards the top of the Poqueira valley at 2500m. It opens year round (book a few days ahead if possible) and costs 1000 ptas per person, with prepared meals available (breakfast 550 ptas, dinner 1600 ptas). Blankets are provided and there are showers. Higher up, just above the Sierra Nevada road, are two 12-place *refugios vivac* – stone shelters with just boards to sleep on and a long table and benches to eat at. They're free, and always open, but reservations are not possible. These are the *Refugio Vivac La Caldera*, below the west flank of Mulhacén, a 1½ hour walk up from Refugio Poqueira; and *Refugio Vivac La Carigüela*, a 2½ hour walk west along the road from Refugio Vivac La Caldera, at the 3200m Collado del Veleta pass below the summit of Veleta.

Wild camping in the mountains is allowed only with official permission. At the time of writing it was necessary to fill in an application form, available at such places as the Centro de Visitantes in Pampaneira, and fax it to the Consejería de Medio Ambiente (fax 958 53 76 21), which would return it immediately if received between 9 am and 2 pm Monday to Friday. You can obtain information on regulations from the Pampaneira or El Dornajo visitor centres or from the office of the Parque Nacional and Parque Natural de Sierra Nevada (☎ 958 48 68 89, fax 958 48 60 72), Carretera Antigua de Sierra Nevada Km 7, Pinos Genil, Granada.

One approach to Veleta and Mulhacén is from the ski station (see Walking in the earlier Estación de Esquí Sierra Nevada section). To continue from Veleta to Mulhacén use the road as far as the Refugio Vivac La Caldera then follow the path up the western flank of Mulhacén, a steep 400m ascent – altogether about eight hours' walking (not counting halts) from the ski resort if you crown Veleta too.

From the Alpujarras side, the two main jumping-off points for Mulhacén are Trevélez and Capileira. From Trevélez you can climb steeply to the Sierra Nevada road near El Chorrillo (2727m), from which the road, then a branch track, and finally a path take you to the summit (five or six hours from Trevélez, plus halts). A more attractive route heads north-westward up to the Cañada de Siete Lagunas, a lake-dotted basin below the eastern side of Mulhacén, then up the rocky Cuesta del Resuello ridge leading to the summit – about seven hours' walking from Trevélez, but you have the option of camping in the Cañada de Siete Lagunas.

From Capileira, you can walk to the Refugio Poqueira in about five hours. Follow the Sierra Nevada road upwards for 7.5km to a bend where a dirt road branches left by a stone house with a swimming pool. Go 800m north-north-west along the branch road to an unfinished house with one high triangular end (drivers can get vehicles this far and park nearby). From here follow the Acequia Baja irrigation channel along its generally northerly course for some 6km. About 400m before the Río Mulhacén, turn right (north-north-east) up the hillside for the 420m ascent to the refugio. From the refugio you can head up the Río Mulhacén valley for 1½ hours to meet the Sierra Nevada road just below the Refugio Vivac La Caldera, then head up the steep west flank of Mulhacén (2½ hours from refugio to summit).

See the earlier Marquesado de Zenete section for a mention of perhaps the toughest Sierra Nevada walking route, the Ruta Integral de los Tresmil.

Pitres & La Taha

Pitres (postcode 18414, population approximately 500, elevation 1250m) is almost as pretty as the Poqueira gorge villages but less touristed. It has a bank and ATM on the main square. The five hamlets in the valley below Pitres are grouped with it in a municipality called La Taha, a name that recalls the Muslim Emirate of Granada, when the Alpujarras was divided into 12 administrative units called *tahas*. Today the lower hamlets below Pitres – Mecina, Mecinilla, Fondales, Ferreirola and Atalbéitar – form a tiny world of their own, where the air seems thick with accumulated centuries. Ancient paths wend their way through some of the Alpujarras' lushest woods and or-

chards, to the ubiquitous tinkle of running water. A few minutes' walk below Fondales is an old Muslim bridge over the Río Trevélez gorge, with a ruined Muslim mill beside it (for directions from Fondales ask for the *puente árabe*).

The good **Camping El Balcón de Pitres** (☎ 958 76 61 11), by the GR-421 on the western side of Pitres, opens year round and charges 1725 ptas plus IVA for two adults with a car and tent. It has a decent restaurant. **Refugio Los Albergues** (☎ 958 34 31 76), two minutes' walk (signposted) down a path from the GR-421 on the eastern side of Pitres, is a small walkers' hostel, with 12 places in a bunk dorm costing 1000 ptas, one double room for 3000 ptas, an equipped kitchen, hot showers and interesting outdoor toilets. It's closed from 10 January to 15 February. The friendly German owner is full of information on the area and its many good walks.

Fonda Sierra Nevada (☎ 958 76 60 17) on Pitres' square has simple singles/doubles costing 1700/3400 ptas. Pitres, Mecina and nearby Pórtugos all have midrange hotels (doubles cost from 5000 to 7500 ptas). There's a handful of cafes and restaurants around Pitres' square.

Trevélez
postcode 18417 • pop 800
• elevation 1476m
Trevélez, set in a gash in the mountainside almost as impressive as the Poqueira gorge, is famous for three reasons: it's a frequent starting point for ascents of the high Sierra Nevada peaks; it produces some of Spain's best *jamón serrano*, with hams trucked in from far and wide for curing in the dry mountain air; and it's often said to be the highest village in Spain. In fact the top of Trevélez is below 1600m, so several other villages – notably Valdelinares, Aragón, which reaches above 1700m – could claim the 'highest' title, but the Trevélez municipality is certainly the highest on the mainland as it includes Mulhacén.

Along the main road you're confronted by a welter of *jamón* and souvenir shops, but a wander into the upper parts reveals a lively village of typical Alpujarran quaint-ness. La General bank just above the main road has an ATM.

Walking Aside from being a starting point for Mulhacén and walks to other Alpujarras villages, Trevélez is also one end of an old pack-animal route up the Trevélez valley and over the 2800m Puerto de Trevélez pass to Jerez del Marquesado, 22km north-east (see the earlier Marquesado de Zenete sec-tion). This could be walked in a long day or you could overnight at the *Refugio Postero Alto* (☎ 958 34 51 54) before Jerez.

Places to Stay & Eat One kilometre south of Trevélez along the GR-421 towards Busquístar, *Camping Trevélez* (☎ 958 85 87 35) is open year round, charging 1665 to 2050 ptas plus IVA for two adults with a car and tent. It also has ecologically-minded owners, cabins at 2500/5500 ptas plus IVA for two/four people and a restaurant.

Restaurante González (☎ 958 85 85 31, *Plaza de Don Francisco Abellán s/n*), by the main road at the foot of the village, has singles/doubles with shared bathrooms for 2000/3000 ptas and doubles with private bathroom for 4500 ptas. Its good restau-rant serves an excellent-value menú for 950 ptas, or chicken, trout or *plato alpujar-reño* for 750 to 1100 ptas. *Hostal Regina* (☎ 958 85 85 64, *Plaza de Don Francisco Abellán 12*) has more comfortable rooms with bathrooms costing 3000/5300 ptas or doubles with shared bath for 4100 ptas.

Hostal Fernando (☎ 958 85 85 65, *Pista del Barrio Medio s/n*), by the road going up towards the top of the village, has clean singles/doubles with bathroom from 2000/3500 to 2500/4500 ptas. A little higher, on Plaza Barrio Medio, signs point to *Hotel La Fragua* (☎ 958 85 86 26, *Calle San Antonio 4*), with Trevélez's most comfortable rooms at 2800/5500 ptas with bath. The good *Mesón La Fragua*, a short walk away, offers relatively exotic fare such as par-tridge in walnut sauce (1500 ptas) and fig ice cream (500 ptas), as well as excellent sir-loin *(solomillo)* available several ways for around 950 ptas. Just down the street, *Café*

Bar Castellón (☎ 958 85 85 07, *Calle Cár-cel*) offers basic rooms with shared bath-room and mostly lacking windows, for 1500/3000 ptas.

Mesón Haraicel just above Plaza de Don Francisco Abellán has a few outside tables and good food, with several trout and meat main courses costing 850 to 1000 ptas. Also good is *Mesón Joaquín* by the main road on the western side of the village. A three-course menú, including a drink, costs 1000 ptas.

Jamón de Trevélez crops up on every menu. If you're tempted to buy some to take away, the shops up in the village tend to be cheaper than those on the main road.

East of Trevélez

Seven kilometres south of Trévelez the GR-421 crosses the low Portichuelo de Cástaras pass and turns east into a barer landscape. Yet there are still oases of greenery around the villages. The central and eastern parts of the Alpujarras are as impressive as the west, but pull in far fewer tourists.

From **Juvíles**, 12km from Trevélez, you can walk in half an hour to the top of Fuerte, a rocky hill rising east of the village which was its fortress in Muslim times. *Café Bar Pensión Tino* (☎ 958 76 91 74), at the south-western end of the village, has pleas-ant rooms with bathroom for just 2000/3500 ptas. *Restaurante Alonso* also has rooms.

Five kilometres farther east is **Bérchules**, in a green valley which stretches a long way back into the hills and offers some attractive walks. *La Posada* (☎ 958 85 25 41, *Plaza del Ayuntamiento 3*) is a sturdy old village house turned into simple but comfortable lodgings, with walkers in mind. Bed and breakfast costs 2000 ptas per person, Eng-lish is spoken and vegetarian dinners are available.

Cádiar, down by the Río Guadalfeo 8km south of Bérchules, is one of the bigger Alpujarras villages (2000 people), and more appealing than it looks from afar. *Café Bar Montoro* (☎ 958 75 00 68, *Calle San Isidro 20*), 200m from the large, typically alpujar-reño church, has doubles with bathroom for

GRANADA PROVINCE

just 2000 ptas plus IVA. Two kilometres south, just off the A-348 towards Órgiva and with great views across the valley towards the mountains, is the excellent *Alquería de Morayma* (☎/*fax 958 34 32 21*) – an old farmstead lovingly renovated and expanded to provide a dozen comfortable and unique rooms and apartments ranging from 7000 to 12,500 ptas plus IVA (the biggest hold four). There's good, moderately priced food, a library of Alpujarras information, and fascinating art and artefacts everywhere. **Yegen**, where Gerald Brenan made his home in the 1920s, is 12km east of Bérchules. His house, just off the main square with the fountain, has a plaque. Parts of the valley below Yegen have a particularly moonlike quality. Several walking routes have been marked out locally including a 2½ hour Ruta de Gerald Brenan. You can pick up a leaflet on them at the friendly *Café-Bar Nuevo La Fuente* (☎ *958 85 10 67*) on the village square, which has singles/doubles for 1300/2600 ptas. *El Rincón de Yegen* (☎ *958 85 12 70*), by the road at the eastern edge of the village, has rooms costing around 5000 ptas, apartments for four from around 10,000 ptas, and a restaurant.

Válor, 5km north-east of Yegen, was the birthplace of Aben Humeya, leader of the 1568 rebellion, and is the setting for the most celebrated of several Moros y Cristianos festivities in Las Alpujarras, recreating events of the 1568–70 rebellion. On 14 and 15 September, colourful, costumed 'armies' battle it out noisily on and off from midday to evening. *Hostal Las Perdices* (☎ *958 85 18 21, Calle Torrecilla s/n*), in the centre, has doubles with bathroom that cost 3500 ptas. *Fonda El Suizo* towards the western end of town also has rooms and meals.

Ugíjar (population 2600), 7km south-east of Válor, is the main market town hereabouts, with two hostales. The A-348 then soon enters Almería province (see the Almería Alpujarras section in the Almería Province chapter) but the A-337 heads north over the Sierra Nevada by the 2000m Puerto de la Ragua pass (occasionally snowbound in winter) to La Calahorra (see the Marquesado de Zenete section, earlier).

The Coast

Granada's 80km coastline is rugged and cliff-lined, with spectacular views from the coastal N-340 highway as it winds up and down between scattered seaside towns and villages. This coast is called the Costa Tropical because of the hot-climate crops such as sugar cane, custard apples, avocados and mangos that are grown where the coastal plain broadens out a bit. The N-323 from Granada arrives near the coast just west of Motril after threading through an impressive gorge carved by the Río Guadalfeo. East of uninspiring Motril, the mountains often come right down to the sea, but the settlements are mostly drab and the beaches pebbly. If you're driving from the east, a road to Las Alpujarras heads north across the Sierra de la Contraviesa from La Rábita.

West of Motril the terrain is a bit less abrupt and there are a few quite attractive beach towns.

SALOBREÑA
postcode 18680 • pop 10,000
Salobreña's huddle of white houses rises on a crag between the N-340 and the sea, 2km west of the N-323 junction. At the top is an impressive Muslim castle and below is a long and wide dark-sand beach. It's a low-key place for most of the year but gets lively in July and August.

Orientation & Information
From the N-340, Avenida Federico García Lorca skirts the eastern and lower part of the town as it heads a kilometre or so south to the seafront. Just 200m along on Plaza de Goya is the helpful tourist office (☎ 958 61 03 14), open 9.30 am to 1.30 pm and 4.30 to 7 pm (5 to 8 pm in summer) Monday to Friday, 9.30 am to 1.30 pm Saturday. The Alsina Graells bus stop is diagonally across the street from the tourist office.

Market days are Tuesday and Friday.

Things to See
A 20-minute walk uphill from the tourist office, the **Castillo Árabe** (Arab Castle) dates

from the 13th century, though the site was fortified as early as the 10th century. The castle, a beautiful sight when floodlit at night, was used as a summer residence by the Granada emirs. Legend has it that Emir Mohammed IX had his three daughters, Zaida, Zoraida and Zorahaida, held captive here too; Washington Irving gives a version of this story in *Tales of the Alhambra*. The inner Alcazaba, a setting for many cultural events, retains much of its Nasrid structure. You can walk along parts of the surrounding parapets. The castle is open 10 am to 2 pm and 4 to 8.30 pm daily. The 400 ptas ticket also includes the **Museo Arqueológico**, nearby in the old town hall, below the church. Open the same hours as the castle, the museum has a model and visual aids illustrating how Salobreña was practically an island until river sediments formed a fertile delta around the rocky outcrop on which the town was built.

Immediately below the castle is the 16th-century Mudéjar **Iglesia de Nuestra Señora del Rosario** with a striking arched doorway. The old Muslim town (the original Albayzín and the later Broval and Bóveda districts) spills out below the castle, ending on one side in steep cliffs. There's a **mirador** in the Albayzín and another on Paseo de las Flores below the castle.

Special Events
Semana Santa processions through the steep old town streets attract a lot of visitors. The Día de la Cruz (Day of the Cross) on 3 May is a lively, colourful affair with horse riders, polka-dot dresses and sevillana dancing, as in Granada. Salobreña's fair takes place in the last week of June. Around 20 August, the one-day Lucero de Alba features rock and flamenco acts in the castle and elsewhere.

Places to Stay
Salobreña has half a dozen hostales, mostly inexpensive. *Pensión Mari Carmen (☎ 958 61 09 06, Calle Nueva 32)* and *Pensión Arnedo (☎ 958 61 02 27, Calle Nueva 15)*, both about a 10 minute walk west of Plaza de Goya, have reasonable doubles with shared bath for less than 3000 ptas. *Hotel Salambina (☎ 958 61 00 37)*, just west of town on the N-340, has better rooms costing 6000 ptas plus IVA a double. The slightly flashier *Hotel Salobreña (☎ 958 61 02 61)*, a couple of kilometres farther west on the N-340, has comfortable doubles for 9200 ptas plus IVA.

Places to Eat
Little *Restaurante Pesetas* on Calle Bóveda, the street opposite the Iglesia de Nuestra Señora del Rosario, serves good tapas and meals. The popular *La Bodega*, with outdoor tables on Plaza de Goya, does a menú for 1300 ptas. A couple of hundred metres down Avenida Federico García Lorca, on Plaza Ramírez de Madrid, *Mesón de la Villa* is another good bet. There are several restaurants, small eateries (*chiringuitos*), bars and even a spot of nightlife on and near the beachfront. *El Peñón*, by the big rock which divides Salobreña's main beach, does good seafood.

Getting There & Away
Alsina Graells (☎ 958 60 00 64) has plenty of buses along the coast in both directions (955 ptas to Málaga; 1145 ptas to Almería), and at least six daily to Granada (735 ptas). There are also daily buses to Lanjarón, Sevilla, Córdoba, Jaén and Madrid.

ALMUÑÉCAR
postcode 18690 • pop 21,000
Fifteen kilometres west of Salobreña, Almuñécar may appear uninviting but there's an attractive old section around its 16th-century castle. Popular with Spanish tourists and with a small community of northern Europeans, it's bright and not too expensive, although the beaches are pebbly.

History
Phoenicians set up a colony called Ex or Sex here in the 8th century BC to obtain oil and wine from interior Andalucía for trade. The Roman Sexi Firmum Iulium was founded in 49 BC. It was here that Abd ar-Rahman I arrived from Damascus in 755, going on to found the Muslim emirate of

Córdoba. Later, the town served as a coastal fortress for the Granada emirate. And it was from Almuñécar that Granada's last emir, Boabdil, with 1130 supporters, finally abandoned Spain for North Africa in 1493.

Orientation & Information

The bus station (☎ 958 63 01 40) is at Avenida Juan Carlos I No 1, just south of the N-340. Plaza de la Constitución, the main square of the old part of town, is a few minutes walk south-west, with little Plaza de la Rosa a few minutes farther south-east. The tourist office (☎ 958 63 11 25) is at the other end of town in the pretty neo-Mudéjar Palacete de La Najarra on Avenida de Europa, just back from the eastern end of Playa de San Cristóbal. It opens 10 am to 2 pm and from 4 to 7 pm (5 to 8 pm in summer) daily.

Almuñécar's beachfront is divided by a rocky outcrop, the Peñón del Santo, with Playa de San Cristóbal, the best of the beaches, to the west, and Playa Puerta del Mar to the east. Farther east is the separate Playa de Velilla with lots of apartment blocks but quite a good beach.

Things to See

Just behind Playa de San Cristóbal is a tropical bird aviary, the **Parque Ornitológico Loro-Sexi** – open 11 am to 2 pm and 4 to 7 pm daily (300 ptas). The top of the hill just inland is occupied by the **Castillo de San Miguel**, built over Muslim and Roman fortifications by the conquering Christians. The climb up through narrow streets to the entrance (on the northern side) is well worthwhile: the castle commands excellent views and contains a museum which has displays that add up to a quick history of Almuñécar. Hours are 10.30 am to 1.30 pm and 4 to 7 pm Tuesday to Saturday, 10.30 am to 2 pm Sunday. The 300 ptas ticket also gives admission to the nearby **Museo Arqueológico**, in 1st century Roman galleries called the Cueva de Siete Palacios. The museum has local Phoenician, Roman and Islamic finds plus a rare 3500-year-old Egyptian amphora, probably brought by the Carthaginians. One hundred metres along Avenida de Europa from the tourist office, in the Parque Botánico El Majuelo, is the **Factoría de Salazones de Pescado**, the remains of a Carthaginian and Roman fish-salting workshop.

Farther afield, off Avenida del Mediterráneo about a half-hour walk west of the old town, is the **Necrópolis Puente de Noy**, a Phoenician and Roman cemetery, where over 200 tombs have been excavated. Out near the N-340 are several lengths of **Roman aqueduct**.

Places to Stay

There are two year-round camping grounds on the N-340 east of the centre. *Camping Carambolo (☎ 958 63 03 22)* at Km 315 is the cheaper of the two and farther from the beach. Farther out, at Km 317.5, *Camping El Paraíso (☎ 958 63 23 70)* is on the coastal side of the N-340. The summer sites at nearby La Herradura are better situated.

Budget hostales are in the streets between the bus station and Plaza de la Rosa. The basic but clean *Hostal Victoria (☎ 958 63 00 22, Plaza de la Victoria 6)* has doubles with bathroom for 4000 ptas, but usually opens only during July and August. The better *Hotel Victoria II (☎ 958 63 17 34, Plaza de Damasco 2)* has doubles costing 6000 ptas. Almost next door in a distinctive neo-Muslim building, the good *Hostal Plaza Damasco (☎ 958 63 01 65, Calle Cerrajeros 16)* has similar prices. *Hotel Goya (☎ 958 63 05 50, Avenida de Europa 31)*, near Playa de San Cristóbal, has doubles costing 6500 ptas plus IVA. These last three places all charge quite a lot less from September to June. Almost on Playa de San Cristóbal, opposite the monument to Abd ar-Rahman I, is the more upmarket *Hotel Casablanca (☎ 958 63 55 75, Plaza San Cristóbal 4)*, with comfortable doubles at 9000 ptas plus IVA.

Places to Eat

Plaza de la Constitución has a few popular restaurants with tables outside. *Bodega Francisco (Calle Real 15)*, between Plaza de la Constitución and Plaza de la Rosa, is a typical bar with a long tapas list and an

850 ptas menú. Just east of Plaza de la Rosa is Plaza Kelibia, which has several bars with tables on the square: *La Trastienda* has excellent tapas. *Pizzería Il Grillo (Plaza de Damasco 5)*, nearby, serves up good Italian food. Directly south of Plaza de la Rosa, Acera del Mar has a line of eateries facing Playa Puerta del Mar. Or you could head for the restaurants opposite Playa de San Cristóbal: *Hotel Casablanca's* restaurant, with tables on the square at the eastern end of Paseo de los Flores, does a menú that costs 900 ptas and serves good meat dishes.

Entertainment
Plaza Kelibia and Acera del Mar buzz at night. The *Auditorio Martín Recuerda*, in the Casa de la Cultura on Calle Puerta de Granada, hosts musical events, theatre, poetry readings and a cine club. *Venta Luciano*, 3km north of Almuñécar on the Carretera Suspiro del Moro, has an all-you-can-eat-and-drink barbecue followed by a flamenco show (3300 ptas, 4300 ptas with transport) at 8.30 pm on Friday. Book on ☎ 958 63 13 79 or at hotels and travel agents in town.

Getting There & Away
Several buses a day run along the coast to Nerja, Málaga and Almería, and inland to Granada. There's also one bus daily to each of Lanjarón, Orgiva, Jaén and Úbeda, and two to Sevilla.

If you're driving to/from Granada, consider going by the Carretera del Suspiro del Moro, a spectacular road across the mountains to the Puerto del Suspiro del Moro on the N-323 Granada–Motril road, via Otívar.

MARINA DEL ESTE
West of Almuñecar, the N-340 winds between the mountains and the coast for 7km to La Herradura. Shortly before La Herradura is the turn-off to Marina del Este on the Punta de la Mona promontory. The 4km road winds uphill then descends steeply to the coast and the beautiful marina with its exclusive feel.

There are a couple of diving outfits: Club Nautique (☎ 958 82 75 14) charges 5500 ptas for a dive including the boat and equipment, or 50,000 ptas for a four-day PADI course. Shortly before the marina is Alcázar (☎ 958 64 01 82), a sports club in a large neo-Muslim building with loads of facilities – ask about paragliding.

El Barco, with main dishes from 1000 to 2000 ptas, does excellent seafood. In summer, *Tradewinds* is a lively spot for a drink and tapas from 6 pm until late.

LA HERRADURA
postcode 18697 • pop 1800
The little resort town of La Herradura, named after its pretty, horseshoe-shaped bay, attracts paragliders from far and wide and is popular locally for water sports (it has a windsurfing school and several dive outfits) and seafront restaurants. Its sheltered beach is packed during July and August. In January the town hosts the Andrés Segovia international classical guitar competition.

Orientation & Information
The Alsina Graells bus stop is at the top of Calle Acera del Pilar, right by the N-340. Calle Acera del Pilar heads south to the seafront Paseo Andrés Segovia, also called Paseo Marítimo, which runs right along the bay. The town, with a few shops and services, spills down the gentle slope between the N-340 and the beach, and along the land side of Paseo Andrés Segovia. On this street, head to Windsurf La Herradura (☎ 958 64 01 43) for windsurfer, canoe, dinghy and catamaran rentals. Dive outfits include Granada Sub (☎ 958 64 02 81) and Mar Azul (☎ 958 88 10 38).

Places to Stay
Two summer camp sites, *Camping La Herradura (☎ 958 64 00 56)* and *Nuevo Camping La Herradura (☎ 958 64 06 34)*, are opposite the beach on Paseo Andrés Segovia. Nuevo Camping is the more expensive at about 2500 ptas for two adults, a tent and a car. On the same street, *Hostal Peña Parda (☎ 958 64 00 66)*, at the western end,

and *Hostal La Caleta* (☎ 958 82 70 07), towards the eastern end, both charge around 7000 ptas for doubles with bathroom in summer and have good restaurants. *Hotel Tryp Los Fenicios* (☎ 958 82 79 00), a few doors east of Hostal La Caleta, has doubles costing 16,000 ptas plus IVA in high season.

Places to Eat

Most restaurants on Paseo Andrés Segovia serve good food at reasonable prices, though they mark up drinks. *Casa Antonio & Evelyn*, east of Calle Acera del Pilar, has a mixed menu; try one of their excellent soups, or *jabalí* (wild boar). Also at the eastern end of Paseo Andrés Segovia are *Café Luciano*, open from 1 pm, a relaxed place to linger over a coffee, and *El Chambao de Joaquín* (☎ 958 64 00 44), with a beachside garden, which does a terrific *paella* at 2.30 pm every Saturday and Sunday (750 ptas including a drink; you need to book for Sunday).

Getting There & Away

Plenty of Alsina Graells buses head east and west along the coast and a few go to Granada.

Jaén Province

There are two special reasons to venture on from Granada or Córdoba to the back-country province of Jaén (ha-**en**). One is the Parque Natural de Cazorla, perhaps the most beautiful of all Andalucía's mountain regions. The other is a wonderful Renaissance architectural heritage dominated by the master Andrés de Vandelvira, at its best in Úbeda but also impressive in Baeza and Jaén.

The Jaén landscape alternates between rolling agricultural *campiña* (countryside under cultivation), covered with olive trees, and impressive mountain ranges. The Río Guadalquivir rises among the Cazorla mountains, then flows west across the province. The Desfiladero de Despeñaperros pass – a gap in the Sierra Morena on Jaén's northern border – has, from time immemorial, been the most important northern gateway to Andalucía.

You'll find lots of interesting information in English, French, German and Spanish on the provincial government's 'Jaén, Paraíso Interior' Web site at www.promojaen.es.

Food

Jaén food is traditional, but richly varied. Many bars still have the endearing habit of serving free tapas with drinks.

The cuisine is based on local products such as olive oil, seasonal vegetables (including wild mushrooms), game, trout, *bacalao* (salted cod; traditionally the only sea fish available in interior Andalucía), pork and ham. *Escabeche* marinade (oil, vinegar and water) is used to preserve perishables.

Ensalada de perdiz (partridge salad) and *choto* (veal) are other favourites and there's a wide range of *revueltos* (scrambled egg dishes). *Lomo de orza* is seasoned pork loin, fried then conserved in oil in a clay pot called an *orza*.

Rin-rán is a traditional concoction of bacalao, potato and dried red peppers mashed up together. *Carruécano* is pumpkin fried with garlic and chillies.

Highlights

- Explore the beautiful Parque Natural de Cazorla – Spain's biggest protected area, a haven for wildlife, with excellent walking among craggy mountains and green river valleys
- Enjoy the wonderful Renaissance architecture of Úbeda, Baeza and Jaén
- Wander around the old-fashioned town of Cazorla, a good starting point for the Parque Natural de Cazorla
- Visit impressive Muslim and Reconquesta castles at Jaén, Baños de la Encina, Cazorla and Segura de la Sierra

In the Cazorla region, venison (of *ciervo*, red deer, or *gamo*, fallow deer) and *jabalí* (wild boar) are widely available. You may even come across *mouflon* (wild sheep).

JAÉN
postcode 23080 • pop 113,000
• elevation 575m

The provincial capital, set among rugged mountains and olive groves, is a likeable, fairly lively place with plenty to keep you interested for a day or two.

Castile's Fernando III ('El Santo', the Saint) took Jaén from the emirate of Granada after a six-month siege in 1246. Fernando agreed to respect the emirate's frontiers in return for tribute of half the emir's annual income. However, in the late

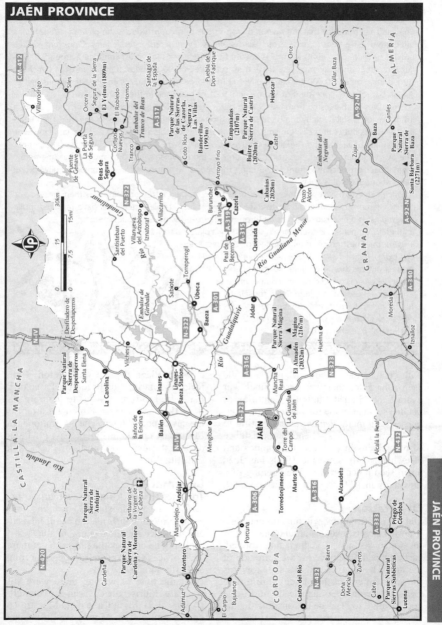

Essential Oil

You can't fail to notice that the favoured crop in the Jaén countryside is the olive *(aceituna)*. Line after line of olive trees *(olivos)* stretch across almost every scrap of fertile land. One-third of Jaén province – more than 4500 sq km – is devoted to olive groves *(olivares)* containing around 40 million olive trees. In an average year these trees produce 900,000 tonnes of olives, most of which are turned into some 200,000 tonnes of olive oil *(aceite de oliva)*. Thus, Jaén provides about half of Andalucía's olive oil, one-third of Spain's and 10% of that used in the entire world.

The olives are harvested from late November to January. Though there's some mechanisation, a lot of the job is still done by the traditional method of spreading nets beneath the tree, then beating the olives out with sticks. On small family plots, this can be quite a festive occasion. However, the majority of Jaén's (and Andalucía's) olive groves are owned by a handful of large landowners. The overwhelming importance of this one crop in the province's economy means that unemployment in Jaén province rises from 10% during the harvest to around 45% in summer. An olive picker earns about 5000 ptas a day.

Once harvested, olives are taken to oil mills to be mashed into a pulp which is then pressed and finally filtered. In recent years up-to-date machinery and stainless steel vats have replaced mule-driven presses which squeezed the oil through esparto-grass mats. Oil considered good enough for immediate consumption is sold as virgin olive oil *(aceite de oliva virgen)*, the finest grade of oil (the best of the best is *virgen extra)*. Refined olive oil *(aceite de oliva refinado)* is made from oil that's not quite so good, and plain *aceite de oliva* is a blend of refined and virgin oil.

Olive oil is used throughout Spain for salads, for frying and for much else besides. Virgin oil is considered a very healthy food, being cholesterol-free and full of vitamins.

NICK KELLY

15th century the Catholic Monarchs made Jaén a base for their successful final war against the Granada emirate. Centuries of decline set in after the Reconquesta (Reconquest), with many *jiennenses* emigrating to the Spanish colonies – hence the existence of other Jaéns in Peru, the Philippines and elsewhere. Only since the 1960s has Jaén again seen much growth. The opening of a university in 1993 livened the city up a lot.

Orientation
Old Jaén, with narrow, winding, often pedestrianised streets, huddles around the foot of the Cerro de Santa Catalina, the wooded, castle-topped hill above the western side of the city. The large cathedral stands towards the southern end of the old city. From here Calle de Bernabé Soriano leads north-east and downhill to Plaza de la Constitución, the focal point of the newer part of the city.

From Plaza de la Constitución, Calle Roldán y Marín, soon becoming Paseo de la Estación, heads north-west to the train station, 1km away. This is the main artery of the newer part of town. The bus station is on Plaza de Coca de la Piñera, east off Paseo de la Estación, 250m north of Plaza de la Constitución.

Information
Tourist Offices A single new tourist office at Calle de la Maestra 13, near the cathedral, providing information on all Jaén city and province and the rest of Andalucía, will probably be open by the time you get there. This office was expected to open morning and afternoon every day.

At the time of writing there were still separate tourist offices run by the city (☎ 953 21 91 16) at Calle de la Maestra 16, open 8 am to 3 pm Monday to Friday, and

JAÉN PROVINCE

by the Junta de Andalucía (☎ 953 22 27 37) at Calle del Arquitecto Berges 1, open 9 am to 7 pm Monday to Friday, and 10 am to 1 pm Saturday.

Money There's no shortage of banks or ATMs around Plaza de la Constitución and on Calle Roldán y Marín.

Post & Communications The main post office on Plaza de los Jardinillos opens 8.30 am to 8.30 pm Monday to Friday and 9.30 am to 2 pm Saturday.

Bookshops Librería Metrópolis in the old town at Calle del Cerón 17 is good for maps and Spanish-language guidebooks.

Medical Services & Emergency The main general hospital is the Hospital Ciudad de Jaén (☎ 953 22 24 08) on Avenida del Ejército Español. The Red Cross (Cruz Roja) is on ☎ 953 25 15 40.

The Policía Municipal station (☎ 953 21 91 05) is on Carrera de Jesús, just behind the city hall. The Policía Nacional station (☎ 953 26 18 50) is at Calle del Arquitecto Berges 11.

Cathedral

Jaén's huge cathedral was built mostly in the 16th and 17th centuries, and mainly to the designs of Andrés de Vandelvira, on the site of Muslim Jaén's main mosque. Its highlight is the superb twin-towered **southwestern facade** on Plaza de Santa María, which is more baroque than Renaissance, with an array of 17th-century statuary, much of it by Sevilla's Pedro Roldán.

The vast but dark interior opens 8.30 am to 1 pm and 5 to 8 pm (4 to 7 pm during winter) Monday to Saturday, 8.30 am to 1.30 pm and 5 to 7 pm Sunday and holidays. Directly behind the main altar, the **Capilla Mayor** (or Capilla del Santo Rostro) houses the Reliquia del Santo Rostro de Cristo, a cloth with an image of Christ's face, with which St Veronica is believed to have wiped Christ's face on the road to Calvary. On Fridays at 11.30 am and 5 pm long queues of the faithful assemble to kiss the cloth.

Palacio de Villardompardo

This handsome Renaissance palace on Plaza de Santa Luisa de Marillac, 500m north-west of the cathedral, houses two museums and what's claimed to be the largest Islamic bathhouse open to visitors in Spain.

The **Baños Árabes** (Arab Baths), in the bowels of the building, are beautified by horseshoe arches and star-shaped skylights. Their most impressive section is the temperate room *(sala templada)*. Built in the 11th century, then turned into a tannery by the Christians, the baths disappeared in the 16th century when the Conde de Villardompardo built a palace over the site. They were rediscovered in 1913.

The **Museo Internacional de Arte Naïf** (International Museum of Naïf Art), opened in 1988, is the only museum in Spain devoted to this very colourful, perspective-free school of painting. The work and collection of the museum's founder, Manuel Moral of Torre del Campo, Jaén, forms the basis of the display. Village life and the countryside are constant themes: the paintings from Haiti are the most vivid.

The **Museo de Artes y Costumbres Populares** (Museum of Popular Art & Customs) is devoted to pre-industrial Jaén province. Old carts and fine 19th-century clothes are the most eye-catching items.

All three sections open 9 am to 8 pm Tuesday to Friday, 9.30 am to 2.30 pm Saturday and Sunday (closed on holidays). Admission is free to all nationalities with a passport or national identity card.

Iglesia de la Magdalena

Jaén's oldest church stands a short walk west of the Palacio de Villardompardo along Calle Santo Domingo. Originally a mosque, it has a Gothic main facade and interior. Its tower is the mosque's minaret, reworked in the 16th century. You can enter the church daily during mass, usually 6 to 8 pm: the outstanding feature inside is the retable by Jacobo Florentino. Behind the church is a lovely Islamic courtyard with Roman tombstones and a pool used for ritual ablutions in Muslim times.

JAÉN PROVINCE

Iglesia de San Ildefonso

The 'home church' of Jaén's patron saint, the Virgen de la Capilla, stands on Plaza de San Ildefonso, 200m north-east of the cathedral. San Ildefonso was founded in the 13th century but remodelled several times. An inscription on the bottom (north-eastern) end of its exterior marks the spot where the Virgin is believed to have appeared on 10 June 1430. Inside, her much-venerated image stands in a special chapel. The church is open 8.30 am to noon and 6 to 8.30 pm daily.

Museo Provincial

Jaén's Provincial Museum, Paseo de la Estación 27, has an excellent archaeological collection covering the cultures of Jaén province from pre-3000-BC hunter-gatherers to Muslim times. The highlight is a room of fine 5th-century-BC Iberian sculpture from Porcuna, Jaén province, showing a clear Greek influence.

The museum opens 3 to 8 pm Tuesday, 9 am to 8 pm Wednesday to Saturday and 9 am to 3 pm Sunday (closed Monday and holidays). Admission costs 100 ptas (free with an EU passport or national identity card).

Castillo de Santa Catalina

Undoubtedly Jaén's most exhilarating spot is this originally Muslim castle perched atop the Cerro de Santa Catalina. If you don't have a vehicle for the circuitous 4km drive up from the city centre, you can take a taxi (800 ptas) or walk (about an hour) using a steep path that leaves the Carretera de Circunvalación almost opposite the top of Calle de Buenavista.

The castle was handed over to Fernando III in 1246 by the emir of Granada. Fernando extended it and it was remodelled in 1808 to house a garrison. It opens 10 am to 1.30 pm (to 2 pm during winter) daily except non-holiday Wednesdays. Admission is free. Inside you can check out the keep, a chapel and some underground water tanks.

Past the castle at the end of the ridge stands a large cross on the spot where

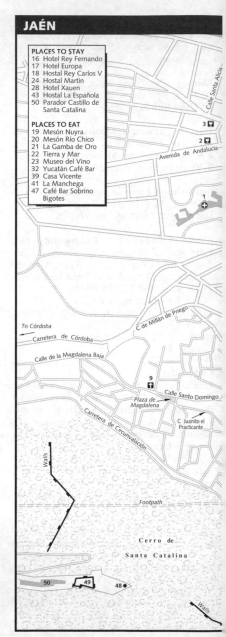

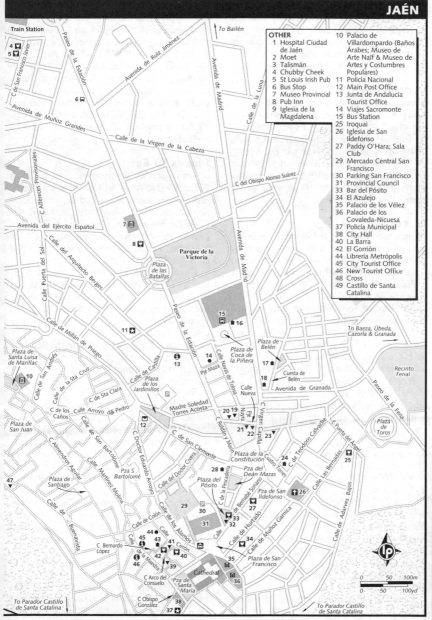

JAÉN

OTHER
1 Hospital Ciudad de Jaén
2 Moet
3 Talismán
4 Chubby Cheek
5 St Louis Irish Pub
6 Bus Stop
7 Museo Provincial
8 Pub Inn
9 Iglesia de la Magdalena
10 Palacio de Villardompardo (Baños Árabes; Museo de Arte Naïf & Museo de Artes y Costumbres Populares)
11 Policía Nacional
12 Main Post Office
13 Junta de Andalucía Tourist Office
14 Viajes Sacromonte
15 Bus Station
25 Iroquai
26 Iglesia de San Ildefonso
27 Paddy O'Hara; Sala Club
29 Mercado Central San Francisco
30 Parking San Francisco
31 Provincial Council
33 Bar del Pósito
34 El Azulejo
35 Palacio de los Vélez
36 Palacio de los Covaleda-Nicuesa
37 Policía Municipal
38 City Hall
40 La Barra
42 El Gorrión
44 Librería Metrópolis
45 City Tourist Office
46 New Tourist Office
48 Cross
49 Castillo de Santa Catalina

euro currency converter €1 = 166 ptas

Fernando III placed a cross after his victory in 1246. The views over the city and the olive groves beyond are magnificent.

If you have walked up, you deserve to treat yourself to a drink in Parador Castillo de Santa Catalina next to the castle!

Special Events

Semana Santa (Holy Week) is celebrated in a big way, with processions through the old city by members of 13 brotherhoods (*cofradías*). The week climaxes in the early hours of Good Friday. Jaén's biggest party is the Feria y Fiestas de San Lucas with concerts, funfairs, bullfights and general merrymaking for about 10 days up to the saint's day, 18 October.

Places to Stay

Mosquitoes can be a nuisance in Jaén hotels, especially the cheaper ones. Prices in several places rise a bit during Semana Santa and the Feria y Fiestas de San Lucas.

Hostal Rey Carlos V (☎ *953 22 20 91, Avenida de Madrid 4)* is the nearest hostal to the bus station, but on a noisy street. Basic singles/doubles cost 2700/3700 ptas.

Hostal Martín (☎ *953 24 36 78, Calle Cuatro Torres 5)* in a narrow street just east of Plaza de la Constitución, has basic but adequate rooms that cost 3000/4000 ptas.

Hostal La Española (☎ *953 23 02 54, Calle Bernardo López 9)*, near the cathedral, has sagging beds and sporadic hot water but more character than the other cheapies – it's a sizeable old house on a narrow street, with an interestingly tilted wooden spiral staircase. Rooms cost 2000/3800 ptas; doubles with shower and toilet cost 4250 or 4750 ptas.

A step up in quality is *Hotel Europa* (☎ *953 22 27 00, Plaza de Belén 1)*, where bright, modern rooms with air-con, TV and bath cost 5300/8650 ptas. It has a garage.

Also good, and more central, is *Hotel Xauen* (☎ *953 24 07 89, Plaza del Deán Mazas 3)*, just off Plaza de la Constitución. Rooms here, again with air-con, TV and bath, cost 5900/8000 ptas.

Hotel Rey Fernando (☎ *953 25 18 40, Plaza de Coca de la Piñera 5)*, next to the bus station, has comfortable rooms for 7700/10,000 ptas plus IVA.

If money is no object and you have a vehicle, stay at the *Parador Castillo de Santa Catalina* (☎ *953 23 00 00, fax 953 23 09 30, ✉ jaen@parador.es)*, which has an incomparable site atop the Cerro de Santa Cata-lina. Built in 1965 in imitation of the castle next door, the parador has spacious, comfortable singles/doubles for 14,000/17,500 ptas plus IVA, a pool and Islamic-style decorative touches.

Places to Eat

Several of the atmospheric old bars on Calles Cerón, Arco del Consuelo and Bernardo López, near the cathedral, serve tapas and *raciones* (meal-sized servings of tapas). One, *La Manchega*, also does good-value *platos combinados* (mixed platters) for 500 ptas, and breakfast coffee and toasted rolls for 130 to 240 ptas.

Casa Vicente, in a restored mansion on nearby Calle Francisco Martín Mora, is one of the best restaurants in town. Its specialities are pork and venison; a three-course a la carte meal will cost around 3000 ptas excluding drinks.

Yucatán Café Bar on Calle de Bernabé Soriano isn't a bad place for breakfast. It also serves reasonable platos combinados for up to 795 ptas.

Short Calle Nueva, off Calle Roldán y Marín, has a string of good places to eat and drink. A top choice is *Mesón Río Chico* (☎ *953 24 08 02, Calle Nueva 2)*, with both a downstairs *taberna* serving excellent tapas and raciones of meat, *revueltos* (scrambled-egg dishes) and fish (try the *solomillo al roquefort* (sirloin with Roquefort) ración for 1200 ptas) and a more expensive restaurant upstairs. *Tierra y Mar* and *La Gamba de Oro* both specialise in seafood. They're bright, lively places with raciones in the 400 to 800 ptas range. *Mesón Nuyra* (☎ *953 27 31 31)*, downstairs in Pasaje Nuyra, a passageway off Calle Nueva, is a bit more formal. Salads cost between 1100 and 1600 ptas; fish and meat main dishes are 1500 to 2200 ptas. Another good taberna-cum-restaurant establishment is the **Museo del Vino** *(Calle Doctor Sagaz Zubelzu 4)*, with main dishes for 1500 ptas-plus and, as its name suggests, good wines.

The **Parador Castillo de Santa Catalina** (see Places to Stay for details) has an excellent restaurant where a three-course meal will cost around 4000 ptas plus drinks. The menu includes many Jaén specialities.

You can buy almost any type of fresh food at the large, modern **Mercado Central San Francisco** on Calle de los Álamos.

Entertainment

Several very atmospheric old bars cluster just north-west of the cathedral on Calle Cerón and narrow Calles Arco del Consuelo and Bernardo López. Among them are **La Barra** *(Calle Cerón 7)*, **El Gorrión** *(Calle de Arco del Consuelo 7)* and **La Manchega**, with entrances on both Calle de Arco del Consuelo and Calle Bernardo López. These last two have both been in action since the 1880s. See Places to Eat for more on Manchega. Several of the establishments on Calle Nueva (see Places to Eat) are also excellent for a drink and tapas.

A little groovier without being pretentious are the cosy, arty **Bar del Pósito** *(Plaza del Pósito 10)*, which spills onto a pleasant little square off Calle de Bernabé Soriano, and **El Azulejo** bar *(Calle de Hurtado 8)*.

For a bit more action, the **Iroquai** *(☎ 953 24 36 74, Calle de Adarves Bajos 53)*, also with an entrance on Calle Las Bernardas, usually has live rock, blues, flamenco or fusion on Thursdays (look out for its posters) and plays good recorded music other nights. **Paddy O'Hara** *(Calle de Bernabé Soriano 30)* purveys that always popular combination, Guinness and Celtic music. **Sala Club** *(Calle de Bernabé Soriano 30)*, next door, offers Thursday night dance sessions with guest house, funk and hip-hop DJs.

The main nightlife zone is farther away, towards the train station and university: **Pub Inn** *(Paseo de la Estación 23)*, **Moët** *(Avenida de Andalucía 10)*, **Talismán** *(Avenida de Muñoz Grandes 5)*, **St Louis Irish Pub** *(Calle de San Francisco Javier 5)*, and **Chubby Cheek** *(☎ 953 27 38 19, Calle de San Francisco Javier 7)*, with live jazz

most weeks, are all places where you'll find a lively scene towards the end of the week.

Things to Buy

The main shopping areas focus on Calle Roldán y Marín, Paseo de la Estación and Calle de San Clemente (off Plaza de la Constitución). A big flea market *(mercadillo)* is held on Thursday mornings at the Recinto Ferial on Avenida de Granada.

Getting There & Away

Bus From the bus station (☎ 953 25 01 06) Alsina Graells runs 11 or more daily buses to Granada (930 ptas, 1½ hours), seven or more to Baeza (465 ptas, 45 minutes) and Úbeda (545 ptas, 1¼ hours), and buses to Cazorla (960 ptas, two hours) at noon and 4.30 pm. The Ureña line travels up to eight times daily to Córdoba and three times to Sevilla. Other buses head for Guadix, Málaga, Almería, Madrid, Valencia, Barcelona and many smaller places in Jaén province.

Train Jaén train station (☎ 953 27 02 02) is at the end of a branch line and there are only four departures most days. One train leaves at 8 am for Córdoba (1175 ptas, 1½ hours), Sevilla (2255 ptas, three hours) and Cádiz. Three go to Madrid.

Car & Motorcycle Jaén is 92km north of Granada by the fast N-323. This road continues to Bailén where it meets the Córdoba–Madrid N-IV. To/from Córdoba, take the A-306 via Porcuna.

Viajes Sacromonte (☎ 953 22 22 12) in Pasaje Maza, an arcade at Paseo de la Estación 12, is a car rental agent.

Getting Around

There's a bus stop on Paseo de la Estación, south of the train station: bus No 1 will take you to Plaza de la Constitución, the central point for all city buses, for 150 ptas.

Parking San Francisco, off Calle de Bernabé Soriano near the cathedral, is always open, it costs 100 ptas per hour or 1400 ptas for 24 hours.

Taxis gather on Plaza de San Francisco, near the cathedral.

THE NORTH-WEST

The N-IV Córdoba–Madrid highway slices across the north-west of Jaén province. If you're travelling this way there are a few places worth your time, not far off the highway.

Parque Natural Sierra de Andújar

This 740 sq km natural park north of Andújar is claimed to have the biggest expanses of natural vegetation in the Sierra Morena. Evergreen oaks grow in sunny areas, gall oaks in shady ones, and the park is home to plenty of bull-breeding ranches and a few wild wolves, lynx and boars, plus deer, mouflon and various birds of prey. Information is available from the park visitor centre (☎ 953 54 90 30) at Km 12 on the road from Andújar to the Santuario de la Virgen de la Cabeza and from the tourist office (☎ 953 50 49 59) on Plaza de Santa María, Andújar.

The Santuario de la Virgen de la Cabeza, within the park and a 31km drive north of Andújar, is a 13th-century shrine, now largely rebuilt after an eight-month siege by Republicans in the civil war. It's the scene of one of Spain's biggest religious events, the Romería de la Virgen de la Cabeza, on the last Sunday of April. Half a million people converge to witness a small statue of the Virgin Mary – known as La Morenita (The Little Brown One) – being carried around the Cerro del Cabezo for about four hours from about 11 am. It's a festive, emotive occasion: children and items of clothing are passed over the crowd to priests who touch them to the Virgin's mantle.

A small hotel, *Hotel la Mirada* (☎ *953 54 91 11*), and *Pensión Virgen de la Cabeza* (☎ *953 12 21 65*) near the sanctuary could be bases for exploring the park at normal times of year. There's also a range of accommodation in Andújar.

At least four buses a day run from Jaén to Andújar and there are buses from Andújar to the sanctuary on Saturday and Sunday.

Baños de la Encina

One of Andalucía's finest Muslim castles dominates the quiet ridge-top town of Baños de la Encina, a few kilometres north of unexciting Bailén. Built in 967 on the orders of the Cordoban caliph Al-Hakim II, the oval castle has 14 wall towers and a large keep entered through a double horseshoe arch. It fell to the Christians in 1212 just after the battle of Las Navas de Tolosa. Tourist information – and the key to the castle – are available at the 16th-century town hall (☎ 953 61 30 04) on the village's main square, Plaza de la Constitución, open 9 am to 1 pm Monday to Friday. Several mansions and churches – including the Ermita del Cristo del Llano, with spectacular rococo decoration almost reminiscent of the Alhambra – make a ramble through Baños' old streets worthwhile.

PARQUE NATURAL SIERRA MÁGINA & HUELMA

This little visited natural park, prominently visible from the Jaén–Granada and Jaén–Baeza roads and crossed by the A-301 south of Úbeda, is full of rugged mountains, topped by 2167m Mágina, the highest peak in Jaén province. There are a number of marked walking trails in the park. In autumn the area is famous for its wild mushrooms, of which 300 kinds grow here. The park visitor centre (☎ 953 78 76 56) is in the castle at Jódar, north-east of the park. The centre is open 6 to 8 pm Thursday and Friday, 10 am to 2 pm and 6 to 8 pm Saturday and Sunday.

The small town of Huelma, in the southern foothills, is one base for a visit. It has an old quarter of typically Muslim narrow winding streets, and its ruined castle remained in Muslim hands till 1438 – much later than places not far north such as Jaén and Baeza. Andrés de Vandelvira and Diego de Siloé both had a hand in the design of the nearby Iglesia de la Inmaculada. *Hostal Marce* (☎ *953 39 10 06, Calle Santa Ana 17*), has doubles with bath for around 3000 ptas.

BAEZA

postcode 23440 • pop 15,000
• elevation 770m

Standing on the northern side of the Guadalquivir valley, 48km north-east of

Las Navas de Tolosa

About 40km north-east of Bailén, the N-IV threads through a rocky gorge, its two carriageways at times as much as 1km apart, and leaves Andalucía. The gorge is called the Desfiladero de Despeñaperros (Defile of the Overthrow of the Dogs) – a name owed to perhaps the most significant battle in Andalucian history, which was fought a few kilometres south in 1212.

The Muslim Almohads' rout of the Christian Castilian army at Alarcos, near Ciudad Real in Castilla-La Mancha, in 1195, and subsequent papal diplomacy, eventually spurred some of the Iberian peninsula's Christian states into an unaccustomed show of unity. In 1212 three Christian armies, led by Alfonso VIII of Castile, Pere II of Aragón and Sancho VII 'El Fuerte' (The Strong) of Navarra, with the help of a few French crusaders, marched south. Waiting for them on the plain of Las Navas de Tolosa, south of the Desfiladero de Despeñaperros, were the Almohad forces of Mohammed II al-Nasir. The Muslims had blocked a narrow canyon where they could ambush the Christians. But a mysterious shepherd called Martín Alhaga appeared and guided the northern armies through an alternative defile unknown to the Almohads.

On 16 July the opposing armies met on Las Navas de Tolosa and the Christians scored an overwhelming victory. Mohammed abandoned his standard on the battlefield and later Alfonso VIII reported to the Pope that the Christian armies camped there had for two days needed no other fuel for their fires than their enemies' discarded spears and arrows. The battle, one of the key events of the Reconquesta, opened the doors of Andalucía to the Christians.

Many arrowheads and hatchets have been found at what's thought to be the battle site, Mesa del Rey, 4 or 5km south of Santa Elena village.

Jaén, this relaxed country town is packed with gorgeous Gothic and Renaissance buildings.

The seat of a bishopric under the Visigoths, Baeza (ba-**eh**-thah) developed into a trade centre renowned for its bazaars during the Muslim period. In 1227 it became the first sizeable Andalucian town to fall to the Christians when it was conquered by Fernando III. Its heyday was during the 16th century when the Baeza nobility, having finally ended centuries of feuding, ploughed much of the profit from booming textile and grain industries into grand buildings.

Orientation & Information

The heart of town is Plaza de España, with the long, wide Paseo de la Constitución stretching to its south-west.

The bus station is about 700m east of Plaza de España on Paseo Arco del Agua (officially called Avenida Alcalde Puche Pardo).

The tourist office (☎ 953 74 04 44) is in a beautiful 16th-century building on Plaza del Pópulo, just south-west of Paseo de la Constitución. It opens 9 am to 2.30 pm Monday to Friday and 10 am to 1 pm on alternate Saturdays. The main post office is at Calle Julio Burell 19.

You'll find banks and ATMs on Paseo de la Constitución and to the east on Calle San Pablo.

You could walk round the following sequence of sights in a leisurely day. The opening hours of some of the buildings are unpredictable.

Plaza de España & Paseo de la Constitución

On Plaza de España stands the **Torre de los Aliatares**, one of the few remaining bits of Muslim Bayyasa, whose walled fortress it helped to fortify. Somehow this tower survived Isabel la Católica's 1476 order to demolish Baeza's fortifications in order to end the feuds between the town's Benavide and Carvajal noble families.

Paseo de la Constitución, once Baeza's marketplace and bullring, is lined with attractive arcades.

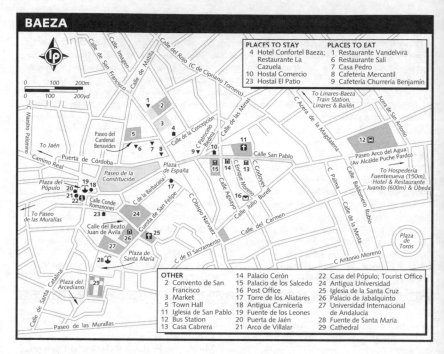

BAEZA

PLACES TO STAY	PLACES TO EAT
4 Hotel Confortel Baeza;	1 Restaurante Vandelvira
Restaurante La	6 Restaurante Sali
Cazuela	7 Casa Pedro
10 Hostal Comercio	8 Cafetería Mercantil
23 Hostal El Patio	9 Cafetería Churrería Benjamín

OTHER	14 Palacio Cerón	22 Casa del Pópulo; Tourist Office
2 Convento de San	15 Palacio de los Salcedo	24 Antigua Universidad
Francisco	16 Post Office	25 Iglesia de la Santa Cruz
3 Market	17 Torre de los Aliatares	26 Palacio de Jabalquinto
5 Town Hall	18 Antigua Carnicería	27 Universidad Internacional
11 Iglesia de San Pablo	19 Fuente de los Leones	de Andalucía
12 Bus Station	20 Puerta de Jaén	28 Fuente de Santa María
13 Casa Cabrera	21 Arco de Villalar	29 Cathedral

Plaza del Pópulo

This beautiful square, a few steps west of Paseo de la Constitución, is also named Plaza de los Leones after the **Fuente de los Leones** (Fountain of the Lions) in its centre. The fountain, constructed with carvings from the Iberian and Roman village of Cástulo, 15km west of Baeza, is topped by a statue that is traditionally believed to represent Imilce, an Iberian princess from Cástulo who was the wife of Carthaginian leader Hannibal. Imilce, if she it be, wears a suitably enigmatic smile.

On the southern side of the square is the lovely plateresque **Casa del Pópulo**, built in about 1540. Formerly a courthouse, it's now Baeza's tourist office. Adjoining it is the 1526 **Arco de Villalar** (Villalar Arch), next to which is the originally Muslim **Puerta de Jaén** (Jaén Gate).

On the eastern side of the square stands the **Antigua Carnicería** (Old Slaughterhouse), a fine 1548 building with a Renaissance gallery and the large two-headed Habsburg eagle shield of Carlos I.

If you have time to spare you could go through the Puerta de Jaén and along the street to the **Paseo de las Murallas**, a path-cum-road which loops round the old city walls to a point near the cathedral and affords good views over the surrounding country.

Antigua Universidad

Baeza's Old University is a short walk south-east of Plaza del Pópulo on Calle del Beato Juan de Ávila. Founded in 1538, the university was a fount of progressive ideas which ran counter to the conservative tendencies of Baeza's dominant families. It was closed in 1824 and since 1875 the building has housed an *instituto de bachillerato* (high school). You can visit 10 am to 1 pm and 4 to 6 pm, Tuesday to Sunday. Admission is free. The main patio has two floors of elegant Renaissance arches and a plaque outside one classroom telling us that the poet Antonio Machado taught French here from 1912 to 1919.

Palacio de Jabalquinto
Round the corner on Calle San Felipe Neri is the finest of Baeza's noble mansions. Probably built in the early 16th century for one of the Benavides clan, it has a spectacular facade in the flamboyant Isabelline Gothic style, topped by a Renaissance gallery. The patio has been under restoration but is normally open the same hours as the Antigua Universidad. Admission is free. It, too, is Renaissance-style, with marble columns, two tiers of elegant arches, a fountain and orange trees. A majestic baroque stairway ascends from one side.

Iglesia de la Santa Cruz
Across the square from the Palacio de Jabalquinto, the mid-13th-century Church of the Holy Cross was one of the first churches built in Andalucía after the Reconquest. It was one of the last in Spain, and one of the very few in Andalucía, to be built in the Romanesque style which was already starting to give way to the Gothic of most early post-Reconquest Andalucian churches. Santa Cruz's round-arched portals and semicircular apse set it quite apart from Gothic. It's supposedly open 11 am to 1 pm Monday to Saturday and noon to 2 pm Sunday and holidays, though these times are not very reliable. Inside are some 15th-century paintings.

Plaza de Santa María
This handsome square south-west of the Palacio de Jabalquinto is dominated by the cathedral, but also worth a pause are the **Fuente de Santa María** in the middle and the **Universidad Internacional de Andalucía** on the northern side. The pretty fountain, built in 1569 by *baezano* Ginés Martínez, is in the form of a miniature Roman triumphal arch. The university, which mainly conducts short courses for postgraduates, is housed in the sober 17th-century Seminario (Seminary) de San Felipe Neri.

Cathedral
Baeza's cathedral is an aesthetic hotchpotch with interesting parts. The predominant style is 16th-century Renaissance, shown in the **main facade** on Plaza de Santa María and the basic design of the three-nave interior (by Andrés de Vandelvira and Jerónimo del Prado). The oldest feature is the 13th-century Gothic-Mudéjar **Puerta de la Luna** (Moon Doorway) at the western end, above which is a nice 14th-century Gothic rose window. The **Puerta del Perdón** (Pardon Doorway) on the southern side is 15th-century Gothic.

The cathedral is open from 10.30 am to 1 pm and 5.15 to 7 pm (4.15 to 6 pm in winter) daily. Admission is free, but donations are welcome. A lavish baroque **retable** backs the main altar and a 13th-century Romanesque-Gothic **Crucifixion sculpture** – rare in Andalucía – stands high on the retable of the adjacent Capilla del Sagrario. At the cathedral's western end, the **grille** on the Antiguo Coro (Old Choir) is one of the masterpieces of Jaén's 16th-century wrought iron supremo, Maestro Bartolomé. The centre of the grille, from the bottom up, depicts with pleasing simplicity St Andrew, the coronation of the Virgin (holding the infant Jesus) and the Crucifixion. To the right of the grille you can pop 100 ptas into a slot by an unremarkable painting: the painting slides noisily aside, a recording of holy music plays and the 18th-century **Custodia del Corpus**, a large silver monstrance used in Baeza's Corpus Christi processions, is revealed in all its glory.

The **cloister** has four Mudéjar chapels with Arabic inscriptions.

Town Hall
The town hall, a block north of Paseo de la Constitución at Paseo del Cardenal Benavides 9, has a marvellous plateresque facade. The four finely carved balcony portals on the upper storey are separated by the coats of arms of Felipe II (in the middle), the magistrate Juan de Borja, who had the place built, and the town. The building was originally a courthouse and prison (entered by the right and left-hand doors respectively).

Convento de San Francisco

The San Francisco convent on Calle de San Francisco, a short walk from the town hall, was apparently one of Andrés de Vandelvira's masterpieces, conceived as the funerary chapel of the Benavides family. But it stood in ruins for a long time after being devastated by an earthquake and sacked by French troops in the early 19th century. It's now partly restored and, at the eastern end, girders trace the outline of its dome over a space adorned with Renaissance carvings. The cloister, occupied by the Restaurante Vandelvira (see Places to Eat for details), is worth a look too.

Calle San Pablo

This street leading east from Plaza de España is strung with handsome 16th-century mansions including No 18, the Palacio de los Salcedo; No 24, the Palacio Cerón (also called the Nuevo Casino), with a nice two-tier patio; and No 30, the Casa Cabrera, with a good plateresque front. Across the street from the Casa Cabrera is the 15th-century Gothic Iglesia de San Pablo.

Special Events

Baeza stages picturesque Semana Santa and Corpus Christi processions and an annual fair from 10 to 15 August. Most renowned is the Romería de La Yedra. On the morning of 7 September the image of the Virgen del Rosell is carried from the Iglesia de San Pablo through Baeza's streets, accompanied by a singing and dancing crowd. In the afternoon, a colourful procession of riders and decorated carts follows the image to La Yedra village, 4km north, to continue celebrations there.

Places to Stay

Some prices go up a few hundred pesetas from about June to September.

The friendly *Hostal El Patio* (☎ 953 74 02 00, Calle Conde Romanones 13) occupies a 17th-century mansion with a fountained and pillared (but covered) patio which boasts one of the most extensive lounge suites you've ever seen. Good, modernised singles/doubles cost 2000/3000 ptas,

or 2500/3500 ptas with shower, and there are doubles with bathroom for 4000 ptas.

Another friendly place, *Hostal Comercio* (☎ 953 74 80 67 or 953 74 01 00, Calle San Pablo 21), has decent rooms with shower and toilet for 2083/3337 ptas (singles with shared toilet for a little less, doubles with bathroom for 3885 ptas). There's heating in winter and plenty of hot water. Antonio Machado stayed in room 215 in 1912.

The most upmarket place in town is *Hotel Confortel Baeza* (☎ 953 74 81 30, fax 953 74 25 19, @ baeza@globalnet.es, Calle de la Concepción 3), in the old Hospital de la Purísima Concepción – very modernised but still with a large, ar caded central patio. Cosy, air-con rooms cost 6700/10,200 ptas plus IVA, including breakfast.

Hospedería Fuentenueva (☎ 953 74 31 00, fax 953 74 32 00, @ fuentenueva@mx4 .redestb.es, Paseo Arco del Agua s/n), about 300m beyond the bus station, used to be a women's prison but is now a beautifully restored and relaxed small hotel. The 12 rooms are comfortable, bright, air-con and mostly large, with marble bathrooms, and cost 6700/10,500 ptas plus IVA, including breakfast. You can book online at www .fuentenueva.com.

Hotel Juanito (☎ 953 74 00 40, fax 953 74 23 24, Paseo Arco del Agua s/n), 450m farther along the street, next to a petrol station, offers rooms with bathroom, air-con, heating and TV for 5050/6050 ptas plus IVA. Its restaurant is the most celebrated in the province (see Places to Eat for details).

Places to Eat

Cafetería Churrería Benjamín (Calle Patrocinio Biedma 1), on the corner of Calle San Pablo, is a fine place for a breakfast of good crisp *churros y chocolate* (deep-fried doughnuts to dip in thick hot chocolate).

Cafetería Mercantil on Plaza de España is busy from morning to night with amiable baezano men (no women, it seems) and serves a long list of generous raciones for 1000 to 1500 ptas, plus *media-raciones* (half-raciones), tapas and *bocadillos* (long, filled white bread rolls). This is your chance to sample *criadillas* (bull or lamb testicles) or *sesos* (brains), but there are plenty of more straightforward things too!

You can eat inexpensively at **Casa Pedro** *(Paseo del Cardenal Benavides 3)* which offers fried eggs and ham for 600 ptas, omelettes for 375 to 700 ptas and a *menú* (fixed-price meal) at 1200 ptas.

The popular **Restaurante La Cazuela** in the Hotel Confortel Baeza (see Places to Stay for details) is a step up in quality and price. Individual main dishes go for 1350 to 1950 ptas, or there's a three-course menú for 1600 ptas.

Restaurante Sali *(Paseo del Cardenal Benavides 9)* does a three-course menú with lots of choice for 1600 ptas. À la carte main dishes range from chicken or pork loin at 800 ptas to *solomillo pimienta* (pepper steak) for 2300 ptas.

Restaurante Vandelvira *(Calle de San Francisco 14)*, in part of the remodelled Convento de San Francisco (see that section earlier in this chapter for details), is one of the classier places in town. The menú costs 2100 ptas and most à la carte mains cost between 1450 and 2350 ptas. If you want to splurge you might go for the partridge pâté salad (1300 ptas) followed by *solomillo al carbón* (char-grilled steak; 2350 ptas). Add IVA to all prices.

The restaurant of the **Hospedería Fuentenueva** (see Places to Stay for details) is good, with Jaén cuisine leavened by exotica such as couscous. A three-course meal should cost 2000 to 3000 ptas, and its bar-cafe has some tasty snacks such as *suelas* (sizeable toasted sandwiches) for around 500 ptas.

People come from far and wide to **Restaurante Juanito** *(☎ 953 74 00 40, Paseo Arco del Agua s/n)* in the Hotel Juanito (see Places to Stay), where Juan Antonio Salcedo and his wife Luisa have been dishing up traditional Jaén fare for four decades. A three-course meal is likely to set you back 4000 ptas or more, plus drinks. Specialities include *alcachofas Luisa* (Luisa's artichokes) or partridge salad as starters, and *cabrito al horno* (roast kid), *lomo de orza*, or *cordoniz/perdiz/faisán* (partridge/quail/pheasant) in *escabeche* to follow. The Juanito is closed Sunday and Monday evenings.

Getting There & Away

From the bus station (☎ 953 74 04 68), Alsina Graells runs up to 11 buses daily to Jaén (465 ptas, 45 minutes), up to 15 to Úbeda, and at least five daily to Granada. There are two buses to Cazorla daily at 1 and 5.30 pm. Other buses go to Madrid, Córdoba, Sevilla and Málaga.

The nearest train station is Linares-Baeza (☎ 953 65 02 02), 13km north-west, where a few trains a day leave for Granada, Córdoba, Sevilla, Málaga, Cádiz, Almería, Madrid and Barcelona. Buses connect with most trains from Monday to Saturday.

ÚBEDA
postcode 23400 • pop 32,000
• elevation 750m

Just 9km east through the olive groves from Baeza, with which it has a neighbourly rivalry, Úbeda (oo-be-dah) has an even larger heritage of marvellous buildings from bygone centuries. Plaza Vázquez de Molina is the finest ensemble of Renaissance buildings in Andalucía.

History

Úbeda was taken from the Muslims by Fernando III in 1234. In the 14th century a group of local knights earned the title Lions of Úbeda for their heroics during the conquest of Algeciras, which is why lions are a common motif on Úbeda buildings.

Just as in Baeza, the town's leading post-Reconquest families, among them the Molinas, the de la Cuevas and the Cobos, spent a deal of energy quarrelling with each other and getting tangled up with the factions competing for the Castilian throne. In 1506 most of Úbeda's fortifications were knocked down, on Isabel la Católica's orders, to put an end to these quarrels. But the Cobos and the Molinas had by now patched things up enough to intermarry, and one of their line, Francisco de los Cobos y Molina, rose to be first secretary to King Carlos I; his nephew Juan Vázquez de Molina succeeded him in

JAÉN PROVINCE

the job and kept it under Felipe II. High office exposed these men to international culture just as the Renaissance was reaching Spain from Italy. Consequently, much of the wealth that they and a flourishing local agriculture brought to 16th-century Úbeda was spent on the profusion of lavish Renaissance mansions and churches that remain its greatest glory today.

Orientation & Information

Most of the architecture – the main reason for visiting Úbeda – is in the warren of narrow, winding streets and expansive squares that constitute the old town, in the southeast. The cheaper accommodation and the bus station are about 1km away, in the drab new town to the west and north. Plaza de Andalucía marks the boundary between the two parts of town.

The tourist office (☎ 953 75 08 97) is in

Andrés de Vandelvira

Born in 1509 at Alcaraz, 150km north-east of Úbeda, Andrés de Vandelvira almost singlehandedly brought the Renaissance to thenwealthy towns of the Jaén region. Influenced by the pioneering Spanish Renaissance architect Diego de Siloé, Vandelvira designed a string of marvellous stone buildings in Úbeda, Baeza, Jaén and elsewhere, which add up to one of the outstanding groupings of Renaissance architecture in Spain.

His work spanned all three main phases of Spanish Renaissance architecture and three of Úbeda's finest buildings illustrate this neatly. In buildings of the ornamental early Renaissance phase known as plateresque, such as the Capilla de El Salvador, a predilection for sculpted coats of arms lingered from the Isabelline Gothic era. A much purer line and more classical proportions emerge in the later Palacio de Vázquez de Molina. In his last building, the Hospital de Santiago (completed the year he died, 1575), Vandelvira displays almost as much sobriety as did Juan de Herrera in El Escorial, the paradigm of the austere Spanish late Renaissance.

---

the 18th-century Palacio Marqués de Contadero, at Calle Baja del Marqués 4 in the old town. It opens 8 am to 3 pm Monday to Saturday.

The post office at Calle Trinidad 4 opens 8.30 am to 2.30 pm Monday to Friday and 9.30 am to 1 pm Saturday. You'll find the biggest concentration of banks and ATMs on Plaza de Andalucía and nearby Calle Rastro.

There's a Health Centre (Centro de Salud; ☎ 953 75 11 03), with an emergency section, in the new part of town on Calle Explanada; and a general hospital (☎ 953 79 71 00) on the north-western edge of town at Carretera de Linares Km 1. The Policía Nacional (☎ 091) occupy the Antiguo Pósito on Plaza Vázquez de Molina.

Plaza Vázquez de Molina

Almost entirely surrounded by beautiful stone buildings from the 15th and 16th centuries, this 180m-long square is Úbeda's crown jewel. After dark, floodlighting makes it even more picturesque than by day. A lookout point (mirador) 150m east of the square along Baja de El Salvador, affords fine views with the Cazorla mountains in the distance to the east.

Capilla de El Salvador Facing along Plaza Vázquez de Molina from its western end, this church was Andrés de Vandelvira's first work in Úbeda. Commissioned by Francisco de los Cobos y Molina as a funerary chapel for his family, it today belongs to the Sevilla-based Duques de Medinaceli, descendants of the Cobos and one of Andalucía's major landowning families. Vandelvira built the chapel in the 1540s to basic designs by Diego de Siloé, but he added plenty of his own touches, including the portals and the sacristy.

The main facade on Plaza Vázquez de Molina is a pre-eminent example of plateresque, modelled on Siloé's Puerta del Perdón at Granada cathedral. The portal is topped by a carving of the transfiguration of Christ, flanked by statues of St Peter and St Paul. On the underside of the arch immediately above the door, the French sculptor

JAÉN PROVINCE

Windmill, Cabo de Gata, Almería province

Muslim castle, Baños de la Encina, Jaén province

Reminiscent of North Africa, Cabo de Gata in Almería is the driest place in Europe.

Chestnuts grow wild in Las Alpujarras, Granada province.

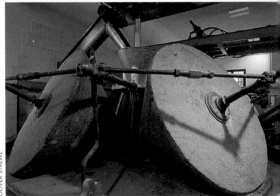

Oak woods in Las Alpujarras

Pressing business in Jaén province – olive oil is a major product

Trees that live 1000 years – one-third of Jaén province is dedicated to olive groves.

Esteban Jamete placed representations of Greek gods – a Renaissance touch which would have been inconceivable a few decades earlier. A Gothic penchant for heraldry lingers, however, in the sculptures flanking the portal. To the left, soldiers bear the five-lion coat of arms of Francisco de los Cobos y Molina; to the right, two women hold the shield of his wife María Manrique.

The church's side portals, though they are smaller, also bear intricate carving including, on the northern Portada del Evangelio, Santiago Matamoros incarnated as Carlos I, beneath a medallion of Christ.

You can visit the inside of the church from 10.30 am to 2 pm and 4.30 to 6 pm daily. Admission costs 350 ptas. The entrance is on the southern side. The sacristy, designed by Vandelvira and with much classical sculpture by Jamete, has a portrait of Francisco de los Cobos y Molina. The richly decorated chancel is modelled on Siloé's Capilla Mayor in Granada cathedral, with a frescoed dome. The main retable, by Alonso Berruguete, was badly damaged in the civil war and only one statue, the *Transfiguración del Monte Tabor* (Transfiguration on Mount Tabor), is original. A fine 1557 grille – some say it's by Jaén's Maestro Bartolomé – divides the chancel from the nave, beneath which is the Cobos family crypt, containing the tomb of Francisco de los Cobos y Molina.

Palacio del Deán Ortega Next to the Capilla de El Salvador stands what was the abode of its chaplains. Their quarters amounted to one of Vandelvira's finest palaces and were at least as big as the church. Partly remodelled in the 17th century, the mansion became Úbeda's parador in 1930 and its typically Vandelvira two-tier courtyard is about the most elegant spot for a drink (beer: 250 ptas) or snack in town.

Palacio de Vázquez de Molina This beautiful mansion, now Úbeda's town hall, dominates the western end of Plaza Vázquez de Molina. Vandelvira built it in about 1562 for Juan Vázquez de Molina, whose coat of arms surmounts the doorway.

The uncluttered facade, deeply Italian-influenced, has superbly harmonious proportions. Horizontally, it's divided into three tiers by slender cornices. Vertically, Esteban Jamete's caryatids, separating the oval windows of the top level, continue the lines of the pilasters flanking the rectangular windows of the middle tier.

You can enter the building from 9 am to 2.30 pm and 5 to 9 pm daily by its northern entrance on Plaza del Ayuntamiento to admire the fine patio, with two storeys of rounded arches on slender pillars.

In one side of the building, the **Museo de Alfarería Artesana** is devoted to Úbeda pottery, a craft that dates back to Muslim times. It opens 10.30 am to 2 pm and 4.30 to 7 pm daily except Sunday afternoon and Monday. Admission costs 230 ptas.

Santa María de los Reales Alcázares This large church facing the Palacio de Vázquez de Molina is one of Úbeda's finest but has been closed for restoration for several years. Built over Muslim Úbeda's main mosque, it has a Renaissance facade but is mainly 15th-century Gothic. Inside are grilles by Maestro Bartolomé and a lovely Gothic cloister occupying what was the mosque's ritual ablutions courtyard.

Other Buildings Next door to Santa María stands the **Cárcel del Obispo** (Bishop's Prison), where nuns who stepped out of line used to be incarcerated. It is now a courthouse. Under the trees in front is a **statue of Andrés de Vandelvira**, the man who made Úbeda worth visiting. By the statue, fronting the main square, the 16th-century **Antiguo Pósito**, originally a communal store for surplus grain, is now a police station. Calle de Santa María Soledad de Torres Acosta leads south from here into the area that was the Muslim fortress.

Plaza del Ayuntamiento & Around

This broad square on the northern side of the Palacio de Vázquez de Molina is overlooked from its north-western corner by the **Palacio de Vela de los Cobos**, with

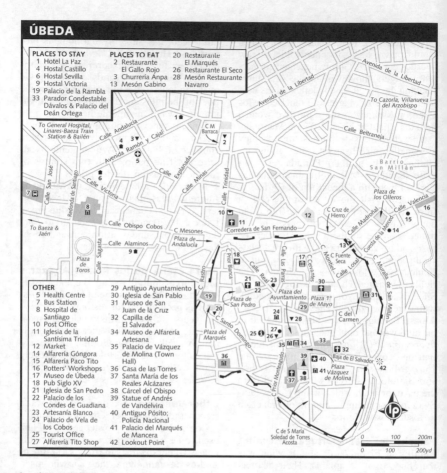

ÚBEDA

PLACES TO STAY
1 Hotel La Paz
4 Hostal Castillo
6 Hostal Sevilla
9 Hostal Victoria
19 Palacio de la Rambla
33 Parador Condestable
   Dávalos & Palacio del
   Deán Ortega

PLACES TO EAT
2 Restaurante
   El Gallo Rojo
3 Churrería Anpa
13 Mesón Gabino

20 Restaurante
   El Marqués
26 Restaurante El Seco
28 Mesón Restaurante
   Navarro

OTHER
5 Health Centre
7 Bus Station
8 Hospital de
  Santiago
10 Post Office
11 Iglesia de la
   Santísima Trinidad
12 Market
14 Alfarería Góngora
15 Alfarería Paco Tito
16 Potters' Workshops
17 Museo de Úbeda
18 Pub Siglo XV
21 Iglesia de San Pedro
22 Palacio de los
   Condes de Guadiana
23 Artesanía Blanco
24 Palacio de Vela de
   los Cobos
25 Tourist Office
27 Alfarería Tito Shop

29 Antiguo Ayuntamiento
30 Iglesia de San Pablo
31 Museo de San
   Juan de la Cruz
32 Capilla de
   El Salvador
34 Museo de Alfarería
   Artesana
35 Palacio de Vázquez
   de Molina (Town
   Hall)
36 Casa de las Torres
37 Santa María de los
   Reales Alcázares
38 Cárcel del Obispo
39 Statue of Andrés
   de Vandelvira
40 Antiguo Pósito;
   Policía Nacional
41 Palacio del Marqués
   de Mancera
42 Lookout Point

handsome middle-floor windows and top-floor gallery – built by Vandelvira for another of the Cobos clan, Francisco Vela de los Cobos.

Three blocks north-west up Calle Real (once Úbeda's main commercial street) stands the 17th-century **Palacio de los Condes de Guadiana**, another of the town's best mansions, with a tower and some good carving round the windows and balconies.

Plaza 1° de Mayo & Around

A couple of blocks north-east of Plaza del Ayuntamiento, this used to be the market square, bullring and site of Inquisition burnings. The kiosk in the south-eastern corner stands where heretics met their fate. Local worthies could watch events from the gallery of the elegantly proportioned 16th-century **Antiguo Ayuntamiento** (Old Town Hall) in the south-western corner. Along the top (northern) side of the square is the **Iglesia de San Pablo**, with a fine late Gothic portal (1511). Its 13th-century western front is in Romanesque-cum-Gothic style, and the tower at the eastern end (1537) is plateresque. You can enter the church between 7 and 9 pm daily: look for the 1530s

JAÉN PROVINCE

Capilla de Camarero Vago, by Vandelvira, and some good grilles.

Just north at Calle Cervantes 4, a 14th-century Mudéjar house with an attractive patio houses the **Museo de Úbeda**, with archaeological exhibits from Neolithic to Muslim times. It opens 3 to 8 pm Tuesday, 9 am to 8 pm Wednesday to Saturday, and 9 am to 3 pm Sunday. Admission is free with EU passport or national identity card; 250 ptas otherwise.

Museo de San Juan de la Cruz

This museum, in the 17th-century Oratorio de San Juan de la Cruz on Calle del Carmen, a block east of Plaza 1° de Mayo, is devoted to the 16th-century mystic, poet and religious reformer St John of the Cross (San Juan de la Cruz).

St John of the Cross, born in Castilla y León in 1542, founded the breakaway monastic order of Carmelitos Descalzos (Barefoot Carmelites – they wore sandals instead of shoes) in an effort to return to the austerity and contemplative life from which he felt mainstream Carmelites had lapsed. He wrote of the 'dark night of the soul', leading to the bright dawn of experience of God, and taught that mysticism was basically understanding and accepting the way things are.

St John's work provoked hefty opposition from the mainstream Carmelites, and he was imprisoned several times. After a stint as rector of a monastery in Baeza, St John came to Úbeda in September 1591, suffering from gangrene in his leg, and died here three months later.

On the museum's ground floor you'll visit the chapel where he was originally buried; an effigy lies on the spot. Upstairs, you see the room in which he died – with some of his bones in a glass case. Other rooms hold prints recording the key events of his life, early editions of his writings, and art connected with his life and teachings. In a reconstructed monk's cell, a lifelike figure of St John sits at a writing table he used – facing a cabinet containing letters written by him and a couple of fingers from his right hand!

It's open 11 am to 1 pm and 5 to 7 pm daily except Monday. Admission is free. Visits, guided by Spanish-speaking monks, last about half an hour.

Hospital de Santiago

Vandelvira's last building, begun in 1562 and completed in 1575, is the farthest from the heart of old Úbeda but one of his masterpieces. The Hospital de Santiago, on Calle Obispo Cobos, is a very sober, grand-scale, late Renaissance building which has been dubbed the Escorial of Andalucía, after Felipe II's contemporary palace-monastery near Madrid.

The lack of decoration focuses attention on the building's fine proportions, from the long facade crowned by end towers to the classic Vandelvira two-level patio with marble columns. Off the patio are a chapel, badly damaged in the civil war but now restored as an auditorium, and a staircase with colourful original frescos.

You can wander into the hospital (not a hospital now – it houses a library, the municipal dance school and an exhibition hall) from 8.30 am to 2 pm and 4 to 10 pm Monday to Friday, 11 am to 2.30 pm and 6 to 9.30 pm Saturday and Sunday.

Special Events

Semana Santa processions are colourful, and Úbeda celebrates early summer with the Festival Internacional de Música y Danza Ciudad de Úbeda, bringing varied music and dance performers to the town through the month of May. The biggest festivities are the Fiestas de San Miguel from 27 September to 4 October, with firework shows, parades, concerts, a bullfight season and more.

Places to Stay

Two hundred metres west of Plaza de Andalucía, *Hostal Victoria* (☎ 953 75 29 52, Calle Alaminos 5) has good singles/doubles, with bathroom, TV, air-con and heating, for 2600/4700 ptas. Farther from the centre and under the same ownership, *Hostal Castillo* (☎ 953 75 04 30, Avenida Ramón y Cajal 16) has similar rooms

JAÉN PROVINCE

without TV for the same price, plus rooms with a washbasin for 2200/3500 ptas.

Hostal Sevilla (☎ 953 75 06 12, Avenida Ramón y Cajal 9) has clean, fairly modern rooms with bathroom and heating for 2000/3800 ptas (a little less without TV).

Hotel La Paz (☎ 953 75 21 40, Calle Andalucía 1) looks bland but the rooms are individually decorated and some are large and stylish. Doubles with bathroom, TV and aircon cost 7200 ptas. The few singles (around 2500 ptas) are small.

In the old town, the 30-room *Parador Condestable Dávalos (☎ 953 75 03 45, fax 953 75 12 59, ℮ ubeda@parador.es)* on Plaza Vázquez de Molina is the old Palacio del Deán Ortega, now comfortably modernised. The privilege of staying here costs 14,800/18,500 ptas plus IVA.

The *Palacio de la Rambla (☎ 953 75 01 96, Plaza del Marqués 1)* is another refined hotel in a 16th-century palace. Large doubles cost 14,000 ptas plus IVA, breakfast included. Still the home of the Marquesa de la Rambla, the eight-room hotel centres on a lovely Vandelvira patio and has a pleasant garden.

Places to Eat

In the new town, *Hostal Castillo* (see Places to Stay for details) serves a reasonable three-course menú, with salad and a drink, for 1100 ptas. *Churrería Anpa* just up the street is a bustling breakfast spot.

Restaurante El Gallo Rojo (Calle Manuel Barraca 3), just off the northern end of Avenida Ramón y Cajal, is one of the best places in the new part of town. It does a three-course menú with lots of choice and a drink for 1300 ptas plus IVA. A la carte meat and fish main dishes range from 900 to 1800 ptas plus IVA, though *tortillas* (omelettes) are less.

In the old town, *Restaurante El Marqués* on Plaza del Marqués, 150m downhill from Plaza de Andalucía, does reasonable-value platos combinados for 700 to 1000 ptas (but 20% more if you eat them at a table).

Mesón Restaurante Navarro (Plaza del Ayuntamiento 2) (the sign just says 'Mesón Restaurante'), has a bar at the front, with

excellent and varied raciones (1200 to 1600 ptas), media-raciones and bocadillos (175 to 600 ptas), and a restaurant serving typical local fare in the back (1200 to 2000 ptas for main dishes).

Mesón Gabino on Calle Fuente Seca is a cellar restaurant with old stone pillars and decent food, including salads, vegetable and egg dishes at 500 to 850 ptas and meat and fish main dishes for 850 to 2000 ptas. Another mid-priced option in the old town is *Restaurante El Seco (Calle Corazón de Jesús 8)*, with tortillas and scrambled egg dishes from 600 to 1200 ptas, meat and fish around 1400 ptas, and a three-course menú including a drink for 1600 ptas.

The finest food is served at the restaurant in the *Parador Condestable Dávalos* (see Places to Stay for details). Lunch or dinner will cost around 4000 ptas, but that's a fair price for some of the excellent local dishes, such as *carruécano*, green peppers stuffed with partridge, local turkey and some scrumptious desserts.

Entertainment

Pub Siglo XV bar on Calle Prior Blanca is an atmospheric place with old stone pillars and sometimes live flamenco or other music.

Shopping

The typical green glaze on Úbeda's varied and attractive pottery, and the tradition of embroidering coloured patterns into esparto-grass mats *(ubedíes)*, both date from Muslim times.

Several workshops in the San Millán barrio, the potters' quarter north-east of the old town, sell pottery and the potters are often willing to explain some of the ancient techniques they use. Alfarería Paco Tito at Calle Valencia 22 is one of the best known, but several others on the same street, and Alfarería Góngora nearby at Cuesta de la Merced 32, are worth a look. Alfarería Tito also has a large shop at Plaza del Ayuntamiento 12.

For esparto mats and baskets, visit Artesanía Blanco at Calle Real 47 in the old town.

The main shopping streets are Calle Mesones and Calle Obispo Cobos, between Plaza de Andalucía and the Hospital de Santiago.

Getting There & Away

Bus The bus station (☎ 953 75 21 57) is at Calle San José 6 in the new part of town. Alsina Graells runs to Baeza up to 16 times daily, to Jaén (545 ptas, 1¼ hours) up to 13 times, to Cazorla three or four times and to Granada up to seven times. Bacoma goes to Córdoba and Sevilla four times daily. Other buses head to Málaga, Madrid, Valencia, Barcelona and small places around Jaén province.

Train The nearest station is Linares-Baeza (☎ 953 65 02 02), 21km north-west, which you can reach by Linares-bound buses. See the Baeza section for information on trains.

CAZORLA

postcode 23470 • pop 8500
• elevation 885m

Cazorla, 45km south-east of Úbeda, is the main gateway to the Parque Natural de Cazorla, which begins in the hills above the town. It's an attractive old place in its own right, with an imposing castle, narrow streets climbing the steep hillside beneath the dramatic Peña de los Halcones (Falcon Crag), and a range of good places to stay, eat and drink. It can get pretty crowded during Spanish holiday times and on fine weekends from spring to autumn.

Orientation & Information

The A-319 from the west winds up into Cazorla as Calle Hilario Marco, which ends at Plaza de la Constitución, the main square of the newer part of town. The second important square is Plaza de la Corredera, 150m south of Plaza de la Constitución along Calle Doctor Muñoz, which probably qualifies as Cazorla's main street. Plaza de Santa María, 300m farther south-east, down through narrow streets, is the heart of the oldest part of town.

The Oficina de Turismo Municipal (☎ 953 71 01 02) at Paseo del Santo Cristo

17, 200m north of Plaza de la Constitución, has information on the Parque Natural as well as Cazorla town but only opens during the summer. Quercus (☎ 953 72 01 15, fax 953 71 00 68) at Calle Juan Domingo 2, just off Plaza de la Constitución, provides some tourist information as well as selling maps, Spanish-language guidebooks and souvenirs and offering excursions into the park (see the Parque Natural de Cazorla section).

The post office is at Calle Mariano Extremera 2 behind the town hall, just off Plaza de la Corredera. You'll find several banks with ATMs on and between Plaza de la Constitución and Plaza de la Corredera.

The health centre, Centro de Salud Dr José Cano Salcedo (☎ 953 72 10 61), is at Calle Ximénez de Rada 1. The Policía Local (☎ 953 72 01 81) are in the town hall just off Plaza de la Corredera.

Plaza de la Corredera

The 17th-century **Iglesia de San José** at the northern end of the square contains six copies of El Greco paintings by Rafael del Real. In the square's top corner, with its landmark clock tower, stands the **town hall**, a former monastery. A theatre occupies the monastery's old church. The **Iglesia del Carmen**, 200m up Calle del Carmen from here, is Cazorla's best-looking church – a mainly 17th- and 18th- century construction, but with an earlier, plateresque tower.

Plaza de Santa María

Calle Gómez Calderón heads south from the town hall to the **Balcón de Zabaleta**, a lookout with fine views over the town and the Castillo de la Yedra. Down to the left is the lovely Plaza de Santa María (or Plaza Vieja). The large, ruined **Iglesia de Santa María** at the square's far end was built by Andrés de Vandelvira in the 16th century, over a river which runs under the square. The church was wrecked by Napoleonic troops in reprisal for Cazorla's tenacious resistance to them and is now an open-air concert venue. Also on the square is a 400-year-old fountain, the **Fuente de las Cadenas**.

JAÉN PROVINCE

Castillo de la Yedra

A short walk up from Plaza de Santa María, the impressive Castle of the Ivy (also called the Castillo de las Cuatro Esquinas, Castle of the Four Corners) is of Roman origin, though it was largely built by the Muslims, then restored in the 15th century, after the Reconquesta. It houses the Museo del Alto Guadalquivir (Museum of the Upper Guadalquivir) with interesting art and relics of local life – including a reconstructed traditional kitchen, models of old oil mills and a chapel with a lifesize Romanesque-Byzantine Crucifixion sculpture. The castle is open 3 to 8 pm Tuesday, 9 am to 8 pm Wednesday to Saturday, and 9 am to 3 pm Sunday and holidays. Admission is free with an EU passport or national identity card; 250 ptas otherwise.

Special Events

On 14 May, in a pilgrimage called La Caracolá, the image of San Isicio (a Christian apostle supposedly stoned to death at Cazorla in Roman times), is carried from the Ermita de San Isicio to the Iglesia de San José, and the streets are lit with oil lamps. Cazorla's main annual fiesta, from 17 to 21 September, features bullfights and music. On the first day a 17th-century painting of the Cristo del Consuelo (Christ of Consolation), which was rescued from the Napoleonic destruction of the Iglesia de Santa María, is carried in procession.

Places to Stay

Tiny *Camping Cortijo San Isicio* (☎ 953 72 12 80), off the Quesada road 4km southwest of central Cazorla, has room for just 54 people, charging 1400 ptas plus IVA for two adults with a tent and car. You should find it open from March to October.

Albergue Juvenil Cazorla (☎ 953 72 03 29, Plaza Mauricio Martínez 6), 200m uphill from Plaza de la Corredera, is a spick-and-span youth hostel, with a pool, in a former 16th-century convent. It has places for 120 people in rooms holding between two and six, most with shared bathrooms. The top-floor doubles, with wood-beamed ceilings, are as attractive as any budget room in town.

The clean, friendly *Hostal Betis* (☎ 953 72 05 40, Plaza de la Corredera 19), has singles costing between 1200 and 1500 ptas and doubles for 2500 to 2800 ptas. Some rooms overlook the square. *Pensión Taxi* (☎ 953 72 05 25, Travesía de San Antón 7), just off Plaza de la Constitución, is another friendly place; singles/doubles with shared bathrooms cost 1800/3500 ptas. *La Cueva de Juan Pedro* (☎ 953 72 12 25, Cale La Hoz 2), on a corner of Plaza de Santa María, has six rooms with bathroom and kitchen for 2000/4000 ptas.

Hotel Guadalquivir (☎/fax 953 72 02 68, Calle Nueva 6), just off Calle Doctor Muñoz, is a step up in quality – a friendly, family-run place where prettily decorated rooms with bathroom, TV, air-con and heating cost 4200/5800 ptas plus IVA. It has a cafe too.

Hotel Andalucía (☎ 953 72 12 68, Calle Martínez Falero 42) looks dull but has nice, sizeable rooms with bath and TV at the decent price of 3600/4700ptas.

The new *Hotel Ciudad de Cazorla* (☎ 953 72 17 00, fax 953 71 04 20, Plaza de la Corredera 9) has 35 rooms with air-con, heating, bath and TV, mostly at 8400/12,000 ptas. It has a restaurant, pool and garage.

Hotel Peña de los Halcones (☎ 953 72 02 11, fax 953 72 13 35, Travesía del Camino de La Iruela 2), 400m uphill from Plaza de la Corredera, has good-sized, pine-furnished rooms, with air-con, bath and TV for 7500/8200 ptas plus IVA. Some have great views. The hotel has a restaurant, cafe and pool.

A few other hotels are a bit of a hike down Calle Hilario Marco. The small *Hotel Parque* (☎ 953 72 18 06, Calle Hilario Marco 62), and the 23-room *Hotel Don Diego* (☎ 953 72 05 31, Calle Hilario Marco 163), almost opposite, have rooms with bath for around 4000/6000 ptas plus IVA.

Rooms at the *Villa Turística de Cazorla* (☎ 953 71 01 00) on Ladera de San Isicio have kitchen and fireplace, for 6500/10,500 ptas plus IVA. It has a good restaurant and a pool too.

JAÉN PROVINCE

Places to Eat

In late summer or autumn, after rain, locals disappear into the woods to gather large, deliciously edible mushrooms that they call *níscalos*. If these appear in restaurants, go for them.

The cheery **Mesón Don Chema** *(Calle Escaleras del Mercado 2)*, down a lane off Calle Doctor Muñoz, serves good, typical local fare at middling prices, with revuelto, meat, fish and various raciones all costing between 700 and 1600 ptas.

If a pizza is what you're after, **La Forchetta** *(Calle de las Escuelas 2)*, just down from Plaza de la Constitución, serves tasty ones costing 500 to 850 ptas, plus pasta at similar prices. **Restaurante La Sarga** *(Plaza del Mercado s/n)* is one of the more upmarket eateries in town, serving a four-course menú for 1700 ptas, and individual mains for 1200 to 1800 ptas. Specialities include *caldereta de gamo* (venison stew).

Over on Plaza de Santa María, the ancient, wood-beamed **La Cueva de Juan Pedro**, hung with countless clumps of garlic and drying peppers, serves up very traditional Cazorla fare such as *conejo* (rabbit), *trucha* (trout), rin-rán, *jabalí* (boar), *venison* (venado) and even mouflon. All are available as raciones, prepared in a variety of ways, for around 800 to 1000 ptas.

Several of the bars on Cazorla's three main squares serve good tapas and raciones – among them **Bar Las Vegas** *(Plaza de la Corredera 17)*, where besides *lomo de jabalí* (loin of wild boar) there's an item called *gloria bendita* (blessed glory), which is a tasty prawn-and-capsicum *revuelto*. The Las Vegas has the town's best breakfast *tostadas* (toasted rolls), too. **La Montería** *(Plaza de la Corredera 18)* has tapas of *choto con ajo* (veal with garlic) and venison. Other tapas stops include bright **Café-Bar Rojas** *(Plaza de la Constitución 2)* and down-to-earth **Taberna Quinito** *(Plaza de Santa María 6)*.

A daily *market* is held on Plaza del Mercado.

Entertainment

Aside from its tapas bars (see Places to Eat), Cazorla has a number of music bars which get lively on weekend nights – among them **La Rana Verde** *(Calle San Juan 12)*, above the youth hostel, and **Pub Liberty** *(Calle Hilario Marco 4)*.

Getting There & Away

Bus Alsina Graells runs two daily buses to/from Úbeda, Baeza, Jaén (960 ptas, two hours) and Granada. The main stop in Cazorla is Plaza de la Constitución; Quercus has timetable information. At our latest check, the buses to Cazorla left Granada at 10.30 am and 3 pm, Jaén 1½ hours later, Baeza 2½ hours later and Úbeda three hours later. Departures from Cazorla were at 5.30 pm daily, 7 am Monday to Saturday and at 8 am Sunday and holidays. A couple more daily buses run just between Úbeda and Cazorla.

AROUND CAZORLA

The village of **La Iruela**, 100m higher than Cazorla on the hill to the east, is less than 1km from Plaza de la Corredera – up Calle del Carmen and its continuation, Camino de la Iruela. The picturesque ruins of La Iruela's Knights Templar castle stand atop a sheer crag at the far (eastern) end of the village. Beside the main A-319 just after the turning up to La Iruela, friendly **Hotel La Finca Mercedes** *(☎ 953 72 10 87)* has doubles with bathroom for 5500 ptas plus IVA, and good views.

For recommended walks and drives in the Cazorla-La Iruela district, see the next section.

PARQUE NATURAL DE CAZORLA

The 2143 sq km Parque Natural de las Sierras de Cazorla, Segura y Las Villas (to give it its full title) is the biggest protected area in Spain. It's a crinkled, pinnacled region of several rugged, complicated mountain ranges – not extraordinarily high, but memorably beautiful – divided by high plains called *navas* and deep river valleys and lakes, and in many places thickly forested. The chief ranges run roughly north to south.

JAÉN PROVINCE

Cazorla Fauna & Flora

In the hills and forests of the Parque Natural de Cazorla you stand a chance of seeing ibex, mouflon, red and fallow deer and wild boar. You may even glimpse deer or boar near some of the main roads. All five species are subject to controlled hunting.

The ibex lives mainly on rocky heights and has made a fair recovery from an outbreak of scabies in the late 1980s that slashed its population from 10,000 to 500. There are now about 2000 ibex in the park. The other four animals prefer forests. The mouflon (a large, wild, reddish-brown sheep) and the fallow deer were introduced for hunting and the red deer and wild boar were reintroduced in the 1960s after being hunted to extinction here. The roe deer, also hunted out of existence here, was not reintroduced.

Your prospects of seeing wildlife increase as you get farther from the beaten track. Chances are higher early and late in the day, when deer are most likely to emerge on to open grassy areas. While walking you'll very likely come across areas of upturned earth where boar have rooted for food.

Some 140 species of birds nest in the park. Rocky crags are the haunt of the golden eagle, Bonelli's eagle, griffon vulture, Egyptian vulture and peregrine falcon. The forests harbour buzzards, short-toed eagles, booted eagles, goshawks, sparrowhawks, hobbies and great spotted woodpeckers.

The lammergeier or bearded vulture, with its majestic 2m-plus wingspan, is something of an emblem of the park, but it's still at an early stage of reintroduction here after disappearing in 1987 from what was its only Spanish habitat outside the Pyrénées. Efforts are being made to breed a new Cazorla population from captive birds brought from Central Europe at a special centre in the park. The first chick born under this program hatched in December 1999. The lammergeier's Spanish name, quebrantahuesos (bone-breaker), reflects its habit of smashing bones by dropping them on to rocks so that it can get at the marrow.

The park's rich vegetation is a delight. In spring the flowers are magnificent; in autumn the deciduous trees provide vivid splashes of colour. Of the park's 2300 plant species, 24 are unique, including the beautiful Cazorla violet (violeta de Cazorla in Spanish), a very bright violet colour, and the Cazorla geranium (geranio cazorlense). Both like rock crevices in the drier areas.

Among trees, pines predominate. The tall black pine (pino laricio in Spanish), with its horizontally-spreading branches typically clustered near the top, likes terrain above 1300m; the maritime pine (pino resinero or pino marítimo), with its typically rounded top, grows at levels up to about 1500m; the Aleppo pine (pino carrasco), with a bushy top and separated, often bare branches, predominates below 1100m. These last two trees were introduced in the 18th and 19th centuries after many of the native oaks had been floated downriver to be made into ships at Cádiz or Cartagena. Some holm oak and gall oak woodlands remain, however, and if you know your trees you'll find many other species including wild olive, juniper, poplar, ash, willow and maple – these last four notably in river valleys.

The park's attractions include fine walking, a good chance of seeing some wildlife, and picturesque villages with historical interest.

Exploring the park is a lot easier if you have your own wheels, but some bus services exist (see Getting There & Away at the end of the section), and there are plenty of places to stay inside the park. Those without vehicles have the option of guided excursions to reach the more remote areas.

The Río Guadalquivir, Andalucía' longest river, rises between the Sierra de Cazorla and Sierra del Pozo in the south of the park and flows northwards into the Embalse del Tranco de Beas reservoir, from which it emerges westbound for the Atlantic Ocean.

The best times to visit the park are April to June, and September and October: the vegetation is at its most colourful and you avoid most of the winter rain and the heat of July and August. In winter a lot of the park is often covered in snow. When walking, go properly equipped, with enough water and appropriate clothes.

Temperatures up in the hills are several degrees lower than down in the valleys, and there's often a wind chill factor.

The park is hugely popular with Spanish tourists and attracts an estimated 600,000 visitors a year – some 50,000 of them during Semana Santa. The other peak periods are July and August, and weekends from April to October.

Maps & Guides

Lonely Planet's *Walking in Spain* details three of the best Cazorla walks.

Editorial Alpina's 1:40,000 maps *Sierra de Cazorla*, covering the southern one-third of the park (costing around 700 ptas), and *Sierra de Segura*, covering the northern two-thirds (costing around 1000 ptas), are the best maps. Both were published in 1998. Selected walking and mountain bike routes are specially marked, and described in accompanying booklets (though we have only seen these in Spanish). You should be able to get the Alpina and other maps and guides at the Torre del Vinagre information centre (for details see The Centre of the Park later in this section) and at some shops in Cazorla town.

Information

Tourist Offices The main park information centre is at Torre del Vinagre. There are seasonal tourist offices at Cortijos Nuevos, Hornos, Santiago de la Espada, Segura de la Sierra, Orcera and Siles. Offices in Cazorla also provide information on the park.

Money You'll find banks with ATMs in Burunchel, Arroyo Frío and Cortijos Nuevos.

Organised Tours

A number of outfits offer guided trips to some of the park's less accessible areas, plus other activities. Hotels and camp sites in the park can often arrange for you to picked up.

The highest-profile operator is Quercus (☎ 953 72 01 15), some of whose guides speak English or French. It has offices at Calle Juan Domingo 2 in Cazorla and at the Torre del Vinagre. Quercus offers 4WD trips from these centres to *zonas restringidas* (areas where vehicles are not normally allowed, with chained-off tracks) for 3000 to 3700 ptas per person a half-day or 5000 to 5500 ptas a full day, as well as guided hikes and '*caza fotográfica*' (photographic hunting) outings.

Excursiones Bujarkay (☎ 953 71 30 11) offers walking, 4WD, biking and horse-riding trips with local guides (*guías nativos*). It's based at Calle Borosa 81 in Coto Ríos but also has a roadside kiosk in Arroyo Frío. Its prices are similar to Quercus'.

Accommodation & Food

The park has plenty of accommodation but few places in the budget range, except for camp sites, of which there are at least 10. During peak visitor periods it's worth booking ahead.

Camping is not allowed outside the organised camp sites. These don't always stick to their published opening dates and from October to April it's always worth ringing ahead or checking with one of the tourist offices.

Virtually all hotels, hostales and camp sites in the park have restaurants, mostly serving local fare. There's also a variety of other restaurants and kiosks around the park.

See the later Places to Stay section for details on what's available.

The South of the Park

The park begins just a few hundred metres up the hill east of Cazorla town, and the footpaths and dirt roads working their way between the pine forests, meadowlands, crags, streams and valleys of the Sierra de Cazorla offer heaps of scope for day walks or drives, with fine panoramas.

The main A-319, north-east from Cazorla, doesn't enter the park until Burunchel, after 7km. From Burunchel it winds 5km up to the 1200m Puerto de las Palomas pass, with the breezy Mirador Paso del Aire lookout a little farther on. Five twisting kilometres downhill from here is Empalme del Valle, a junction where the A-319 turns north towards Arroyo Frío to pick up the north-flowing Guadalquivir.

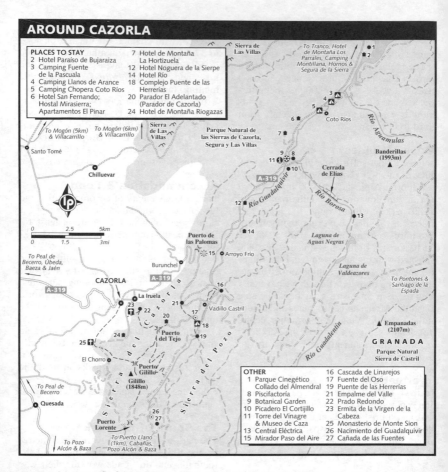

AROUND CAZORLA

PLACES TO STAY
2 Hotel Paraíso de Bujaraiza
3 Camping Fuente
   de la Pascuala
4 Camping Llanos de Arance
5 Camping Chopera Coto Ríos
6 Hotel San Fernando;
   Hostal Mirasierra;
   Apartamentos El Pinar
7 Hotel de Montaña
   La Hortizuela
12 Hotel Noguera de la Sierpe
14 Hotel Río
18 Complejo Puente de las
   Herrerías
20 Parador El Adelantado
   (Parador de Cazorla)
24 Hotel de Montaña Riogazas

OTHER
1 Parque Cinegético
   Collado del Almendral
8 Piscifactoría
9 Botanical Garden
10 Picadero El Cortijillo
11 Torre del Vinagre
   & Museo de Caza
13 Central Eléctrica
15 Mirador Paso del Aire
16 Cascada de Linarejos
17 Fuente del Oso
19 Puente de las Herrerías
21 Empalme del Valle
22 Prado Redondo
23 Ermita de la Virgen de la
   Cabeza
25 Monasterio de Monte Sion
26 Nacimiento del Guadalquivir
27 Cañada de las Fuentes

JAÉN PROVINCE

Sierra de Cazorla by Car This itinerary of about 60km is a good introduction to the parts of the park nearest Cazorla town for those with wheels. Much of it is on unpaved roads but it's all quite passable for ordinary cars, if bumpy in places.

Head first up to La Iruela (see Around Cazorla for details) and turn right along Carretera Virgen de la Cabeza soon after entering La Iruela (a sign says 'Ermita' and 'Merendero de Riogazas'). You reach the **Merenderos de Cazorla** lookout, with fine views over Cazorla, after about 700m. After another 4km, during which the road ceases

to be paved, you pass the Hotel de Montaña Riogazas (see Places to Stay for details); 3km farther south is **El Chorro**, a gorge which is a good spot for watching Egyptian and griffon vultures.

Just beyond El Chorro, the road meets another dirt road coming up from the southwest. A left turn here (initially southwards) will wind you round over the **Puerto Lorente** pass and down to a junction after 12km. Fork right here and after a couple of hundred metres a 'Nacimiento del Guadalquivir' sign points down some steps towards the river on your left. A plaque on the

euro currency converter 1000 ptas = €6.01

far bank marks the official **source of the Guadalquivir**. In dry periods you can apparently identify the stream emerging from underground, but if there has been rain it will be overwhelmed by another coming down from higher in the hills.

The road heads a short distance past the source to the **Cañada de las Fuentes** picnic area. (Those with extra time and energy could continue 8km from here to Cabañas, see the later Cabañas Walk section.)

From Cañada de las Fuentes and the Nacimiento del Guadalquivir, head northwards following the infant Guadalquivir – a beautiful trip down the wooded valley with the river bubbling to one side and rugged crags rising all around. It's 11km to the **Puente de las Herrerías**, a bridge over the Guadalquivir supposedly built in one night for Queen Isabel La Católica to cross during her campaigns against Granada. Here the road becomes paved, and 3km farther, past the large Complejo Puente de las Herrerías camp site (see Places to Stay for details), you reach a T-junction. Go left and after 400m, opposite the turning to Vadillo Castril village, is the start of the **Sendero de la Cerrada del Utrero**, a beautiful 2km loop walk (see under Empalme del Valle for details). One kilometre farther is the turning to the Parador El Adelantado hotel (which is 5km up a paved side-road) and after another 2.5km you're at the Empalme del Valle junction, from which it's 17km back to Cazorla by the A-319 via the Puerto de las Palomas and Burunchel.

Sierra de Cazorla Walk This 18km walk from Cazorla town takes six or seven hours plus stops and involves a total ascent of just over 1000m. It passes through beautiful woods, across breezy mountain heights, near idyllic-looking farms and an abandoned monastery, and offers superb vistas and a good chance of spotting some wildlife.

Leave Cazorla's Plaza de Santa María by Camino de San Isidro, between the Fuente de las Cadenas and La Cueva de Juan Pedro. After five minutes, veer left up a dirt road, then go left at a one-spout fountain.

Thirty minutes later, at the top of a zigzag rise, go left. You pass the 17th-century **Monasterio de Monte Sión** after 10 minutes. The path rounds the monastery orchard and climbs into woods. Thirty minutes later you will emerge on the Riogazas–El Chorro dirt road. Go 50m to the right, then left up a faint path marked by a green paint arrow. The path, immediately more distinct, climbs eastwards, and after 15 minutes meets a path from the left at a stone with green and blue paint daubs. Go right and in 40 minutes upwards you reach the 1750m **Puerto Gilillo** pass, with a small stone shelter just below it. To cap **Gilillo** (1848m), the highest peak in this area of the park, head south up from the pass – a 15-minute ascent.

Back down at Puerto Gilillo, take the northwards path from beside the stone hut, wending north-north-east along **Loma de los Castellones** ridge. The path is clear most of the way but you have to look for it going round the left side of the second hump (marked 1732m on the Alpina map). A few minutes later follow a green arrow down to the left: you'll soon be continuing in your previous direction. After 35 minutes, cross a grassy basin to join a track coming from the right, and after 10 more minutes you're at **Puerto del Tejo** (1556m), with a path junction. The right-hand (northwards) option winds 2km down to the Parador El Adelantado hotel (1325m). For Cazorla, go left. The path winds round Cerro de la Laguna then descends northwards. About an hour from Puerto del Tejo you reach an old, little-used farmstead, **Prado Redondo**, surrounded by woods and grassy lawns.

From Prado Redondo head west through the trees. Your path bends a little to the right, climbing, then curves gradually left and finally, within 10 minutes from Prado Redondo, descends into a gully beneath power lines. Follow the path down (it diverges from the gully after a few minutes) and you'll pass above La Iruela to reach the **Ermita de la Virgen de la Cabeza** chapel after 25 minutes. Continue five minutes down to the El Chorro–La Iruela road, turn right, and you emerge on La Iruela's main street in 15 minutes more. Turn left, then fork left downhill after five minutes. This brings you into Cazorla in another 15 minutes.

Empalme del Valle–Puente de las Herrerías–Cerrada del Utrero Walk
This loop walk of 12km, ending back at Empalme del Valle, includes about 7km of road walking, but it's accessible in a day trip by the bus from Cazorla to Empalme del Valle and back. It's also a way of getting to the accommodation at Puente de las Herrerías.

From Empalme del Valle (1100m), the signposted **Sendero de El Empalme del Valle** strikes 1.5km north-west over the 1230m Collado del Oso pass to the Fuente del Oso, a shady fountain beside the Parador El Adelantado approach road. From the Fuente del Oso the **Sendero de la Fuente del Oso** goes 1.4km south-east down to the **Puente de las Herrerías** (1000m). Now follow the route from the Puente de las Herrerías described in the earlier Sierra de Cazorla by Car section, as far as the start of the Sendero de la Cerrada del Utrero. (Note that two similarly-named paths, the Sendero de la Cerrada del Utrero and Sendero de la Central de Utrero, start from the one point: when we checked, the maps of the two walks posted at the start were juxtaposed.)

The 2km **Sendero de la Cerrada del Utrero** takes you around under imposing cliffs to the Cascada de Linarejos waterfall, which falls a long way into a pool just below a small dam on the Guadalquivir. Most of the year, when the river is low, you can cross the river to the waterfall and explore the paths on that side. The main path *(sendero)* continues above the Embalse de la Cerrada del Utrero, the narrow reservoir formed on the Guadalquivir by the dam, and returns to the road at a bridge 300m below the start of the path. Return to that start and continue 3.5km to Empalme del Valle.

Cabañas Walk This 2028m peak, one of the highest in the park, is a two-hour round-trip walk from the road at Puerto Llano, 8km south of Cañada de las Fuentes (see the Sierra de Cazorla by Car section). The route loops round the southern end of the hill and approaches the summit, which offers superb views, from the south-east.

Sierra del Pozo & Barranco del Guadalentín Walks Further good walks in the south of the park are to be had in the Sierra del Pozo, which rises above the eastern side of the upper Guadalquivir valley, and in the Barranco del Guadalentín, a deep river valley farther east. The latter is particularly rich in wildlife, but you need either your own vehicle, or a guide with one, to reach these areas.

Places to Stay Accommodation options in the southern part of the park are limited.

Hotel de Montaña Riogazas (☎ 953 12 40 35, ✉ hotelriogazas@cibercentro.es), at Km 4.5 on the road from La Iruela to El Chorro, is an old hunting lodge converted into an attractive little hotel with 12 pleasant rooms, a dining room and pool. It closes from November to May, except for the Christmas and Semana Santa holiday periods. Singles/doubles cost 4000/5800 ptas plus IVA.

Complejo Puente de las Herrerías (☎/fax 953 72 70 90) is the largest camp site in the park, with room for about 1000 people at 475 ptas plus IVA for each adult, tent and car. It also has a small hotel with 11 double rooms with bath at 6500 ptas plus IVA, and cabins with fireplace, bathroom, kitchen and living room costing from 6500 ptas plus IVA for two people to 20,500 ptas plus IVA for 10. Facilities include a restaurant and pool, and you can arrange activities such as horse riding, canoeing, canyoning and climbing.

Parador El Adelantado or *Parador de Cazorla* (☎ 953 72 70 75, fax 953 72 70 77, ✉ cazorla@parador.es) offers all the parador comforts in a pine forest setting, with a grassy garden and fine pool. The 33 rooms cost 12,000/15,000 ptas plus IVA, but only nine of them have outside views.

The Centre of the Park
From Empalme del Valle the A-319 heads north down the Guadalquivir valley to the

unspectacular villages of Arroyo Frío (6km) and Coto Ríos (22km) and the Embalse del Tranco de Beas. The main concentration of accommodation and visitor facilities in the park is dotted along this road and the most popular day hike, up the Río Borosa, is accessible from it. The bus from Cazorla goes as far as Coto Ríos.

Torre del Vinagre Sixteen kilometres north-east of Empalme del Valle, the roadside Centro de Interpretación Torre del Vinagre (☎ 953 71 30 40) was built as a hunting lodge for Spain's high and mighty, including Franco, in the 1950s. Today it offers displays and information on the park, with opening hours that vary by the year and season: it usually closes on winter Mondays but otherwise expect it to open 11 am to 2 pm year-round and 5 to 8 pm in summer, 4 to 7 pm in spring and autumn, and 4 to 6 pm in winter. In an adjoining building, open the same hours, is the **Museo de Caza** (Hunting Museum), with stuffed park wildlife and some impressive antlers and tusks. Just up the road is a **botanical garden** exhibiting the park's flora, with limited opening hours. Admission to the museum and the garden is free.

Picadero El Cortijillo (☎ 953 72 72 51), just across the Guadalquivir on the road to the Río Borosa walk (see the following section) offers horse riding (from one hour to a day) and rents out mountain bikes.

Río Borosa Walk Though it can get very busy at weekends and holiday times, this seven-hour walk (return, not counting stops) is popular for good reason. It follows the Río Borosa upstream, through scenery that progresses from the pretty to the majestic, via a gorge and two tunnels (a torch is highly beneficial) to two beautiful mountain lakes – an ascent of 500m in the course of 12km from Torre del Vinagre. Using the bus to Torre del Vinagre (see Getting There & Away at the end of this section), you can do it as a day trip from Cazorla. The route is dotted with good trackside springs, the last of them at the Central Eléctrica. Carry a water bottle that you can fill there with enough water for three hours.

A road signed 'Central Eléctrica', east off the A-319 opposite the information centre, crosses the Guadalquivir after about 500m and within 1km from the river reaches a fish farm (*piscifactoría*), with parking areas close by. The marked start of the walk is on your right, shortly past the fish farm.

The first section is an unpaved road, crisscrossing the tumbling, trout-rich river on bridges. After 40 minutes, diverge to the right along a path signed 'Cerrada de Elias'. This takes you through a beautiful 30-minute section where the valley narrows to a gorge (the **Cerrada de Elías**) and the path takes to a wooden walkway to save you from swimming. You reemerge on the dirt road and continue for 40 minutes to the **Central Eléctrica**, a small hydroelectric station.

The path passes between the power station and river and crosses a footbridge, where a 'Nacimiento de Aguas Negras, Laguna de Valdeazores' sign directs you on upwards. Forty minutes from the station, the path turns left and zigzags up into a **tunnel** cut inside the cliff for water flowing to the power station. A narrow path, separated from the watercourse by a fence, runs through the tunnel, which takes about five minutes to walk through. Then there's five minutes in the open air before you enter a **second tunnel**, one minute long. From this you emerge just below the dam holding back the **Laguna de Aguas Negras**, a picturesque little reservoir surrounded by beautiful hills and trees. A 15-minute walk south brings you to a similar-sized natural lake, the **Laguna de Valdeazores** – altogether about 3½ hours walking from Torre del Vinagre.

Parque Cinegético Collado del Almendral & Tranco Seven kilometres north of the Coto Ríos turning, on a spur of land between the A-319 and the Embalse del Tranco de Beas, the *parque cinegético* (game park) is a large enclosed area where ibex, mouflon and deer are kept. A 1km footpath leads from the parking area to three lookout points where you might see animals – your chances are highest at dawn and dusk.

JAÉN PROVINCE

Fifteen kilometres farther north, the A-319 crosses the dam that holds back the reservoir. The small village of Tranco stands on the northern side of the dam.

Places to Stay In Arroyo Frío two modern, medium-sized hotels, *Hotel Cazorla Valle* (☎ 953 72 71 00, fax 953 72 06 09) and *Hotel Montaña* (☎ 953 72 70 11, fax 953 72 70 01) both have doubles in the 8500 ptas region. At the northern end of the village *Complejo Turístico Los Enebros* (☎ 953 72 71 10, fax 953 72 71 34) has a hotel, apartments and a small camp site. In the hotel singles/double rooms with bathroom, TV and heating cost 5500/7000 ptas plus IVA; apartments for six are 14,000 ptas plus IVA. There are also two pools and a playground.

About 1km north of Arroyo Frío, a turning to the east leads 2km to the comfortable, pine-panelled, 21-room *Hotel Río* (☎ 953 71 30 33, fax 953 72 13 35), with doubles with bathroom costing 6900 ptas plus IVA, and a pool.

Five kilometres farther along the A-319 from Arroyo Frío is *Hotel Noguera de la Sierpe* (☎ 953 71 30 21, fax 953 71 31 09), a favourite of the hunting community and decked with trophies (some of which, such as the entire stuffed lion in the lobby, clearly aren't of local origin). The rooms are comfortable without being exactly cosy. They cost 7000/9500 ptas plus IVA. The large gardens contain a swimming pool and a small lake. There's also a horse-breeding ranch here.

Two kilometres north of Torre del Vinagre is the turning to the 27-room *Hotel de Montaña La Hortizuela* (☎/fax 953 71 31 50), a cosy hotel in a tranquil setting 1km off the main road. The medium-sized rooms, with bath, cost 4500/5500 ptas plus IVA. The hotel has a good restaurant, with a 1400-ptas menú. A group of wild boar comes to the garden to dine on the slops thrown out after lunch.

A farther 1km north on the A-319 are the comfortable, modern *Hotel San Fernando* (☎ 953 71 30 69), with rooms costing 6700/8475 plus IVA, and the older *Hostal Mirasierra* (☎/fax 953 71 30 44), charging

4200/5200 ptas plus IVA; both have pools. Adjoining the Mirasierra is *Apartamentos El Pinar* (☎ 953 71 30 68) which has four-person apartments for 8700 ptas.

Within the next 4km on (or just off) the A-319 are three medium-sized camp sites beside the Guadalquivir: first *Camping Chopera Coto Ríos* (☎ 953 71 30 05), with a rather tight but shady site by the side road into Coto Ríos; then *Camping Llanos de Arance* (☎ 953 71 31 39), just across the Guadalquivir; and finally *Camping Fuente de la Pascuala* (☎ 953 71 30 28), beside the A-319. All charge around 1100 ptas for two adults with a car and tent.

Just before the Parque Cinegético Collado del Almendral, *Hotel Paraíso de Bujaraiza* (☎ 953 12 41 14) is on the shores of the reservoir and has doubles with bathroom costing 5000 ptas.

North of Tranco along the road towards Hornos are the stone-built *Hotel de Montaña Los Parrales* (☎ 953 12 61 70), overlooking the reservoir, with a pool and doubles with bath for 5350 ptas including breakfast, and *Camping Montillana* (☎ 953 12 61 94) which charges 325/450/325 ptas plus IVA per adult/tent/car.

The North of the Park
North of the Embalse del Tranco de Beas the main valley widens out and the hills are less rugged.

Hornos & Around Twelve kilometres north of the dam at Tranco, the A-319 runs into a T-junction from which the A-317 winds 4km up to Hornos (postcode 23292, pop 800, elevation 870m), a village atop a high rock outcrop with panoramic views. Hornos' castle, which dates from Islamic times, looks more impressive from a distance than it really is.

The A-317 winds 45km south-east across the Sierra de Segura from Hornos to the small town of Santiago de la Espada near the park's eastern boundary. About 10km northeast of Hornos on the A-317 is the Puerto de Horno de Peguera pass and junction. One kilometre up the road to the north (towards Siles), a dirt road turns left at some ruined houses to the top of **El Yelmo** (1809m), one of the most distinctive mountains in the northern part of the park. It's 5km to the top, an ascent of 360m. At a fork after 1.75km, go right (the left fork goes down to El Robledo and Cortijos Nuevos). Both the climb and the summit of El Yelmo afford superb long-distance views. You should see griffon vultures wheeling around the skies – and, at the weekend and holidays, paragliders and hang-gliders. The road is OK for cars, if narrow, but is also a good walk.

Segura de la Sierra Easily the most spectacular and interesting village in the park, Segura de la Sierra (postcode 23379, pop 2000, elevation 1115m) sits atop a high hill crowned by a castle which dominates the countryside. By road it's 20km north of Hornos: turn east off the A-317 4km after the village of Cortijos Nuevos.

Segura, a small place of just a few narrow streets, is possibly of Phoenician origin. The Romans mined silver in the area. In Muslim times Segura was briefly the capital of a small kingdom. When taken in 1214 by the Knights of Santiago, it was one of the very first Christian conquests in Andalucía.

As you approach the upper, older part of the village, there's a tourist office (☎ 953 48 02 80), open during Semana Santa and summer only, beside the Puerta Nueva, an arch which was one of four gates in Segura's Muslim walls. In other seasons tourist information is available 8 am to 3 pm Monday to Friday from the town hall (☎ 953 48 02 80), just through the arch. The two main attractions, the castle and the Baño Moro, are normally left open all day every day, but you might want to check this before proceeding.

Along and across the street from the town hall is the **Iglesia de Nuestra Señora del Collado**, the parish church, built about 1400 but much reconstructed since. The deconsecrated **Iglesia de los Jesuitas**, adjoining it below, has a good Renaissance facade. Continue down from here, then left along Calle Caballeros Santiaguistas, to the **Baño Moro** (Muslim Bath), built about 1150, probably for the local ruler Ibn ben Hamusk. It has three rooms (for cold, temperate and hot

baths), a barrel vault with skylights, and horseshoe arches. Nearby is the **Puerta Catena**, the best preserved of Segura's four Muslim gates.

If you're walking up to the **castle**, at the top of the village, take the first narrow street up to the right after the parish church, Calle de las Ordenanzas del Común. After a few minutes you'll come out beside Segura's tiny, sort-of-rectangular bullring, with the castle track heading up to the right. Alternatively, you can drive most of the way up by heading past the parish church and round the perimeter of the village.

The main feature of the castle is its three-storey keep from which there are great views across to El Yelmo and far to the west. There's also a chapel with supposedly marvellous acoustics, if you find it open. The castle's origins are Muslim or earlier. It took its most recent knocks in a siege during the Napoleonic wars, but the first documented restoration was made by the Knights of Santiago. (The most recent was in the 1970s.)

Places to Stay & Eat In Hornos, *Bar El Cruce* (☎ 953 49 50 03, Puerta Nueva 27), at the entrance to the village, has half a dozen decent single/doubles with bathroom at 3100/3700 ptas, and good food. Round the corner into the village, *El Mirador* restaurant (☎ 953 49 50 19, Puerta Nueva 11) also has eight rooms with bath for 2700/3900 ptas.

Camping El Robledo (☎ 953 12 61 56) is at El Robledo, about 4km east of Cortijos Nuevos on a road leading up to El Yelmo.

The only accommodation in Segura de la Sierra is *Mesón Jorge Manrique* (☎ 953 48 03 80, Calle de las Ordenanzas del Común 2), with just a few rooms at 1800/3500 ptas, or 4000 ptas for a double with private bathroom. It has a small restaurant with most dishes at 1100 ptas or less.

Getting There & Around
Bus Carcesa (☎ 953 72 11 42) runs buses daily, except Sunday, from Cazorla's Plaza de la Constitución to Empalme del Valle, Arroyo Frío, Torre del Vinagre and Coto Ríos. The timetable changes from time to

JAÉN PROVINCE

time so you should check with the company or with Quercus in Cazorla (see under Orientation & Information in the earlier Cazorla section for details). At our last check, the buses left Cazorla at 5.45 am (6.30 am from late June to mid-September and on Saturday year round) and 2.30 pm. The bus takes about 30 minutes to Empalme del Valle, one hour to Torre del Vinagre and 1¼ hours to Coto Ríos. Buses back to Cazorla left Coto Ríos at 7.10 am (8 am from late June to mid-September and on Saturday all year) and 4.15 pm.

No buses link the northern part of the park with the centre or south, but coming from Jaén, Baeza or Úbeda, you could get an Alsina Graells bus to La Puerta de Segura (leaving Jaén daily at 9.30 am). From the same stop in La Puerta de Segura, Gil San (☎ 953 49 60 27) runs a bus at 1.30 pm daily, except Saturday, Sunday and holidays, to Segura de la Sierra and Cortijos Nuevos.

Car & Motorcycle Approaches to the park include the A-319 from Cazorla, roads into the north from Villanueva del Arzobispo and Puente de Génave on the N-322, and the A-317 to Santiago de la Espada from Puebla de Don Fadrique in northern Granada province.

There are at least seven petrol stations in the park.

Almería Province

Andalucía's easternmost province is its sunniest and driest, with over 3000 hours of sunshine each year and large expanses of rocky semi-desert, particularly north and east of Almería city. This stark landscape meets the coast in majestic fashion on the hilly Cabo de Gata promontory, where excellent beaches are strung between dramatic cliffs and headlands. Farther north, a succession of 2000m-plus mountain ranges, generally oriented east–west, are divided by the valleys of often-dry rivers. Minor roads across these ranges provide plenty of scope for drivers with a taste for adventure, but it makes sense to avoid them when the mountains are covered in cloud or snow.

In recent decades Almería has used its sunshine to stage a comeback from oblivion and poverty through tourism and intensive cultivation of vegetables, fruit and flowers in plastic greenhouses.

ALMERÍA
postcode 04080 • pop 168,000
The large Islamic fort dominating the city, the Alcazaba, is the chief reminder of Almería's distant heyday. Islamic Al-mariya, initially a port for the Córdoba caliphate, grew wealthy as capital of an 11th-century *taifa* (small kingdom), thriving on silk-weaving from Alpujarras thread and international trade. The city was taken by the Catholic Monarchs in 1489 and its Muslim populace expelled a year later. Devastated by an earthquake in 1522, Almería only began to recover in the 19th century. Today it's a likeable and lively port city, and the increasingly prosperous hub of a horticultural and mining region.

Orientation & Information
The city centre lies between the Alcazaba in the west and Rambla de Belén, a *paseo* (walk) created from a dry river bed, in the east. Paseo de Almería, cutting north from Rambla de Belén to the intersection called

Highlights

- Spend time exploring the beaches, coastal walks and villages of rugged, dry Cabo de Gata
- Marvel at the Alcazaba of Almería, one of Andalucía's most impressive Muslim castles
- Admire the colourful Níjar pottery
- Make the trip to Los Vélez, a little-visited area with fascinating historical relics and beautiful mountain scenery

Puerta de Purchena, is the main artery. The bus and train stations are a few hundred metres east of Rambla de Belén.

The Patronato Provincial de Turismo's helpful tourist information office (☎ 950 62 11 17) on Plaza Bendicho opens 10 am to 2 pm and 5 to 8 pm Monday to Friday. The Junta de Andalucía tourist office (☎ 950 27 43 55) at Parque de Nicolás Salmerón s/n opens 9 am to 7 pm Monday to Friday, 10 am to 2 pm at weekends.

There are numerous banks on Paseo de Almería. The post office is at Plaza de Juan Cassinello 1. Travel agencies cluster along Paseo de Almería and Avenida de la Estación.

The main public hospital is Hospital Torrecárdenas (☎ 950 21 21 00) on Pasaje Torrecárdenas, 4km north-east of the city centre. The Policía Local station (☎ 950 21 00 19) is at Calle Santos Zárate 11.

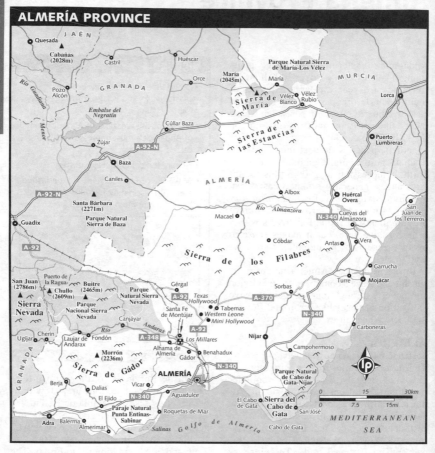

ALMERÍA PROVINCE

Alcazaba

Earthquakes and other ravages of time have spared little of the Alcazaba's internal splendour, but its hefty walls and towers still dominate the city and command great views. The entrance is on Calle Almanzor, up the hill west of Calle de la Reina.

The Alcazaba was founded in 955 by the Córdoba caliph Abd ar-Rahman III to defend this coast against Fatimid raids from North Africa, and it was around the fort that the city grew. The lowest of the Alcazaba's three compounds, the **Primer Recinto**, is today mainly gardens. Originally it served

as a military camp and refuge for the population during sieges. From its top corner, the **Muralla de la Hoya** (or Muralla de Jairán) – a wall built in the early 11th century by Jairán, Almería's first kingdom ruler – descends the valley on the northern side of the Alcazaba and climbs the Cerro de San Cristóbal on the far side.

The **Segundo Recinto** was the heart of the Alcazaba. Built against the wall at its eastern end are the Aljibes Califales (Caliphal Water Cisterns) and a chapel, the Ermita de San Juan, converted from a mosque by the Catholic Monarchs. On the northern side of the enclosure are the remains of the Muslim rulers' palace, the Palacio de Almotacín – named after the ruler under whom medieval Almería reached its peak, Almotacín (1051–91). The Ventana de la Odalisca (Concubine's Window) here gets its name from a slave girl who, legend says, jumped to her death from it after her Christian prisoner lover had been thrown from it.

The **Tercer Recinto**, at the north-western end of the Alcazaba, is a fortress that was added by the Catholic Monarchs. Its sturdy stone walls and towers are in better shape than the rest of the Alcazaba.

The Alcazaba opens 10 am to 2 pm and 5 to 8.30 pm daily from mid-June to September, and 9 am to 6.30 pm daily (except 25 December and 1 January) from October to mid-June. Admission is free for EU citizens with a passport or identity card, and costs 250 ptas for others.

Down in the valley north of the Alcazaba you may notice a number of pens containing gazelle and other un-Spanish wildlife. This is the Estación Experimental de Zonas Áridas, a research centre into threatened Saharan fauna.

Cathedral

Almería's weighty cathedral is at the heart of the old part of the city, a tangle of narrow streets below the Alcazaba. Begun in 1524, it's mainly a mixture of late Gothic and Renaissance styles. Its fortress-like appearance, with six towers, was dictated by pirate raids from North Africa. Don't miss the Sol de Portocarrero, a splendid 16th-century stone sun, carved on the eastern end of the building on Calle del Cubo.

The spacious interior, open 6 to 8 pm daily, has a Gothic ribbed ceiling and uses jasper and local marble in some of its baroque and neo-classical trimmings. The chapel behind the main altar contains the tomb of Bishop Diego Villalán, founder of the cathedral, whose broken-nosed image is a work of 16th-century architect and sculptor, Juan de Orea, as are the choir, with its walnut stalls, and the Sacristía Mayor, with its carved stone roof, windows and arches. Admission is free.

Museums & Exhibitions

The **Centro Andaluz de la Fotografía** (Andalucian Photography Centre), on Plaza Pablo Cazard, puts on good photo exhibitions in a beautiful patio – it opens 9 am to 2 pm and 4 to 9 pm Monday to Friday, 6 to 9 pm Saturday, and admission is free.

Almería's Archaeological Museum is currently divided between two temporary sites. Finds from nearby Los Millares and other prehistoric material are in the **Biblioteca Pública** on Calle Hermanos Machado – open 9 am to 2 pm Tuesday to Saturday. The Iberian and Roman collections are in the **Archivo Histórico Provincial** at Calle Infanta 12, open 9 am to 2 pm Monday to Friday. Admission to both is free.

The **Centro de Arte – Museo de Almería** on Plaza de la Estación exhibits visiting art shows and the city's permanent art collection. It opens 11 am to 4 pm daily except Saturday and 7 to 9 pm (6 to 8 pm in winter) daily except Sunday. Admission is free.

Beach

A long, grey-sand beach fronts the palm-lined Paseo Marítimo, east of the city centre.

Special Events

Almería's big bash is the summer *feria* (fair) in late August – 10 days and nights of music, bullfights, fairground rides, exhibitions and full-on partying.

Places to Stay – Budget

Camping On the coast 4km west of town on the Aguadulce road is *Camping La Garrofa* (☎ 950 23 57 70). It opens year round with room for 200 people and costs 550 ptas for each adult, car and tent.

Hostels The spick-and-span *Albergue Juvenil Almería* (☎ 950 26 97 88, Calle Isla de Fuerteventura s/n) can accommodate 170 people, nearly all in double rooms. It's 1.5km east of the city centre, beside the Estadio de la Juventud stadium and three blocks north of Avenida del Cabo de Gata. Take bus No 1 'Universidad' from the eastern end of Rambla del Obispo Orbera and ask the driver for the *albergue* or the stadium.

ALMERÍA

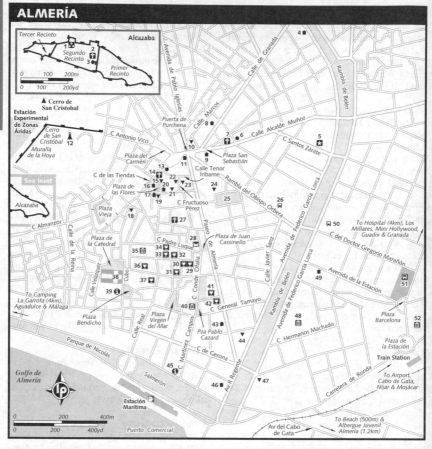

Hostales & Hotels A good choice near the bus and train stations is *Hostal Americano* (☎ 950 28 10 15, Avenida de la Estación 6). Well-kept, decent-sized singles/doubles cost from 2665/5175 ptas plus IVA with washbasin to 3660/5990 ptas plus IVA with bathroom.

Hostal Universal (☎ 950 23 55 57, Puerta de Purchena 3), in the centre of town, has about 20 simple but sizeable rooms, with shared bathrooms, costing 2000/4000 ptas. The building was once a minor mansion, as the broad staircase suggests.

The better *Hostal Sevilla* (☎ 950 23 00 09, Calle de Granada 23), nearby, has clean, air-con rooms with TV and private bathroom for 3600/5500 ptas plus IVA. *Hostal Bristol* (☎ 950 23 15 95, Plaza San Sebastián 8) is similar but slightly more expensive. *Hostal Maribel* (☎ 950 23 51 66, Avenida de Federico García Lorca 153), 600m north-east of Puerta de Purchena, has clean if small rooms with TV costing 3250/6000 ptas with shared bathroom or 3650/6700 ptas with private bathroom. Double rooms with air-con cost 7000 ptas.

ALMERÍA

PLACES TO STAY
4   Hostal Maribel
8   Hostal Sevilla
9   Hostal Bristol
11 Hostal Universal
16 Hotel Torreluz (Three
    Star)
17 Hotel Torreluz (Two Star)
20 Hotel Torreluz (Four Star)
43 Hotel Costasol
46 Gran Hotel Almería
49 Hostal Americano

PLACES TO EAT
10 Restaurante Alfareros
15 Torreluz Mediterráneo
18 Casa Puga
19 Cafetería Torreluz
21 Tasca Restaurante Torreluz
22 Asador Torreluz
23 Bodega Las Botas
24 Restaurant Sol de Almería

44 Calle Mayor
47 Cafetería Central

OTHER
1   Ruins of Palacio de
    Almotacín
2   Ermita de San Juan
3   Aljibes Califales
5   Police Station (Policía Local)
6   RENFE Office
7   Templo de San Sebastián
12 Christ Statue
13 Aljibes Árabes; Peña El
    Taranto
14 Templo de Santiago
25 Covered Market
26 Buses for Albergue Juvenil
    Almería
27 Iglesia de San Pedro
28 Post Office
29 Cortabón; Taberna Postigo
30 El Cafetín

31 Velvet
32 Pub Venue
33 Irish Tavern
34 Georgia Café Bar
35 Archivo Histórico
    Provincial
36 Vértice Pub
37 Vhada
38 Cathedral
39 Patronato Provincial de
    Turismo
40 Centro Andaluz de la
    Fotografía
41 La Clásica
42 Molly Malone
45 Junta de Andalucía Tourist
    Office
48 Biblioteca Pública
50 Bus for Airport
51 Bus Station
52 Centro de Arte – Museo de
    Almería

Places to Stay – Mid-Range & Top End

In this range you can count on a private bathroom, satellite TV, air-con in summer and heating in winter. *Hotel Torreluz* (☎ 950 23 43 99) on Plaza de las Flores is actually three separate hotels, of two, three and four stars, with prices to suit a range of pockets. The two-star hotel has good singles/doubles for 5000/8250 ptas plus IVA; the three-star hotel charges 6900/10,675 ptas plus IVA; and a double in four-star luxury is 18,000 ptas plus IVA.

Hotel Costasol (☎ 950 23 40 11, Paseo de Almería 58) has attractive rooms for 8340/10,425 ptas plus IVA; it also has a restaurant.

The top place is the *Gran Hotel Almería* (☎ 950 23 80 11, Avenida Reina Regente 8), with doubles costing around 20,000 ptas plus IVA.

Places to Eat

A bustling local breakfast favourite is *Cafetería Torreluz* on Calle de las Flores, where varied *tostadas* (toasted rolls or slices of toast) and *mini bocadillos* (small sandwiches) cost from 115 ptas to 230 ptas, and a *desayuno continental* (continental

breakfast) of orange juice, coffee and tostada costs 400 ptas. Several other good eateries called Torreluz cluster around Plaza de las Flores. Head for *Tasca Restaurante Torreluz* on Calle Concepción Arenal for tapas, *raciones* (meal-sized servings of tapas) from 700 ptas to 3000 ptas, or *platos combinados* (mixed platters) such as *patatas con huevos estrellados* (fried eggs and chips; 875 ptas) or *solomillo de cerdo al ajo* (pork sirloin in garlic; 1550 ptas). For full meals, the classy *Torreluz Mediterráneo* (Plaza de las Flores) and the *Asador Torreluz* grill (Calle Fructuoso Pérez) offer fish and meat dishes costing between 1500 ptas and 3000 ptas.

Bodega Las Botas (Calle Fructuoso Pérez 3) is an atmospheric sherry bar serving varied tapas, *media-raciones* (half a *ración*) from 600 ptas to 1100 ptas and raciones (1000 ptas to 2000 ptas).

The simple *Restaurante Alfareros* (Calle Marcos 6), near Puerta de Purchena, serves a good three-course lunch and dinner menú (fixed-price meal), including wine and a decent choice of fish and meat main courses, for 1000 ptas. It opens daily.

Restaurant Sol de Almería on Calle Circunvalación, by the covered market, offers several daily menús for 900 ptas, including a drink. It opens for lunch and dinner.

On Avenida de Federico García Lorca beside Rambla de Belén, the bright *Cafetería Central* does pasta and salads for around 700 ptas, and platos combinados and main dishes from 700 ptas to 2000 ptas.

Casa Puga (Calle Jovellanos 7) has few rivals as Almería's best tapas bar. Shelves of ancient wine bottles set the tone, and the tasty tapas – from mushrooms/chicken breast/swordfish *a la plancha* (grilled) to *anchoa con alcachofa* (anchovy and artichoke) or *revuelto de jamón* (scrambled eggs with ham) – cost a reasonable 100 ptas to 125 ptas each. *Calle Mayor (Calle General Segura 12)*, a little more modern, offers good tapas (for example salmon and cheese) for 100 ptas to 125 ptas, baked potatoes for 350 ptas and raciones.

Entertainment

A dozen or so music bars cluster in the streets between the post office and the cathedral. Some open from late afternoon. *Georgia Café Bar (☎ 950 25 25 70, Calle Padre Luque 17)*, running for more than 20 years, sometimes stages live jazz. See the map for locations of some of the other most popular ones. *La Clásica (☎ 950 26 70 25, Calle Poeta Villaespesa 4)*, a little away from the main group, stays open later than most, with dancing to salsa and pop in its patio. The *Molly Malone (Paseo de Almería 56)*, despite its famous Irish name, has 'English Bar' engraved on its windows and unmistakably Andalucian tiles and wrought iron inside. Needless to say, it's fun.

Peña El Taranto (☎ 950 23 50 57), in the renovated Aljibes Árabes (Arab Water Cisterns) on Calle Tenor Iribarne, is Almería's top flamenco club. Live performances open to the public often happen at weekends: you may be lucky enough to catch the local celebrity, guitarist Tomatito, in action.

Getting There & Around

Air Almería airport (☎ 950 21 37 00) receives charter flights from several European countries. Scheduled services go to/from Dusseldorf by LTU International Airways

(☎ 950 21 37 80), Barcelona and Madrid by Iberia (☎ 950 21 37 90 at the airport) and Melilla by Binter Mediterráneo (also ☎ 950 21 37 90). You can pick up inexpensive outbound international fares from agencies such as Viajes Cemo (☎ 950 62 70 19 in Roquetas de Mar, ☎ 950 47 28 35 in Mojácar, ☎ 950 21 38 47 at the airport) or Tarleton Direct (☎ 950 33 37 34 in Roquetas, ☎ 950 47 22 48 in Mojácar, ☎ 950 21 37 70 at the airport).

Bus Daily departures from the bus station (☎ 950 21 00 29, but it is unlikely to be answered) include nine or more buses to Guadix (1300 ptas, 1¼ hours); five or more to Granada (1300 ptas, 2¼ hours); eight to Málaga (1945 ptas, 3¼ hours); three to Sevilla (5100 ptas, five hours); and 10 or more to Murcia (2150 ptas). There's also at least one bus daily each to Jaén, Úbeda, Córdoba, Madrid, Valencia, Barcelona and – except Sunday – Ugíjar (via Berja) and Bérchules (via Adra).

For buses to places within Almería province, see the Getting There & Away information for individual destinations.

Train You can buy tickets at the town centre RENFE office (☎ 950 23 18 22) at Calle Alcalde Muñoz 7, open 9.30 am to 1.30 pm Monday to Friday and 9.30 am to 1 pm Saturday, as well as at the train station (☎ 950 25 11 35). Direct trains run to/from Granada (1610 ptas to 1775 ptas, 2¼ to three hours, four times daily), Sevilla (4260 ptas, five to 5½ hours, three times daily) and Madrid (4000 to 4200 ptas, 6¾ to 10 hours, twice daily). All trains go through Guadix (920 to 1400 ptas, 1¼ to 1¾ hours).

Car & Motorcycle There are several car rental agencies in the city. Avis, Europcar, Hertz and local company Atesa (☎ 950 29 31 31) have desks at the airport.

Boat From the Estación Marítima, Trasmediterránea (☎ 950 23 61 55 or ☎ 902 45 46 45) sails to/from Melilla six days a week and three times daily from mid-June to late August or early September. The trip takes up to eight hours. The cheapest passenger accommodation, a *butaca* (seat), costs 4020 ptas one way; the fare for a car is 16,125 ptas. You can buy tickets at the Estación Marítima. The Moroccan lines Ferri Maroc (☎ 950 27 48 00) and Limadet (☎ 950 27 12 80) both sail to/from Nador, the Moroccan town neighbouring Melilla, with similar frequency and prices.

To/From the Airport The airport is 9km east of the city, off the N-344; the No 14 'Aeropuerto' bus (110 ptas) runs between the city (the end of Calle del Doctor Gregorio Marañón) and airport every 30 to 45 minutes from 7 am (7.30 am on Saturdays) to 9.30 pm.

AROUND ALMERÍA
West of Almería
There are two neat but run-of-the-mill beach resorts to the west: **Aguadulce**, 11km from Almería, and **Roquetas de Mar**, a few kilometres farther around the coast. Both with a sizeable northern-European package holiday trade. Almerimar, farther west, is popular with Spanish vacationers. The wetlands of the **Paraje Natural Punta Entinas-Sabinar**, between Roquetas and Almerimar, are a good place to see greater flamingo and other water birds – around 150 species have been recorded there.

A vast area west of Almería and a lesser one to its east are covered in ugly plastic-sheeting greenhouses which, with the aid of fertiliser and water pumped up from as deep as 100m, have turned wildernesses into some of Europe's most intensive horticultural zones and, since the 1970s, brought wealth to parts of Almería province. Most of the produce is trucked out early in the year to northern Europe. The capital of *'plasticultura'* is the sprawling town of **El Ejido**, west of Almería. El Ejido reputedly has Spain's highest ratio of bank branches to population, but is also the scene of considerable tension between Spaniards and the Moroccan labourers on whom the greenhouse industry relies. This boiled over in 2000 in a violent wave of attacks on Moroccans and their property after three Spaniards were murdered by Moroccans.

Los Millares
Archaeology fans will enjoy a trip to this site, 17km north-west of Almería on the N-324 between the villages of Gádor and Santa Fé de Mondújar – you need a vehicle as public transport is virtually nonexistent.

Los Millares, occupied from about 2700 to 1800 BC, was the site of what's thought to be Spain's first metalworking culture. Its copper-smelting people, numbering up to 2000, also made pottery and jewellery, hunted, bred domestic animals and grew crops. The site, almost 1km long on a spur between the Río Andarax and Rambla de Huéchar, contains four lines of defensive walls (reflecting successive enlargements of the village), round dwelling huts and over 100 tombs. The tombs typically comprise a domed chamber reached by a low corridor: a few have been reconstructed.

At our last check, Los Millares was open 9.30 am to 4.30 pm Wednesday to Saturday, 9.30 am to 2 pm Sunday and holidays – but it's advisable to check with the Almería tourist offices or by phoning the site (☎ 608 95 70 65). Admission is free.

Take the A-92 north from Almería to Benahadux, then head north-west on the A-348. Signs indicate the Los Millares turning, shortly before Alhama de Almería.

Wild West Towns
North of Benahadux, Almería's desertified landscape takes on a particularly Arizona-like aspect. In the 1960s and 70s, makers of Western movies spotted the resemblance and shot dozens of films here – some now classics, others best forgotten. Locals played Indians, outlaws and cavalry while Clint Eastwood, Raquel Welch, Charles Bronson and co did the talking bits. Movie makers come here less often now, but three Wild West town sets remain as tourist attractions.

Mini Hollywood (☎ 950 36 52 36), the best-known and best-preserved of these, is 24km from Almería on the Tabernas road. Parts of more than 100 films, including *A Fistful of Dollars*, *The Magnificent Seven* and *The Good, the Bad and the Ugly*, were shot here. Mini Hollywood normally opens 10 am to 9 pm daily from April to October, and 10 am to 7 pm daily except Monday in other months. Admission costs 1200 ptas (children 850 ptas). At noon and 5 pm (and 8 pm from mid-June to mid-September) a mock bank hold-up and shootout is staged – a great hit with kids. Also here, and open the same hours, is a Reserva Zoológica (☎ 950 36 29 31), with lions, elephants and 100-odd other species of African and Ibérian fauna. Combined tickets for both attractions cost 2395 ptas (children 1200 ptas).

Three kilometres farther towards Tabernas, then a few minutes along a track to the north, **Texas Hollywood** (☎ 950 16 54 58) boasts a Western town, a stockaded fort, a Mexican village and Indian tepees. There's also **Western Leone** (☎ 950 16 54 05), on the A-92 about 1km north of the A-370 turning. Both places took a hand in some of the same films as Mini Hollywood.

A Mini Hollywood bus service runs from hotels in Roquetas de Mar and Aguadulce, but otherwise you will need your own vehicle.

Níjar

Some of Andalucía's most attractive and original glazed pottery, and colourful striped cotton rugs known as *jarapas*, are made in this small town 4km north of the N-340, 31km north-east of Almería. It's well worth a detour if you're passing, though bus schedules make a day trip from Almería impossible. Shops and workshops selling the products, many of which are quite affordable, are dotted along Calle García Lorca, which leads up towards the old town centre, and in the 'Barrio Alfarero' (Potters' Quarter) along Calle Las Eras off Calle García Lorca. Níjar has two *hostales*.

LAS ALPUJARRAS

West of the small spa town of Alhama de Almería, the A-348 winds up the Andarax valley into the Almerian Alpujarras. (See the Las Alpujarras section in the Granada Province chapter for introductory information on this series of valleys below the Sierra Nevada; the Almería section of Las Alpujarras is much less visited than the Granada Alpujarras.) The landscape is at first unbelievably barren, with arid, serrated ridges stretching to infinity – but becomes gradually more vegetated as you approach Fondón, where the small *Camping Puente Colgante* (☎ 950 51 42 90) opens mid-June to mid-September.

For information on walking routes and refuges in the mountain range, visit the Centro de Visitantes Laujar de Andarax (☎ 950 51 35 48), just west of Laujar de Andarax on the A-348.

Laujar de Andarax
postcode 04470 • pop 1800
• elevation 920m

This pleasant 'capital' of the Almería Alpujarras is where Boabdil, the last emir of Granada, settled briefly after losing Granada. It was also the headquarters of Aben Humeya, the first leader of the 1568–70 Morisco uprising, until he was assassinated by his cousin Aben Aboo. Today it produces Almería's best wine.

Things to See & Do The handsome **Casa Consistorial** (town hall) on the central Plaza Mayor de la Alpujarra was built in 1792 with a facade of three tiers of arches. The large 17th-century brick **Iglesia de la Encarnación** has a minaret-like square tower and a lavish golden retable. A signposted road leads 1km north to **El Nacimiento**, a series of waterfalls in a deep valley, with a couple of restaurants nearby. The falls are the starting point for some walking trails which the Centro de Visitantes, just west of town, can tell you about.

Places to Stay & Eat The good *Hostal Fernández* (☎ 950 51 31 28, Calle General Mola 4), just off Plaza Mayor de la Alpujarra, has doubles with bathroom costing 4500 ptas plus IVA. *Fonda Nuevo Andarax* (☎ 950 51 31 13, Calle Canalejas 27), 300m west along the main street, costs 5000 ptas with bathroom. *Hotel Almirez* (☎ 950 51 35 14), 1km west of town on the A-348, is more comfortable; doubles with bathroom cost 5000 ptas and it has a restaurant. The *Villa Turística de Laujar* (☎ 950 51 30 27), on a hill above the eastern end of

JANE SMITH

The Faro de Cabo de Gata lights the way for ships passing between Andalucía and Africa.

the village, offers comfy 'villa-apartments' (for two people, they cost 11,355 ptas including breakfast) and has a restaurant, a pool and tennis courts in large gardens.

Getting There & Away A bus to Laujar (845 ptas) leaves Almería bus station at 8.30 am daily, starting back from Laujar at 4.15 pm. Between Laujar and the Granada Alpujarras, you'd have to get one bus to Berja, then another to Ugíjar or beyond.

CABO DE GATA

The stark landscape of eastern Almería meets the Mediterranean most dramatically where the Sierra del Cabo de Gata, of volcanic origin, plunges towards the azure and turquoise waters around this promontory east of Almería city. Some of Spain's most beautiful and least crowded beaches are strung between awesome cliffs and capes, and the whole area has a rare, elemental feel. With just 100mm of rain in an average year, Cabo de Gata is the driest place in Europe and, dotted with low white houses, sometimes seems like a piece of North Africa that has floated across to Europe. Though certainly not undiscovered, Cabo de Gata is far enough from the beaten track to feel pretty empty by Andalucian coastal standards. There are no real towns here, just a scattering of villages which – with a couple of exceptions in Easter, July and August – remain very low-key.

You can walk along, or not far from, the coast all the way from Retamar in the northwest to Agua Amarga in the north-east, but in summer there's very little shade (the route is described in Lonely Planet's *Walking in Spain*). The western side of the promontory is straight and flat, with a sandy beach stretching most of its length; the south and east are more rugged, but still have plenty of good beaches. There's worthwhile snorkelling in several places.

It's worth calling ahead for accommodation anywhere on Cabo de Gata during Easter, July and August. Camping is only allowed in the four organised camp sites.

The IGN 1:50,000 map *Parque Natural de Cabo de Gata-Níjar* is the best for the area.

Getting There & Away

Bus Schedules from Almería bus station are:

Agua Amarga (615 ptas) – 7.45 pm Monday and Friday by Autocares Bergarsan (☎ 950 26 42 92); buses leave Agua Amarga for Almería at 6.15 am Monday and Friday

El Cabo de Gata (300 ptas) – four or more daily by Autocares Becerra (☎ 950 22 44 03)

La Isleta del Moro (415 ptas) – 6.30 pm Monday, 2.15 pm Saturday, by Autocares Bernardo (☎ 950 25 04 22); on other days drivers of San José buses might be persuaded to detour; buses leave La Isleta del Moro for Almería at 6.30 am Monday and Saturday

Las Negras (500 ptas) – 5.30 pm Monday to Friday, 1 pm Saturday, by TM (☎ 950 22 81 78); departures from Las Negras at 7.30 am Monday to Saturday

San José (355 ptas) – 1.15 and 6.30 pm Monday to Friday, 2.15 pm Saturday, by Autocares Bernardo (☎ 950 25 04 22); departures from San José are at 7 am and 3 pm Monday to Saturday, and 7.30 pm Monday to Friday; from June to September there's an extra bus on Saturday and one on Sunday

From Mojácar there's nothing better than one bus on Thursday and two on Saturday to/from Carboneras, 9km north of Agua Amarga, by Autocares Baraza (☎ 950 39 00 53).

Car & Motorcycle The only petrol station on Cabo de Gata is halfway along the Ruescas–San José road. San José has a couple of car rental agencies.

Centro de Interpretación Las Amoladeras

About 2.5km before Ruescas on the road from Almería, this is the main information centre for the Parque Natural de Cabo de Gata-Níjar, which covers Cabo de Gata's 60km coast, plus a thick strip of hinterland. The centre (☎ 950 16 04 35) has displays on the area's fauna, flora and human activities, as well as tourist information. You can expect it to be open 10 am to 2 pm and 5 to 9 pm daily from mid-July to mid-September, and 10 am to 3 pm daily except Monday at other times.

El Cabo de Gata

Officially called San Miguel de Cabo de Gata, this is the main village on the western side of the promontory. Fronted by a sandy beach, it's composed largely of one- and two-storey holiday homes, but has an old nucleus with a small fishing fleet at the southern end. A bank on Calle Iglesia has an ATM.

South of the village are the **Salinas de Cabo de Gata**, salt-extraction lagoons. In spring, many greater flamingos and other water birds call in here while migrating from Africa or the Doñana area to breed-

ing grounds farther north (France's Camargue, in the case of the flamingos). A few flamingos and many other species stay on here to breed, then others arrive in summer: by late August there can be 1000 flamingos here. Autumn brings the biggest numbers of migratory birds as they pause on their return south. A good place to watch the birds is the hide in a wood-fenced area just off the road 3km south of the village. You should see a good variety of birds any time of year, except winter, when the salinas are drained after the autumn salt harvest.

Another flamingo-viewing spot, where in fact you'll probably get closer to the birds, is the small lagoon where the stream **Rambla de Morales** reaches the beach, 2km north-west of El Cabo de Gata village.

Places to Stay & Eat Near the beach, 2km down a side road south-west of Ruescas, or 2km north by dirt road from El Cabo de Gata village, is *Camping Cabo de Gata* (☎ *950 16 04 43*). It's open year-round and has a pool, a restaurant and 250 sites. It costs 550 ptas plus IVA for each adult, car and tent; electrical hook-up costs 425 ptas.

Hostal Las Dunas (☎ *950 37 00 72, Calle Barrio Nuevo 58*), 250m from the beach at the northern end of the village, has clean, modern rooms with bathroom for 4500/6500 ptas plus IVA. *Hostal Chiri-Bus* (☎ *950 37 00 36, Calle La Sardina 2*), on the left as you enter the village from Ruescas, has a handful of nice, modern rooms with bathroom costing 3500/5000 ptas for singles/doubles. Nearby *Pizzeria Pedro* (*Calle Islas de Tabarca 2*) serves fine pizzas and pasta at middling prices. *Restaurante Mediterráneo* (☎ *950 37 11 37*), on Calle Iglesia towards the southern end of the village seafront, has a few rooms with shared bathrooms costing 4000/6000 ptas. It serves decent food with many seafood and meat main dishes for 750 ptas to 1100 ptas.

Faro de Cabo de Gata & Around

The salt collected from the salinas is piled up in great heaps at **La Almadraba de Mon-**

CABO DE GATA

televa, a drab village at their southern end with a curious towered church. South of La Almadraba the coast becomes rapidly more rugged and the road winds round the cliffs to the Faro de Cabo de Gata, the lighthouse on the promontory's southern tip. A turning by Bar José y María, just before the light-house, leads up to the **Torre Vigía Vela Blanca**, an 18th-century watchtower atop 200m cliffs, with awesome views. Here the road ends but a walking and cycling track continues down to Playa de Mónsul (about one hour away), Playa de los Genoveses and San José.

Places to Stay & Eat At La Almadraba de Monteleva *Hotel Las Salinas* (☎ 950 37 01 03) has a classy restaurant and very comfy rooms costing 10,000 ptas to 15,000 ptas for a double. *Bar José y María*, near the lighthouse, does platos combinados from 650 ptas and seafood raciones from 750 ptas.

San José & Around
postcode 04118 • pop 175

Spreading around a bay towards the south-ern end of the eastern side of Cabo de Gata, San José becomes a mildly chic little resort in summer, but out of season its permanent population seems decidedly sparse as most of the holiday villas and flats stand empty. Despite gradual growth, it's still a small, pleasant, low-rise place.

Orientation & Information The road from the north becomes San José's main street, Calle Correo, with the beach a cou-ple of blocks down to the left. On Calle Correo you'll find a natural park informa-tion office (☎ 950 38 02 99), open 10 am to 2 pm and 5.30 to 9.30 pm daily from June to September, 9.30 am to 2.30 pm daily except Tuesday in other months. It sells maps. A municipal tourist office, with the same telephone number and hours, stands nearby on the square behind Restaurante El

ALMERÍA PROVINCE

Emigrante (see Places to Eat). Also on Calle Correo in the centre are a Caja Rural bank, an ATM and a Spar supermarket. Farther on up the hill is the post office.

Beaches San José has a sandy central beach, with a harbour at its eastern end, but two of the finest beaches on Cabo de Gata lie along a dirt road to the south-west. **Playa de los Genoveses**, a broad, 1km strip of fine yellow sand, with shallow waters, and rocky headlands at each end, is 4.5km from San José. **Playa de Mónsul**, 2.5km farther on, is a shorter length of grey sand backed by huge lumps of volcanic rock. Two kilometres west of Playa de Mónsul, the road is blocked to motor vehicles – but not to walkers or bicycles – as it climbs to the Torre Vigía Vela Blanca (see Faro de Cabo de Gata & Around earlier in this chapter).

Activities The information offices can tell you about bicycle rental, horse riding, boat trips, 4WD tours and diving.

Places to Stay – Budget Open from April to September, *Camping Tau* (☎ 950 38 01 66) has a shady site 400m back from the beach, with room for 185 people. It costs around 500 ptas for each person, tent and car. Follow the 'Tau' sign pointing left along Camino de Cala Higuera as you approach central San José from the north, and go about 800m.

Albergue Juvenil de San José (☎ 950 38 03 53, Calle Montemar s/n) is a friendly, non-Inturjoven youth hostel run by the local municipality. It has room for 86 people in bunk rooms holding ones to eight, at 1300 ptas a night. It opens 1 April to 1 October, and also for Christmas–New Year and long weekends. There's a small terrace cafe serving breakfast and, in busy periods, dinner. To find it, head towards Camping Tau but turn right after crossing a dry river bed, then take the first left up the hill.

Bar El Refugio Cala Higuera (☎ 950 52 56 25, @ albergerar@larural.es) is on Cala Higuera, a pebbly bay 1.25km by dirt road beyond Camping Tau. Its 10 rustic but cosy

rooms and studios for two to five people, some with kitchen, cost from 3000 ptas to 8000 ptas in high season. The friendly people here prefer guests who stay two nights or more and usually offer a discount if you stay several days. There's also a terrace restaurant just above the sea. To get there, continue 200m past Camping Tau to a T-junction, then go right and follow the signs.

Places to Stay – Mid-Range & Top End
In the centre of San José *Hostal Bahía* (☎ 950 38 03 07), on Calle Correo, and its sister establishment *Hostal Bahía Plaza* (same telephone number), across the street, have 34 attractive, clean singles/doubles with bathroom and TV, in bright, modern buildings, for 5000/7500 ptas. There are several other medium-sized hostales, slightly more expensive, at the entrance to San José from the north, including *Hostal Las Gaviotas* (☎ 950 38 00 10), *Hostal Ágades* (☎ 950 38 03 90), and *Hostal Puerto Genovés* (☎ 950 38 03 20), on Calle Arrastre just east of the main road.

The French-run *Hostal Eldorado* (☎ 950 38 01 18), above the road towards Playa de los Genoveses, has pretty, well-equipped rooms costing 9000 ptas a double, all with good views, and a French/Spanish/Mexican restaurant.

Top of the range is the often-full eight-room *Hotel San José* (☎ 950 38 01 16), up the hill past the post office. Doubles cost 15,000 ptas plus IVA.

Plenty of apartments are available for rent (ask the tourist offices or look for signs); two people can pay as little as 2500 ptas a day for a few days' stay off season, though it's more like 8000 ptas in high summer.

Places to Eat With good service and tasty food, *Restaurante El Emigrante* on Calle Correo is clean and attractive. Fish and meat main courses cost around 850 ptas to 1400 ptas, tortillas or a mixed salad cost 400 ptas to 500 ptas.

Just back from the eastern end of the beach, *Cafetería Restaurante El Ancla* is a popular seafood restaurant, with most main dishes costing between 1200 ptas and 2100 ptas, though some shellfish is less. Just beyond, near the harbour, is a line of eateries with outdoor tables including two Italian places (pizza or pasta 650 ptas to 1100 ptas) and *El Tempranillo* with platos combinados for 700 ptas to 800 ptas.

The Hotel San José's *Restaurant El Borany* is a good place for a splurge.

San José to Las Negras

The rugged coast north-east of San José allows only two small settlements, the odd fort and a few beaches before the slightly bigger village of Las Negras, 17km away as the crow flies. The road spends most of its time ducking inland.

The hamlet of **Los Escullos** has a short, mainly sandy beach and a restored old fort, the Castillo de San Felipe. You can walk here from San José along a track from Cala Higuera. The large, moderately shaded *Camping Los Escullos* (☎ *950 38 98 11*), 900m back from the beach, opens year-round and has a pool, a grocery store, an ATM and bikes to hire. High-season cost for two adults with a car, tent and electrical hook-up is 2800 ptas plus IVA. Near the beach are two reasonable small mid-range hotels: *Hotel Los Escullos* (☎ *950 38 97 33*), charging 8000 ptas or 9000 ptas a room, and *Casa Emilio* (☎ *950 38 97 32*) with singles/doubles for 4500/6500 ptas. All three places have restaurants.

La Isleta del Moro, 1km farther north-east, is a tiny village with a couple of fishing boats and Playa del Peñón Blanco stretching to the east. *Hostal Isleta del Moro* (☎ *950 38 97 13*) has rooms with bathroom costing 3000/5000 ptas, and a restaurant with fresh seafood. *Casa Café de la Loma* (☎ *950 52 52 11*) on a small hill above the village with great views, run by a friendly English-speaking German, has six nice rooms costing 3500/4500 ptas, or 5800 ptas for a double with bathroom (all 1000 ptas more in August). In summer a vegetarian restaurant opens here with excellent weekly flamenco nights.

From here, the road climbs to the **Mirador de la Amatista** before heading inland

past the former gold-mining village of Rodalquilar. About 1km past Rodalquilar is the turning for **Playa del Playazo**, 2km away along a level track. This good sand beach stretches between two headlands, one topped by the Batería de San Ramón fortification (now a private home). From here you can walk near the coast to Camping La Caleta and Las Negras.

The village of **Las Negras**, on a pebbly beach stretching towards an imposing headland of volcanic rock, Cerro Negro, attracts a vaguely trendy holiday clientele. *Camping La Caleta* (☎ *950 52 52 37*), open year-round, is 1km south in a separate cove. It has little shade – but a nice pool and a restaurant. It costs 550 ptas for each adult, 500 ptas per car and 600 ptas per tent, plus IVA. *Hostal Arrecife* (☎ *950 38 81 40, Calle Bahía 6*), on the main street, has singles/doubles with bathroom costing 4000/6000 ptas. Other accommodation is mostly holiday apartments and houses to let, but you may find a few signs offering rooms by the night. *Restaurante La Palma* by the beach serves good medium-priced food.

Las Negras to Agua Amarga

There's no road along this cliff-lined and most secluded stretch of the Cabo de Gata coast, but walkers can take an up-and-down path of 11km. **Playa San Pedro**, one hour's walk from Las Negras, is the site of a ruined hamlet whose buildings (including a castle) house an international colony of two or three dozen hippies. It's 1½ hours' walk on from San Pedro to **Cala del Plomo** a beach, with another tiny settlement, then 1½ hours more to Agua Amarga. You could stop at the nice little Cala de Enmedio beach half an hour after Cala del Plomo.

Drivers from Las Negras to Agua Amarga must head inland through Hortichuelas. From the bus shelter on the eastern side of the road in Fernán Pérez, you can head north-east cross-country for 10km by a mostly unpaved but reasonable road (keep to the main track all the way), to meet the paved road running down to Agua Amarga from the N-341.

Agua Amarga

The most northerly settlement on the eastern side of Cabo de Gata, Agua Amarga is a pleasant, more-tourist-than-fishing village stretched along a good sandy beach. It has a supermarket and a post office.

Three kilometres east up the Carboneras road is a turning to a clifftop lighthouse, the Faro de la Mesa Roldán (1.25km), with an old watchtower for a neighbour. The views up here are marvellous. From the car park by the turning you can walk down to the nudist Playa de los Muertos. The road continues north through Carboneras, a minor resort with a big cement factory, to Mojácar.

Places to Stay & Eat At the eastern end of the beach *Hostal Restaurante La Palmera* (☎ 950 13 82 08, Calle Aguada s/n) has 10 pleasant rooms with bathroom costing 7000 ptas to 11,000 ptas plus IVA depending on their views. On Calle La Lomilla just up from the western end of the beach, *Hotel Family* (☎ 950 13 80 14), run by a friendly French family, has nine lovely rooms with bathroom costing between 8000 ptas and 12,000 ptas including a big breakfast. An excellent four-course menú,

for 2000 ptas including drinks, is served in the restaurant nightly at 7 pm, also at weekends at 1 pm.

Other accommodation options include *Hotel Las Calas* (☎ 950 13 82 35), behind Chiringuito Las Tarahis at the western end of the beach, with doubles for 19,260 ptas, and houses and apartments for rent. *Chiringuito Las Tarahis* serves tortillas from 500 ptas and fish and meat dishes from 1200 ptas. *Pizzeria Sotavento* on Calle La Noria in the village is also popular.

MOJÁCAR
postcode 04638 • pop 4000

Mojácar, up the coast north-east of Cabo de Gata and 85km from Almería, is two towns: the old Mojácar Pueblo, a jumble of white cube-shaped houses on a hilltop 2km inland, and the new Mojácar Playa, a modern coastal resort strip 7km long but only a few blocks wide. Even though the Pueblo is dominated by tourism, it is very picturesque, especially in the dim after-dark lighting. Mojácar Playa has few high-rise buildings, a good, long, clean beach, and quite a lively summer scene. The whole place is pretty quiet from October to Easter.

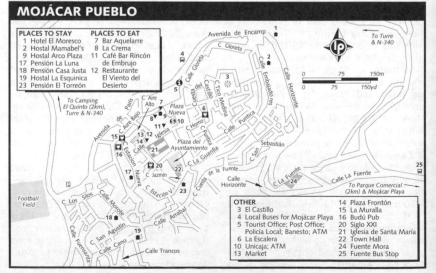

MOJÁCAR PUEBLO

PLACES TO STAY
1 Hotel El Moresco
2 Hostal Mamabel's
9 Hostal Arco Plaza
17 Pensión La Luna
18 Pensión Casa Justa
19 Hostal La Esquinica
23 Pensión El Torreón

PLACES TO EAT
7 Bar Aquelarre
8 La Crema
11 Café Bar Rincón de Embrujo
12 Restaurante El Viento del Desierto

OTHER
3 El Castillo
4 Local Buses for Mojácar Playa
5 Tourist Office; Post Office; Policía Local; Banesto; ATM
6 La Escalera
10 Unicaja; ATM
13 Market
14 Plaza Frontón
15 La Muralla
16 Budú Pub
20 Siglo XXI
21 Iglesia de Santa María
22 Town Hall
24 Fuente Mora
25 Fuente Bus Stop

From the 13th to 15th centuries, Mojácar Pueblo stood on the Granada emirate's eastern frontier and suffered several Christian attacks, including a notorious massacre in 1435, before finally succumbing to the Catholic Monarchs in 1488. Tucked away in an isolated corner of one of Spain's most backward regions, it was decaying and almost abandoned by the mid-20th century before its mayor lured artists and others with give-away property offers.

Orientation & Information
Mojácar Playa and Mojácar Pueblo are joined by a road which heads uphill from a junction by the Parque Comercial shopping centre, towards the northern end of Mojácar Playa.

The tourist office (☎ 950 47 51 62) is on Calle Glorieta in Mojácar Pueblo, just north of the main square, Plaza Nueva. It's open 10 am to 2 pm and 5 to 8 pm Monday to Friday (9 am to 4 pm from about November to May), and 10 am to 1 pm Saturday. A summer information booth (☎ 950 47 87 26), on Paseo del Mediterráneo opposite the Parque Comercial in Mojácar Playa, opens similar hours to the Pueblo office from about June to October. In the same building as the Pueblo office are a post office and the Policía Local station (☎ 950 47 20 00). Banesto, next door, and Unicaja, across the square, have ATMs, as does Banco de Andalucía in the Parque Comercial. There's another post office in the Parque Comercial too.

Things to See & Do
Seeing the Pueblo is mainly a matter of wandering the quaint streets with their flower-decked balconies, and nosing into the craft shops, galleries and boutiques. **El Castillo,** at the very top of the village, is private property (and not a castle), but there are great views from the public terraces around it. The fortress-style **Iglesia de Santa María** on Calle Iglesia, just south of Plaza Nueva, dates from 1560 and may previously have been a mosque.

Apart from the long, sandy main **beach,** a number of more secluded beaches are

A Plea for Tolerance

The most touching spot in Mojácar is the **Fuente Mora** (Moorish Fountain), on Calle La Fuente in the lower part of the Pueblo. Though remodelled in modern times, the fountain maintains the Spanish Muslim tradition of turning water into art. Flowing from 12 spouts into marble troughs, the water tinkles along a courtyard decked with hanging plants. An inscription here records the speech made, according to legend, on this spot in 1488 by Alavez, the last Islamic governor of Mojácar, to Garcilaso, the envoy of the conquering Catholic Monarchs. It translates, in part, as follows:

> I am just as much a Spaniard as you. Though my people have lived in Spain for more than 700 years, you say to us: 'You are foreigners, go back to the sea.' In Africa an inhospitable coast awaits us, where they will surely tell us, as you do – and certainly with more reason – 'You are foreigners: cross the sea by which you came and go back to your own land.' Treat us like brothers, not enemies, and let us continue working the land of our ancestors.

strung south of the town. Some of those beyond the Torre de Macenas, an 18th-century fortification, are nudist beaches.

Special Events
The Moros y Cristianos festival, on the weekend nearest 10 June, re-enacts the Christian conquest of Mojácar, along with dances, processions and other festivities.

Places to Stay
Mojácar Pueblo Two kilometres west of the Pueblo on the Turre road, *Camping El Quinto* (☎ 950 47 87 04) is small but pleasant. It opens year round, charging 1900 ptas plus IVA for two adults with a car and tent. *Pensión Casa Justa* (☎ 950 47 83 72, Calle Morote 7) is reasonable value with singles/double rooms costing 2500/5000 ptas, or 6000 ptas to 7000 ptas for

euro currency converter €1 = 166 ptas

doubles with bathroom. *Hostal La Esquinica* (☎ *950 47 50 09, Calle Cano 1*), nearby, charges 2500/4500 ptas. *Pensión La Luna* (☎ *950 47 80 32, Calle Estación Nueva 11*) has 11 comfortable, uniquely decorated doubles with bathroom for 6000 ptas, including breakfast. *Hostal Arco Plaza* (☎ *950 47 27 77, Calle Aire 1*), just off Plaza Nueva, has 16 pretty rooms painted a variety of pastel shades with bathroom, TV, aircon and heating for 6000/8000 ptas.

Hostal Mamabel's (☎ *950 47 24 48, Calle Embajadores 5*) is a charming place to stay, with a fine restaurant and just eight excellent, spacious rooms, costing 9000 ptas plus IVA a double. All are individually and tastefully decorated and have sea views, bathroom, heating and TV. Some enjoy their own terraces.

Pensión El Torreón (☎ *950 47 52 59, Calle Jazmín 4*) has great views from its bougainvillea-draped balcony, and just five rooms, with shared bathroom, at 6000 ptas a double. According to a persistent Mojácar belief, Walt Disney was born in this house in about 1901. Originally named José Guirao, he emigrated as a child with his parents to the US. When young José's parents died, he was adopted by a Californian family called Disney, and renamed Walt.

Doubles at the 147-room *Hotel El Moresco* (☎ *950 47 80 25, Avenida de Encamp*) are 14,000 ptas plus IVA.

Mojácar Playa Almost everything here is on Paseo del Mediterráneo, the main road running along the back of the beach. *Camping El Cantal* (☎ *950 47 82 04*), 1km south of the Parque Comercial (near El Cantal bus stop), opens year-round, with room for 800 people at 2300 ptas plus IVA for two adults with a car and tent. *Hostal Bahía* (☎ *950 47 80 10*), just to its south, has doubles with bathroom for 6500 ptas.

Hotel El Puntazo (☎ *950 47 82 65, Paseo del Mediterráneo 257*), 2km south of the Parque Comercial, is a decent medium-sized hotel with a range of singles/doubles costing from 5640/7050 ptas to 13,185/16,480 ptas, plus a pool and a restaurant.

At *Hotel Playa Río Abajo* (☎ *950 47 89 28*) at the northern end of town, the 18 nice rooms are set in chalets in a pleasant garden fronting the beach. They cost up to 9000 ptas plus IVA. The hotel has its own pool, restaurant and bar. From La Rumina bus stop, head towards the beach and you'll find it.

Mojácar's *Parador* (☎ *950 47 82 50, fax 950 47 81 83,* @ *mojacar@parador.es*), a few hundred metres south of the Parque Comercial, is modern, with nice gardens. Rooms cost 12,000/15,000 ptas plus IVA.

Places to Eat
Mojácar Pueblo On Plaza Frontón by the church *Restaurante El Viento del Desierto* is good value; fish soup is 400 ptas and main courses such as beef bourguignon or rabbit in mustard cost 650 ptas to 800 ptas. At *Café Bar Rincón de Embrujo* (*Calle Iglesia 4*), down the street, platos combinados and seafood raciones start from only 500 ptas.

Bar Aquelarre, up in the shopping precinct above Plaza Nueva, serves up reasonable meat and seafood dishes – some costing 600 ptas to 800 ptas, others dearer. *La Crema*, in the same precinct, is one of the few places offering an early breakfast out of season.

Hostal Mamabel's (see Places to Stay) serves up probably the best food in Mojácar, with main courses costing from 1500 ptas to 2500 ptas and a three-course menú for 1800 ptas (excluding drinks), all plus IVA.

Mojácar Playa There are dozens of places to eat along Paseo del Mediterráneo, especially south of the Parque Comercial. *Restaurante Chino La Gran Muralla*, 2km south of the Parque Comercial, near the Pueblo Indalo bus stop, serves fair-value set meals from 625 ptas to 1750 ptas. *Antonella*, with a fine position just above the beach near the Cueva del Lobo bus stop, pulls in the customers with its medium-priced pizzas and pasta. Out of season it only opens during the evening and for Sunday lunch. *Mesón Casa Egea*, towards the southern end of Mojácar Playa (Las Ventánicas bus stop), is popular for its fish and meat main courses costing from about 600 ptas to 1000 ptas.

Entertainment

Lively bars in Mojácar Pueblo include *La Escalera* on Calle Horno, *Budú Pub* on Calle Estación Nueva, *La Muralla* on Calle Aire Alto and *Siglo XXI* on Calle Enmedio. On weekends and holidays from Easter to October you can burn energy after midnight by heading for one of Mojácar's open-air discos such as *Master*, halfway between Mojácar Pueblo and Playa; *Pascha*, on the beach just north of Camping El Cantal; or *Tuareg*, amid oasis-like gardens on the Carboneras road 3.5km south of Mojácar Playa. At *Tito's* bar, near Las Ventánicas bus stop towards the southern end of Mojácar Playa, you can sit on outdoor steps overlooking the beach, sometimes to the sound of live music.

Getting There & Away

Bus Long-distance buses stop at the Parque Comercial and at the Fuente stop at the foot of Mojácar Pueblo. The tourist office has timetables.

Two or more buses run daily to/from Murcia (1295 ptas, two to three hours) Al-mería (815 ptas, 1¾ hours), Granada (2080 ptas, 4¼ hours) and Madrid (4225 ptas, eight hours). There's a bus to Málaga daily except Sunday and holidays. For Almería, Granada and Murcia you buy tickets on the bus; for Málaga and Madrid you must book at a travel agency such as Viajes Cemo (☎ 950 47 28 35) on Paseo del Mediterráneo 2km south of the Parque Comercial (Pueblo Indalo bus stop). Buses to Alicante, Valencia and Barce-lona go from Vera, 16km north, which is served by several daily buses from Mojácar.

Car & Motorcycle Mojácar is 14km east of the N-340. A winding, scenic coastal road approaches Mojácar from Agua Amarga and Carboneras to the south.

Getting Around

A local bus service (100 ptas) runs a circuit from the southern to northern ends of Mojácar Playa (Hotel Indalo to La Rumina stop), then back to the Parque Comercial, up to the Pueblo (stopping on Calle Glori-

eta near the tourist office), then back down to the Parque Comercial and Hotel Indalo. It starts about every half-hour from 9 am to 11.30 pm in summer, and about every hour from 9.30 am to 7.30 pm in winter, reaching the Pueblo in about 15 minutes.

VÉLEZ BLANCO & AROUND

postcode 04830 • pop 2300
• elevation 1070m

The intriguing district called Los Vélez is north of the A-92-N Granada–Murcia road in the north of the province. It's focused on three small towns – Vélez Rubio, Vélez Blanco and María – and the scenic Sierra de María mountain range whose highest peak is María (2045m). Easily the most attractive and interesting of the towns is tile-roofed Vélez Blanco. Much of the mountains and countryside are under protection in the Parque Natural Sierra de María-Los Vélez.

Information

Information on walking routes, and refuges and other attractions is available at Vélez Blanco's Centro de Visitantes Almacén del Trigo (☎ 950 41 56 51) on Avenida del Marqués de los Vélez (the road leading out towards María), which opens 10 am to 2 pm daily. Another natural park visitor centre, the Centro de Visitantes Mirador Umbría de María (☎ 950 52 70 05), is 2km west of María off the A-317.

Things to See

Vélez Blanco is crowned by the very imposing **Castillo de los Fajardo**. The castle, built over an earlier Muslim fort, was designed by 16th-century Italian Renaissance architect F Florentini for Don Pedro Fajardo, the Marqués de los Vélez. Its interior is now rather bare (its impoverished owners sold off the decorations around 1900), but don't despair – you can see the lovely marble main patio next time you're in New York, as it has ended up, reconstructed, in that city's Metropolitan Museum of Art! The castle opens 11 am to 1 pm and 4 to 6 pm Monday, Tuesday, Thursday and Friday, 11 am to 4 pm at weekends and holidays. Admission costs 150 ptas.

Just south of Vélez Blanco on the A-317 from Vélez Rubio, signs point to the **Cueva de los Letreros**, an ancient rock shelter with the most outstanding of several groups of 7000-year-old rock paintings in the district. The paintings, which would have had a sacred or magical purpose, show abstract symbols and animals and people in a hunting context. Though they're not very big and not all very distinct, they exert a curious fascination. For a close-up look, contact the Centro de Visitantes Almacén del Trigo and arrange a time for them to open the iron fence around the shelter for you; admission is free. From the A-317 you can drive 500m along the signposted dirt track, then it's a 10-minute walk up to the shelter.

Vélez Rubio centres on the handsome Plaza de la Constitución, which is dominated by the lavish baroque Iglesia de la Encarnación. There's an archaeological, geological and ethnographic museum, the Museo Miguel Guirao, at Carrera del Carmen 27.

Places to Stay & Eat

In the centre of Vélez Blanco, *Hostal La Sociedad* (☎ *950 41 50 27, Calle Corredera 5)* has good double rooms with bathroom costing 4000 ptas (but you might find it closed in winter). *Bar Sociedad* across the street serves tapas and meals. The new *Hotel Velad Al-Abyadh* (☎ *950 41 51 09, Calle Balsa Parra 28)*, at the entrance to Vélez Blanco from Vélez Rubio, has comfortable singles/doubles costing 6000/7000 ptas plus IVA at the back and 7000/8000 ptas plus IVA at the front. For meals try *Restaurante Los Vélez* *(Calle Balsa Parra 15)* along the street.

In Vélez Rubio, *Hotel Jardín* (☎ *950 41 01 06)* on the old main road, the N-342, at the eastern end of town, has doubles with bathroom costing 4200 ptas; *Hostal Zurich* (☎ *950 41 03 35)*, on the N-342 near the western end of town at the junction of the A-317 to Vélez Blanco, has doubles costing 5000 ptas to 6000 ptas plus IVA. Both have restaurants. *Cafetería Gaspar*, on the N-342 a few hundred metres east of Hostal Zurich, serves good-value platos combinados.

In María, *Hostal Torrente* (☎ *950 41 73 99, Camino Real 23)*, on the main road, and *Hostal Sevilla* (☎ *950 41 74 10)*, on the Plaza de la Encarnación, are both cheap.

Getting There & Away

Alsina Graells (☎ 968 29 16 12) runs three or four buses daily each way through Vélez Rubio en route between Granada (1515 ptas), Guadix (1005 ptas) and Murcia (955 ptas). Other Alsina services run to/from Sevilla and Córdoba. Bacoma/ Enatcar (☎ 902 42 22 42) also runs daily buses to Vélez Rubio from Granada, Guadix and Alicante (1620 ptas).

From Almería, Enatcar goes daily, except Sunday, at 1.30 and 3.30 pm to Vélez Rubio (1585 ptas), Vélez Blanco (1640 ptas) and María (1715 ptas).

Autobuses Giménez Garciá (☎ 968 44 19 61) has a bus from María (7.30 am Monday to Friday, 9.30 am Saturday) to Vélez Blanco, Vélez Rubio and Lorca. Returning, these stop at Vélez Rubio at 3.40 pm Monday to Friday and 12.55 pm Saturday.

The bus stop in Vélez Rubio is at the Hostal Zurich.

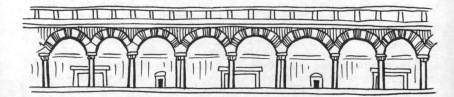

Language

Spanish, or Castilian *(castellano)*, as it is often and more precisely called, is spoken throughout Andalucía. English isn't as widely spoken as many travellers expect, though you are more likely to find people who speak some English in the main cities and tourist areas. Generally, however, you'll be better received if you try to communicate in the local language.

Andalucian Pronunciation
Pronunciation of Spanish isn't difficult, given that many Spanish sounds are similar to their English counterparts, and there's a clear and consistent relationship between pronunciation and spelling. However, few Andalucians pronounce Castilian as it is used in other parts of Spain or as it is taught to foreigners. Local accents vary too but if you stick to the following rules you should have very few problems making yourself understood.

Vowels
Unlike English, each of the vowels has a uniform pronunciation which doesn't vary. For example, the letter *a* has one pronunciation rather than the numerous ones we find in English, such as in 'cake', 'care', 'cat', 'cart' and 'call'. Many words have a written accent. This acute accent (as in *días*) indicates a stressed syllable; it doesn't change the sound of the vowel. Vowels are pronounced clearly even if they are in unstressed positions or at the end of a word.

a	similar to the 'a' in 'art' but shorter
e	as in 'met'
i	between the 'i' in 'marine' and the 'i' in 'flip'
o	similar to the 'o' in 'hot'
u	as in 'put'

Consonants
Some consonants are the same as their English counterparts. The pronunciation of other consonants varies according to which vowel follows. The Spanish alphabet also contains the letter ñ, which is not found in the English alphabet. Until recently, the clusters **ch** and **ll** were also officially separate consonants, and you're likely to encounter many situations – eg, in lists and dictionaries – in which they are still treated that way.

b	soft, as the 'v' in 'van'; also (less commonly) as in 'book' when word-initial or when preceded by a nasal such as 'm' or 'n'
c	as 'k' before 'a', 'o' and 'u'; as 's' when followed by 'e' or 'i' (not 'th' as in standard Castilian)
ch	as in 'choose'
d	when word-initial it's as in 'do'; elsewhere as the 'th' in 'then', and sometimes not pronounced at all – thus *partido* (divided) becomes 'partio'
g	as in 'go' when initial or before 'a', 'o' or 'u'; elsewhere much softer. Before 'e' or 'i' it's a harsh, breathy sound, similar to the 'ch' in Scottish *loch*
h	always silent
j	a harsh, guttural sound similar to the 'ch' in Scottish *loch*
ll	similar to the 'y' in 'yellow' but often closer to a 'j' in Andalucía
ñ	a nasal sound like the 'ni' in 'onion' or the 'ny' in 'canyon'
q	always followed by a silent 'u' and either 'e' (as in *que*) or 'i' (as in *aquí*); the combined sound of 'qu' is like the 'k' in 'kick'
r	a rolled 'r' sound; longer and stronger when initial or doubled
s	often not pronounced at all, especially when not initial; thus *pescados* (fish) can be pronounced 'pecao' in Andalucía

v same sound as Spanish **b** (see above)

x as the 'x' in 'taxi' when between two vowels; as the 's' in 'say' before a consonant

z pronounced as 's' (not 'th' as in standard Castilian); often silent when at the end of a word

Semiconsonant
Andalucian Spanish also has the semiconsonant **y**. It's pronounced as **i** when at the end of a word or when it stands alone as a conjunction. As a consonant, its sound is somewhere between the 'y' in 'yonder' and the 'g' in 'beige', depending on the region.

Greetings & Civilities
Hello.	*¡Hola!*
Goodbye.	*¡Adiós!*
Yes.	*Sí.*
No.	*No.*
Please.	*Por favor.*
Thank you.	*Gracias.*
That's fine/ You're welcome.	*De nada.*
Excuse me.	*Perdón/Perdóneme.*
Sorry/Excuse me.	*Lo siento/ Discúlpeme.*

Useful Phrases
Do you speak English?	*¿Habla inglés?*
Does anyone speak English?	*¿Hay alguien que hable inglés?*
I understand.	*Entiendo.*
I don't understand.	*No entiendo.*
Just a minute.	*Un momento.*
Could you write it down, please?	*¿Puede escribirlo, por favor?*
How much is it?	*¿Cuánto cuesta/vale?*

Getting Around
What time does the ... leave/arrive?	*¿A qué hora sale/ llega el ...?*
boat	*barco*
bus (city)	*autobús/bus*
bus (intercity)	*autocar*
train	*tren*
metro/ underground	*metro*

Signs
Entrada	Entrance
Salida	Exit
Información	Information
Abierto	Open
Cerrado	Closed
Prohibido	Prohibited
Comisaria	Police Station
Servicios/Aseos	Toilets
Hombres	Men
Mujeres	Women

next	*próximo*
first	*primer*
last	*último*

I'd like a ... ticket.	*Quisiera un billete ...*
one-way	*sencillo*
return	*de ida y vuelta*
1st-class	*de primera clase*
2nd-class	*de segunda clase*

Directions
Where is the bus stop?	*¿Dónde está la parada de autobús?*
I want to go to ...	*Quiero ir a ...*
Can you show me (on the map)?	*¿Me puede indicar (en el mapa)?*
Go straight ahead.	*Siga/Vaya todo derecho.*
Turn left.	*Gire a la izquierda.*
Turn right.	*Gire a la derecha.*
near	*cerca*
far	*lejos*

Around Town
I'm looking for ...	*Estoy buscando ...*
a bank	*un banco*
the city centre	*el centro de la ciudad*
the consulate	*el consulate*
the embassy	*la embajada*
my hotel	*mi hotel*
the market	*el mercado*
the police	*la policía*
the post office	*los correos*
public toilets	*los servicios/ aseos públicos*
a telephone	*un teléfono*
the tourist office	*la oficina de turismo*

the beach	la playa
the bridge	el puente
the castle	el castillo
the cathedral	la catedral
the church	la iglesia
the hospital	el hospital
the lake	el lago
the main square	la plaza mayor
the mosque	la mezquita
the old city	la ciudad antigua/ el casco antiguo
the palace	el palacio
the ruins	las ruinas
the sea	el mar
the square	la plaza
the tower	la torre

Accommodation

Where is a cheap hotel?	¿Dónde hay un hotel barato?
What's the address?	¿Cuál es la dirección?
Could you write it down, please?	¿Puede escribirla, por favor?
Do you have any rooms available?	¿Tiene habitaciones libres?

I'd like ...	Quisiera ...
a bed	una cama
a single room	una habitación individual
a double room	una habitación doble
a room with a bathroom	una habitación con baño
to share a dorm	compartir un dormitorio

How much is it ...?	¿Cuánto cuesta ...?
per night	por noche
per person	por persona

Can I see it?	¿Puedo verla?
Where is the bathroom?	¿Dónde está el baño?

Time & Dates

What time is it?	¿Qué hora es?
today	hoy
tomorrow	mañana
in the morning	de la mañana
in the afternoon	de la tarde
in the evening	de la noche

Emergencies

Help!	¡Socorro/Auxilio!
Call a doctor!	¡Llame a un doctor!
Call the police!	¡Llame a la policía!
Go away!	¡Vete!

Monday	lunes
Tuesday	martes
Wednesday	miércoles
Thursday	jueves
Friday	viernes
Saturday	sábado
Sunday	domingo

January	enero
February	febrero
March	marzo
April	abril
May	mayo
June	junio
July	julio
August	agosto
September	setiembre/septiembre
October	octubre
November	noviembre
December	diciembre

Health

I'm ...	Soy...
diabetic	diabético/a
epileptic	epiléptico/a
asthmatic	asmático/a

I'm allergic to ...	Soy alérgico/a a ...
antibiotics	los antibióticos
penicillin	la penicilina

antiseptic	antiséptico
aspirin	aspirina
condoms	preservativos/ condones
contraceptive	anticonceptivo
diarrhoea	diarrea
medicine	medicamento
nausea	náusea
sunblock cream	crema protectora contra el sol
tampons	tampones

Numbers

0	*cero*
1	*uno, una*
2	*dos*
3	*tres*
4	*cuatro*
5	*cinco*
6	*seis*
7	*siete*
8	*ocho*
9	*nueve*
10	*diez*
11	*once*
12	*doce*
13	*trece*
14	*catorce*
15	*quince*
16	*dieciséis*
17	*diecisiete*
18	*dieciocho*
19	*diecinueve*
20	*veinte*
21	*veintiuno*
22	*veintidós*
23	*veintitrés*
30	*treinta*
31	*treinta y uno*
40	*cuarenta*
50	*cincuenta*
60	*sesenta*
70	*setenta*
80	*ochenta*
90	*noventa*
100	*cien/ciento*
1000	*mil*

one million	*un millón*

FOOD

breakfast	*desayuno*
lunch	*almuerzo/comida*
dinner	*cena*
menu	*carta*
waiter/waitress	*camarero/a*

I'd like the set lunch.	*Quisiera el menú del día.*
Is service included in the bill?	*¿El servicio está incluido en la cuenta?*
I'm a vegetarian.	*Soy vegetariano/a*

Food Glossary

Andalucía has such a variety of foods and food names that you could travel for years and still find unfamiliar items on almost every menu. The following guide should at least help you sort out what's what.

Basics

botella – bottle
cocina – kitchen
comida – lunch, meal, food
copa – glass, especially a wine glass
cuchara – spoon
cuchillo – knife
cuenta – bill (check)
media-ración – half a *ración*
menú del día – fixed-price set meal
mesa – table
plato – plate
ración – meal-sized serving of a *tapa* dish
taza – cup
tenedor – fork
vaso – glass

aceite (de oliva) – (olive) oil
azúcar – sugar
caliente – hot
confitura – jam
frío/a – cold
hierba buena/menta – mint
mayonesa – mayonnaise
mermelada – jam
miel – honey
picante – hot (spicy)
pimienta – pepper
sal – salt
salsa – sauce
soja – soy
vegetal – vegetable (adjective)
vinagre – vinegar

arroz – rice
bollo – bread roll
empanada – pie
espagueti – spaghetti
fideo – vermicelli noodle
harina – flour
macarrones – macaroni
mollete – soft bread roll

pan – bread
panecillo – bread roll
tostada – toasted roll
trigo – wheat

Cooking Methods & Common Dishes

a la brasa – grilled
a la parrilla – grilled
a la plancha – grilled on a hotplate
adobo – a marinade of vinegar, salt, lemon and spices, usually for fish before frying
ahumado/a – smoked
albóndiga – meatball or fishball
aliño – in a vinegar and oil dressing
alioli – garlic mayonnaise
asado/a – roasted
caldereta – stew
caldo – broth, stock
casero/a – home-made
cazuela – casserole
cocido – cooked; also hotpot/stew
croqueta – croquette
crudo – raw
escabeche – a marinade of oil, vinegar and water for pickling perishables, usually fish or seafood
espeto – (roasting) spit
estofado – stew
flamenquín – rolled and crumbed veal or ham, deep fried
frito/a – fried
gratinado/a – au gratin
guiso – stew
horneado/a – baked
horno – oven
migas – simple dish basically composed of fried flour and water
olla – pot
paella – rice, seafood and meat dish
pavía – battered fish or seafood
pil pil – garlic sauce usually spiked with chilli
potaje – stew
rebozado/a – battered and fried
relleno/a – stuffed
salado/a – salted, salty
seco/a – dry, dried
tierno/a – tender, fresh
zarzuela – fish stew

Soups, Starters & Snacks – *Sopas, Entremeses & Meriendas*

bocadillo – bread roll with filling
ensalada – salad
gazpacho – cold, blended soup of tomatoes, peppers, cucumber, onions, garlic, lemon and breadcrumbs
montadito – small bread roll with filling, or a small sandwich, or an open sandwich – often toasted
pincho – a tapa-sized portion of food, or a *pinchito* (see Meat & Poultry)
pitufo – small filled baguette or roll
sopa de ajo – garlic soup
tabla – selection of cold meats and cheeses on a board
tapa – snack on a saucer

Fruits – *Frutas*

aceituna – olive
aguacate – avocado
cereza – cherry
chirimoya – custard apple, a tropical fruit
frambuesa – raspberry
fresa – strawberry
granada – pomegranate
higo – fig
lima – lime
limón – lemon
mandarina – tangerine
manzana – apple
manzanilla – camomile (also a type of olive or a type of sherry)
melocotón – peach
melon – melon
naranja – orange
pasa – raisin
piña – pineapple
plátano – banana
sandía – watermelon
uva – grape

Vegetables – *Vegetales/Verduras/ Hortalizas*

ajo – garlic
alcachofa – artichoke
apio – celery
berenjena – aubergine, eggplant
calabacín – courgette, zucchini

calabaza – pumpkin
cebolla – onion
champiñones – mushrooms
col – cabbage
coliflor – cauliflower
espárragos – asparagus
espinacas – spinach
guindilla – chilli pepper
guisante – pea
hongo – wild mushroom
judías blancas – butter beans
judías verdes – green beans
lechuga – lettuce
maíz – sweet corn
patata – potato
patatas a lo pobre – 'poor man's potatoes', a potato dish with peppers and garlic
patatas bravas – spicy fried potatoes
patatas fritas – chips, French fries
pimiento – pepper, capsicum
pipirrana – salad of diced tomatoes and red peppers
puerro – leek
seta – wild mushroom
tomate – tomato
verdura – green vegetable
zanahoria – carrot

Pulses & Nuts – *Legumbres & Nueces*
almendra – almond
alubia – dried bean
anacardo – cashew nut
cacahuete – peanut
garbanzo – chickpea
haba – broad bean
lentejas – lentils
nuez (pl: *nueces*) – nut, walnut
piñón – pine nut
pipa – sunflower seed

Fish – *Pescados*
aguja – swordfish
anchoa – anchovy
atún – tuna
bacalao – salted cod; it's soaked before cooking, prepared many different ways and can be succulent
boquerones – anchovies
caballa – mackerel

cazón – dogfish
chanquetes – whitebait (illegal, but not uncommon)
dorada – sea bass
lenguado – sole
merluza – hake
mero – halibut, grouper, sea bass
mojama – cured tuna
pescadilla – whiting
pescaíto frito – small fried fish
pez espada – swordfish
platija – flounder
rape – monkfish
rosada – ocean catfish, wolf-fish
salmón – salmon
salmonete – red mullet
sardina – sardine
trucha – trout

Seafood – *Mariscos*
almejas – clams
bogavante – lobster
búsano – sea snail, whelk
calamares – squid
camarón – shrimp
cangrejo – crab
chipirón – small squid
choco – cuttlefish
cigala – crayfish
conchas finas – Venus shell
frito variado – a mixture of deep-fried seafood
fritura – same as *frito variado*
gamba – prawn
langosta – lobster
langostino – large prawn
mejillones – mussels
ostra – oyster
peregrina – scallop
pulpo – octopus
puntillita/o – small squid, fried whole
quisquilla – shrimp
sepia – cuttlefish
venera – scallop

Meat & Poultry – *Carne & Aves*
beicon – bacon (usually thin-sliced and pre-packaged; see *tocino*)
bistek – thin beef steak

butifarra – thick sausage (to be cooked)
cabra – goat
cabrito – kid, baby goat
callos – tripe
caracol – snail
carne de monte – 'mountain meat' such as venison or wild boar
caza – hunt, game
cerdo – pig, pork
chacinas – cured pork meats
charcutería – cured pork meats
chorizo – red sausage
choto – veal
chuleta – chop, cutlet
codorniz – quail
conejo – rabbit
cordero – lamb
embutidos – the many varieties of sausage
faisán – pheasant
filete – fillet
hamburguesa – hamburger
hígado – liver
jabalí – wild boar
jamón (serrano) – (mountain-cured) ham
lengua – tongue
lomo – loin (of pork unless specified otherwise – usually the cheapest meat dish on the menu)
morcilla – black pudding
paloma – pigeon
pato – duck
puvo – turkey
pechuga – breast, of poultry
perdiz – partridge
picadillo – minced meat
pierna – leg
pinchito – Moroccan-style kebab
pollo – chicken
rabo (de toro) – (ox) tail
riñón – kidney
salchicha – fresh pork sausage
salchichón – cured sausage
sesos – brains
solomillo – sirloin (usually of pork)
ternera – beef, veal
tocino – bacon (usually thick; see *beicon*)
vaca, carne de – beef
venado – venison

Dairy Products & Eggs – *Productos Lácteos & Huevos*
leche – milk
mantequilla – butter
nata – cream
queso – cheese
revuelto de ... – eggs scrambled with...
tortilla – omelette
tortilla española – potato omelette
yogur – yoghurt

Desserts & Sweet Things – *Postres & Dulces*
bizcocho – sponge cake
churro – long, deep-fried doughnut
galleta – biscuit, cookie
helado – ice cream
natillas – custards
pastel – pastry, cake
tarta – cake
torta – round flat bun, cake
turrón – almond nougat or rich chocolatey sweets that appear at Christmas
yema – yolk, or candied yolk

DRINKS
Nonalcoholic
water	*agua*
fizzy mineral water	*agua mineral con gas*
plain mineral water	*agua mineral sin gas*
tap water	*agua de grifo*
almond drink	*tiger nut drink*
fruit juice	*zumo*
soft drinks	*refrescos*
coffee ...	*café ...*
with liqueur	*carajillo*
with a little milk	*cortado*
with milk	*con leche*
iced coffee	*café helado*
black coffee	*café solo*
long black	*doble*
decaffeinated	*café descafeinado*
tea	*té*
hot chocolate	*chocolate*

Alcoholic
anisette	*anís*
beer	*cerveza*

champagne	*champán/cava*	whisky	*güisqui*
cider	*sidra*		
cocktail	*combinado*	a glass of … wine	*un vino …*
brandy	*coñac*	red	*tinto*
rum	*ron*	white	*blanco*
sangría (red wine punch)	*sangría*	rosé	*rosado*
		sweet	*dulce*
sherry	*jerez*	sparkling	*espumoso*

Glossary

abierto – open
acequia – irrigation channel
alameda – avenue or boulevard, originally planted with poplar *(álamo)* trees
albergue juvenil – youth hostel; not to be confused with *hostal*
alcalde – mayor
alcázar – Muslim-era fortress
alfiz – rectangular frame about the top of an arch in Islamic architecture
altar mayor – high altar
andaluz – Andalucian
años de hambre – years of hunger (1940s)
apartado de correos – post office box
apnea – snorkelling
armadura – wooden *Mudéjar* ceiling, especially one like an inverted ship's hull
arroyo – stream
artesonado – *Mudéjar* wooden ceiling with interlaced beams leaving a pattern of spaces for decoration
auto da fe – elaborate execution ceremony staged by the Inquisition
autonomía – autonomous community or region; Spain's 50 *provincias* are grouped into 17 of these
autopista – motorway (toll charged)
autovía – toll-free motorway
AVE – Alta Velocidad Española; the high-speed train between Madrid and Sevilla
ayuntamiento – city or town hall
azulejo – glazed tile

bailaor/a – flamenco dancer
baile – flamenco dance
bakalao – ear-splitting Spanish techno music (not to be confused with *bacalao*, salted cod)
balneario – bathing place, usually an inland spa
barrio – district or quarter (of a town or city)
biblioteca – library
bici todo terreno – mountain bicycle
bodega – cellar (especially a wine cellar), winery or traditional wine bar likely to serve wine from the barrel

bota – sherry cask or animal-skin wine vessel
botijo – jug, usually an earthenware one
BTT – abbreviation for *bici todo terreno*
buceo – scuba diving
bulería – upbeat type of flamenco song

cajero automático – automatic teller machine (ATM)
calle – street
callejón – lane
cama – bed
cambio – in general, change; also currency exchange
campo – countryside, field
caña –small beer in a glass; also a cane
cantaor/a – flamenco singer
cante jondo – 'deep song', the essence of flamenco
capilla – chapel
capilla mayor – chapel containing the high altar of a church
carmen – walled villa with gardens, in Granada
carnaval – carnival; a pre-Lent period of fancy-dress parades and merrymaking
carpa – marquee or piece of material strung over an area for shade or shelter; in Andalucía, marquees are often in Moroccan style
carretera – road, highway
carta – menu
casa de huéspedes – guesthouse
casa rural – a village house or farmstead with rooms to let
casco – literally 'helmet'; often used to refer to the old part of a city (more correctly, *casco antiguo*)
castellano – Castilian; the language also called Spanish
castillo – castle
catedral – cathedral
caza – hunting
cercanías – local trains serving suburbs and nearby towns
cerrado – closed
cervecería – beer bar

chiringuito – small, often makeshift bar or eatery, usually in the open air
Churrigueresque – ornate style of baroque architecture named after the brothers Alberto and José Churriguera
claustro – cloister
cofradía – same as *hermandad*
colegiata – collegiate church, a combined church and college
comarca – district, grouping of *municipios*
comedor – dining room
comisaría – National Police station
comunidad autónoma – same as *autonomía*
consejo de gobierno – cabinet of the Junta de Andalucía
consigna – left-luggage office or lockers
converso – Jew who converted to Christianity in medieval Spain
copa – glass, drink; *ir de copas* is to go out for a few drinks
copla – flamenco song
cordillera – mountain chain
cordobés/a – person from Córdoba
coro – choir (part of a church, usually in the middle)
correos – post office
corrida de toros – bullfight
cortes – parliament
cortijo – country property
costa – coast
costumbristas – 19th-century Andalucian painters and writers who dealt with local customs and manners
coto – area where hunting rights are reserved to a specific group of people
cuenta – bill (check)
cuesta – sloping land, road or street
custodia – monstrance (receptacle for the consecrated Host)

dehesa – woodland pastures with evergreen oaks
dólmen – prehistoric megalithic tomb
ducha – shower
duende – the spirit or magic possessed by great flamenco performers
duro – literally 'hard'; also a common name for a 5 ptas coin

embalse – reservoir

embarcadero – pier, landing stage
encierro – running of bulls Pamplona-style (also happens in many other places around Spain)
entrada – entrance
ermita – hermitage or chapel
escalada – climbing
estación de autobuses – bus station
estación de esquí – ski station or resort
estación de ferrocarril – train station
estanco – tobacconist
estípite – pilaster

farmacia – pharmacy
faro – lighthouse
feria – fair; can refer to trade fairs as well as to city, town or village fairs, which are basically several days of entertainment and merrymaking
ferrocarril – railway
fiesta – festival, public holiday or party
finca – piece of land or building, usually in the country
fin de semana – weekend
flamenco – means flamingo and Flemish as well as flamenco music and dance
fonda – basic eatery and inn combined
fuente – fountain, spring

gaditano – person from Cádiz
garum – a spicy, vitamin-rich sauce made from fish entrails in Roman Andalucía, used as a seasoning or tonic
gitano – the Spanish word for Roma people, formerly called Gypsies
glorieta – big roundabout

hermandad – brotherhood, in particular one that takes part in religious processions
hispalense – person or thing from Sevilla
hospedaje – guesthouse
hostal – simple guesthouse or small place offering hotel-like accommodation; not a youth hostel
humedal – wetland

iglesia – church
infanta – princess
infante – prince
IVA – *impuesto sobre el valor añadido*; value-added tax (VAT)

jardín – garden
jiennense – person from Jaén
judería – Jewish *barrio* in medieval Spain
Junta de Andalucía – executive government of Andalucía

laberinto – maze
latifundio – huge estate
lavabo – washbasin
lavandería – laundry
librería – bookshop
lidia – the art of bullfighting
lista de correos – poste restante
litera – bunk or (on a train) couchette
llegada – arrival
lucio – pond or pool in the Doñana *marismas*

madrileño – person from Madrid
madrugada – the 'early hours', from around 3 am to dawn – a pretty lively time in some Spanish cities!
marcha – action, life, 'the scene'
marismas – wetlands, marshes
marisquería – seafood eatery
medina – Arabic word for town or inner city
menú del día – fixed-price meal available at lunchtime, sometimes in the evening
mercadillo – flea market
mercado – market
mezquita – mosque
mihrab – prayer niche in a mosque indicating the direction of Mecca
mirador – lookout point
morería – former Islamic quarter in a town
morisco – Muslim converted (often only superficially) to Christianity in medieval Spain
moro – 'Moor' or Muslim (usually in a medieval context)
movida – similar to *marcha*; a *zona de movida* is an area of a town where young people gather to drink and have a good time
mozárabe – Mozarab; Christian living under Muslim rule in medieval Spain
mudéjar – Muslim living under Christian rule in medieval Spain; also refers to their decorative style of architecture
muelle – wharf, pier
muladí – Muwallad; Christian who converted to Islam, in medieval Spain

municipio – municipality, Spain's basic local administrative unit
museo – museum

oficina de turismo – tourist office
onubense – person from Huelva

palo – literally a stick; also refers to the catagories of flamenco song
panadería – bakery
papelería – stationery shop
parador – one of the Paradores de Turismo, a chain of luxurious hotels, often in historic buildings
paseo – avenue; park-like strip
paso – literally 'step'; also means the platform an image is carried on in a religious procession
peña – a club, usually supporters of a football club or flamenco enthusiasts; sometimes a dining club
pescadería – fish shop
pícaros – dice tricksters and card sharps, rogues
pinsapar – forest of Spanish firs
piscina – swimming pool
plateresque – early phase of Renaissance architecture noted for its decorative facades
plato combinado – literally 'combined plate', a fairly large serving of meat/seafood/omelette with trimmings
playa – beach
plaza de toros – bullring
porrón – jug with a long, thin spout through which you (try to) pour wine into your mouth
presa – dam
provincia – province; Spain is divided into 50 of them
pueblo – village, town
puente – bridge; also means the extended break from work that many people take when a holiday falls close to a weekend
puerta – gate, door
puerto – port, mountain pass

quinto real – the royal fifth: the 20% of the bullion from the New World to which the Spanish Crown was entitled

ración – meal-sized serving of tapas

rambla – stream
rastro – flea market, car-boot (trunk) sale
Reconquista – the Christian reconquest of the Iberian Peninsula from the Muslims (8th to 15th centuries)
reembolso – reimbursement
refugio – shelter or refuge, especially a mountain refuge with basic accommodation for hikers
reja – grille, especially a wrought-iron one over a window or dividing a chapel from the rest of a church
RENFE – Red Nacional de los Ferrocarriles Españoles, Spain's national rail network
reserva – reserve
retablo – retable (altarpiece)
ría – estuary
río – river
romería – festive pilgrimage or procession
ronda – ring road

s/m – on menus, an abbreviation for *según mercado*, meaning 'according to market price'
s/n – sin numero (without number), sometimes seen in addresses
sacristía – sacristy, the part of a church in which vestments, sacred objects and other valuables are kept
saeta – outburst of adoration by an onlooker at Santa Semana processions
salida – exit, departure
salinas – salt lagoons
Semana Santa – Holy Week, the week leading up to Easter Sunday
sendero – path or track
sevillana – a woman from Sevilla; also a popular Andalucian dance
sevillano – a man from Sevilla; also means Sevillan (adjective)
sida – AIDS
sierra – mountain range
Siglo de Oro – Spain's cultural 'Golden Century', beginning in the 16th century and ending in the 17th century

supermercado – supermarket

taifa – small Muslim kingdom in medieval Spain
tapas – bar snacks, traditionally served on a saucer or lid *(tapa)*
taquilla – ticket window
tarjeta de crédito – credit card
tarjeta de residencia – residence card
tarjeta telefónica – phonecard
techumbre – roof or, specifically, a common type of *armadura*
terraza – terrace; often means an area with outdoor tables at a bar, cafe or restaurant
tetería – teahouse, often in Middle Eastern style with low seats around low tables
tienda – shop, tent
tocaor/a – flamenco guitarist
torno – revolving counter in a convent where nuns sell cakes, sweets and other products to the public without being seen
trascoro – screen behind the *coro*
trono – throne; can also mean the platform on which an image is carried in a religious procession
turismo – means both tourism and saloon car; *el turismo* can also mean the tourist office
turismo rural – rural tourism; usually refers to accommodation in *casas rurales* and associated activities such as walking and horse riding

urbanización – urban housing development

v.o.s. (versión original subtitulada) – foreign-language film subtitled in Spanish
valle – valley

zoco – large market in Muslim cities
zona de acampada – country camp site with no facilities, no supervision and no charge
zonas restringidas – restricted areas

LONELY PLANET

You already know that Lonely Planet publishes more than this one guidebook, but you might not be aware of the other products we have on this region. Here is a selection of titles that you may want to check out as well:

Barcelona
ISBN 1 86450 143 X
US$14.99 • UK£8.99

Canary Islands
ISBN 1 86450 310 6
US$15.99 • UK£9.99

Europe on a shoestring
ISBN 1 86450 150 2
US$24.99 • UK£14.99

Madrid
ISBN 1 86450 123 5
US$14.99 • UK£8.99

Mediterranean Europe
ISBN 1 86450 154 5
US$27.99 • UK£15.99

Read This First: Europe
ISBN 1 86450 136 7
US$14.99 • UK£8.99

Spain
ISBN 1 86450 192 8
US$24.99 • UK£14.99

Spanish phrasebook
ISBN 0 86442 475 2
US$5.95 • UK£3.99

Walking in Spain
ISBN 0 86442 543 0
US$17.95 • UK£11.99

Western Europe
ISBN 1 86450 163 4
US$27.99 • UK£15.99

World Food Spain
ISBN 1 86450 025 5
US$12.95 • UK£7.99

Available wherever books are sold.

Lonely Planet Guides by Region

onely Planet is known worldwide for publishing practical, reliable and no-nonsense travel information in our guides and on our Web site. The Lonely Planet list covers just about every accessible part of the world. Currently there are 16 series: Travel guides, Shoestring guides, Condensed guides, Phrasebooks, Read This First, Healthy Travel, Walking guides, Cycling guides, Watching Wildlife guides, Pisces Diving & Snorkeling guides, City Maps, Road Atlases, Out to Eat, World Food, Journeys travel literature and Pictorials.

AFRICA Africa on a shoestring • Botswana • Cairo • Cairo City Map • Cape Town • Cape Town City Map • East Africa • Egypt • Egyptian Arabic phrasebook • Ethiopia, Eritrea & Djibouti • Ethiopian Amharic phrasebook • The Gambia & Senegal • Healthy Travel Africa • Kenya • Malawi • Morocco • Moroccan Arabic phrasebook • Mozambique • Namibia • Read This First: Africa • South Africa, Lesotho & Swaziland • Southern Africa • Southern Africa Road Atlas • Swahili phrasebook • Tanzania, Zanzibar & Pemba • Trekking in East Africa • Tunisia • Watching Wildlife East Africa • Watching Wildlife Southern Africa • West Africa • World Food Morocco • Zambia • Zimbabwe, Botswana & Namibia
Travel Literature: Mali Blues: Traveling to an African Beat • The Rainbird: A Central African Journey • Songs to an African Sunset: A Zimbabwean Story

AUSTRALIA & THE PACIFIC Aboriginal Australia & the Torres Strait Islands •Auckland • Australia • Australian phrasebook • Australia Road Atlas • Cycling Australia • Cycling New Zealand • Fiji • Fijian phrasebook • Healthy Travel Australia, NZ & the Pacific • Islands of Australia's Great Barrier Reef • Melbourne • Melbourne City Map • Micronesia • New Caledonia • New South Wales • New Zealand • Northern Territory • Outback Australia • Out to Eat – Melbourne • Out to Eat – Sydney • Papua New Guinea • Pidgin phrasebook • Queensland • Rarotonga & the Cook Islands • Samoa • Solomon Islands • South Australia • South Pacific • South Pacific phrasebook • Sydney • Sydney City Map • Sydney Condensed • Tahiti & French Polynesia • Tasmania • Tonga • Tramping in New Zealand • Vanuatu • Victoria • Walking in Australia • Watching Wildlife Australia • Western Australia
Travel Literature: Islands in the Clouds: Travels in the Highlands of New Guinea • Kiwi Tracks: A New Zealand Journey • Sean & David's Long Drive

CENTRAL AMERICA & THE CARIBBEAN Bahamas, Turks & Caicos • Baja California • Belize, Guatemala & Yucatán • Bermuda • Central America on a shoestring • Costa Rica • Costa Rica Spanish phrasebook • Cuba • Cycling Cuba • Dominican Republic & Haiti • Eastern Caribbean • Guatemala • Havana • Healthy Travel Central & South America • Jamaica • Mexico • Mexico City • Panama • Puerto Rico • Read This First: Central & South America • Virgin Islands • World Food Caribbean • World Food Mexico • Yucatán
Travel Literature: Green Dreams: Travels in Central America

EUROPE Amsterdam • Amsterdam City Map • Amsterdam Condensed • Andalucía • Athens • Austria • Baltic States phrasebook • Barcelona • Barcelona City Map • Belgium & Luxembourg • Berlin • Berlin City Map • Britain • British phrasebook • Brussels, Bruges & Antwerp • Brussels City Map • Budapest • Budapest City Map • Canary Islands • Catalunya & the Costa Brava • Central Europe • Central Europe phrasebook • Copenhagen • Corfu & the Ionians • Corsica • Crete • Crete Condensed • Croatia • Cycling Britain • Cycling France • Cyprus • Czech & Slovak Republics • Czech phrasebook • Denmark • Dublin • Dublin City Map • Dublin Condensed • Eastern Europe • Eastern Europe phrasebook • Edinburgh • Edinburgh City Map • England • Estonia, Latvia & Lithuania • Europe on a shoestring • Europe phrasebook • Finland • Florence • Florence City Map • France • Frankfurt City Map • Frankfurt Condensed • French phrasebook • Georgia, Armenia & Azerbaijan • Germany • German phrasebook • Greece • Greek Islands • Greek phrasebook • Hungary • Iceland, Greenland & the Faroe Islands • Ireland • Italian phrasebook • Italy • Kraków • Lisbon • The Loire • London • London City Map • London Condensed • Madrid • Madrid City Map • Malta • Mediterranean Europe • Milan, Turin & Genoa • Moscow • Munich • Netherlands • Normandy • Norway • Out to Eat – London • Out to Eat – Paris • Paris • Paris City Map • Paris Condensed • Poland • Polish phrasebook • Portugal • Portuguese phrasebook • Prague • Prague City Map • Provence & the Côte d'Azur • Read This First: Europe • Rhodes & the Dodecanese • Romania & Moldova • Rome • Rome City Map • Rome Condensed • Russia, Ukraine & Belarus • Russian phrasebook • Scandinavian & Baltic Europe • Scandinavian phrasebook • Scotland • Sicily • Slovenia • South-West France • Spain • Spanish phrasebook • Stockholm • St Petersburg • St Petersburg City Map • Sweden • Switzerland • Tuscany • Ukrainian phrasebook • Venice • Vienna • Wales • Walking in Britain • Walking in France • Walking in Ireland • Walking in Italy • Walking in Scotland • Walking in Spain • Walking in Switzerland • Western Europe • World Food France • World Food Greece • World Food Ireland • World Food Italy • World Food Spain **Travel Literature:** After Yugoslavia • Love and War in the Apennines • The Olive Grove: Travels in Greece • On the Shores of the Mediterranean • Round Ireland in Low Gear • A Small Place in Italy

Lonely Planet Mail Order

onely Planet products are distributed worldwide. They are also available by mail order from Lonely Planet, so if you have difficulty finding a title please write to us. North and South American residents should write to 150 Linden St, Oakland, CA 94607, USA; European and African residents should write to 10a Spring Place, London NW5 3BH, UK; and residents of other countries to Locked Bag 1, Footscray, Victoria 3011, Australia.

INDIAN SUBCONTINENT & THE INDIAN OCEAN Bangladesh • Bengali phrasebook • Bhutan • Delhi • Goa • Healthy Travel Asia & India • Hindi & Urdu phrasebook • India • India & Bangladesh City Map • Indian Himalaya • Karakoram Highway • Kathmandu City Map • Kerala • Madagascar • Maldives • Mauritius, Réunion & Seychelles • Mumbai (Bombay) • Nepal • Nepali phrasebook • North India • Pakistan • Rajasthan • Read This First: Asia & India • South India • Sri Lanka • Sri Lanka phrasebook • Tibet • Tibetan phrasebook • Trekking in the Indian Himalaya • Trekking in the Karakoram & Hindukush • Trekking in the Nepal Himalaya • World Food India **Travel Literature:** The Age of Kali: Indian Travels and Encounters • Hello Goodnight: A Life of Goa • In Rajasthan • Maverick in Madagascar • A Season in Heaven: True Tales from the Road to Kathmandu • Shopping for Buddhas • A Short Walk in the Hindu Kush • Slowly Down the Ganges

MIDDLE EAST & CENTRAL ASIA Bahrain, Kuwait & Qatar • Central Asia • Central Asia phrasebook • Dubai • Farsi (Persian) phrasebook • Hebrew phrasebook • Iran • Israel & the Palestinian Territories • Istanbul • Istanbul City Map • Istanbul to Cairo • Istanbul to Kathmandu • Jerusalem • Jerusalem City Map • Jordan • Lebanon • Middle East • Oman & the United Arab Emirates • Syria • Turkey • Turkish phrasebook • World Food Turkey • Yemen **Travel Literature:** Black on Black: Iran Revisited • Breaking Ranks: Turbulent Travels in the Promised Land • The Gates of Damascus • Kingdom of the Film Stars: Journey into Jordan

NORTH AMERICA Alaska • Boston • Boston City Map • Boston Condensed • British Columbia • California & Nevada • California Condensed • Canada • Chicago • Chicago City Map • Chicago Condensed • Florida • Georgia & the Carolinas • Great Lakes • Hawaii • Hiking in Alaska • Hiking in the USA • Honolulu & Oahu City Map • Las Vegas • Los Angeles • Los Angeles City Map • Louisiana & the Deep South • Miami • Miami City Map • Montreal • New England • New Orleans • New Orleans City Map • New York City • New York City City Map • New York City Condensed • New York, New Jersey & Pennsylvania • Oahu • Out to Eat – San Francisco • Pacific Northwest • Rocky Mountains • San Diego & Tijuana • San Francisco • San Francisco City Map • Seattle • Seattle City Map • Southwest • Texas • Toronto • USA • USA phrasebook • Vancouver • Vancouver City Map • Virginia & the Capital Region • Washington, DC • Washington, DC City Map • World Food New Orleans **Travel Literature:** Caught Inside: A Surfer's Year on the California Coast • Drive Thru America

NORTH-EAST ASIA Beijing • Beijing City Map • Cantonese phrasebook • China • Hiking in Japan • Hong Kong & Macau • Hong Kong City Map • Hong Kong Condensed • Japan • Japanese phrasebook • Korea • Korean phrasebook • Kyoto • Mandarin phrasebook • Mongolia • Mongolian phrasebook • Seoul • Shanghai • South-West China • Taiwan • Tokyo • Tokyo Condensed • World Food Hong Kong • World Food Japan **Travel Literature:** In Xanadu: A Quest • Lost Japan

SOUTH AMERICA Argentina, Uruguay & Paraguay • Bolivia • Brazil • Brazilian phrasebook • Buenos Aires • Buenos Aires City Map • Chile & Easter Island • Colombia • Ecuador & the Galapagos Islands • Healthy Travel Central & South America • Latin American Spanish phrasebook • Peru • Quechua phrasebook • Read This First: Central & South America • Rio de Janeiro • Rio de Janeiro City Map • Santiago de Chile • South America on a shoestring • Trekking in the Patagonian Andes • Venezuela **Travel Literature:** Full Circle: A South American Journey

SOUTH-EAST ASIA Bali & Lombok • Bangkok • Bangkok City Map • Burmese phrasebook • Cambodia • Cycling Vietnam, Laos & Cambodia • East Timor phrasebook • Hanoi • Healthy Travel Asia & India • Hill Tribes phrasebook • Ho Chi Minh City (Saigon) • Indonesia • Indonesian phrasebook • Indonesia's Eastern Islands • Java • Lao phrasebook • Laos • Malay phrasebook • Malaysia, Singapore & Brunei • Myanmar (Burma) • Philippines • Pilipino (Tagalog) phrasebook • Read This First: Asia & India • Singapore • Singapore City Map • South-East Asia on a shoestring • South-East Asia phrasebook • Thailand • Thailand's Islands & Beaches • Thailand, Vietnam, Laos & Cambodia Road Atlas • Thai phrasebook • Vietnam • Vietnamese phrasebook • World Food Indonesia • World Food Thailand • World Food Vietnam

ALSO AVAILABLE: Antarctica • The Arctic • The Blue Man: Tales of Travel, Love and Coffee • Brief Encounters: Stories of Love, Sex & Travel • Buddhist Stupas in Asia: The Shape of Perfection • Chasing Rickshaws • The Last Grain Race • Lonely Planet ... On the Edge: Adventurous Escapades from Around the World • Lonely Planet Unpacked • Lonely Planet Unpacked Again • Not the Only Planet: Science Fiction Travel Stories • Ports of Call: A Journey by Sea • Sacred India • Travel Photography: A Guide to Taking Better Pictures • Travel with Children • Tuvalu: Portrait of an Island Nation

Index

Text

N

Bold indicates maps.

Boxed Text

MAP LEGEND

BOUNDARIES

.... International
.... Provincial
.... Regional

HYDROGRAPHY

.... Coastline
.... River, Creek
.... Lake
.... Canal
.... Swamp

.... Building, Hotel
.... University Campus

◉ **MALAGA** .... Provincial Capital
● Marbella .... Large Town, City
● Cártama .... Town
● Pizarra .... Village
● .... Point of Interest
🛏 .... Place to Stay
▲ .... Camping Ground
⛺ .... Caravan Park
🏠 🏠 ...... Hut or Chalet, Shelter
▼ .... Place to Eat
🍺 .... Pub or Bar
✈ .... Airport
.... Ancient or City Wall
⑤ .... Bank
↗ .... Beach
🚌 🚏 ...... Bus Station, Bus Stop

ROUTES & TRANSPORT

.... Freeway
.... Highway
.... Major Road
.... Minor Road
.... Unsealed Road
.... City Freeway
.... City Highway
.... City Road

.... City Street, Lane
.... Pedestrian Mall
.... Tunnel
.... Train Route & Station
.... Cable Car or Funicular
.... Walking Track
.... Walking Tour
.... Ferry Route

AREA FEATURES

✿ .... Park, Gardens
× × .... Cemetery
.... Market
.... Beach
.... Forest
.... Urban Area

MAP SYMBOLS

🏛 .... Cathedral or Church
⌂ .... Cave
.... Cliff or Escarpment
🏢 .... Embassy
⛲ .... Fountain
⛳ .... Golf Course
✚ .... Hospital
🖥 .... Internet Service
🗼 .... Lighthouse
※ .... Lookout
⚑ .... Monument
▲ ～ .... Mountain, Range
🏛 .... Museum
🏞 .... National Park
🅿 .... Parking
)(........................ Pass

⊙ .... Petrol or Gas Station
★ .... Police Station
✉ .... Post Office
🏚 .... Ruins
⛷ .... Ski Field
🏠 .... Stately Home
🏊 .... Swimming Pool
✡ .... Synagogue
🚕 .... Taxi Rank
☎ .... Telephone
🎭 🎬 .... Theatre, Cinema
🚻 .... Toilet
ℹ .... Tourist Information
🚍 .... Transport
🏄 .... Windsurfing
🦁 .... Zoo

LONELY PLANET OFFICES

Australia
Locked Bag 1, Footscray, Victoria 3011
☎ 03 8379 8000 fax 03 8379 8111
email: talk2us@lonelyplanet.com.au

USA
150 Linden St, Oakland, CA 94607
☎ 510 893 8555 TOLL FREE: 800 275 8555
fax 510 893 8572
email: info@lonelyplanet.com

UK
10a Spring Place, London NW5 3BH
☎ 020 7428 4800 fax 020 7428 4828
email: go@lonelyplanet.co.uk

France
1 rue du Dahomey, 75011 Paris
☎ 01 55 25 33 00 fax 01 55 25 33 01
email: bip@lonelyplanet.fr
www.lonelyplanet.fr

World Wide Web: www.lonelyplanet.com or AOL keyword: lp
Lonely Planet Images: lpi@lonelyplanet.com.au